ARISTOTLE

XV

LCL 316

ARISTOTLE

PROBLEMS

BOOKS 1–19

EDITED AND TRANSLATED BY

ROBERT MAYHEW

HARVARD UNIVERSITY PRESS

CAMBRIDGE, MASSACHUSETTS

LONDON, ENGLAND

2011

First published 2011

LOEB CLASSICAL LIBRARY® is a registered trademark
of the President and Fellows of Harvard College

Library of Congress Control Number 2011925635
CIP data available from the Library of Congress

ISBN 978-0-674-99655-7

Composed in ZephGreek and ZephText by
Technologies 'N Typography, Merrimac, Massachusetts.
Printed on acid-free paper and bound by
The Maple-Vail Book Manufacturing Group

CONTENTS

CONTENTS

vi

To Allan Gotthelf

PREFACE

The present work began as a revision of W. S. Hett's 1936–1937 Loeb *Problems*, but it soon became apparent to myself and the Loeb editor that in fact a new edition was needed. Hett's text was based on Ruelle's 1922 Teubner edition, but significant advances in our knowledge of the history and nature of the text of the *Problems* have since been made, especially by Gerardo Marenghi and Pierre Louis. Further, Hett relied too heavily on Forster's 1927 Oxford translation; moreover, his rendering of the Greek is often unreliable, and key terms are frequently translated inconsistently (sometimes within the same chapter). Finally, the *Problems* is a difficult work, and a first-time reader requires a fair amount of guidance, but Hett's edition offered little of it: the introduction is brief and not terribly helpful, and there are too few notes to the text and translation (Book 19 being an exception). I have sought to remedy these limitations by providing a more up-to-date text and a more reliable translation, a lengthier introduction to the entire work, and many more notes to both the text and the translation; and I have written a brief introduction to each of the thirty-eight books of the *Problems*, describing its nature and subject matter.

This volume (LCL 316) contains *Problems* 1–19; LCL 317 contains books 20–38 and indexes to the entire work, along with a new edition of the *Rhetoric to Alexander*, attributed to Aristotle, edited and translated by David Mirhady.

I am grateful to Seton Hall University for a University Research Council Summer Stipend, which allowed me to devote summer 2008 to this project, and to the Loeb Classical Library Foundation for a grant that provided similar support the following year.

I wish to thank my daughter Tessa for creating electronic versions of the three mathematical figures accompanying Book 15 and of the wind rose in the introduction to Book 26.

Alan Bowen gave me extensive comments on the text and translation of Book 15, and Andrew Barker did the same for Books 11 and 19. I am extremely grateful to both of them for guiding me through material on two subjects about which I am quite ignorant: ancient Greek mathematics and music. I wish to thank Gregory Salmieri as well for his helpful comments on my translation of Book 30. For the past three years, Jeffrey Henderson, the Loeb Classical Library general editor, has answered a constant stream of questions and has provided comments on the whole *Problems*, book by book, as I finished them. I wish to thank him for improving every aspect of this work. (The *Problems* is a long and difficult text, sometimes in wretched condition, covering a vast array of topics. There are no doubt errors in the final product, and I am solely responsible for all of them.)

Allan Gotthelf sparked my interest in Aristotle's biology while I was a graduate student in the 1980s, and although the fire has dimmed occasionally while working on unrelated projects, it has never gone out. A few years ago, when I mentioned to Allan my interest in the *Problems* and my suspicion that it may have much to tell us about the state of natural philosophy (including biology) in the Lyceum after Aristotle, he was enthusiastic and gently suggested—as one way to pursue this interest—investigating the possibility of revising or replacing the original Loeb *Problems*. For his encouragement and support, and for his passionate devotion to Aristotelian philosophy ancient and modern, I dedicate this work to him.

GENERAL INTRODUCTION

The *Problemata* or *Problems* is the third longest work in the *corpus Aristotelicum*, and one of the least studied. It consists of thirty-eight books, and over nine hundred chapters. Nearly all of these chapters begin with a question—and specifically with the words διὰ τί ("why")—followed by one or more (often provisional) answers and/or follow-up questions.[1]

The books of the *Problems* have been roughly organized as follows: 1–11 living things; 12–19 miscellaneous; 20–22 plants; 23–26 meteorological topics; 27–30 ethical and intellectual virtues; and 31–38 parts of the human body. As an overview, here is a list of the book titles:

1. Medical Problems
2. Problems Concerning Sweat
3. Problems Concerning Wine-Drinking and Drunkenness

[1] To be precise, according to my edition of the text, there are 903 chapters, 98 percent of which begin with διὰ τί. A dozen chapters open with a different kind of question (e.g., *Pr.* 2.21 begins: "Should one induce sweating more in the summer than in the winter?"), four chapters seem to open with a statement, not a question (e.g., *Pr.* 1.55 begins: "In fevers one should provide drink often and in small quantities"), and seven chapters seem to be missing their opening line(s).

The individual books themselves, however, lack even this rough sort of organization. For example, here are the opening questions from the first ten chapters of *Pr.* 4 (on sexual intercourse):

1. Why do the one who is having sex and the one who is dying cast their eyes up, whereas the one who is sleeping casts them down?
2. Why do both the eyes and the haunches of those who engage in sex a great deal sink in very noticeably, though the latter are near the sexual organs and the former are far from them?
3. Why do both those who have sex and the eunuchs, who do not engage in sex, alike deteriorate with respect to the sharpness of their eyes?
4. Why does the human alone grow hair when he begins to be capable of having sex, whereas none of the other animals that have hair do?
5. Why is being barefoot not good with a view to sexual intercourse?
6. Why is a human more exhausted after having sex than other animals?

7. Why, although having sex occurs because of heat, and being afraid and dying cause cooling, do some people when they are in these conditions emit seed?

8. Why should one neither have sex nor vomit nor sneeze nor let out breath unless one is in a turgid state?

9. Why do those who are fasting have sex more quickly?

10. Why do the young, when they first begin to have sex, after the act loathe those with whom they had intercourse?

The first three chapters are on the supposed connection between sexual intercourse and the eyes; but aside from this initial loose grouping, there is absolutely no plan or method behind the order of chapters. Further, there is a fair amount of overlap both within Book 4 (cf. 3 and 32, 6 and 21, 12 and 24, 19 and 22, 25 and 28) and between Book 4 and the rest of the *Problems* (cf. 4.7 and 3.33, 4.16 and 1.50, 4.30 and 30.1, 4.31 and 10.24).

The random order of the chapters typical of virtually all the books, and the frequent repetitions and occasional contradictions among them, strongly suggest that the content of the *Problems* is the result of an accumulation of material over time, in layers, and the product of more than one hand. This must be kept in mind when inquiring into its authenticity, authorship, and date. For example, by contrast, take the *On Colors* in the *corpus Aristotelicum*. It is a fairly unified treatise, of which it makes perfect sense to ask: Was it written by Aristotle? If not, then by whom? And when? (Scholars tend to reject Aristotelian authorship, claiming instead that Theophrastus or some other early Peripatetic was the author. When it was written depends of course on who wrote it.)[2] But if one takes this approach to the *Problems*, the answers cannot be as straightforward.[3]

Was the Problems *written by Aristotle*? Some of the chapters in some of the books very likely were, and he may himself have directed the compilation of (early versions of) some of the books; but he certainly did not write the whole work. This follows from the above reasons for rejecting any one hand authoring the *Problems*, and it finds further support from these considerations: that some of its vocabulary is post-Aristotelian, that some of the views expressed contradict those expressed in Aristotle's authentic works, and that some chapters seem to be raising questions about passages in the works of Theophrastus, who followed Aristotle as the head of the Lyceum.

If it was not written by Aristotle, then by whom? By no one author, but by a number of Peripatetic philosophers working during the century or two following Aristotle's establishment of the Lyceum—perhaps including well-known ones, such as Theophrastus.[4] But this is not to deny

---

[2] See H. B. Gottschalk, "The *de Coloribus* and Its Author," *Hermes* 92, no. 1 (1964): 59–85.

[3] Much of what follows is speculative.

[4] Here, in alphabetical order, are the major figures in the Lyceum after Aristotle, from the fourth to the second century, and thus I believe some of the possible authors of the chapters of the *Problems*: Aristo of Ceos, Aristoxenus of Tarentum, Chamaeleon, Clearchus of Soli, Critolaus of Phaselis, Demetrius of Phalerum, Dicaearchus of Messana, Eudemus of Rhodes, Heraclides of Pontus, Hieronymous of Rhodes, Lyco of Troas, Phaenias of Eresus, Praxiphanes, Strato of Lampsacus, Theophrastus of Eresus.

that an entirely different person or series of people may have organized the work into its present form.

When was it written? Scholarly estimates for the date of the *Problems* range from the third century BC to the sixth century AD.[5] For example, E. S. Forster writes: "As to the date at which the *Problems* reached their final form, it is difficult to dogmatize. The best criterion is that of language, and such forms as πυκνάκις (872a22), ῥᾳδιέστερον (870b37), and εἰδῆσαι (921b26), to take only three examples, point to a date certainly not much earlier than the first century B.C., and probably a good deal later."[6] This may be; but it is important to keep in mind the distinction between when most of the books of the *Problems* were *written* and when it reached its final form. As indicated in the previous paragraph, I believe that the bulk of the material in the *Problems* that has come down to us was likely written from the latter half of the fourth century (when Aristotle was active) to the second century BC. But this does not rule out the possibility or even likelihood that the work was put into its present form much later, and that some of its chapters were added much later as well (though the sixth century AD seems highly improbable).

Much of this is speculative. What more can we say

[5] See the discussions of this issue in Flashar, pp. 356–58, and Louis, vol. 1, pp. xxiii–xxv, and in the work cited in the following note. (Where bibliographical information is not provided, see the list of references to works cited in the notes, on pp. xxx–xxxiii.)

[6] E. S. Forster, "The Pseudo-Aristotelian *Problems*: Their Nature and Composition," *Classical Quarterly* 22, no. 3/4 (1928): 163–65.

about the nature and authorship of this work? There is abundant ancient evidence that Aristotle wrote a work called *Problems*—or, to give the full title that has come down to us in the manuscript tradition, *Physical Problems Arranged According to Kind* (Φυσικὰ προβλήματα κατ' εἶδος συναγωγῆς). First, there is the ancient biographical evidence. For example, Diogenes Laertius attributes to Aristotle a work entitled *Physical (problems) arranged alphabetically*, thirty-eight books—Φυσικῶν (sc. προβλημάτων) κατὰ στοιχεῖον λή (5.26, no. 121)— as does the *Vita Hesychii* (no. 110); and Ptolemy el-Garib attributes to Aristotle a *Problems* in sixty-eight (or twenty-eight) books—Προβλήματα ξή (or κή) (no. 75).

More important, in the *corpus Aristotelicum* there are eight references to a work called the *Problems*. At the opening of *Meteorology* 2.6, Aristotle writes: "Let us now speak about the position of the winds, and which ones are opposite to which, and which can blow simultaneously and which cannot, and what sort and how many there happen to be, and in addition to these about any other conditions that have not been discussed in the *Problems* arranged according to part (μὴ συμβέβηκεν ἐν τοῖς προβλήμασιν εἰρῆσθαι τοῖς κατὰ μέρος)" (363a21–25). This seems to refer to *Pr. 26*, a long book devoted to the winds. Later in the *Meteorology*, Aristotle discusses animals generated in excrement, and adds: "For there is concoction in the upper stomach, but the excretion putrefies in the lower; and the reason for this has been explained in others (ἐν ἑτέροις)"— i.e., in other works or places (381b12–13). According to Alexander of Aphrodisias, in his commentary on the *Meteorology*, the other works are the *Problems* (ἐν τοῖς Προβλήμασι) (*In mete.* 197, 10–20)—and he may be right, as this could refer to *Pr.* 20.12. And in the *Generation of Animals*, in a discussion of the production of many offspring, in contrast to one or a few, Aristotle ends by referring to what "was said in the *Problems*" (εἴρηται . . . ἐν τοῖς προβλήμασιν) (4.4, 772b6–12). Most scholars deny that this is a reference to anything in the extant *Problems*, but I think it might point to *Pr.* 10.14. The five other references in the *corpus*,[7] however, cannot be traced to anything in the extant *Problems*. Further, there are nearly fifty references in other ancient authors to a *Problems* by Aristotle (see frs. 711–12, 721–68 Gigon), most of them in Plutarch, Galen, Apollonius (the paradoxographer), and Aulius Gellius.[8] Though many of these can be traced to the extant *Problems* (I indicate such references in the notes to the translation), most of them cannot.

There seem to be two possibilities, then, in light of the fact that only some of the ancient references (including Aristotle's own) refer to passages in the extant *Problems*. (1) There were two works with (something like) the title *Problems*, one by Aristotle (now lost), and one (by other Peripatetics?) which came down to us in the *corpus Aristotelicum*. On this interpretation, those references to the *Problems* in Aristotle and other ancient authors which cannot be traced to the extant *Problems* must refer to this lost

---

[7] *Somn.Vig.* 2 (456a24–29), *Juv.* 5 (470a15–18), *PA* 3.15 (676a19–21), *GA* 2.8 (747a34–b6), *GA* 4.7 (775b25–776a8).

[8] This number does not include the passages in which Aristotle is referred to but the title of the work is not, though it is likely or certainly the *Problems*. For instance: Cicero *Tusc.* 1.33 and Plutarch *Lys.* 2.5 refer to passages in *Pr.* 30.1, and Plutarch *QC* 3.10 (*Mor.* 659D) might contain a reference to *Pr.* 1.35.

work.[9] But it seems on the face of it odd that some of the *Problems* references in Aristotle would refer to his own (now lost) *Problems* and others to the extant work. This lends support to a second possibility. (2) The *Problems* began as a work by Aristotle—who authored some chapters and perhaps directed the authorship of others—and over the years, and beyond his death, some material was added to this work and other material was removed or otherwise lost.[10] On this interpretation, all of the ancient references are to the same work, but not all of that work survives.

In light of the goal-directed nature of Aristotle's works and the sophistication of the methodology he employs in them, surprisingly little can be said about the purpose and methodology of the *Problems*.[11] But here are a couple of general observations:

1. In the broadest terms, the purpose of the chapters of the *Problems* is to raise questions—about passages in the works of Aristotle or Theophrastus or other Peripatetic philosophers and scientists, about passages in the works of

9 See Flashar, pp. 303–16, and Louis, vol. 1, pp. xxv–xxx.

10 Why would material have been cut? If a specific set of problems was raised as a preliminary stage in writing a treatise on some topic, the material could have been removed after the treatise was written. Louis (vol. 1, pp. xxvi–xxvii) argues that a book of problems concerning fire may have been replaced by Theophrastus' *On Fire*. But this is highly speculative.

11 According to Aristotle's logical works, the concept "problem" has a fairly specific nature and set of functions; see James G. Lennox, *Aristotle's Philosophy of Biology* (Cambridge, 2001), ch. 3, "Aristotelian Problems." But it is not clear that the problems raised in the *Problems* have the same nature or that they serve any specific set of functions.

medical writers (and especially the Hippocratic treatises), and in general about *endoxa* (the reputable opinions in the air at the time, on any number of subjects). But there is no easily discernible deeper purpose that explains—in the case of each book of the *Problems*—why these particular questions were raised. Given the random and repetitive (and at times contradictory) nature of the questions and answers making up the books of the *Problems*, they clearly were not *organized* with a view to any purpose or to achieve any specific methodological goals. That is, the questions and answers never, taken together over the course of a book, represent a progression that achieves some overall aim.

2. As noted earlier, virtually all of the chapters of the *Problems* begin by asking "why" or "on account of what" (διὰ τί); they never ask whether something exists or whether some proposition is true. So the *Problems* is limited in its aims at least to this extent. What are being sought are causal explanations of one sort or another: why certain things are the case; why certain things occur as they do; why certain things have the attributes they do; why people tend to hold certain beliefs; etc. For example: "Why are males, on the whole, larger than females?" (10.8); "Why does the nighttime Boreas wind cease on the third day?" (26.14); "Why is sweat salty?" (2.3); "Why is it considered more just to defend those who have died than those who are living?" (29.9). Further, what is being sought, in most cases, is specifically *material* explanation. For example, in answer to the question why is sweat salty, the author continues: "Is it because it comes from motion and heat, which

separate out what is foreign in the assimilation of the nourishment into blood and flesh? For this is very quickly removed owing to its not belonging, and it evaporates out" (2.3). Or: "Why does one sneeze twice in most cases, and neither once nor many times? Is it because there are two nostrils? So the vessel through which breath flows is divided along to each nostril" (33.3). There is no reference to how perspiration benefits the person or what purpose sneezing twice serves. Nevertheless, in the discussions of living things there is occasional interest in teleological explanation. For example: "Why is having sex the most pleasant activity, and is it so for animals out of necessity or for the sake of something (ἐξ ἀνάγκης ἢ ἕνεκά τινος)?" (4.15); "Why is the tongue of animals never fat? Is it because what is fat is dense, but the tongue is naturally porous, so that it may recognize flavors?" (10.19).

To make further progress on these issues—authorship and date, nature and aim, sources and influences, connections to the works of Aristotle and other philosophers and scientists—what are needed are scholarly commentaries on all of the books of the *Problems*, focusing on language, content, methodology, philosophical presuppositions, similarities and differences with other ancient thinkers, etc. Unfortunately, in the past century commentaries have been written (and none of them recent) only on Books 11 (on voice) and 19 (on music). There have been advances in our understanding of the text and manuscript tradition of the *Problems*, but there is nothing like a scholarly consensus on the nature, authorship, and date for each of its books, and the *Problems* as a whole remains something of a mystery. But if this work receives the scholarly attention given to the rest of the *corpus Aristotelicum*, I believe it has much to tell us about the nature of intellectual activity in the Lyceum, especially after Aristotle.

TRANSLATION

As there was, in my view, no entirely reliable and up-to-date English translation of the *Problems*, I aimed to get mine as close to the original as possible while remaining within the bounds of decent English—though at times I suspect I pushed these limits. I especially sought to remedy one major defect of Hett's original Loeb, by translating key scientific and philosophic terms consistently—at least within the same book.

I have for the most part limited the notes to the translation to the following: (1) indication of textual problems; (2) clarification of especially unclear passages; (3) identification of quotes, obscure locations, uncommon plants, etc.; and (4) identification of *sources*—i.e., the particular texts that (possibly) gave rise to the questions raised.[12] I could not, however, point out every connection between some line and a similar passage(s) in the *corpus Aristotelicum*, as that would have generated far too many notes for a Loeb volume.

[12] In the notes to the translation, "source" is shorthand for "possible or likely or definite source." For example, the note at the outset of *Pr.* 1.23 includes "Source: Thphr. *Vent.* 57," which means that Theophrastus' *On Winds*, ch. 57, is the (likely) source for *Pr.* 1.23. (Abbreviations of ancient authors and texts are, where possible, taken from Liddell-Scott-Jones.)

TEXT

Introducing his collection of notes on the text of the *Problems*, which make up ch. 15 of his *Aristotelica*, Herbert Richards (1915, p. 133) writes:

> The text, which is at present in a very poor way, rests mainly on the Oxford edition of Bekker (1837),[13] and Bussemaker's edition (1857) in the Firmin Didot Aristotle. My notes will show some of the things which they allowed to pass not only without correction but without any indication of discontent.

Building on the work of Bekker and Bussemaker, Richards' notes did contribute to making the text a little less poor. Progress was also made, and brought to light a few years after Richards' complaint, in the form of the 1922 Teubner edition of the text (Ruelle being the main editor, though he was succeeded after his death by Knoellinger, who was in turn succeeded by Klek).[14] Forster's 1927 translation contains scores of notes that are useful to anyone trying to make sense of this text. Flashar's 1962 German translation, with an extensive introduction and useful commentary, advanced our knowledge of the nature of the work and made some contributions to improving the text. Further and significant advances were made by Pierre

13 A one-volume version of Bekker's edition of the *Problems* was published by Oxford University Press in 1837.

14 In my textual notes, I always refer to Ruelle, though in the Teubner *apparatus criticus*, sometimes a reading or emendation is attributed specifically to one of the other editors.

Louis and especially by Gerardo Marenghi, in their preparations of new editions of the text.

In my work on the *Problems*, I often found the text to be—whatever advances made since 1915—still "in a very poor way." I myself did little to advance our understanding of the text.[15] I did not consult any manuscripts but relied exclusively on the work of other scholars (see References for details). Marenghi's edition is my base text where available, i.e., for the following twenty books: 1, 6–9, 11–14, 19, 27–28, 31–38. For the rest, Louis is my base text.[16] In important cases, where the reports of Marenghi and Louis conflict, I mention both in the textual notes. Further, I sometimes mention manuscript readings reported by Ferrini but not mentioned elsewhere.[17] Divider lines in my text mark (|) the beginning of every fifth line of a Bekker column and (||) the beginning of a new column (a or b); when Bekker's lineation would otherwise split a word, the divider appears after that word.

[15] Occasionally I think I had something original to suggest. Indications of these suggestions can be found in the notes to the text, though some of them require lengthier explanation than the Loeb format allows. I may eventually discuss them elsewhere.

[16] Louis relies for the most part on the four major manuscripts—Y^a C^a X^a Ap—though he occasionally cites others (Q K^a N^a O^a r s t u v w x). Marenghi makes use of a broader range of texts. Scholars agree that the oldest manuscript (Y^a) is the most important.

[17] The primary value of Ferrini's 2003 essay, for my purposes, is its reports on readings in the *recentiores* which anticipated certain emendations of modern scholars, who did not rely on these manuscripts.

For a history of the text and the nature of the manuscripts, see Louis (vol. 1, pp. xxxv–lii), Ferrini, and the works of Marenghi.[18] The following division of the manuscripts into four families is Marenghi's.

SIGLA

α

Y^a = *Parisinus gr.* 2036 (saec. X)
N^a = *Marcianus gr.* 215 (saec. XV)
C^a = *Laurentianus gr.* 87, 4 (saec. XIII)
H = *Hauniensis gr.* 1628 (saec. XIV)
Q = *Marcianus gr.* 200 (saec. XV)
w = *Laurentianus gr.* 87, 15 (saec. XVI)
E = *Oxoniensis Collegii Corporis Christi* 113 (saec. XV)
R = *Roman. Angelicanus gr.* 78 (saec. XV)
A = *Londinensis Additional gr.* 23927 (saec. XV)
v = *Laurentianus gr.* 87, 20 (saec. XIV)

β

K^a = *Marcianus gr.* IV, 58 (saec. XIII)
O^a = *Marcianus gr.* 216 (saec. XV)
s = *Vaticanus Palatinus gr.* 164 (saec. XV)

---

18 In addition to the introductions to his works cited in the References, see also G. Marenghi, "La tradizione manoscritta dei *Problemata Physica* Aristotelici," *Bolletino del Comitato per la Preparazione della Edizione Nazionale dei Classici Greci e Latini* 9 (1961): 47–57.

γ

G = *Berolinensis* 890 (saec. XIV)
r = *Vaticanus Urbinas gr.* 50 (saec. XV)
M = *Mutinensis gr.* 135 (saec. XV)
Ap = *perditus quo Apostolios scriptor usus est*[19]
    Ap^a = *Parisinus suppl. gr.* 204 (saec. XV)
    Ap^b = *Parisinus gr.* 1865 (saec. XV)
X^a = *Vaticanus gr.* 1283 (saec. XV)
c = *Neapolitanus gr.* 320 (saec. XVI)
u = *Vaticanus Reginensis gr.* 124 (saec. XV)
a^m = *Ambrosianus gr.* 750 (saec. XVI)
p = *Vaticanus gr.* 1480 (saec. XVI)
d = *Neapolitanus gr.* 322 (saec. XVI)

δ

B = *Bononiensis* 3635 (saec. XIV)
x = *Marcianus gr.* 259 (saec. XIV)
D = *Oxoniensis Collegii Novi* 233 (saec. XV)
A^m = *Ambrosianus gr.* 67 (saec. XV)
L = *Harleianus gr.* 6295 (saec. XIV)
t = *Vaticanus Palatinus gr.* 295 (saec. XV–XVI)

---

[19] I follow Louis, who uses "Ap" to designate the reading common to Ap^a and Ap^b. But in Marenghi's list, Ap = *Parisinus gr.* 1865 and S = *Parisinus suppl. gr.* 204.

Manuscripts cited in this volume but not mentioned and placed in a family by Marenghi:

Monac.361 = *Monacensis gr.* 361 (saec. XIII)
Lambeth.1204 = *Lambethanus* 1204 (saec. XIV)
Alex.175 = *Alexandrinus* 175 (saec. XIV–XV)
Y^e = *Parisinus gr.* 985 (saec. XV)
P^c = *Parisinus gr.* 1884 (saec. XVI)
Berol.148 = *Berolinensis* 148 (saec. XVI)
Vat.1904 = *Vaticanus gr.* 1904 (saec. XVI)
Marc.604 = *Marcianus gr.* 604 (saec. XVI)
Burnel.67 = *Burnelianus* 67 (saec. XVII)

Miscellaneous Sources

[Arist./Alex.] *Sup.Pr.* = *Pseudo-Aristoteles (Pseudo-Alexander), Supplementa Problematorum*, edited by Sophia Kapetanaki and Robert W. Sharples (Berlin: Walter de Gruyter, 2006)

Nicasius = Nicasius Ellebodius, textual citations in his notes to the Latin translations in *Ambrosianus* 609 and 739 (saec. XVI) [see Ferrini, p. 118]

PPA = *Problemata Physica Arabica*—the version of Hunain ibn Isḥāq (saec. IX) [=*Pr.* 1–15], in L. Filius, ed. *The* Problemata Physica *Attributed to Aristotle: The Arabic Version of Hunain ibn Isḥāq and the Hebrew Version of Moses ibn Tibbon* (Leiden, 1999) [Arabic text with English translation, pp. 1–661]

Superscript Abbreviations

[ac] = ante correctiones
[pc] = post correctiones
[mg] = in margines
[s] = supra vel sub lineam

REFERENCES

A. Pre-Eighteenth Century
(in Chronological Order)

Barth. = Bartholomew of Messina (thirteenth-century Latin translation)

Trap. = George of Trebizond (G. Trapezuntius) (1452 Latin translation)

Gaza = Theodore of Gaza (1454 Latin translation; rev. ed. 1475)

Aldine = Aldus Manutius (1497 editio princeps)

Erasmus = D. Erasmus (1531 edition of the text)

Sylburg = F. Sylburg (1585 edition of the text)

Casaubon = I. Casaubon (1590 edition of the text, with Latin translation of Gaza)

Septalius = L. Septalius (1632 edition of the text, with Latin translation)

B. Eighteenth–Twenty-First Century
(in Alphabetical Order)

Barker = A. Barker, private correspondence (2009)

Barnes = J. Barnes, ed., *The Complete Works of Aristotle:*

The Revised Oxford Translation, vol. 2 (Princeton, 1984)

Bekker = I. Bekker, *Aristotelis Opera*, vol. 2 (Berlin, 1831)

Bojesen = E. F. Bojesen, *De problematis Aristotelis scripsit et sectionem XIX commentario instruxit* (Copenhagen, 1836)

Bonitz = H. Bonitz, *Aristotelische Studien*, vol. 4 (Vienna, 1866)

Bowen = A. Bowen, private correspondence (2009)

B.-St.H. = J. Barthélémy-Saint Hilaire, *Les Problèmes d'Aristote* (Paris, 1891)

Bussemaker = U. C. Bussemaker's edition of the *Problemata*, in Dübner, Bussemaker, and Heitz, eds., *Aristotelis Opera Omnia Graeca et Latine* IV (Paris, 1869)

Chabanon = M. P. G. de Chabanon, *Mémoires sur la Problèmes d'Aristote Concernant la Musique* (Paris, 1779)

D-K = H. Diels, *Die Fragmente der Vorsokratiker* (Berlin, 1903), revised by Walther Kranz, 6th ed. (Berlin, 1952)

Eichtal-Reinach = E. d'Eichtal and T. Reinach, "Notes sur les problèmes musicaux attribués à Aristote," *Revue des Études Grecques* 5 (1892)

Ferrini = M. F. Ferrini, "Nota al testo dei *Problemata* che fanno parte del *Corpus Aristotelicum*. La Tradizione Manoscritta." *Annali dell'Istituto Universitario Orientale di Napoli: Sezione Filologica-Letteraria* 25 (2003)

Flashar = H. Flashar, *Aristoteles: Problemata Physica—Aristoteles Werke in Deutscher Übersetzung Herausgegaben von E. Grumach*, vol. 19 (Berlin, 1962)

Forster = E. S. Forster, *Problemata—The Works of Aris-*

totle Translated into English Under the Editorship of W. D. Ross, vol. 7 (Oxford, 1927)

Gevaert-Vollgraff = F. A. Gevaert and J. C. Vollgraff, *Les problèmes musicaux d'Aristote* (Ghent, 1903)

Graf = E. Graf, *De Graecorum veterum re musica* (Marburg, 1889)

Heath = T. Heath, *Mathematics in Aristotle* (Oxford, 1949)

Hett = W. S. Hett, *Aristotle: Problems*, 2. vols. Loeb Classical Library (Cambridge, MA, 1936–1937)

Jan = C. von Jan, *Musici scriptores Graeci* (Leipzig,1895)

Louis = P. Louis, *Aristote: Problèmes*, 3. vols. (Paris, 1991–1994) [Budé/Les Belles Lettres]

Marenghi[1] = G. Marenghi, *Aristotele: Problemi di musicali* (Florence, 1957) [Greek text with Italian translation of Book 19]

Marenghi[2]= G. Marenghi, *Aristotele: Problemi di fonazione e di acustica* (Naples, 1962) [Greek text with Italian translation of Book 11]

Marenghi[3] = G. Marenghi, *Aristotele: Problemi di medicina* (Milan, 1965; rev. 1999) [Greek text with Italian translation of Books 1, 6–9, 14, 27–28, 31–38]

Marenghi[4] = G. Marenghi, "Per un'edizione critica dell' Ἀριστοτέλους Προβλημάτα Ἐπιτομὴ Φυσικῶν," *Bollettino del Comitato per la Preparazione dell'Edizione Nazionale dei Classici Greci e Latini* 19 (1971–1972): 101–29 [discussion of textual problems in Book 10]

Marenghi[5] = G. Marenghi, *[Aristotele]: Profumi e miasmi* (Naples, 1991) [Greek text with Italian trans. of Books 12–13]

Monro = D. B. Monro, "On Arist. *Prob.* 19.12," *Journal of Philology* 1 (1868)

Platt = A. Platt, "Notes on Aristotle," *Journal of Philology* 32 (1913)

Prantl = C. Prantl, *Über die Probleme des Aristoteles* (Munich, 1850)

Richards = H. Richards, *Aristotelica* (London, 1915)

Ruelle = C. Ruelle, H. Knoellinger, and J. Klek, eds., *Aristotelis Quae Ferunter Problemata Physica* (Leipzig, 1922) [Teubner]

Stumpf = C. Stumpf, *Die pseudo-arist. Probleme über Musik* (Berlin, 1896)

ARISTOTLE'S
PHYSICAL PROBLEMS
ARRANGED ACCORDING TO
KIND

BOOK I

INTRODUCTION

In the opening chapter of the *Parva Naturalia*, Aristotle writes that "the natural scientist should know the first principles concerning health and disease" (φυσικοῦ . . . περὶ ὑγιείας καὶ νόσου τὰς πρώτας ἰδεῖν ἀρχάς) (*Sens.* 436a17–18). In another treatise in this collection, he promises to speak later "concerning disease and health" (*Long.* 464b32–33); and in the final chapter, he says: "Concerning health and disease, not only a physician but also a natural scientist should to some extent speak of their causes" (*Resp.* 480b22–24). So it seems Aristotle wrote, or planned to write, something on medicine (perhaps entitled *On Health and Disease*). In the *Parts of Animals*, after describing how certain physiological processes can give rise to diseases in the brain, he says: "It is appropriate to speak of these matters in the *Origins [or 'Principles'] of Diseases* (ἐν ταῖς τῶν νόσων ἀρχαῖς),[1] to the extent that the natural philosopher should speak about them" (653a8–10). Diogenes Laertius' list of Aristotle's works mentions a *Medicine* (Ἰατρικά) in two books (5.25); the *Vita Hesychii* refers to an *On Medicine* (Περὶ ἰατρικῆς) in two books and another *On Medicine* in six books (nos. 98 and 167). Most interesting in the present context, the *Vita Marciana* at-

[1] This is likely, but need not be, the title of a work.

3

tributes to Aristotle a work called *Medical Problems* (τὰ ἰατρικὰ προβλήματα) (4).[2] None of Aristotle's medical treatises is extant.[3]

One might be tempted to equate this last item with *Pr.* 1 (Ὅσα ἰατρικά);[4] but I think the most we can reasonably conclude is that remnants of *Medical Problems* may survive in Book 1, and that Aristotle's medical writings generally could have been the source for some of its fifty-seven chapters. This is all the more likely given that, so far as we know, there were no *medical* writings by other early Peripatetics that could have served as sources for these chapters.[5]

What else can we say about its sources? Various Hippocratic writings prompted the discussions in some of these

---

[2] Aristotle mentions well over a dozen times a treatise of his called *Dissections* (Ἀνατομαί) (e.g., *Somn. Vig.* 456b2, *PA* 666a9), though this was likely more a work of biology than of medicine. See DL 5.25 and frs. 295–324 Gigon. In *Acute Affections*, Caelius Aurelianus (Roman, fifth century AD) refers to a work by Aristotle entitled *On Remedies* (*De adiutoriis*) (2.13, 87).

[3] Although its authenticity is disputed, one exception may be *HA* 10 (also known as "On Sterility"; cf. DL 5.25). See P. van der Eijk, *Medicine and Philosophy in Classical Antiquity* (Cambridge, 2005), ch. 9, "On Sterility ('Hist. an.' 10)," a medical work by Aristotle?" The "fragments" of Aristotle placed under the heading Ἰατρικά (frs. 353–62 Gigon) are meager.

[4] G. Marenghi, *Aristotele: Problemi di medicina* (Milan, 1965; rev. 1999), 7–14, and P. Louis, *Aristote: Problèmes*, vol. 1 (Paris, 1991), 1–8, argue for the authenticity of the bulk of *Pr.* 1.

[5] But note the *Anonymi Londinensis Iatrica*, a papyrus containing a Peripatetic doxography of ancient medicine adapted from a work by Aristotle or his student Meno.

chapters (e.g., *Aër* 10 is probably the source for *Pr.* 1.8–12 and 19–20). Three chapters were possible responses to works of Theophrastus (e.g., *Lass.* 17 is the source for *Pr.* 1.39). The medical writings of Diocles of Carystus (fourth century) may have been another source. There seem to be few connections between *Pr.* 1 and the extant works of Aristotle.

Book 1 is the second longest in the *Problems*. It can be divided into two parts: chs. 1–29 (diseases and their causes) and chs. 30–57 (the treatment of diseases). In fact, the manuscripts have—between chs. 29 and 30—some version of a subtitle: "Those [*problems*] helpful with a view to healing" (ὅσα βοηθηματικὰ πρὸς ἴασιν).[6]

---

[6] There may be some connection between the second part of *Pr.* 1 and the *On Remedies* (*De adiutoriis*) attributed to Aristotle (see n. 2). The only other subtitle in the *Problems* is in Book 15 (in some mss.).

ΟΣΑ ΙΑΤΡΙΚΑ

1. Διὰ τί αἱ μεγάλαι ὑπερβολαὶ νοσώδεις; ἢ ὅτι ὑπερβολὴν ἢ ἔλλειψιν ποιοῦσιν; τοῦτο δ᾽ ἦν ἡ νόσος.

2. Διὰ τί δὲ τὰς νόσους πολλάκις ὑγιάζουσιν ὅταν |
5 πολὺ ἐκστῇ τις; καὶ ἐνίων ἰατρῶν τοιαύτη ἡ τέχνη·
ὑπερβολαῖς γὰρ ἰῶνται οἴνου ἢ ὕδατος ἢ ἄλμης ἢ
σίτου ἢ λιμοῦ. ἢ ὅτι ἐναντία ἀλλήλοις τὰ τὴν νόσον
ποιοῦντα; εἰς τὸ μέσον οὖν ἄγει θάτερον ἑκάτερα.[1]

3. Διὰ τί αἱ τῶν ὡρῶν μεταβολαὶ καὶ πνεύματα
10 ἐπιτείνουσιν | ἢ παύουσι καὶ κρίνουσι τὰς νόσους καὶ
ποιοῦσιν; ἢ ὅτι θερμαὶ καὶ ψυχραί εἰσι καὶ ὑγραὶ καὶ
ξηραί, αἱ δὲ νόσοι τούτων εἰσὶν ὑπερβολαί, ἡ δ᾽ ὑγεία
ἰσότης; ἐὰν οὖν δι᾽ ὑγρότητα καὶ ψύξιν, ἡ ἐναντία ὥρα
παύει· ἐὰν δὲ μὴ[2] ἐναντία ὥρα ἔχηται, ἡ ὁμοία κρᾶσις
15 ἐπιγενομένη ἐπέτεινε καὶ ἀνεῖλεν. | διὰ ταῦτα δὲ καὶ
νοσίζουσι τοὺς ὑγιαίνοντας, ὅτι μεταβάλλουσαι λύ-
ουσι τὴν κρᾶσιν· ἅμα γὰρ ταῖς οἰκείαις ὥραις καὶ

---

[1] ἑκάτερα β aᵐ : ἑκατέρου cett. codd. : ἑκάτερον Louis ex Gaza

[2] μὴ Kᵃ² Xᵃ u² aᵐ Barth. : om. cett. codd.

---

[1] For Pr. 1.1–2, see Pr. 5.33, 30.8 (936a37), Top. 139b21,

MEDICAL PROBLEMS

1.[1] Why are great excesses disease-producing? Is it because they produce either excess or defect? And these *are* disease.

2. But why do people often cure diseases by making the patient go through a great deal of change? Indeed, this is the technique of some physicians; for they heal by excesses of wine, water, salt, food, or hunger. Is it because the things that produce disease are the opposites of one another? Therefore each excess or defect leads the other to the mean.

3.[2] Why do the changes of season and the winds intensify or check, and bring to a crisis and produce, diseases? Is it because they are hot and cold, wet and dry, and diseases are excesses of these, whereas health is their equilibrium? Therefore, if a disease is due to moisture or cold, the opposite season checks it; but if a season that is not opposite follows, the addition of a mixture of similar qualities intensifies the disease and produces death. This is why such seasons even cause disease in the healthy, because by changing they disturb the mixture; for at the same time health is

145b8, *GA* 738a27–33, *EN* 1104a11–18, *Rh.* 1361b3–6. See also Pl., *Ti.* 86a, and Hp. *Vict.* 1.2, *Flat.* 1.

2 See Hp. *Aër* 1–11, *Aph.* 3, *Hum.* 12–16, *Vict.* 3.68.

ἡλικίαις καὶ τόποις αὐξάνεται. διὸ δεῖ ἐν ταῖς μεταβολαῖς μάλιστα διακυβερνᾶν. ὁ δὲ καθόλου περὶ τῶν
ὡρῶν εἴρηται, καὶ κατὰ μέρος τὸ αὐτὸ αἴτιον. αἱ γὰρ
20 τῶν πνευμάτων | μεταβολαὶ καὶ τῶν ἡλικιῶν καὶ τό-
πων ὥρας τινός εἰσι μεταβολαί. διὸ καὶ ταῦτα ἐπιτείνει καὶ παύει καὶ κρίνει καὶ ποιεῖ, ὥσπερ αἱ ὧραι,
καὶ ἐπιτολαὶ τῶν ἄστρων, ὥσπερ Ὠρίων καὶ Ἀρκτοῦ-
ρος καὶ Πλειὰς καὶ Κύων, [ὥσπερ][3] πνευμάτων καὶ
ὑδάτων καὶ εὐδιῶν καὶ χειμώνων καὶ ἀλέας.[4] |

25 4. Διὰ τί ἐν ταῖς μεταβολαῖς τῶν ὡρῶν ἐμέτοις οὐ
δεῖ χρῆσθαι; ἢ ἵνα μὴ γένηται συντάραξις διαφόρων
γινομένων τῶν περιττωμάτων διὰ τὰς μεταβολάς; ||

859b 5. Διὰ τί καὶ οἱ κιβδηλιῶντες καὶ οἱ ὑπὸ λιμοῦ
πονοῦντες[5] τοὺς πόδας οἰδοῦσιν; ἢ διὰ τὴν σύντηξιν
ἀμφότεροι; συντήκονται δ᾽ οἱ μὲν διὰ λιμὸν διὰ τὸ
ὅλως μὴ λαμβάνειν τροφήν, οἱ δὲ κιβδηλιῶντες διὰ τὸ
μηδὲν ἀπολαύειν ἧς λαμβάνουσι τροφῆς. |

---

³ [ὥσπερ] Ruelle : ὥσπερ codd : αἰτίαι οὖσαι Forster ex
Gaza : αἰτίαι Hmg   ⁴ ὥσπερ—ἀλέας secl. Flashar
⁵ πονοῦντες Yª : om. cett. codd.

---

3 From the translation of Gaza.

4 See Thphr.(?), Sign. 1–7.   5 See Hp. Aph. 1.2.

6 "Residue" (περίττωμα, περίττωσις) is a technical term in
Aristotle's biology (contrasted with "colliquation"). In GA 1.18, he
writes: "I call residue that which is left over from nourishment,
but colliquation that which has been secreted out of the growth
material by a dissolving that is contrary to nature" (724b26–28).

7 I retain Hett's "those with jaundice" (οἱ κιβδηλιῶντες),

improved by suitable seasons, ages and places. This is why one should carefully steer one's course especially at such changeable seasons. And what has been said about the seasons generally, the same cause applies in particular cases. For changes of wind, ages and places are in some respects changes of season. And this is why these things intensify and check and bring to a crisis and produce diseases, just as seasons and the rising of the stars do, such as Orion, Arcturus, the Pleiades, and the Dog Star, (which are also the causes of)[3] winds, rain, fair weather, storms, and warmth.[4]

4.[5] Why shouldn't one use emetics at the changes of the seasons? Is it in order that there may be no disturbance when the residues[6] are varying because of these changes?

5. Why should both those with jaundice[7] and those suffering from starvation have swollen feet? Are both due to colliquation?[8] Now those who have swollen feet owing to starvation undergo colliquation because they receive no nourishment at all, whereas the jaundiced do so because they derive no benefit from the nourishment they take.

---

though to whom this actually refers is unclear. The word derives from κιβδήλος ("false")—often used in connection with counterfeit currency (see EN 1165b12), which has led to the idea that it here refers to people who look like adulterated gold. According to the Suda (K 1574), ὠχροί ("pale") is a synonym for κιβδηλιῶντες; so both "who are pale" and "who are anemic" are possible alternatives to "with jaundice." Flashar thinks the term refers to Addison's disease (Bronzekrankheit), symptoms of which include darkening of the skin, vomiting, and diarrhea.

[8] "Colliquation" (σύντηξις, σύντηγμα) is a technical term in Aristotle's biology. See n. 6. "Colliquation" can refer to the material secreted, or to the process (as it does here).

5   6. Διὰ τί τῶν ἀπὸ χολῆς νοσημάτων ⟨ὄντων⟩[6] ἐν τῷ
θέρει (πυρέττουσι γὰρ μάλιστα ἐν τῷ θέρει) τὰ ὀξέα
ἀπὸ χολῆς ὄντα[7] ἐν τῷ χειμῶνι γίνεται μᾶλλον; ἢ ὅτι[8]
μετὰ πυρετοῦ ὄντα ὀξέα ἐστὶ διὰ τὸ βίαια εἶναι, ἡ δὲ
βία παρὰ φύσιν; ὑγραινομένων γάρ τινων τόπων
10   θερμὴ φλεγμασία γίνεται· ἡ δὲ | φλεγμασία ὑπερ-
βολὴ θερμότητος οὖσα ποιεῖ τοὺς πυρετούς. ἐν μὲν οὖν
τῷ θέρει ξηραὶ καὶ θερμαί εἰσιν αἱ νόσοι, ἐν δὲ τῷ
χειμῶνι ὑγραὶ καὶ θερμαί, διὸ ὀξεῖαι· ταχέως γὰρ
ἀναιροῦσιν· οὐ γὰρ θέλει πέττεσθαι διὰ τὸ πλῆθος τοῦ
περιττώματος. |

15   7. Διὰ τί ποτε ὁ λοιμὸς μόνη τῶν νόσων μάλιστα
τοὺς πλησιάζοντας τοῖς θεραπευομένοις προσαναπίμ-
πλησιν; ἢ ὅτι μόνη τῶν νόσων κοινή ἐστιν ἅπασιν,
ὥστε διὰ τοῦτο πᾶσιν ἐπιφέρει τὸν λοιμόν, ὅσοι φαύλως ἔχοντες προϋπάρχουσιν. καὶ γὰρ διὰ τὸ ὑπέκ-
20   καυμα τῆς νόσου τῆς παρὰ τῶν θεραπευομένων | γινο-
μένης ταχέως ὑπὸ τοῦ πράγματος ἁλίσκονται.

8. Διὰ τί τοῦ χειμῶνος βορείου γενομένου, ἐὰν τὸ
ἔαρ ἔπομβρον γένηται καὶ νότιον, τὸ θέρος νοσῶδες

---

6 ⟨ὄντων⟩ Forster ex Gaza
7 [ἀπὸ χολῆς ὄντα] Marenghi[3]
8 ὅτι Cᵃ : διότι Yᵃ mg et cett. codd.

---

9 Hp. *Acut.* 5 lists the acute diseases as follows: pleurisy, pneu-
monia, phrenitis, and intense fever. Acute diseases, it is claimed,
cause many more deaths than all the other diseases combined.

6. Why, although diseases due to bile occur in the summer (for people have fevers especially in the summer), are acute diseases[9] that are due to bile more frequent in the winter? Is it because, as they occur with fever, they are acute through being violent, and violence is contrary to nature? For feverish inflammation occurs when certain regions are moist, and inflammation, being an excess of heat, produces fevers. In the summer, therefore, diseases are dry and hot, and in the winter moist and hot, which is why they are acute; for they quickly cause death, because they will not admit of concoction,[10] owing to the quantity of residues.

7. Why does the plague alone among diseases particularly infect those who come close to people being treated for it? Is it because it alone among diseases is common to all people, so that for this reason it carries the plague to all those who are in poor health to begin with? Indeed, because of the inflamed material arising from those who are being treated for the disease, they are quickly attacked by this.

8.[11] Why, when the winter comes with a Boreas,[12] if the spring comes rainy and with a Notos,[13] is the summer dis-

---

[10] The process of concoction (πέττειν, "to concoct/cook/digest/ripen") is an important one in Aristotle's biology (especially in the *GA*). It refers, for example, to the way in which an animal's natural heat processes nourishment (in the case of digestion) or transforms blood into semen.

[11] The likely source for *Pr.* 1.8–12 is Hp. *Aër* 10. See also *Aph.* 3.11–14.

[12] I.e., with a prevalent north wind.

[13] I.e., with a prevalent south wind.

11

γίνεται πυρετοῖς καὶ ὀφθαλμίαις; ἢ ὅτι τά τε σώματα
ἐκδέχεται τὸ θέρος πολλὴν ἔχοντα ἀλλοτρίαν ὑγρό-
25 τητα, καὶ ἡ γῆ καὶ ὁ τόπος | ἐν ᾧ ἂν οἰκῶσι, γίνεται
ἔφυδρος καὶ τοιοῦτος οἷοι λέγονται οἱ ἀεὶ νοσώδεις
τόποι; πρῶτον μὲν οὖν ὀφθαλμίαι γίνονται τηκομένης
τῆς περὶ τὴν κεφαλὴν περιττώσεως, ἔπειτα πυρετοί. ‖
860a δεῖ γὰρ νοῆσαι ὅτι τὸ αὐτὸ καὶ θερμότατον γίνεται καὶ
ψυχρότατον, οἷον ὕδωρ καὶ λίθος τὸ μὲν ζεῖ, ὁ δὲ κάει⁹
μᾶλλον. ἔν τε οὖν ἀέρι πνίγη γίνεται θερμαινομένου
τοῦ ἀέρος διὰ πάχος, καὶ ἐν τοῖς σώμασιν ὡσαύτως
5 πνίγη καὶ καύματα, | τὸ δ' ἐν σώματι καῦμα πυρετός
ἐστιν, ἐν δ' ὀφθαλμοῖς ὀφθαλμίαι. ὅλως δὲ καὶ ἡ
μεταβολὴ ἰσχυρὰ οὖσα τὰ σώματα φθείρει, ὅταν τοῦ
ἔαρος¹⁰ ὑγροῦ ὄντος εὐθὺς ἐπιλαμβάνῃ τὸ θέρος θερμὸν ὂν καὶ ξηρόν. ἔτι δὲ χαλεπώτερον, ἐὰν καὶ τὸ
10 θέρος ἔπομβρον γένηται. ἔχει γὰρ ὁ ἥλιος ὕλην | ἣν
ποιήσει ζεῖν καὶ ἐν τοῖς σώμασιν καὶ ἐν τῇ γῇ καὶ
ἀέρι· διὸ γίνονται πυρετοὶ καὶ ὀφθαλμίαι.

9. Διὰ τί, ἐὰν ὁ χειμὼν νότιος γένηται καὶ ἔπομ-
βρος, τὸ δ' ἔαρ αὐχμηρὸν καὶ βόρειον, νοσῶδες γίνεται καὶ τὸ ἔαρ καὶ τὸ θέρος; ἢ ὅτι ἐν μὲν τῷ χειμῶνι
15 διὰ τὴν ἀλέαν καὶ | ὑγρότητα ὁμοίως τὰ σώματα
διάκειται τῇ ὥρᾳ; ὑγρὰ γὰρ ἀνάγκη εἶναι καὶ οὐ
συνεστηκότα. οὕτω δ' ἐχόντων, τὸ ἔαρ ψυχρὸν ὂν
ἔπηξεν καὶ ἐσκλήρυνεν αὐτὰ διὰ τὸν αὐχμόν, ὥστε
ταῖς μὲν κυούσαις ὁ τόκος ὁ ἐαρινὸς εἰς ἐκτρώσεις
γίνεται διὰ τὴν θερμασίαν καὶ τὸν σφακελισμὸν τὸν
20 γινόμενον | ὑπὸ τῆς ξηρᾶς ψυχρότητος, ἄτε οὐκ ἐκκρι-

ease-producing, with fevers and eye disease? Is it because the summer receives bodies that contain much foreign moisture, and the earth (and so the place in which people live) becomes waterlogged and of the kind described as permanently disease-producing? First, eye disease occurs when the residues around the head melt, and then there is fever. For one must realize that the same thing can come to be both very hot and very cold—for instance water and stone, of which the former boils and the latter heats up more (*than other things*). Therefore, in the air it is stifling when the air grows hot due to its density, and similarly in bodies there is stifling and intense heat, and intense heat in the body is fever and in the eyes it is eye disease. In general, change that is powerful destroys bodies, when a summer that is hot and dry immediately follows a spring that has been moist. But it is more dangerous still, if the summer is also rainy. For the sun encounters matter which it will cause to boil both in bodies and in the earth and air; this is why fevers and eye disease occur.

9. Why, if the winter comes rainy and with a Notos, and the spring comes dry and with a Boreas, are both the spring and the summer disease-producing? Is it because in winter, owing to warmth and moisture, bodies are in a state similar to the season? For they must be moist and not compacted. In these conditions, the spring—being cold—solidifies and hardens the bodies owing to its dryness. Consequently, in pregnant women childbirth in spring tends toward miscarriage owing to the heating and the mortification that come from the dry cold, because the moisture

---

9 τὸ μὲν ζεῖ, ὁ δὲ κάει Forster ex Gaza : ὁ μὲν ζεῖ, τὸ δὲ κάει codd. : τὸ μὲν ζεῖ, τὸ δὲ κάει Marenghi³

10 ἔαρος β : ἀέρος cett. codd.

13

νομένης τῆς ὑγρότητος, τὰ δὲ κυόμενα παιδία ἀσθενῆ
γίνεται καὶ πηρὰ διὰ τὴν ὑπερβολὴν τοῦ ψύχους·
συμβέβηκε γὰρ τότε γεννώμενα ἐν εὐδίᾳ καὶ συστῆ-
ναι καὶ τραφῆναι ἐν τῇ τεκούσῃ. τοῖς δ' ἄλλοις, ἅτε ἐν
25   τῷ ἔαρι οὐκ ἀποκαθαρθέντος τοῦ φλέγματος | ⟨διὰ⟩[11]
τὴν ὑπερβολήν, ὃ συμβαίνει ὅταν ἀλεεινὸν γένηται,
ἀλλὰ διὰ ψύχος συστάντος, ὅταν ἐπιλάβῃ τὸ θέρος
καὶ ἡ ἀλέα τήκουσα βίᾳ, τοῖς μὲν χολώδεσι καὶ
ξηροῖς, διὰ τὸ μὴ διερὰ εἶναι τὰ σώματα αὐτοῖς ἀλλὰ
τὴν φύσιν αὖον ἔχειν, γίνονται μὲν ὑγρότητες, αὗται
30   δὲ λεπταί, ὥστε ὀφθαλμίαις | ξηραῖς ἁλίσκονται, οἱ δὲ
φλεγματώδεις βράγχοις καὶ εἰς τὸν πνεύμονα κατάρ-
ροις. ταῖς γυναιξὶ δὲ δυσεντερίαι γίνονται διὰ τὴν
ὑγρότητα καὶ ψυχρότητα τῆς φύσεως, τοῖς δὲ γεραι-
τέροις ἀποπληξίαι, ὅταν ἀθρόον λυθὲν ὑγρὸν ἐπιπέσῃ
καὶ δι' ἀσθένειαν τοῦ συμφύτου θερμοῦ παγῇ. |

35   10. Διὰ τί, ἐὰν μὲν τὸ θέρος αὐχμηρὸν γένηται καὶ
βόρειον,[12] τὸ δὲ μετόπωρον ἐναντίον, ὑγρὸν καὶ νότιον,[13] ἐν τῷ χειμῶνι κεφαλαλγίαι τε γίνονται καὶ βράγ-
860b   χοι καὶ βῆχες, ‖ καὶ τελευτῶσιν εἰς φθίσεις; ἢ ὅτι
λαμβάνει ὕλην πολλὴν ὁ χειμών, ὥστ' αὐτῷ ἔργον
ἐστὶ πῆξαι τὴν ὑγρότητα καὶ φλέγμα ποιῆσαι; ἐν μὲν
οὖν ταῖς κεφαλαῖς ὅταν ὑγρασία γένηται, βάρη ποιεῖ,
5   ἐὰν δ' ᾖ πολλὴ καὶ | ψυχρά, σφακελισμούς· ἐὰν δὲ διὰ
πλῆθος μὴ πήξῃ, ῥεῖ εἰς τὸν ἐχόμενον τόπον, ὅθεν αἱ
βῆχες καὶ οἱ βράγχοι καὶ αἱ φθόαι γίνονται.

11 ⟨διὰ⟩ Nicasius

is not secreted and the embryo becomes weak and deformed owing to the excess of cold; for children born at this time in fine weather are congealed and nourished in the mother. But in other cases, because in spring the phlegm is not cleared away owing to its excess (as happens when the weather is warm) but congeals owing to the cold, when summer comes and the warmth violently melts the phlegm, fluids form in those who are bilious and dry, because their bodies are not wet but are arid by nature. But these fluids are slight, so that they suffer only from dry eye disease, while those who are phlegmatic suffer from sore throats and discharges in the lungs. And dysentery occurs among women owing to the moisture and coldness of their nature, while apoplexy occurs among the elderly when the collected moisture is released and accumulates, and solidifies owing to the weakness of their natural heat.

10. Why, if the summer comes dry and with a Boreas, whereas the autumn is the opposite—wet and with a Notos—do headaches, sore throats, and coughs occur in the winter, and end in consumption? Is it because the winter encounters matter in a large quantity (*in the body*), so that it is a job to solidify the moisture and produce phlegm? Therefore, when moisture appears in the head, it produces heaviness, and if it is in large quantity and cold, mortification; but if owing to the quantity it does not solidify, it flows into the neighboring place,[14] from which come coughs, sore throats, and consumption.

[14] I.e., the throat and lungs.

[12] βόρειον γ δ : νότιον α β Barth. PPA
[13] νότιον γ δ PPA : βόρειον α β Barth.

15

11. Διὰ τί δέ,[14] ἐὰν βόρειον γένηται τὸ θέρος καὶ
αὐχμῶδες, καὶ τὸ μετόπωρον, συμφέρει τοῖς φλεγμα-
10 τώδεσι καὶ ταῖς | γυναιξίν; ἢ ὅτι ἡ φύσις ἐπὶ θάτερα
ἀμφοῖν ὑπερβάλλει, ὥστε εἰς τοὐναντίον ἡ ὥρα ἑλκύ-
σασα καθίστησιν εἰς τὴν εὐκρασίαν; καὶ παραχρῆμά
τε ὑγιαίνουσιν, ἐὰν μή τι δι᾽ ἑαυτοὺς ἁμαρτάνωσι, καὶ
εἰς τὸν χειμῶνα οὐχ ὑγροὶ ἀφικνοῦνται, ἔχοντες πεκ-
καύματα τῷ ψύχει. |

15 12. Διὰ τί τοῖς χολώδεσι νοσῶδές ἐστι τὸ βόρειον
καὶ αὐχμῶδες θέρος καὶ μετόπωρον; ἢ ὅτι ἐπὶ ταὐτὸ
ῥέπει αὐτοῖς τὸ σῶμα καὶ αἱ ὧραι, ὥστε ὥσπερ πῦρ
ἐπὶ πυρὶ γίνεται; ξηραινομένων γὰρ τῶν σωμάτων,
καὶ τοῦ γλυκυτάτου μὲν ἐξικμαζομένου ἐξ αὐτῶν,
20 ὑπερθερμαινομένων δὲ | λίαν, ἀνάγκη διὰ μὲν τὰς
συντήξεις[15] ὀφθαλμίας ξηρὰς γίνεσθαι, διὰ δὲ τὸ
χολῶδεις[16] τοὺς ὑπολειπομένους εἶναι χυμούς, ὑπερ-
θερμαινομένων δὲ καὶ τούτων πυρετοὺς ὀξεῖς γίνεσθαι
ἅτε ὑπ᾽ ἀκράτου τῆς χολῆς, ἐνίοις δὲ μανίας, οἷς ἂν
μέλαινα χολὴ φύσει ἐνῇ· αὕτη γὰρ ἐπιπολάζει ἀναξη-
25 ραινομένων | τῶν ἐναντίων χυμῶν.

13. Διὰ τί τὸ τὰ ὕδατα μεταβάλλειν νοσῶδές φασιν
εἶναι, τὸ δὲ τὸν ἀέρα οὔ; ἢ ὅτι τοῦτο γίνεται τροφή,
καὶ ἔχοντες καὶ ἀπολελαυκότες τοῦ ὕδατος ἀπέρχον-
ται, τοῦ δ᾽ ἀέρος οὐδέν; ἔτι ὕδατος μὲν πολλὰ εἴδη

[14] δέ om. γ (praeter X^a p) L
[15] συντήξεις : συμπήξεις Forster
[16] χολώδεις δ : χολῶδες cett. codd.

11. But why, if the summer and the autumn come dry and with a Boreas, does this benefit those who are phlegmatic, and women? Is it because the nature of both is excessive in one direction, so that the season, dragging in the opposite direction, establishes a good temperament? And they are healthy at that time, unless they commit some error themselves, and they do not reach the winter moist, having inflamed material as resistance against the cold.

12. Why is the summer and autumn together being dry and with Boreas winds disease-producing in the bilious? Is it because their bodies and the seasons are inclined to be the same, so that it is just like fire added to fire?[15] For as the bodies become dry, and the sweetest part is evaporated out of them, by becoming excessively hot, dry eye disease necessarily arises because of colliquation;[16] but because the remaining humors are bilious, by becoming excessively hot, acute fevers occur because of the unmixed bile, and in some cases madness, when black bile is naturally present;[17] for this surfaces as the opposite humors dry up.

13.[18] Why do people say that change of water is disease-producing, but that change of air is not? Is it because water becomes nourishment, and after drinking and enjoying water people leave it, but they never leave the air?[19] Fur-

---

[15] On the expression "fire added to fire," see *Pr.* 1.17 (861a31–32), 4.28 (880a21), and 34.3 (963b32), as well as *Mete.* 375a20 and *Resp.* 472b5. Cf. Pl. *Lg.* 666a.   [16] Translating συντήξεις with the mss. Forster's conjecture yields "solidification."

[17] On black bile (i.e., melancholy) and madness, see *Pr.* 30.1.
[18] See *GA* 767a28–35 and Hp. *Aër* 7–9.   [19] I.e., people leave one source of water for another, from which they drink at another time, but they never change their source of air.

30 ἐστὶ καὶ διάφορα[17] | καθ᾽ αὑτά, ἀέρος δ᾽ οὔ, ὥστε καὶ
τοῦτο αἴτιον. ἐν μὲν γὰρ τῷ ἀέρι σχεδὸν τῷ αὐτῷ
συμβαίνει διατελεῖν καὶ ἀποδημοῦντας, ἐν δ᾽ ὕδασιν
ἄλλοις· διὸ καλῶς δοκεῖ νοσώδης ἡ τοῦ ὕδατος μεταβολὴ εἶναι.

14. Διὰ τί μᾶλλον ἡ τοῦ ὕδατος ἢ ἡ τῶν σιτίων
35 μεταβολὴ | νοσώδης; ἢ ὅτι πλεῖστον ἀναλίσκομεν τὸ
ὕδωρ; ἔν τε γὰρ τοῖς σιτίοις ὑπάρχει καὶ ὄψοις, καὶ ἐν
τῷ πόματι τὸ πλεῖστον ὕδωρ. ‖

861a 15. Διὰ τί δ᾽ ἡ μεταβολὴ νοσώδης; ἢ ὅτι πᾶσα μὲν
ἡ μεταβολὴ καὶ ὥρας καὶ ἡλικίας εὐκίνητον; εὐκίνητα
γὰρ τὰ ἄκρα, οἷον καὶ αἱ ἀρχαὶ καὶ αἱ τελευταί. ὥστε
καὶ αἱ τροφαὶ ἕτεραι οὖσαι ἀλλήλας φθείρουσιν· αἱ
5 μὲν γὰρ ἄρτι, | αἱ δ᾽ οὔπω προσπεφύκασιν. ἔτι δ᾽
ὥσπερ ἡ ποικίλη τροφὴ νοσώδης (ταραχώδης γὰρ καὶ
οὐ μία πέψις), οὕτω συμβαίνει μεταβάλλουσιν τὸ[18]
ὕδωρ ποικίλῃ πόματος χρῆσθαι τῇ τροφῇ· καὶ ἡ
τοιαύτη τροφὴ κυριωτέρα τῆς ξηρᾶς ἐστὶ τῷ πλεῖστον
εἶναι καὶ ἐξ αὐτῶν τῶν σιτίων τὸ ὑγρὸν γίνεσθαι
τροφήν. |

10 16. Διὰ τί ἡ τῶν ὑδάτων μεταβολὴ τοῖς ἔχουσι
φθεῖρας ποιεῖ πολλοὺς ἔχειν; ἢ ὅτι ἀπεψία γινομένη
τοῦ ὑγροῦ διὰ τὴν ταραχήν, ἢ γίνεται διὰ τὴν ποι-
κιλίαν τοῦ ὕδατος πυκνὰ μεταβάλλουσιν, ὑγρότητα
ἐμποιεῖ, καὶ μάλιστα ἐν τῷ ἐπιτηδείως ὑπάρχοντι
15 τόπῳ; ὁ δ᾽ ἐγκέφαλος ὑγρός· διὸ καὶ | ἡ κεφαλὴ ἀεὶ

---

[17] διάφορα γ : διαφοραὶ cett. codd.
[18] τὸ Cᵃ : om. cett. codd.

18

ther there are many forms of water, differing essentially from each other, but there is no difference in air, so that this too is a reason. For we happen to live, even when we leave home, in much the same air, but with different water; this is why the change of water is correctly thought to be disease-producing.

14. Why is the change of water more disease-producing than the change of food? Is it because we consume water most? For water is present in food, even in cooked food, and in drink there is mostly water.

15.[20] But why is change disease-producing? Is it because all change, both of season and of age, is volatile? For the limits are volatile, such as the beginnings and the ends. So, because the forms of nourishment are different they corrupt each other; for some nourishment has recently grown into (*the body*), while some has not yet done so. Further, just as varied nourishment is disease-producing (for concoction is then disordered and not uniform), so those who change water are supplied with varied nourishment in what they drink. And such nourishment is more powerful than dry nourishment, both by being a great quantity and because the moisture from the foods themselves are nourishment.

16.[21] Why does the change of waters in those who have lice cause them to have more? Is it because there is a lack of concoction of the moisture owing to the disturbance, which is due to the variation in those who change their water frequently, which produces moisture, especially in the region most suitable (*for the spread of lice*)? Now the brain is moist; this is why the head too is always especially moist.

[20] See Hp. *Hum.* 15.
[21] See *HA* 557a19–21.

μάλιστα. δηλοῖ δέ, ὅτι αἱ τρίχες ἔνεισι μάλιστα ἐν
αὐτῇ. ἡ δὲ τοῦ τόπου τούτου ὑγρότης φθειρῶν ποι-
ητική. δηλοῖ δ᾽ ἐπὶ τῶν παίδων· ὑγροκέφαλοί τε γάρ
εἰσιν, καὶ πολλάκις ἢ κορυζῶσιν ἢ αἷμα ποιεῖ ῥεῖν,
καὶ φθεῖρας πλείους οἱ ἐν ταύτῃ τῇ ἡλικίᾳ ἔχουσιν. |

20 17. Διὰ τί ἀπὸ Πλειάδος μέχρι ζεφύρου οἱ τὰς
μακρὰς νόσους κάμνοντες μάλιστα ἀναιροῦνται, καὶ
οἱ γέροντες μᾶλλον τῶν νέων; πότερον ὅτι δύο ἐστὶ τὰ
φθαρτικώτατα, ὑπερβολή τε καὶ ψῦχος; τὸ γὰρ ζῆν
θερμόν, ἡ δ᾽ ὥρα αὕτη ἄμφω ταῦτ᾽ ἔχει· ψυχρά τε γάρ
25 ἐστι, καὶ ἀκμαιότατος | ὁ χειμών· τὸ λοιπὸν γὰρ ἔαρ
ἐστίν. ἢ ὅτι ὁμοίως μὲν διάκεινται τοῖς γέρουσι τῶν
καμνόντων οἱ τὰς μακρὰς κάμνοντες ἀσθενείας; οἷον
γὰρ ἤδη γῆρας ἡ μακρὰ ἀσθένεια συμβαίνει· τὸ γὰρ
σῶμα ἀμφοῖν ξηρὸν καὶ ψυχρόν ἐστιν, τῶν μὲν δι᾽
30 ἡλικίαν, τῶν δὲ διὰ νόσον. ὁ δὲ χειμὼν | καὶ οἱ πάγοι
ὑπερβολή ἐστι ψυχρότητος καὶ ξηρότητος. μικρᾶς οὖν
δεομένοις αὐτοῖς ῥοπῆς, γίνεται οἷον πῦρ ἐπὶ πυρὶ ὁ
χειμών, καὶ φθείρει διὰ ταῦτα.

18. Διὰ τί ἐν τοῖς ἑλώδεσι τὰ μὲν ἐν τῇ κεφαλῇ
ἕλκη ταχὺ ὑγιάζεται, τὰ δ᾽ ἐν ταῖς κνήμαις μόλις; ἢ
35 ὅτι | βαρεῖα ἡ ὑγρότης διὰ τὸ γεώδης εἶναι, τὰ δὲ
βαρέα εἰς τὸ κάτω ἀποχωρεῖ; τὰ μὲν οὖν ἄνω ἔκκριτα[19] διὰ τὸ ἀποκεχωρηκέναι εἰς τὰ κάτω, τὰ δὲ
κάτω πολλῆς γέμει περιττώσεως καὶ εὐσήπτου. ‖

---

[19] ἔκκριτα : εὔπεπτα Prantl ex *Pr.* 14.6, 909a38

This is clear, because hair is present especially on this part. And the moisture of this region is conducive to the production of lice. This is clear in the case of children: for they are moist-headed, and often either have a runny nose or cause blood to flow there, and those in this age group have many lice.

17.[22] Why do those suffering from diseases of long standing mostly die between the rising of the Pleiades and the coming of the Zephyr,[23] and the old more than the young? Is it because two things are most destructive, excess and cold? For living is hot, but this season possesses both of these qualities: it is cold, and winter is at its height (for spring is the following season). Or is it because those suffering from long-standing illnesses are in a condition similar to what is suffered by the old? For long-standing illness occurs, as it were, as premature old age; for in both, the body is dry and cold, in the latter because of age, in the former because of disease. But winter and frost are excesses of coldness and dryness. Therefore, to those requiring little to turn the scale, winter is like fire added to fire and so destroys them.

18.[24] Why is it that in marshy regions, wounds on the head heal quickly, whereas those on the legs heal slowly? Is it because the moisture is heavy owing to its being earthy, and what is heavy withdraws downward? So the upper parts are cleared out[25] because the moisture has withdrawn to the lower parts, whereas the lower parts are full of a great deal of residue and easily putrefied.

[22] Cf. Diocl. fr. 183a6 (v.d. Eijk).   [23] I.e., the west wind.
[24] This chapter is virtually identical to *Pr.* 14.6.
[25] The parallel text of *Pr.* 14.6 has "easily concocted" (εὔ-πεπτα).

861b   19. Διὰ τί, ἐὰν τοῦ χειμῶνος γενομένου βορείου καὶ
τοῦ ἔαρος νοτίου καὶ ἐπόμβρου τὸ θέρος λίαν αὐχμηρὸν γένηται, θανατῶδες γίνεται τὸ μετόπωρον πᾶσιν,
μάλιστα δὲ τοῖς παιδίοις, καὶ τοῖς ἄλλοις δὲ δυσεν-
5   τερίαι καὶ τεταρταῖοι | χρόνιοι γίνονται ἐν αὐτῷ; ἢ ὅτι
μετρίου μὲν ἐπιγενομένου ὕδατος θερινοῦ καταψυχθὲν
τὸ ζέον ὑγρὸν ἐν ἡμῖν λωφᾷ, ὅσον ἠθροίσθη ἐν τῷ ἦρι
γενομένῳ τῷ²⁰ ὑγρῷ, εἰ δὲ μή, τὰ μὲν παιδία διὰ τὸ
ὑγρὰ εἶναι φύσει καὶ θερμὰ ὑπερζεῖ τῷ πάθει, διὰ τὸ
10 μὴ καταψυχθῆναι; ὅσα δὲ μὴ τοῦ θέρους, | τοῦ μετ-
οπώρου [ὅσον]²¹ ἐκζεῖ. αἱ δὲ περιττώσεις ἐὰν μὴ εὐθὺς
ἀνέλωσι, περὶ πνεύμονα καὶ ἀρτηρίαν γινόμεναι (ἄνω
γὰρ πρῶται συνίστανται διὰ τὸ ὑπὸ τοῦ ἀέρος ἡμᾶς
θερμαίνεσθαι· διὰ γὰρ ταῦτα καὶ ὀφθαλμίαι πυρετῶν
πρότερον γίνονται ἐν τῷ νοσερῷ θέρει). ἐὰν οὖν μὴ ἐν
15 τοῖς ἄνω, | καθάπερ εἴρηται, τὰ περιττώματα εὐθὺς
ἀνέλῃ, καταβαίνουσιν εἰς τὰς κοιλίας ἄπεπτα ὄντα,
τοῦτο δέ ἐστι δυσεντερία, διὰ τὸ μὴ ἐκκρίνεσθαι ὑπὸ
πλήθους τὸ ὑγρόν. καὶ ἐὰν παύσωνται, τεταρταῖοι
γίνονται τοῖς σῳζομένοις· ἡ γὰρ τοῦ ἀπέπτου ὑπό-
20 στασις μονιμωτάτη ἐστὶ καὶ σύντονος γίνεται | τῷ
σώματι, καθάπερ ἡ μέλαινα χολή.

20. Διὰ τί, ἐὰν τὸ θέρος ἔπομβρον γένηται καὶ
νότιον, καὶ τὸ μετόπωρον, ὁ χειμὼν νοσερὸς γίνεται; ἢ

²⁰ τῷ secl. Marenghi³
²¹ [ὅσον] Hett : ὅσον plur. codd. : ὅσων β : οἷον Forster

19.[26] Why, when the winter comes with a Boreas and the spring comes rainy and with a Notos, if the summer comes very dry, the autumn is deadly to all and especially to children, while in others dysentery and chronic quartan fevers[27] occur during the same period? Is it because when there is a moderate rainfall in the summer, the boiling moisture in us, which accumulated during the moist spring, cools and abates, but if this does not happen, the children, owing to their moist and hot nature, boil over with afflictions, because they are not cooled? And all that does not boil out in summer does so in autumn.[28] These residues, if they do not kill right away, settle in the lung and windpipe (for they collect above first because we are heated by the air; for it is owing to this too that eye disease occurs before fevers in the summer in which disease is prevalent). If, therefore, as has been said, the residues in the upper parts do not kill (*the patient*) right away, they descend unconcocted into the bowels, and this is dysentery, because the moisture owing to its quantity is not excreted. Even if (*these symptoms*) cease, quartan fevers occur in the survivors; for the sediment of what is unconcocted is very fixed and becomes intense in the body, just like black bile.

20. Why, if the summer and autumn are rainy and with Notos winds, is the winter disease-filled? Is it because

[26] The likely source for *Pr.* 1.19–20 is Hp. *Aër* 10. See also *Aph.* 3.11–14.

[27] Quartan fever is intermittent, with outbreaks every seventy-two hours. It is often associated with malaria.

[28] Or perhaps "And all that does not (*cool*) during the summer boils out in autumn."

ὅτι σφόδρα ὑγρὰ τὰ σώματα ὁ χειμὼν λαμβάνει, καὶ
ἡ μεταβολὴ ἔτι μεγάλη γίνεται ἐξ ἀλέας πολλῆς καὶ
25 οὐκ ἐκ προσαγωγῆς, | διὰ τὸ καὶ τὸ μετόπωρον γίνε-
σθαι ἀλεεινόν, ὥστε τοῖς μὲν γίνεσθαι ἀνάγκη τὰ
ὀξέα νοσήματα, μὴ ἀραιοῖς οὖσιν; τοῖς γὰρ τοιούτοις
ἄνω μᾶλλον τὰ ὑγρὰ περιττώματα ἀθροίζεται, διὰ τὸ
τούτους μὲν τοὺς τόπους ἔχειν χώραν, τοὺς δὲ κάτω
ἑτέρους εἶναι. οἱ οὖν ὄντες πυκνόσαρκοι οὐ πολλὰ |
30 περιττώματα δέχονται. ψυχομένης οὖν τῆς περιττώσεως τῆς ἐν τοῖς ἄνω μέρεσιν τοῦ σώματος, ὥσπερ
τοῖς οἰνωμένοις ὅταν ῥιγῶσι, τὰ εἰρημένα νοσήματα
συμβαίνει γίνεσθαι. τοῖς δ' ἀραιοτέροις πυρετῶν
γινομένων, τοὺς ἀπὸ πλείστης ἀπεψίας γινομένους
35 πυρετοὺς καύσους συμβαίνει γίνεσθαι, | διὰ τὸ τοῖς
τοιούτοις ἐσκεδάσθαι μὲν μᾶλλον κατὰ πᾶν τὸ σῶμα
τὰ ὑγρὰ ἢ τοῖς πυκνοσάρκοις, συνισταμένης δὲ τῆς
σαρκὸς αὐτῶν ὑπὸ τοῦ χειμῶνος θερμαινόμενα τὰ
ὑγρὰ πυρετοὺς ποιεῖν. ἡ γὰρ παντὸς τοῦ σώματος
862a ὑπερβάλλουσα ‖ θερμότης ἐστὶ πυρετός· ἐπιτεινομένη
δὲ διὰ τὸ πλῆθος τῆς ἐνυπαρχούσης αὐτοῖς ὑγρότητος
καῦσος γίνεται.

21. Διὰ τί, ὅταν ἐκ γῆς ἀτμὸς ἀνίῃ πολὺς ὑπὸ τοῦ
5 ἡλίου, | τὸ ἔτος λοιμῶδες γίνεται; ἢ ὅτι ὑγρὸν ἀνάγκη
καὶ ἔπομβρον τὸ ἔτος σημαίνειν, καὶ τὴν γῆν ὑγρὰν
ἀνάγκη εἶναι; οἷον οὖν ἐν ἑλώδει τόπῳ ἡ οἴκησις
γίνεται, νοσώδης δ' ἡ τοιαύτη ἐστίν. καὶ τὰ σώματα
δὴ τότε ἀνάγκη περίττωμα πολὺ ἔχειν, ὥστε ἐν τῷ
θέρει ἔχειν ὕλην νοσώδη. |

24

the winter encounters bodies that are very moist, and the change from great warmth is considerable and not gradual, because the autumn has also been warm, so that some necessarily suffer from acute diseases, unless their bodies are porous? For in such people the moist residues collect above, because these regions have space, but the lower ones are different. So those with solid flesh do not receive many residues. Therefore, when the residue in the upper parts of the body becomes cold, as in wine drinkers when they shudder, the aforementioned diseases occur. But when fevers occur in more porous bodies, those coming from a great deal of unconcocted material become burning fevers, because in such people the moisture has been scattered throughout the whole body more than in those with solid flesh, and when their flesh has condensed owing to the cold of winter, the moisture is heated and produces fevers. For excessive heat of the whole body is fever; and when this is intensified owing to the amount of moisture present in them, it becomes burning fever.

21. Why, when a great deal of vapor rises from the earth because of the sun, is the year pestilential? Is it because this necessarily signifies that the year is moist and rainy, and that the earth is necessarily moist? So it is like residing in a marshy region, and such a region is disease-producing. And bodies then necessarily contain considerable residues, so that during the summer they contain disease-producing matter.

10   22. Διὰ τί γίνεται τὰ ἔτη νοσώδη, ὅταν γένηται
φορὰ τῶν μικρῶν βατράχων τῶν φρυνοειδῶν; ἢ ὅτι
ἕκαστον εὐθενεῖ[22] ἐν τῇ οἰκείᾳ χώρᾳ τῆς φύσεως; καὶ
ταῦτα δὴ φύσει ἐστὶν ὑγρά, ὥστε ἔπομβρον καὶ ὑγρὸν
σημαίνειν τὸν ἐνιαυτὸν γίνεσθαι. τὰ δὲ τοιαῦτα ἔτη
15 νοσώδη ἐστίν· ὑγρὰ | γὰρ τὰ σώματα ὄντα πολὺ ἔχει
τὸ περίττωμα, ὅ ἐστι τῶν νόσων αἴτιον.

    23. Διὰ τί οἱ νότοι οἱ ξηροὶ καὶ μὴ ὑδατώδεις
πυρετώδεις εἰσίν; ἢ ὅτι ὑγρότητα καὶ θέρμην ἀλλοτρίαν ποιοῦσιν; εἰσὶ γὰρ ὑγροὶ καὶ θερμοὶ φύσει,
20 τοῦτο δ' ἐστὶ πυρετῶδες· ὁ | γὰρ πυρετὸς ἐξ ἀμφοτέρας
τῆς τούτων ἐστὶν ὑπερβολῆς. ὅταν μὲν οὖν ἄνευ ὕδατος πνέωσι, ταύτην ἐν ἡμῖν ποιοῦσι τὴν διάθεσιν,
ὅταν δ' ἅμα ὕδατι, τὸ ὕδωρ καταψύχει ἡμᾶς. οἱ δ' ἐκ
θαλάττης νότοι καὶ συμφέρουσι τοῖς φυτοῖς· ἐψυγμέ-
25 νοι γὰρ ἀπὸ τῆς θαλάττης ἀφικνοῦνται πρὸς | αὐτά. αἱ
δ' ἐρυσίβαι γίνονται ὑπὸ ὑγρότητος καὶ θέρμης ἀλλο-
τρίας.

    24. Διὰ τί ἐν τοῖς νότοις βαρύτερον ἔχουσι καὶ
ἀδυνατώτερον οἱ ἄνθρωποι; ἢ ὅτι ἐξ ὀλίγου πολὺ
ὑγρὸν γίνεται διατηκόμενον διὰ τὴν ἀλέαν, καὶ ἐκ
30 πνεύματος κούφου | ὑγρὸν βαρύ; ἔτι δ' ἡ δύναμις
ἡμῶν ἐν τοῖς ἄρθροις ἐστί, ταῦτα δ' ἀνίεται ὑπὸ τῶν
νοτίων. δηλοῦσι δ' οἱ ψόφοι τῶν κεκολλημένων. τὸ
γὰρ γλίσχρον ἐν τοῖς ἄρθροις πεπηγὸς μὲν κινεῖσθαι
κωλύει ἡμᾶς, ὑγρὸν δὲ λίαν ὂν συντείνεσθαι. |

    [22] εὐθενεῖ α β Barth. : εὐσθενεῖ δ γ

22. Why are the years disease-producing when there is a succession of small toadlike frogs? Is it because each thing prospers in an area suitable to its nature? And these frogs are by nature moist, so that they signify that the year is rainy and moist. Now such years are disease-producing, for the bodies (*of humans*), being moist, contain a great deal of residue, which is a cause of diseases.

23.[29] Why are the Notos winds that are dry and not rainy fever-producing? Is it because they produce extraneous moisture and heat? For they are moist and hot by nature, and this is fever-producing; for fever comes from the excess of both of these. Therefore, when these winds blow without rain, they produce this condition in us; but when they come with water, the water cools us. Now the Notos winds from the sea are also beneficial to plants; for they have been cooled by the sea when they reach them. But mildew[30] comes from extraneous moisture and heat.

24.[31] Why do people feel heavier and more powerless in the Notos winds? Is it because moisture melted by the warmth becomes abundant instead of slight, and light breath is replaced by heavy moisture? Besides, our power lies in our joints, and these are made slack by the Notos winds. Now the creaking of things glued together shows this. For the sticky material in the joints, having been solidified, prevents us from moving, but if it is too moist it prevents us from exerting ourselves.

---

29 Cf. *Pr.* 26.17 and 50. Source: Thphr. *Vent.* 57.

30 Or blight.

31 Cf. *Pr.* 26.42. Source: Thphr. *Vent.* 56. See also Hp. *Morb.Sacr.* 13.

35   25. Διὰ τί ἀρρωστοῦσι μὲν μᾶλλον τοῦ θέρους,
ἀποθνήσκουσι δὲ μᾶλλον οἱ ἀρρωστοῦντες τοῦ χειμῶνος; ἢ ὅτι τοῦ χειμῶνος διὰ τὴν πυκνότητα ἐντὸς τῶν
σωμάτων συνεσταλμένου τοῦ θερμοῦ, καὶ πονοῦντες
μᾶλλον, εἰ μὴ πέττοιμεν, τῶν[23] ἐν ἡμῖν συνισταμένων
862b1   περιττωμάτων, ἰσχυρὰν ἀνάγκη τὴν ἀρχὴν ‖ εἶναι τῆς
νόσου, τοιαύτην δ᾽ οὖσαν φθαρτικὴν εἰκός ἐστιν αὐτὴν εἶναι; ἐν δὲ τῷ θέρει, μανοῦ καὶ κατεψυγμένου
παντὸς τοῦ σώματος καὶ ἐκλελυμένου πρὸς τοὺς πόνους ὄντος, ἀρχὰς νόσων ἀνάγκη πλείους μὲν γίνε-
5   σθαι διά τε κόπους | καὶ ἀπεψίαν τῶν εἰσφερομένων
(καὶ γὰρ οἱ νέοι καρποὶ τότε εἰσίν), ἀλλ᾽ οὐχ οὕτως
ἰσχυράς, διὸ εὐβοήθητοι.

26. Διὰ τί μετὰ τὰς τροπὰς ἀμφοτέρας μέχρι ἑκα-
τὸν ἡμερῶν ἀποθνήσκουσι μάλιστα; ἢ ὅτι ἄχρι τοσ-
ούτου ἑκατέρα ἡ ὑπερβολὴ διέχει, ἥ τε τοῦ θερμοῦ καὶ
10   τοῦ ψυχροῦ; ἡ δ᾽ ὑπερβολὴ | τοῖς ἀσθενέσι ποιεῖ τὰς
νόσους καὶ τὰς φθοράς.

27. Διὰ τί τὸ ἔαρ καὶ τὸ φθινόπωρον νοσώδη; ἢ ὅτι
αἱ μεταβολαὶ νοσώδεις; τὸ δὲ μετόπωρον τοῦ ἔαρος
νοσωδέστερον, ὅτι μᾶλλον τοῦ θερμοῦ ψυχομένου ἢ
τοῦ ψυχροῦ θερμαινομένου νοσοῦμεν. ἐν μὲν οὖν τῷ
15   ἔαρι τὸ ψυχρὸν θερμαίνεται, | ἐν δὲ τῷ μετοπώρῳ τὸ
θερμὸν ψύχεται.

28. Διὰ τί ἐν τῷ χειμῶνι ἐλάττω μὲν τὰ ἀρρω-
στήματα ἢ ἐν τῷ θέρει, θανάσιμα δὲ μᾶλλον; ἢ ὅτι ἐν

---

[23] ante τῶν add. ⟨διὰ⟩ Forster

28

25.[32] Why are people more likely to be ill in the summer, whereas those who are ill are more likely to die in the winter? Is it because in the winter the heat is drawn together in our bodies owing to its density, and, as we suffer more if we cannot concoct the residues when they are collected in us, the onset of the disease is necessarily severe, and being of this sort it is likely to be fatal? But in the summer, when the whole body is loose, cooled down, and slack with respect to exertion, there is necessarily the onset of more diseases, because of our fatigue and the lack of concoction of what we swallow (for there are fresh fruits at this time); but the diseases are not so strong, which is why they are easy to treat.

26.[33] Why do people die especially during the hundred days after each of the solstices? Is it because each excess—of heat and of cold—extends to this period? And excess produces diseases and death in those who are weak.

27.[34] Why are spring and late autumn disease-producing? Is it because changes are disease-producing? But the autumn is more disease-producing than the spring, because we succumb to disease more when the hot is cooled than when the cold is heated. Now in the spring, the cold is heated, whereas in the autumn the hot is cooled.

28.[35] Why are illnesses fewer in the winter than in the summer, but more deadly? Is it because in the summer ill-

32 Cf. *Pr.* 1.28.
33 Source: Hp. *Aër* 11.
34 For *Pr.* 1.27–29, see Hp. *Aph.* 3.9–10, 18–23.
35 Cf. *Pr.* 1.25.

μὲν τῷ θέρει ἀπὸ μικρᾶς προφάσεως τὰ ἀρρωστή-
ματα, ἐν δὲ τῷ χειμῶνι οὔ; πεπτικώτεροι γὰρ καὶ
20 ὑγιεινότεροι ἡμῶν αὐτῶν, | ὥστε εἰκότως τὰ ἀπὸ μείζο-
νος προφάσεως γινόμενα μείζω καὶ ἀναιρετικώτερα.
ταὐτὸ δὲ τοῦτο καὶ ἐπὶ τῶν ἀθλητῶν καὶ ὅλως ἐπὶ τῶν
ὑγιεινῶς διακειμένων ὁρῶμεν· ἢ γὰρ οὐ λαμβάνονται
νόσῳ, ἢ ταχὺ συναπίασιν· μεγάλης γὰρ αἰτίας δέον-
ται. |

25   29. Διὰ τί τοῦ μὲν φθινοπώρου καὶ τοῦ χειμῶνος οἱ
καῦσοι μᾶλλον γίνονται ἐν ταῖς ψυχραῖς ὥραις, τοῦ δὲ
θέρους τὰ ῥίγη ἐνοχλεῖ καυμάτων ὄντων; ἢ ὅτι τῶν
κατὰ τὸν ἄνθρωπον ἡ χολὴ μέν ἐστι θερμόν, τὸ δὲ
φλέγμα ψυχρόν; ἐν μὲν οὖν τῷ θέρει τὸ ψυχρὸν ἀναλύ-
30 εται, καὶ διαχυθὲν ῥίγη | καὶ τρόμους παρασκευάζει·
ἐν δὲ τῷ χειμῶνι τὸ θερμὸν ὑπὸ τῆς ὥρας κρατεῖται
κατεψυγμένον. οἱ δὲ καῦσοι μᾶλλον ἐνοχλοῦσι τοῦ
χειμῶνος καὶ τοῦ φθινοπώρου, ὅτι διὰ τὸ ψῦχος τὸ
θερμὸν εἴσω συστέλλεται, ὁ δὲ καῦσος ἔσωθέν ἐστι
καὶ οὐκ ἐπιπολῆς· εἰκότως οὖν οἱ καῦσοι ταύτην τὴν
35 ὥραν | γίνονται. καταμάθοι δ' ἄν τις τοῦτο ἀκρι-
βέστερον ἐπὶ τῶν ψυχρολουτρούντων τοῦ χειμῶνος
καὶ τῶν τοῦ χειμῶνος λουομένων τῷ θερμῷ, ὅτι οἱ μὲν
τῷ ψυχρῷ λουόμενοι, ἀπορριγώσαντες ὀλίγον χρόνον
863a ἕως λούονται, τὴν λοιπὴν ἡμέραν ‖ οὐδὲν πάσχουσιν
ὑπὸ τοῦ ψυχροῦ, οἱ δὲ τῷ θερμῷ ὕδατι χρησάμενοι
δυσριγότερως διάγουσι. τῶν μὲν γὰρ τῷ ψυχρῷ λουομένων πυκνοῦται ἡ σὰρξ καὶ συστέλλεται εἴσω τὸ

nesses are from minor causes, but not in the winter? For we ourselves are better with respect to concoction and healthier, so that it is reasonable that illnesses coming from greater causes are greater and more destructive. Now we see this same thing in athletes and generally in those who are in a healthy condition: either they are not afflicted by disease or (if they are) they quickly depart; for they require a great cause (to make them ill).

29.[36] Why do burning fevers occur more in the cold seasons of late autumn and winter, whereas chills[37] are trouble in the summer when there is burning heat? Is it because, of the (humors) in man, bile is hot, but phlegm is cold? So in summer, the cold is dispersed, and when dissipated produces chills and trembling; but in the winter the heat is mastered by the season and cools. But the burning fevers of winter and late autumn are more trouble, because the heat is collected within owing to the cold, and burning fever is internal and not on the surface. It is reasonable, therefore, that burning fevers occur in this season. Now one could examine this more precisely in the case of those who wash in cold water in winter and those who wash in hot water in winter, because those who wash in cold water have chills for a short time while they are washing, but they are not affected by the cold for the rest of the day, whereas those who use hot water spend the day experiencing bad chills. For the flesh of those who wash in cold water solidifies and the heat is collected within, whereas the flesh of

36 Cf. *Pr.* 1.20 and 14.3, and see also Hp. *Morb.* I 29.
37 Or "shivering."

θερμόν, τῶν δὲ θερμολουτρούντων ἡ σὰρξ ἀραιοῦται
5 καὶ τὸ | θερμὸν ἕως τοῦ ἔξω τόπου περισπᾶται.[24]

30. Τίς καταπλάσματος ἀρετή; ἢ διὰ τὸ χυτικὸν
εἶναι κἂν ἱδρῶτα ποιοῖ καὶ ἀποπνοήν;

31. Τῷ δῆλον ὅταν ἔμπυον; ἢ ἐὰν καταχεομένου τοῦ
θερμοῦ ἀλλαγῇ, ἔμπυον, εἰ δὲ μή, οὔ; |

10 32. Ποῖα δεῖ καίειν ἢ ποῖα δεῖ τέμνειν; ἢ ὅσα μὲν
ἔχει στόμα μέγα καὶ οὐ ταχὺ συμφύεται, ταῦτα καίειν
δεῖ, ὅπως ἡ ἐσχάρα ἐκεῖ πέσῃ; οὕτω γὰρ οὐκ ἔσται
ὕπουλα.

33. Τίς ἐναίμου ἀρετή; ἢ τὸ ξηραντικὸν εἶναι καὶ
τῆς ἐπιούσης περιττώσεως σταλτικὸν ἄνευ ἐσχαρώ-
15 σεως καὶ σήψεως | τῆς σαρκός; οὕτω γὰρ ἂν ἀφλέ-
γμαντον εἴη καὶ συμφυτικόν. μὴ ἐπιρρέοντος μὲν γὰρ
ἀφλέγμαντον ἔσται, ξηρὸν δ' ὂν συμφύσεται· ἕως δ'
ἂν ὑγρορροῇ, οὐ συμφύσεται. διὰ τοῦτο οὖν δριμέα τὰ
πλεῖστα, ὥστε ἀποστύφειν.

34. Ποῖα τέμνειν δεῖ καὶ ποῖα καίειν, καὶ ποῖα οὔ,
20 ἀλλὰ | φαρμάκοις; ἢ τὰ μὲν ἐπὶ ταῖς μασχάλαις καὶ
βουβῶσι φαρμάκῳ; μετὰ γὰρ διαίρεσιν τὰ μὲν ἐπί-

---

[24] post περισπᾶται hunc titul. praebent codd., ὅσα βοηθηματικὰ πρὸς ἴασιν (βοηθήματα Xᵃ x aᵐ, βοηθητικὰ L, προβλήματα add. Oᵃ), sed numeri (δ excipias) continuatur : nov.
part. PPA

---

[38] According to the manuscript tradition, there should be a
subtitle between the end of ch. 29 and the beginning of ch. 30,
which (ignoring certain variations) can be translated "Those problems helpful with a view to healing."

those who wash in hot water becomes porous and the heat is drawn off to the outside.[38]

30.[39] What is the virtue of a poultice? Can it produce sweat and evaporation through its dissolving power?

31. By what is it clear that there is suppuration?[40] If it changes when hot water is poured over it, there is suppuration, whereas if it doesn't, there is not?

32.[41] Which (wounds) should one cauterize and which should one cut? Should all those that have a large opening and do not close be cauterized, so that a scab may form there? For in this way there will not be festering.

33. What is the virtue of a styptic?[42] Is it that it has a drying effect and is capable of stanching the overflow of residues, without producing scabbing or the putrefaction of flesh? In this case (the wound) would not be inflamed and would be inclined to heal. For if it does not flow, it will not be inflamed, and being dry it will heal. But as long as there is a flow of moisture, it will not heal. Therefore, because of this most styptics are acrid, so as to be astringent.[43]

34.[44] Which (wounds) should one cut and which should one cauterize, and which neither of these, but (one should treat) with drugs? Should those in the armpits and groin be treated with drugs? For after surgery, such wounds

39 See Hp. *Medic.* 12 and Anon. Lond. 36.55–37.6.

40 I.e., the formation of pus.

41 Cf. *Pr.* 1.34 and see also Hp. *Aph.* 7.87.

42 I.e., a drug to stop the flow of blood. See, e.g., Hp. *Epid.* 5.96, 7.34.

43 Or "so as to cause contraction."

44 See Hp. *Aph.* 6.27, 7.44–45.

πονα, τὰ δὲ ἐπικίνδυνα. καίειν δὲ τὰ πλατέα τῶν
φυμάτων καὶ πολὺ πρόβλημα ἔχοντα, καὶ ἐν φλεβώ-
δεσι καὶ μὴ εὐσάρκοις. τέμνειν δὲ τὰ εἰς ὀξὺ συν-
ηγμένα καὶ τὰ μὴ ἐν στερεοῖς. |

25   35. Διὰ τί, ἐὰν χαλκῷ τις τμηθῇ, ῥᾷον ὑγιάζεται ἢ
σιδήρῳ; πότερον ὅτι λειότερον, ὥσθ᾽ ἧττον σπαράττει
καὶ ποιεῖ πληγήν; ἢ εἴπερ ἀκμὴν μᾶλλον ὁ σίδηρος
λαμβάνει, ῥᾷων καὶ ἀπαθεστέρα ἡ διαίρεσις; ἀλλὰ
μὴν φαρμακῶδες ὁ χαλκός, ἡ δ᾽ ἀρχὴ ἰσχυρόν.[25] τὸ[26]
30   οὖν εὐθὺς ἅμα τῇ τομῇ | θᾶττον τὸ φάρμακον[27] ποιεῖ
τὴν σύμφυσιν.

36. Διὰ τί δὲ καὶ τὰ διὰ χαλκοῦ καύματα θᾶττον
ὑγιάζεται; ἢ ὅτι μανότερον καὶ ἧττον σωματικόν, ἐν δὲ
τοῖς στερεωτέροις πλείων ἡ θερμότης;

37. Πότερον ἡ πτισάνη κουφοτέρα ἡ κριθίνη καὶ
35   βελτίων | πρὸς τὰ ἀρρωστήματα ἢ ἡ πυρίνη; δοκεῖ
863b γάρ τισιν αὕτη ‖ σημεῖον ποιουμένοις τοὺς μεταχειρι-
ζομένους, ὅτι πολὺ εὐχρούστεροι οἱ περὶ τὴν τῶν
ἀλεύρων ἐργασίαν ἢ τὴν τῶν ἀλφίτων. εἶθ᾽ ὅτι ὑγρότερον ἡ κριθή, τὸ δ᾽ ὑγρότερον πλέονος ⟨δεῖται⟩[28]

[25] ἀρχὴ : ἀκμὴ δ aᵐ ‖ ἰσχυρόν : ἰσχυρά γ δ
[26] τὸ : fort. τῷ Bekker
[27] τὸ φάρμακον secl. Marenghi[3]
[28] ⟨δεῖται⟩ Nicasius : ⟨οὔσης⟩ Ruelle

---

[45] Plutarch attributes this chapter (or perhaps its lost source)
to Aristotle: see QC 3.10 (Mor. 659D). According to Plutarch, its

are sometimes painful and sometimes dangerous. But one should cauterize flat growths and those having a large protuberance, as well as those in regions that are venous or not fleshy. And one should cut those gathering in a sharp point and those that are not in the solid parts.

35.[45] Why, if someone is cut with bronze, does he heal more quickly than if he is cut with iron? Is it because it is smoother, so that it tears and makes less of an impact? Or even if iron takes an edge better, the division (*by bronze*) is easier and less painful?[46] And certainly, bronze is medicinal[47] and the beginning is crucial.[48] Therefore, by acting at the moment of cutting, the drug produces healing more quickly.

36. But why do burns owing to bronze heal more quickly? Is it because bronze is more porous and less corporeal, and heat is greater in things that are more solid?

37.[49] Is barley gruel lighter and better with a view to illnesses than wheat gruel? For it seems so to some, who present as a sign of this those who handle (*barley and wheat*), in that those who work around barley meal have a much better complexion than those who work around wheat flour. Next, (*they argue*) that barley is moister, and

topic is wounds caused by spearheads and swords, and not surgery, as the previous chapter would suggest.

[46] Forster takes the same text to be contradicting the assumption of the opening question. If he is correct, we should rather render it "Or if indeed iron takes an edge better, the division (*by iron*) is easier and less painful?" Cf. *PPA* 2.5.   [47] On the purported curative powers of bronze, see *Pr.* 9.6 and *Mir.* 834b28–31.

[48] Or, with the reading of some mss., "its edge is strong."

[49] Cf. *Pr.* 21.24 and 38.10.

πέψεως. ἢ οὐθὲν κωλύει ἔνια ἔχειν δυσπεπτότερα καὶ
5 ἔνια | πρὸς κουφότητα χρησιμώτερα; οὐ γὰρ μόνον
ὑγροτέρα ἐστὶν ἡ κριθὴ τοῦ πυροῦ, ἀλλὰ καὶ ψυχρο-
τέρα. δεῖ δὲ τὸ ῥόφημα καὶ τὸ προσφερόμενον τοιοῦτον εἶναι τῷ πυρέττοντι, ὃ τροφήν τε βραχεῖαν
ποιήσει καὶ καταψύξει. ἡ δὲ πτισάνη τοῦτο ἔχει ἡ
κριθίνη· διὰ γὰρ τὸ ὑγρότερον ἢ σωματωδέστερον |
10 εἶναι ὀλίγον δίδωσι, καὶ τοῦτο ψυκτικόν.

38. Διὰ τί τὴν αἱμωδίαν παύει ἡ ἀνδράχνη καὶ
ἅλες;ἢ ὅτι ἡ μὲν ὑγρότητά τινα ἔχει; φανερὰ δ' αὕτη
μασωμένοις τε, καὶ ἐὰν συνθλασθῇ χρόνον τινά· ἕλκεται γὰρ ἡ ὑγρότης. τὸ δὴ γλίσχρον εἰσδυόμενον
15 ἐξάγει τὸ ὀξύ. καὶ | γὰρ ὅτι συγγενής, ἡ ὀξύτης
σημαίνει· ἔχει γάρ τινα ὀξύτητα ὁ χυμός. ὁ δ' ἅλς
συντήκων ἐξάγει καὶ τὴν ὀξύτητα. διὰ τί οὖν ἡ κονία
καὶ τὸ νίτρον οὔ; ἢ ὅτι στύφει καὶ οὐ τήκει;

39. Διὰ τί τοὺς μὲν θερινοὺς κόπους λουτρῷ ἰᾶσθαι
20 δεῖ, | τοὺς δὲ χειμερινοὺς ἀλείμματι; ἢ τοὺς μὲν ἀλείμ-
ματι διὰ τὰς φρίκας καὶ τὰς γενομένας μεταβολάς;
θέρμῃ γὰρ λύειν δεῖ, ἢ ποιήσει ἀλεάζειν· τὸ δ' ἔλαιον
θερμόν. ἐν δὲ τῷ θέρει καθυγραίνειν· ἡ γὰρ ὥρα ξηρά,
καὶ οὐ φοβεραὶ αἱ φρῖκαι διὰ τὴν εἰς ἀλέαν ἔκκλισιν.
25 ὀλιγοσιτία δὲ καὶ | κωθωνισμὸς θέρους, τὸ μὲν ὅλως,

---

50 This chapter is virtually identical to *Pr.* 7.9.
51 A plant in the genus *Portulaca*.
52 I.e., an affinity between purslane and bleeding gums.
53 The word translated "juice" (χυμός) is elsewhere rendered

what is moister requires more concoction. Or does nothing prevent barley from having some qualities that make it more difficult to concoct and some that make it more useful, because of its lightness? For barley is not only moister than wheat, but also colder. Now porridge and such things offered to the one who has a fever should provide a bit of nourishment and cause cooling. And barley gruel has these qualities: for by being more moist than substantial it provides a little nourishment, and this produces cooling.

38.[50] Why do purslane[51] and salt stop bleeding gums? Is it because purslane contains moisture? This is obvious to anyone who chews it, or if it is crushed together for some time; for moisture is drawn from it. The sticky material sinks in and draws out the acidity. And indeed, the acidity is a sign that there is an affinity;[52] for the juice[53] contains a certain acidity. But salt too drives out the acidity, by melting it. Why, then, don't lye and soda do this? Is it because they cause contraction and not melting?

39.[54] Why should summer fatigue be treated by baths, but winter fatigue by anointing? Is the latter treated by anointing because of shivering and the changes that occur? For it[55] must be released by means of heat, which produces warming; and oil is hot. But in the summer, it is necessary to moisten; for the season is dry, and the shivering is not to be feared because of the tendency toward warmth. Now little food and ample liquids are appropriate for summer;

"humor"—in effect, the juice of animals (see, e.g., *Pr.* 1.12); it can also mean "flavor" (see, e.g., 3.8).

[54] This chapter is virtually identical to *Pr.* 5.38. Source: Thphr. *Lass.* 17.

[55] Either the fatigue or the cold.

τὸ δὲ μᾶλλον, ὁ μὲν πότος θέρους ὅλως διὰ τὴν
ξηρότητα, ἡ δ' ὀλιγοσιτία κοινὸν μέν, μᾶλλον δὲ
θέρους· ἐκθερμαίνεται γὰρ διὰ τὴν ὥραν ὑπὸ τῶν
σιτίων.

40. Διὰ τί τῶν φαρμάκων τὰ μὲν τὴν κοιλίαν λύει,
30 τὴν ‖ δὲ κύστιν οὔ, τὰ δὲ τὴν μὲν κύστιν λύει, τὴν
κοιλίαν δ' οὔ; ἢ ὅσα μέν ἐστιν ὑγρὰ τὴν φύσιν καὶ
ὕδατος μεστά, ταῦτα ἂν ᾖ φαρμακώδη, λύει τὴν
κύστιν; ἐκεῖ γὰρ ὑφίσταται τὰ ἄπεπτα τῶν ὑγρῶν·
ὑποδοχὴ γάρ ἐστιν ἡ κύστις τοῦ μὴ πεττομένου ὑγροῦ
35 ἐν τῇ κοιλίᾳ, ὃ οὐ μένει, ἀλλὰ πρὶν ποιῆσαί ‖ τι ἢ
864a παθεῖν ὑποχωρεῖ. ὅσα δ' ἐκ γῆς τὴν φύσιν ἐστίν, ‖ ἂν
ᾖ φαρμακώδη, ταῦτα δὲ τὴν κοιλίαν λύει· εἰς ταύτην
γὰρ ἡ φορὰ τῶν γεωδῶν. ὥστε ἂν ᾖ κινητικόν, ταράττει.

41. Διὰ τί δὲ τὰ μὲν τὴν ἄνω κοιλίαν, τὰ δὲ τὴν
κάτω κινεῖ, οἷον ἐλλέβορος μὲν τὴν ἄνω, σκαμμωνία
5 δὲ τὴν κάτω, ‖ τὰ δ' ἄμφω, οἷον ἐλατήριον καὶ τῆς
θαψίας ὁ ὀπός; ἢ ὅτι τὰ μέν ἐστι θερμά, τὰ δὲ ψυχρὰ
τῶν φαρμάκων τῶν τὴν κοιλίαν κινούντων; ὥστε τὰ
μὲν διὰ τὴν θερμότητα εὐθὺς ἐν τῇ ἄνω κοιλίᾳ ὄντα
φέρεται ἐξ αὐτῆς πρὸς τὸν ἄνω τόπον, κἀκεῖθεν συν-
10 τήξαντα μάλιστα μὲν τὰ ἀλλοτριώτατα ‖ καὶ ἥκιστα

---

56 Any of a number of species of plant in the genus *Helleborus*.
For its use as a purgative, see, e.g., Hp. *Epid.* 6.5.15.
57 The plant *Convolvulus scammonia*, the resin of which is a
strong purgative.

the former is generally the case, the latter more so (*in the summer*). Drinking (*a lot*) should generally be the case in summer because of the dryness, whereas little food should be common (*to all seasons*), but more so in summer: for one is heated by food in accordance with the season.

40. Why do some drugs loosen the stomach, but not the bladder, while others loosen the bladder, but not the stomach? Does anything that is moist by nature and full of water, if it is medicinal, loosen the bladder? For the unconcocted moisture settles there, since the bladder is the receptacle of the moisture that is not concocted in the stomach, and this does not remain there, but withdraws before causing or experiencing anything. But anything earthy in nature, if it is medicinal, loosens the stomach; for the passage of earthy materials is into the stomach. Consequently, if it is capable of producing motion, it upsets the stomach.

41. But why do some move the upper part of the stomach, and some the lower, for instance hellebore[56] moves the upper part, scammony[57] the lower, while some move both, for instance elaterium[58] and the sap of the thapsia?[59] Is it because some of the drugs that move the stomach are hot, while others are cold? So the former, owing to their heat, right away when in the upper stomach, are carried from it to the upper region, and there they melt especially what is foreign and least natural to it; and if the drug is

[56] According to Pliny (*HN* 20.1.3), this is a drug derived from the wild cucumber (*Ecballium elaterium*). For its use as a purgative, see, e.g., Hp. *Epid.* 6.5.15.

[59] I.e., the resin from the root of *Thapsia garganica*. See Thphr. *HP* 9.9.1 and Plin. *HN* 13.43.124. For its use as a purgative, see, e.g., Hp. *Epid.* 7.79.

συμπεφυκότα, ἂν δ᾽ ἰσχυρὸν ᾖ τὸ φάρμακον ἢ πλέον
δοθῇ τῆς φύσεως, κατάγει εἰς τὴν ἄνω κοιλίαν ταῦτά
τε καὶ ἐάν τι περίττωμα ᾖ, καὶ διὰ τὴν θερμότητα
ταράττον τὸ πνεῦμα πολὺ γινόμενον ὑπ᾽ αὐτοῦ, προσ-
ιστὰν τοὺς ἐμέτους ποιεῖ. τὰ δὲ ψυχρὰ τὴν φύσιν

15   αὐτῶν | διὰ βάρος καὶ πρὶν παθεῖν τι ἢ ποιῆσαι κάτω
φέρεται, κἀκεῖθεν ὁρμῶντα τὸ αὐτὸ δρᾷ τοῖς ἄνω· κατὰ
γὰρ τοὺς πόρους ἀνιόντα ἐκεῖθεν, καὶ κινήσαντα ὧν
ἂν κρατήσῃ περιττωμάτων καὶ συντηγμάτων, λαβόν-
τα τὴν αὐτὴν ἄγει ὁδόν. ὅσα δ᾽ ἀμφοῖν μετέχει καὶ

20   ἐστὶ μικτὰ τῶν φαρμακωδῶν | ἐκ θερμοῦ καὶ ψυχροῦ,
ταῦτα δὲ δι᾽ ἑκατέραν τὴν δύναμιν ἀπεργάζεται ἄμφω,
ὥσπερ καὶ νῦν παρασκευάζουσιν οἱ ἰατροὶ μιγνύντες
ἀλλήλοις.

42. Διὰ τί τὰ φάρμακα καθαίρει, ἄλλα δὲ πικρότερα
ὄντα καὶ στρυφνότερα καὶ τοῖς ἄλλοις τοῖς τοιούτοις

25   ὑπερβάλλοντα | οὐ καθαίρει; ἢ διότι οὐ διὰ τὰς τοι-
αύτας δυνάμεις καθαίρει, ἀλλ᾽ ὅτι ἄπεπτά ἐστιν; ὅσα
γὰρ δι᾽ ὑπερβολὴν θερμότητος ἢ ψυχρότητος, μικρὰ
ὄντα τοὺς ὄγκους, ἄπεπτά ἐστι καὶ οἷα κρατεῖν ἀλλὰ
μὴ κρατεῖσθαι ὑπὸ τῆς τῶν ζῴων θερμότητος, εὐδι-

30   άχυτα ὄντα ὑπὸ τῶν δύο κοιλιῶν, | ταῦτα φάρμακά
ἐστιν. ὅταν γὰρ εἰς τὴν κοιλίαν εἰσέλθωσι καὶ διαχυ-
θῶσι, φέρονται καθ᾽ οὕσπερ ἡ τροφὴ πόρους εἰς τὰς
φλέβας, οὐ πεφθέντα δ᾽ ἀλλὰ κρατήσαντα ἐκπίπτει

---

60 I.e., the foreign and unnatural materials.

strong or more is given than what is natural, it carries these[60] down into the upper stomach, as well as any residues that there may be. And owing to the heat, the abundant breath that is generated by the drug causes a disturbance, and by creating a blockage it produces vomiting. But the drugs that are cold by nature, because of their weight, are carried downward before experiencing or causing anything, and there, setting things in motion, it does the same thing (*that the other drugs do*) in the upper part; for rising from there along the passages, and moving the residues and colliquations that they master, they carry them taking the same road. But those drugs that share in both qualities and are a mixture of hot and cold, these produce both results according to their particular powers, so that even now physicians prepare these by mixing them with each other.

42. Why do drugs purge, but other things that are bitterer and more astringent or have an excess of other such qualities do not purge? Is it because they purge not owing to these qualities, but because they are unconcocted? For those things are drugs which, owing to an excess of hot or cold, though they are small in bulk, are unconcocted, and are such as to master but not be mastered by the heat characteristic of animals,[61] being easily dissolved by the two stomachs. For when they go into the stomach and are dissolved, they are carried along the same passages as nourishment into the veins, and not being concocted but

[61] Concoction occurs when the natural heat of an animal is able to process (or "master") the ingested material. (See n. 10 above.) In the case of drugs, however, the body cannot process the substance but is in turn affected (or "mastered") by it.

φέροντα τὰ ἐμπόδια αὐτοῖς· καὶ καλεῖται τοῦτο κάθαρ-
σις. χαλκὸς δὲ καὶ ἄργυρος καὶ τὰ τοιαῦτα ἄπεπτα |
35 μέν ἐστιν ὑπὸ τῆς τῶν ζῴων θερμότητος, ἀλλ' οὐκ
εὐδιάχυτα ταῖς κοιλίαις. ἔλαιον δὲ καὶ μέλι καὶ γάλα
864b καὶ τὰ || τοιαῦτα τῆς τροφῆς καθαίρει, ἀλλ' οὐ τῷ ποιῷ
ἀλλὰ τῷ ποσῷ· ὅταν γὰρ διὰ πλῆθος ἄπεπτα γένηται,
τότε καθαίρει, ἄνπερ καθαίρῃ. διὰ δύο γὰρ αἰτίας
ἄπεπτά ἐστιν, διὰ τὸ ποιὰ αὐτὰ εἶναι ἢ διὰ τὸ ποσά.
5 διόπερ οὐ φάρμακόν ἐστιν οὐδὲν | τῶν εἰρημένων· οὐδὲ
γὰρ διὰ δύναμιν καθαίρει. στρυφνότης δὲ καὶ πικρό-
της συμβέβηκε τοῖς φαρμάκοις καὶ δυσωδία, τῷ ἐναντίον εἶναι τῇ τροφῇ τὸ φάρμακον. τὸ μὲν γὰρ πεφθὲν
ὑπὸ τῆς φύσεως, τοῦτο προσφύεται τοῖς σώμασι καὶ
καλεῖται τροφή· τὸ δὲ μὴ πεφυκὸς κρατεῖσθαι, εἰσιὸν
10 δ'[29] | εἰς τὰς φλέβας καὶ δι' ὑπερβολὴν θερμότητος ἢ
ψυχρότητος ταράττον, αὕτη δὲ φαρμάκου φύσις ἐστίν.
    43. Διὰ τί τὸ μὲν πέπερι πολὺ μὲν ὂν τὴν κύστιν
λύει, ὀλίγον δὲ τὴν κοιλίαν, ἡ δὲ σκαμμωνία πολλὴ
οὖσα τὴν κοιλίαν λύει, ὀλίγη δὲ καὶ παλαιὰ τὴν
15 κύστιν; ἢ διότι | ἑκάτερον ἑκατέρας ἐστὶ κινητικώ-
τερον;[30] τὸ μὲν γὰρ πέπερι οὐρητικόν ἐστιν, ἡ δὲ
σκαμμωνία καθαρτικόν.[31] τὸ μὲν οὖν πέπερι πολὺ μὲν
ὂν φέρεται εἰς τὴν κύστιν καὶ οὐ διαχεῖται ἐν τῇ
κοιλίᾳ,[32] ὀλίγον δ' ὂν κρατηθὲν διαλύει καὶ γίνεται

[29] εἰσιὸν δ' : εἰσιόντα Yᵃ Cᵃ : εἰσιόν τε Ruelle
[30] κινητικώτερον Yᵃ Apᵇ : κινητικώτερα cett. codd.

achieving mastery, they fall out carrying the obstructions with them; and this is called purgation. Now bronze and silver and such things are unconcocted by the heat characteristic of animals; nevertheless they are not easily dissolved by the stomachs. But olive oil and honey and milk and other such nourishment purge, not by their quality but by their quantity; for when they are unconcocted owing to their quantity, they purge, if ever they do purge. For things are unconcocted for two reasons: because of their quality or because of their quantity. This is why none of the above-mentioned (*kinds of nourishment*)[62] are drugs: for it is not owing to a power that they purge. But astringency and bitterness and malodor are characteristic of drugs, a drug being the opposite of nourishment. For what is concocted by its nature grows into the body and is called nourishment; what is not of a nature to be mastered, however, but enters into the veins and because of an excess of heat or cold causes trouble—this is the nature of a drug.

43. Why does pepper, when there's a lot of it, loosen the bladder, but when there's little the stomach, whereas scammony, when there's a lot of it, loosens the stomach, and when there's little or it's old, the bladder? Is it because each substance produces motion more in each of these parts? For pepper is a diuretic, whereas scammony is a purgative. Therefore pepper, when there's a lot of it, travels into the bladder and is not dissolved in the stomach, but when there's little it is mastered, and loosening the stom-

---

[62] I.e., oil, honey, milk, etc.

---

31 καθαρτικόν Sylburg : κατωρετικόν codd. (praeter L, καταρυτικόν) 32 ἐν τῇ κοιλίᾳ : εἰς τὴν κοιλίαν L Am

φάρμακον αὐτῆς. ἡ δὲ σκαμμωνία πολλὴ μὲν οὖσα
20 εἰς | τοῦτο κρατεῖται ὥστε διαχυθῆναι, διαχυθεῖσα δὲ
γίνεται φάρμακον διὰ τὴν εἰρημένην ἐν τοῖς ἀνωτέρω
αἰτίαν· ὀλίγη δ' οὖσα μετὰ τοῦ ποτοῦ ἀναπίνεται εἰς
τοὺς πόρους, καὶ ταχὺ πρὶν ταράξαι καταφέρεται εἰς
τὴν κύστιν, καὶ ἐκεῖ τῇ αὑτῆς δυνάμει ἀπάγει τὰ
25 περιττώματα καὶ τὰ συντήγματα | ὅσα <ἐξ>³³ ἐπιπο-
λῆς ἐστίν. ἡ δὲ πολλή, ὥσπερ εἴρηται, διὰ τὴν ἰσχὺν
πολὺν χρόνον ἐμμείνασα κατάγει πολλὴν κάθαρσιν
καὶ γεώδη.

44. Διὰ τί τὰς αὐτὰς φλεγμασίας οἱ μὲν ψύχοντες
ὑγιάζουσιν, οἱ δὲ θερμαίνοντες πέττουσιν; ἀλλ' οἱ μὲν
30 ἀλλοτρίᾳ | θερμότητι, οἱ δὲ καταψύχοντες τὴν οἰκείαν
συνάγουσιν.

45. Διὰ τί μεταβάλλειν δεῖ τὰ καταπλάσματα; ἢ
ὅπως³⁴ μᾶλλον αἰσθάνηται; τὰ γὰρ συνήθη ὥσπερ ἐπὶ
τῶν ἐδεσμάτων οὐκέτι φάρμακα ἀλλὰ τροφὴ γίνεται,
35 οὕτω | καὶ ἐπὶ τῶν τοιούτων.

46. Διὰ τί ὑγιεινὸν τὸ τῆς τροφῆς μὲν ὑποστέλ-
865a λεσθαι, ‖ πονεῖν δὲ πλείω; ἢ ὅτι τοῦ νοσεῖν αἴτιον
περιττώματος πλῆθος; τοῦτο δὲ γίνεται, ἡνίκα τροφῆς
ὑπερβολὴ ἢ πόνων ἔνδεια.

47. Διὰ τί τὰ φάρμακα καὶ τὰ πικρὰ ὡς ἐπὶ τὸ πολὺ
καὶ τὰ δυσώδη καθαίρει; ἢ ὅτι ἅπαντα τὰ δυσώδη καὶ |
5 πικρὰ ἄπεπτά ἐστι; διὸ καὶ τὰ φάρμακα πικρὰ καὶ

---

³³ <ἐξ> Bekker
³⁴ ὅπως β : ὅτι ὡς cett. codd.

44

ach becomes a drug with respect to it. But scammony, when there's a lot of it, is mastered to the point that it is dissolved, and being dissolved it becomes a drug for the reason stated above; whereas when there's little, it is absorbed into the passages with what is drunk, and quickly carried down into the bladder before it causes trouble, and there by its own power it leads off all the residue and colliquation that are ‹out› of the surface. But a large quantity of scammony, as has been said, owing to its strength remains a long time and leads down an abundant purgation of earthy material.

44. Why do some treat the same inflammations by cooling, which others "concoct"[63] by heating? In fact, the latter bring the inflammation to a head with a foreign heat, while the former cool its own heat.

45. Why should poultices be changed? Is it so that they may be felt more? For as in the case of the things we eat, the things one is used to are no longer drugs, but become nourishment, and similarly in such cases.

46.[64] Why is a *reduction* of nourishment healthy, but an *increase* in exertion? Is it because a quantity of residue is a cause of being diseased? Now this occurs when there is an excess of nourishment or a lack of exertion.

47.[65] Why do drugs that are bitter and malodorous usually purge? Is it because all malodorous and bitter things are unconcocted? This is why drugs are bitter and mal-

---

[63] Here "concoct" likely means "bring to a head," as the author describes in the following line.   [64] This chapter is virtually identical to *Pr.* 5.33. Possible sources for these chapters are Hp. *Flat.* 7 and the views of Herodicus of Selimbria (see Pl. *R.* 406a–c, *Phdr.* 227d).   [65] Cf. *Pr.* 1.42.

δυσώδη· τῷ γὰρ ἄπεπτα εἶναι καὶ κινητικὰ μετὰ
πικρότητος φάρμακά ἐστιν. καὶ ἐὰν δοθῇ πλείω, δια-
φθείρει. ὅσα δέ, κἂν μικρὰ δοθῇ, διαφθαρτικά, ταῦτα
οὐ φάρμακα λέγεται εἶναι ἀλλὰ θανατηφόρα. οὐδ᾽

10 ὅσα μὴ τῷ ποιῷ καθαίρει, | οὐκ ἔστι φάρμακα. καὶ
γὰρ τῆς τροφῆς πολλὰ μὲν ταὐτὸ ποιεῖ, ἐὰν ποσὰ
δοθῇ, οἷον γάλα, ἔλαιον, γλεῦκος· ἅπαντα δὲ ταῦτα
διὰ τὸ μὴ εἶναι εὔπεπτα καθαίρει, καὶ τούτοις οἷς μὴ
εὔπεπτα καθαίρει [καὶ τούτους].[35] ἔστι γὰρ ἄλλα ἄλ-

15 λοις εὔπεπτα καὶ δύσπεπτα. διὸ οὐ πᾶσι | ταὐτὰ
φαρμακώδη, ἀλλ᾽ ἐνίοις ἴδια. ὅλως γὰρ τὸ φάρμακον
δεῖ οὐ μόνον μὴ πέττεσθαι ἀλλὰ καὶ κινητικὸν εἶναι,
ὥσπερ καὶ τὸ γυμνάσιον ἔξωθεν ἧκον ἢ ἔσωθεν τῇ
κινήσει ἐκκρίνει τὰ ἀλλότρια.

48. Διὰ τί τὰ μὲν εὐώδη οὐρητικὰ καὶ σπέρματα

20 καὶ | φυτά; ἢ ὅτι θερμὰ καὶ εὔπεπτα, τὰ δὲ τοιαῦτα
οὐρητικά; ταχὺ γὰρ λεπτύνει ἡ ἐνοῦσα θερμότης, καὶ
ἡ ὀσμὴ οὐ σωματώδης, ἐπεὶ καὶ τὰ ὀσμώδη, οἷον σκόροδα, διὰ τὴν θερμότητα οὐρητικά, μᾶλλον μέντοι
συντηκτικά. θερμὰ δὲ τὰ εὐώδη σπέρματα. |

25 49. Διὰ τί δεῖ πρὸς μὲν τὰ μὴ καθαρὰ καὶ φαῦλα
τῶν ἑλκῶν ξηροῖς καὶ δριμέσι καὶ στρυφνοῖς χρῆσθαι
φαρμάκοις, πρὸς δὲ τὰ καθαρὰ καὶ ὑγιαζόμενα ὑγροῖς
καὶ μόνοις;[36] ἢ διότι ἀπὸ μὲν τῶν μὴ καθαρῶν δεῖ

---

[35] καὶ τούτοις secl. Marenghi[3] ‖ καὶ τούτους seclusi
[36] μόνος codd. (praeter aᵐ, δριμέσι) : μάνοις Monro :
λείοις Bonitz

46

odorous; for a drug exists by being unconcocted and capable of producing motion, along with bitterness. And if too much is given, the patient dies. Now those things that are deadly, even if a small amount is given, are not called drugs but poisons. Nor are those things drugs, which do not purge by their quality. For many forms of nourishment produce the same effect, if large amounts are given, such as milk, olive oil, and grape juice: all of these purge, because they are not easily concocted, and they do so in those for whom they are not easily concocted. For to different persons some things are concocted easily and some concocted with difficulty. This is why the same things are not druglike to all people, but some are specific to certain people. For in general, the drug should not only be unconcocted, but also capable of producing motion, just as exercise—coming outside or inside—secretes foreign matter by movement.

48.[66] Why are fragrant seeds and plants diuretic? Is it because they are hot and easily concocted, and such things are diuretic? For the internal heat liquefies quickly and the smell is not corporeal, since even the odorous ones, like garlic, are diuretic owing to their heat, though they are more productive of colliquation. And fragrant seeds are hot.

49.[67] Why should one use dry, sharp, and astringent drugs on unclean and foul sores, but moist drugs alone on sores that are clean and healing? Is it because something

66 Cf. *Pr.* 12.12 and 20.16.
67 See Hp. *Ulc.* passim.

ἀφαιρεῖν τι; τοῦτο δ' ἐστὶν ὑγρότης ἀλλοτρία, ἣν
30 ἀφαιρεῖν δεῖ. τὰ δηκτικὰ | δὲ καὶ δριμέα καὶ στρυφνὰ
τοιαῦτα, καὶ τὸ ξηρὸν μᾶλλον τοῦ ὑγροῦ. τὰ δὲ καθαρὰ συνεπουλώσεως δεῖται μόνον.

50a. Διὰ τί συμφέρει πρὸς τὰ ἀπὸ φλέγματος
νοσήματα ⟨ἡ⟩[37] λαγνεία; ἢ ὅτι τὸ σπέρμα περιττώματος[38] ἀπόκρισις καὶ φύσει ὅμοιον φλέγματι, ὥστε
35 ἀφαιροῦσα πολὺ φλεγματῶδες | ὠφελεῖ ἡ συνουσία;

50b.[39] .... πότερον δὲ τροφὴν προσφέρειν ἀρχομένῳ βέλτιον ἢ ὕστερον; ἢ ἀρχομένῳ, ὅπως μὴ
προεξησθενηκότι ἡ φλεγμασία ἐπιπίπτῃ; ἢ [οὖν][40]
ἀπισχναντέον εὐθύς; ἢ οὕτω προσοιστέον· ἀναλαμ-
865b βάνειν χρὴ πρῶτον τοῖς ῥοφήμασι· ‖ πραότερα γὰρ
καὶ λειότερα καὶ εὐτηκτότερα, καὶ ἐκδέξασθαι τὴν
τροφὴν ἐκ τούτου ῥάδιόν ἐστιν ἀσθενεῖ σώματι. οὐ[41]
γὰρ ἐν τῇ κοιλίᾳ δεῖ παθεῖν τὰ σῖτα πρῶτον, διαχυ-
θῆναί τε καὶ θερμανθῆναι, μετὰ πόνου τῷ σώματι |
5 ταῦτα πέπονθεν.

51. Διὰ τί δεῖ σκοπεῖν τὰ περὶ τὸ οὖρον σημεῖα,
ἀπολαμβάνοντα τὴν οὔρησιν, εἰ ἤδη πέπεπται ἢ μή,
μᾶλλον ἢ[42] συνεχῶς οὐροῦντα; ἢ διότι σημεῖον μὲν
τοῦ πεπέφθαι, ἐὰν ᾖ πυρρόν; τοῦτο δὲ γίνεται μᾶλλον
10 διαλαμβάνουσιν. | ἢ διότι ἔνοπτρον γίνεται ἅπαν

---

[37] ⟨ἡ⟩ Marenghi[3] (cf. Pr. 4.16, 878b14)
[38] περιττώματος : περιττώσεως γ
[39] nov. cap. α u PPA Barth. ‖ lac. ante πότερον indicavi
[40] οὖν seclusi   [41] οὐ : ἃ β : οὗ Bussemaker· ὃ Richards
[42] ἢ Vat.1904[mg] : καὶ codd.

48

must be removed from unclean sores? And that which must be removed is foreign moisture. Now the ones that will do this are biting, sharp, and astringent, and the dry more than the moist. But clean sores need only to be scarred over.

50a.[68] Why is lustfulness beneficial with a view to diseases caused by phlegm? Is it because the seed is a separation of residue and in nature similar to phlegm, so that sexual intercourse helps by removing a lot of phlegmlike material?

50b.[69] . . . But is it better to introduce nourishment at the beginning rather than later? Is it better at the beginning, so that the inflammation does not attack an already weakened patient? Or should the patient be reduced right away? Or should it be administered in this way: he should at first take in porridge, for this is milder, smoother, and more easily dissolved, and it is easy for a weak body to receive nourishment from it? For the food should not be acted on in the stomach first, as being dissolved and heated are experienced in the body with pain.

51.[70] Why should one investigate the signs pertaining to urine by interrupting the flow of urine to see whether it is already concocted, and not rather urinating continuously? Is it because it is a sign of having been concocted, if it is red? And this appears more when it is stopped at intervals. Or is it because all moisture becomes a mirror of color

---

68 Cf. *Pr.* 4.16. Source: Hp. *Epid.* 6.5.15.

69 This appears to be part of a new chapter (a division with some manuscript support), though I doubt it is the *beginning* of a new chapter. On 50b, see Hp. *Aph.* 1.10.

70 See Hp. *Prog.* 12.

μᾶλλον ὑγρὸν χρόας ὀλίγον ἢ πολὺ ὄν; ἐν μὲν γὰρ τῷ
πολλῷ ὑγρῷ τὰ σχήματα ἐνορᾶται, ἐν δὲ τῷ ὀλίγῳ τὰ
χρώματα, οἷον καὶ ἐπὶ τῆς δρόσου καὶ τῶν ῥανίδων
καὶ ἐπὶ τῶν δακρύων τῶν ἐπὶ ταῖς βλεφαρίσιν. συν-
15 εχῶς μὲν οὖν ἀφιέμενον γίνεται πλεῖον, | διασπώμενον
δὲ δέχεται μᾶλλον· ὥστε κἂν ᾖ αὐτὸ τοιοῦτον ἤδη διὰ
τὴν πέψιν, καὶ φαίνεται μᾶλλον τῆς ἀνακλάσεως γινομένης καὶ ἐνόπτρου ἔνοπτον διὰ τὴν διαίρεσιν.

52. ... ὅτι[43] οὐ δεῖ πυκνοῦν τὴν σάρκα πρὸς ὑγείαν,
ἀλλ᾽ ἀραιοῦν· ὥσπερ γὰρ πόλις ὑγιεινὴ καὶ τόπος
20 εὔπνους (διὸ | καὶ ἡ θάλασσα ὑγιεινή), οὕτω καὶ σῶμα
τὸ εὔπνουν μᾶλλον ὑγιεινόν. δεῖ γὰρ ἢ μὴ ὑπάρχειν
μηθὲν περίττωμα, ἢ τούτου ὡς τάχιστα ἀπαλλάτ-
τεσθαι, καὶ ἀεὶ οὕτως ἔχειν τὸ σῶμα ὥστε λαμβάνον
εὐθὺς ἐκκρίνειν τὴν περίττωσιν, καὶ εἶναι ἐν κινήσει
25 καὶ μὴ ἠρεμεῖν. τὸ μὲν γὰρ μένον σήπεται,[44] | ὥσπερ
ὕδωρ τὸ μὴ κινούμενον, σηπόμενον δὲ νοσοποιεῖ· τὸ δὲ
ἐκκρινόμενον πρὸ τοῦ διαφθαρῆναι χωρίζεται. τοῦτο
οὖν πυκνουμένης μὲν τῆς σαρκὸς οὐ γίνεται (ὥσπερεὶ
γὰρ ἐμφράττονται οἱ πόροι), ἀραιουμένης δὲ συμβαίνει. διὸ καὶ οὐ δεῖ ἐν τῷ ἡλίῳ γυμνὸν βαδίζειν·

---

[43] ante ὅτι lac. indic. Flashar : ante ὅτι add. διὰ τί Sylburg
ex Gaza   [44] σήπεται Bussemaker (cf. *Pr.* 5.34, 884a33 and
37.3, 966a20–21) : σήπει codd.

---

[71] I.e., red color.   [72] Some scholars take "division" here
to refer to refraction; I think it more likely refers to the "division"
in the flow of urine referred to earlier in the chapter.

more in small than in large amounts? For shapes are seen in a large quantity of moisture, but colors in a small quantity, for instance even in the case of dew and raindrops, and in tears on the eyelids. Therefore, when it is discharged continuously it becomes greater in quantity, but when (*the flow of urine*) is broken up it takes on colors more, so that if owing to the concoction it has this character,[71] it is more obvious when reflection occurs and it is visible in a mirror owing to division.[72]

52.[73] . . . because with a view to health one should not thicken the flesh, but make it porous; for just as a city or a region with a good flow of air is healthy (and this is why the sea is healthy), so too a body is healthier if it has a good flow of air. For either there should be no residue, or the body should release it as quickly as possible, and so the body should always be such as to excrete the residue immediately upon receiving it, and be in motion and not at rest. For what stays still becomes putrid, like water that doesn't move, and what is putrid produces disease; but what is excreted is separated before there is decay. So if the flesh is thickened, this[74] does not occur (for the passages are, so to speak, blocked), but it does happen when the flesh is porous. And this is why one should not walk naked in the

[73] This chapter is virtually identical to *Pr.* 5.34 and to part of 37.3 (966a13–34). If its opening was originally like that of 5.34, then we should omit the "because" (ὅτι) and begin the chapter "Why (διὰ τί) with a view to health should one not thicken" etc. If it was originally more like 37.3, however, we should retain the "because" and assume that the preceding text is lost, or similar or identical to what we find at 37.3, 965b36–966a13.

[74] I.e., the excretion of residue.

30 συνίσταται γὰρ ἡ σὰρξ | καὶ κομιδῇ ἀποσαρκοῦται,[45]
καὶ ὑγρότερον τὸ σῶμα γίνεται· τὸ μὲν γὰρ ἐντὸς
διαμένει, τὸ δ᾽ ἐπιπολῆς ἀπαλλάττεται, ὥσπερ καὶ τὰ
κρέα τὰ ὀπτὰ τῶν ἐφθῶν μᾶλλον. οὐδὲ τὰ στήθη
γυμνὰ ἔχοντα βαδίζειν· ἀπὸ γὰρ τῶν ἄριστα ᾠκοδομημένων τοῦ σώματος ὁ ἥλιος ἀφαιρεῖ ἃ ἥκιστα
35 δεῖται | ἀφαιρέσεως, ἀλλὰ μᾶλλον τὰ ἐντός. ἐκεῖθεν
μὲν οὖν διὰ τὸ πόρρω εἶναι, ἐὰν μὴ μετὰ πόνου, οὐκ
ἔστιν ἱδρῶτα ἀγαγεῖν, ἀπὸ τούτου δὲ διὰ τὸ πρόχειρον
ῥᾴδιον.

53. Διὰ τί ποτε τοῖς χιμέτλοις καὶ τὸ ψυχρὸν ὕδωρ ‖
866a συμφέρει καὶ τὸ θερμόν; ἢ ὅτι τὰ χίμετλα δι᾽ ὑπερβολὴν γίνεται ὑγροῦ; τὸ μὲν οὖν ψυχρὸν συνίστησι
καὶ τραχύνει τὸ ὑγρόν, τὸ δὲ θερμὸν ἐκπνευματοῖ καὶ
ἔξοδον ποιεῖ τῷ πνεύματι, ἀραιοῦν τὴν σάρκα. |

5 54. Διὰ τί τὸ ψυχρὸν καὶ ποιεῖ καὶ παύει τὰ χίμετλα, καὶ τὸ θερμὸν τὰ πυρίκαυστα; ἢ διὰ τὸ αὐτό;
ποιεῖ μὲν συντήκοντα, παύει δὲ μᾶλλον ξηραίνοντα.

55. Ἐν τοῖς πυρετοῖς διδόναι δεῖ τὸ ποτὸν πολλάκις
καὶ κατ᾽ ὀλίγον. τὸ μὲν γὰρ πολὺ παραρρεῖ, τὸ δ᾽
10 ὀλίγον | μὲν, πολλάκις δὲ, διαβρέχει καὶ εἰς τὰς
σάρκας χωρεῖ. οἷα γὰρ τὰ ἐν τῇ γῇ, ἐὰν μὲν κατὰ
πολὺ ἔλθῃ τὸ ὕδωρ, παραρρεῖ, ἐὰν δὲ κατ᾽ ὀλίγον,
βρέχει μόνον, τὸ αὐτὸ καὶ ἐν τοῖς πυρετοῖς. τὰ γὰρ

---

[45] ἀποσαρκοῦται : ἀποστρακοῦται Nicasius (cf. Gaza con-
calescit)

52

sun, for the flesh congeals and becomes very fleshy,[75] and
the body becomes moister; for what moisture is inside remains, whereas what is on the surface is released, just like
meat that is roasted rather than boiled. Nor should one
walk with a bare chest; for the sun then removes from the
best constructed parts of the body what least requires to be
removed, rather than the inside parts. Therefore, because
they are farther, it is not possible to lead sweat away (*from
them*), except with exertion, but from the outside parts it is
easy, because they are close at hand.

53.[76] Why are both cold and hot water beneficial to chilblains? Is it because chilblains occur owing to an excess
of moisture? So cold congeals and hardens the moisture,
while heat vaporizes it and provides an exit to the breath by
making the flesh porous.

54.[77] Why does cold both produce and stop chilblains,
and heat both produce and stop burns? Is it owing to
the same thing? They produce by means of colliquation,
whereas they stop by means of drying.

55.[78] In fevers one should provide drink often and in
small quantities. For a large quantity flows past, whereas a
small quantity taken often soaks through and moves into
the flesh. For regarding what goes into the earth, if water
comes in a large quantity, it flows past, but if it comes in a
small quantity, it merely soaks in, and the same thing oc-

[75] Louis's conjecture yields "and becomes very hard."

[76] Cf. Hp. *Epid.* 5.57, 7.76a.   [77] Cf. Hp. *Epid.* 5.57, 7.76a.

[78] The remaining chapters do not raise problems, but rather
describe medical treatments. They were probably taken from a
medical treatise (of Aristotle's?) and added here, to be trans-
formed into or made the basis of genuine problems.

ῥέοντα ὕδατα ἐάν τις κατ' ὀλίγον ἄγῃ, ὁ ὀχετὸς
15 ἐκπίνει· ἐὰν δὲ τὸ ἴσον ἀθρόον ἄγῃ, ὅπου ‖ ἂν ἄγῃ,
χωρεῖ. ἔπειτα κατακείσθω ἀκίνητος ὡς μάλιστα, ἀκίνητος μέν, ὅτι καὶ τὸ πῦρ φανερῶς, ἐάν τις μὴ κινῇ,[46]
καταμαραίνεται. πρὸς πνεῦμα δὲ μὴ κατακείσθω, διότι
ὁ ἄνεμος τὸ πῦρ ἐξεγείρει καὶ ῥιπιζόμενον τὸ πῦρ ἐξ
20 ὀλίγου πολὺ γίνεται. περιστελλέσθω[47] δὲ τούτου ἕνεκεν, ὅτι πυρὶ ‖ ἐὰν ἀναπνοὴν μὴ διδῷς, σβέννυται. καὶ
τὰ ἱμάτια μὴ ἀπογυμνούσθω, ἕως ἂν νοτὶς ἐγγένηται·
τὸ φανερὸν γὰρ πῦρ τὸ ὑγρὸν σβέννυσιν. κατὰ ταῦτα[48] δὲ καὶ ἐν τῇ φύσει. ἐπὶ δὲ τῶν διαλειπόντων
πυρετῶν προπαρασκευάζειν δεῖ καὶ ἐκλύοντα[49] καὶ
25 πυριάματα πρὸς τοὺς πόδας παρατιθέντα, ‖ καὶ περι-
εσταλμένον ἀναπαύεσθαι, ὅπως ὅτι θερμότατος ᾖ πρὸ
τοῦ τὴν λῆψιν εἶναι. καὶ γὰρ ὅπου πολὺ πῦρ, λύχνος
οὐ δυνήσεται καίεσθαι· τὸ γὰρ πῦρ τὸ πολὺ τὸ ὀλίγον
ἄγει πρὸς ἑαυτό. τούτου ἕνεκα πολὺ πῦρ ἐν τῷ σώματι
παρασκευάζειν δεῖ, ὅτι ὀλίγον ὁ πυρετὸς πῦρ ἔχει, ‖
30 ὥστε τὸ πολὺ πῦρ τὸ ὀλίγον πρὸς ἑαυτὸ ἄγει.

56. ⟨Ἐν⟩ τοῖς[50] τεταρταίοις πυρετοῖς δεῖ μὴ λεπτύ-
νειν, ἀλλὰ πῦρ ἐν τοῖς σώμασιν ἐμποιεῖν εἰσάγοντα.
δεῖ δὲ καὶ τοῖς γυμνασίοις χρῆσθαι. ᾗ δ' ἡμέρᾳ ἡ
λῆψις, λουσάμενον ὕπνον μὴ ζητεῖν. διὰ δὲ τοῦτο καὶ

---

[46] κινῇ : ἐγκινῇ β Χ[a2] a[m] p
[47] περιστελλέσθω β : περιστέλλεσθαι cett. codd.
[48] ταῦτα : ταὐτὰ Sylburg
[49] ἐκλύοντα a β δ : ἐκλούοντα γ   [50] ⟨ἐν⟩ Sylburg (cf.
Pr. 1.55, 866a8) ‖ ante τεταρταίοις add. τοῖς P[c] L

curs in fevers. For if one brings forth the flowing water in a small quantity, the channel drains; but if one brings forth the same quantity all at once, it spreads everywhere.[79] Next, let the patient lie as motionless as possible—motionless, because fire also obviously dies down, if one does not move it. And let him not lie in a draft, because wind stirs up the fire, and being fanned, the fire grows from small to large. And let the patient be well wrapped up for this reason: because if you do not give the fire a chance to breathe, it is quenched. And let the clothes not be removed until dampness appears; for the moisture quenches the open fire. Along these lines, this also occurs in nature. In the case of intermittent fevers, one should make preparations beforehand by relaxing[80] the patient and applying compresses to his feet, and he should rest well covered, in order that he may be very hot before the seizure comes. Indeed, a lamp cannot burn where there is a great fire, for the great fire absorbs the small one into itself. For this reason one should prepare a great fire in the body, because the fever has a small fire, so that the great fire absorbs the little one into itself.

56. In quartan fevers one should not grow thin, but fire should be created and introduced into the body.[81] And one should also employ exercises. Now on the day in which the seizure (*is expected*), one should bathe but should not attempt to sleep. And for this reason too, a heating regimen

[79] The author is likely referring to irrigation.

[80] Or "bathing," if the alternative reading is correct.

[81] I.e., the body should be heated. The author is continuing to use the language of fire.

35 συμφέρει θερμαίνουσα δίαιτα, | ὅτι ἀσθενὴς ὁ τεταρ-
ταῖος πυρετός· εἰ γὰρ μὴ ἦν ἀσθενής, οὐκ ἂν τεταρ-
ταῖος ἐγένετο. ὁρᾷς; ὅπου πῦρ πολύ, λύχνος οὐ δύναται καίεσθαι· τὸ γὰρ πολὺ τὸ ὀλίγον πρὸς ἑαυτὸ ‖
866b ἁρπάζει. τούτου δ᾿ ἕνεκεν πολὺ πῦρ ἐν τῷ σώματι
ἐμποιεῖν, ὅτι ὀλίγον ὁ πυρετὸς πῦρ ἔχει. ἔστι δὲ τὸ
καθ᾿ ἡμέραν διαίτημα τὸ μὲν πῦρ τὸ δὲ νοτίδα εἰς τὸ
σῶμα εἰσάγοντα.

57. Εἰσὶ δὲ νόσοι αἱ μὲν ἀπὸ πυρός, αἱ δ᾿ ἀπὸ
5 νοτίδος. ἰατρεύονται | δ᾿ αἱ μὲν ἀπὸ πυρὸς νόσοι
νοτίδι, αἱ δ᾿ ἀπὸ νοτίδος πυρί· νοτίδα γὰρ ξηραίνει.

is beneficial, because the quartan fever is weak; for if it were not weak, it would not occur only every four days. Do you see? A lamp cannot burn where there is a great fire, for the great fire seizes the small one into itself. For this reason, one should produce a great fire in the body, because the fever has a small fire. So the daily regimen is to introduce on the one hand fire, on the other hand dampness into the body.

57.[82] Now some diseases come from fire, whereas others come from dampness. Those diseases that come from fire are cured by dampness, whereas those that come from dampness are cured by fire, for it dries the dampness.

[82] According to Forster, this chapter is in fact part of the previous one.

BOOK II

INTRODUCTION

Most of the chapters in *Pr.* 2 have as their source Theophrastus' *On Sweat*.[1] The similarity between much of *On Sweat* and *Pr.* 2 is undeniable; but can we be certain that the latter relied on the former (as most scholars believe) and not vice versa?[2] The best I can do in an introduction is present a representative pair of passages and point out why I believe the standard view is correct. Consider *Sud.* 30 and *Pr.* 2:

> *Sud.* 30: People don't sweat on the parts of the body borne down below the water, because the water prevents melting. Sweat is a certain melting, as of

[1] See W. W. Fortenbaugh's edition of the Greek text, with translation and commentary, in W. W. Fortenbaugh, R. Sharples, and M. G. Sollengberger, eds., *Theophrastus of Eresus: On Sweat, On Dizziness and On Fatigue* (Leiden, 2003). In the works of Aristotle that have come down to us, sweat is rarely discussed; but see *Mete.* 2.1, 353b12, 2.3, 357a24–b7, *HA* 3.19, 521a14, and *PA* 3.5, 668b3. None of the chapters in *Pr.* 2 seems to be replying to or drawing on these passages.

[2] Scholars nearly all agree that Theophrastus' *On Sweat* is the prior work. See, for example, Forster (p. 165), Flashar (pp. 335–38), and Fortenbaugh, *On Sweat* (pp. 12–15). Louis argues for the opposite position (vol. 1, pp. 31–37).

poorly constructed additions to the flesh, when they are secreted owing to heat.

Pr. 2.2: Why don't the parts (*of the body*) in hot water sweat, even though they are hot? Is it because the water prevents them from being melted, and sweat is the poorly constructed addition in the flesh, when it is secreted owing to heat?

If Thphr. *Sud.* 30 were written in answer to *Pr.* 2.2, then it is an extremely feeble, unoriginal answer indeed—simply affirming and repeating what is contained in the question. As this pair is typical,[3] the alternative interpretation would have us attribute to Theophrastus a work that is hardly worthy of a mind like his. So I think it is much more reasonable to maintain that *Pr.* 2 was composed in large part to raise questions in the Lyceum about the *On Sweat*. Another source seems to have been the Hippocratic corpus.

---

[3] Not every chapter in *Pr.* 2 is this brief, however, and many go beyond what is contained or implied in the corollary chapter in *On Sweat*. This makes an even stronger case for the priority of *On Sweat*.

ΟΣΑ ΠΕΡΙ ΙΔΡΩΤΑ

1. Διὰ τί οὔτε συντείνουσιν οὔτε κατέχουσι τὸ
πνεῦμα | γίνεται ἱδρώς, ἀλλὰ μᾶλλον ἀνιεῖσιν; ἢ ὅτι τὸ
πνεῦμα κατεχόμενον πληροῖ τὰς φλέβας, ὥστε κωλύει
ἐξιέναι, ὥσπερ τὸ ὕδωρ τὸ ἐκ τῶν κλειβυδρῶν, ὅταν
πλήρεις οὔσας ἐπιλάβῃ τις; ὅταν δὲ ἐξέλθῃ, πολὺς
γίνεται διὰ τὸ ἐν αὐτῇ ⟨τῇ⟩[1] ἐπιληψίᾳ ἀθροισθῆναι
κατὰ μικρόν. |

2. Διὰ τί οὐχ ἱδροῦσι τὰ ἐν θερμῷ ὕδατι μέρη, οὐδ᾽
ἂν θερμὰ ᾖ; ἢ διότι κωλύει τὸ ὕδωρ τήκεσθαι, ὁ δὲ
ἱδρὼς τὸ κακῶς προσῳκοδομημένον ἐστὶν ἐν τῇ σαρκί[2] ὅταν ἐκκρίνεται διὰ θερμότητα.

3. Διὰ τί ὁ ἱδρὼς ἁλμυρόν; ἢ διότι γίνεται ὑπὸ
κινήσεως | καὶ θερμότητος, ἀποκρινούσης ὅσον ἀλλό-
τριον ἔνεστιν ἐν τῇ προσφύσει τῆς τροφῆς πρὸς αἷμα
καὶ τὰς σάρκας; τοῦτο γὰρ τάχιστα ἀφίσταται διὰ τὸ
μὴ οἰκεῖον εἶναι καὶ ἔξω ἐξικμάζει. ἁλμυρὸς δ᾽ ἐστὶ

[1] ⟨τῇ⟩ Bussemaker
[2] post σαρκί add. κωλύει τήκεσθαι X[a] (ante κωλύει add. ὁ Bekker)

PROBLEMS CONCERNING
SWEAT

1.[1] Why does sweat appear neither when people make tense nor hold their breath, but rather when they release it? Is it because holding one's breath fills the veins, so that it prevents sweat from exiting—just like the water from clepsydras, when someone shuts them off when they're full?[2] But when sweat does come out, a great deal appears because it has collected gradually during the blockage.

2.[3] Why don't the parts (*of the body*) in hot water sweat, even though they are hot? Is it because the water prevents them from being melted, and sweat is the poorly constructed addition in the flesh, when it is secreted owing to heat?

3.[4] Why is sweat salty? Is it because it comes from motion and heat, which separate out what is foreign in the assimilation of the nourishment into blood and flesh? For this is very quickly removed owing to its not belonging, and it evaporates out. Now it is salty because what is sweetest

---

[1] Source: Thphr. *Sud.* 25.   [2] These clepsydras (κλεψ-ύδραι) are not water clocks but devices for picking up and moving liquids (like modern pipettes). Cf. *Resp.* 7.   [3] Source: Thphr. *Sud.* 30. Athenaeus cites this chapter, attributing it to Aristotle (1.24E).   [4] Source: Thphr. *Sud.* 2–3.

διὰ τὸ τὸ³ γλυκύτατον καὶ κουφότατον εἰς τὸ σῶμα
25 ἀνηλῶσθαι, τὸ δὲ ἀλλοτριώτατον | καὶ ἀπεπτότατον
ἀπολύεσθαι. τὸ τοιοῦτον δὲ ἐν μὲν τῇ κάτω ὑποστάσει
οὖρον καλεῖται, ἐν δὲ σαρκὶ ἱδρώς· ἄμφω δὲ ἁλμυρὰ
διὰ τὴν αὐτὴν αἰτίαν.

4. Διὰ τί τὰ ἄνω ἱδροῦσι μᾶλλον τῶν κάτω; πότερον
τὸ θερμὸν ἄνω καὶ ἀνέρχεται καὶ ἔστιν ἄνω, τοῦτο δὲ
30 ἄνω | φέρει τὸ ὑγρόν; ἢ ὅτι πνεῦμα ποιεῖ τὸν ἱδρῶτα,
τοῦτο δὲ ἐν τοῖς ἄνω; ἢ διότι ἄπεπτον ὑγρὸν ὁ ἱδρώς
ἐστι, τοιοῦτο δὲ ἐν τοῖς ἄνω; ἡ γὰρ κρᾶσις ἄνω.

5. Διὰ τί τὰς χεῖρας γυμναζομένοις μάλιστα ἱδρὼς
γίνεται, ἐὰν τὰ ἄλλα ὁμοιοσχημονῶμεν; ἢ διότι ἰσχύ-
35 ομεν | μάλιστα τούτῳ τῷ τόπῳ; τούτῳ γὰρ τὸ πνεῦμα
κατέχομεν τῷ ἔγγιστα τοῦ ἰσχύοντος· πονοῦντες δὲ
μᾶλλον ἰσχύομεν· οὕτω δὲ ἔχοντες τὸ πνεῦμα μᾶλλον
867a κατέχομεν. ‖ εἶτα καὶ τῇ τριβομένῃ ⟨χειρὶ⟩⁴ συμ-
πονοῦμεν μᾶλλον ἢ ὅταν ἄλλο μέρος τριβώμεθα· τῇ
γὰρ καθέξει τοῦ πνεύματος καὶ τριβόμενοι γυμνα-
ζόμεθα καὶ τρίβοντες.

6. Διὰ τί ὁ ἱδρὼς ἐκ τῆς κεφαλῆς ἢ οὐκ ὄζει ἢ
5 ἧττον | τοῦ ἐκ τοῦ σώματος; ἢ ὅτι εὔπνους ὁ τῆς
κεφαλῆς τόπος; δηλοῖ δὲ μανὸς ὢν τῇ τῶν τριχῶν
ἐκφύσει. δυσώδεις δὲ οἱ τόποι καὶ τὰ ἐν αὐτοῖς γίνεται
ὅσα μὴ εὔπνοα.

---

3 alt. τὸ Ap.ᵇ : om. cett. codd.
4 ⟨χειρὶ⟩ Forster ex Thphr. *Sud.* 34, 214

5 The corresponding passage in Thphr. *Sud.* (2, 9–10) specifies
the bladder (κύστις).

and lightest (*of the nourishment*) is absorbed into the body, while what is most foreign and most difficult to concoct is released. And such material, when it is sediment in the lower part,[5] is called "urine," but in the flesh it is called "sweat"; and both are salty for the same reason.

4.[6] Why do the upper parts sweat more than the lower? Does the heat in the upper parts rise and exist above, and this carries the moisture upward? Or is it because breath produces sweat, and this is in the upper parts? Or is it because sweat is unconcocted moisture, and *this* is in the upper parts? For the mixing takes place above.[7]

5.[8] Why does sweat occur most of all[9] by exercising the arms, if we keep the other limbs at rest? Is it because we are strongest in this region? For in this part, which is nearest to the strongest part, we hold our breath, and we are stronger by exerting ourselves; and in this condition we hold our breath more. Then too in being rubbed ⟨on the arm⟩ we share the exertion more than when we are rubbed on another part; for by holding our breath we get exercise both when being rubbed and when rubbing.

6.[10] Why does sweat from the head either have no odor or less than sweat from the body? Is it because the region of the head has a good flow of air? Now its porous nature is shown by the growth in it of hair. But those regions of the body and what is in them are malodorous when they do not have a good flow of air.

---

[6] Source: Thphr. *Sud.* 24.

[7] This mixing could refer to the formation of sweat or to the concoction of moisture (of which sweat is a by-product).

[8] Source: Thphr. *Sud.* 34. Cf. Hp. *Vict.* 2.64.

[9] Either most often or in the greatest quantity.

[10] Source: Thphr. *Sud.* 9. Cf. *Pr.* 13.8.

7. Διὰ τί οἱ γυμναζόμενοι ἐὰν διαναπαυσάμενοι
παλαίωσιν, μᾶλλον ἱδροῦσιν ἢ ἐὰν συνεχῶς; ἢ διὰ
10 τὸ ἀθροίζεσθαι | διαναπαυομένων; ἔπειτα τοῦτον τὸν
ἱδρῶτα ἐξάγει ὕστερον ἡ πάλη. ἡ δὲ συνεχὴς ἀναξηραίνει ὥσπερ ὁ ἥλιος.

8. Διὰ τί μᾶλλον ἱδροῦσιν, ὅταν μὴ διὰ πολλοῦ
χρόνου χρῶνται ταῖς ἀφιδρώσεσιν; ἢ διότι οἱ ἱδρῶτες
γίνονται οὐ μόνον δι' ὑγρότητα, ἀλλὰ καὶ διὰ τὸ τοὺς
15 πόρους ἀνεῷχθαι | μᾶλλον καὶ ἀραιὰ τὰ σώματα εἶναι;
τοῖς μὲν οὖν μὴ χρωμένοις συμμεμύκασιν οἱ πόροι,
τοῖς χρωμένοις δ' ἀναστομοῦνται.

9. Διὰ τί τοῦ ἡλίου μᾶλλον θερμαίνοντος τοὺς
γυμνοὺς ἢ τοὺς ἀμπεχομένους, ἱδροῦσι μᾶλλον οἱ
20 ἀμπεχόμενοι; | πότερον ὅτι τοὺς πόρους συμμύειν
ποιεῖ ἐκκαίων ὁ ἥλιος; ἢ διότι τὰς ἀτμίδας ξηραίνει;
ἀμπεχομένοις δὲ ταῦτα ἧττον συμβαίνει.

10. Διὰ τί ἱδροῦσι μάλιστα τὰ πρόσωπα; ἢ ⟨ὅτι⟩[5]
ὅσα ἀραιὰ καὶ ὑγρὰ μάλιστα, διὰ [δὲ][6] τούτων ὁ ἱδρὼς
25 διαπορεύεται; | δοκεῖ δὲ πηγὴ εἶναι ἡ κεφαλὴ τοῦ
ὑγροῦ· διὸ καὶ αἱ τρίχες, διὰ τὸ πολὺ ὑγρόν. ὁ δὲ
τόπος ἀραιὸς καὶ ἰσχνός· δίεισιν ἄρα κατὰ φύσιν.

11. Διὰ τί οὔτ' ἀθρόου ὄντος τοῦ πυρὸς μᾶλλον
ἱδροῦσιν, οὔτ' ἐλάττονος ἀεί, ἀλλὰ πλείονος ἐπεισ-

---

5 ⟨ὅτι⟩ addidi (cf. *Pr.* 10.35, 894b14)
6 [δὲ] Ross apud Forster

---

11 Source: Thphr. *Sud.* 31.   12 Source: Thphr. *Sud.* 22.

66

7.[11] Why do those who are exercising, if they rest a bit and then wrestle, sweat more than if they wrestle continuously? Is it because the sweat collects while they are resting? Then the wrestling brings out this latter sweat. But continuous wrestling dries up the sweat, just as the sun does.

8.[12] Why do people sweat more when they have not engaged in sweating off[13] for a long time? Is it because sweats arise not merely owing to moisture, but also owing to the passages being more open and the bodies being porous? In those who have not engaged in sweating off, then, the passages are closed, while in those who have engaged in it, they are open.

9.[14] Why, though the sun heats the naked more than the dressed, do the dressed sweat more? Is it because the sun by its scorching causes the passages to close? Or is it because it dries the vapors? And these occur less in those who are dressed.

10.[15] Why does the face sweat most? Is it because those parts that are porous and moist sweat most, the sweat passing right through them? Now the head seems to be the source of moisture; and this is why there is hair there, because of the considerable moisture. And this region is porous and rare, so the moisture naturally passes through it.

11.[16] Why do people sweat more not when the fire is ⟨made large⟩[17] all at once nor when it is gradually

[13] By visiting a steam room. [14] Sources: Thphr. *Sud.* 27 and/or Hp. *Aër* 8. Cf. *Pr.* 1.52 and 2.37.

[15] Source: Thphr. *Sud.* 33. Cf. *Pr.* 2.17 and 36.2.

[16] Source: Thphr. *Sud.* 28. Cf. *Pr.* 2.32.

[17] See Thphr. *Sud.* 28.

30 φερομένου; οἱ γὰρ | ἐν τοῖς πυριατηρίοις ἱδροῦσι
μᾶλλον ἢ εὐθὺς εἰ εἴη τοσοῦτον. ἢ ὅτι τὸ σύμμετρον
ἕκαστον ἐργάζεται; οὐκοῦν εἰ τοσοῦτον[7] ποιεῖ, τὸ
πλεῖον οὐ ποιήσει πλεῖον ἢ μᾶλλον τοὐναντίον, ὅτι τῷ
σύμμετρον εἶναι ἐργάζεται τὸ ἔργον. διὰ μὲν οὖν
τοῦτο οὐχὶ πρὸς πλεῖον μᾶλλον ἱδροῦσιν, διὰ δὲ τὸ
35 πρὸς | ἕκαστον ἄλλην εἶναι συμμετρίαν, καὶ τὸ πεποι-
ηκὸς μηκέτι ποιεῖν προστιθεμένου μᾶλλον. οὐ γὰρ
ταὐτὸ προοδοποιεῖται εἰς ἕκαστον καὶ ἐπιτηδείως
ἔχειν παρασκευάζει, καὶ ἤδη τοῦτο ἐργάζεται, ἀλλ'
ἕτερον. τὸ μὲν οὖν ὀλίγον μᾶλλον ἢ πολὺ προωδο-
867b ποίησεν καὶ παρεσκεύασεν τὸ σῶμα πρὸς ‖ τὸ ἱδροῦν·
ἄλλης δὲ δεῖ συμμετρίας καὶ πλείονος πρὸς τὸ ποιῆσαι. τοῦτο δὲ οὐκέτι ποιεῖ ὃ πεποίηκεν, ἀλλὰ μετ'
αὐτὸ ὕστερον, ἄλλο τῆς συμμετρίας γινόμενον.

12. Διὰ τί ἀποστλεγγισαμένοις μᾶλλον ῥεῖ ὁ ἱδρὼς
5 ἢ | ἐῶσιν ἐπιμεῖναι; πότερον διὰ τὸ καταψύχεσθαι ὑπὸ
τοῦ ἔξω; ἢ ὅτι ὥσπερ πῶμα γίνεται ὁ ἔξω ἱδρὼς ἐπὶ
τοῖς πόροις, ὥστε κωλύει τοῦ ἔσωθεν τὴν ὁρμήν;

13. Διὰ τί τὸ πήγανον δυσώδεις τοὺς ἱδρῶτας ποιεῖ,

---

7 τοσοῦτον : ante τοσοῦτον add. τὸ Yᵃ : τὸ τόσον Ruelle

18 The implication being that in steam rooms, fires are gradually made large or intense.
19 Source: Diocles frs. 185–86 (v.d. Eijk).
20 This chapter is virtually identical to Pr. 20.33; see also 13.9.
Source: Thphr. Sud. 10. Cf. Thphr. Od. 10.
21 Rue is a genus (Ruta) of shrub, many species of which have

made smaller, but only when it is (*gradually*) brought to be larger? For those in steam rooms sweat more than if the fire were such right away.[18] Is it because the proper proportion produces each effect? If, therefore, (*heat*) produces some effect, more will not produce a greater effect or rather will produce an opposite one, because the effect is accomplished by there being a proportion. Because of this, therefore, people do not sweat more in the presence of greater heat, but because a different proportion relates to each increase, and what has produced its effect produces no greater effect when more is added. For it is not the same thing that leads the way to each effect and prepares a suitable condition, *and* further produces the effect, but something different. Therefore, something small rather than great leads the way to and prepares a condition in the body suitable for sweating; but to *produce* sweat requires a different and greater proportion. And this no longer does what it has already done, but it is later, coming after this, and having a different proportion.

12.[19] Why does the sweat flow more when people are scraped clean with a strigil than when they allow it to remain? Is it because there is cooling down by the outside sweat? Or is it because the outside sweat comes to be like a cover over the passages, such that it prevents the rush of sweat from the inside?

13.[20] Why do rue and certain perfumes[21] make sweat

medicinal and culinary uses. The word translated "perfumes" (μύρων) might also be rendered "ointments" or "unguents" or "myrrh oil." If the author has in mind specifically this last, then he is referring to the oil derived from the dried sap of trees in the genus *Commiphora*, which is used primarily in perfume.

καὶ ἔνια τῶν μύρων; ἢ ὅτι ὧν ἐν τῇ ὀσμῇ βαρύτης ἔνι,
10 ταῦτα | κεραννύμενα ταῖς περιττωματικαῖς ὑγρότησι
κακωδεστέραν ποιεῖ τὴν ὀσμήν;

14. Διὰ τί ἱδροῦμεν τὸν νῶτον μᾶλλον ἢ τὰ
πρόσθεν; ἢ ὅτι ἐν μὲν τῷ πρόσθεν ἐστὶ τόπος ἐντός,
εἰς ὃν ἀποχετεύεται τὸ ὑγρόν, ἐν δὲ τῷ ὄπισθεν οὐκ
15 ἔστιν, ἀλλ᾽ ἔξω τὴν | ἔκκρισιν ἀναγκαῖον γίνεσθαι; τὸ
δ᾽ αὐτό ἐστιν αἴτιον καὶ ὅτι τὴν κοιλίαν ἧττον ἱδροῦμεν ἢ τὸ στῆθος. ἔτι δὲ ὅτι μᾶλλον διαφυλακτικόν
ἐστι τοῦ ἱδρῶτος τὰ νῶτα καὶ τὰ ὄπισθεν ἢ τὰ
πρόσθεν διὰ τὸ μᾶλλον τὰ ἔμπροσθεν τῶν ὄπισθεν
ἀποψύχεσθαι. ὅπερ ἐστὶν αἴτιον καὶ τοῦ τὰς μασχά-
20 λας | ἱδροῦν τάχιστα καὶ μάλιστα· ἥκιστα γὰρ ψύ-
χονται. ἔτι δὲ σαρκωδέστερά ἐστι τὰ περὶ τὸν νῶτον
τῶν πρόσθεν, ὥστε ὑγρότερα. πλείων δὲ ὑγρότης
ἐστὶν ἐν τοῖς ὄπισθεν· ὁ γὰρ μυελὸς κατὰ τὴν ῥάχιν
ὢν ὑγρασίαν πολλὴν παρέχει. |

25 15. Διὰ τί ἐφ᾽ ἃ κατακείμεθα οὐχ ἱδροῦμεν; ἢ ὅτι
θερμὸς ὢν ὁ τόπος ᾧ ἁπτόμεθα, κωλύει διεξιέναι τὸν
ἱδρῶτα, ἀναξηραίνει γὰρ αὐτόν; ἔτι δὲ θλίβεται, θλιβόμενον δὲ διαχεῖται τὸ αἷμα, οὗ συμβαίνοντος καταψύχεται μᾶλλον. σημεῖον δὲ ἡ νάρκη· κατάψυξίς τε
30 γάρ ἐστι τὸ πάθος, | καὶ γίνεται ἐκ θλίψεως ἢ πληγῆς.

16. Διὰ τί οἱ καθεύδοντες μᾶλλον ἱδροῦσιν; ἢ διὰ
τὴν ἀντιπερίστασιν; ἀθροισθὲν γὰρ τὸ θερμὸν ἐντὸς
ἐξελαύνει τὸ ὑγρόν.

malodorous? Is it because things that have a heavy scent, when mixed with residual moisture, make the scent have a more evil odor?

14.[22] Why do we sweat more in the back than in front? Is it because in the front there is a place within into which the moisture drains, but there isn't behind, and the secretion must have an exit? And this is the same reason that we sweat less on the stomach than on the chest. A further reason is that the back and hind parts are more retentive of sweat than the front parts, because the parts in front are cooled off more than the hind parts. This is the reason the armpits sweat most quickly and most of all; for they are cooled the least. Further, the areas around the back are fleshier than those in front, and so they are moister. But there is more moisture in the hind parts (*in any case*), for the marrow in the spine provides considerable moisture.

15. Why do we not sweat in the parts on which we lie? Is it because the region we touch, being hot, prevents the sweat from dispersing, for this dries it? Further, this region is under pressure, and the blood is dispersed under pressure; and when this happens, the part cools down more. Now numbness is a sign of this: for this condition is a sort of cooling down, and it comes from pressure or a blow.

16.[23] Why do those who are sleeping sweat more? Is it due to the compression (*of heat*)?[24] For the heat being collected within drives out the moisture.

[22] Source: Thphr. *Sud.* 32. [23] Source: Thphr. *Sud.* 40. Cf. *Pr.* 2.28 and Hp. *Epid.* 6.4.12. [24] The term ἀντιπερί-στασις is found elsewhere in the *corpus Aristotelicum* and in the works of Theophrastus, and usually refers to the compression or concentration of heat. See, e.g., *Som.* 457b2, Thphr. *Ign.* 18.

17. Διὰ τί τὸ πρόσωπον μάλιστα ἱδροῦσιν ἀσαρ-
35 κότατον | ὄν; ἢ ὅτι εὐίδρωτα μὲν ὅσα ὕφυγρα καὶ
ἀραιά, ἡ δὲ κεφαλὴ τοιαύτη; ὑγρότητα γὰρ οἰκείαν
ἔχει πλείστην. δηλοῦσι δὲ αἱ φλέβες τείνουσαι ἐντεῦθεν, καὶ οἱ κατάρροι ἐξ αὐτῆς, καὶ ὁ ἐγκέφαλος ὑγρός,
καὶ οἱ πόροι πολλοί. σημεῖον δὲ αἱ τρίχες ὅτι πολλοὶ
868a οἱ πόροι εἰσί περαίνοντες || ἔξω. οὔκουν ἐκ τῶν κάτω ὁ
ἱδρώς, ἀλλ' ἐκ τῆς κεφαλῆς γίνεται. διὸ ἱδροῦσι καὶ
πρῶτον καὶ μάλιστα τὸ μέτωπον· ὑπόκειται γὰρ πρῶ-
τον· τὸ δὲ ὑγρὸν κάτω ῥεῖ ἀλλ' οὐκ ἄνω. |

5 18. Διὰ τί οἱ ἱδροῦντες ἐὰν ψυχθῶσιν ἢ ὕδατι ἢ
πνεύματι, ναυτιῶσιν; πότερον τὸ ὑγρὸν ψυχθὲν ἔστη
ἀθρόον, ἔμπροσθεν οὐκ ἠρεμοῦν διὰ τὸ ῥεῖν; ἢ καὶ τὸ
πνεῦμα διὸν ἔξω γινόμενον ἱδρὼς διὰ τὴν ψύξιν,
τοῦτο ἔσω ψυχθὲν πρὶν ἐξελθεῖν ὑγρὸν ἐγένετο, καὶ
προσπεσὸν[8] ποιεῖ τὴν ναυτίαν; |

10 19. Διὰ τί ποτε ἐκ τῆς κεφαλῆς καὶ τῶν ποδῶν
μάλιστα οἱ ἱδρῶτες γίνονται θερμαινομένων; ἢ ὅτι τὸ
θερμαινόμενον ἐφέλκει ἐφ' ἑαυτὸ τὸ ὑγρόν, τὸ δὲ
ὑγρὸν οὐκ ἔχει ὅπῃ καταναλίσκηται διὰ τὸ εἶναι τοὺς
τόπους τούτους ὀστώδεις; ἐκπίπτει οὖν ἔξω. |

---

[8] post προσπεσὸν add. τῷ ἀναπνευστικῷ τόπῳ Forster ex
Thphr. Sud. 38, 240

---

25 This chapter is virtually identical to Pr. 36.2. Source: Thphr.
Sud. 33. Cf. Pr. 2.10.   26 Source: Thphr. Sud. 38.
27 Or "by wind" (πνεύματι), though the term elsewhere in the
passage refers to breath.

17.[25] Why do people sweat most on the face, though it is least fleshy? Is it because parts that are moist and porous are inclined to sweat, and the head is like this? For it contains a great deal of natural moisture. Now this is shown by the veins extending from here, and the discharges coming from it, and the brain being moist, and there being many passages. And the hair is a sign that there are many passages extending outward (*from the head*). Therefore, sweat does not come from the lower parts, but from the head. This is why people sweat first and most on the forehead: for it lies in the first place; and moisture flows downward, but not upward.

18.[26] Why do those who sweat feel nausea if they are cooled either by water or by breathing?[27] Does the moisture when cooled collect and stand still, having previously not been at rest because it was flowing? Or does the breath while passing through to the outside become sweat, because of the cooling, but having been cooled within before exiting has become moisture, and attacking (*the region in which breathing occurs*)[28] produces nausea?

19.[29] Why does sweat come from the head and the feet most of all when they grow hot? Is it because what grows hot draws moisture to itself, but the moisture has no place in which it can be dissipated because these parts are bony? Therefore it escapes outside.

[28] The text does not include an object of "attacking" (προσ-πεσὸν). Hett took it to be implied, and wrote "the patient." This is plausible; but I have supplied the object included in Thphr. *Sud.* 38, translating τῷ ἀναπνευστικῷ τόπῳ.

[29] Cf. Thphr. *Sud.* 33, 35–37.

15   20. Διὰ τί οἱ πονοῦντες, ὅτε παύσονται,[9] ἱδροῦσιν;
ἔδει γάρ, εἴπερ ὁ πόνος αἴτιος, ὅταν πονῶσιν. πότερον
ὅτι πονούντων μὲν ὑπὸ τοῦ πνεύματος αἱ φλέβες
ἐμφυσώμεναι τοὺς πόρους συμμεμυκέναι ποιοῦσι,
παυσαμένων δὲ συνίζουσιν, ὥστε δι᾿ εὐρυτέρων γινο-
20   μένων τῶν πόρων ῥᾷον διέρχεται | τὸ ὑγρόν. ἢ ὅτι
πονούντων μὲν ἀποκρίνει ἡ κίνησις ἐκ τοῦ συμπεφυ-
κότος ὑγροῦ πνεῦμα, καὶ διὰ θερμότητα τὴν ἀπὸ τῆς
κινήσεως γίνεται τὸ ὑγρὸν πνεῦμα ἐπιπολῆς· ὅταν δὲ
παύσηται πονῶν, ἅμα καὶ ἡ θερμότης λήγει, καὶ ἐκ
τοῦ πνεύματος πυκνουμένου ὑγρότης γίνεται, ὁ καλού-
25   μενος | ἱδρώς.
      21. Πότερον δεῖ μᾶλλον τοῦ θέρους παρασκευάζειν
τὸ ἱδροῦν ἢ τοῦ χειμῶνος; ἢ ὅτε μᾶλλον ὑγροὶ καὶ
χαλεπώτεροι ἄνευ ἐπιμελείας γένοιντ᾿ ἄν, ὥστε τοῦ
χειμῶνος[10] ἂν δέοι μᾶλλον, ᾗ μεγάλη ἡ μεταβολὴ καὶ
30   τὰ περιττώματα | οὐ συνεκπέττεται; πάλιν ψυχθέντος
ἔτι παρὰ φύσιν τὸ τοῦ χειμῶνος. δῆλον ἄρα ὅτι τοῦ
θέρους μᾶλλον. καὶ γὰρ τὰ ὑγρὰ σήπεται μᾶλλον
ἅπαντα τοῦ θέρους· διὸ τότε δεῖ ἀπαντλεῖν. διὰ τοῦτο
δὲ καὶ οἱ ἀρχαῖοι πάντες οὕτως ἔλεγον. |
35   22. Διὰ τί ἀεὶ τοῦ σώματος ῥέοντος καὶ τῆς ἀπορροῆς γινομένης ἐκ τῶν περιττωμάτων, οὐ κουφίζεται
τὸ σῶμα, ἐὰν μὴ ἀφιδρώσῃ; ἢ ὅτι ἐλάττων ἡ ἔκκρισις;

9 ὅτε παύσονται : ὅταν παύσωνται Bekker (cf. Thrpr. Sud.
25, 166)
10 χειμῶνος : θέρους Forster

20.[30] Why do those exerting themselves sweat when they stop? For if the exertion is the cause they should sweat while they are exerting themselves. Is it because when they exert themselves, the veins, being inflated with breath, cause the passages to close up, but when they stop, the veins contract, so that the moisture more easily passes through the passages that are becoming wider? Or is it because when they exert themselves, the motion separates the breath from the natural moisture, and owing to the heat from the motion the moisture becomes breath on the surface? But when they stop the exertion, the heat ceases at the same time, and moisture comes from the condensation of the breath, which is called sweat.

21.[31] Should one induce sweating more in the summer than in the winter? Should it be done when the bodies become, in the absence of care, moister and difficult to deal with, so that one should do so more in the winter, at which time the change is great and the residues are not easily concocted? Then again, sweating in winter, when the body is cooled, is against nature. Therefore, it is clear that one should induce sweating more in the summer. And indeed, everything moist putrefies more in the summer; so that is when the moisture should be drawn off. This is why even the ancients expressed this opinion.

22.[32] Why, though the body has a continuous flow and there is an efflux of residues, does the body not grow lighter unless it sweats? Is it because the secretion is too

[30] Source: Thphr. *Sud*. 25–26. Cf. *Pr*. 2.7 and 23.
[31] Source: Thphr. *Sud*. 23. Cf. *Pr*. 2.33 and 42.
[32] This chapter is virtually identical to *Pr*. 37.1–2.

ὅταν γὰρ ἐξ ὑγροῦ μεταβάλλῃ[11] εἰς ἀέρα, πλεῖον
868b γίνεται ἐξ ἐλάττονος· ‖ τὸ γὰρ ὑγρὸν διακρινόμενον
πλεῖον, ὥστε πλείονι χρόνῳ ἡ ἔκκρισις, διὰ δὲ τοῦτο
καὶ ὅτι δι' ἐλαττόνων πόρων ἡ ἔκκρισίς ἐστιν. ἔτι τὸ
γλίσχρον καὶ τὸ κολλῶδες μετὰ μὲν τοῦ ὑγροῦ ἐκ-
5 κρίνεται διὰ τὴν κατάμιξιν, μετὰ | δὲ τοῦ πνεύματος
ἀδυνατεῖ. μάλιστα δὲ τοῦτ' ἐστὶ τὸ λυποῦν. διὸ καὶ οἱ
ἔμετοι τῶν ἱδρώτων κουφίζουσι μᾶλλον, ὅτι συνεξ-
άγουσι τοῦτο ἅτε παχύτεροι καὶ σωματωδέστεροι ὄντες, καὶ ὅτι τῇ μὲν σαρκὶ πόρρω ὁ τόπος οὗτος, ἐν ᾧ τὸ
γλίσχρον καὶ τὸ κολλῶδες, ὥστε ἔργον μεταστῆσαι,
10 τῇ δὲ | κοιλίᾳ ἐγγύς· ἢ γὰρ ἐν αὐτῇ ἐγγίνεται ἢ
πλησίον· διὸ καὶ δυσεξάγωγον ἄλλως.

23. Διὰ τί ἧττον ἱδροῦσιν ἐν αὐτῷ τῷ πονεῖν ἢ
ἀνέντες; ἢ ὅτι πονοῦντες μὲν ποιοῦσι, πεπονηκότες δὲ
πεποιήκασιν; εἰκότως οὖν ἐκκρίνεται πλέον· ὁτὲ μὲν
15 γὰρ γίνεται, ὁτὲ | δὲ ἐστίν. ἢ ὅτι πονούντων μὲν
συγκλείονται τῆς σαρκὸς οἱ πόροι διὰ τὴν κάθεξιν τοῦ
πνεύματος, ὅταν δ' ἀνῶσιν, ἀνοίγονται; διὸ καὶ τὸ
πνεῦμα κατέχοντες ἧττον ἱδροῦσιν.

24. Διὰ τί οὐχὶ ὅταν τροχάζωμεν, ὁ ἱδρὼς πλείων,
καὶ ὅταν ἐν κινήσει ᾖ τὸ σῶμα, ἀλλ' ὅταν παύσωνται;
20 ἢ ὅτι | τότε μὲν ὥσπερ ὑπὸ τῆς χειρὸς ἢ ἄλλου τινὸς

---

[11] μεταβάλλῃ : μεταβάλῃ Υ^a P^c

---

33 I.e., the volume of moisture.
34 I.e., the sticky and viscous material.

small? For when there is a change from moisture to air, a great amount of air comes to be from a small amount of moisture. For the amount of moisture separated out is great, so that the secretion takes a great deal of time—for this reason[33] and because the secretion is through small passages. Further, what is sticky and viscous is secreted with the moisture, because it is mixed with it, but it cannot be secreted with the breath. Now it is particularly this[34] that causes pain. And this is why vomiting lightens more than sweats do, because being denser and more corporeal it takes out this material with it, and because the region containing what is sticky and viscous is far away from the flesh, so that it is hard work to move it, but near the stomach. For it is formed in or close to the stomach; and this is why it is difficult to remove it otherwise.

23.[35] Why do people sweat less during the very act of exertion than when they have ceased? Is it because while exerting themselves they are *doing* something, but having exerted themselves they *have done* something? So it is reasonable that it is secreted in greater amounts in the latter case: for at the one time sweat is coming to be, while at the other it exists. Or is it because while they are exerting themselves, the passages of the flesh are closed because they hold their breath, but when they cease, the passages open? And this is why they sweat less while they are holding their breath.

24.[36] Why is the sweat plentiful not when we run fast and the body is in movement, but when we stop? Is it because it is just like running water which, blocked by the

35 Source: Thphr. *Sud*. 25–26. Cf. *Pr*. 2.7 and 20.
36 Source: Thphr. *Sud*. 29. Cf. *Pr*. 2.1.

ἔστιν ὕδωρ ῥέον ἀποφράξαι πανταχόθεν συναθροι-
ζόμενον, ὅταν δὲ ἀφεθῇ, πλέον ἢ ὅσον ἐξ ἀρχῆς· ὡς δὲ
ὑπὸ τῆς χειρός, οὕτω καὶ ὑπὸ τοῦ πνεύματος ἔστιν
ἀποληφθῆναι, ὥσπερ ἐν τῇ κλεψύδρᾳ, καὶ πάλιν πρὸς
25 τὴν κύστιν· ἀπολαμβάνει γὰρ ἐντός. | ὁμοίως οὖν
πολλῆς κινήσεως οὔσης τὸ πνεῦμα ἐναπολαμβάνεται·
διὸ καὶ αἱ φλέβες διατείνονται τοῦ ὑγροῦ οὐ δυνα-
μένου ἐξιέναι. ἀπολαμβανόμενον δὲ ἀθρόον τὸ ὑγρόν,
ὅταν ἀνεθῇ τὸ πνεῦμα, ἀθρόον ἐξέρχεται.

25. Διὰ τί, ὅταν πίωσιν, ἧττον ἱδροῦσιν ἐπιφαγόν-
30 τες; ἢ | διότι τὰ σιτία ἐπισπᾶται μὲν τὴν ὑγρότητα
καθαπερεὶ σπόγγος ἐμπεσών; ἔστι δὲ κωλῦσαι τὴν
ὁρμὴν οὐ μικρὸν μέρος, ὥσπερ ἐν τοῖς ῥεύμασι, τῷ[12]
ἐπιλαβεῖν τοὺς πόρους προσενεγκάμενον τὴν τροφήν.

26. Διὰ τί οἱ ἀγωνιῶντες ἱδροῦσι τοὺς πόδας, τὸ δὲ
35 πρόσωπον | οὔ; μᾶλλον γὰρ εὔλογον, ὅταν πᾶν ἱδρῶσι
τὸ σῶμα, τότε μᾶλλον καὶ τοὺς πόδας· ψυχρότατος
γὰρ ὁ τόπος, διὸ ἥκιστα ἱδροῦσιν. καὶ οἱ ἰατροὶ ἐν
ταῖς ἀρρωστίαις μάλιστα περιστέλλειν τοὺς πόδας
869a παραγγέλλουσιν, ὅτι εὔψυκτοί εἰσιν, ‖ ὥστε ἀρχὴν
ῥᾳδίως ῥίγους ποιοῦσι καὶ τῷ ἄλλῳ σώματι. ἢ ὅτι καὶ
ἡ ἀγωνία ἐστὶ θερμότητος οὐ μετάστασις ὥσπερ ἐν
τῷ φόβῳ ἐκ τῶν ἄνω τόπων εἰς τοὺς κάτω (διὸ καὶ αἱ
κοιλίαι λύονται τῶν φοβουμένων), ἀλλ' αὔξησις θερ-
5 μοῦ, ὥσπερ | ἐν τῷ θυμῷ; καὶ γὰρ ὁ θυμὸς ζέσις τοῦ

[12] τῷ Forster : τὸ codd.

78

hand or some other means, collects on all sides, and when it is released it is more plentiful than it was at the beginning? But just as water can be checked by the hand, so too can sweat be checked by breath, as in the clepsydra,[37] and it goes back toward the bladder; for this breath checks it within. Similarly, when there is a lot of movement the breath is checked; and this is why the veins are distended, the moisture being unable to escape. But being checked the moisture collects, and when the breath is released, it[38] comes out all at once.

25. Why, when people drink, do they sweat less if they are also eating? Is it because the food absorbs the moisture, just as if a sponge were put on it? And it is possible to hinder the flow in no small part, just as in streams, by seizing the passages through the addition of nourishment.

26.[39] Why do those who are anxious sweat in the feet, but not in the face? For it is more reasonable, that when the whole body sweats, then the feet too would sweat more: for this region is the coldest, which is why it sweats least. And the physicians, in the case of illnesses, give orders particularly to wrap the feet, because they are easily cooled, such that at the beginning they readily produce shivering even in the rest of the body. Is it also because anxiety is not a transference of heat from the upper regions to the lower, as in the case of fear (and this is why the bowels are loosened in those who are afraid), but an increase of heat, as in the case of anger? Indeed, anger is a boiling of

37 See n. 2 above.
38 I.e., the collected moisture.
39 Source: Thphr. Sud. 36. Cf. Pr. 2.31.

θερμοῦ ἐστι τοῦ περὶ τὴν καρδίαν· καὶ ὁ ἀγωνιῶν οὐ
διὰ φόβον καὶ διὰ ψύξιν πάσχει, ἀλλὰ διὰ τὸ μέλλον.[13]

27. Διὰ τί τὸ πρόσωπον ἐξέρυθροι γίνονται, οὐχ
ἱδροῦσι δέ; ἢ διὰ τὸ μᾶλλον θερμαίνεσθαι, ὥστε τὸ
10 μὲν ἐν τῷ προσώπῳ | ὑγρὸν ξηραίνει ἡ θερμότης
ἐπιπολάζουσα, τὸ δὲ ἐν τοῖς ποσὶ συντήκει διὰ τὸ
ἐλάττων μὲν εἶναι, πλείων δὲ τῆς ἐμφύτου καὶ προ-
ϋπαρχούσης;

28. Διὰ τί καθεύδοντες ἱδροῦσι μᾶλλον ἢ ἐγρηγο-
ρότες; ἢ ὅτι ἔσωθεν ἡ ἀρχὴ τοῦ ἱδρῶτος, θερμότερα δὲ
15 τὰ ἐντός, ὥστε | καὶ ἐκκρίνει διαχέουσα ἡ ἐντὸς θερ-
μότης τὸ ἐντὸς ὑγρόν; ⟨ἢ⟩[14] ὅτι ἀεὶ ἔοικεν ἀπορρεῖν τι
τοῦ σώματος, ἀλλὰ διὰ τὸ μηθὲν εἶναι πρὸς ὃ προσπῖπτον ἀλισθήσεται λανθάνει; σημεῖον δέ· τὰ γὰρ
κοῖλα τοῦ σώματος ἀεὶ ἱδροῖ.

29. Διὰ τί ἐν τοῖς πυριατηρίοις μᾶλλον ἱδροῦσιν
20 ὅταν ᾖ | ψῦχος; ἢ ὅτι τὸ θερμὸν οὐ βαδίζει ἔξω διὰ τὴν
τοῦ ψυχροῦ περίστασιν (κωλύεται γὰρ ὑπὸ τούτου),
ἀλλ' ἐντὸς κατειλούμενον καὶ μένον διαλύει τὰ ἐν ἡμῖν
ὑγρά, καὶ ἱδρῶτα ποιεῖ ἐξ αὐτῶν;

30. Διὰ τί ὠφελιμώτερός ἐστιν ὁ ἱδρώς, κἂν ἐλάτ-
25 των | ἐπέλθῃ, ὁ γυμνοῦ τροχάζοντος γενόμενος ἢ ὁ ἐν
ἱματίῳ; ἢ ⟨ὅτι⟩[15] τὸ μὲν πονεῖν τοῦ μὴ πονεῖν βέλτιόν

---

[13] τὸ μέλλον : τὸ μᾶλλον ἐκθερμαίνεσθαι Forster ex Thphr.
Sud. 36, 232
[14] ⟨ἢ⟩ Bonitz   [15] ⟨ὅτι⟩ addidi

the heat around the heart; and the one who is anxious is affected not by fear or by cold, but by what is going to happen.[40]

27.[41] Why do people become very red in the face, but do not sweat? Is it through being heated more, so that the surface heat dries the moisture in the face, but causes a colliquation in the feet because it is less, though more than what is natural and already present?[42]

28.[43] Why do people sweat more when sleeping than when awake? Is it because the origin of sweat is internal, and the inner parts are hotter, so that the inner heat dissolves and secretes the inner moisture? Or is it because it is likely that something is always flowing from the body, but it escapes notice because there is nothing onto which it can fall so that it will be collected. And there is a sign of this: the hollow parts of the body always sweat.

29.[44] Why do people sweat more in steam rooms when it is cold out? Is it because the heat cannot go outside owing to the surrounding of cold (for it is prevented by this), but being cooped up inside and remaining there it dissolves the moisture in us, and produces sweat from it?

30.[45] Why is sweat more beneficial, even if it comes in a small quantity, from a runner who is naked than from one who is wearing a cloak? Is it because in general exerting

[40] Or, with Forster (based on the parallel passage in Thphr. *Sud.*), "but by being heated more."

[41] Source: Thphr. *Sud.* 37.

[42] The meaning of this second line is difficult to decipher.

[43] Source: Thphr. *Sud.* 40. Cf. *Pr.* 2.16.   [44] Cf. *Pr.* 2.11 and 32.   [45] Source: Thphr. *Sud.* 39. Cf. *Pr.* 38.3. See also Hp. *Vic.* 2.63 and Diocl. frs. 182 and 184 (v.d. Eijk).

ἐστι καθόλου, καὶ ὁ ἱδρὼς δὲ ὁ μετὰ πόνου τοῦ ἄνευ
πόνου βελτίων ἐστί, καὶ ὁ μᾶλλον δὲ μετὰ πόνου τοῦ
ἧττον βελτίων· μᾶλλον δ' ἐστὶ μετὰ πόνου ὁ γυμνοῦ
30 τροχάζοντος γινόμενος. ἐὰν γὰρ | μὴ πολλῇ συντονίᾳ
τροχάσῃ, οὐ δύναται ἱδρῶσαι γυμνὸς ὤν· ἐν ἱματίῳ
γὰρ κἂν πάνυ μετρίως τροχάσῃ, ταχὺ ἱδροῖ διὰ τὴν
ἀπὸ τοῦ ἱματίου ἀλέαν. καὶ εὐχρούστεροι δὲ γίνονται
οἱ γυμνοὶ τρέχοντες τοῦ θέρους τῶν ἐν ἱματίοις, ὅτι
ὥσπερ ἅπαντες οἱ ἐν τοῖς εὐπνουστέροις τόποις οἱ-
35 κοῦντες | εὐχρούστεροί εἰσι τῶν ἐν τοῖς καταπεπνιγμέ-
νοις οἰκούντων, οὕτω καὶ αὐτὸς αὑτοῦ ὁ ἄνθρωπος,
ὅταν ὥσπερ ἐν εὐπνοίᾳ ᾖ, τότε εὐχρούστερός ἐστιν ἢ
ὅταν καταπεπνιγμένος ᾖ καὶ περιεχόμενος ὑπό τινος
869b ἀλέας πολλῆς, ὃ συμβαίνει μᾶλλον ‖ τῷ ἐν ἱματίῳ
τρέχοντι. διὰ ταῦτα δὲ καὶ οἱ πολὺν χρόνον καθεύδοντες ἀχρούστεροί εἰσι τῶν μέτριον χρόνον καθευ-
δόντων· καταπέπνικται γὰρ καὶ ὁ καθεύδων.

31. Διὰ τί οἱ ἀγωνιῶντες ἱδροῦσι τοὺς πόδας, τὸ δὲ
5 πρόσωπον | οὔ, ἐν τῷ ἄλλῳ βίῳ ἱδρούντων ἡμῶν
μάλιστα μὲν τὸ πρόσωπον, ἥκιστα δὲ τοὺς πόδας; ἢ
ὅτι ἡ ἀγωνία φόβος τίς ἐστι πρὸς ἀρχὴν ἔργου, ὁ δὲ
φόβος κατάψυξις τῶν ἄνω; διὸ καὶ ὠχριῶσι τὰ πρόσωπα οἱ ἀγωνιῶντες. κινοῦνται δὲ καὶ σκαίρουσι τοῖς
10 ποσίν· ποιοῦσι γὰρ τοῦτο οἱ | ἀγωνιῶντες καὶ καθάπερ
γυμνάζονται· διόπερ εἰκότως ἱδροῦσι ταῦτα οἷς πονοῦσιν. καὶ τρίβουσι δὲ τὰς χεῖρας καὶ συγκαθιᾶσι καὶ
ἐκτείνονται καὶ ἐξάλλονται καὶ οὐδέποτε ἠρεμοῦσιν·

oneself is better than not exerting oneself, and so the sweat that comes with exertion is better than that which comes without exertion, and more sweat that comes with exertion is better than less? Now the sweat of a naked runner is more the sweat that comes with exertion. For unless he runs with a great deal of intense exertion, he cannot sweat if he is naked; for in a cloak, even if he runs at a very moderate pace, he would quickly sweat because of the warmth from the cloak. And those who run naked in the summer acquire a better complexion than those who run in cloaks, because just as all those who live in places with a good flow of air have a better complexion than those who live in stifling places, so a person himself too has a better complexion when he is as it were in a place with a good flow of air than when he is stifled and surrounded by a great deal of warmth, which happens more to the one who runs in a cloak. This is also why those who sleep for a long time have a worse complexion than those who sleep for a moderate time; for the one who sleeps is also stifled.

31.[46] Why do those who are anxious sweat in the feet and not in the face, whereas in the other circumstances in life we sweat most in the face and least in the feet? Is it because anxiety is a certain fear with respect to the beginning of a task, and fear is a cooling of the upper parts? And this is why those who are anxious grow pale in their faces. And they move and bounce on their feet; for those who are anxious act in this way, as if they were exercising; therefore, it is reasonable that they sweat in those parts with which they exert themselves. And they also rub their hands, stoop, stretch, fidget, and are never still; for they are eager with

[46] Source: Thphr. *Sud.* 36. Cf. *Pr.* 2.26.

ὁρμητικοὶ γάρ εἰσι πρὸς τὸ ἔργον διὰ τὸ τὸ θερμὸν
αὐτῶν ἠθροῖσθαι εἰς τὸν περὶ τὸ στῆθος τόπον ὄντα
15 εὐσωματωδέστερον· | ὅθεν πάντῃ διάττοντος αὐτοῦ τε
καὶ τοῦ αἵματος συμβαίνει πυκνὴν καὶ ποικίλην γίνεσθαι κίνησιν. μάλιστα δὲ ἱδροῦσι τοὺς πόδας, ὅτι
οὗτοι μὲν συνεχῶς πονοῦσι, τὰ δὲ ἄλλα μέρη τοῦ
σώματος ἀναπαύσεως τυγχάνει ταῖς τῶν σχημάτων
καὶ κινήσεων μεταβολαῖς. |

20   32. Διὰ τί ἐν τοῖς πυριατηρίοις οὔτε ἀθρόου τοῦ
πυρὸς ὄντος μᾶλλον ἱδροῦσιν, οὔτ' ἐλάττονος ἀεὶ γινομένου, ἀλλὰ πλείονος; ἐπεισφερομένου γὰρ ⟨εἰς⟩[16] τὰ
πυριατήρια μᾶλλον ἱδροῦσιν ἢ εἴπερ εὐθὺς ἐξ ἀρχῆς
τοσοῦτον ἦν τὸ πῦρ. ἢ τὸ μὲν πολὺ ἐκ πρώτης ξηρὰν
25 λαμβάνον τὴν ἐπιπολῆς σάρκα | καὶ δέρμα καίει καὶ
ὀστρακοῖ, γενομένη δὲ τοιαύτη στέγει[17] τοὺς ἱδρῶτας;
τὸ δὲ ὀλίγον μᾶλλον τὴν σάρκα ἀνιὲν αὐτήν τε ἀραιοῖ,
καὶ τὰ ἐντὸς καθάπερ ὀργάζει πρὸς τὴν διάκρισιν καὶ
ἐξαγωγήν. οὕτω δ' ἐχούσης αὐτῆς, ἐπεισενεχθὲν
πλέον πῦρ καὶ εἰσδυόμενον εἰς βάθος τῆς σαρκὸς δι' |
30 ἀραιότητα ἐξατμίζει τε τὰ προμαλαχθέντα ὑγρά, καὶ
τὰ λεπτὰ αὐτῶν ἀποκρίνον ἐξάγει μετὰ τοῦ πνεύματος.

33. Πότερον δεῖ μᾶλλον τοῦ θέρους παρασκευάζειν
τὸ ἱδροῦν ἢ τοῦ χειμῶνος; ἢ τοῦ μὲν χειμῶνος συστελλόμενον ἐντὸς τὸ θερμὸν ἐκπέττει καὶ πνευματοῖ τὰ ἐν

16 ⟨εἰς⟩ Richards
17 στέγει Nicasius (tegit Barth.) : τέγγει codd.

respect to their task owing to the heat that has collected in the region around the chest, which is rather substantial. As this heat and the blood rush in all directions from there, movement becomes frequent and varied. And they sweat most in the feet, because these exert themselves continually, while the other parts of the body get a rest by the changes of position and movement.

32.[47] Why do people in steam rooms sweat more not when the fire is (*made large*)[48] all at once nor when it gradually becomes smaller, but when it (*gradually becomes*) larger? For they sweat more when (*the fire is gradually*) introduced into the steam room than if the fire is large right from the beginning. Or does a large one at the outset, finding the flesh dry on the surface, burn the skin and make it hard as baked clay, and when it's in this condition it contains the sweat? But in smaller quantities the fire loosens the flesh and makes it porous, and softens the inner parts, as it were, with a view to the separation and expulsion (*of the sweat*). And when the flesh is in this condition, more fire is introduced, and penetrating into the depth of the flesh (owing to the flesh being more porous), it vaporizes the moisture from the softened parts, and separating off the lighter parts expels them with the breath.

33.[49] Should one induce sweating more in the summer than in the winter? In the winter, does the heat collecting within concoct and aerate the moisture within us (which is

[47] Source: Thphr. *Sud.* 28. Cf. *Pr.* 2.11.

[48] The parallel passage in Thphr. *Sud.* 28 refers to making the fire large all at once.

[49] Source: Thphr. *Sud.* 23. Cf. *Pr.* 2.21 and 42.

35 ἡμῖν ὑγρά | (διὸ πάντων αὐτῶν ἢ τῶν πλείστων ἀναλι-
σκομένων οὐδὲν δεῖται συγγενοῦς ἀποκρίσεως), τοῦ
δὲ θέρους δι᾽ ἀραιᾶς τῆς σαρκὸς ἐκπίπτοντος τοῦ
θερμοῦ ἧττον πέττεται τὰ ἐν ἡμῖν ὑγρά, διὸ δεῖται
870a ἀπαντλήσεως; ἐμμείναντα γὰρ διὰ τὴν || ὥραν σήπε-
ται καὶ νοσοποιεῖ. σήπεται γὰρ πᾶν τὸ σηπόμενον ὑπ᾽
ἀλλοτρίου θερμοῦ, ὑπὸ δὲ τοῦ οἰκείου πέττεται. ἐν μὲν
οὖν τῷ θέρει τὸ ἀλλότριον ἰσχύει, διὸ σήπεται πάντα
5 μᾶλλον ἐν αὐτῷ· ἐν δὲ τῷ χειμῶνι τὸ οἰκεῖον, | διὸ οὐ
σήπει ὁ χειμών.

34. Διὰ τί τῶν ἱδρώτων γινομένων ὑπὸ τῆς ἐντὸς
θερμασίας ἢ ὑπὸ τῆς ἐκτὸς προσπιπτούσης, πρὸς
ἐνίων ἱδρώτων φρίττομεν; ἢ διότι ὑπὸ μὲν τῆς ἐντὸς
θερμασίας ὅταν ἐκπίπτωσιν ἐκ πολλοῦ τόπου εἰς ὀλί-
10 γον, συστελλομένοις[18] πρὸς | τὴν περιοχὴν παντελῶς
τὰς τοῦ θερμοῦ περιόδους ἀποφράττουσιν, εἶτα ἡ
φρίκη ἐγγίνεται; ἔτι τῆς σαρκὸς παντελῶς διαβρόχου
γινομένης καὶ τοῦ θερμοῦ διεξιόντος. ἡ δὲ ἐκτὸς θερ-
μασία προσπίπτουσα ἀραιοῖ τὸν χρῶτα πρῶτον, εἶτα
τὸ ἐντὸς τῆς φύσεως θερμὸν ἀποκρινάμενον τὴν φρί-
κην ἐποίησεν. |

15 35. Διὰ τί τῶν ἱδρώτων οἱ θερμοὶ κρίνονται βελ-
τίους εἶναι τῶν ψυχρῶν; ἢ ὅτι πᾶς μὲν ἱδρὼς περιττώ-
ματός τινος ἔκκρισίς ἐστιν· εἰκὸς δὲ τὸ μὲν ὀλίγον
περίττωμα ἐκθερμαίνεσθαι, τὸ δὲ πλεῖον μὴ ὁμοίως,
ὥστε ὁ ψυχρὸς ἱδρὼς πολλοῦ περιττώματος ἂν εἴη
20 σημεῖον· διὸ καὶ μακροτέρας | τὰς νόσους δηλοῖ.

18 συστελλομένοις : συστελλόμενοι Nicasius

why, as all or most of this is expended, there is no need for an inborn form of secreting it), but in the summer, owing to the porousness of the flesh, when the heat comes out the moisture within us is less concocted, which is why it needs to be drawn off? For if it remains, owing to the time of year it putrefies and causes disease. For all that becomes putrid is putrefied by foreign heat, but it is concocted by its own heat. Therefore, in the summer the foreign heat is strong, which is why all the moisture in the body tends to become putrid; but in the winter its own heat is strong, which is why the winter does not cause putrefaction.

34. Why, although sweat is brought about by inner heat or by heat applied from without, in some cases do we shiver when we sweat? Is it because, when owing to inner heat sweat passes from a large area into a small one, by collecting on the surface it completely blocks the circuits of the heat, and then shivering occurs? Further, when the flesh becomes completely sodden the heat flows out. But the heat applied from without first makes the skin porous, then the natural inward heat is given off and causes shivering.

35.[50] Why are hot sweats judged to be better than cold ones? Is it because all sweat is the excretion of some residue? Now it is reasonable that a small amount of residue should be heated, but a larger amount not to the same extent, so that cold sweat would be a sign of a lot of residue; and this is why it would show that the diseases[51] are longer-lasting.

[50] The question in this chapter is raised in connection with a widespread Hippocratic view; see, e.g., Hp. *Epid*. 7.25, *Prog*. 6. Cf. *Pr*. 31.23.

[51] I.e., those giving rise to or accompanied by cold sweats.

36. Διὰ τί τῶν ἱδρώτων διὰ θερμασίαν γινομένων πρὸς τὸ πολὺ πῦρ ἧττον ἱδροῦμεν; ἢ διότι ἤτοι σφόδρα θερμαινομένου τοῦ σώματος εἰς πνεύματα ⟨τὰ⟩[19] ὑγρὰ διαλύεται, ἢ ἐκπίπτοντος τοῦ ὑγροῦ καὶ ταχὺ 25 περιξηραινομένου τὴν αἴσθησιν | οὐ λαμβάνομεν;

37. Διὰ τί τοῦ ἡλίου μᾶλλον θερμαίνοντος, ἐὰν μηδὲν περίβλημα ἔχωμεν, ἱδρῶτες[20] γίνονται τοῖς ἱματίοις περιστελλομένοις; καὶ περὶ τούτου ταὐτὰ ἐροῦμεν τῷ προτέρῳ.

38. Διὰ τί τῶν ὀξειῶν κινήσεων μᾶλλον θερμαίνειν 30 δοκουσῶν, | τῶν δὲ νωθρῶν ἧττον, αἱ πρὸς τὸ σιμὸν πορεῖαι νωθρότεραι οὖσαι ἱδρῶτάς τε μᾶλλον ἐκκρίνουσιν καὶ τὸ πνεῦμα προσιστᾶσιν, ὡς θερμαίνουσαι μᾶλλον τῶν κατάντων; ἢ ὅτι τοῖς βάρεσιν εἰς τὸ κάτω φέρεσθαι κατὰ φύσιν ἐστίν, εἰς δὲ τὸ ἄνω παρὰ 35 φύσιν; | ἡ οὖν τοῦ θερμοῦ φύσις ἡ φέρουσα ἡμᾶς πρὸς μὲν τὰ κατάντη οὐθὲν συμπονεῖ, πρὸς δὲ τὰ σιμὰ φορτηγοῦσα διατελεῖ. ὥστε διὰ μὲν τὴν τοιαύτην κίνησιν ἐκθερμαίνεται, καὶ μᾶλλον τοὺς ἱδρῶτας ἐκκρίνει, καὶ τὸ πνεῦμα προσίστησιν. συμβάλλεται δέ 870b τι || ἐν ταῖς πορείαις καὶ ἡ τοῦ σώματος σύγκαμψις πρὸς τὸ μὴ εὐθυπορεῖν τὸ πνεῦμα προσιστᾶσα.

39. Διὰ τί τῶν ἱδρώτων γινομένων, ὅσῳ ἂν ἐπιβάλληταί τις μᾶλλον, οὐχ οἱ τὰ πλεῖστα τῶν ἱματίων 5 ἐπιβαλλόμενοι | ἱδροῦσιν; καὶ περὶ τούτου ταὐτὰ ἐροῦμεν τῷ ἐπάνω.

---

[19] ⟨τὰ⟩ Forster
[20] post ἱδρῶτες add. ⟨μᾶλλον⟩ Forster (cf. Pr. 2.9, 867a19)

36.[52] Why, although sweat occurs owing to heat, do we sweat less before a big fire? Is it because when the body is heated a great deal, the moisture (*in it*) is dissolved into breath, or because when moisture comes out and is quickly dried, we do not grasp the sensation?

37.[53] Why, though the sun heats us more if we wear no clothing, does sweat come (*more readily*) when we are wrapped in cloaks? To this we shall give the same answer that we gave to the former problem.[54]

38. Why, though quick movements seem to produce more heat, and sluggish ones less, does a walk uphill, which is more sluggish, secrete more sweat and obstruct the breathing, as though it produced more heat than a walk downhill? Is it because for heavy bodies, being carried downward is according to nature, but upward is contrary to nature? Therefore, the nature of the heat carrying us downhill is not labored, but going uphill involves continually bearing a burden. So owing to such movement it[55] is heated further and secretes more sweat and obstructs the breathing. And in walking (*uphill*) the bending of the body contributes somewhat to preventing the free passage of the breath by obstructing it.

39. Why, though sweat is produced to the extent that one puts on more clothes, do those who put on the most clothes not sweat (*the most*)? To this we shall give the same answer that we gave to the one above.[56]

[52] Source: Thphr. *Sud*. 28. Cf. *Pr*. 2.11 and 32.
[53] Cf. *Pr*. 2.9 and 39.
[54] I.e., *Pr*. 2.36.
[55] The body or "the nature of the heat" in the body.
[56] I.e., *Pr*. 2.36.

40. Διὰ τί τῶν σωμάτων ξηροτέρων ὄντων τοῦ θέρους ἢ τοῦ χειμῶνος, ἱδρωτικωτέρως διακείμεθα τοῦ θέρους; ἢ ὅτι τοῦ μὲν θέρους ἀραιῶν τῶν σωμάτων ὄντων τὸ τῆς φύσεως θερμὸν οὐ πολὺ κατέχεται,
10 διαλύει οὖν τὰ ὑγρὰ εἰς πνεῦμα; | τοῦ δὲ χειμῶνος πεπυκνωμένων ἐκτὸς τῶν σωμάτων, πολὺ κατειλημμένον τὸ τῆς φύσεως θερμὸν εἰς πνεῦμα οὐ διαλύει τὰ ὑγρά. ἔτι δὲ καὶ τοῦ μὲν θέρους πολὺ προσφερόμεθα τὸ ὑγρόν, τοῦ δὲ χειμῶνος²¹ τοὐναντίον.

41. Διὰ τί οἱ ἀπὸ τοῦ αὐτομάτου γινόμενοι τοῖς
15 ὑγιαίνουσιν | ἱδρῶτες φαυλότεροι δοκοῦσιν εἶναι τῶν ὑπὸ τῶν πόνων; ἢ ὅτι οἱ μὲν πόνοι ἀπαντλοῦντες ἀεὶ τὸ περιττεῦον ὑγρὸν ξηροτέραν τὴν σάρκα παρασκευάζουσιν, ὥστε τὰς κοιλίας τῶν πόρων ὑγιεινὰς εἶναι καὶ τῇ τοῦ θερμοῦ ἠθίσει μηδεμίαν ἔμφραξιν γίνε-
20 σθαι· οἱ δ' αὐτόματοι μὲν προσαγορευόμενοι | ἱδρῶτες, γινόμενοι δ' ἐξ ἀνάγκης, ὅταν ὑπὸ πλείονος ὑγρασίας συγχεομένων τῶν τῆς φύσεως πόρων τὸ θερμὸν²² μὴ παντελῶς καταλαμβάνηται, ἀλλ' ἔτι ἀπομάχεσθαι καὶ ἐκκρίνειν αὐτὸ δύνηται, εὐλόγως νόσου σημεῖα φαί-
25 νεται. τότε γὰρ ὑπὸ πλείονος ὑγρασίας ἢ τοῦ | συμμέτρου κατὰ φύσιν ψύχεται, ἥ τε σὰρξ δίομβρος γενομένη τὴν κακίστην πρὸς ὑγείαν διάθεσιν λαμβάνει.

42. Διὰ τί τοῦ χειμῶνος ἱδρῶτες ἧσσον γίνονται, καὶ ἡμεῖς οὐχ ὁμοίως παρασκευάζειν βουλόμεθα,

40. Why, though bodies are drier in the summer than in the winter, are we in such a condition as to sweat more in the summer? Is it because in the summer, when bodies are porous, the natural heat is not contained in large quantities, so it dissolves the moisture into breath? But in the winter, when bodies are thickened on the outside, the natural heat being captured in great quantities does not dissolve the moisture into breath. And further, in the summer we take in a great deal of moisture, but in the winter we do the opposite.

41. Why are the sweats that occur automatically among the healthy thought to be worse than those which are due to exertion? Is it because the exertions that continually draw off the residual moisture make the flesh drier, so that the hollows of the passages are healthy and there is no blockage to the draining of the heat? But the sweats that are named automatic, and that occur by necessity when the heat is not completely captured because the natural passages are disturbed by large amounts of moisture, but still can resist and secrete it, are reasonably regarded as a sign of disease. For then the body is cooled by moisture that is greater than a naturally proportionate amount,[57] and the flesh becoming soaked takes on a most unhealthy condition.

42.[58] Why do sweats occur less in the winter, and we do not want to produce them to same extent, although the

[57] Or "is naturally cooled by the moisture being greater than a proportionate amount."   [58] Cf. *Pr.* 2.21, 33, 40.

---

21 δὲ χειμῶνος : χειμῶνος δὲ Yᵃ Ap. Xᵃ Pᶜ
22 τὸ θερμὸν Sylburg : τὰ θερμὰ codd.

ὑγροτέρων ὄντων τῶν σωμάτων τοῦ χειμῶνος; ἢ ἧσ-
30 σον μὲν ἱδροῦμεν, | ὅτι τὰ ὑγρὰ τοῦ χειμῶνος πέπηγε
καὶ συνέστηκε σφόδρα, δυσδιαλυτώτερα οὖν; οὐχ
ὑπολαμβάνομεν δὲ δεῖν ἱδρωτοποιεῖσθαι τοῦ χειμῶνος, διότι ἡ τοιαύτη διάθεσις ὑγιεινή. ὁ δὲ τοὺς ἱδρῶτας ἐμποιῶν τήκει καὶ συγχεῖ τὴν ἕξιν· ἔτι τε καὶ
ἀραιοτέραν τοῦ προσήκοντος ἐμποιῶν τό τε ἐντὸς |
35 θερμὸν ἀποκρίνων ἔλαττον ποιεῖ, ὥστε μὴ ὁμοίως
δύνασθαι τῷ περιέχοντι ψυχρῷ ἀντιτετάχθαι· τό τε
ἐκτὸς ὑγρὸν ῥᾳδιέστερον παρεμπεσεῖται τοῖς σώμασιν, ἀραιῶν τῶν πόρων διὰ τὰς ἱδρωτοποιίας ὄντων.[23]

[23] ὄντων B x D L Aᵐ Pᶜ H : om. cett. codd.

body is moister in winter? Or do we sweat less, because in the winter the moist parts are solidified and condensed a great deal, so they are less liable to be dissolved? Now we do not suppose that it is necessary to induce sweat in the winter, because then our condition is healthy. But the one who produces sweat causes melting and disturbs that condition; and further, by making the body more porous than it should be and secreting the internal heat, he produces less, so that it cannot offer similar resistance to the surrounding cold. And the external moisture will more easily penetrate the body, when the passages are more porous owing to the production of sweat.

BOOK III

INTRODUCTION

There was a great deal of intellectual interest among early Peripatetics in wine-drinking and drunkenness. Aristotle, Theophrastus, Chamaeleon, and Hieronymous each wrote (or is said to have written) a work *On Drunkenness* (Περὶ μέθης). None of these is extant, but a number of "fragments" survive.[1] There are no clear, specific connections between the meager remains of these works and the 36 chapters that make up *Pr.* 3, on wine-drinking and drunkenness (περὶ οἰνοποσίαν καὶ μέθη). But as there is virtually no evidence of any other sources for *Pr.* 3, I think it likely that the main sources were (some of) these Peripatetic treatises.[2]

This view gains support by comparing the content of *Pr.* 3 with the remains of the various treatises entitled *On Drunkenness*. The topics of the former include: the effects of wine and drunkenness—on judgment, on the

---

[1] Aristotle frs. 666–77 Gigon (to which should be added Plu. *QC* 3.3 (*Mor.* 650A) = fr. 1015 Gigon); Theophrastus frs. 569–79 FHSG; Chamaeleon frs. 9–13 Wehrli; Hieronymous frs. 28–30 White. On wine and drunkenness in the *corpus Aristotelicum*, see Bonitz, *Index Aristotelicus* 449b3–11, 450a40–58, 501a35–b37. Theophrastus also wrote a work *On Wine and Oil* (DL 5.45).

[2] Medical texts may have been another source. See, e.g., chs. 1, 4, 12 (with notes).

senses, on emotional control, on sleep, on sexual potency and fertility; the effects of different kinds of wine—mixed, unmixed, sweet; the effects of wine on different kinds of people—children, the brave, Scythians, the elderly, those who exercise; hangovers and their treatment. The topics of the treatises entitled *On Drunkenness* include: the effects of wine and drunkenness—on mental states, on sexual potency; the effects of different kinds of wine—mixed, boiled, spiced, Samagorean; the effects of wine on different kinds of people—the young, the elderly; the unusual drinking habits of certain individuals; the rituals associated with wine-drinking; various laws concerning wine-drinking; the terminology and etymology of words associated with wine-drinking and drunkenness.

This comparison reveals an obvious overlap of subject matter. The main difference—that the set of topics treated in *Pr.* 3 is narrower—is best explained by the nearly exclusive focus, in many books of the *Problems*, on natural philosophy and science. It is of course possible that passages from the *On Drunkenness* of Aristotle or another Peripatetic might be imbedded in *Pr.* 3, but we have no way of knowing that given the evidence that survives.

ΟΣΑ ΠΕΡΙ
ΟΙΝΟΠΟΣΙΑΝ ΚΑΙ
ΜΕΘΗΝ

871a   1. Διὰ τί οἱ μεθύοντες θερμοῦ ὄντος τοῦ οἴνου
δύσριγοί εἰσιν, καὶ τάχιστα ἁλίσκονται ὑπὸ πλευ-
ρίτιδος καὶ τῶν τοιούτων;[1] ἢ διότι πολὺ ὑγρὸν ἐὰν
5   ψυχθῇ, πολὺ ψυχρὸν | γίνεται, ὥστε κρατεῖν τῆς φυσι-
κῆς θερμότητος; γίνεται γὰρ ὅμοιον ὥσπερ ἂν εἰ
ἐσθὴς βεβρεγμένη εἴη ὑγρῷ ψυχρῷ, οὕτως ἡ σὰρξ
ἔνδοθεν.

2. Διὰ τί οὐχ οἱ σφόδρα μεθύοντες παροινοῦσιν,
ἀλλ᾽ οἱ ἀκροθώρακες μάλιστα; ἢ ὅτι οὔθ᾽ οὕτως ὀλί-
10   γον πεπώκασιν | ὥστε ὁμοίως ἔχειν τοῖς νήφουσιν,
οὔθ᾽ οὕτως ὥστε διαλύεσθαι, ὅπερ πάσχουσιν οἱ πολὺ
πεπωκότες; ἔτι οἱ μὲν νήφοντες μᾶλλον ὀρθῶς κρί-
νουσιν, οἱ δὲ σφόδρα μεθύοντες οὐδ᾽ ἐγχειροῦσι κρί-
νειν· οἱ δὲ ἀκροθώρακες κρίνουσι μὲν διὰ τὸ μὴ
σφόδρα μεθύειν, κακῶς δὲ διὰ τὸ μὴ νήφειν, καὶ ταχὺ |
15   τῶν μὲν καταφρονοῦσιν, ὑπὸ τῶν δὲ λιγωρεῖσθαι
δοκοῦσιν.

[1] τοιούτων : cf. Pr. 3.6, 871b34, τοιούτων νόσων

PROBLEMS CONCERNING
WINE-DRINKING AND
DRUNKENNESS

1.[1] Why, though wine is hot, are those who are drunk sensitive to cold, and are quickly overcome by pleurisy and other such (*diseases*)? Is it because a quantity of liquid, if cooled, becomes a quantity of cold, and so masters the natural heat? For a similar thing occurs: if a garment is drenched in cold liquid, so does the flesh within (*become cold*).

2.[2] Why do those who are very drunk not act inebriated, but those who are tipsy especially do? Is it because they have neither drunk so little that they are like the sober, nor so much that they become undone, just as those who have drunk a great deal experience? Further, those who are sober are better able to judge correctly, whereas those who are very drunk do not *attempt* to judge. But those who are tipsy do judge, because they are not very drunk, whereas they do so poorly, because they are not sober—and they quickly look down upon some people, and think they are slighted by others.

---

[1] Cf. *Pr.* 3.6. See also Hp. *Mor.* 1.26.
[2] Cf. *Pr.* 3.27. See also Plu. *QC* 3.8 (*Mor.* 656C–D).

3. Διὰ τί μᾶλλον κραιπαλῶσιν οἱ ἀκρατέστερον πίνοντες ἢ οἱ ὅλως ἄκρατον; πότερον διὰ τὴν λεπτότητα ὁ κεκραμένος μᾶλλον εἰσδύεται εἰς πλείους τόπους καὶ στενωτέρους, ὁ δὲ ἄκρατος ἧττον, ὥστε
20 δυσεξαγωγότερος ὁ κεκραμένος; | ἢ διότι ἐλάττω πίνουσιν ἄκρατον διὰ τὸ μὴ δύνασθαι, καὶ ἀπεμοῦσι μᾶλλον; ἔτι δὲ συμπέττει τὰ λοιπὰ θερμότερος ὤν, καὶ αὐτὸς αὑτόν· ὁ δὲ ὑδαρὴς τοὐναντίον.

4. Διὰ τί τῶν οἰνοφλύγων τὸ σπέρμα οὐ γόνιμον ὡς ἐπὶ τὸ πολύ; ἢ ὅτι ἡ κρᾶσις τοῦ σώματος ἐξύγρανται; |
25 τὰ δὲ ὑγρὰ σπέρματα οὐ γόνιμα, ἀλλὰ τὰ συνεστῶτα καὶ πάχος ἔχοντα.

5. Διὰ τί οἱ οἰνόφλυγες τρέμουσιν, καὶ μᾶλλον ὅσῳ ἂν ἀκρατοποτῶσιν; ἔστιν δὲ ὁ μὲν οἶνος θερμαντικόν, ὁ δὲ τρόμος γίνεται μάλιστα ἀπὸ ψυχροῦ (διὸ οἱ
30 ῥιγῶντες μάλιστα | τρέμουσιν). πολλοῖς δ᾽ ἤδη χρωμένοις μόνον ἀκράτῳ τροφῆς χάριν τρόμοι ἰσχυροὶ συνέβησαν, ὥστε ἀπορρίπτειν τοὺς θλίβοντας,[2] καὶ τῷ θερμῷ ὕδατι λουόμενοι ἀναισθήτως εἶχον. ἢ ὅτι γίνεται μὲν ὁ τρόμος διὰ κατάψυξιν, γίνεται δὲ ἢ περισταμένου ἐντὸς τοῦ θερμοῦ διὰ τὸ ἐκτὸς ψύχος, |
35 οἷον τοῦ χειμῶνος, ἢ σβεννυμένου τοῦ κατὰ φύσιν θερμοῦ, σβεννυμένου μὲν τῷ ἐναντίῳ, ἢ διὰ χρόνον,

[2] θλίβοντας Nicasius Barth. : φλιβολίτας Yᵃ Cᵃ : φιλοβολίτας Ap. : φλίβοντας Ruelle

[3] Cf. *Pr.* 3.14 and 22. See also Plu. *QC* 6.9 (*Mor.* 696D).

3.[3] Why do those who drink wine somewhat unmixed[4] have a worse hangover than those who drink it completely unmixed? Is it because wine that is mixed, owing to its lightness, penetrates more into farther and narrower regions, but unmixed wine does so less, so that the mixed wine is more difficult to get rid of? Or is it because people drink less unmixed wine (*when they do*) because they are unable to (*drink more*), and they vomit more? Further, being hotter, it causes concoction in the other parts and in itself; but watery wine does the opposite.

4.[5] Why is the seed of drunkards[6] not fertile in most cases? Is it because the mixture of the body has become moistened? Now moist seeds[7] are not fertile, but only those that are congealed and have density.

5.[8] Why do drunkards tremble, and more so according to how much unmixed wine they drink? Now wine is capable of heating, whereas trembling comes mostly from cold (which is why those with chills tremble most of all). But powerful trembling is already experienced by many who use unmixed wine alone for nourishment, so that they throw off those who are restraining them, and when they wash in hot water they have no perception of it. Is it because trembling occurs owing to cooling, and this occurs either when the internal heat is surrounded by external cold, as in winter, or when the natural heat is extinguished, being extinguished by its opposite or owing to time, as in

[4] The Greeks normally drank wine mixed with water.

[5] Cf. Hp. *Superf.* 30. See also Ath. 10.434f–35a.

[6] Or perhaps "winos" (τῶν οἰνοφλύγων).

[7] I.e., seeds that are too moist, or more moist than normal.

[8] Cf. *Pr.* 3.26.

οἷον γῆρας, ἢ τῇ τοῦ ἀλλοτρίου θερμοῦ ὑπερβολῇ, ὃ
συμβαίνει τῷ ἐν τῷ ἡλίῳ ἢ πυρὶ καιομένῳ; συμβαίνει
δὲ τοῦτο καὶ τοῖς τῷ ἀκράτῳ οἴνῳ χρωμένοις. ὧν γὰρ
871b θερμός,[3] ὅταν ὑπερτείνηται[4] ‖ δυνάμει τῇ τοῦ σώματος
οἰκείᾳ θερμότητι μιγνύμενος, ἀποσβέννυσιν αὐτό·
σβεσθέντος δὲ καὶ ψυχθέντος τοῦ σώματος συμβαίνει
τοὺς τρόμους γίνεσθαι. ἔστιν δὲ καὶ παρὰ πάντα τὰ
5 εἰρημένα ἄλλος τρόπος καταψύξεως· ‖ ἀναιρεθείσης
δὴ[5] τῆς ὕλης, ᾗ τὸ θερμὸν ἑκάστῳ τρέφεται, συμβαίνει καὶ τὸ θερμὸν φθείρεσθαι. τοῦτο δὲ ἐπὶ μὲν τῶν
ἀψύχων ἐπὶ τοῦ λύχνου ἐστὶ φανερόν (τοῦ γὰρ ἐλαίου
ἀναλωθέντος συμβαίνει σβέννυσθαι τὸ φῶς), ἐπὶ δὲ
τῶν ἐμψύχων τό τε γῆρας ταὐτὸ ποιεῖ τοῦτο καὶ τῶν
10 νόσων ‖ αἱ μακραὶ καὶ συντηκτικαί. ἀναιρουμένης γὰρ
ἢ λεπτυνομένης τῆς τοῦ θερμοῦ τροφῆς ἐκλείπειν[6]
αὐτὸ συμβαίνει. ὑγρῷ μὲν γὰρ τρέφεται τὸ θερμόν,
τούτῳ δὲ οὐ τῷ τυχόντι, ἀλλὰ λείῳ καὶ πλείονι.[7] διὸ
τοῖς νοσοῦσι τὰς εἰρημένας νόσους καὶ πρεσβυτέροις
15 φθειρομένου τοῦ τοιούτου καὶ ‖ ἀλλοιουμένου (δριμὺ
γὰρ καὶ αὐχμηρὸν ἀντὶ λείου καὶ λιπαροῦ γίνεται)
συμβαίνει ἐκλείπειν αὐτό. σημεῖον δὲ τῶν εἰρημένων
ἐστὶν αἱ γινόμεναι βοήθειαι τοῖς μαράνσει τὸν βίον
ἐκλείπουσιν· ὅ τι γὰρ ἂν ἐπιστάξῃ τις αὐτοῖς τῶν
τροφωδῶν ὑγρῶν, προσαναφέρεσθαι συμβαίνει τὸ ‖
20 ζωτικὸν[8] αὐτῶν, ὡς τῇ τοῦ τοιούτου ἐκλείψει γινομένης

---

[3] post θερμός add. τις Y[a], τις ὁ οἶνος X[a]
[4] ὑπερτείνηται : ὑπερτείνῃ τῇ Bonitz

old age, or by the excess of foreign heat, which happens to
what is burning in the sun or in fire? And this also happens
to those who use unmixed wine. For (*wine*), being hot,
whenever its power is increased by mixing with the heat
proper to the body, extinguishes it;[9] and when it is extinguished and the body is cooled, trembling occurs. But
there is also, besides all that has been said, another manner
of cooling: indeed, when the matter by which the heat in
each individual is nourished has been withdrawn, the heat
too is destroyed. Now in inanimate things this is evident in
the case of the lamp (for when the oil is used up the light is
extinguished), and in the case of animate things old age
produces this same effect, as do long and wasting diseases.
For when that which nourishes the heat is removed or reduced, the result is that it fails. For heat is nourished by
moisture, and not by any chance moisture, but by moisture
that is smooth and abundant.[10] This is why in those who are
suffering from the aforementioned diseases and in the elderly, as this moisture decays and changes (for it becomes
harsh and dry instead of smooth and oily), the result is that
the heat fails. A sign of what has been said is the things that
are helpful to those whose life is failing by wasting; for
if one provides them with any nutritive moisture, their
vitality is restored, so that their dissolution occurs due to

[9] I.e., the heat from the unmixed wine extinguishes the heat
from the body.   [10] Or, with Bekker's conjecture, "fat."

---

[5] δὴ Ross apud Forster : δὲ codd.

[6] ἐκλείπειν Forster ex Gaza (cf. 871b16) : ἐκλύειν codd.

[7] πλείονι : πίονι Bekker   [8] τὸ ζωτικὸν Richards : τὸ δὲ
ὀπτικὸν codd. : τὸ πεπτικὸν Nicasius

τῆς διαλύσεως. ἔοικεν δὲ τοῖς ἀκρατοποτοῦσι τοῦτ᾽
εἶναι αἴτιον. ὧν γὰρ θερμὸς ὁ οἶνος μετὰ τῆς φύσει
ὑπαρχούσης θερμότητος μᾶλλον ἀναλίσκει τὰ ἐν τῷ
σώματι ὑπάρχοντα ἐφόδια τῷ οἰκείῳ θερμῷ. διὸ συμ-
25 βαίνει τοὺς μὲν ὑδρωπικοὺς | αὐτῶν γίνεσθαι, τοὺς δὲ
ῥευματικούς, τοὺς δὲ εἰς τὴν κοιλίαν. τά τε γὰρ λοιπὰ
αὐτοῖς ὑγρὰ δριμέα ἐστίν, καὶ τὰ εἰσιόντα δι᾽ ἀσθένειαν τοῦ οἰκείου θερμοῦ ἁπαλὰ ὄντα οὐ παχύνεται.
ἀσθενὲς δέ ἐστι τὸ θερμὸν τῷ τὴν ὕλην εἶναι τοιαύτην
30 ἐν ᾧ ἔτι σώζεται, καθάπερ τὸ καλάμινον | πῦρ· καὶ γὰρ
τοῦτο διὰ τὴν τῆς ὕλης ἀσθένειαν ἀσθενέστερόν ἐστι
τοῦ ξυλίνου.

6. Διὰ τί οἱ μεθύοντες θερμοῦ ὄντος τοῦ οἴνου
δύσριγοί εἰσιν, καὶ τάχιστα ἁλίσκονται ὑπὸ πλευ-
ρίτιδος καὶ τῶν τοιούτων νόσων; ἢ ὅτι τὸ πολὺ ὑγρὸν
35 ἐὰν ψυχθῇ, πολὺ | ψυχρὸν γίνεται, ὥστε κρατεῖν τῆς
φυσικῆς θερμότητος; πάντα δὲ τὰ ὑγρότερα ψυχό-
τερα[9] ἐστι τὴν φύσιν. σημεῖον δέ· θερμαίνεται μὲν
γὰρ τοῖς ἐκτός, ὑγραίνεται δὲ οὔ. εἰ δ᾽ ἧττόν ἐστι
θερμά, καὶ ἀπολείπει δῆλον ὅτι θᾶττον αὐτὰ[10] ἢ θερμότης ἢ ὑγρότης, ὥστε λειφθέντων ψυχρῶν ὑγρῶν ‖
872a εἰκότως ῥιγοῦσίν τε μᾶλλον οἱ μεθύοντες καὶ τὰ τοῦ
ῥίγους οἰκεῖα πάσχουσι πάθη.

9 ψυχότερά Xᵃ : θερμότερά cett. codd.
10 αὐτὰ : fort. αὐτὴ

the cessation of such moisture. Now this seems to be the cause in those who drink unmixed wine. For the wine, which is hot, together with the heat already present by nature, tends to use up the supply (*of such moisture*) already present in the body for its own heat. This is why the result is that some become dropsical,[11] others rheumatic, and with others (*the problem*) is in the stomach. For the moisture remaining in them is harsh, and what enters,[12] being soft because of the weakness of their own heat, does not thicken. Now the heat is weak because the matter in which it is still preserved is weak, just like with a reed fire: for this too because of the weakness of its matter is weaker than a wood fire.

6.[13] Why, though wine is hot, are those who are drunk sensitive to cold, and are quickly overcome by pleurisy and other such diseases? Is it because the quantity of liquid, if cooled, becomes a quantity of cold, and so masters the natural heat? Now the moister anything is the colder[14] it is in its nature. And here is a sign of this: it is heated by external causes, but not moistened. But if there is less heat, it is also clear that the heat itself leaves more quickly than the moisture, so that, when the cold moisture is left, it is reasonable that those who are drunk should have chills more and experience the usual symptoms of cold.

---

[11] "Dropsy" (from ὕδρωψ; ὑδρωπικός = "dropsical") is an obsolete medical term, referring to swelling in the body owing to an accumulation of excess water.

[12] Likely any food or drink the person consumes.

[13] Cf. *Pr.* 3.1.

[14] Most mss. have "hotter."

7. Διὰ τί οἱ μὲν παῖδες θερμοὶ ὄντες οὐ φίλοινοί
εἰσι, Σκύθαι δὲ καὶ οἱ ἄνδρες οἱ ἀνδρεῖοι θερμοὶ ὄντες
5 φίλοινοι; ἢ ὅτι οἱ μὲν θερμοὶ ὄντες καὶ ξηροί (ἡ γὰρ
τοῦ ἀνδρὸς ἕξις τοιαύτη), οἱ δὲ παῖδες ὑγροὶ καὶ
θερμοί; ἡ δὲ φιλοποσία ἐστὶν ἐπιθυμία ὑγροῦ τινός. ἡ
οὖν ὑγρότης κωλύει διψητικοὺς εἶναι τοὺς παῖδας·
ἔνδεια γάρ τις ἐστὶν ἡ ἐπιθυμία.

8. Διὰ τί μεθύοντες μᾶλλον διαισθανόμεθα τὰ ἁλυ-
10 κὰ | καὶ τὰ μοχθηρὰ ὕδατα, νήφοντες δὲ ἧττον; ἢ ὅτι
τὸ οἰκεῖον ὑπὸ τοῦ οἰκείου ἐστὶν ἀπαθές, καὶ τὸ ὁμοίως
διακείμενον, τὰ δὲ ἐναντία τῶν ἐναντίων ἐστὶν αἰσθη-
τικώτατα· ὁ μὲν οὖν μεθύων γλυκεῖς ἐν αὑτῷ χυμοὺς
ἔχει (τοιοῦτο γὰρ ὁ οἶνος δοκεῖ), καὶ τῶν φαύλων
15 χυμῶν αἰσθητικώτερός | ἐστιν, ὁ δὲ νήφων δριμεῖς καὶ
ἁλυκούς. τῆς τροφῆς οὖν πεπεμμένης οἱ περιττωμα-
τικοὶ ἐπιπολάζουσιν. οὗτοί τε οὖν εἰσὶν ἀπαθεῖς ὑπὸ
τῶν ὁμοίων, καὶ τὸν ἔχοντα ποιοῦσιν.

9. Διὰ τί τοῖς μεθύουσι σφόδρα κύκλῳ πάντα
φαίνεται φέρεσθαι, καὶ ἤδη ἁπτομένης τῆς μέθης
20 ἀθρεῖν τὰ πόρρω | οὐ δύνανται; διὸ καὶ σημεῖον τῆς
μέθης αὐτὸ ποιοῦνταί τινες. ἢ ὅτι κινεῖται ὑπὸ τῆς
θερμότητος τοῦ οἴνου ἡ ὄψις πυκνάκις; διαφέρει οὖν
οὐθὲν τὴν ὄψιν κινεῖν ἢ τὸ ὁρώμενον· ταὐτὸ γὰρ ποιεῖ
πρὸς τὸ φαίνεσθαι τὰ εἰρημένα. ἐπεὶ δὲ καὶ περὶ τὰ

---

15 On children, see *Som.* 457a14ff.; on the courageous, see *Pr.*
27.4; on the Scythians, see Hdt. VI 84, Hieronym. fr. 29 White,
Chamael. fr. 10 Wehrli.

7.[15] Why are children, who are hot, not wine lovers, while Scythians and courageous males, who are hot, *are* wine lovers? Is it because the latter are hot and dry (for such a state is characteristic of the male), whereas children are moist and hot? Now the love of drinking is a desire for something moist. Therefore, their moisture prevents children from being thirsty; for desire is a sort of lack.

8.[16] Why do we distinctly perceive salty and bad water more when we are drunk, but less when we are sober? Is it because like (and what is similarly situated) is unaffected by like, but opposites are most perceptible to opposites? Now the one who is drunk has in himself sweet flavors[17] (for wine seems to be such), and so he is more able to perceive foul flavors, whereas the one who is sober has in himself harsh and salty flavors. So when the nourishment is concocted, the residues rise to the surface. Therefore, these are unaffected by those like them, and make the one possessing them (*similarly unaffected*).

9.[18] Why does everything appear to be traveling in a circle to those who are very drunk, and as soon as drunkenness has grabbed them they are unable to observe things far away? And this is why some make this a sign of drunkenness. Is it because the vision[19] is frequently moved by the heat of the wine? Therefore, it makes no difference whether the vision or the object seen is moved; for with respect to the phenomena referred to either one produces

---

[16] Cf. *Pr.* 3.19.

[17] Or "juices" or "humors" (χυμοὺς).

[18] Cf. *Pr.* 3.20 and 15.6.

[19] ἡ ὄψις can be (and in this chapter is) translated a number of ways, e.g., "vision," "sight," "organ of sight."

25 πλησίον ὄντα διαψεύδεσθαι τὴν ὄψιν συμβαίνει | τῶν
μεθυόντων, καὶ περὶ τὰ πόρρω μᾶλλον εἰκὸς ταῦτα
πάσχειν. διόπερ ἐκεῖνα μὲν ὅλως οὐχ ὁρᾶται, τὰ δ'
ἐγγὺς οὐκ ἐν ᾧ τόπῳ ἐστὶν ὁρᾷ. κύκλῳ δὲ φαίνεται
φέρεσθαι, καὶ οὐκ ἐγγὺς καὶ πόρρω, ὅτι εἰς μὲν τὸ
πόρρω διά τε τὴν κύκλῳ κίνησιν ἀδυνατωτέρα ἐστὶ
30 φέρεσθαι ἡ | ὄψις. ἅμα γὰρ τἀναντία ποιεῖν οὐ ῥάδιον.
ἔστι δὲ ἡ μὲν πόρρω ἐπ' εὐθείας φορά,[11] ἡ δὲ κύκλῳ ἐν
ᾧ τοὔνομα σημαίνει σχήματι. διά τε οὖν τὰ εἰρημένα
πόρρω οὐ φέρεται· καὶ εἰ φέροιτο τὸ ἐγγὺς καὶ πόρρω,
οὐκ ἂν ταῦθ' ὁρῴη. ἀπολείποι γὰρ ἂν ἐν θατέρῳ
35 χρόνῳ αὐτῶν τὸ ὁρώμενον | ἐν ταὐτῷ τόπῳ, ἀπολείπων
δὲ οὐκ ἂν ὁρῴη. κύκλῳ δὲ φέρεται διὰ τὸ ὑπάρχον
σχῆμα τῆς ὄψεως. ἔστι γὰρ κῶνος, οὗ ἡ βάσις κύ-
872b κλος, ἐν ᾧ κινουμένη ὁρᾷ μὲν τοῦτο διὰ ‖ τὸ μηδέποτε
ἀπολείπειν αὐτό, διέψευσται δὲ τῷ τόπῳ διὰ τὸ μὴ τὴν
αὐτὴν ὄψιν ἐπιβάλλειν ἐπ' αὐτό. ταὐτὸν γὰρ ἂν ἦν ἢ
τοῦτο πρὸς τὴν ὄψιν κινεῖν ἢ τὴν ὄψιν πρὸς τοῦτο.

10. Διὰ τί τοῖς μεθύουσιν ἐνίοτε πολλὰ φαίνεται τὸ
5 ἓν | ὁρῶσιν; ἢ καθάπερ εἴρηται, κινουμένης τῆς ὄψεως
συμβαίνει μηθένα χρόνον τὴν αὐτὴν ἐπὶ ταὐτοῦ ἠρεμεῖν ὄψιν, τὸ δ' ἐν ταὐτῷ χρόνῳ ἑτέρως ὁρώμενον
ὀψιαίτερον εἶναι δοκεῖ; ἁφῇ γὰρ ὄψεως ὁρᾶται τὸ
ὁρώμενον, ἅπτεσθαι δὲ πλείοσιν ἅμα τοῦ αὐτοῦ ἀδύ-

---

11 ἐπ' εὐθείας φορά Bonitz : ἐπιθυμία σφοδρά codd. : ἐπ'
ἰθὺ μία σφοδρά Bussemaker

the same result. Now since the vision of those who are drunk is deceived about objects that are near, it is reasonable that it should be more affected in this way about distant objects. So, while the latter are not seen at all, the one who is drunk sees the objects that are near, but not in the place in which they are. But they appear to be traveling in a circle, and not to be near or far, because the vision is less able to travel into the distance owing to its movement in a circle. For it is not easy to do opposite movements at the same time. But the distant vision is movement in a straight line, whereas vision in a circle is in the figure signified by its name. Therefore, the vision does not travel a distance, owing to the reasons mentioned; and if it were to travel to both near and distant objects, it would not see them. For what was seen in the same place one would lose sight of in the next instant, and losing sight of it one could not see it. Now it travels in a circle owing to the shape belonging to the organ of sight. For it is a cone, the base of which is a circle, moving in which (*the eye*) sees the object because it never loses sight of it, but it is deceived as to its position because the same vision does not strike it. For moving the object toward the sight and moving the sight toward the object is the same thing.

10.[20] Why, to those who are drunk, does the one thing that they are looking at sometimes appear to be many? Is it, as we have said,[21] that when the organ of sight is moved, the same vision does not remain on the same spot for any time, but that which is seen differently at the same time seems to be later? For what is seen is seen by contact with sight, and it is impossible to be in contact with several

[20] Cf. *Pr.* 3.30.   [21] See *Pr.* 3.9, 872a34–35.

10 νατον. ὄντος δὲ ἀναισθήτου τοῦ μεταξὺ | χρόνου, ἐν ᾧ
ἡ ὄψις ἥπτετο καὶ παρήλλαττεν τὸ ὁρώμενον, εἷς εἶναι
δοκεῖ χρόνος ἐν ᾧ τε ἧπται καὶ παρήλλαχεν· ὥστ᾽ ἐν
τῷ αὐτῷ χρόνῳ ταὐτοῦ πλειόνων ἁπτομένων ὄψεων
πλείω δοκεῖ εἶναι τὰ ὁρώμενα, διὰ τὸ ταὐτοῦ[12] κατὰ
τὸν αὐτὸν χρόνον[13] ἀδύνατον εἶναι ἅπτεσθαι. |

15   11. Διὰ τί οἱ μεθύοντες ἀφροδισιάζειν ἀδύνατοί
εἰσιν; ἢ ὅτι δεῖ τινὰ τόπον ἐκθερμανθῆναι μᾶλλον τοῦ
ἄλλου σώματος, τοῦτο δὲ ποιεῖν διὰ τὸ πλῆθος τῆς ἐν
ὅλῳ τῷ σώματι θερμασίας ἀδυνατοῦσιν; ἀποσβέννυται γὰρ τὸ ὑπὸ τῆς κινήσεως γινόμενον θερμὸν ὑπὸ
20 τοῦ περιέχοντος μᾶλλον, ὅτι | πολύ ἐστιν ἐν αὐτοῖς τὸ
ὑγρὸν καὶ ἄπεπτον. ἔτι δὲ τὸ σπέρμα ἐκ τροφῆς,
τροφὴ δὲ πᾶσα πέττεται· ἧς πληρωθέντες ὁρμητικοί
εἰσι πρὸς τὰ ἀφροδίσια. διὸ καὶ κελεύουσί τινες πρὸς
τὴν πρᾶξιν τὴν τοιαύτην ἀριστᾶν μὲν πολύ, δειπνεῖν
25 δὲ ὀλίγον, ἵνα ᾖ αὐτοῖς ἐλάττω τὰ ἄπεπτα τῶν | πε-
πεμμένων.

    12. Διὰ τί ὁ γλυκὺς καὶ ἄκρατος καὶ ὁ κυκεὼν
μεταξὺ διαπινόμενοι ἐν τοῖς πότοις νήφειν ποιοῦσιν,
καὶ διὰ τί ἧττον μεθύσκονται ταῖς μεγάλαις κωθωνι-
ζόμενοι; ἢ πάντων τὸ αὐτὸ αἴτιόν ἐστιν, ἡ κατάκρου-
30 σις[14] τοῦ ἐπιπολῆς θερμοῦ· τὸ | γὰρ μεθύειν ἐστίν,
ὅταν ᾖ τὸ θερμὸν ἐν τοῖς περὶ τὴν κεφαλὴν τόποις.

---

[12] ταὐτοῦ Richards : ταῦτα codd.
[13] χρόνον Kᵃ : τρόπον cett. codd.
[14] κατάκρουσις Bonitz ex Pr. 3.25a, 874b12 : παράκρουσις
codd.

things at the same time. But as the intervening time, in which the sight was in contact with and passed on from what is seen, is imperceptible, the time in which it has been in contact and passed on *seems* to be one moment; so that, when many visions are in contact with the same thing during the same time, what are seen seem many, because it is impossible *(for the many visions)* to be in contact with the same thing at the same time.

11.[22] Why are those who are drunk unable to have sex? Is it because a certain region of the body must be heated more than the rest, but they cannot do this owing to the quantity of heat in the whole body? For the heat generated by the movement is extinguished by the more abundant surrounding heat, because there is a great deal of uncon-cocted moisture in them. Moreover, seed comes from nourishment, and all nourishment is concocted: those who have had their fill are more inclined to sexual intercourse. And this is why, with a view to such an act, some recom-mend a large breakfast, but a light dinner, so that the unconcocted nourishment in them may be less than the concocted.

12.[23] Why do sweet wine and unmixed wine and *kykeon*,[24] when consumed at intervals during a drinking bout, make people sober, and why are people less drunk when they drink from large *(wine cups)*?[25] Is the cause of all these the same, the downward pressure of the surface heat? For there is drunkenness, when the heat is in the regions around the head.

---

[22] Cf. *Pr.* 3.33.   [23] Cf. *Pr.* 3.25a. See also Hp. *Epid.* 2.6.30, and Plu. *QC* 3.7 (*Mor.* 655E).   [24] A drink con-sisting (with some variations) of wine, honey, barley, and cheese.

[25] Translating ταῖς μεγάλαις (sc. κύλιξι).

13. Διὰ τί τοῦ γλυκέος ἐπιπολαστικοῦ ὄντος, ἐάν
τις μεθύων ἤδη ἐπιπίῃ γλυκύ, καταπέττεται ὁ ἐνυπάρ-
χων οἶνος καὶ ἧττον ἐνοχλεῖ; ἢ ὅτι τὸ μὲν γλυκὺ
35 λεαντικόν τέ ἐστι | καὶ γλίσχρον (ἐμφράττει οὖν τοὺς
πόρους), τὸ δὲ αὐστηρὸν τραχυντικόν, καὶ τὸ μὲν
εὐπετῆ ποιεῖ τῷ θερμῷ τὴν ἀναφοράν, ὁ δὲ γλυκὺς
873a στέγει αὐτό, τοὺς πόρους ἐμφράττων; ‖ ὅτι δὲ τῶν ἄνω
θερμανθέντων ἐστὶν ἡ μέθη, εἴρηται. ἔτι δὲ ὁ μὲν
γλυκὺς ἄνοδμος, ὁ δὲ αὐστηρὸς οὔ· ὀσμὴ δὲ πᾶσα
βαρύνει κεφαλήν.

14. Διὰ τί ἀπὸ τοῦ κεκραμένου μὲν, ἀκρατεστέρου
5 δὲ, ἔωθεν | μᾶλλον πονοῦσι τὴν κεφαλὴν ἢ ἀπὸ τοῦ
ἀκράτου; ἢ ὅτι ὁ μὲν ἄκρατος παχυμερὴς ὢν εἰς τοὺς
περὶ τὴν κεφαλὴν πόρους στενοὺς ὄντας αὐτὸς μὲν
οὐκ εἰσπίπτει, ἡ δὲ δύναμις αὐτοῦ, ἡ ὀσμὴ καὶ θερμότης; ὁ δὲ κεκραμένος μιχθεὶς λεπτῷ τῷ ὕδατι αὐτὸς
10 εἰσδύεται, ἔχων δὲ σῶμα καὶ | τῆς δυνάμεως πολὺ τῆς
τοῦ ἀκράτου, δυσπεπτότερός ἐστιν. τά τε γὰρ ὑγρὰ
πάντων δυσπεπτότατα, καὶ τὰ σώματα τῶν ἐν αὑτοῖς
δυνάμεων.

15. Διὰ τί μᾶλλον δύνανται πιεῖν εἰς μέθην οἱ
ἀγύμναστοι τῶν γεγυμνασμένων, καὶ ῥᾷον ἀπαλλάτ-
15 τουσιν; ἢ ὅτι | οἱ ἔχοντες περίττωμα καὶ ὑγρὸν ἐν
αὑτοῖς οὐρητικοὶ γίνονται; ὅπερ ποιεῖ δύνασθαι πίνειν
καὶ ὕστερον κούφως ἔχειν διὰ τὸ μὴ ἐμμένειν πολὺ
ὑγρὸν οἰνῶδες. οἱ μὲν οὖν ἀγύμναστοι ὑγροὶ καὶ
περιττωματικοί εἰσιν, οἱ δὲ γεγυμνασμένοι ξηροί,

13. Why, although what is sweet rises to the surface, if someone who is already drunk drinks sweet wine in addition, the wine that is already present is concocted and causes less trouble? Is it because what is sweet is soothing and sticky (therefore it obstructs the passages), whereas what is bitter produces roughness, and the latter makes it easy for the heat to rise, whereas what is sweet contains it by blocking the passages? Now, that drunkenness is due to the upper parts being heated has been stated.[26] Further, sweet wine is odorless, whereas bitter wine is not; and every odor weighs down the head.

14.[27] Why do people have a worse headache in the morning from wine that is mixed, but closer to unmixed, than from unmixed wine? Is it because unmixed wine, which consists of thick parts, cannot itself pass into the passages around the head, which are narrow, though its power—the odor and heat—can? But mixed wine, being mingled with water, which is light, itself penetrates, and having the body and a great deal of the power of unmixed wine, it is more difficult to concoct? For moist things are the most difficult of all to concoct, and the bodies more than the powers in them.

15. Why are those who don't exercise better able to drink to a state of drunkenness than those who do exercise, and why do they more easily get free of it? Is it because those who have residues and moisture within them are inclined to urinate? This makes them able to drink and later to be empty, because not much vinous moisture remains. Now those who do not exercise are moist and full of residues, whereas those who do exercise are dry, so

20 ὥστ᾽ εἰς τὸ σῶμα τούτοις ἡ ὑγρότης ἡ | οἰνηρὰ
ἀφικνεῖται. εὐθύς τε οὖν ἀντισπᾷ τῇ οὐρήσει ἡ φορὰ
αὕτη, καὶ ὕστερον ἐμμένον τὸ ὑγρὸν τοῦτο ἐν τῷ
σώματι βάρος ποιεῖ.

16. Διὰ τί ὁ οἶνος καὶ τετυφωμένους ποιεῖ καὶ
μανικούς; ἐναντία γὰρ ἡ διάθεσις· ὁ μὲν γὰρ μᾶλλον
25 ἤδη ἐν κινήσει, | ὁ δὲ ἧττον. ἢ ὥσπερ Χαιρήμων εἶπεν·
"τῶν χρωμένων γὰρ τοῖς τρόποις κεράννυται"; τἀναντία οὖν ποιεῖ οὐ ταὐτὰ ἀλλὰ τὰ μὴ ὁμοίως ἔχοντα,
ὥσπερ καὶ τὸ πῦρ τὰ μὲν ξηραίνει, τὰ δὲ ὑγραίνει,
ἀλλ᾽ οὐ ταὐτά· καὶ τήκει τὸν κρύσταλλον καὶ πήγνυσι
30 τοὺς ἅλας. καὶ ὁ οἶνος | (ὑγρὸς γάρ ἐστι τὴν φύσιν)
τοὺς μὲν βραδυτέρους ἐπιτείνει καὶ θάττους ποιεῖ,
τοὺς δὲ θάττους ἐκλύει. διὸ ἔνιοι τῶν μελαγχολικῶν τῇ
φύσει ἐν ταῖς κραιπάλαις ἐκλελυμένοι γίνονται πάμπαν. ὥσπερ γὰρ τὸ λουτρὸν τοὺς μὲν συνδεδεμένους
35 τὸ σῶμα καὶ σκληροὺς εὐκινήτους ποιεῖ, τοὺς δὲ | εὐκι-
νήτους καὶ ὑγροὺς ἐκλύει, οὕτως ὁ οἶνος, ὥσπερ λούων
τὰ ἐντός, ἀπεργάζεται ταὐτό.[15]

17. Διὰ τί ἡ κράμβη παύει τὴν κραιπάλην; ἢ ὅτι
873b τὸν ‖ μὲν χυλὸν γλυκὺν καὶ ῥυπτικὸν ἔχει (διὸ καὶ
κλύζουσιν αὐτῷ τὴν κοιλίαν οἱ ἰατροί), αὐτὴ δ᾽ ἐστὶ
ψυχρά; σημεῖον δέ· πρὸς γὰρ τὰς σφοδρὰς διαρροίας
χρῶνται αὐτῇ οἱ ἰατροί, ἕψοντες σφόδρα καὶ ἀποχυ-

---

[15] ταὐτό Richards : τοῦτο codd.

[28] "The rush itself" (ἡ φορὰ αὕτη) refers to the motion de-

that in them the moisture of the wine goes into the body. Therefore, the rush itself[28] holds back the urine right away, and later this moisture, remaining in the body, produces weight.

16. Why does wine make people both stupefied and frenzied? For these dispositions are opposite: the latter actually involves more movement, the former less. Is it just as Chaeremon said: "Wine is mixed with the characters of the users"?[29] Therefore, it produces opposite results not with respect to the same things, but to things that are not similar, just as fire dries some things, and makes others moist, but not the same things: it melts ice and solidifies salt. Wine as well (for it is moist by nature) tightens the slow and makes them quicker, but relaxes the quick. This is why some of those who are melancholic by nature become completely relaxed during drinking bouts.[30] For just as a bath makes those who are stiff in body and hard able to move more easily, while it relaxes those who move easily and are moist, so wine, as if bathing the inside, accomplishes the same thing.

17. Why does cabbage prevent hangovers? Is it because it has juice that is sweet and able to cleanse (and this is why physicians rinse out the stomach with it), whereas in itself it is cold? Here's a sign of this: physicians use it in severe cases of diarrhea, boiling it thoroughly, drawing off the

scribed in the previous line: the moisture of the wine going into the body, in those whose bodies are dry owing to exercise.

29 Fr. 16 (*TGF*). On the tragic poet Chaeremon (active mid-fourth century), see Arist. *Rh.* 1413b13ff.

30 On melancholy and wine-drinking, see *Pr.* 30.1, 953a33–b34, 954b36–55a11.

5 λίζοντες[16] καὶ ψύχοντες. | συμβαίνει δὴ τῶν κραιπα-
λώντων τὸν μὲν χυλὸν αὐτῆς εἰς τὴν κοιλίαν κατασπᾶν τὰ ἐν αὐτοῖς ὑγρά, οἰνηρὰ καὶ ἄπεπτα ὄντα,
αὐτὴν δὲ ὑπολειπομένην ἐν τῇ ἄνω κοιλίᾳ ψύχειν τὸ
σῶμα. ψυχομένου δὲ ὑγρὰ λεπτὰ συμβαίνει εἰς τὴν
κύστιν φέρεσθαι. ὥστε κατ' ἀμφότερα τῶν ὑγρῶν
10 ἐκκρινομένων | διὰ τοῦ σώματος, καὶ καταψυχομένου,
εἰκότως ἀκραίπαλοι γίνονται· ὁ γὰρ οἶνος ὑγρὸς καὶ
θερμός ἐστιν. ἔτι δὲ συμβαίνει τῶν ὑγρῶν κατασπω-
μένων καὶ ἐκκρινομένων κάτω καὶ πνεῦμα ἐπάγεσθαι
αὐτοῖς, ὅπερ[17] μόνον ἀπὸ τοῦ οἴνου εἰς τὴν κεφαλὴν
15 φερόμενον τὸν κάρον καὶ τὴν | κραιπάλην ποιεῖ. κάτω
δὲ ὁρμήσαντος καὶ καταψυχομένου τοῦ σώματος διὰ
τὰ εἰρημένα, λύεται ὁ τῆς κραιπάλης πόνος. ἔστι γὰρ
ἡ κραιπάλη ζέσις τις καὶ φλεγμασία λήγουσα. λυπεῖ
δὲ μᾶλλον τῆς μέθης, ὅτι ἐκείνη μὲν ἐξίστησιν, ἡ δὲ
20 κραιπάλη ἐν αὐτοῖς οὖσι τὸν πόνον παρέχει· | καθάπερ
οὖν καὶ ὑπὸ τῶν πυρετῶν οἱ λαμβανόμενοι παίζουσι
μᾶλλον ἢ ἀλγοῦσι, παρ' αὑτοῖς δὲ γενόμενοι οἱ αὐτοί,
κουφισθέντες τοῦ πάθους, ἀλγοῦσιν. ταὐτὰ γὰρ καὶ
ἐπὶ τῆς κραιπάλης καὶ ἐπὶ τῆς μέθης συμβαίνει.

18. Διὰ τί μᾶλλον ἐμετιᾶν ποιεῖ ὁ ὑδαρὴς οἶνος ἢ
25 τὸ | ὕδωρ καὶ ὁ ἄκρατος; ἢ ὅτι ἐμεῖν μὲν μάλιστα ποιεῖ

16 ἀποχυλίζοντες u[mg] : ἀποξυλίζοντες codd.
17 ὅπερ Bekker : ὅθεν codd.

---

31 If the mss. reading is correct, this should be rendered "removing the fibrous material."

juice,[31] and cooling it. Indeed, in the case of those suffering from a hangover, the juice of the cabbage draws the moisture in them, which is vinous and unconcocted, down into the stomach, and remaining itself in the upper part of the stomach,[32] it cools the body. And as it cools, moist and light material is carried into the bladder. So, the moisture is secreted through the body in both ways, and as the body cools down, it is reasonable that people cease to have a hangover; for wine is moist and hot. Further, the drawing off and secretion of this moisture results in the breath being led down to these parts—the very material that alone, when carried from the wine up into the head, produces stupor and hangover. But when the breath rushes downward and the body is cooled in the ways mentioned, the pain of the hangover is relieved. For the hangover is a sort of boiling and inflammation as it abates. And it is more painful than drunkenness, because this utterly changes them,[33] whereas the hangover produces pain in those who are themselves. They are therefore just like those who are attacked by fevers, who are amused rather than suffering, but when they come to themselves and are freed from their disease, they suffer. For the same things happen in the case of the hangover and in the case of drunkenness.

18. Why does watery wine produce vomiting more easily than either water or unmixed wine? Is it because what

[32] Instead of "stomach" and "the upper part of the stomach," the author could have in mind "the bowels" and "the stomach," as κοιλία can refer to both stomach and bowels.

[33] The word translated "utterly changes them" (ἐξίστησιν) could also be rendered by something like "drives them out of their senses."

117

τὰ ἐπιπολαστικὰ καὶ ὅσα ἀηδῆ ἐστίν; ἔστι δὲ ὁ μὲν
οἶνος κατακρουστικός, τὸ δὲ ὕδωρ λεπτὸν καὶ οὐκ
ἀηδές. διὰ μὲν οὖν τὸ λεπτὸν [καὶ οὐκ ἀηδὲς][18] εἶναι
κάτω διέρχεται ταχύ, διὰ δὲ τὸ μὴ ἀηδὲς οὐ ποιεῖ
30 καρδιώττειν. ὁ δὲ κεκραμένος λίαν | οὐκ ἔστι λεπτὸς
ὥστε διαρρεῖν ταχύ, διὰ δὲ τὸ μικρὸν ἔχειν οἴνου
ἀηδής ἐστιν· ταράττει γὰρ τὴν αἴσθησιν τῷ πλείους
ἐν αὐτῇ τὰς κινήσεις ἐμποιεῖν, τήν τ' ἀπὸ τοῦ οἴνου
καὶ τοῦ ὕδατος· αἰσθηταὶ γὰρ ἄμφω γίνονται. ὁ δ'
εὔκρατος τὴν μὲν τοῦ ὕδατος αἴσθησιν ἀφανίζει, οἴ-
35 νου δὲ μαλακοῦ ποιεῖ | αἴσθησιν· διὸ ἡδέως πίνεται.
ἀηδὴς δὲ ὢν ὁ ὑδαρὴς οἶνος ἐπιπολαστικός ἐστιν· τὸ
δὲ τοιοῦτον ἐμετικόν ἐστιν.

19. Διὰ τί μεθύοντες μᾶλλον διαισθανόμεθα τὰ
874a ἁλυκὰ ‖ καὶ τὰ μοχθηρὰ ὕδατα, νήφοντες δ' ἧττον; ἢ
ὅτι τὰ λυπηρὰ μᾶλλον δῆλα τοῖς μὴ ἐπιθυμοῦσι, τοὺς
δ' ἐπιθυμοῦντας διαλανθάνει; ὁ μὲν οὖν ἐνδεῶς[19] ἔχων
ὁμοίως τῷ ἐπιθυμοῦντι ἔχει, ὁ δὲ νήφων οὕτως ἔχει· ὁ
δὲ μεθύων πλήρης. |

5   20. Διὰ τί τοῖς μεθύουσι σφόδρα κύκλῳ πάντα
φαίνεται φέρεσθαι, καὶ ἤδη ἀπτομένης μᾶλλον τῆς
μέθης ἀριθμεῖν τὰ πόρρω οὐ δύνανται; διὸ καὶ σημεῖον τῆς μέθης ποιοῦνται αὐτό τινες. ἢ ὅτι κινεῖται
ὑπὸ τῆς θερμότητος τοῦ οἴνου ἡ ὄψις πυκνάκις; ὥσπερ

18 καὶ οὐκ ἀηδὲς del. Bekker ex Gaza
19 ἐνδεῶς Kᵃ Oᵃ s Vat.1904ᵐᵍ : ἡδέως cett. codd.

---

34 I.e., watery wine.   35 Cf. *Pr.* 3.8.

comes to the surface and is unpleasant most of all produces vomiting? Now wine exerts downward pressure, whereas water is light and not unpleasant. Therefore, because it is light it passes through quickly, and because it is not unpleasant it does not cause heartburn. But wine mixed too much[34] is not so light as to pass through quickly, but it is unpleasant because it contains little wine; for it confuses the perception by producing multiple movements in it: one from the wine and one from the water. For both are perceptible. But well-mixed wine obscures the perception of water, and produces a perception of soft wine, which is why it is drunk with pleasure. But watery wine, being unpleasant, rises to the surface, and this sort of thing produces vomiting.

19.[35] Why do we distinctly perceive salty and bad water more when we are drunk, but less when we are sober? Is it because offensive things are more obvious to those not feeling desire,[36] but they escape the notice of those feeling desire? So the one who is in need is similar to the one who feels desire, and the sober person is in this condition; but the one who is drunk is satiated.

20.[37] Why does everything appear to those who are very drunk to be traveling in a circle, and as soon as drunkenness has seized them more they cannot count[38] things far away? And this is why some make this a sign of drunkenness. Is it because the vision is frequently moved by the heat of the wine? Therefore, just as when one places some-

---

[36] I take the author to be referring here to the desire to quench one's thirst, not the desire for wine specifically.

[37] Cf. *Pr.* 3.9.   [38] The parallel line at *Pr.* 3.9 has "observe" ($\dot{\alpha}\theta\rho\epsilon\hat{\imath}\nu$) in place of "count" ($\dot{\alpha}\rho\iota\theta\mu\epsilon\hat{\imath}\nu$).

10 οὖν ὅταν ὑποθῇ <τί>[20] τις ὑπὸ τὸν ὀφθαλμόν, | δύο
φαίνεται, οὕτω καὶ τοῖς μεθύουσιν. οὐδὲν γὰρ διαφέρει, ἐὰν μὲν ὑποθῇ, κινῇ δὲ τὴν ὄψιν, οὐδ᾽ ἐὰν
ἔξωθεν ἢ ἔσωθεν· ἀμφοτέρως γὰρ τὸ αὐτὸ πάσχει ἡ
ὄψις. ὥστε οὐ δόξει μένειν τὸ ὁρώμενον, καὶ τὸ πόρρωθεν ἔτι μᾶλλον· ἔτι γὰρ ἧττον κρατεῖ ἀποτεινο-
15 μένης τῆς ὄψεως, καὶ πλέον τὸ | διάστημα ἐπὶ τῷ ἄκρῳ
ποιεῖ ἡ ἐγγὺς αὕτη κίνησις. ἂν δὲ σφόδρα κινῆται καὶ
ὁμαλῶς ἄνω καὶ κάτω, ἧττον κρατήσει τοῦ πόρρω.
πάντα δὲ ἀποτεινόμενα κύκλῳ φέρεται, οἷον οἱ ἱστοὶ[21]
καὶ τὰ καταρτώμενα. καὶ ἡ ὄψις οὖν δι᾽ ἀσθένειαν
ταὐτὸ πάσχει ὥσπερ ἂν εἰ πόρρω ἐφέρετο. διαφέρει |
20 δ᾽ οὐδὲν τὴν ὄψιν κινεῖν ἢ τὸ ὁρώμενον· ταὐτὸ γὰρ
ποιεῖ πρὸς τὸ φαίνεσθαι.

21. Διὰ τί, ὅταν ἀθρόως πίνωσι, ξηρότεραι αἱ
κοιλίαι γίνονται, ὅτε δεῖ ὑγραίνεσθαι μᾶλλον ὑπὸ τοῦ
πλείονος; ἢ ὅτι τοῦ μὲν πολλοῦ καὶ ἀθρόου οὐ κρατεῖ ἡ
25 κοιλία, ἀλλ᾽ εἰς | τὸν αὐτοῦ ἔρχεται τόπον ἀπαθές;
ἔστιν δὲ ὑγροῦ τόπος ἀπέπτου ἡ κύστις. τοῦ δὲ ὀλίγου
κρατεῖ καὶ πέττει, ὥστε μένον ὑγραίνει.

22. Διὰ τί μᾶλλον κραιπαλῶσιν οἱ εὔκρατον πίνοντες ἢ οἱ ἄκρατον; ἢ διὰ τὴν λεπτότητα εἰς πλείους

---

20 <τί> Richards   21 οἱ ἱστοὶ C[a] Y[a] Ap (antennae Barth.) :
ὄϊστοὶ X[a] (οἱ add. Bekker)

---

39 The subject of this sentence is unclear. It could be the person who is seeing or the object of sight, though what follows
strongly suggests that the implied subject is the eye itself.

thing under the eye, it appears to be two, so also with those who are drunk. For it makes no difference whether one places something under the eye, or moves the eye, nor whether the movement is from outside or from inside, since the sight experiences the same thing in both cases. Consequently, the object seen will not seem to stand still, and the farther away it is the more this is the case; for it[39] has less control when the vision is extended to a distance, and this nearby movement produces an even greater variation at the limit of vision. Now if (*the eye*) is moved exceedingly and regularly up and down, it will have less control over the distant object. And everything that is extended to a distance moves in a circle, for example masts[40] and suspended objects. Therefore the vision too, because of its weakness, experiences the same thing as if it were moved to a distance. And it makes no difference whether the vision or the object seen is moved; for with respect to what appears, either one produces the same result.

21. Why, when people drink incessantly, do their stomachs become drier, whereas they should become moister owing to the large quantity? Is it because the stomach does not take control of a large quantity arriving at once, but (*what is drunk*) goes to its own place unaffected? And the bladder is the place for unconcocted moisture. But it does take control of and concoct a little moisture, so that it remains and makes the stomach moist.

22.[41] Why do those who drink well-mixed wine suffer from hangovers more than those who drink it unmixed? Is it because the mixed wine, owing to its lightness, goes into

---

[40] Or "arrows" if the other mss. reading is correct.
[41] Cf. *Pr.* 3.3 and 14.

30 τόπους ὁ κεκραμένος | εἰσέρχεται, καθάπερ ἐν τοῖς
ἱματίοις, καὶ ἔστι δυσεξαγωγότερος; τὸ δὲ ὕδωρ
λεπτομερέστερον μέν, ἀλλ' εὐέξοδον. ἢ διότι ἔλαττον
πίνουσιν ἄκρατον διὰ τὸ μὴ δύνασθαι, καὶ μᾶλλον
ἀπεμοῦσιν; ἔτι δὲ συμπέττει τὰ λοιπά. ταὐτὸ δ' ἐστὶ
πρόβλημα.[22] |

35 23. Διὰ τί ὑπὸ τοῦ ἀκράτου ἀποθνήσκουσιν, ἐάν τις
προϊσχνάνας πολὺ πίῃ; καὶ μὴ προϊσχνάναντες δὲ
πολλοὶ τῶν φιλοπότων ἀθρόον πολὺ πίνοντες ξηροὶ
γίνονται· δοκεῖ γὰρ ὅ τε οἶνος τῶν θερμῶν εἶναι τὴν
874b φύσιν καὶ τὸ ζῆν, τὸ δὲ ‖ ἀποθνήσκειν κατάψυξις. ἢ
ὥσπερ καὶ ἀπὸ τοῦ κωνείου, σβεννυμένου κατὰ μικρὸν
τοῦ θερμοῦ τοῦ οἰκείου, ἀλλὰ τρόπον ἕτερον; τὸ μὲν
γὰρ τῇ ψυχρότητι πήγνυσιν τὸ ὑγρὸν καὶ θερμόν, ὁ δ'
5 οἶνος τῇ θερμότητι τῇ αὑτοῦ μαραίνει τὴν | φυσικὴν
θερμότητα. ὥσπερ οὖν ὑπὸ τοῦ πολλοῦ πυρὸς καὶ
ἡλίου τὸ ὀλίγον πῦρ ἀποσβέννυται, οὕτω καὶ[23] ἡ ἐν
τοῖς σώμασιν θερμότης ὑπὸ τῆς ἐν τῷ οἴνῳ, ἐὰν
ὑπερβάλῃ.[24]

24. Διὰ τί οἱ μεθύοντες ἀριδάκρυοι μᾶλλον; ἢ ὅτι
θερμοὶ καὶ ὑγροὶ γίνονται; ἀκρατεῖς οὖν εἰσίν, ὥστε
10 ὑπὸ μικρῶν | κινεῖσθαι.

25a. Διὰ τί ἧττον μεθύσκονται ταῖς μεγάλαις κω-

---

[22] ταὐτὸ δ' ἐστὶ πρόβλημα om. Forster, non vertit Gaza
[23] οὕτω καὶ Yᵃ : οὕτως cett. codd.
[24] ὑπερβάλῃ Yᵃ : ὑπερβάλλῃ cett. codd.

more places, just as it does into cloaks, and so is more difficult to get rid of? Now water has lighter parts, but it goes away easily. Or is it because people drink less unmixed wine, because they are unable (*to drink much of it*), and (*those who do drink it*) are more likely to vomit? Further, (*unmixed wine*) also concocts the rest.[42] This is the same problem.

23. Why do people die from unmixed wine, if one who is lean beforehand[43] drinks a great deal? And many of those who love drinking wine, even when they are not lean beforehand, become dry by drinking a great deal at once; for both wine and living seem to be by nature among the things that are hot, whereas dying is a process of cooling. Or is it just like (*death*) from hemlock, when the heat proper (*to the body*) is gradually extinguished, but in another way? For hemlock solidifies what is moist and hot by coldness, whereas wine by its own heat causes the natural heat to waste away. Therefore, just as a little fire is extinguished by a large fire or by the sun, so too the heat in the body is extinguished by that in the wine, if the latter surpasses it.

24. Why are those who are drunk more prone to tears? Is it because they become hot and moist? Therefore they lack control, such that they are moved by small matters.

25a.[44] Why are people less drunk when they drink from

---

[42] I.e., everything else besides itself.

[43] Or perhaps "one who is parched beforehand"; the verb is based on ἰσχνός ("withered" or "dry" or "lean").

[44] *Pr.* 3.25, as preserved by the manuscript tradition, is almost certainly a conflation of what were originally two chapters (reconstructed here as 25a and 25b). Ch. 25a seems to be a mangled and/or incomplete version of *Pr.* 3.12.

θωνιζόμενοι; πάντων γὰρ ταὐτὸ αἴτιον, ἡ κατάκρουσις
τοῦ θερμοῦ[25] ἐπιπολῆς. τὸ μὲν γὰρ μεθύειν ἐν τοῖς
περὶ κεφαλὴν τόποις.

25b. Διὰ τί τοῖς μεθύουσιν οὐκ ἐγγίνεται ὕπνος;[26] ἢ
ὅτι δεῖ πρὸς τοὺς ὕπνους ὑγρότητα ἐνυπάρχειν θερ-
15 μήν; | αὕτη γὰρ εὔπεπτος. ἂν δὲ μὴ ἐνῇ ὑγρότης ⟨ἢ⟩[27]
ὀλίγη ἢ δύσπεπτος, οὐ γίνεται ὕπνος. διὸ ἐν τοῖς
κόποις καὶ μετὰ τὰ σιτία καὶ τοὺς πότους ὑπνωτι-
κώτατοι γίνονται ὑπὸ τῆς θέρμης. τοῖς δὲ μελαγχο-
λικοῖς καὶ τοῖς μεγάλως πυριῶσιν[28] ἀγρυπνία, τοῖς
20 μὲν ὅτι κατέψυκται τὸ ὑγρόν, τοῖς δὲ ὅτι | οὐκ ἔστιν ἢ
ὀλίγον. φανερὸν οὖν ὅτι εἰς ταῦτα βλεπτέον καθ᾽
ἕτερον τῶν παθῶν.

26. Διὰ τί οἱ οἰνόφλυγες τρέμουσιν, καὶ μᾶλλον
ὅσῳ ἂν ἀκρατοποτῶσιν; ἔστι δὲ ὁ μὲν οἶνος θερ-
μαντικός, ὁ δὲ τρόμος γίνεται μάλιστα ἀπὸ[29] ψυχροῦ
25 (διὸ οἱ ῥιγῶντες μάλιστα | τρέμουσιν). πολλοῖς δ᾽ ἤδη
χρωμένοις μόνῳ ἀκράτῳ τροφῆς χάριν τρόμοι τε
ἰσχυροὶ συνέβησαν, ὥστε ἀπορρίπτειν τοὺς θλίβοντας, καὶ τῷ θερμῷ ὕδατι λουόμενοι ἀναισθήτως εἶχον.
ἕτεροι δὲ τοῦτον τὸν τρόπον διαιτώμενοι, καὶ τρίψεσι

---

25 τοῦ θερμοῦ conieci (cf. Pr. 3.12, 872b29) : τουτέστιν codd.

26 διὰ τί—ὕπνος Y[a mg] : om. codd. (et Bekker) : διὰ τί οἱ
μέθυσοι οὐκ ὑπνίζονται Sylburg   27 ⟨ἢ⟩ Bonitz

28 μεγάλως πυριῶσιν Sylburg ex Gaza : μεγάλας πυρίας
codd. : post μεγάλας πυρίας add. προσλαμβάνουσι Bussemaker, add. ἔχουσι Hett

29 ἀπὸ Ap (cf. Pr. 3.5, 871a29) : ὑπὸ cett. codd.

large *(wine cups)*?[45] Indeed, the cause of all these is the same,[46] the downward pressure of the surface heat. For drunkenness is in the regions around the head.

25b. Why does sleep not come to those who are drunk? Is it because in order to sleep, hot moisture must be present? For this is easily concocted. But if no or little moisture is present or if it is poorly concocted, sleep doesn't come. This is why in a state of fatigue, and after food and drink, people become most inclined to sleep, owing to the heat. Now sleeplessness exists among the melancholic and those who burn with a high fever, in the former because the moisture in them has cooled, and in the latter because there is no or little moisture. Therefore, it is evident that in each case we must look to these things *(for an explanation)*.

26.[47] Why do drunkards tremble, and more so according to how much unmixed wine they drink? Now wine is capable of heating, whereas trembling comes mostly from cold (which is why those with chills tremble most of all). But powerful trembling is already experienced by many who use unmixed wine alone for nourishment, so that they throw off those who are restraining them, and when they wash in hot water they have no perception of it. And others who live in this manner, and also have massages and meat

---

[45] This line is identical to the second half of the opening question of *Pr.* 3.12. As in 3.12, "large *(wine cups)*" translates ταῖς μεγάλαις (sc. κύλιξι).

[46] The word "all" (πάντων) suggests that something has dropped out of the beginning of the chapter. Cf. the opening question of *Pr.* 3.12.

[47] Cf. *Pr.* 3.5.

χρώμενοι καὶ τροφῇ κρέασι, πρὸς ἀποπληκτικὰς ἀρ-
30 ρωστίας | ἤλασαν· ⟨οἷς⟩[30] τρόμοι μὲν διὰ τὴν ἀκινη-
σίαν ἧττον ἐνέπιπτον, πόνος δὲ ἰσχυρὸς καὶ τὸ μὴ
δύνασθαι ἡσυχάζειν ἤδη. ἔτι τοῦ μὲν τρόμου αἰτία ἡ
ψυχρότης· φαίνονται γάρ, ὥσπερ εἴρηται, οἵ τε ῥιγῶντες τοῦτο πάσχοντες καὶ οἱ σφόδρα γέροντες.
ἀμφοτέρων δὲ τούτων τῶν μὲν τὸ πάθος ψυχρόν, τῶν
35 δὲ ἡ | ἡλικία· ὁ δὲ οἶνος θερμαντικώτατος, ὥσθ᾽ ὑπ-
εναντίον ἄν τι συμβαίνοι. ἢ οὐθὲν κωλύει γίνεσθαι
ταὐτὸ ὑπὸ ἐναντίων, μὴ ὡσαύτως δὲ ποιούντων; οἷον
καὶ ὑπὸ τῶν πάγων ἀποκάεται καὶ ὑπὸ θερμοῦ, ὅταν ὁ
875a πάγος ἀθρόον ποιήσῃ τὸ ‖ θερμόν· ὥστ᾽ ἔστι μὲν ὡς
ὑπ᾽ ἐναντίων τὸ πάθος τὸ αὐτὸ συμβαίνειν, ἔστι δὲ ὡς
ὑπὸ τοῦ αὐτοῦ τὸ αὐτό. ὁ δὲ τρόμος γίνεται μὲν ὑπ᾽
ἐνδείας θερμοῦ, οὐ παντός, ἀλλὰ τοῦ οἰκείου. φθεί-
ρεται δὲ τὸ θερμὸν ἢ μαράνσει ἢ σβέσει, σβέσει μὲν |
5 ὑπὸ τῶν ἐναντίων, ὑπὸ ψυχροῦ καὶ ὑγροῦ, μαράνσει δὲ
ἐνδείᾳ τροφῆς, οἷον οἱ λύχνοι, ὅταν μὴ ἔχωσιν ὑπέκ-
καυμα μηδ᾽ ἔλαιον, ἢ ὑπὸ θερμοῦ ἀλλοτρίου, οἷον τὸ
πῦρ ἐν τῷ ἡλίῳ καὶ οἱ λύχνοι παρὰ τῷ πυρί.[31] οἱ μὲν
οὖν ῥιγῶντες ὑπὸ ψυχροῦ σβεννυμένου τοῦ θερμοῦ
10 τρέμουσιν. διὸ καὶ τοῖς προσχεομένοις | τὸ θερμὸν αἱ
φρῖκαι γίνονται· ἐγκατακλειόμενον γὰρ τὸ ψυχρὸν
εἴσω καὶ ἀντιπεριιστάμενον ἵστησι τὰς τρίχας· καὶ τῷ
ἀρχομένῳ πυρέττειν τὸ γινόμενον ῥῖγος δι᾽ ὁμοίαν
αἰτίαν γίνεται. ἐν δὲ τῷ γήρᾳ τὸ θερμὸν μαραίνεται

30 ⟨οἷς⟩ Sylburg   31 τῷ πυρί : τὸ πῦρ Yª Cª

for nourishment, are seized with apoplectic fits; trembling afflicts them less, owing to their immobility, but there is still severe pain and an inability to remain at rest.[48] The cause of trembling is cold; for as was said, it is evident that both those with chills and the very old experience this. In the former of these two cases the cause is their cold condition, and in the latter it is their age; but wine is capable of a great deal of heating, so that the opposite should happen. Or does nothing prevent the same effect coming from opposite causes, but not acting in the same way? For example, something is burned off both by frost and by heat, when the frost causes the heat to collect; so it is that the same effect results from opposite causes, and the same effect results from the same cause. Now trembling occurs because of a lack of heat—not any heat, but that proper (*to the body*). Heat is destroyed by dying out or by extinguishing: extinguishing by opposites, by cold and moist, dying out through a lack of nourishment, for example, when lamps have neither fuel nor oil, or by an external heat, for example, a fire in the sun[49] and lamps near a fire.[50] So those who have chills tremble owing to the cold, when the heat is extinguished. And this is why shivering occurs in people when hot water is poured over them. For the cold being enclosed within and compressed makes the hair stand on end; and the chills occurring in the one who is beginning to suffer from a fever occurs for a similar reason. And in old age the heat dies out when the nourishment falls short. For

[48] "To remain at rest" (ἡσυχάζειν) might also be translated "to keep quiet."

[49] I.e., during the day, in sunlight.

[50] Cf. the discussion of extinguishing and dying out in *Pr.* 3.23.

ARISTOTLE

τῆς τροφῆς ὑπολειπούσης. τροφὴ μὲν γὰρ ὑγρὸν τῷ
15 θερμῷ, | τὸ δὲ γῆρας ψυχρόν.[32] οἱ δὲ οἰνόφλυγες
μαραινομένης μὲν τῆς οἰκείας θερμότητος τρέμουσι,
κἂν εἴ τινες ἄλλοι τοῦτο πάσχουσι διὰ τὸν οἶνον, οὐ
τὸν αὐτὸν δὲ τρόπον τοῖς διὰ γῆρας, ἀλλ' ἔτι τρίτος ἦν
τρόπος τῆς τοῦ θερμοῦ φθορᾶς. ὅταν γὰρ ὑπερβάλ-
20 λοντι χρῶνται ἐν τῷ σώματι, πολλὴ | οὖσα ἡ θερμότης
ἢ ἀποσβέννυσιν ἢ ἀσθενῆ ποιεῖ τὴν οἰκείαν θερμότητα ἢ ἰσχύομεν· ἔστι γὰρ ὅταν μὴ κρατῇ τὸ κινοῦν
τοῦ κινουμένου, οἷον ὅταν ξύλον μακρὸν καὶ μέγα μὴ
ἐγκρατῶς[33] ἔχῃ τις, τὸ ἄκρον τρέμει. γίνεται δὲ τοῦτο
ἢ τῷ τὸ ἐχόμενον μεῖζον εἶναι ἢ τῷ τὸ κινοῦν ἔλαττον.
25 συμβαίνει | δὲ σβεννυμένου τοῦ θερμοῦ (δοκεῖ γὰρ
αἴτιον τοῦτο εἶναι τοῦ κινεῖσθαι τοῖς ζῴοις) μὴ κρατεῖν τὴν φύσιν. σημεῖον δ' ὅτι διὰ ψυχρότητα γίνεται
τὸ πάθος τοῖς οἰνόφλυξιν καὶ τοῖς πρεσβύταις, ὅτι
ἄνευ ῥίγους γίνεται ὁ τρόμος.

27. Διὰ τί ὁ ἀκροθώραξ μᾶλλον παροινεῖ τοῦ μᾶλ-
30 λον | μεθύοντος καὶ τοῦ νήφοντος; ἢ ὅτι ὁ μὲν νήφων
εὖ κρίνει, ὁ δὲ παντάπασιν μεθύων διὰ τὸ τὰς αἰσθή-
σεις ἐπιπεπλασμένας εἶναι, οὐ δυνάμενος τὸ βάρος
φέρειν, οὐ κρίνει; οὐ κρίνων δὲ οὐ παροινεῖ. ὁ δὲ
ἀκροθώραξ κρίνει τε καὶ διὰ τὸν οἶνον κακῶς κρίνει,
35 ὥστε παροινεῖ· ὥσπερ καὶ Σάτυρον τὸν | Κλαζομένιον
ὄντα φιλολοίδορον, φεύγοντα δίκην, ἵνα ὑπὲρ τοῦ

32 ψυχρόν : ξηρόν Sylburg ex Gaza
33 ἐγκρατῶς Richards : εὐκρατῶς codd.

128

moisture is the nourishment of heat, and old age is cold.[51] But drunkards tremble because the proper heat dies out, and if some others experience this owing to wine, it is not in the same way as those who do so owing to old age, but there is still a third way in which the heat is destroyed. For when people have an excess (*of wine*) in the body, its heat, which is considerable, either extinguishes or weakens the proper heat, wherein we are strong; for when the mover cannot control what is moved, for example, when one does not have control over a long and large plank, the extreme end trembles. And this occurs either when what is being held is too large or when the mover is too weak. So it happens that when the heat is extinguished (for this seems to be the cause of being moved among living beings), it is not in control of its nature. A sign that this condition occurs in drunkards and the elderly owing to cooling is that the trembling occurs without chills.

27.[52] Why does the one who is tipsy act more inebriated than both the one who is drunker and the one who is sober? Is it because the one who is sober judges well, while the one who is completely drunk—because his senses are blocked and he is unable to bear the heaviness—does not judge at all? And because he does not judge, he does not act inebriated. But the one who is tipsy does judge, and because of the wine he judges poorly, such that he acts inebriated. This is just like Satyrus of Clazomenae,[53] who was fond of abuse: when he was defending a case, in order that

51 Or, with Gaza and Sylburg, "is dry"—an alternative with a great deal of plausibility.
52 Cf. *Pr.* 3.2.
53 See Plu. *Cohib.Ira* 10 (*Mor.* 458F–59A).

πράγματος λέγῃ καὶ μὴ λοιδορῆται, τὰ ὦτα ἐπέπλα-
σαν, ἵνα μὴ ἀκούων εἰς λοιδορίαν τρέπηται· παυο-
μένου δὲ τοῦ ἀντιδίκου ἀφεῖλον· μικρὰ δὲ ἀκούσας ἔτι
λέγοντος οὐκ ἀπέσχετο, ἀλλὰ κακῶς ἔλεγεν, διὰ τὸ
40 αἰσθάνεσθαι μὲν, κακῶς | δὲ κρίνειν. ‖

875b   28. Διὰ τί πρὸς τὸν γλυκὺν οἶνον ἡδίω ὄντα οὐ
γίνονται οἰνόφλυγες; ἢ ὅτι οὐκ ἴδιον χυμὸν ἔχει ὁ
γλυκύς, ἀλλ᾽ ἀλλότριον; φιλόγλυκυς οὖν μᾶλλον ἢ
φίλοινος ἔσται ὁ κεκρατημένος. |

5   29. Διὰ τί οἱ οἰνόφλυγες ὑπὸ τοῦ ἡλίου θερμαινόμενοι μάλιστα χαίρουσιν; ἢ ὅτι δέονται πέψεως; ἔτι
δὲ καὶ διὰ τὸ κατεψῦχθαι· διὸ καὶ αἱ ἀποπληξίαι καὶ αἱ
ἀπονακρώσεις τάχιστα μετὰ τοὺς πότους γίνονται.

30. Διὰ τί τοῖς μεθύουσιν ἐνίοτε πολλὰ φαίνεται τὸ
10 ἓν | ὁρῶσιν; ἢ ὅτι αἱ ἀρχαὶ τῶν ὄψεων ἔσω μὲν
κινοῦνται ὑπὸ τοῦ οἴνου, καθάπερ ἡ ὅλη κεφαλή,
κινουμένων δὲ τῶν ἀρχῶν οὐκ εἰς ταὐτὸ συμβάλ-
λουσιν αἱ ὄψεις, ἀλλ᾽ οἷον ἐπὶ μέρος ἑκάτερον τοῦ
ὁρωμένου· διὸ δύο φαίνεται; ταὐτὸ δὴ τοῦτο γίνεται
15 καὶ ἐάν τις κάτωθεν πιέσῃ τὴν ὄψιν· ἐκίνησεν | γὰρ
τὴν ἀρχὴν τῆς ὄψεως, ὥστε μηκέτι εἰς ταὐτὸ συμ-
βάλλειν τῇ ἑτέρᾳ. ἡ μὲν οὖν τοιαύτη κίνησις ἔξωθεν
γίνεται, ἡ δὲ ἀπὸ τοῦ οἴνου ἔσωθεν. διαφέρει δ᾽ οὐθέν·
ταὐτὰ γὰρ ποιήσει ὁπωσοῦν κινηθεῖσα.

---

[54] "Offensively" and "poorly" translate the same word
(κακῶς).   [55] Cf. *Pr.* 3.32.   [56] Cf. *Pr.* 3.10.
[57] The "internal principles (or sources) of sight" are the eyes.

he might speak about the matter and not be abusive, he blocked up his ears lest he hear something and be turned to abuse; but just as his opponent was finishing, people removed (*what blocked his ears*), and after hearing his opponent say a few words, he could not hold back, but spoke offensively, because though he was using his senses, he was judging poorly.[54]

28. Why don't people become drunkards with respect to sweet wine, which is more pleasant? Is it because sweet wine has a flavor that is not peculiar (*to wine*), but to something else? Therefore, the one who is overpowered by it is a sweet lover rather than a wine lover.

29.[55] Why do drunkards in particular enjoy being warmed by the sun? Is it because they need concoction? Further, is it also due to the fact that they are cooled; and this is why apoplexy and torpor quickly occur after drinking.

30.[56] Why, to those who are drunk, does the one thing that they are looking at sometimes appear to be many? Is it because the internal principles of sight[57] are moved by the wine, as is the whole head, and when the principles are moved the sight from both eyes[58] cannot meet at the same spot, but as it were at each part of the object seen, which is why it appears double? Indeed, this same thing also occurs if one presses the eye from below; for this moves the principle of sight, so that (*the sight from this eye*) no longer meets the other at the same spot. Now such a movement is from outside, but that due to wine is from inside. But this makes no difference; for however the eye is moved, it will produce the same result.

---

[58] Literally, "the sights" (αἰ ὄψεις).

31. Διὰ τί τῶν μεθυόντων ἡ γλῶττα πταίει; πότερον
20 ὅτι | καθάπερ τὸ ὅλον σῶμα ἐν τῇ μέθῃ σφάλλεται,
οὕτω καὶ ἡ γλῶττα σφαλλομένη πταίει καὶ οὐ δύναται
τὴν λέξιν διαρθροῦν; ἢ σπογγώδης ἐστὶν ἡ τῆς γλώττης σάρξ; βρεχομένη οὖν ἐξαίρεται· τούτου δὲ συμβαίνοντος διὰ τὸ πάχος τὸ ἀπὸ τοῦ ὄγκου δυσκι-
25 νητοτέρα οὖσα οὐ δύναται διακριβοῦν. | ἢ διότι οὔτε ἐν
τῷ ὑγρῷ δυνάμεθα λαλεῖν διὰ τὴν ἀπουσίαν τοῦ
ἀέρος, οὔθ᾽ ὅταν εἰς τὸ στόμα λάβωμεν ὑγρόν; ἐν τῇ
μέθῃ οὖν ἐν ὑγρῷ πολλῷ τῆς γλώττης οὔσης οὐκ
ἀκριβοῦμεν· τὸ δὲ μὴ ἀκριβοῦν ἐστι τὸ πταίειν. ἢ
διότι ἐν ταῖς μέθαις ἡ ψυχὴ συμπαθὴς γινομένη
30 πταίει; τῆς ψυχῆς οὖν τοῦτο πασχούσης | εἰκὸς καὶ
τὴν γλῶτταν ταὐτὸ πάσχειν· ἀπ᾽ ἐκείνης γὰρ ἡ τοῦ
λέγειν ἀρχή. διὸ καὶ χωρὶς τῆς μέθης, ὅταν ἡ ψυχὴ
πάθῃ τι, συμπάσχει καὶ ἡ γλῶττα, οἷον τῶν φοβουμένων.

32. Διὰ τί οἱ οἰνόφλυγες καὶ οἱ περὶ τὴν θάλατταν
35 χαίρουσιν | ἡλίῳ; ἢ διότι οἱ μὲν οἰνόφλυγες δέονται
πέψεως, καὶ ἅμα συμβαίνει τινὰς τόπους κατεψῦχθαι;
διὸ καὶ ἀποπληξίαι καὶ ἀπονάρκωσεις μετὰ τοὺς πότους. οἱ δὲ θαλάττιοι διὰ τὸ ἀεὶ ἐν ὑγρῷ εἶναι τοῦτο
ποιοῦσιν.

33. Διὰ τί οἱ μεθύοντες ἀδύνατοι ἀφροδισιάζειν; ἢ
40 ὅτι | δεῖ μᾶλλόν τινα τόπον ἐκθερμανθῆναι τοῦ ἄλλου
876a σώματος, ‖ οἱ δὲ διὰ τὸ πλῆθος τῆς θερμασίας ἀδυνα-

59 Cf. Pr. 8.14.   60 Cf. Pr. 3.29.

31.[59] Why does the tongue of those who are drunk stumble? Is it because, just as the whole body staggers in the state of drunkenness, so also the tongue, staggering, stumbles and is unable to articulate speech? Or is it because the flesh of the tongue is spongy? It therefore swells when it gets wet; and when this happens, owing to the thickness from its (increased) bulk it is more difficult to move, and cannot do so with precision. Or is it because, just as we cannot talk under water owing to the absence of air, neither can we talk when we take moisture into the mouth? Therefore, in the state of drunkenness, we cannot be precise because the tongue is in a quantity of moisture; and (in the case of speech) to be imprecise is to stumble. Or is it because in the state of drunkenness, the soul, being affected along with (the body), stumbles? So when the soul is in this condition, it is reasonable that the tongue is also in the same condition; for the source of speaking is from the soul. And this is why, apart from drunkenness, when the soul is affected in some way, the tongue is also affected with it, for example, in those who are afraid.

32.[60] Why do drunkards and those who are around the sea enjoy the sun? Is it because drunkards need concoction, and at the same time certain regions (in them) have become cooled? And this is why apoplexy and torpor occur after drinking. But seamen do this[61] because they are continually amid moisture.

33.[62] Why are those who are drunk unable to have sex? Is it because a certain region of the body must be heated more than the rest, but this is impossible owing to the

[61] I.e., enjoy the sun.
[62] Cf. Pr. 3.11.

τοῦσιν; ἀποσβέννυται οὖν τὸ ἀπὸ τῆς κινήσεως θερμὸν γινόμενον ὑπὸ τοῦ περιέχοντος. ἢ διότι δεῖ μὲν
ἐκθερμανθῆναι τοὺς κάτω τόπους, ὁ δ' οἶνος ἄνω
5 πέφυκε φέρεσθαι, ὥστε ἐκεῖ ποιεῖ τὴν | θερμασίαν,
ἐντεῦθεν δὲ ἀπάγει; καὶ μετὰ τὰ σιτία ἥκιστα ἀφρο-
δισιαστικοί, καὶ κελεύουσιν ἀριστᾶν μὲν πολύ, δειπνεῖν δὲ ὀλίγον. ἀπέπτων μὲν γὰρ ὄντων ἄνω φέρεται,
πεπεμμένων δὲ κάτω τὸ θερμὸν καὶ τὸ ὑγρόν· ἡ δὲ τοῦ
σπέρματος γένεσις ἐκ τούτων. καὶ οἱ κοπιῶντες ἐξ-
10 ονειρώττουσιν, | ὅτι ὑγρὸς καὶ θερμὸς ὁ κόπος· ἐὰν οὖν
ἐν τῷ τόπῳ τούτῳ γένηται ἡ περίττωσις, συμβαίνει
ἐξονειρώττειν. διὰ ταὐτὸ δὲ καὶ ἐπὶ τοῖς ἀρρωστή-
μασιν, ὅσοις γίνεται, συμβαίνει. καὶ τοῖς φοβουμέ-
νοις καὶ τοῖς ἀποθνήσκουσι συμβαίνει ὡσαύτως. |

15   34. Διὰ τί νέοι ὄντες ἐνουροῦσι μᾶλλον, ὅταν μεθ-
υσθῶσιν, ἢ πρεσβύτεροι; ἢ διὰ τὸ θερμοὺς καὶ ὑγροὺς
εἶναι πολὺ τὸ συρρυὲν γίνεται περίττωμα, διὰ τὸ μὴ
ἀναλίσκειν τὸ σῶμα τὸ ὑγρόν, ὥστε ὑπερχεῖται· πρεσβυτέροις δὲ γινομένοις διὰ ξηρότητα τὴν ὑπερβολὴν
20 ἀντισπᾷ τὸ σῶμα; ἢ ὅτι μᾶλλον | ὑπνωτικώτεροί εἰσιν
οἱ νέοι τῶν πρεσβυτέρων; διὸ τοὺς μὲν νέους καθ-
ύπνους ὄντας λανθάνει ἡ ὁρμὴ τοῦ οὔρου ἐκπίπτουσα
πρὶν διεγερθῆναι, τοὺς δὲ πρεσβυτέρους οὔ, καθάπερ
οὐδὲ τῶν ἔξωθεν κινήσεων οὐδὲν ἧττόν τι λανθάνει
αὐτοὺς ἢ τοὺς νέους. δῆλον δέ· καὶ γὰρ αὐτοὶ οἱ νέοι ἐν
25 τοῖς βαθυτάτοις | ὕπνοις μάλιστα ἐνουροῦσιν.

---

    63 Cf. *Pr.* 5.31.

quantity of heat? So the heat coming to be from the movement is extinguished by the surrounding heat. Or is it because (*in order to have sex*) the lower regions must be heated, whereas wine naturally travels upward, so that it produces heat there, but takes it away from the lower regions? And after meals, people are least inclined to have sex, and so they recommend a large breakfast, but a light dinner. For when (*food*) is unconcocted, heat and moisture travel upward, but when it is concocted, they travel downward; and the generation of seed is from these. And those who are fatigued have nocturnal emissions, because fatigue is a moist and hot condition; therefore, if residue forms in this region, nocturnal emission occurs.[63] And what happens to them, for the same reason also happens in those who are ill. It also happens in the same way in those who are frightened and in those who are dying.

34. Why do those who are young urinate in bed, when they are drunk, more than the elderly? Is the residue that has flowed together abundant because they are hot and moist, (*and*) because the body does not use up the moisture, so that it overflows; but in the elderly, because of their dryness, the body draws in the excess? Or is it because the young are much more inclined to sleep than the elderly? This is why when the young are asleep, the flow of urine going out escapes their notice before they can wake up, but not with the elderly, just as no outside movement escapes their notice as much as it does the young. And this is clear: for the young themselves[64] urinate in bed most in the deepest sleep.

[64] Perhaps this is meant to indicate the young by their very nature, apart from when they are drunk.

35. Διὰ τί τὸ ἔλαιον πρὸς τὰς μέθας συμφέρει, καὶ τοῦ δύνασθαι πίνειν τὸ καταρροφεῖν; ἢ διότι οὐρητικόν ἐστι καὶ τῷ πόματι προοδοποιεῖ;

35. Why is olive oil beneficial against drunkenness, and why does sipping it enable one to drink?[65] Is it because it is a diuretic and so prepares the way for the drink?

[65] I.e., to drink more wine than one otherwise could.

BOOK IV

INTRODUCTION

Aristotle and other Peripatetic philosophers had a serious interest in the erotic. Relevant titles attributed to Aristotle are *Theses on Erotic Love* (Θέσεις ἐρωτικαί) (DL 5.24 and *Vit.Hsch.* 66) and *On Erotic Love* (Ἐρωτικός) (*Vit.Hsch.* 12; cf. Ἐρωτικῶν, *Vit.Hsch.* 182).[1] Diogenes Laertius lists two such works in his account of Theophrastus: *On Erotic Love* (Ἐρωτικός) and *Another Work on Erotic Love* (Ἄλλο περὶ ἔρωτος) (5.43).[2] Similar works are attributed to Hieronymous of Rhodes, Aristo of Ceos, Demetrius of Phalerum, and Clearchus of Soli.[3] But given the title of these works, and the little surviving evidence of their content, it is unlikely that they are a source for much of *Pr.* 4 (though 4.10 and 27 may be exceptions). For though the subject of *Pr.* 4 is sexual intercourse, its focus is largely biological.

The discussion in *Pr.* 4 of sexual intercourse employs material explanation nearly exclusively. This emphasis

---

[1] See frs. 41–46 Gigon.

[2] See frs. 557–68 FHSG.

[3] Hieronymous, Περὶ ἐρωτικῶν (frs. 33–36 White); Aristo, Ἐρωτικὰ ὅμοια (*Erotic Examples*) (frs. 10–14 SFOD); Demetrius, Ἐρωτικός (DL 5.81); and, Clearchus, Ἐρωτικά (frs. 21–35 Wehrli).

could be explained by the overall or predominate aim (to the extent that there is one) of this set of problems. Moreover, there is one chapter that explicitly inquires into the final cause of a central aspect of sexual intercourse. *Pr.* 4.15 opens as follows:

> Why is having sex the most pleasant activity, and is it so for animals out of necessity or for the sake of something? Is it pleasant either because the seed comes from the entire body, as some claim, or indeed it does not come from the entire body, but through that region into which all the pores of the veins extend?

Note too that the second question reveals an openness to the Hippocratic "pangenesis" theory according to which seed is drawn from the entire body—a view Aristotle attempted to refute in *GA* 1.17–18.

Pr. 4 reveals a typical lack of organization. The first three chapters are on the connection between sexual intercourse and the eyes (as is the last chapter); but after this initial grouping, there seems to be no method behind the ordering of chapters. For the most part, *Pr.* 4 focuses on sexual intercourse in humans (though they are sometimes compared to other animals). In some cases, the author is discussing humans generally, in others he seems to be or clearly is discussing males (or males compared to females). With two exceptions, the subject is heterosexual intercourse (and this is not surprising given the focus on generation). The longest chapter, however—ch. 26—is concerned with male homosexual intercourse, as is ch. 27. On the whole, the chapters of *Pr.* 4 raise questions about the

Aristotelian conception of generation and the mechanics of sexual intercourse. The sources are in large part Aristotle's biological treatises (especially the *Generation of Animals*), but also include the Hippocratic writings that deal with this subject.

ΟΣΑ ΠΕΡΙ ΑΦΡΟΔΙΣΙΑ

1. Διὰ τί ὁ ἀφροδισιάζων καὶ ὁ ἀποθνήσκων ἀνα-
βάλλει τὰ ὄμματα, καθεύδων δὲ καταβάλλει; ἢ διότι
ἄνωθεν τὸ θερμὸν ἐξιὸν ἀναστρέφει ἵνα περ ὁρμᾷ, ἐν
δὲ τῷ ὕπνῳ κάτω συνάγεται (διὸ ῥέπει κάτω); συγ-
35 κλείονται δ᾽ | οἱ ὀφθαλμοὶ παρὰ τὸ μὴ ὑπάρχειν ἔτι
νοτίδα.

2. Διὰ τί τῶν πλείοσιν ἀφροδισίοις χρωμένων
ἐπιδηλότατα ἐνδίδωσιν[1] τὰ ὄμματα καὶ τὰ ἰσχία, τὰ
μὲν ἐγγὺς ὄντα, τὰ δὲ πόρρω; πότερον ὅτι καὶ ἐν αὐτῇ
τῇ συνουσίᾳ ἐπιδηλότατα συμπονεῖ ταῦτα τῇ ἐργασίᾳ
876b συνιόντα περὶ || τὴν πρόεσιν τοῦ σπέρματος; συνεκ-
θλίβεται οὖν μάλιστα ἐντεῦθεν ὅσον εὔτηκτον τῆς
τροφῆς ἔνεστι διὰ τὴν θλῖψιν. ἢ διότι παραθερμαι-
νόμενα τήκεται μάλιστα, ὁ δ᾽ ἀφροδισιασμὸς θερμό-

---

[1] ἐνδίδωσι Sylburg (cf. *GA* 747a16) : συνδίδωσι codd.

---

[1] Re. "above," "below," "upward," "downward": in his study of
animals, Aristotle takes the upright human as the standard per-
spective (see *PA* 656a3–14).

PROBLEMS CONCERNING
SEXUAL INTERCOURSE

1. Why do the one who is having sex and the one who is dying cast their eyes up, whereas the one who is sleeping casts them down? Is it because the heat exiting from above turns the eyes in the direction in which it rushes out, while in sleep the heat collects below, which is why it inclines (*the eyes*) downward?[1] But the eyes *close* from dampness no longer being present.

2. Why do both the eyes and the haunches[2] of those who engage in sex a great deal sink in very noticeably, though the latter are near (*the sexual organs*) and the former are far from them? Is it because even during intercourse itself these parts very noticeably cooperate in the act by contracting around the time of the emission of seed? Therefore, it is especially from here that any easily melted nourishment that is present is pressed out through pressure. Or is it because things that are overheated melt most

---

[2] It is clear that by "the haunches" (τὰ ἰσχία) the author of *Pr.* 4 includes the buttocks, for he later refers to τὰ περὶ τὴν ἕδραν ("the buttocks"—literally, "the area around the seat") and ἀρχός ("rectum").

5 τητα² ἐργάζεται, μάλιστα δὲ ταῦτα θερμαίνεται, | ἃ
κινεῖται ἐν τῇ ἐργασίᾳ; οἱ δ' ὀφθαλμοὶ καὶ τὰ περὶ τὴν
ἕδραν ἐπιδήλως συμπονεῖ. οὔτε γὰρ μὴ συναγαγόντι
τὰ περὶ τὴν ἕδραν ἐνδέχεται προέσθαι, οὔτε [μὴ]³ τῶν
ὀφθαλμῶν καταβληθέντων· τὰ μὲν γὰρ περὶ τὴν
ἕδραν συνιόντα θλίβει, οἷον ἐκ κύστεως τῇ χειρὶ τὸ
10 ὑγρόν, ἡ δὲ | τῶν ὀφθαλμῶν συναγωγὴ τὰ ἀπὸ τοῦ
ἐγκεφάλου. ὅτι δὲ μεγάλην ἔχουσι τὰ ὄμματα τὴν
δύναμιν καὶ ὁ τόπος αὐτῶν πρὸς γένεσιν, δηλοῖ ἡ τῶν
ἀτέκνων καὶ γονίμων⁴ γυναικῶν τοῖς ἐναλείμμασι πεῖ-
ρα, ὡς δέον ταύτῃ διελθεῖν εἰς τὸ σπέρμα δύναμιν.
15 πίονα δὲ ἄμφω τυγχάνει ὄντα | πάντων ἀεί, ἀρχός τε
καὶ ὄμματα· διὰ μὲν οὖν τὴν συνεργίαν κοινωνεῖ τῆς
θερμασίας, διὰ δὲ ταύτην λεπτύνεται καὶ συναποκρί-
νεται πολὺ εἰς τὸ σπέρμα. οὔτε γάρ, ἂν μὴ πῖον ᾖ,
ὁμοίως τήξει⁵ ἡ θερμότης, οὔτε πῖον ὂν μὴ συμπονοῦν,
οἷον ἐν τῇ κοιλίᾳ· ἀλλὰ οἱ νεφροὶ τῶν ἄλλων μάλιστα |
20 αἰσθάνονται διὰ τὴν γειτνίασιν. καὶ αὐτὴ δ' ἡ τοῦ
σπέρματος πάροδος παρὰ τοὺς τόπους τούτους οὖσα
ἐπιδηλότατα ἱκανή ἐστι λεπτύνειν· ἀφαιρεῖ γάρ, ἀλλ'
οὐ προστίθησι πλησιάζουσα.

---

² θερμότητα : θερμότητι Yᵃ Barth.
³ [μὴ] Platt
⁴ γονίμων : ἀγόνων Forster
⁵ τήξει conieci (cf. Barth. *solvet* and *Pr.* 5.4, 880b37, 14,
882a17–18, 882a24–25) : τρήσει Ap : γρύσει cett. codd.

of all, and having sex produces heat, and those parts which are moved in the act are most heated? Now the eyes and the buttocks noticeably cooperate in sex. For it is not possible to emit seed without bringing the buttocks together nor when the eyes have been cast down; for the contraction of the buttocks exerts pressure, just as the moisture (*can be emitted*) from the bladder by (*pressure from*) the hand, while the closing of the eyes exerts pressure on the matter from the brain. It is clear, from the experiment with ointments[3] of both childless and fruitful women, that the eyes and the region around them have a great potential with a view to generation, as potency must pass this way into the seed. Now both the rectum and the eyes always are fat in everyone; so owing to their cooperation in sex they share in the heat (*it produces*), and for this reason they become leaner and much (*of this material*) is secreted into the seed. For unless a part is fat, the heat will not melt it to the same extent, nor will it do so if the part is fat but does not cooperate in sex, as in the case of the stomach; but the kidneys perceive much more than other parts, owing to their proximity (*to the sexual organs*). And the mere passage of the seed through these regions, being very noticeable, is sufficient to make them lean; for it[4] removes something, but although it is near does not add anything.

[3] In *GA* 2.7, Aristotle describes the practice of women rubbing ointment in and around their eyes to determine whether they are pregnant (747a7–19). In both *GA* 2.7 and *Pr.* 4.2 the references to seed include seed produced by females. In the *Generation of Animals* it is clear that Aristotle did not deny that females contribute seed to generation, though it is different from that emitted by the male.   [4] Either the seed or the heat.

3. Διὰ τί καὶ οἱ ἀφροδισιάζοντες καὶ οἱ εὐνοῦχοι οὐ

25 χρώμενοι | ἀφροδισίοις ὁμοίως[6] ἀμφότεροι τὰ ὄμματα
πρὸς ὀξυωπίαν βλάπτονται; ἢ ὅτι τοῖς μὲν διὰ λαγνεί-
αν, τοῖς δὲ διὰ τὴν πήρωσιν τὰ ἄνω ξηρὰ γίνεται
μᾶλλον τοῦ δέοντος, ἐπιδηλότατα δ᾽ ἐν τούτοις, ὅσων
τὸ ἔργον ἐστὶν ἀκριβές, ἡ δ᾽ ὄψις τοιοῦτον; κατασπω-

30 μένων δὲ τῶν ὑγρῶν τὰ ἄνω ξηραίνεται. | ὁ μὲν οὖν
ἀφροδισιασμὸς δῆλον ὅτι τοῦτο ποιεῖ· τοῖς δὲ εὐνούχοις τά τε σκέλη οἰδεῖ καὶ αἱ κοιλίαι εὔλυτοι ὡς κάτω
μεθισταμένου τοῦ ὑγροῦ.

4. Διὰ τί ἄνθρωπος μόνον, ὅταν ἄρχηται δύνασθαι
ἀφροδισιάζειν, ἡβᾷ, τῶν δὲ ἄλλων ζῴων ὅσα τρίχας

35 ἔχει οὐθέν; | ἢ ἐπειδὴ κατὰ τὰς ἡλικίας μεταβάλλει τὰ
ζῷα εἰς τοὐναντίον; φωνή τε γὰρ βαρεῖα ἐξ ὀξείας
γίνεται, καὶ δασύνεται ἐκ ψιλῶν· δῆλον οὖν ὡς καὶ τὰ
ἐκ γενετῆς δασέα ζῷα ψιλοῖτ᾽ ἄν, οὐ δασύνοιτο, σπερ-
ματικὰ γινόμενα. οὐ πάσχει δὲ τοῦτο διὰ τὸ τὰ σπερ-

877a μαίνοντα ξηρότερα γίνεσθαι καὶ || ἀραιότερα, ἐξ ὧν
θρὶξ φύεται. δῆλον δὲ ἐκ τοῦ μὴ ἐν ταῖς οὐλαῖς
φύεσθαι τρίχας· στεγαναὶ γὰρ αἱ οὐλαί, ἀλλ᾽ οὐκ
ἀραιαί. μηδὲ τοῖς παιδίοις καὶ γυναιξίν· ὑγρὰ γὰρ καὶ
ἄμφω, ἀλλ᾽ οὐ ξηρά. |

6 ὁμοίως : ὁμῶς Yᵃ Cᵃ Pᶜ

---

5 Cf. *Pr.* 4.32.

6 In the *corpus Aristotelicum*, the most sustained discussions
of eunuchs are in the *Problems*: see 10.36, 42, 57; 11.16, 34, 62.
Among the authentic works of Aristotle, see *HA* 8(9).50, the topic
of which is animal castration.

3.[5] Why do both those who have sex and the eunuchs,[6] who do not engage in sex, alike deteriorate with respect to the sharpness of their eyes? Is it because in the one case owing to lust, and in the other owing to the mutilation, the upper parts[7] become drier than they ought to be, and this is most noticeable in those parts for which the function is precise, and such is the organ of sight? When the moisture is drawn downward, the upper parts become dry. Now it is clear that having sex does this; but in eunuchs the legs swell and the bowels are easily relaxed, as the moisture is moved down.

4. Why does the human alone grow hair[8] when he begins to be capable of having sex, whereas none of the other animals that have hair do? Is it because on approaching maturity animals change to their opposite? For voice goes from shrill to deep, and they become hairy from being bald; so it is clear that even the animals that are hairy from birth would become bald, and would not continue growing hair when they become seed-producing. But this does not happen, because the animals that produce seed become drier and more porous, conditions under which hair grows. This is clear from hair not growing on scars; for scars are watertight, but not porous. Nor does it grow on children and women; for both are moist and not dry.

---

[7] Neither Aristotle nor the authors of the *Problems* ever indicate what precisely "the upper parts" refers to. In *GA* 4.9, however, Aristotle seems to hold that (in the case of a human fetus) the upper parts are those above the umbilical cord, the lower parts those below it.

[8] Literally, "reach puberty" (ἡβᾷ). The verb ἡβάω can mean both "reach puberty" and "show the outward signs of puberty" (in the present case, the hair growth that accompanies puberty).

5   5. Διὰ τί ἡ ἀνυποδησία οὐ συμφέρει πρὸς ἀφρο-
δισιασμούς; ἢ ὅτι τὸ μέλλον ἀφροδισιάζειν σῶμα δεῖ
τὰ ἐντὸς θερμὸν εἶναι καὶ ὑγρόν; τοιοῦτον δὲ ἐν τοῖς
ὕπνοις μᾶλλον ἢ ἐν τῷ ἐγρηγορέναι· διὸ καὶ ταχὺ καὶ
ἄνευ ἐργασίας οἱ ἐξονειρωγμοὶ γίνονται, ἐγρηγοροῦσι
10   δὲ μετὰ πόνου. ἅμα δὲ | τὸ σῶμα τοιοῦτον καὶ οἱ πόδες
ὑγρότεροι καὶ θερμότεροι· σημεῖον δέ, ὅτι καθευδόντων θερμοί, ὡς ἅμα τοῖς ἐντὸς οὕτως ἔχοντες. ἡ δ'
ἀνυποδησία τοὐναντίον ποιεῖ· ξηραίνει γὰρ καὶ ψύχει.
ὥστ', εἴτε ἀδύνατον μὴ θερμῶν ὄντων ἀφροδισιάσαι
15   εἴτε χαλεπόν, ἀνάγκη ἀσύμφορον εἶναι πρὸς | τὴν τῶν
ἀφροδισίων χρῆσιν.

      6. Διὰ τί ἐκλύεται μάλιστα τῶν ζῴων ἀφροδι-
σιάσας ἄνθρωπος; ἢ διότι πλεῖστον προΐεται σπέρμα
κατὰ λόγον τοῦ σώματος; διὰ τί δὲ πλεῖστον προΐεται;
ἢ ὅτι ἥκιστα ἐκπονεῖ τὴν τροφὴν καὶ φύσει ὑγρὸν καὶ
20   θερμόν ἐστι τῶν | ζῴων μάλιστα; ὧν τὸ μὲν ποιεῖ
σπέρμα πολύ, τὸ δὲ τὴν φύσιν σπερματικὴν ποιεῖ· καὶ
γὰρ τὸ σπέρμα τοιοῦτόν ἐστιν, ἕως ἂν σῴζηται.

      7. Διὰ τί τοῦ ἀφροδισιάζειν γινομένου διὰ θερμό-
τητα, τοῦ δὲ φόβου ὄντος ψυκτικοῦ καὶ τοῦ ἀποθνή-
25   σκειν, ἐνίοις, ὅταν | γένωνται ἐν τούτοις τοῖς πάθεσι,
σπέρμα προέρχεται; ἢ ὅτι ψυχομένων ἐνίων τόπων
ἕτεροι ὑποθερμαίνονται, τήν τ' οἰκείαν ἔχοντες θερμό-

---

9 I.e., moist and hot.   10 Cf. *Pr.* 4.21 and *HA* 636b24–39.
11 Or "relaxed."   12 Cf. *GA* 750a13: "The seed-producing animal should be hot and moist" (τὸ σπερματικὸν ζῷον δεῖ

5. Why is being barefoot not good with a view to sexual intercourse? Is it because the body that is about to have sex should be hot and moist within? This condition obtains more in sleep than in the one who is awake; and this is why nocturnal emissions take place quickly and without effort, whereas (*people emit seed*) with labor while awake. At the same time the body is in this condition,[9] the feet too are moister and hotter; and a sign of this is the fact that the feet of those who are sleeping are hot, being at the same time in this condition on the inside. Now being barefoot produces the opposite condition; for it dries and cools. So, as it is either impossible or difficult to have sex when they are not hot, (*being barefoot*) is necessarily unfavorable with a view to the performance of sex.

6.[10] Why is a human more exhausted[11] after having sex than other animals? Is it because in proportion to the size of his body he emits more seed? But why does he emit more? Is it because he uses less effort in digesting nourishment and is by nature much moister and hotter than other animals? While moisture produces a lot of seed, heat produces what is seed-producing in nature;[12] and indeed, the seed is such, as long as it is preserved.

7.[13] Why, although having sex occurs because of heat, and being afraid and dying cause cooling, do some people, when they are in these conditions, emit seed? Is it because when some regions are being cooled, others heat up, because they have their own heat and also receive it from the

θερμὸν καὶ ὑγρὸν εἶναι). The crucial role of heat in the body's concoction of seed, according to Aristotle's conception of generation, runs throughout the *Generation of Animals*.
13 Cf. *Pr.* 3.33.

τητα καὶ δεχόμενοι τὴν τῶν καταψυχομένων τόπων,
ὥστε καταψυχομένων μὲν συμβαίνει, οὐ διὰ τὸ ψύχε-
30 σθαι μέντοι, ἀλλὰ [καὶ]⁷ διὰ τὸ θερμαίνεσθαι; | δῆλον
δὲ καὶ τῇ ὄψει· τῶν γὰρ φοβουμένων τὰ ἄνω λειφαι-
μεῖ, τὰ δὲ κάτω ὑγραίνεται, καὶ κοιλία καὶ κύστις
λύεται. ὑπιὸν οὖν τὸ θερμὸν ἐν μὲν τῷ φόβῳ κάτω, ἐν
δὲ τῷ θανάτῳ κάτωθεν ἄνω, ἐξυγραῖνον τῇ θερμότητι
ποιεῖ τὴν τοῦ σπέρματος ἔξοδον. |

35   8. Διὰ τί οὐ δεῖ μὴ ὀργῶντα οὔτε ἀφροδισιάζειν
οὔτ᾽ ἐμεῖν οὔτε πτάρνυσθαι οὔτε φῦσαν ἀφιέναι; ἢ ὅτι
μὴ ὀργῶντες ὁμοίως ἔχομεν τοῖς ἐκ τῆς γῆς ἀνασπω-
μένοις, οἷς προσεκσπᾶταί τι ἀλλότριον ἢ ἐγκαταλεί-
πεται ἀποσπασθέν; ἅπαν δ᾽ ὃ δεῖ μὲν ἐξαρθῆναι,
877b κολοβὸν δὲ ὑπολείπεται, ‖ πλείω χρόνον παρέξει πόνον. ἐάν τέ τις κινήσῃ τι ἀλλότριον, τοῦτο πόνον
παρέξει, οὐκ ἐν τῇ αὑτοῦ χώρᾳ ὄν· ἃ συμβήσεται τοῖς
μὴ ὀργῶσι ποιοῦσί τι τῶν εἰρημένων.

       9. Διὰ τί νήστεις θᾶττον ἀφροδισιάζουσιν; ἢ διότι
5 οἱ πόροι | κενώτεροι οἱ τοῦ σώματος νήστεσι, πλήρεσι
δὲ πλήρεις; κωλύουσιν οὖν τὴν εἰς τὸ σπέρμα ὑγρότητα διεξιέναι. δῆλον δ᾽ ἐπὶ τῆς κύστεως· οὐ γὰρ
δύνανται πλήρους οὔσης ταχὺ ἀφροδισιάζειν.

       10. Διὰ τί οἱ νέοι, ὅταν πρῶτον ἀφροδισιάζειν

⁷ [καὶ] Bekker

14 The verb translated "is in a turgid state" (ὀργῶντα) can also
mean "swells with moisture" and "is excited." In the *History of An-*

regions that are cooling down, so that *(the emission of seed)* occurs when there is cooling down—not because of the cooling, however, but because of the heating? This is clear even from observation: for the upper parts of those who are frightened lose blood, while the lower parts become moist, and the bowels and bladder are relaxed. So in the case of fear the heat moves downward, while it moves upward from below in the case of death, and causing moisture by its heat, it produces an emission of seed.

8. Why should one neither have sex nor vomit nor sneeze nor let out breath unless one is in a turgid state?[14] Is it because unless we are turgid we are like *(plants)* torn from the earth to which something foreign is attached or from which something is torn off and left behind? Now anything that should be removed but is curtailed and left behind will cause trouble for a long time. And if someone moves something foreign, this will also cause trouble, by not being in its proper place—which will occur when people perform any of the acts that were mentioned when they are not in a turgid state.

9. Why do those who are fasting have sex more quickly? Is it because the passages of the body are emptier in those who are fasting, but full in those who are full? So *(the full passages)* prevent the moisture passing through into the seed. This is clear in the case of the bladder: for when this is full, it is not possible to have sex quickly.

10. Why do the young, when they first begin to have sex,

imals, ὀργάω is used to refer to the sexual excitement of both males and females (542a32) and (more specifically) to the excitement of mares and cows in heat (572b1–7, 573a6).

10 ἄρχωνται, | αἷς ἂν ὁμιλήσωσι, μετὰ τὴν πρᾶξιν μι-
σοῦσιν; ἢ διὰ τὸ μεγάλην γίνεσθαι τὴν μεταβολήν;
τῆς γὰρ συμβαινούσης ὕστερον ἀηδίας μεμνημένοι,
ὡς αἰτίαν ᾗ ἐπλησίασαν φεύγουσιν.

11. Διὰ τί οἱ ἱππεύοντες συνεχῶς ἀφροδισιαστι-
15 κώτεροι γίνονται; | ἢ ὅτι διὰ τὴν θερμότητα καὶ τὴν
κίνησιν ταὐτὸ πάσχουσιν ὅπερ ἐν τῇ ὁμιλίᾳ; διὸ καὶ
τῇ τῆς ἐπεχούσης ἡλικίας ἐπιδόσει περὶ τὰ αἰδοῖα
μείζω τὰ μόρια ταῦτα γίνεται. ἀεὶ οὖν τῇ κινήσει
ταύτῃ χρωμένων εὔροα τὰ σώματα γίνεται καὶ προ-
ωδοπεποιημένα πρὸς τὸν ἀφροδισιασμόν. |

20 12. Διὰ τί, ὅταν ἄρξωνται ἀφροδισιάζειν δύνασθαι,
οἱ χρῶτες ὄζουσι, πρότερον δ' οὐκ ὄζουσι πρὸ ἥβης
οὔθ' οἱ ἄνδρες οὔτε αἱ γυναῖκες; ἢ ὅτι τὰ ἄπεπτα τούς
τε χυμοὺς ἀεὶ χείρους ἔχει (ἢ γὰρ ὀξυτέρους ἢ ἁλμυ-
ρωτέρους ἢ πικροτέρους) καὶ τὰς ὀσμὰς δυσωδεστέ-
25 ρας, τὰ δὲ πεπεμμένα ἢ γλυκεῖς | ἢ ἧττον ἀγλευκεῖς,
καὶ τὰς ὀσμὰς εὐωδεστέρας ἢ ἧττον δυσώδεις· τοῦτο
δ' ἐστὶ δῆλον ἐπὶ πάντων θεωμένοις καὶ φυτῶν καὶ
ζῴων. ἀφαιρεθέντων δὴ τῶν εὐπέπτων, τὰ ὑπολειπό-
μενα ἄπεπτα, οἷον δὴ καὶ ἐπὶ τῆς τέφρας ἀναλωθέντος
τοῦ γλυκέος πικρὰ ἡ κονία, καὶ ὁ ἱδρὼς ἁλμυρός. |
30 πέττει δ' ἡ φυσικὴ θερμότης τὸ σπέρμα, ὃ μικρὸν ὂν
πολλὴν ἔχει δύναμιν· ἐκ πολλοῦ γὰρ ὀλίγον συγκε-
κεφαλαίωται. διὸ ὅταν ἀπέλθῃ, ἐκλύονται ὡς ἐπὶ τὸ

---

15 The Greek seems to be saying that the one who feels this
loathing is male, and the object of this loathing is female.

after the act loathe those with whom they had intercourse?
Is it because the change brought about is great? For re-
membering the corresponding disgust that comes after,
they avoid the one with whom they associated, as being the
cause.[15]

11.[16] Why do those who ride horses continually become
more desirous of sex? Is it because owing to the heat and
the motion, they experience the same thing they do during
intercourse? This is also why in the progress involved in
reaching maturity, with respect to the genitals, these parts
become larger. So as they are always engaged in this sort of
movement, their bodies become free-flowing and so well
disposed toward sex.

12.[17] Why does the skin smell when people begin to be
able to have sex, but neither men nor women smell before
puberty? Is it because what is unconcocted always has a
worse taste (for it is more pungent or saltier or more bitter)
and a very ill-smelling odor, whereas what is concocted has
a sweet (or less unpleasant) flavor and a pleasant-smelling
(or less ill-smelling) odor? Now this is clear to observers in
the case of all plants and animals. When what is well concocted is removed, what remains is unconcocted, for example in the case of ash, when the sweet part has been consumed, the cinder (*that remains*) is bitter; and, sweat is
salty. Now the natural heat concocts the seed, which although small in quantity has great potency; for a small
quantity has been distilled from a lot. So when it leaves,[18]

---

[16] Source: Hp. *Aër* 21.

[17] Cf. *Pr.* 4.24 and Thphr. *Od.* 7.

[18] I.e., when seed leaves the body.

ARISTOTLE

πολὺ μᾶλλον καὶ καταψύχονται· ὥστ᾽ ἀπεπτότεροι οἱ
χυμοὶ γίνονται μᾶλλον, ἀναστομουμένων τῶν πόρων
35 διὰ τὴν ἔκκρισιν | αὐτοῦ. ἁλμυρώτεροι οὖν ἢ οἷ[8] τῶν
παίδων ἱδρῶτες καὶ δυσωδέστεροι διὰ τὴν ἀπεψίαν·
καὶ ἐὰν τύχῃ τοιαύτη ἡ φύσις οὖσα ὥστε δυσώδη
ἔχειν τὴν ὑπόστασιν τοῦ ἱδρῶτος, τούτοις μᾶλλον
ἐπισημαίνει καὶ ἐν τοῖς τόποις τούτοις μάλιστα, οἷον
μασχάλῃ, ἐν ᾧ μάλιστα καὶ τοῖς ἄλλοις. ‖

878a   13. Διὰ τί, ἐὰν μὲν ἐκ τοῦ σπέρματος τοῦ ἡμετέρου
γένηται τὸ ζῷον, τοῦτο ἡμέτερον ἔκγονόν ἐστιν, ἐὰν δὲ
ἐξ ἄλλου τινὸς ἢ μέρους ἢ ἀποκρίσεως, οὐχ ἡμέτερον;
γίνεται γὰρ σηπομένων πολλὰ καὶ ἐκ τοῦ σπέρματος.
5 τί δὴ οὖν, ἐὰν μὲν | τοιοῦτον οἷον ἡμεῖς, ἡμέτερον, ἐὰν
δὲ ἀλλότριον, οὔ; ἢ γὰρ ἅπαντα προσήκει ἢ οὐθέν. ἢ
πρῶτον μέν, ὅτι οὕτω μὲν ἐξ ἡμετέρου γίνεται, ἐκείνως
δ᾽ ἐξ ἀλλοτρίου, ὅσα ἐξ ἀποκαθάρματος γίνεται καὶ
ἐκκρίσεως, καὶ ὅλως οὐθὲν τῶν τοῦ ζῴου ζῷον γεννᾷ
10 ἀλλ᾽ ἢ τὸ σπέρμα; τὸ δὲ βλάπτον καὶ | τὸ κακὸν
οὐθενός ἐστιν οἰκεῖον, οὐδὲ τὸ ἀλλότριον· οὐ γὰρ
ταὐτὸ τούτου τι εἶναι καὶ τούτου ἀλλότριον ἢ ἕτερον ἢ
κακόν. αἱ δὲ ἐκκρίσεις καὶ σήψεις οὐχ ἡμέτερα, ἀλλ᾽
ἕτερα καὶ ἀλλότρια τῆς φύσεως ἡμῶν εἰσιν. οὐ γὰρ
ὅσα ἐν τῷ σώματι γίνεται, τοῦ σώματος θετέον, ἐπεὶ
15 καὶ φύματα γίνεται, | ἃ αἴρουσι[9] καὶ ἐκβάλλουσιν. καὶ
ὅλως ὅσα παρὰ φύσιν, πάντα ἀλλότρια· παρὰ φύσιν

8 ἢ οἱ Yᵃ Pᶜ : οἱ cett. codd.
9 αἴρουσι Sylburg : φέρουσι codd. : ἀφαιροῦσι Nicasius

156

in most cases one becomes more exhausted and cools down; as a result, the juices[19] are more unconcocted, while the passages are opened because of its excretion. Therefore, the sweat (*of adults*) is saltier and more ill-smelling than that of children, because it is unconcocted; and if their nature is such that the sediment of their sweat is ill-smelling, it is evident more in such people, and especially in those regions (for example, the armpit) in which it is especially evident in other people, too.

13. Why, if the animal is born from our seed, is it our offspring, but if it comes from some other part or excretion, it is not ours? For many things come to be from what is putrefying as well as from seed. So why, then, if something is like us, is it more our own, but if it is like another, it is not? For either all should belong to us or none. Is it, in the first place, because in the former case it *does* come from what is our own, whereas in the latter it comes from something foreign, namely, from purgation or excretion; and in general, nothing from an animal generates an animal except for seed? And nothing that is harmful or bad is one's own, nor is anything foreign; for it is not the same thing to be some part of something and to be foreign to or different from or bad for something. But excretions and putrefactions are not our own, but are different from and foreign to our nature. For not everything that comes to be in the body should be considered part of the body, since even tumors appear in it, which are removed and thrown away. In general, anything whatsoever that is contrary to

[19] The same word ($\chi \upsilon \mu \acute{o} \varsigma$) has been translated "taste" and "juice" in this chapter.

δὲ πολλὰ καὶ τῶν συγγινομένων ἐστίν. εἰ οὖν ἐκ μόνου
τούτου τῶν ἡμετέρων γίνεται ζῷον, ὀρθῶς ἂν τὸ ἐκ
τούτου γινόμενον ἔκγονον ἡμέτερον εἴη μόνον. καὶ ἐκ
20 τοῦ σπέρματος δ᾽ ἄν τι ἄλλο γένηται, | οἷον σκώληξ
σαπέντος, ἢ καὶ ἐν τῇ μήτρᾳ διαφθαρέντος, οἷον ἃ
λέγεται τέρατα, οὐκ ἔκγονα λεκτέον. ὅλως γὰρ ἐκ
διεφθαρμένου γινόμενα οὐκέτι ἐξ ἡμετέρου ὄντος γίνεται, ἀλλ᾽ ἐξ ἀλλοτρίου, ὥσπερ τὰ ἐκ τῶν ἀποκρίσεων,
οἷον τὸ ἐκ τῆς κόπρου. σημεῖον δ᾽ ὅτι ἐκ διεφθαρμένου |
25 πάντα τὰ τοιαῦτα γίνεται· μὴ ἐκ διαφθειρομένου γὰρ
τοιοῦτον πέφυκε γίνεσθαι οἷον ἂν ᾖ ἐξ οὗ τὸ σπέρμα,
ἐὰν ἐξ ἵππου, ἵππος, ἐὰν δὲ ἐξ ἀνθρώπου, ἄνθρωπος.
καὶ αὐτό τε οὐ τιμῶμεν τὸ σπέρμα, οὐδὲ πᾶν τὸ ἐν τῇ
γενέσει περαινόμενον. καὶ γὰρ ὑγρὸν καὶ ὄγκος τις
30 καὶ σὰρξ γίνεται | ποτέ [δὲ],[10] διὰ τὸ μήπω ἔχειν τὴν
φύσιν, ἀλλ᾽ ἢ τοσοῦτον μόνον τῆς φύσεως, ὅτι οὕτω
διάκειται ὥστε γενέσθαι ἐξ αὐτοῦ τοιοῦτον οἷον ἡμεῖς·
ἐκ δὲ διεφθαρμένου οὐδὲ τοιοῦτον. διὰ ταῦτα οὔτ᾽ ἐξ
ἑτέρου τῶν ἐν ἡμῖν οὔτ᾽ ἐκ τούτου διεφθαρμένου ἢ
ἀτελῶς ἔχοντος τὸ ἔκγονόν ἐστιν ἡμέτερον. |

35 14. Διὰ τί ἐν τῷ ὕδατι ἧττον δύνανται ἀφροδισιάζειν οἱ ἄνθρωποι; ἢ ὅτι ἐν ὕδατι οὐθὲν τήκεται, ὅσα
ὑπὸ πυρὸς τήκεται, οἷον μόλιβδος ἢ κηρός; ἡ δὲ γονὴ

---

[10] ποτέ : ἀτελές Nicasius ‖ [δέ] Forster ‖ post ποτέ lac. indic.
Louis

---

[20] The point is that if seed is the only substance that one pro-

nature is foreign; and many of the things that grow in the body are contrary to nature. Therefore, if an animal is born from this alone (*i.e., seed*) among what is ours, then it is correct that what is born from this would alone be our offspring. And anything else that comes from the seed—like a worm from putrefying seed, or even from seed corrupted in the womb, which are called monsters—should not be called offspring.[20] For in general, what comes to be from corruption is no longer what comes to be from what is ours, but from what is foreign, just like what is from an excretion (for example, what comes from feces). And there is a sign that all such things come to be from corruption: for when something does not come from what is corrupted, it comes to be naturally like that from which the seed came—if from a horse, a horse, if from a human, a human. And we do not honor the seed itself, nor everything that is completed in the process of generation. Indeed, sometimes moisture and some mass and flesh comes to be, because it does not yet have its nature, but only so much of its nature that it is in a condition in which to beget *something* from it like us;[21] but such does not come from what is corrupted. These are the reasons why neither what is from anything else in us (*besides seed*) nor what is from corrupted or incomplete (*seed*) is our offspring.

14. Why are humans less able to have sex in water? Is it because nothing that is melted by fire melts in water, such as lead and wax? Now semen is obviously melted by fire;

duces that generates something *according to nature*, then only that which comes (1) from one's seed and (2) according to nature should be considered one's offspring.

[21] The text seems to be corrupt here.

τηκομένη φαίνεται πυρί· πρὶν μὲν γὰρ ἡ τρῖψις ἐκθερμάνῃ, οὐ τήκεται. οἱ δὲ ἰχθύες οὐ τρίψει ὀχεύουσιν. ‖

878b   15. Διὰ τί τὸ ἀφροδισιάζειν ἥδιστον, καὶ πότερον ἐξ ἀνάγκης ἢ ἕνεκά τινος ὑπάρχει τοῖς ζῴοις; ἢ ἡδὺ μέν ἐστιν ἤτοι διὰ τὸ ἀπὸ παντὸς τοῦ σώματος ἀπιέναι τὸ σπέρμα, ὥσπερ τινές φασιν, ἢ καὶ ἀπὸ
5   παντὸς μὲν μὴ ἀπιέναι, διὰ δὲ | τοιούτου εἰς ὃ πάντες συντείνουσιν οἱ πόροι τῶν φλεβῶν; οὔσης οὖν τῆς ἡδονῆς ὁμοίας τῆς ἐν τῷ κνησμῷ, τοῦτο συμβαίνει γίνεσθαι ὥσπερ δι᾽ ὅλου τοῦ σώματος. ὁ δὲ κνησμὸς ἡδύς ἐστιν, ὑγροῦ ἔξοδος πνευματώδους ἐγκατακεκλεισμένου παρὰ φύσιν. ἡ δὲ γονὴ τοιούτου εἰς τὸ
10   κατὰ φύσιν ἔξοδος. | ἔστι δὲ καὶ ἐξ ἀνάγκης ἡδὺ καὶ ἕνεκά τινος, ἐξ ἀνάγκης μὲν ὅτι ἡ εἰς τὸ κατὰ φύσιν ὁδὸς ἡδύ ἐστιν, ἐὰν ᾖ αἰσθητή, ἕνεκα δέ τινος ἵνα γένεσις ᾖ ζῴων· διὰ γὰρ τὴν ἡδονὴν μᾶλλον ὁρμᾷ πρὸς τὴν μῖξιν τὰ ζῷα.

16. Διὰ τί ἡ λαγνεία πρὸς νοσήματα ἔνια τῶν ἀπὸ
15   φλέγματος | συμφέρει; ἢ ὅτι περιττώματός ἐστιν ἔξοδος, ὥστε συνεκκρίνεται πολλὴ περίττωσις; τὸ δὲ φλέγμα περίττωμα.

17. Διὰ τί τὰ ἀφροδίσια τὴν κοιλίαν ψύχει καὶ ξηραίνει; ἢ ψύχει μέν, ὅτι ἐκκρίνεται τὸ θερμὸν ἐν τῇ μίξει; ξηραίνει δ᾽ ἡ μῖξις· ἐξατμίζεται γὰρ τοῦ θερμοῦ
20   ἐξιόντος, ἐξέρχεται | δὲ ψυχομένου. ἔτι καὶ ἡ θερμότης ἐν τῇ ὁμιλίᾳ ξηραίνει.

for until the friction heats it, it does not melt. But fish copulate without friction.

15. Why is having sex the most pleasant activity, and is it so for animals out of necessity or for the sake of something? Is it pleasant either because the seed comes from the entire body, as some claim, or indeed it does not come from the entire body, but through that region into which all the passages of the veins extend? Therefore, as the pleasure from the rubbing is similar (*in both cases*), this happens just as if it came from the entire body. Now the rubbing is pleasant, as is the exiting of pneumatic moisture[22] that has been enclosed contrary to its nature. But the (*emission of*) semen is the exiting of such moisture in accordance with nature. And it is pleasant both from necessity and for the sake of something: from necessity, because the path that is according to nature is pleasant, if it is perceived; for the sake of something, in order that there is a generation of animals—for owing to this pleasure, animals are more roused to copulate.

16.[23] Why is lustfulness good for some diseases that come from phlegm? Is it because lustfulness involves the exiting of a residue, such that a great deal of residue is ejected with it? And phlegm is a residue.

17. Why does sexual intercourse cool and dry the stomach? Does it cool it because heat is excreted during copulation? But copulation also dries: for evaporation takes place as the heat exits, and (*the heat*) escapes as (*the stomach*) is cooled. And further, the heat produced during intercourse dries.

[22] See n. 30 below.   [23] This chapter is similar to the first part of *Pr.* 1.50. Source: Hp. *Epid.* 6.5.15.

18. Διὰ τί, ὅσοις αἱ βλεφαρίδες ῥέουσι, λάγνοι; ἢ
διὰ τὸ αὐτὸ καὶ διότι οἱ φαλακροί; ἔστι γὰρ μόρια
ἄμφω ταῦτα τοῦ αὐτοῦ. ἔστι δὲ τὸ αἴτιον· ὁπόσαι
25 πρεσβυτέρου | γινομένου μὴ αὐξάνονται τῶν συγγενι-
κῶν τριχῶν, ἅπασαι τοῦτο πάσχουσιν ἐν ταῖς λαγνεί-
αις. κεφαλὴ γὰρ καὶ ὀφρὺς καὶ βλεφαρὶς συγγενικαὶ
τρίχες. τούτων δὲ μόνον ἐνίοις αἱ ὀφρύες δασύνονται
πρεσβυτέροις γινομένοις (δι᾽ ἣν δὲ αἰτίαν, εἴρηται ἐν
ἄλλοις), αἱ ἕτεραι δὲ διὰ τὸ αὐτὸ ἄμφω λείπουσιν. |
30 αἴτιον δὲ ὅτι καταψύχει τὰ ἄνω ἡ λαγνεία ὀλίγαιμα
ὄντα, ὥστ᾽ οὐ πέττει τὴν τροφὴν ὁ τόπος· οὐ λαμ-
βάνουσαι δὲ τροφὴν ἐκρέουσιν αἱ τρίχες.

19. Διὰ τί οὐρητιῶντες οὐ δύνανται ἀφροδισιάζειν;
ἢ ὅτι πλήρεις γίνονται οἱ πόροι; τὸ δὲ πλῆρες ὑγροῦ
35 οὐ δέχεται | ἄλλο ὑγρόν.

20. Διὰ τί αἱ ἰξίαι τοὺς ἔχοντας κωλύουσι γεννᾶν,
καὶ ἀνθρώπους καὶ τῶν ἄλλων ζῴων ὅ τι ἂν ἔχῃ; ἢ ὅτι
ἡ ἰξία γίνεται μεταστάντος πνεύματος; διὸ καὶ ὠφελεῖ
πρὸς τὰ μελαγχολικά. ἔστι δὲ καὶ ὁ ἀφροδισιασμὸς
879a μετὰ πνεύματος ‖ ἐξόδου. εἰ οὖν ὁδοποιεῖται ἡ ὁρμὴ
γινομένου αὐτοῦ, οὐ ποιεῖ ὁρμᾶν τὸ σπέρμα, ἀλλὰ
καταψύχεται· μαραίνει οὖν τὴν συντονίαν τοῦ αἰδοίου.

---

24 Source: GA 783b26–32.   25 Eyelashes and head hair.
26 I.e., will fall out.   27 See PA 658b19.
28 Cf. Pr. 4.22.   29 An enlargement of the spermatic
veins in the scrotum.   30 In Pr. 4, I transliterate πνεῦμα
rather than translate it "breath," as it is a technical term in Aristotle's theory of generation. He claims that what makes seed fer-

18.[24] Why are those whose eyelashes fall off lustful? Is it for the same reason the bald are lustful? For these parts[25] are both from the same thing. Now this is the reason: all of the congenital hair that does not grow as one gets older will experience this[26] in cases of lustfulness. For head hair and eyebrow and eyelash are congenital hair. And of these, the eyebrows alone grow bushier in some men as they get older (the reason for which has been stated in other places),[27] but the others both fail for the same reason. The reason is that the lustfulness cools down the upper parts of the body, which have little blood, such that this region does not concoct the nourishment; and as the hairs do not receive nourishment, they fall out.

19.[28] Why are those who want to urinate unable to have sex? Is it because the passages become full? And what is full of moisture does not receive more moisture.

20. Why do varicocele[29] prevent those who have them from procreating—both humans and any other animals that have them? Is it because the varicocele arise when the *pneuma*[30] is displaced? This is also why they are beneficial in cases of melancholy.[31] Now sexual intercourse too is accompanied by an exiting of *pneuma*. So if its onrush makes a path during intercourse, it does not cause the seed to rush out, but instead to be cooled; therefore, it withers the rigidness of the penis.

---

tile is heat, in the form of a special refined kind of hot air (the *pneuma*) "enclosed within the seed" (*GA* 736b33–37). Male seed is a combination of water and *pneuma* (736a1), and this latter contains "soul heat" ($\theta\epsilon\rho\mu\acute{o}\tau\eta\tau\alpha$ $\psi\nu\chi\iota\kappa\acute{\eta}\nu$) (762a20).

[31] I.e., afflictions connected with melancholy ($\tau\grave{\alpha}$ $\mu\epsilon\lambda\alpha\gamma$-$\chi o\lambda\iota\kappa\acute{\alpha}$). See *Pr.* 30.1.

21. Διὰ τί οἱ ἀφροδισιάζοντες ἐκλύονται καὶ
5 ἀσθενέστεροι | γίνονται ὡς ἐπὶ τὸ πολύ; πότερον διὰ
τὸ ἀπὸ πάντων ἔκκρισιν εἶναι τὸ σπέρμα, ὥσθ' οἷον
οἰκοδομήματος αἱ ἁρμονίαι, καὶ τοῦ σώματος οὕτω
σειομένη ἡ σύνθεσίς ἐστι τῷ ἀπεληλυθέναι τι, οἷον εἰ
τὸ αἷμα ἐξέλθοι ἢ πᾶν ὅ τι ἄλλο[11] μέρος; οὕτω σφόδρα
10 ἐπίκαιρον τὸ ἐξιόν ἐστι, καὶ ὃ ἐκ πολλῆς | γίνεται
τροφῆς ὀλίγον, οἷον τὸ ἀμύλιον ἐκ τοῦ σταιτός.

22. Διὰ τί οἱ ἀφροδισιάζοντες καὶ οὐρητιῶντες
ἐντείνουσιν; ἢ ὅτι πληρουμένων τῶν πόρων ὑγρότητος, τὸ σπέρμα ὑπεξιὸν ἐν ἐλάττονι τόπῳ πλείονά τ'
ὄγκον ποιεῖ καὶ αἴρει; ἐπίκειται γὰρ τὸ αἰδοῖον ἐπὶ
τοῖς πόροις. |

15 23. Διὰ τί ἡ σύντασις γίνεται τοῦ αἰδοίου καὶ ἡ
αὔξησις; ἢ διὰ δύο, διά τε τὸ βάρος ἐπιγίνεσθαι ἐν τῷ
ὄπισθεν τῶν ὄρχεων αἴρεσθαι (ὑπομόχλιον γὰρ οἱ
ὄρχεις γίνονται) καὶ διὰ τὸ πνεύματος πληροῦσθαι
τοὺς πόρους; ἢ τοῦ ὑγροῦ αὐξανομένου καὶ μεθιστα-
20 μένου ἢ ἐξ ὑγροῦ γινομένου ὁ ὄγκος | μείζων γίνεται;
τὰ λίαν δὲ μεγάλα ἧττον αἴρεται διὰ τὸ πορρωτέρω τὸ
βάρος τοῦ ὑπομοχλίου γίνεσθαι.

24. Διὰ τί οἱ ἀφροδισιάζοντες ἢ οἱ τοιοῦτοι δυσώδεις, οἱ δὲ παῖδες οὔ; καὶ τοῦ καλουμένου γράσου

11 om. ἢ Forster ex Gaza || ὅ : ἤ Y[a] C[a] : om. Flashar || ἄλλο
secl. Hett

21.[32] Why do those who have sex usually become exhausted and weaker? Is it because the seed is an excretion from the entire body, such that, like the harmonies of a building, the composition of the body too is thus disturbed by losing something, for example if the blood or all of some other part[33] were to escape? What exits (*the body during sex*) is so very important, i.e., what is little in quantity comes from a great deal of nourishment, like a cake comes from flour.

22.[34] Why do those who have sex and want to urinate have erections?[35] Is it because, as the passages are full of moisture, the seed withdrawing into a smaller space makes the bulk (*of the penis*) fuller and raises it? For the penis is near the passages.

23. Why does tension and growth of the penis occur? Is it for two reasons: because through weight being added behind the testicles, it is raised (for the testicles become a fulcrum), and because the passages become full of *pneuma*? Or does the bulk become greater as the moisture increases and changes position, or from the formation of moisture? Now very large things are less easily raised because the weight is farther away from the fulcrum.

24.[36] Why are those who have sex or such people (*as are able to*) ill-smelling, but children are not? Indeed

---

[32] Cf. *Pr.* 4.6.   [33] Depending on which manuscript reading we accept, this could also be translated "all of the blood or some other part" or "either all or some of the blood."

[34] Cf. *Pr.* 4.19.   [35] The author is often taken to be asking why those who desire to urinate while having sex have erections. But the question could be: Why do those capable of having sex have erections when they need to urinate?   [36] Cf. *Pr.* 4.12.

ὄζουσιν. ἢ τῶν πνευμάτων, ὥσπερ εἴρηται, τὰ μὲν τῶν
25 παιδίων πέττει τὸ | ὑγρὸν καὶ τοὺς ἱδρῶτας, οἱ δὲ τῶν
ἀνδρῶν ἄπεπτοι;

25. Διὰ τί ἐν τῷ θέρει οἱ μὲν ἄνδρες ἧττον δύνανται
ἀφροδισιάζειν, αἱ δὲ γυναῖκες μᾶλλον, καθάπερ καὶ ὁ
ποιητὴς λέγει ἐπὶ τῷ σκολύμῳ "μαχλόταται δὲ γυναῖκες, ἀφαυρότατοι δέ τοι ἄνδρες"; πότερον ὅτι οἱ ὄρχεις
30 καθίενται | μᾶλλον ἢ ἐν τῷ χειμῶνι; ἀνάγκη δέ, εἰ
μέλλει ἀφροδισιάζειν, ἀνασπάσαι. ἢ ὅτι αἱ θερμαὶ
φύσεις ἐν τῷ θέρει συμπίπτουσιν ὑπερβάλλοντος τοῦ
θερμοῦ, αἱ δὲ ψυχραὶ θάλλουσιν;[12] ἔστι δὲ ὁ μὲν ἀνὴρ
ξηρὸς καὶ θερμός, ἡ δὲ γυνὴ ψυχρὰ καὶ ὑγρά. τοῦ μὲν
35 οὖν ἀνδρὸς ἠμαύρωται ἡ δύναμις, | τῶν δὲ θάλλει
ἐπανισουμένη τῷ ἐναντίῳ.

26. Διὰ τί ἔνιοι ἀφροδισιαζόμενοι χαίρουσι, καὶ οἱ
μὲν ἅμα δρῶντες, οἱ δ᾽ οὔ; ἢ ὅτι ἔστιν ἑκάστῃ περιτ-
879b τώσει τόπος ‖ εἰς ὃν πέφυκεν ἀποκρίνεσθαι κατὰ
φύσιν, καὶ πόνου ἐγγινομένου τὸ πνεῦμα ἐξιὸν ἀνοι-
δεῖν ποιεῖ, καὶ συνεκκρίνει αὐτήν, οἷον τὸ μὲν οὖρον
εἰς κύστιν, ἡ δ᾽ ἐξικμασμένη τροφὴ εἰς κοιλίαν, τὸ δὲ
5 δάκρυον εἰς ὄμματα, μύξαι δ᾽ εἰς μυκτῆρας, | αἷμα δὲ
εἰς φλέβας; ὁμοίως δὴ τούτοις καὶ ἡ γονὴ εἰς ὄρχεις
καὶ αἰδοῖα. οἷς δὴ οἱ πόροι μὴ κατὰ φύσιν ἔχουσιν,
ἀλλ᾽[13] ἢ διὰ τὸ ἀποτυφλωθῆναι τοὺς εἰς τὸ αἰδοῖον,

---

12 θάλλουσιν Richards : θάλπουσιν codd.
13 ἀλλ᾽ secl. Hett

they reek of what is called goat smell. Is it because of the *pneuma*, as has been said: that of children concocts the moisture and the sweat, whereas (*the moisture and sweat*) of men is unconcocted?

25.[37] Why are men less able to have sex in the summer and women more so, just as the poet says of the time when the thistle blooms: "Women are more wanton, while men are more feeble"?[38] Is it because the testicles drop down more than in winter? But it is necessary, if one is going to have sex, for them to be drawn up. Or is it because hot natures collapse in the summer, when the heat is excessive, but the cold ones thrive?[39] Now man is dry and hot, while woman is cold and moist. So the potency of the man is diminished, while that of the women thrives, being equalized by its opposite.

26. Why do some men enjoy submitting to sex, and some at the same time enjoy being active, whereas others do not? Is it because for each residue there is a place into which it is naturally secreted according to nature, and when there is an exertion the *pneuma*, on exiting, causes swelling and ejects it, for example, urine into the bladder, digested nourishment into the stomach, tears into the eyes, mucus into the nostrils, and blood into the veins? In the same way as these, then, the semen is naturally secreted into the testicles and penis. Now in those in whom the passages are not according to nature, either because the passages that go to the penis have been blocked off (as

---

[37] Cf. *Pr.* 4.28.   [38] Hes. *Op.* 586. Hesiod mentions thistle blooming (which occurs in mid-July) at 582.

[39] Translating Richards' conjecture ("thrive") rather than the reading of the mss. ("soften," "warm up").

οἷον συμβαίνει τοῖς εὐνούχοις καὶ εὐνουχίαις, ἢ καὶ
ἄλλως, εἰς τὴν ἕδραν συρρεῖ ἡ τοιαύτη ἰκμάς· καὶ γὰρ
10 διεξέρχεται ταύτῃ. σημεῖον | δ᾽ ἐν τῇ συνουσίᾳ ἡ
συναγωγὴ τοῦ τοιούτου τόπου καὶ ἡ σύντηξις τῶν
περὶ τὴν ἕδραν. ἐὰν οὖν ὑπερβάλλῃ τις τῇ λαγνείᾳ,
τούτοις ἐνταῦθα συνέρχεται, ὥστε ὅταν ἡ ἐπιθυμία
γένηται, τοῦτ᾽ ἐπιθυμεῖ τῆς τρίψεως εἰς ὃ συλλέγεται.
ἡ δ᾽ ἐπιθυμία καὶ ἀπὸ σιτίων καὶ ἀπὸ διανοίας γίνεται.
15 ὅταν | γὰρ κινηθῇ ὑφ᾽ ὁτουοῦν, ἐνταῦθα τὸ πνεῦμα
συντρέχει, καὶ τὸ τοιοῦτο περίττωμα συρρεῖ οὗ πέφυκεν. κἂν μὲν λεπτὸν ᾖ ἢ πνευματῶδες, τούτου ἐξελθόντος, ὥσπερ αἱ συντάσεις τοῖς παισὶ καὶ τοῖς ἐν
ἡλικίᾳ ἐνίοτε, οὐθενὸς ὑγροῦ ἐκκριθέντος, παύονται,
ὅταν τε[14] κατασβεσθῇ τὸ ὑγρόν.[15] ἐὰν δὲ μηδέτερον |
20 τούτων πάθῃ, ἐπιθυμεῖ ἕως ἄν τι τούτων συμβῇ. οἱ δὲ
φύσει θηλυδρίαι οὕτω συνεστᾶσιν ὥστ᾽ ἐκεῖ μὲν μὴ
ἐκκρίνεσθαι ἢ ὀλίγην, οὗπερ τοῖς ἔχουσι κατὰ φύσιν
ἐκκρίνεται, εἰς δὲ τὸν τόπον τοῦτον. αἴτιον δὲ ὅτι παρὰ
φύσιν συνεστᾶσιν· ἄρσενες γὰρ ὄντες οὕτω διάκεινται
25 ὥστε ἀνάγκη τὸν τόπον | τοῦτον πεπηρῶσθαι αὐτῶν.
πήρωσις δὲ ἡ μὲν ὅλως ποιεῖ φθόρον, ἡ δὲ διαστρο-
φήν. ἐκείνη μὲν οὖν οὐκ ἔστιν· γυνὴ γὰρ ἂν ἐγένετο.
ἀνάγκη ἄρα παρεστράφθαι καὶ ἄλλοθί που ὁρμᾶν τῆς
γονικῆς ἐκκρίσεως. διὸ καὶ ἄπληστοι, ὥσπερ αἱ γυ-
ναῖκες· ὀλίγη γὰρ ἡ ἰκμάς, καὶ οὐ βιάζεται ἐξιέναι,

14 ante ὅταν lac. indic. Louis ‖ τε Forster : δὲ codd.
15 post ὑγρόν lac. indic. Ruelle

168

happens to eunuchs and eunuchlike men)[40] or for some other reason, such fluid flows into the anus;[41] for indeed, it passes in this direction. A sign of this is the contraction of this region of the body during intercourse and the colliquation of the buttocks. Therefore, if someone is excessive in his lust, (*the semen*) collects there, such that when the desire arises, the region in which it is collected desires friction. Now the desire arises both from food and from thought. For when one is moved by anything, the *pneuma* races there, and this residue flows to its natural region. So if (*the semen*) is light or full of *pneuma*, when it goes out the erections cease, just as they sometimes do in boys and in older men when no moisture is excreted and when the moisture dries up. But if one experiences neither of these, desire continues until one of these happens. Now the effeminate by nature are so constituted that little or no semen is excreted in the place in which it is excreted in those whose condition is according to nature, but into this region.[42] And the reason is that they are constituted contrary to nature; for though they are male, they are in such a state that this region in them is necessarily deformed. The deformity causes either complete destruction or distortion. But it is not the former; for then a woman would come to be. So it is necessary that the secretion of semen be perverted and moved toward some other place. This is why they are insatiable, like women; for there is little fluid, and

[40] Aristotle notes that some men born with deformed genitalia are sterile from birth, and that as a result they "never grow a beard, but remain eunuchlike" (*GA* 746b20–24).

[41] The Greek is τὴν ἕδραν (literally, "the seat"). See n. 2 above. [42] I.e., in and around the anus.

30 καὶ | καταψύχεται ταχύ. καὶ ὅσοις μὲν ἐπὶ τὴν ἕδραν,
οὗτοι πάσχειν ἐπιθυμοῦσιν, ὅσοις δ᾽ ἐπ᾽ ἀμφότερα,
οὗτοι καὶ δρᾶν καὶ πάσχειν· ἐφ᾽ ὁπότερα δὲ πλεῖον,
τούτου μᾶλλον ἐπιθυμοῦσιν. ἐνίοις δὲ γίνεται καὶ ἐξ
ἔθους τὸ πάθος τοῦτο. ὅσα γὰρ ἂν ποιῶσι, συμβαίνει
35 αὐτοῖς χαίρειν καὶ προΐεσθαι | τὴν γονὴν οὕτως.
ἐπιθυμοῦσιν οὖν ποιεῖν οἷς ἂν ταῦτα γίνηται, καὶ
μᾶλλον τὸ ἔθος ὥσπερ φύσις γίνεται. διὰ τοῦτο ὅσοι
ἂν μὴ πρὸ ἥβης ἀλλὰ περὶ ἥβην ἐθισθῶσιν ἀφρο-
880a δισιάζεσθαι, ‖ διὰ τὸ γίνεσθαι αὐτοῖς ἐν τῇ χρείᾳ τὴν
μνήμην, ἅμα δὲ τῇ μνήμῃ τὴν ἡδονήν, διὰ [δὲ][16] τὸ
ἔθος ὥσπερ πεφυκότες ἐπιθυμοῦσι πάσχειν· τὰ μέντοι
πολλὰ καὶ τὸ ἔθος ὥσπερ πεφυκόσι γίνεται. ἐὰν δὲ
5 τύχῃ λάγνος | ὢν καὶ μαλακός, καὶ θᾶττον ἕκαστα
τούτων συμβαίνει.

27. Διὰ τί μάλιστ᾽ αἰσχύνονται ὁμολογεῖν οἱ ἐπιθυμοῦντες ἀφροδισιάζεσθαι, ἀλλ᾽ οὐ πιεῖν οὐδὲ φαγεῖν οὐδὲ ἄλλο τῶν τοιούτων οὐδέν; ἢ ὅτι τῶν μὲν
πλείστων ἀναγκαῖαι αἱ ἐπιθυμίαι, ἔνια δὲ καὶ ἀναιρεῖ
10 τοὺς μὴ τυγχάνοντας; ἡ δὲ τῶν | ἀφροδισίων ἐκ
περιουσίας ἐστίν.

28. Διὰ τί οἱ μὲν ἄνδρες τοῦ χειμῶνος, αἱ δὲ
γυναῖκες τοῦ θέρους ὁρμητικώτεραι πρὸς τὰ ἀφροδίσια; ἢ ὅτι οἱ μὲν ἄνδρες θερμοὶ μᾶλλον καὶ ξηροὶ
τὰς φύσεις, αἱ δὲ γυναῖκες ὑγραὶ καὶ κατεψυγμέναι;
15 τοῖς μὲν οὖν τὸ ὑγρὸν καὶ | τὸ θερμὸν αὔταρκες πρὸς

16 [δὲ] Forster

170

it is not forced to exit[43] and is cooled quickly. Those in whom (*the semen collects*) in the anus desire to be passive, while those in whom it (*collects*) in both regions desire to be both active and passive; and in whichever of the two it (*collects*) more, they desire (*the corresponding role*) more. Now in some this condition even comes to be from habit. For people do whatever they happen to enjoy and they emit semen accordingly. So they desire to do that by which this comes to be, and the habit becomes more like a nature. For this reason, whoever has not been accustomed to submit to sex before puberty, but around puberty, owing to the memory arising in them during the act, and with the memory the pleasure, because of their habit, as if naturally, they desire to be passive; to be sure, numerous actions and habit come to be just like nature. And if one happens to be lustful and soft, each of these comes about more quickly.

27.[44] Why are those who desire to submit to sex most of all ashamed to admit it, but they are not ashamed to admit to a desire for drinking or eating or any such actions? Is it because the desires for most things are necessary, and some even destroy those who do not satisfy them? But the desire for sexual pleasures comes from what's superfluous.

28.[45] Why do men have a stronger impulse for sex in the winter and women in the summer? Is it because men are hotter and drier in their natures, whereas women are moist and cooled? Therefore, in men the moisture and the heat

---

[43] I.e., it is not released through ejaculation.
[44] Cf. *Rh.* 1384b17–22.
[45] Cf. *Pr.* 4.25.

τὴν ὁρμὴν τοῦ χειμῶνος (ἡ δὲ τοῦ σπέρματος γένεσις
ἐκ τούτων), ταῖς δὲ τὸ θερμὸν ἔλαττον καὶ τὸ ὑγρόν
ἐστι πεπηγὸς διὰ τὴν ἔνδειαν τοῦ πυρός· τοῦτο δὲ
θέρους. ταῖς μέν οὖν σύμμετρον τὸ θερμόν, τοῖς δὲ
πλέον τοῦ ἱκανοῦ· τὸ γὰρ ἄγαν πολὺ ἐκλύει τῆς
20 δυνάμεως. | διὸ καὶ τὰ παιδία τοῦ θέρους λεπτότερα·
συμβαίνει γὰρ πῦρ ἐπὶ πῦρ φέρειν.

29. Διὰ τί ὅσοι θερμοὶ τὴν φύσιν, ἐὰν ἰσχυροὶ ὦσι
καὶ εὐτραφεῖς, ἐὰν μὴ ἀφροδισιάσωσι, χολή τε προ-
ίσταται[17] αὐτοῖς πολλάκις καὶ ἔκπικρον ὑποχωρεῖ καὶ
25 φλέγμα ἁλμυρὸν | γίνεται, καὶ ἀλλοχροοῦσιν; ἢ ὅτι
μετὰ τοῦ σπέρματος ἀεὶ περίττωμα συναπέρχεται; διὸ
καὶ ἐνίοις τῶν περιττωματικῶν[18] ἰχθύων πλύντρου ὄζει
ἡ γονή. ἀφροδισιάζουσι μὲν οὖν τοῦτο συναπέρχεται,
ὥστ' οὐ λυπεῖ· μὴ ἁπτομένοις δὲ τῆς ὁμιλίας τὸ
περίττωμα ἐκπικροῦται ἢ ἁλμυρὸν γίνεται. |

30 30. Διὰ τί ἀφροδισιαστικοὶ οἱ μελαγχολικοί; ἢ ὅτι
πνευματώδεις, τὸ δὲ σπέρμα πνεύματος ἔξοδός ἐστιν;
οἷς οὖν πολὺ τὸ τοιοῦτον, ἀνάγκη πολλάκις ἐπιθυμεῖν
τούτους ἀποκαθαίρεσθαι· κουφίζονται γάρ.

31. Διὰ τί καὶ οἱ ὄρνιθες καὶ οἱ δασεῖς ἄνθρωποι
35 λάγνοι; | πότερον ὅτι ὑγρότητα ἔχουσι πολλήν; ἢ οὔ

---

[17] προΐσταται : προσίσταται Bussemaker
[18] περιττωματικῶν Sylburg ex Gaza : πνευματικῶν codd.

---

[46] Or "a lot of *pneuma*," if we follow the manuscript tradition.
[47] Galen (*In Hp. Epid.* 6 p. 138,19–139,18 [CMG v. 10,2,2])

are sufficient with respect to this impulse in the winter (and the generation of seed comes from these), but in women the heat is less and the moisture is solidified owing to the lack of fire; and this occurs in summer. Therefore, in women the heat is balanced (*in the summer*), while in men it is more than what is sufficient; for the excess exhausts much of their capacity. This is also why children are thinner in summer; for it is a case of adding fire to fire.

29. Why are those who are hot by nature, if they are strong and well nourished, often overpowered by bile if they do not have sex, and what they evacuate is bitter, and salty phlegm appears, and their complexion changes? Is it because residue always passes out with the seed? And this is why in some of those who have a lot of residue[46] the semen smells of water in which fish have been washed. Therefore, when they have sex, this passes out with the seed, so that no harm is done; but in those not engaging in intercourse, the residue is bitter or becomes salty.

30.[47] Why are the melancholic highly sexual? Is it because they are full of *pneuma*,[48] and the seed is an exiting of *pneuma*? Therefore, those in whom there is a lot of this material must necessarily often desire to purge themselves; for they are thereby relieved.

31.[49] Why are birds and hairy humans lustful? Is it because they contain much moisture? Or is this not so (for

seems to refer to this chapter (see also *Pr.* 30.1, 953b30–54a5) and attributes it to Aristotle's *Problems*. See also *Pr.* 18.1 and 7, *Insom.* 461a22, and Diocl. fr. 110 (v.d. Eijk).

[48] Πνευματώδεις ("full of *pneuma*") can also be rendered "flatulent."

[49] Cf. *Pr.* 10.24.

(τὸ γὰρ θῆλυ ὑγρὸν μέν, ἀλλ᾽ οὐ δασύ), ἀλλ᾽ ὅτι
ἀμφότεραι αἱ φύσεις πεπτικαὶ πολλῆς ὑγρότητος διὰ
θερμότητα; σημεῖον δ᾽ αἱ τρίχες καὶ τὰ πτερά. ἢ ὅτι
πολὺ τὸ ὑγρόν, καὶ κρατεῖται ὑπὸ τοῦ θερμοῦ; οὔτε
880b γὰρ ἂν μὴ πολλῆς οὔσης τῆς ὑγρότητος ‖ οὔτε μὴ
κρατουμένης ἐξεφύετο τοῖς μὲν αἱ τρίχες τοῖς δὲ τὰ
πτερά. τὸ δὲ σπέρμα γίνεται ἐν τοῖς τοιούτοις πλεῖστον καὶ τόποις καὶ ὥραις, οἷον ἐν τῷ ἔαρι· ἡ γὰρ
5 φύσις αὐτοῦ ὑγρὰ καὶ θερμή. διὰ ταὐτὸ δὲ καὶ | οἱ
ὄρνιθες λάγνοι καὶ οἱ χωλοί· ἡ γὰρ τροφὴ ἀμφοτέροις
κάτω μὲν ὀλίγη διὰ τὴν ἀναπηρίαν τῶν σκελῶν, εἰς δὲ
τὸν ἄνω τόπον ἔρχεται καὶ εἰς σπέρμα συγκρίνεται.

32. Διὰ τί, ἐὰν ἀφροδισιάζῃ ὁ ἄνθρωπος, οἱ ὀφθαλμοὶ ἀσθενοῦσι μάλιστα; ἢ δῆλον ὅτι ἀπολείποντος
10 τοῦ ὑγροῦ τοῦτο | γίνεται; τεκμήριον δ᾽ ὅτι ἡ γονὴ
ψυχρά ἐστιν· οὐ γὰρ γίνεται ὑγρά, ἐὰν μὴ διαθερμάνῃ
τὰ θερμά. οὐδὲ δεῖται τήξεως· κέχυται γὰρ ἐν τῷ
ἀνθρώπῳ ὥσπερ τὸ αἷμα.

the female is moist, but not hairy), but it is because both natures[50] concoct a lot of moisture owing to heat? A sign of this is the hair and the feathers. Or is it because there is a lot of moisture, and it is mastered by the heat? For if there were not a lot of moisture or if it were not mastered, then hair would not grow on the one or feathers on the other. Now the seed comes to be plentiful in such places and seasons, for example in the spring; for its nature is moist and hot. And for the same reason, both birds and the lame are lustful; for in both, the nourishment below is meager owing to the deficiency[51] of their legs, but (*more nourishment*) goes to the upper region and is condensed into seed.

32.[52] Why, if a human has sex, do the eyes become very weak? Is it clear that this occurs when moisture is wanting? Now evidence for this is that the semen is cold; for it does not become moist unless the heat heats it thoroughly. Nor does it need melting; for it is spread throughout the human just like blood.

[50] I.e., birds and hairy humans.
[51] Literally, "deformity."
[52] Cf. *Pr.* 4.3.

175

BOOK V

INTRODUCTION

Judging by its title, the topic of Book 5 is fatigue (κόπος), including its causes and consequences. Of its forty-two chapters, however, only a dozen mention fatigue (1, 6–8, 10–12, 23, 26, 31, 35, 38). But a number of other chapters are nonetheless connected to the topic (however tenuously at times), as they discuss exercise, exertion, and stress[1]—fatigue, so to speak, in the sense of both weariness and physical fatigue (2–5, 9, 14–22, 24–25, 27–30, 32–34, 36, 39–41).

There are only three chapters that, in their present form, have nothing to do with this topic, however broadly conceived (13, 37, 42). All three deal with horseback riding (see also ch. 1, 880b20). Perhaps these were included, in some earlier form, to mark a contrast with a major subject thread running throughout Book 5, namely, walking and running, which half the chapters discuss (1, 9–12, 15–20, 23–26, 29, 35–36, 39–41). Four chapters (3–5, 14) deal with body fat (especially around the abdomen) and have at most an indirect connection to fatigue.

---

[1] The word πόνος has been translated, depending on the context, as "stress" or "exertion."

There is only one clear major source for much of Book 5: Theophrastus' *On Fatigue*.[2] Fourteen chapters clearly seem to be responding to or otherwise influenced by this work (1, 8, 10–12, 19–20, 23–24, 26, 31, 35, 38, 40).[3] Aristotle's *On the Progression of Animals* and the Hippocratic *Regimen* (2.61–66) are two other possible sources.[4]

[2] See M. G. Sollengberger's edition of the Greek text, with translation and commentary, in W. W. Fortenbaugh, R. Sharples, and M. G. Sollengberger, eds., *Theophrastus of Eresus: On Sweat, On Dizziness and On Fatigue* (Leiden, 2003).

[3] And Thphr. *Ign.* 36 was a likely source for *Pr.* 5.36.

[4] Especially interesting are Hipp. *Vict.* 2.62–63 (on walking and running) and 66 (on fatigue).

ΟΣΑ ΑΠΟ ΚΟΠΟΥ

880b
15
1. Διὰ τί μακροὶ μὲν ὄντες οἱ περίπατοι ἐν τοῖς ὁμαλέσιν κοπιαρώτεροί εἰσιν τῶν ἀνωμάλων, βραχεῖς δὲ ἀκοπώτεροι; ἢ ὅτι ἥ τε πολλὴ κίνησις ποιεῖ κόπον καὶ ἡ ἰσχυρά; τοιαύτη δὲ ἡ σπασματώδης, πολλὴ δὲ ἡ συνεχὴς καὶ μία. ἐν μὲν οὖν τοῖς ἀνάντεσιν, ἐὰν ᾖ
20 μακρά, ἀνάπαυσις γίνεται | ἡ μεταβολή, καὶ οὐ μακρὰ ἡ κίνησις, οὐδὲ ἵππων αὐτῶν, διὰ τὴν μεταβολήν· ἐν δὲ τοῖς ὁμαλέσιν ἡ ὁμοιότης τοῦ σχήματος οὐ διαλαμβάνει οὐδὲ ἀναπαύει τὰ μέρη, ἀλλὰ συνεργάζεται πρὸς τὸ συνεχῆ τὴν κίνησιν εἶναι. ὅταν δὲ ᾖ βραχεῖα,
25 διὰ μὲν τὸ πλῆθος τῆς κινήσεως ἐν τοῖς ἐπιπέδοις | οὐ γίνεται κόπος· ἐν δὲ τοῖς ἀνάντεσιν διὰ τὸ τὴν μεταβολὴν ἰσχυρὰν γίνεσθαι καὶ ἐναντίαν, ὁτὲ μὲν ἄνω ὁτὲ δὲ κάτω, ποιεῖ κόπον. τοιαύτη δέ, ὡς φαμέν, ἐν τοῖς ἀνάντεσιν, ἐν δὲ τοῖς πεδινοῖς τοὐναντίον.

2. Διὰ τί τοῖς λειποψυχοῦσι καὶ τοῖς ἐκ τῶν γυμνα-
30 σίων | διαλυομένοις ἐλάττους τε οἱ ὄγκοι καὶ ὀξύτεραι δοκοῦσιν εἶναι αἱ φωναί; ἢ ὅτι αἵ τε φωναὶ ἐλάττους φαινόμεναι ὀξύτεραι φαίνονται (σημεῖον δὲ ὅτι μιμού-

180

PROBLEMS ARISING
FROM FATIGUE

1.[1] Why are long walks on level ground more fatiguing than over uneven ground, but short ones are less fatiguing? Is it because prolonged and vigorous movement produces fatigue? Now spasmodic motion is of this kind,[2] and continuous and uniform motion is prolonged. So in the case of walks over hills, if they are long, the change[3] constitutes a rest, and the motion is not a long one, even with horses, because of the change; but on level ground the similarity of position does not divide (*the walk*) into intervals (*of uphill and downhill*) and does not rest the limbs, but contributes to making the motion continuous. But when it is short, no fatigue occurs because of the length of the motion on flat ground; but over hills, because the change is vigorous and into the opposite, sometimes upward and sometimes downward, it produces fatigue. Such, we claim, is the motion over hills, whereas on level ground it is the opposite.

2. Why does the bulk seem to be smaller in those who faint and in those who collapse from gymnastic exercise, and the voices shriller? Is it because their voices, appearing to be less, appear shriller (and a sign of this is the fact

---

[1] Source: Thphr. *Lass*. 15.   [2] I.e., vigorous.
[3] I.e., from walking uphill to walking downhill.

μένοι τοὺς πόρρωθεν ὀξὺ φθέγγονται) καὶ οἱ ὄγκοι
ἐλάττους;[1]

3. Διὰ τί ἡ γαστὴρ μόνον λεπτύνεται τῶν γυμνα-
35 ζομένων; | ἢ ὅτι πλείστη ἡ πιμελὴ περὶ τὴν γαστέρα;

4. Διὰ τί τὸ πῖον τετριμμένον γίνεται τοῖς πονοῦσιν; ἢ διότι τὸ πῖον τήκεται θερμαινόμενον, ἡ δὲ
κίνησις θερμαίνει; ἡ δὲ σὰρξ οὐ τήκεται.

5. Διὰ τί δὲ τὰ περὶ τὴν κοιλίαν πιότατα; πότερον
881a ὅτι ‖ ἐγγύς ἐστι τῆς τροφῆς; ἐν ὅσῳ οὖν τἆλλα παρ᾽
ἐκείνης λαμβάνει, αὐτὴ πολλάκις λαμβάνει. ἢ ὅτι
ἥκιστα πονεῖ; καμπὰς γὰρ οὐκ ἔχει.

6. Διὰ τί οἱ κόποι μᾶλλον παύονται, ὅταν τις τῷ
5 ἐλαίῳ | ὕδωρ συμμίξας ἀνατρίψηται; ἢ ὅτι μᾶλλον
εἰσδύεται τὸ ἔλαιον μετὰ τοῦ ὕδατος; ἐὰν δὲ αὐτὸ καθ᾽
αὑτὸ ᾖ, οὐχ ὁμοίως παρεισδύνει διὰ τὸ ἐπιπολαστικὸν
εἶναι. μᾶλλον οὖν μαλάττεται τὸ σῶμα εἰσδυομένου,
ἐπεὶ τὸ ἔλαιόν ἐστι φύσει θερμόν, τὰ δὲ θερμὰ καὶ
10 ξηραίνει καὶ σκληρύνει. | πρὸς δὲ τοὺς κόπους ἀξύμ-
φορόν ἐστιν ἡ ξηρασία καὶ ἡ σκληρότης· μετὰ δὲ τοῦ
ὕδατος ἀνατριφθὲν ἧττον ξηραίνει.

7. Διὰ τί τοῖς κοπιῶσι προστάττουσιν ἐμεῖν, εἴπερ
ὁ ἔμετος κοπῶδές ἐστιν; ἢ κόπος γίνεται ὀστῶν θλω-
μένων καὶ πιεζομένων καὶ κοπιωμένων; ταῦτα δὲ ὑπὸ
15 τῶν ἐκτός τινος | πάσχοι ἂν ἢ τῶν ἐν τῷ σώματι, καὶ
τοῦτο διττῶς· ἢ γὰρ σαρκῶν ὑπερτεινουσῶν τὴν δύνα-

---

[1] post ἐλάττους add. quod sanguis a summis corporis parti-
bus sevocat ad imas Gaza

that when people imitate those at a distance they speak shrilly) and their bulk appears smaller?[4]

3. Why does the abdomen alone become thinner in those who exercise? Is it because there is the most fat around the abdomen?

4. Why is the fat worn away in those who exert themselves? Is it because fat melts when it is heated, and movement produces heat? But flesh does not melt.

5. But why are the parts around the stomach fattest? Is it because they are near the nourishment? Now to the degree to which the other parts receive something from the stomach, the stomach itself receives it just as often. Or is it because the stomach exerts itself least of all? For it does not have joints.

6. Why is fatigue stopped more readily when someone, mixing water with oil, rubs it in? Is it because the oil mixed with water penetrates farther? But by itself, the oil does not penetrate to the same extent because it is on the surface. Therefore, the body is softened more when (*the oil mixed with water*) penetrates, since oil is hot by nature, and what is hot both dries and hardens. Now dryness and hardness are both useless for fatigue; but when oil is rubbed in mixed with water there is less drying.

7. Why do they order those who are fatigued to vomit, if vomiting is itself fatiguing? Does fatigue occur when the bones are bruised, crushed, and fatigued? Now these are caused by something external or by things within the body, and this latter in two ways: for either the flesh extends be-

---

[4] Gaza adds "because the blood separates from the upper parts of the body to the lower."

μιν αὐτῶν, ἢ σώματος μιχθέντος συχνοῦ τῷ ἄλλῳ
σώματι χώραν οἰκείαν οὐκ ἔχοντος, οἷα τὰ περιττώ-
ματά ἐστιν. πάντα γὰρ τὰ ἐκτὸς ἡμῖν περιαπτόμενα
20 βάρη κοπωδέστερα τῶν τοῦ σώματος μερῶν, | κἂν
τύχῃ σταθμῷ ὄντα αὐτῶν ἐλαφρότερα. σημεῖον δὲ τῶν
εἰρημένων· οἱ γὰρ πλεῖον βεβρωκότες καὶ πεπωκότες,
ἔλαττον πονήσαντες ἢ νήστεις ὄντες, μᾶλλον κοπιῶσι
διὰ τὸ μὴ τὴν οἰκείαν χώραν ἔχειν τὰ σιτία ὄντα
ἄπεπτα. ἐπεὶ δὲ ὁ κόπος σύντηξιν ποιεῖ, ἡ δὲ σύντηξις
25 περίττωμά ἐστιν, τοῦτό | ἐστιν ὃ τὸν κόπον ἐν ἡμῖν
ποιεῖ, πλανώμενον ἀτάκτως καὶ προσπῖπτον ὀστοῖς τε
καὶ νεύροις καὶ τοῖς ἐντὸς τῆς σαρκὸς ἀραιοῖς οὖσι
καὶ ἀνεῳγμένοις. ὁ οὖν ἔμετος ἐξάγων αὐτὸ ὃν αἴτιον
τοῦ κόπου, εἰκότως ἀκόπους ποιεῖ· λείπει γὰρ οἷον ἦν
ἐν ἀρχῇ τοῦ πόνου τὸ σῶμα. κοπῶδες δ' ἐστὶν ὁ ἔμετος |
30 οὐ τῇ τῆς γινομένης ἐν αὐτῷ κινήσεως ὑπερβολῇ, ἀλλ'
ὅταν συμβῇ μὴ καλῶς ἐξεμέσαι· λειφθέντων γὰρ
πολλῶν σιτίων, καὶ περιττωμάτων τούτοις ἐνόντων,
τὸν τοῦ ἐμέτου κόπον γίνεσθαι συμβαίνει, καθάπερ
ἐπὶ τῶν πεπληρωμένων εἴρηται. εἰ οὖν μηδ' ἐκείνοις ὁ
35 πόνος ἐστὶ τοῦ κόπου αἴτιος, | ἀλλὰ τὸ οὕτως ἔχοντας
πονῆσαι, οὐδ' ἂν τοῖς μὴ ἐξαιροῦσι τὰ σιτία ὁ ἔμετος
εἴη τοῦ κόπου αἴτιος· χρὴν γὰρ πᾶσι τοῖς ἐμοῦσι
γίνεσθαι κόπον, γίνονται δὲ ἀκοπώτεροι πολλοὶ ἐμέ-
σαντες.

8. Διὰ τί κοπιαρώτερόν ἐστι τῷ βραχίονι τὸ διὰ
881b κενῆς ‖ ῥίπτειν ἢ λιθάζοντα; ἢ ὅτι σπασμωδέστερον

yond its own power, or part of the body mixes in a large quantity with the rest of the body and does not keep its proper place, as is the case with residues. For any loads that are attached to us from the outside are more fatiguing than the parts of the body, even if they are lighter than these in weight. And there is a sign of what was said: for those who have eaten and drunk a lot, even though they have exerted themselves less than if they were fasting, become more fatigued because the food being unconcocted does not keep to its own proper place. Now since fatigue causes colliquation, and colliquation is a residue, this is what causes fatigue in us, wandering about disorderly and attacking the bones and sinews and the parts of the flesh within, which are porous and open. Therefore vomiting, by ejecting what is the cause of the fatigue, reasonably makes people less weary; for it leaves the body just as it was at the beginning of the exertion. But vomiting is fatiguing, not because of the excess of movement that occurs during it, but when it happens to vomit forth insufficiently; for when a lot of food is left behind, and there are residues in it, fatigue arises from vomiting, as has been said in the case of those who are full of food.[5] Therefore, if in the latter cases, the exertion is not the cause of the fatigue, but their exerting themselves in this condition, then vomiting could not be the cause of fatigue in those who do not eject all the food; for fatigue must then occur in all those who vomit, but many become less fatigued after vomiting.

8.[6] Why is it more fatiguing for the arm to throw with an empty hand than to hurl a stone? Is it because to throw

[5] Early in this chapter, at 881a21.
[6] Source: Thphr. *Lass*. 13. See also Arist. *IA* 705a16–19.

τὸ διὰ κενῆς ἐστίν; οὐ γὰρ ἀπερείδεται πρὸς οὐδέν,
ὥσπερ ὁ βάλλων πρὸς τὸ ἐν τῇ χειρὶ βέλος. ὁμοίως δὲ
τούτῳ καὶ ὁ πένταθλος πρὸς τοὺς ἁλτῆρας καὶ ὁ θέων

5 παρασείων πρὸς τὰς | χεῖρας. διὸ ὁ μὲν μεῖζον ἅλλεται
ἔχων ἢ μὴ ἔχων ἁλτῆρας, ὁ δὲ θᾶττον θεῖ παρασείων
ἢ μὴ παρασείων.

9. Διὰ τί ἡ ταχυδρομία καὶ ἐπ᾽ ἀνθρώπου καὶ ἐπὶ
τῶν ἄλλων ζῴων νοσηματικοὺς ποιεῖ τὰ περὶ τὴν
κεφαλήν; καίτοι ὅλως ὁ δρόμος κατασπᾶν δοκεῖ κάτω

10 τὰ περιττώματα, | ὥσπερ ὁ περίπατος· διὸ καὶ παχύ-
νονται τὰ σκέλη οἱ πολλὰ περιπατοῦντες, ὅτι εἰς τὰ
κάτω ὑπονοστεῖ ἄνωθεν καὶ ἡ τροφὴ καὶ τὰ περιττώματα. <ἢ>[2] ἡ μὲν κίνησις ταὐτὸ ποιεῖ, ἀλλ᾽ ἡ ταχεῖα
διὰ τὴν συντονίαν καὶ τὴν ἀπνευστίαν ἐκθερμαίνει

15 τὴν κεφαλήν, καὶ τὰς φλέβας ἐμφυσᾷ τὰς | ἐν αὐτῇ,
καὶ σπαστικὰς τῶν θύραθεν ποιεῖ δυνάμεων, οἷον
ψύχους καὶ ἀλέας καὶ τῶν ἐκ τοῦ θώρακος, ὧν εἰσιόν-
των νοσεῖν ἀναγκαῖον τὸν τόπον ἐστίν;

10. Διὰ τί κοπιῶσι μὲν μᾶλλον ἐν τοῖς ὁμαλοῖς ἢ ἐν
τοῖς ἀνωμάλοις τόποις, θᾶττον δὲ βαδίζουσιν τὴν

20 ὁμαλὴν ὁδὸν ἢ | τὴν ἀνώμαλον; ἢ ὅτι ἀκοπώτερον μέν
ἐστι τὸ μὴ ἀεὶ ἐν τῷ αὐτῷ σχήματι ποιεῖσθαι τὴν
κίνησιν, ὃ συμβαίνει ἐν τῇ ἀνωμάλῳ πορείᾳ μᾶλλον;
θᾶττον δὲ πορεύονται, ὅτι ἧττον παρὰ φύσιν κινοῦνται. ἐν μὲν οὖν τῷ ὁμαλῷ μικρὰ ἡ ἄρσις καὶ θέσις καὶ

2 <ἢ> Sylburg

with an empty hand is more spasmodic? For it does not receive support from anything, such as the thrower receives from the missile in his hand. And similar to this, the pentathlete receives support from the *halteres*[7] and the runner from his arms, which he swings. This is why the one jumps farther when he has the *halteres* than when he has not, and the other runs faster when he swings his arms than when he does not swing them.

9. Why does running quickly produce a tendency to disease in the regions around the head both in the case of humans and of other animals? Yet in general, running seems to draw down the residues, just as walking does; and this is why those who walk a great deal grow thick in the legs, because both the nourishment and the residues go down from above. Does movement produce the same result, whereas quickness, owing to the tension and the holding of the breath (*it involves*), heats the head and inflates the veins in it, and causes them to draw in external powers, such as cold and heat and what comes from the torso, and when these enter the region must become diseased?

10.[8] Why do people grow more fatigued on level than on uneven ground, though they walk more quickly on a level than on an uneven road? Is it because not making continuous movements in the same position, which occurs more in an uneven walk, is less fatiguing? But they go more quickly (*on level ground*), because they are moving less contrary to nature. So on level ground the raising and

---

[7] The five events of the pentathlon were jumping, running, discus throwing, javelin throwing, and wrestling. The *halteres* were weights held by the competitor in the jumping event.

[8] Cf. Pr. 5.23. Source: Thphr. *Lass.* 14–15.

25 πυκνή ἐστιν, ἐν δὲ τῷ ἀνωμάλῳ τοὐναντίον. | ἔστι δὲ
τὸ αἴρειν παρὰ φύσιν· βίᾳ γάρ ἐστι πᾶσα ἄρσις. τὸ δὲ
παρ' ἑκάστην βάσιν γινόμενον μικρὸν πολὺ γίνεται
παρὰ πολλάς.

11. Διὰ τί τὰ ἐπίπεδα κοπιαρώτερα ἐγκατακεῖσθαι
τῶν κοίλων ἐστίν; ἢ διὰ τὸ αὐτὸ καὶ τὰ κυρτὰ τῶν
30 ἐπιπέδων; | ἐφ' ἕνα γὰρ τόπον συναθροιζόμενον τὸ
βάρος ἐν τῇ καθέδρᾳ ἢ κατακλίσει τῇ θλίψει ποιεῖ
πόνον. τὸ μὲν οὖν κυρτὸν τοῦ εὐθέος, τοῦτο δὲ τοῦ
κοίλου μᾶλλον τοιοῦτόν ἐστιν· τὸ γὰρ σῶμα ἡμῶν
ἐστι περιφερέστερον ἢ εὐθύτερον, τῶν δὲ τοιούτων
κατὰ πλέον ἅπτεται τὰ κοῖλα ἢ τὰ ἐπίπεδα. διὰ ταῦτα |
35 δὲ καὶ τὰ ἐνδιδόντα τῶν μὴ ἐνδιδόντων ἀκοπώτερά
ἐστι καὶ ἐγκατακλιθῆναι καὶ ἐνέζεσθαι.

12. Διὰ τί οἱ βραχεῖς περίπατοι κοπώδεις εἰσίν; ἢ
ὅτι ἀνώμαλοί εἰσιν; πολλάκις γὰρ ἵστασθαι ποιοῦσιν.
τὸ δ' ἐκ τοῦ ἐναντίου εἰς τοὐναντίον πυκνὰ μεταβάλ-
882a λειν κοπῶδές ‖ ἐστιν· συνήθειαν γὰρ οὐδετέρῳ ποιεῖ, ὅ
ἐστιν ἄκοπον. ἀμφοῖν δ' ἅμα οὐκ ἐνδέχεται συνήθειαν
γίνεσθαι.

13. Διὰ τί οἱ ἐπὶ τῶν ἵππων ὀχούμενοι, ὅσῳ ἂν
μᾶλλον θέῃ ὁ ἵππος, τοσούτῳ μᾶλλον δακρύουσι τὰ
5 ὄμματα; πότερον | διὰ τὸ ψυχρότερον εἶναι τὸν ἀεὶ
προσπίπτοντα ἀέρα, ὅσῳ ἂν ἐλάττω χρόνον ἅπτηται
τοῦ σώματος, ὅπερ ἐπὶ τῶν γυμνῶν θεόντων συμβαίνει; τὸ δὲ ψῦχος δάκρυον[3] ποιεῖ. ἢ διὰ τοὐναντίον; καὶ

---

3 δάκρυον : δακρύειν Richards

planting (*of the foot*) is slight but frequent, whereas on uneven ground it is the opposite. Now raising (*the foot*) is contrary to nature; for any raising involves force. But the occurrence, though slight with respect to each step, becomes great with respect to many of them.

11.[9] Why is it more fatiguing to lie down on flat surfaces than on concave ones? Is it for the same reason that makes convex surfaces more fatiguing than flat ones? For the weight being collected into one place, whether sitting or lying down, produces stress owing to the pressure. So the convex surface is more (*fatiguing*) than the straight, while the straight is more than the concave; for our body is more curved than straight, and as such concave surfaces touch it at more points than flat ones. For this reason too what yields (*to pressure*) is less fatiguing than what does not yield, in the case of both lying down and sitting.

12.[10] Why are short walks fatiguing? Is it because they are uneven? For they cause one to stand still often. Now to change frequently from one contrary position to another is fatiguing; for it causes neither to become habitual, and the habitual is not fatiguing. But it is not possible to become habituated to both positions at the same time.

13.[11] Why is it that for those who ride horses, the faster the horse runs the more the rider's eyes shed tears? Is it because the air that continuously strikes them is colder, as it touches the body for a shorter time, which also happens in the case of naked runners? But cold produces tears.[12] Or is it for the contrary reason? For heat also causes us to shed

---

[9] Source: Thphr. *Lass*. 7 and 9.   [10] Source: Thphr. *Lass*. 14–15.   [11] Cf. *Pr*. 5.37.   [12] Or, if Richards is right, "causes us to shed tears" (as in the following line).

189

γὰρ τὸ θερμὸν ποιεῖ δακρύειν, οἷον ὁ ἥλιος· ἡ δὲ
10 κίνησις θερμότητα ποιεῖ. ἢ διὰ τὴν ὑπὸ | τοῦ ἀέρος
πληγήν; ὡς γὰρ οἱ ἄνεμοι ταράττουσιν οἱ ἐξ ἐναντίας
τὰ ὄμματα, οὕτως ὁ ἀὴρ προσπίπτων, ὅσῳ ἂν θᾶττον
ἐλαύνῃ, τοσούτῳ μᾶλλον ποιεῖ πληγὴν μαλακήν.[4]

14. Διὰ τί τὰ μὲν ἄλλα τριβόμενα σαρκοῦνται
μέρη, ἡ δὲ γαστὴρ λεπτοτέρα γίνεται; ἢ οὐδὲ αὐτὴ ἐκ
15 προσαγωγῆς, | ἀλλὰ στιφροτέρα; οὐ μὴν ἀλλ᾽ οὐχ
ὁμοίως γε καὶ ἡ σάρξ, διὸ καὶ τὸ πρόβλημά ἐστιν.
ὅλως γὰρ ἐν τοῖς γυμνασίοις καὶ πόνοις μάλιστα
λεπτύνεται ἡ γαστήρ. αἴτιον δ᾽ ὅτι τὰ πίονα θερμαινόμενα τήκεται, καὶ τὰ φύσει τάσιν ἔχοντα μᾶλλον. τὸ
20 δὲ δέρμα ἐστὶ φύσει ἔχον τάσιν· ἀλλὰ διὰ | τὸ πιαίνε-
σθαι τάχιστα ἀεί τινα ἔχει πιότητα, ἐὰν μὴ κάμνῃ
τινὰ νόσον. αἴτιον δὲ τούτου ὅτι ἐγγύς ἐστι τῆς
τροφῆς. ἐπεὶ οὖν ὅλως ἡ πιμελὴ οὐκ ἔστι φύσει ἀλλ᾽
ἐπίκτητον, καὶ οὐ τῶν ἀναγκαίων μερῶν ὥσπερ ἡ
σάρξ, καὶ ἡ τῶν γυμνασίων κίνησις καὶ ἡ τῆς τρίψεως
25 θερμαίνουσαι τήκουσιν | αὐτὴν καὶ τὴν τροφὴν ἐκπλε-
ονάζουσαν νέμουσιν τοῖς ἄλλοις μορίοις. διὸ αἱ μὲν
καθέδραι τὴν κοιλίαν πιαίνουσι, τὸ δ᾽ ἄλλο σῶμα
λεπτύνουσιν, αἱ δὲ κινήσεις καὶ αἱ τρίψεις τὴν μὲν
κοιλίαν λεπτύνουσι, τὸ δ᾽ ἄλλο σῶμα παχύνουσιν.

15. Διὰ τί ἐκ τῶν μακρῶν καὶ σφοδρῶν ὁδῶν καὶ
30 δρόμων, | ὅταν στῇ τις ἐπ᾽ ἄκρων τῶν δακτύλων,
σείονται τῶν ποδῶν αἱ πτέρναι καὶ σπῶνται[5] κάτω
προπετῶς; ἢ διὰ τὴν συνέχειαν καὶ σφοδρότητα τῆς

tears, as for instance the sun does; and movement produces heat. Or is it due to the impact of the air? For as the
winds from an opposite direction disturb the eyes, so the
air strikes the faster one rides, and all the more produces a
soft blow.[13]

14. Why do the other parts become fleshier by being
rubbed, whereas the abdomen becomes thinner? Or does
it not (*become thinner*) from the introduction (*of rubbing*),
but firmer? In any case, the flesh is not in the same situa-
tion, and this is why there is the problem. For in general,
the abdomen becomes very thin through exercise and exertion. The reason is that the fat parts, and those that
by nature expand more, melt when heated. Now the skin
expands by nature; but because it fattens very quickly, it
always contains some fat, unless one is suffering from a disease. And the reason for this is that it is near the nourishment. Therefore, since the fat is generally not by nature
but an addition, and is not one of the necessary parts, as the
flesh is, both the movement of exercise and the movement
of rubbing heat and melt it, and distribute the superfluous
nourishment to the other parts. This is why sitting down
fattens the stomach, whereas the rest of the body becomes
thinner, and movement and rubbing make the stomach
thinner, but make the rest of the body thicker.

15. Why, when one stands on the tips of the toes after
long and intense walking or running, do the heels shake
and are quickly drawn down? Does the shaking of the sin-

---

[13] Or, if Louis (following Gaza) is right, "a great blow."

⁴ ante πληγὴν add. τὴν Bekker ‖ μαλακήν : μεγάλην Louis
ex Gaza   ⁵ σπῶνται Forster : σπᾶται codd.

κινήσεως οὐκ ἀναπαύεται ὁ σεισμὸς τῷ ἀνθρώπῳ τῶν
νεύρων; τοῦ μὲν γὰρ ὅλου σώματος κρατεῖ ἡ ψυχὴ
35   πολλάκις, μορίων δ' οὔ, ὁπόταν πως | κινηθῇ, οἷον καὶ
καρδίας καὶ αἰδοίου. αἴτιον δ' ὅτι πνεῦμα πολὺ περὶ τὰ
νεῦρα ἐκκαίεται, ὃ οὐχ ἅμα ἐκψύχεται στάντι. τοῦτο
οὖν σεῖον ὥσπερ ὑποσπῶν τῇ κινήσει κατασπᾶται καὶ
τοῦ πορρωτάτω ἥκιστα ποιεῖ κρατεῖν· τοιοῦτον δὲ αἱ
πτέρναι, οἷον τοῖς ὀργιζομένοις τὸ κάτω χεῖλος. ||

882b   16. Διὰ τί οἱ μὴ σφόδρα συντόνως τρέχοντες ἐν τῷ
ῥυθμῷ ἀναπνέουσιν; πότερον ὅτι πᾶς ῥυθμὸς ὡρισμέ-
νη μετρεῖται κινήσει, τοιαύτη δ' ἐστὶν ἡ δι' ἴσου οὖσα,
ὅπερ οἱ τροχάζοντες ποιοῦσιν; ἅμα οὖν ἀρχόμενοι
5   τροχάζειν ἀναπνέουσιν, | ὥστε τὴν ἀναπνοὴν δι' ἴσου
γινομένην, διὰ τὸ τῇ ἴσῃ κινήσει μετρεῖσθαι, ῥυθμὸν
ποιεῖν. ἢ ὅτι πᾶσα μὲν ἁπλῶς ἀναπνοὴ δι' ἴσου
γίνεται τοῖς κατὰ φύσιν αὐτῇ χρωμένοις καὶ μὴ κατέχουσιν; καθημένοις μὲν οὖν καὶ βαδίζουσι μετρίας
οὔσης τῆς τοῦ σώματος κινήσεως, οὐκ εὔδηλος ὁ
10   ῥυθμὸς | γίνεται· συντόνως δὲ τρέχουσιν, οὐ παρακο-
λουθούσης τῇ κινήσει τῆς αἰσθήσεως, οὐ δυνάμεθα
συνορᾶν τὸν τῆς ἀναπνοῆς ῥυθμόν. ἐν δὲ τῷ μετρίως
τροχάζειν μέτρον ἡ κίνησις αἰσθητὸν τῆς ἀναπνοῆς
ποιοῦσα τὸν ῥυθμὸν δηλοῖ.

17. Διὰ τί ἐν τῷ τροχάζειν ἐκπνευματοῦσθαι δοκεῖ
15   ἡμῖν | ὁ ἀήρ; πότερον ὅτι κινούμενοι διὰ τοῦ τροχάζειν

---

14 It is unclear how precisely to understand ἐκπνευματοῦσθαι
(the passive infinitive of the rare ἐκπνευματόω). Hett renders it

ews in the person not stop because of the continuity and intensity of the movement? For often, although the soul controls the whole body, it does not control (*certain*) parts, such as the heart and the privates, when they have been moved in some way. Now the reason is that a lot of breath —which does not cool off the moment one stands still— is heated around the sinews. So this breath goes on shaking, as if drawn down from below by the movements, and makes one less able to control the extremities—such are the heels, like the lower lip in those who are angry.

16. Why do those who are not running under great strain breathe rhythmically? Is it because all rhythm is measured by definite movement, and the kind of movement that runners make is regular? So as soon as they begin to run they breathe, and as their breathing is coming regularly because it is measured by regular movement, it produces a rhythm. Or is it because all breathing without qualification is regular in those who employ it naturally and do not hold their breath? So in those sitting or walking, as the movement of the body is moderate, the rhythm is not obvious; while in those running intensely, as our perception cannot follow the movement, we are unable to observe the rhythm of the breathing. But in the one running moderately, the movement, making the measure of breathing perceptible, reveals its rhythm.

17. Why, in running, does the air seem to us to be vaporized?[14] Is it because, when we move on account of

---

"to vaporize" (which I retain but make passive), Forster "to turn into breath." Cf. *Pr.* 1.53. But keep in mind that $\pi\nu\epsilon\hat{\upsilon}\mu\alpha$ can mean "wind" as well as "breath," and that the author may here be referring to the air around us becoming like wind.

τὸν συνεχῆ τοῖς σώμασιν ἡμῶν ἀέρα κινοῦμεν, ὅ ἐστι
πνεῦμα; διόπερ οὐ δοκεῖ μόνον, ἀλλὰ καὶ κατ᾽ ἀλή-
θειαν ἐκπνευματοῦται ὁ ἀήρ. ἢ διότι τροχάζοντες
προσκόπτομεν τῷ ἀέρι, τούτου δὲ συμβαίνοντος μᾶλ-
20 λον αἴσθησιν λαμβάνομεν | τοῦ ἀέρος διὰ τῆς κινή-
σεως; εἰκότως οὖν ἡμῖν ἐκπνευματοῦσθαι δοκεῖ· τοῦτο
γὰρ συμβαίνει διὰ τὴν φοράν.

18. Διὰ τί μᾶλλον θέοντες ἢ βαδίζοντες πίπτουσιν;
⟨ἢ⟩[6] ὅτι μᾶλλον πρὶν κινεῖσθαι αἴρουσιν; τὸ γὰρ θέειν
τοῦ βαδίζειν τούτῳ διαφέρει. |

25 19. Διὰ τί ποτε ἀναβαίνοντες μὲν τὰ γόνατα πονοῦμεν, καταβαίνοντες δὲ τοὺς μηρούς; ἢ ὅτι ὅταν μὲν
ἀναβαίνωμεν, ἀναρριπτοῦμεν ἄνω τὸ σῶμα, καὶ ἡ
σπάσις πολλὴ τοῦ σώματος καὶ [ἡ][7] ἀπὸ τῶν γονάτων
γίνεται, διὸ πονοῦμεν τὰ γόνατα; ἐν δὲ τοῖς κατάντεσι,
30 διὰ τὸ ὑποφέρεσθαι τοῖς | σκέλεσι, τοῖς μηροῖς ἀπο-
στηριζόμενοι πονοῦμεν αὐτούς. εἶθ᾽ ἅπαν τὸ παρὰ
φύσιν γινόμενον πόνον καὶ λύπην παρασκευάζει. ἔστι
δὲ τὸ κατὰ φύσιν τοῖς μὲν γόνασιν ἡ εἰς τὸ πρόσθεν
κλάσις, τοῖς δὲ μηροῖς ἡ εἰς τοὐπισθεν. ἐν μὲν οὖν
τοῖς ἀνάντεσι τὰ γόνατα κλᾶται εἰς τοὐπισθεν διὰ τὸ
35 ἀποστηρίζεσθαι | βούλεσθαι, ἐν τοῖς κατάντεσι δ᾽ οἱ
μηροὶ εἰς τοὔμπροσθεν κλῶνται διὰ τὸ προπετὲς ἡμῶν
εἶναι τὸ σῶμα.

20. Διὰ τί ποτε ἐν ταῖς ὁδοῖς τῶν μηρῶν τὸ μέσον

6 ⟨ἢ⟩ Sylburg
7 καὶ [ἡ] Hett : [καὶ] ἡ Bonitz : καὶ ἡ codd.

running, we move air that is continuous with our bodies, and this is breath? Consequently the air does not merely seem, but also in truth *is*, vaporized. Or is it because when running we strike the air, and when this happens we perceive the air more because of the movement? Therefore, it reasonably seems to us to be vaporized; for this happens owing to the rapid motion.

18. Why do people fall more when they run than when they walk? Is it because they raise (*their feet*) more before moving themselves? Indeed, running differs from walking in this way.

19.[15] Why do we feel stress in our knees when we go uphill, but in our thighs when we go down? Is it because when we go uphill we throw our bodies upward, and the extension of the body is great and comes from the knees, which is why we feel stress in the knees? But in going downhill, because we are carried by our legs we are supported by our thighs, and so we feel stress in them. Further, whatever occurs contrary to nature produces stress and pain. Now bending forward is, according to nature, in the knees, while bending backward is in the thighs. In going uphill, however, the knees are bent backward because of the need for support, whereas in going downhill the thighs are bent forward because our body is thrown forward.

20.[16] Why, on journeys, do we feel stress most in the

[15] Cf. *Pr.* 5.24. Source: Thphr. *Lass.* 11–12.

[16] Source: Thphr. *Lass.* 10. Note that Theophrastus refers to fatigue rather than stress.

μάλιστα πονοῦμεν; ἢ ὅτι παντὸς μακροῦ καὶ ἑνὸς
ὄντος, ἐστηριγμένου δέ, τοῦ μέσου ὁ πόνος μάλιστα
γίνεται; διὸ καὶ κατάγνυται ‖ μάλιστα ἐντεῦθεν. ὁ δὲ
μηρός ἐστι τοιοῦτον· διὸ καὶ τὸ μέσον αὐτοῦ μάλιστα
πονοῦμεν.

21. Διὰ τί οἱ ὑγροὶ ταχὺ πνίγονται πονήσαντες καὶ
ὑπὸ τοῦ καύματος; ἢ ὅτι ἐκθερμαινόμενον τὸ ὑγρὸς
ἀὴρ γίνεται, | καὶ κάει μᾶλλον τὸ πλέον; ὅταν οὖν μὴ
δύνηται ὑπεξάγειν διὰ τὸ πλῆθος, οὐ γίνεται κατάψυξις, ὥστε ταχὺ ἐκπυροῦται ὑπὸ τοῦ συμφύτου καὶ
ἐπικτήτου θερμοῦ. διὸ καὶ οἱ γινόμενοι ἱδρῶτες τοῖς
γυμναζομένοις καὶ ὅλως τοῖς πονοῦσιν καὶ ἡ τοῦ
πνεύματος ἔξοδος ὠφέλιμον· διακρινομένου γὰρ καὶ
λεπτυνομένου | τοῦ ὑγροῦ πνεῦμα γίνεται.

22. Διὰ τί τὰ σύμμετρα τῶν σωμάτων κάμνει τε
πολλάκις καὶ ἀπαλλάττει ῥᾷον; ἢ διὰ ταὐτὸ ἄμφω;
ὁμαλὸν γὰρ τὸ σύμμετρον, τὸ δὲ ὁμαλὸν ὁμοπαθέ-
στερον· ἐὰν οὖν τι πονήσῃ μέρος, εὐθὺς συμπονεῖ τὸ
ὅλον. τὸ δὲ ἀσύμμετρον, | ἅτε μᾶλλον ἀπηρτημένον,
οὐ συναπολαύει τῶν μερῶν. κάμνει μὲν οὖν πολλάκις
διὰ τοῦτο, ῥᾷον δὲ ἀπαλλάττει, ὅτι πᾶν κοινωνεῖ τὸ
σῶμα· εἰς πλείω γὰρ διανεμόμενον τὸ πάθος γίνεται
ἀσθενέστερον, ὥστε εὐαπαλλακτότερον. τὸ δὲ ἀσύμμετρον, ἅτε οὐ κοινωνοῦν τοῖς μέρεσιν, ἐλαττονάκις
μὲν | κάμνει, χαλεπώτερον δὲ ἀπαλλάττει· σφοδρὸν
γὰρ τὸ πάθος.

middle of the thighs? Is it because when anything is long and a unity, and fixed, the stress occurs most in the middle? And this is why it is most likely to break here. Now the thigh is such a part; and this is why we feel the stress most in the middle of it.

21. Why do those who are moist quickly choke when exerting themselves and on account of heat? Is it because their moisture when heated becomes air and the more there is the more it heats up? Therefore, when it is impossible to draw off (*the moisture*) because of its quantity, no cooling takes place, such that it quickly burns up owing to both the natural and acquired heat. And this is why the sweat that comes to those who exercise and generally to those who exert themselves, as well as the expulsion of breath, are advantageous; for when the moisture separates and rarefies, breath is formed.

22. Why do well-proportioned bodies both feel weary often *and* shake off (*this weariness*) easily? Is it for the same reason in both cases? For what is well proportioned is uniform, and the uniform is more similarly affected; so if any part is feeling stress, the whole immediately feels stress with it. But what is ill proportioned, being more disunited, does not feel something in all its parts at once. Therefore, for this reason (*the well-proportioned body*) feels weary often, but shakes it off easily, because the whole body shares (*the weariness*): the experience, being distributed to more parts, becomes weaker and so more easily shaken off. But what is ill proportioned, not sharing (*the weariness*) with all the parts, feels weary less often, but shakes it off with greater difficulty; for the experience is strong.

23. Διὰ τί κοπιῶσι μὲν μᾶλλον ἐν τοῖς ὁμαλοῖς ἢ ἐν τοῖς ἀνωμάλοις, θᾶττον δὲ βαδίζουσιν τὴν ὁμαλὴν ἢ τὴν ἀνώμαλον; ἢ ὅτι ἀκοπώτερον μὲν τὸ μὴ ἀεὶ . . . [8] ἐν 25 τῇ ἀνωμάλῳ πορείᾳ | μᾶλλον; θᾶττον δὲ πορεύονται, ὅπου ἐν τῷ ἴσῳ χρόνῳ ἐλάττων ἡ ἀναφορά. ἐν μὲν οὖν τῷ ὁμαλῷ μικρὰ ἡ ἄρσις καὶ πυκνή, ἐν δὲ τῷ ἀνωμάλῳ τοὐναντίον. τὸ δὲ παρ' ἑκάστην βάσιν γινόμενον[9] πολὺ γίνεται παρὰ πολλάς.

24. Διὰ τί καταβαίνοντες μὲν τὰ κατάντη τοὺς 30 μηροὺς μάλιστα | πονοῦμεν, ἀναβαίνοντες δὲ τὰς κνήμας; ἢ ὅτι ἀναβαίνοντες μὲν τῷ αἴρειν τὸ σῶμα; ἅπαν γὰρ γίνεται φορτίον τὸ σῶμα. ᾧ οὖν ἅπαν ἐπίκειται καὶ ᾧ αἴρομεν, τοῦτο μάλιστα πονεῖ. ἡ δὲ κνήμη τοῦτο. ἔσχατον γάρ, μῆκος ἔχον, καὶ οὐχ 35 ὥσπερ ὁ ποὺς πλάτος ἔχει· διὸ σαλεύεται. ὥστε | οἷον τῷ ὤμῳ τὰ βάρη κινοῦμεν, καὶ ἐπὶ τούτῳ ἔχομεν. τοιγαροῦν καὶ πονοῦμεν τὸν ὦμον μάλιστα. καταβαίνοντες δὲ τῷ ἐμπίπτειν τὸ σῶμα κάτω καὶ προωθεῖν παρὰ φύσιν ὁ πόνος ἐστίν, ὥστε ᾧ μάλιστα ἐμπίπτει καὶ σαλεύει, τοῦτο παρέχει τὸν πόνον. ἡ μὲν οὖν 40 κνήμη μένει, τὸ δὲ βάρος ὁ | θώραξ γίνεται· ὁ δὲ

[8] post ἀεὶ lac. indic., suppl. e.g. ⟨ἐν τῷ αὐτῷ σχήματι ποιεῖσθαι τὴν κίνησιν, ὃ συμβαίνει⟩ ex Pr. 5.10, 881b20–21 Bonitz (cf. Gaza)

[9] post γινόμενον add. ⟨μικρὸν⟩ ex Pr. 5.10, 881b26 Bonitz

[17] This chapter is a condensed version of Pr. 5.10. Source: Thphr. Lass. 14–15.

23.[17] Why do people grow more fatigued on level than on uneven ground, though they walk more quickly on level than on uneven ground? Is it because not (*making*) continuous (*movements in the same position, which occurs*)[18] more in an uneven walk, is less fatiguing? But they go more quickly, when in an equal time the raising (*of the foot*) is less. So on level ground the raising is slight but frequent, whereas on uneven ground it is the opposite. But the occurrence, (*though slight*)[19] with respect to each step, becomes great with respect to many of them.

24.[20] Why do we feel stress most in our thighs when we go downhill, but in our calves when we go up? Is it because going up requires raising the body? For the whole body becomes a burden. So that upon which the whole rests and by which we raise it feels stress the most. And this is the calf. For it is an extremity, having length, but not having breadth (like the foot); this is why it is shaken.[21] Just as, for example, we move weights with the shoulder, and rest them on it. Accordingly, we also feel stress most in the shoulder.[22] But in going downhill, the stress is due to the body falling downward and thrusting us forward contrary to nature, so that what receives the stress is that which falls forward and is shaken most. Therefore, the calf stays still, while the torso becomes the weight; but the thigh receives

---

[18] Filling in the lacuna with material from the parallel passage in *Pr.* 5.10, 881b20–21. [19] Translating a word from the parallel passage in *Pr.* 5.10, 881b26.

[20] Cf. *Pr.* 5.19. Source: Thphr. *Lass.* 11–12 (in fact the text of 5.24 and Thphr. *Lass.* 11 is often identical).

[21] Hett translates σαλεύεται "it sustains the shock," which may be the author's meaning. [22] I.e., when we carry weights.

883b μηρὸς δέχεταί τε καὶ σαλεύεται διὰ || τὸ μῆκός τε
ἔχειν καὶ στρέφεσθαι ἄνωθεν, ᾗ ὁ θώραξ ἐμπίπτει.

25. Διὰ τί πλείων δοκεῖ ἡ ὁδὸς εἶναι, ὅταν μὴ
εἰδότες βαδίζωμεν πόση τις, ἢ ὅταν εἰδότες, ἐὰν τἆλλα
5 ὁμοίως | ἔχοντες τύχωμεν; ἢ ὅτι τὸ εἰδέναι πόση τὸ
εἰδέναι ἐστὶ τὸν ἀριθμὸν αὐτοῦ, καὶ πλεῖον ἀεὶ τὸ
ἀόριστον τοῦ ὡρισμένου; ὥσπερ οὖν εἰ ᾔδει ὅτι τοσήδε,
πεπερασμένην ἀνάγκη εἶναι, οὕτω καὶ εἰ μὴ οἶδεν,
ὡς ἀντιστρέφοντος παραλογίζεται ἡ ψυχή, καὶ φαί-
10 νεται εἶναι ἄπειρος. ἔτι τὸ ποσὸν ὡρισμένον | καὶ τὸ
ὡρισμένον ποσόν. ὅταν τοίνυν μὴ φαίνηται ὡρισμένον, ὥσπερ ἄπειρον φαίνεται εἶναι, διὰ τὸ τὸ πεφυκὸς
ὡρίσθαι, ἐὰν μὴ ᾖ ὡρισμένον, ἄπειρον εἶναι, ὥστε καὶ
τὸ φαινόμενον μὴ ὡρίσθαι φαίνεσθαι ἀνάγκη πως
ἀπέραντον.

26. Διὰ τί τοὺς μηροὺς μᾶλλον ἢ τὰς κνήμας
15 κοπιῶσιν; | πότερον ὅτι ἐγγὺς τοῦ τόπου τοῦ ἔχοντος
τὸ περίττωμα, ὥστ᾽ ἂν ὑπερβάλλῃ διὰ τὴν κίνησιν τῇ
θερμότητι, συσπῶσιν οἱ μηροὶ μᾶλλον καὶ πλεῖον ἢ αἱ
κνῆμαι; ἢ διὰ τὸ συμφυεῖς[10] εἶναι μᾶλλον τοὺς μηρούς; μάλιστα γὰρ πονοῦσιν τῇ τοῦ συνεχοῦς δια-
στάσει. καὶ γὰρ ἂν μηδὲν ἔχοντες περίττωμα κοπι-
20 άσωσιν, | ὅμως τοὺς μηροὺς καὶ τὴν ὀσφὺν πονοῦσι

10 συμφυεῖς Forster : συμφυὲς codd.

23 Cf. Pr. 30.4.
24 I.e., to be able to specify its length arithmetically.

this and is shaken, because it has length and is bent from above, on which (*the weight of*) the torso falls.

25.[23] Why does the road seem to be longer, when we walk without knowing how long it is, than when we know, if we are the same with respect to other factors? Is it because to know how long it is, is to know its number,[24] and the infinite is always greater than the determinate? Therefore, just as if one knows that it is such a length, it must be limited, so too if one does not know, as though converting (*the proposition*)[25] the soul is led to a false conclusion, and it appears to be infinite. Further, a quantity is determinate and what is determinate is a quantity. So when something does not appear to be determinate, it appears to be as it were infinite, because that which is naturally determinate, if it is not determinate, appears to be infinite, so that what appears not to be determinate must appear in a sense infinite.

26.[26] Why do we feel fatigue more in the thighs than in the calves? Is it because (*the thighs*) are near the region containing the residue, so that if it is excessive in its heat due to movement, the thighs contract more and to a greater extent than the calves? Or is it because the thighs are more naturally connected?[27] For they feel stress most through the separation of this continuity. Indeed, if they feel fatigue even when there is no residue, nevertheless they feel stress more in the thighs and the loin. Or is it be-

---

[25] The word translated here is a form of the standard term in Aristotle's logical works for "to convert" (ἀντιστρέφειν), e.g., to convert "every A is B" into "every B is A" (see, e.g., *A.Pr.* 25a6).

[26] Cf. Thphr. *Lass.* 10

[27] To each other, presumably.

μᾶλλον. ἢ ὅτι καθάπερ οἱ βουβῶνες γίνονται πληγέντες[11] διὰ τὴν συνάρτησιν τῶν φλεβῶν καὶ νεύρων,
οὕτω καὶ οὗτος; ἐγγυτέρω δὲ τῆς ἀρχῆς ὁ μηρός. ἢ
διότι μᾶλλον ἐν τῷ αὐτῷ σχήματι ὁ μηρὸς τῆς κνή-
25 μης; τοῦτο δὲ κοπιαρώτερον. ἢ ὅτι σαρκώδης, ὥστε
πολὺ τὸ κατὰ φύσιν ⟨θερμὸν⟩[12] ἔχον ἐν αὐτῷ;

27. Διὰ τί ἐνίοις,[13] ὅταν πονήσωσιν, ἕλκη ἐκφύου-
σιν; ἢ ὅταν τὸ σῶμα ἀκάθαρτον ᾖ, ἡ κίνησις θερμαί-
νουσα καὶ ἄλλα περιττώματα συνεξικμάζει μετὰ τοῦ
ἱδρῶτος; παχέα δὲ ὄντα καὶ χυμοὺς ἔχοντα μοχθη-
30 ρούς, ὀξεῖς καὶ πικροὺς καὶ | ἁλμυρούς, τὰ περιττώ-
ματα ἐκκρίνεσθαι μὲν οὐ δύναται διὰ τὸ[14] πάχος,
ἐξαίρεται δὲ διὰ τῆς σαρκὸς καὶ ἐξελκοῖ διὰ πικρό-
τητα τοῦ χυμοῦ.

28. Διὰ τί τοῖς ἐκ τῶν γυμνασίων καὶ φαρμακοπο-
σιῶν οὐκ εὐθὺς προσφέρουσι τροφήν; ἢ διότι καθαί-
35 ρεται τὸ σῶμα | ἔτι, καὶ οὐκ ἀναπέπαυται πονοῦν, καὶ
ἀποκέκριται τὰ περιττώματα;

29. Διὰ τί χαλεπώτερον θεῖν ἢ βαδίζειν; ἢ ὅτι πλεῖον φορτίον φέρει ὁ θέων; ὅταν γὰρ ᾖ μετέωρος, ἅπαν
ἐφ᾿ αὐτῷ ἔχει. ὁ δὲ βαδίζων, οἷον οἱ ἐπὶ τοῖς τειχίοις
40 ἀναπαυόμενοι, | ἐπιθεὶς ἔχει ἐπὶ τῷ ἠρεμοῦντι. ‖

884a 30. Διὰ τί ἐκ τῶν γυμνασίων οὐ πεινῶσιν[15] εὐθύς;
πότερον διὰ τὴν ὑπόλειψιν τῆς συντήξεως, ἕως ἄν τι

---

11 πληγέντες : πληγέντος Bonitz
12 ⟨θερμὸν⟩ Richards   13 ἐνίοις : ἔνιοι Richards
14 τὸ Ap Cᵃ : om. cett. codd.
15 πεινῶσιν : πίνουσιν Ap. Xᵃ

cause, just as swelling of the groin occurs when struck owing to the connection of nerves and sinews, so too in the case of the thigh? For the thigh is nearer to the source.[28] Or is it because the thigh is in the same position more than the calf? And this is more fatiguing. Or is it because it is fleshy, so that the natural <heat> is great in them?

27.[29] Why do sores develop in some people when they exert themselves? When the body is impure, does movement produce heat and exude other residues along with the sweat? Now these residues, being thick and containing unpleasant humors[30] (sharp, bitter, and salty), cannot be secreted, because of their thickness, but rise up through the flesh and produce sores because of the bitterness of the humor.

28.[31] Why do they not give nourishment to people right after exercise and taking medicine? Is it because the body is still being purged and has not stopped its exertion, and the residues are still being secreted?

29.[32] Why is it more difficult to run than to walk? Is it because the runner carries a greater burden? For when he is off the ground, he holds the whole burden by himself. But the walker—like those resting against walls—holds it, setting it on the part standing still.[33]

30. Why aren't people hungry right after exercise? Is it because the colliquation persists, until anything (*remain-*

---

[28] I.e., the source of the veins, namely, the heart. See *PA* 665b15.   [29] See Hp. *Epid.* 6.5.15.

[30] Or "flavor."

[31] Cf. [Arist./Alex.] *Sup.Pr.* 2.122.

[32] Cf. *Pr.* 5.18.

[33] I.e., on the leg momentarily planted on the ground.

πεφθῇ·[16] ἢ διὰ τὸ πνεῦμα ὃ ποιεῖ ὁ πόνος ἐκ τοῦ ὑγροῦ;
ἢ διὰ τὴν δίψαν ἣ γίνεται ἐκ τοῦ θερμαίνεσθαι πο-
5 νοῦντας; πάντα γὰρ συμβαίνει | ταῦτα.

31. Διὰ τί ἐξονειρωκτικοί εἰσιν οἱ κοπιῶντες καὶ
φθισιῶντες; ἢ ὅτι ὅλως ἐξονειρωκτικοὶ οἱ θερμοὶ καὶ
ὑγροί; τὸ γὰρ σπέρμα τοιοῦτόν ἐστι τὴν φύσιν. τὸ
τοιοῦτο δὲ ἐξ οὕτω διακειμένων μάλιστα γίνεται, ὅταν
10 ἡ ἀπὸ τοῦ ὕπνου θερμότης | προσγένηται· μικρᾶς γὰρ
ῥοπῆς τὰ σώματα δεῖται, καὶ ταύτης ἔσωθεν ἀλλ' οὐκ
ἔξωθεν. οἱ δὲ φθισικοὶ καὶ κοπιῶντες οὕτω διάκεινται·
οἱ μὲν γὰρ κοπιῶντες διὰ τὸν κόπον καὶ τὴν κίνησιν
συντήγματος θερμοῦ πλήρεις εἰσίν, οἱ δὲ φθισικοὶ διὰ
15 τὸν κατάρρουν καὶ τὴν γινομένην θέρμην ὑπὸ | τῆς
φλεγμασίας.

32. Διὰ τί τὸ ἀριστερὸν σκέλος χαλεπώτερον τρί-
βεσθαι ὑφ' ἑαυτοῦ πολὺν χρόνον ἢ τὸ δεξιόν; ἢ ὅτι
τοῖς δεξιοῖς πονεῖν δυνάμεθα; ἐν δὲ τοῖς παρὰ φύσιν ἡ
τοῦ ἀριστεροῦ σκέλους τρῖψις ἐξεστραμμένως γίνε-
20 ται. τὰ δὲ παρὰ φύσιν | ποιούμενα χαλεπά. τῇ δὲ
ἀριστερᾷ τὰ δεξιὰ οὐθὲν ἐπίδηλον διὰ τὸ μηθετέρως
ἰσχύειν.

33. Διὰ τί ὑγιεινὸν τὸ τροφῆς μὲν ὑποστέλλεσθαι,
πονεῖν δὲ πλείω; ἢ ὅτι τοῦ νοσεῖν αἴτιον περιττώματος

16 ἄν τι πεφθῇ Bussemaker ex Barth. : ἀντιπεφθῇ codd.

---

34 Source: Thphr. *Lass.* 16. Cf. *Pr.* 3.33.

ing in the stomach) has been concocted? Or is it due to the breath, which the exertion produces from the moisture? Or is it due to the thirst, which comes from being heated during exertion? For all of these occur.

31.[34] Why are those who are fatigued and those who are consumptive[35] prone to having nocturnal emissions? Is it because in general those who are hot and moist are prone to having nocturnal emissions? For such is the nature of seed. But this occurs most in those in this condition, when the heat from sleep is added; for the body merely requires a slight influence, and this is internal and not external. Now the consumptive and those who are fatigued are in this condition; for those who are fatigued are full of hot colliquation owing to their fatigue and movement, while the consumptive (*are full of this*) owing to the discharge and to the heat coming from inflammation.

32. Why is it more difficult for the left leg to be rubbed (*with the right hand*), by oneself and for a long time, than the right? Is it because we are able to exert ourselves with our right sides? Now the rubbing of the left leg, involving as it does contortion, is among the things that are contrary to nature. And what is done contrary to nature is difficult. But (*the difficulty in rubbing*) the right side with the left hand is not obvious, because (*the left hand*) is strong on neither side.

33.[36] Why is a *reduction* of nourishment healthy, but an *increase* in exertion? Is it because a large amount of resi-

---

[35] Or "those suffering from phthisis" (φθισιῶντες).

[36] This chapter is virtually identical to *Pr.* 1.46. Possible sources for these chapters are Hp. *Flat.* 7 and the views of Herodicus of Selimbria (see Pl. *R.* 406a–c, *Phdr.* 227d).

πλῆθος; τοῦτο δὲ γίνεται ἢ διὰ τροφῆς ὑπερβολὴν ἢ
25 διὰ πόνων | ἔνδειαν.

34. Διὰ τί οὐ δεῖ πυκνοῦν τὴν σάρκα πρὸς ὑγίειαν,
ἀλλ᾽ ἀραιοῦν; ὥσπερ γὰρ πόλις ὑγιεινὴ καὶ τόπος
εὔπνους (διὸ καὶ ἡ θάλαττα ὑγιεινή), οὕτω καὶ σῶμα
τὸ εὔπνουν μᾶλλον ὑγιεινόν. δεῖ γὰρ ἢ μὴ ὑπάρχειν
30 μηθὲν περίττωμα, | ἢ τούτου ὡς τάχιστα ἀπαλλάτ-
τεσθαι, καὶ δεῖ[17] οὕτως ἔχειν τὰ σώματα ὥστε λαμ-
βάνοντα εὐθὺς ἐκκρίνειν τὴν περίττωσιν, καὶ εἶναι ἐν
κινήσει καὶ μὴ ἠρεμεῖν. τὸ μὲν γὰρ μένον σήπεται,
ὥσπερ ὕδωρ, τὸ δὲ σηπόμενον καὶ μὴ κινούμενον
νοσοποιεῖ· τὸ δὲ ἐκκρινόμενον πρὸ τοῦ διαφθαρῆναι |
35 χωρίζεται. τοῦτο οὖν πυκνουμένης μὲν τῆς σαρκὸς οὐ
γίνεται (ὥσπερεὶ γὰρ ἐμφράττονται οἱ πόροι), ἀραιουμένης δὲ συμβαίνει. διὸ καὶ οὐ δεῖ ἐν τῷ ἡλίῳ γυμνὸν
βαδίζειν· συνίσταται γὰρ ἡ σάρξ, καὶ κομιδῇ ἀποσαρ-
κοῦνται,[18] καὶ ὑγρότερον τὸ σῶμα γίνεται. τὸ μὲν γὰρ
884b ἐντὸς δὴ μένει,[19] τὸ δ᾽ ‖ ἐπιπολῆς ἀπαλλάττεται,
ὥσπερ καὶ τὰ κρέα τὰ ὀπτὰ τῶν ἑφθῶν[20] μᾶλλον. οὐδὲ
τὰ στήθη γυμνὰ ἔχοντα βαδίζειν· ἀπὸ γὰρ τῶν ἄριστα ᾠκοδομημένων ὁ ἥλιος ἀφαιρεῖ ὃ ἥκιστα δεῖται
5 ἀφαιρέσεως, ἀλλὰ μᾶλλον τὰ ἐντός. ἐκεῖθεν | μὲν οὖν
διὰ τὸ πόρρω εἶναι, ἂν μὴ μετὰ πόνου, οὐκ ἔστιν

[17] δεῖ : ἀεὶ Pr. 1.52, 865b22 et Gaza   [18] ἀποσαρκοῦν-
ται Bekker : ἀποσαρκοῦται codd. : ἀποστρακοῦται Louis

[19] δὴ μένει : δεῖ μένειν C[a] : διαμένει Forster ex Pr. 1.52,
865b31   [20] ὀπτὰ τῶν ἑφθῶν Forster ex Pr. 1.52, 865b32,
37.3, 966a28 et Gaza : ἑφθὰ τῶν ὀπτῶν codd.

due is a cause of being diseased? Now this occurs either through an excess of nourishment or through a lack of exertion.

34.[37] Why, for the sake of health, should one not thicken the flesh, but make it porous? For just as a city or a region with a good flow of air is healthy (which is why the sea too is healthy), so also a body is healthier if it has a good flow of air. For either there should be no residue, or the body should release it as quickly as possible, and the bodies should therefore be in such a condition as to excrete the residue right as they receive it, and be in motion and never at rest. For what stands still becomes putrid, like (*stagnant*) water, and what is putrid and does not move produces disease; but what is excreted is separated before any decay takes place. So if the flesh is thickened, this[38] does not occur (for the passages are, as it were, blocked), but it does happen when the flesh is porous. And this is why one should not walk naked in the sun; for then the flesh congeals and becomes very fleshy, and the body becomes moister. For what (*moisture*) is inside remains, and what is on the surface is released, just like meat that is roasted rather than boiled. Nor should one walk with the chest bare; for the sun then draws off from the best-built parts what least requires to be drawn off, rather than the inside parts. Therefore, because they are more remote, it is not possible to draw up sweat from them, except with exertion,

---

[37] This chapter is virtually identical to *Pr.* 1.52 and to part of 37.3 (966a13–34).

[38] I.e., the excretion of residue.

ἱδρῶτα ἀναγαγεῖν, ἀπὸ τούτου δὲ διὰ τὸ πρόχειρον
εἶναι ῥᾴδιον.

35. Διὰ τί κοπώδεις οἱ βραχεῖς τῶν περιπάτων; ἢ
ὅτι πολλάκις συνίστανται καὶ οὐχ ὁμαλῶς κινοῦνται
10 περὶ τὰς | καμπάς; τὸ δὲ τοιοῦτον κοπῶδες.

36. Διὰ τί ἑστηκότες ἐν τῷ ἡλίῳ μᾶλλον θερμαί-
νονται ἢ κινούμενοι, καὶ ταῦτα τῆς κινήσεως θερμαντικῆς οὔσης; ἢ οὐ πᾶσα κίνησις θερμαίνει, ἀλλ᾽ ἐνία
ψύχει, οἷον καὶ ἐπὶ τῶν τὰς χύτρας τὰς ἐψημένας
15 φυσώντων καὶ κινούντων συμβαίνει; | εἰ οὖν ἑστηκότι
μὲν προσμένει τὸ θερμόν, προσμένον δὲ μᾶλλον θερμαίνει ἢ κινούμενον (ἀεὶ γὰρ τὸ σῶμα ἴδιον ἡμῶν
ἀτμίδα τινὰ χλιαρὰν ἀφίησιν ἀφ᾽ ἑαυτοῦ, ἢ θερμαίνει
τὸν ἐγγὺς ἀέρα ὥσπερ δαλὸς παρών), ἠρεμούντων μὲν
ἡμῶν θερμὸς γίνεται ὁ περιέχων ἡμᾶς ἀὴρ διὰ τὰ
20 εἰρημένα, | κινουμένων δὲ πνεῦμα γίνεται, ὃ καταψύχει
ἡμᾶς· πᾶν γὰρ πνεῦμα ψυχρόν ἐστιν.

37. Διὰ τί οἱ ἐπὶ τῶν ἵππων ὀχούμενοι, ὅσῳ ἂν
θᾶττον θέῃ ὁ ἵππος, τοσούτῳ μᾶλλον δακρύουσι τὰ
ὄμματα, καὶ οἱ πεζοί, ὅσῳ ἂν μᾶλλον τρέχωσιν; πό-
25 τερον διὰ τὸ ψυχρὸν | εἶναι τὸν προσπίπτοντα ἀέρα; τὸ
γὰρ ψῦχος δακρύειν ποιεῖ· συστέλλον γὰρ καὶ πυκνοῦν τὴν σάρκα ἐκκαθαίρει τὸ ὑγρόν. ἢ διὰ τοὐναντίον; τὸ γὰρ θερμὸν ποιεῖ ἱδρῶτας, τὸ δὲ δάκρυον
ἱδρώς τίς ἐστι. διὸ καὶ γίνονται ὑπὸ θερμασίας ἄμφω
30 ταῦτα, καὶ ἁλυκά ἐστιν ὁμοίως. ἡ δὲ κίνησις | θερ-
μότητα ποιεῖ. ἢ διὰ τὴν ὑπὸ τοῦ ἀέρος πληγήν; ὡς
γὰρ οἱ ἄνεμοι ταράττουσιν οἱ ἐξ ἐναντίας τὰ ὄμματα,

but from the outside parts it is easy, because they are close at hand.

35.[39] Why are short walks fatiguing? Is it because (*the walkers*) come to a standstill often and they move around their joints irregularly? And this is fatiguing.

36.[40] Why does one become hotter when standing in the sun than when moving, and this when movement is heat-producing? Or is it that not every movement produces heat, but some produce cooling, as occurs, for instance, in the case of blowing upon and thus creating movement over a pot on the boil? Therefore, if heat remains in one who is standing, and remaining (*at a standstill*) produces more heat than moving (for our own body is always giving off warm steam by itself, which heats the neighboring air as if a torch were present), when we are at rest the air surrounding us becomes hot for the reasons given, whereas when we move a wind is generated, which cools us; for every wind is cold.

37.[41] Why is it that for those who ride horses, the faster the horse runs the more the rider's eyes shed tears, and for those on foot, the faster *they* run? Is it because the air that strikes them is cold? For the cold causes tears to flow; and drawing together and thickening the flesh cleans out the moisture. Or is it for the contrary reason? For heat produces sweat, and the tear is a kind of sweat. And this is why both come from heat, and similarly both are salty. But movement produces heat. Or is it due to the impact of the air? For as the winds from an opposite direction disturb

39 Cf. *Pr.* 5.12 and Thphr. *Lass.* 14–15.
40 Cf. Thphr. *Ign.* 36, *Pr.* 24.12 and 38.6.
41 *Pr.* 5.13.

οὕτω καὶ ὁ ἀὴρ ὁ προσπίπτων, ὅσῳ ἂν θᾶττον ἐλαύνῃ
ἢ αὐτὸς τρέχῃ, τοσούτῳ μᾶλλον ποιεῖ πληγὴν μαλακήν, δι' ἣν γίνεται δακρύειν, ἀραιουμένων τῶν τοῦ
35 ὀφθαλμοῦ πόρων ὑπὸ τῆς | πληγῆς· πᾶσα γὰρ πληγὴ
διαιρετικόν ἐστιν ἢ θλαστικόν.

38. Διὰ τί δεῖ τοὺς μὲν θερινοὺς κόπους λουτρῷ
ἰᾶσθαι, τοὺς δὲ χειμερινοὺς ἀλείμματι; ἢ τούτους μὲν
διὰ τὰς φρίκας καὶ τὰς γινομένας μεταβολὰς θερμῷ
δεῖ λύειν, ὃ ποιήσει ἀλεαίνειν (τὸ δὲ ἔλαιον θερμόν); ἐν
885a δὲ τῷ θέρει καθυγραίνειν· ‖ ἡ γὰρ ὥρα ξηρά, καὶ οὐ
γίνονται φρῖκαι διὰ τὴν ἀλέαν. ὀλιγοσιτία δὲ καὶ
κωθωνισμὸς θέρους, τὸ μὲν ὅλως, τὸ δὲ μᾶλλον, ὁ μὲν
πότος θέρους ὅλως διὰ τὴν ξηρότητα, ἡ δὲ ὀλιγοσιτία
5 κοινὸν μέν, μᾶλλον δὲ θέρους· ἐκθερμαίνεται | γὰρ
μᾶλλον διὰ τὴν ὥραν ὑπὸ τῶν σιτίων.

39. Διὰ τί οἱ θένοντες εὐτόνως μάλιστα λαμβάνουσι σπάσματα, ὅταν τις θέουσιν αὐτοῖς ὑποστῇ; ἢ ὅτι
ταῦτα μάλιστα διασπᾶται, ἃ εἰς τοὐναντίον τε καὶ
ἰσχυρῶς ἕλκεται καὶ κινεῖται; ὅταν οὖν θέοντος καὶ
10 σφοδρῶς ὠθουμένων τῶν | μορίων εἰς τὸ πρόσθεν
ὑποστῇ τις, συμβαίνει ἅμα ἀντισπᾶν εἰς τοὐναντίον,
ἔτι φερομένων εἰς τοὔμπροσθεν, ὥστε ἡ σπάσις τοσούτῳ ἰσχυροτέρα γίνεται, ὅσῳ ἂν θέωσι σφοδρότερον.

40. Διὰ τί τῶν περιπάτων οἱ κατὰ τὰς ὁδοὺς ἀκο-
15 πώτεροί | εἰσιν, οἱ ἀνώμαλοι τῶν εὐθέων; ἢ διὰ τὸ τὴν

---

42 This chapter is virtually identical to *Pr.* 1.39. Source: Thphr.
Lass. 17.   43 Or "sprains" or "spasms."

the eyes, so the air strikes the faster one rides or runs, and all the more produces a soft blow, because of which tears flow, as the passages of the eye become porous because of the blow; for every blow produces either splitting or bruising.

38.[42] Why should summer fatigue be treated by baths, but winter fatigue by anointing? Is it that the latter, because of shivering and the changes that occur, must be released by means of heat, which produces warming (and oil is hot)? But in the summer, it is necessary to moisten; for the season is dry, and shivering does not occur because of the warmth. Now little food and ample liquids are appropriate for summer; the former is generally the case, the latter more so (*in the summer*). Drinking (*a lot*) should generally be the case in summer because of the dryness, whereas little food should be common (*to all seasons*), but more so in summer: for one is heated by food in accordance with the season.

39. Why do those who are running vigorously most of all experience muscle tears[43] when someone impedes them in the course of their run? Is it because things tear apart most which are powerfully pulled and moved in the opposite direction? So when someone impedes one who is running and whose parts are being thrust forward intensely, there is at the same time a countertear in the opposite direction, while his parts are still traveling forward, so that the tear is more powerful the more intensely he is running.

40.[44] Why is walking on an uneven road less fatiguing than on a straight one? Is it because an upright position is

44 Sources: Thphr. *Lass*. 11–12, 14–15

φορὰν ὀρθὴν εἶναι κατὰ φύσιν παντὶ τῷ σώματι; οἱ δ᾽
ἐν τοῖς ὁμαλοῖς τῶν ἀνωμάλων κοπιωδέστεροι· τοῖς
γὰρ αὐτοῖς μέρεσι τοὺς πόνους παρέχουσιν, οἱ δ᾽ ἐν
τοῖς ἀνωμάλοις διαμερίζουσι μᾶλλον εἰς ἅπαν τὸ
20 σῶμα. αἱ δὲ ἀλέαι μᾶλλον ἰσχνοῦσι | τῶν ἐν τοῖς
ψύχεσιν· τοῖς γὰρ ἔξω μέρεσι πλείονα τὸν πόνον
παρέχονται. διὸ καὶ τοὺς ἱδρῶτας ἐμποιοῦντες ἰσχναί-
νουσιν. οἱ δ᾽ ἐν τοῖς ψύχεσι στιφροτέραν τὴν σάρκα
ποιοῦσι καὶ τῶν σιτίων ἐπιθυμητικωτέρους· τοῖς γὰρ
ἔσω μέρεσι τὴν αὔξησιν τοῦ θερμοῦ ποιοῦνται, καὶ
25 δυσκινήτων γινομένων | ὑπὸ τοῦ ψύχους τὸν μὲν ἔσω
τόπον καθαίρουσι, τὴν θερμασίαν αὐξάνοντες ἐν αὐτῷ, τὴν δὲ σάρκα στερεὰν ποιοῦσιν, οὐ δυνάμενοι
κρατεῖν διὰ πάσης αὐτῆς. ὁμοίως οἱ ἀνάντεις τῶν
κατάντων ἐπιπονώτεροι καὶ ἰσχναντικώτεροι. οἱ μὲν
γὰρ ἀνάντεις τὴν ὀσφὺν μάλιστα ποιοῦσι πονεῖν, οἱ
30 δὲ κατάντεις | τοὺς μηρούς· τοῖς γὰρ μηροῖς τὸ βάρος
πᾶν ἐμπῖπτον ⟨κόπους⟩[21] εἴωθε παρέχειν. ἄνω γὰρ
παρὰ φύσιν [ὑπὸ τοῦ θερμοῦ][22] βίᾳ φερόμενος ἐκθερμαίνει. διὸ τούς τε ἱδρῶτας ἐμποιοῦσι, καὶ τὸ πνεῦμα
μετεωρίζοντες ἰσχναίνουσι, καὶ τὴν ὀσφὺν ὀδυνῶσιν·
35 τὰ γὰρ σκέλη χαλεπῶς ἀναγόμενα | τὴν ὀσφὺν κάμ-
πτουσί τε καὶ ἀνασπῶσιν, ὑφ᾽ ὧν ἀναγκάζονται μάλιστα πονεῖν. οἱ δ᾽ ἐν ἀντιτύποις περίπατοι τοῖς τε μυσὶ
καὶ τοῖς τεταμένοις τῶν σκελῶν παρέχουσι κόπους·
συντάσεις γὰρ ἐμποιοῦσι τοῖς νεύροις καὶ τοῖς μυσί,
885b βιαίας ‖ γενομένης τῆς ἀπερείσεως αὐτοῖς. οἱ δ᾽ ἐν
τοῖς μαλακοῖς τοῖς ἄρθροις κοπιώδεις εἰσίν· τῶν γὰρ

natural to every body? Now walking on level ground is
more fatiguing than on uneven ground; for (*those walking
on level ground*) receive stress in the same parts, whereas
those walking on uneven ground distribute (*the stress*)
over the whole body. And walking in warm weather causes
thinness more than in cold; for it causes a greater amount
of stress in the outer parts. And this is why the production of sweat causes thinness. But walking in cold weather
makes the flesh harder and produces a greater desire for
food; for it produces an increase of heat in the inner parts,
and since they become less liable to be affected by the
cold, it cleanses the inner region by increasing the heat
therein, while it makes the flesh firm because it cannot
master the whole of it. In the same way walking uphill is
more stressful and tends to cause thinness. For walking
uphill puts the greatest stress on the loins, and downhill on
the thighs; for all the weight falling on the thighs usually
produces ⟨fatigue⟩. For when (*the thigh*) is carried upward by force [by the heat], contrary to nature, it generates
heat. This is why walking uphill produces sweat, and the
breath rising causes thinness, and there is pain in the loins;
for the legs, being raised with difficulty, bend and draw up
the loin, as a result of which they necessarily feel great
stress. Now walking on resistant ground produces fatigue
in the muscles and tendons of the legs; for it causes tension
in the sinews and muscles, when the pressure on them is
forced. But walking on soft ground is also fatiguing to the

---

21 ⟨κόπους⟩ Sylburg
22 [ὑπὸ τοῦ θερμοῦ] Forster

ἄρθρων πυκνὰς τὰς κάμψεις ποιοῦσιν, ἄτε ἐνδιδούσης
τῆς βάσεως. τὸ δ' αὐτό ἐστι πρόβλημα. |

5   41. Διὰ τί πρὸς τὰ σιμὰ χαλεπῶς βαδίζομεν; ἢ
διότι πᾶσα πορεία ἐξ ἄρσεως καὶ θέσεως συντελεῖται;
τὸ μὲν οὖν ἆραι παρὰ φύσιν, τὸ δὲ θεῖναι κατὰ φύσιν,
τὸ δὲ προθεῖναι²³ μεσότης· ἐν δὲ τῷ πρὸς τὰ σιμὰ
βαδίζειν πολὺ τὸ παρὰ φύσιν. |

10   42. Διὰ τί οἱ ἀφ' ἵππων ἧττον πίπτουσιν; ἢ διὰ τὸ
φοβεῖσθαι φυλάττονται μᾶλλον;²⁴

²³ προθεῖναι B Aᵐ D : προσθεῖναι cett. codd.
²⁴ διὰ τί—μᾶλλον om. Cᵃ

joints; for it produces frequent bending of the joints, as the surface gives way. And this is the same problem.

41. Why do we walk up a steep hill with difficulty? Is it because all progression[45] is accomplished by raising and lowering (*the feet*)? Now raising them is contrary to nature, whereas lowering them is according to nature, and putting them forward is a mean between the two; but in walking up a steep hill, the contrary to nature is more frequent.

42. Why do those on horseback fall less often? Are they more careful because they are afraid?

[45] "Progression" (πορεία) likely refers to both walking and running.

BOOK VI

INTRODUCTION

At just over half a Bekker page, Book 6 is the third shortest in the *Problems*. Its eight chapters[1] cover sitting, lying down (with body bent or straight, and on the right side or the left), stretching the limbs, dizziness from standing, and numbness. As for sources, chs. 3 and 5 may be responding to medical writings and chs. 4 and 6 to works of Theophrastus.

---

[1] I follow Louis in including the eighth chapter, which is virtually identical to *Pr.* 6.1. It is not found in some mss., and was omitted by Bekker.

ΟΣΑ ΕΚ ΤΟΥ ΠΩΣ ΚΕΙΣΘΑΙ
ΚΑΙ ΕΣΧΗΜΑΤΙΣΘΑΙ
ΣΥΜΒΑΙΝΕΙ

885b
15 1. Διὰ τί ἡ καθέδρα τοὺς μὲν παχύνει τῶν ἀνθρώ
πων, τοὺς δὲ ἰσχναίνει; πότερον[1] αἱ ἕξεις διαφέρουσιν;
οἱ μὲν γὰρ θερμοί εἰσιν, οἱ δὲ ψυχροί. οἱ μὲν οὖν
θερμοὶ παχύνονται (κρατεῖ γὰρ τὸ σῶμα τῆς τροφῆς
διὰ τὴν θερμασίαν)· οἱ δὲ ἐψυγμένοι, διὰ τὸ δεῖσθαι
20 ἐπεισάκτου θερμότητος καὶ τοῦτο | πάσχειν μάλιστα
τὸ σῶμα ὑπὸ τῶν κινήσεων, οὐ δύνανται πέττειν
ἠρεμοῦντες. ἢ ὅτι οἱ μὲν περιττωματικοί εἰσι, καὶ
δέονται κινήσεως ἢ ἀναλώσει ταῦτα, οἱ δὲ οὔ;

2. Διὰ τί δεῖ ποιεῖν διάτασιν τῶν μερῶν, ὃ ποιεῖ ὁ
γυμναζόμενος; ἢ ὅτι δεῖ τῷ οἰκείῳ πνεύματι καθαί
25 ρεσθαι τοὺς | πόρους;

3. Διὰ τί συγκεκαμμένον βέλτιον κατακεῖσθαι, καὶ
πολλοί γε παραγγέλλουσι τοῦτο καὶ τῶν ἰατρῶν; ἢ ὅτι
ἀλεαίνουσα ἡ κοιλία θᾶττον πέττει; οὕτω δὲ καὶ[2] ἀλε

[1] post πότερον add. ὅτι Sylburg
[2] om. καὶ Bekker

PROBLEMS RESULTING FROM THE MANNER OF LYING DOWN AND ASSUMING A POSITION

1.[1] Why does sitting down[2] make some people fat, whereas others it makes thin? Do their constitutions differ? For some are hot, others cold. So the hot ones become fat[3] (for the body masters the nourishment by means of heat); but those who are cold, because they need external heat and the body derives this mostly from movement, cannot concoct their nourishment when they are at rest. Or is it because the former are full of residues, and need movement to expend them, whereas the latter do not?

2. Why should one stretch the parts of the body, as the person who exercises does? Is it because the passages should be cleansed by the natural breath?

3.[4] Why is it better to lie down with the body bent, and why do many physicians advise this? Is it because the stomach concocts more quickly when it is warm? And in this po-

---

[1] Cf. *Pr.* 6.8.

[2] Marenghi[3] may be closer to the author's meaning, rendering ἡ καθέδρα "*la vita sedentaria.*"

[3] Either by sitting or regardless of whether they sit.

[4] Sources: Hp. *Prog.* 3 and Diocl. fr. 185 [8] (v.d. Eijk).

αἴνει μᾶλλον. ἔτι δεῖ τοῖς πνεύμασι τόπον διδόναι εἰς
30 ὃν ἀπερείσονται· οὕτω γὰρ | ἥκιστα λυπήσουσιν αἱ
φῦσαι. διὰ τοῦτο γὰρ καὶ ἰξίαι καὶ τὰ ἄλλα ἀποστή-
ματα ὑγιεινόν, ὅτι ἔχουσι κοιλίας εἰς ἃς ἀποδέχονται
τὰ πνεύματα. ἐκτεταμένου μὲν οὖν οὐ γίνεται κοιλία
(ἅπαντα γὰρ τὸν τόπον τὰ σπλάγχνα κατέχει), συγ-
καμφθέντος δὲ γίνεται. |

35   4. Διὰ τί ἀνισταμένοις ἴλιγγος μᾶλλον γίνεται ἢ
καθιζάνουσιν; ἢ διότι ἠρεμοῦσι τὸ ὑγρὸν εἰς ἓν μόριον
ἀθρόον ἀποκλίνει; διὸ καὶ τὰ ὠμὰ ᾠὰ οὐ δύναται
δινεῖσθαι, ἀλλὰ καταπίπτει. κινούμενον δὲ τὸ ὑγρὸν
886a ὁμοίως ἔχει. ἀνίστανται μὲν || οὖν ἠρεμήσαντες, ὅτε
οὕτως διάκεινται· καθιζάνουσι δὲ ⟨ἐν⟩³ κινήσει γενόμενοι, ὅτε ὁμαλῶς ἔχει τὸ ὑγρὸν καὶ ἐσκέδασται.

     5. Διὰ τί ἐπὶ τὰ δεξιὰ κατακειμένοις μᾶλλον ἐπέρ-
χεται ὕπνος; πότερον ὅτι ἐναντίως ἔχοντες ἐγρηγό-
5 ρασιν καὶ καθεύδουσιν; | ἐπεὶ οὖν ἐγρηγορότες ἐπὶ τὰ
ἀριστερὰ κατάκεινται, τοὐναντίον ἔσται ἐπ' ἄλλης
ἀρχῆς καὶ τῆς ἐναντίας. ἢ ὅτι ἀκινησία ὁ ὕπνος; τὰ⁴
οὖν κινητικὰ μέρη δεῖ ἠρεμεῖν, τὰ δὲ δεξιὰ κινητικά.
οὕτω δὲ κατακειμένων, οἷον δέδεται ἀρχή τις ἐπεγερ-
τική. |

10   6. Διὰ τί ναρκῶσιν; καὶ διὰ τί χεῖρας καὶ πόδας
μᾶλλον; ἢ ὅτι κατάψυξίς ἐστιν ἡ νάρκη;⁵ διὰ στέρησιν
γὰρ αἵματος γίνεται καὶ μετάστασιν. ἀσαρκότατα δὲ

---

³ ⟨ἐν⟩ Aldine (cf. Barth.) : om. codd.   ⁴ τὰ α δ : τὰ
μὲν cett. codd.   ⁵ νάρκη : νάρκωσις β Xᵃ aᵐ p

sition it produces more warmth. Further, one should give the breath a place in which it can settle; for in this way the winds will cause less pain. For this is why varicocele and the other abscesses restore health, because they have hollows in which they receive breath. Therefore, when one lies stretched out a hollow does not form (for the internal organs occupy all the space), but when the body is bent a hollow does form.

4.[5] Why does dizziness come to those who stand more than to those who sit? Is it because when they are at rest the moisture inclines all together to one part? And this is why raw eggs cannot be spun, but fall over. Now moisture that is moved is in the same state. So people stand up, after having been at rest, when they are in this condition; but they sit down, after having been in motion, when the moisture is even and spread out.

5.[6] Why does sleep come more to those lying on the right side? Is it because being awake and being asleep are opposite conditions? Therefore, since people when awake lie on their left side, the opposite will be the case owing to the opposite principle. Or is it because sleep implies a lack of movement? So the motive parts need to rest, and the parts on the right are motive. And when one is lying in this way, a waking principle is, as it were, bound.

6.[7] Why do people feel numb? And why more in the hands and feet? Is it because numbness implies cooling? For it occurs owing to the loss and displacement of blood.

[5] Source: Thphr. *Vert.* 13; cf. [Arist./Alex.] *Sup.Pr.* 2.49.
[6] Source: Diocl. fr. 185 [8] (v.d. Eijk).
[7] Cf. *Pr.* 2.15 and Thphr. fr. 346 (FHSG).

ταῦτα καὶ νευρωδέστατα, μάλιστα δὲ οἱ πόδες. ὥστε προοδοποιεῖται ὑπὸ τῆς φύσεως πρὸς τὸ καταψύχεσθαι ταχέως. |

15   7. Διὰ τί κατακείμεθα μὲν ἐπὶ τὰ ἀριστερὰ ἡδέως, καθεύδομεν δὲ ἐπὶ τὰ δεξιὰ μᾶλλον; πότερον ὅτι ἀποστραφέντες πρὸς τὸ φῶς οὐ βλέπομεν; ἐν γὰρ τῷ σκότει θᾶττον ὕπνος λαμβάνει. ἢ διότι ἐγρηγόραμεν κατακείμενοι ἐπὶ τοῖς ἀριστεροῖς, καὶ αἱ χρήσεις ἡμῖν
20   οὕτω πρόχειροι, ὥστε πρὸς τὸ | ἐναντίον <τὸ ἐναντίον>[6] σχῆμα πρὸ ἔργου; παρακαλεῖ δὲ ἕκαστον πρὸς[7] τὸ ἔργον τὸ σχῆμα μᾶλλον.

8. Διὰ τί αἱ καθέδραι τινὰς μὲν παχύνουσι, τινὰς δὲ ἰσχναίουσιν; ἢ διὰ τὰς ἕξεις τὰς τοῦ σώματος; οἱ μὲν γὰρ θερμότεροι παχύνονται· κρατεῖ γὰρ τὸ σῶμα τῆς τροφῆς διὰ τὴν θερμότητα οὐκ ἀφαιρουμένην·[8] οἱ δὲ ἐψυγμένοι, διὰ τὸ δεῖσθαι ἐπεισάκτου θερμότητος, οὐ δύνανται πέττειν τὰς τροφὰς ἠρεμοῦντες.[9]

---

[6] <τὸ ἐναντίον> Bussemaker ex Gaza
[7] fort. πρὸς om.
[8] ἀφαιρουμένην Forster : ἀφαιρούμενον codd.
[9] διὰ τί—ἠρεμοῦντες a β Xᵃ aᵐ Barth. : om. cett. codd.

And these parts are the least fleshy and the most sinewy, and especially the feet. So they are predisposed by nature to be cooled quickly.

7. Why do we lie pleasantly on our left side, but sleep better on our right? Is it because by turning over we do not look toward the light? For in the dark, sleep takes over more quickly. Or is it because we stay awake lying on our left side, and the things we do in this position are easy, so that with a view to the opposite, <the opposite> position is functional? Each position tends to call for what is functional.[8]

8.[9] Why does sitting down make some people fat, while others it makes thin? Is it because of the constitutions of their bodies? For those who are hotter grow fat, for the body masters the nourishment by means of heat, which is not lost; but those who are cold, because they need external heat, cannot concoct their nourishment when they are at rest.

[8] There may be a problem with the text here. One possible solution is to omit πρὸς and translate: "Each function tends to call for the position."

[9] Cf. *Pr* 6.1. Bekker did not include this chapter, no doubt because it is omitted in some mss. and is a condensed version of ch. 1.

BOOK VII

INTRODUCTION

The relatively brief seventh book deals with conceptual problems arising from the phenomenon of *sympathy*, to transliterate the key word from the title. The noun συμπάθεια, however, does not appear elsewhere in the *corpus Aristotelicum*—not even in the body of *Pr.* 7. The topic of this book is more accurately described as *the contagious*, broadly understood. Chs. 4 and 8 deal with infectious disease; but far more attention is given to the mentally contagious, so to speak, by which I mean both involuntary imitation and feelings of sympathy. Chs. 1–3 and 6 deal with yawning in response to the yawning of others, and urinating in response to being near water or perceiving others urinating. Ch. 5 discusses shuddering in response to perceiving unpleasant actions, and ch. 7 mental suffering in response to seeing others suffering physically.[1]

There are no clearly identifiable sources for these chapters, though many of the ten words that appear in *Pr.* 7 but

---

[1] Ch. 9, which is identical to *Pr.* 1.38, does not belong in *Pr.* 7. It asks "Why do purslane and salt check bleeding gums?" and was probably included here because of the claim that "there is an affinity" between purslane and bleeding gums, as both are said to be acidic.

nowhere else in the *corpus Aristotelicum* are technical medical terms,[2] which suggests that the author may be raising questions about topics discussed in medical treatises now lost.

[2] See Louis, vol. 1, p. 121.

ΟΣΑ ΕΚ ΣΥΜΠΑΘΕΙΑΣ

1. Διὰ τί τοῖς χασμωμένοις ἀντιχασμῶνται ὡς ἐπὶ τὸ | πολύ; ἢ διότι, ἐὰν ἀναμνησθῶσιν ὀργῶντες, ἐνεργοῦσιν, μάλιστα δὲ τὰ εὐκίνητα, οἷον οὐροῦσιν; ἡ δὲ χάσμη πνεῦμα καὶ ὑγροῦ κίνησίς ἐστιν. πρόχειρον οὖν, ἐὰν μόνον νοήσῃ· ἔστι γὰρ πλησίον.

2. Διὰ τί, ἐὰν μέν τινα ἴδωμεν τὴν χεῖρα ἐκτείνοντα ἢ | τὸν πόδα ἢ ἄλλο τι τῶν τοιούτων, οὐκ ἀντιποιοῦμεν τὸ αὐτό, ἐὰν δὲ χασμώμενον, ἀντιχασμώμεθα; ἢ οὐδὲ τοῦτο ἀεί, ἀλλ' ἐὰν ὀργῶν τύχῃ τὸ σῶμα καὶ οὕτω διακείμενον ὥστε τὸ ὑγρὸν ἀναθερμαίνεσθαι; τότε γὰρ ἡ μνήμη τὴν κίνησιν ποιεῖ, ὥσπερ καὶ πρὸς ἀφροδίσια καὶ ἐδωδήν· τὸ γὰρ ποιῆσαν | μνήμην εἶναι τὸ ἔχον ὁρμὴν πρὸς τὸ φαντασθὲν πάθος.

3. Διὰ τί, ἐπειδὰν πρὸς τὸ πῦρ στῶμεν, οὐρητιῶμεν, καὶ ἐὰν πρὸς ὕδωρ, οἷον ἐὰν πρὸς ποταμόν, οὐροῦσιν; ἢ ὅτι τὸ πᾶν ‖ ὕδωρ ὑπόμνησιν δίδωσιν τῆς ἐν τῷ σώματι ὑγρότητος, καὶ ἐκκαλεῖται τὸ προσιόν· αὐτὸ δὲ τὸ πῦρ διαχαλᾷ τὸ πεπηγὸς ἐν τῷ σώματι, ὥσπερ ὁ ἥλιος τὴν χιόνα.

PROBLEMS ARISING
FROM SYMPATHY

1.[1] Why, in response to others yawning, do people usually yawn in return? Is it because, if they are reminded of something when they feel an urge, they act on it, especially with what is easily moved, for instance urinating? Now yawning is a breath and a movement of moisture. So it is always at hand, if only one thinks of it; for it is nearby.

2. Why, if we see someone stretching out a hand or a foot or any other such thing, we do not do the same thing in return, but if we see someone yawning, we yawn in return? Or do we not always do this, but only if the body happens to feel an urge and is in such a condition that its moisture is heated? For then memory produces movement, just as it does with respect to sexual intercourse and eating; for that which causes a memory to exist is that which provides an impulse toward the imagined condition.

3.[2] Why, when we stand near the fire, do we desire to urinate, and if we stand near water, for instance a river, we *do* urinate? Is it because all water reminds us of the moisture in the body, and the nearby (*water*) calls out for it? Further, the fire itself dissolves what is solidified in the body, just as the sun does the snow.

[1] Cf. *Pr.* 7.2 and 6.   [2] Gell. 19.4 quotes from this chapter and attributes it to Aristotle.

4. Διὰ τί ἀπὸ μὲν νόσων ἐνίων νοσοῦσιν οἱ πλη-
5 σιάζοντες, | ἀπὸ δὲ ὑγιείας οὐδεὶς ὑγιάζεται; ἢ ὅτι ἡ
μὲν νόσος κίνησις, ἡ δὲ ὑγίεια ἠρεμία; ἡ μὲν οὖν κινεῖ,
ἡ δ' οὐθέν. ἢ διότι τὸ μὲν ἄκοντι, τὸ δ' ἑκόντι γίνεται;
καὶ ἄρα τὰ ἀκούσια τῶν ἑκουσίων καὶ τῶν ἐκ προνοίας
διαφέρει.

5. Διὰ τί τῶν μὲν διὰ τῆς ἀκοῆς λυπηρῶν ἔνια
10 φρίττειν | ἡμᾶς ποιεῖ, οἷον πρίων ἀκονώμενος καὶ
κίσηρις τεμνομένη καὶ λίθος ἀλούμενος, τὰ δὲ διὰ τῆς
ὄψεως σημεῖα τῶν παθῶν αὐτὰ ἡμῖν τὰ πάθη ἐμποιεῖ;
αἱμωδιῶμέν τε γὰρ τοὺς ὀξὺ ὁρῶντες ἐσθίοντας, καὶ
τοὺς ἀπαγχομένους ἔνιοι ὁρῶντες ἐκψύχουσιν. ἢ διότι
15 φωνὴ μὲν πᾶσα καὶ ψόφος πνεῦμά[1] | ἐστιν; τοῦτο δὲ
εἰσδυόμενον ἡμῖν πέφυκε κινεῖν. κινήσει δὲ μᾶλλον ἢ
διὰ μέγεθος ἢ διὰ πληγὴν σφοδροτέραν, ποιοῦν ἢ
ἀλλοιοῦν τι τῶν ἐν ἡμῖν. τὰ μὲν οὖν μεγάλα καὶ λεῖα
πνεύματα τὸν τῆς αἰσθήσεως τόπον αὐτὸν[2] κινεῖ, διὸ
καὶ ἡδύνει τὰ τοιαῦτα· τὰ δὲ τραχέα, πληγὴν ποιοῦντα
20 σφοδράν, | σείει τε τὸν τόπον καὶ πόρρω διαδίδωσιν
τῇ τῆς πληγῆς δυνάμει. διαδίδωσι δὲ καὶ τὰ ψυχρὰ
πόρρω· δύναμις γάρ τίς ἐστιν ἡ ψυχρότης. αὕτη μὲν
οὖν ὅτι φρίττειν ποιεῖ, εἴρηται. τὰ δὲ τραχέα τῷ
πληγὴν ποιεῖν πυκνήν, προσκόπτοντα τῇ ἀρχῇ τῶν
25 τριχῶν, ἀπωθεῖ αὐτὴν εἰς τοὐναντίον· | ἀπωθουμένης
δὲ, ἀνάγκη τὴν κορυφὴν τῆς τριχὸς ἀνάπαλιν γίνε-

---

[1] ante πνεῦμα add. ἔν γ
[2] τόπον αὐτὸν Yᵃ Ap : τόπον τὸν αὐτὸν cett. codd.

4.[3] Why do those who get too close become infected by certain diseases, whereas no one becomes healthy from contact with health? Is it because disease is motion, whereas health is rest? Therefore, the one moves, but the other does not. Or is it because the one occurs involuntarily, the other voluntarily? And what is involuntary differs from what is voluntary and what is due to forethought.

5.[4] Why do some things painful to hear make us shudder[5]—for instance, sharpening a saw, cutting a pumice stone, and grinding a stone—but the visual signs of their effects (on others) produce those very effects in us? For we clench our teeth when we see people eating something bitter, and some faint when they see people strangled. Is it because every voice and sound is a breath? And entering into us, this naturally produces movement. And this will move even more either because of its quantity or because of a violent blow, producing or altering something in us. Therefore, breaths that are great in quantity yet soft move the region of sensation itself, and this is why they are such as to cause pleasure; but breaths that are rough, producing a violent blow, shake this region and spread farther by the power of the blow. Now cold things also spread farther; for coldness is a certain power. That this makes us shudder has already been said. But breaths that are rough, by repeatedly producing blows that strike the source of the hair, thrust it in the opposite direction; and when this thrust occurs, the ends of the hair must necessarily go the wrong

[3] Cf. *Pr.* 7.8 and 29.10.
[4] Cf. *Pr.* 7.7 and 35.3. Source: Hp. *Hum.* 9.
[5] The same word ($\phi\rho i\tau\tau\epsilon\iota\nu$) can also mean "shiver."

σθαι, διὸ συμβαίνει ἵστασθαι αὐτάς· πᾶσαι γὰρ νε-
νεύκασι κάτω. ἡ δὲ φορὰ τοῦ διὰ τῆς ἀκοῆς πνεύματος
εἰς τὸ σῶμα ἄνωθεν κάτω ἐστίν. ὄντων οὖν τραχέων
τῶν εἰρημένων ψόφων, ἡ φρίκη γίνοιτ᾽ ἂν διὰ τὰ
30 εἰρημένα. γίνονται δ᾽ | αὗται μᾶλλον τῷ ἄλλῳ σώματι
ἢ ἐν τῇ κεφαλῇ, διὰ τὸ τὰς ἐνταῦθα τρίχας ἀσθενε-
στέρας εἶναι, καὶ τὸ πάθος ἀσθενές. τῆς μὲν οὖν
ἀκοῆς οὔσης ἀμβλυτέρας αἰσθήσεως ἢ τῆς ὄψεως,
ἐπιπόλαια καὶ τὰ πάθη γίνεται ἀπ᾽ αὐτῆς· ἡ δὲ φρίκη
τοιοῦτον, διὸ καὶ ἀπὸ πολλῶν καὶ ἀνομοίων γίνεται. |
35 τῆς δὲ ὄψεως ἐναργεστάτης οὔσης αἰσθήσεως, ἀνάλογον καὶ τὰ συμβαίνοντα γίνεται ἀπ᾽ αὐτῆς· διὸ ταῦτα
μὲν τὰ ἀπὸ τῆς ἀληθείας πάθη συμβαίνει γίνεσθαι
887a ἀπ᾽ αὐτῆς, ἐλαφρότερα ‖ δὲ τῆς ἀληθείας. ἀπὸ δὲ τῆς
ἀκοῆς αὐτὰ μὲν οὔ, τὴν δ᾽ ἀπ᾽ αὐτῶν προσδοκίαν
φρίττομεν· ἀλγεινοῦ γὰρ κακοῦ προσδοκία ἐστίν.

6. Διὰ τί χασμησαμένοις ἀντιχασμῶνται, καὶ ὅταν |
5 οὐροῦντα ἴδωσιν, οὐροῦσι, καὶ μάλιστα τὰ ὑποζύγια;
ἢ διὰ τὴν μνήμην; ὅταν γὰρ μνησθῇ, κινεῖται τοῦτο τὸ
μέρος. τοῖς μὲν οὖν ἀνθρώποις, διὰ τὸ εὐαισθητοτέ-
ροις³ εἶναι, ἰδοῦσιν εὐθὺς συμβαίνει καὶ κινεῖσθαι καὶ
ἀναμιμνήσκεσθαι· τοῖς δὲ ὑποζυγίοις οὐκ αὐταρκές τὸ
10 ἰδεῖν, ἀλλὰ προσδέονται καὶ ἄλλης | αἰσθήσεως· διὸ
καὶ ὀσφρανθέντα, ὅτι εὐκινητοτέρα αὕτη ἡ αἴσθησις
τοῖς ἄνευ λόγου. καὶ διὰ τοῦτο εἰς τὸν αὐτὸν τόπον
ἅπαντα οὐρεῖ, οὗ ἂν τὸ πρῶτον οὐρήσῃ. τότε γὰρ

---

³ εὐαισθητοτέροις γ : εὐαισθητοτέρους α β δ

234

way, and so the hair stands upright; for it had all inclined downward. Now the direction the breath travels by hearing into the body is downward from above. Therefore, as the aforementioned sounds are rough, the shuddering must be due to what has been said. And these have more effect on the rest of the body than on the head, because the hair there is weaker and so the effect is weak. Now, as hearing is a duller perception than sight, the effects arising from it are also on the surface; shuddering is such an effect, and this is why it arises from many different causes. But as sight is the sharpest of the senses, the effects produced by it are also correspondingly (*great*); which is why the very effects are produced by it as occur in reality, but slighter than in reality. This is not the case from hearing, however; instead, we shudder at the expectation that comes from them, for it is an expectation of a grievous ill.

6.[6] Why, in response to yawning, do they[7] yawn in return, and when they see urinating, they urinate, and especially yoke animals? Is it due to memory? For when one remembers, the relevant part is moved. In humans, therefore, due to their senses being better, when they see they are straightaway moved and recollect; but in yoke animals, seeing is not sufficient, but they need another sense as well; and this is why (*they respond in this way*) having smelled, because this sense is more easily moved in animals that lack reason. And because of this, they all urinate at the same place, where the first one urinated. For

[6] Cf. *Pr.* 7.1 and 2, and [Arist./Alex.] *Supl.Pr.* 2.46.

[7] I.e., animals, including humans. Had there been no reference to animals, I would have rendered this "people yawn in return" (as I did in *Pr.* 7.1).

μάλιστα κινοῦνται, ὅταν ὀσφρανθῶσιν· ὀσφραίνονται
δ' ὅταν πλησιάσωσιν. |

15   7. Διὰ τί, ἐπειδὰν τεμνόμενόν τινα ἴδωμεν ἢ καιόμε-
νον ἢ στρεβλούμενον ἢ ἄλλο τι τῶν δεινῶν πάσχοντα,
συναλγοῦμεν τῇ διανοίᾳ; ἢ ὅτι ἡ φύσις ἡμῖν[4] κοινὴ
ἅπασιν; συνήλγησεν οὖν, ἐπειδάν τι τοιοῦτον ἴδῃ, τῷ
πάσχοντι διὰ τὴν οἰκειότητα. ἢ ὅτι ὥσπερ αἱ ῥῖνες καὶ
20   αἱ ἀκοαὶ λαμβάνουσί τινας ἀπορροίας | κατὰ τὰς
οἰκείας δυνάμεις, οὕτω καὶ ἡ ὄψις ταὐτὸ[5] πάσχει καὶ
ἀπὸ τῶν ἡδέων καὶ λυπηρῶν;

8. Διὰ τί ἀπὸ φθίσεως καὶ ὀφθαλμίας καὶ ψώρας οἱ
πλησιάζοντες ἁλίσκονται, ἀπὸ δὲ ὕδρωπος καὶ πυρετῶν καὶ ἀποπληξίας οὐχ ἁλίσκονται, οὐδὲ τῶν ἄλλων;
25   ἢ ἡ μὲν ὀφθαλμία, | ὅτι εὐκινητότατον ὁ ὀφθαλμός,
καὶ μάλιστα ὁμοιοῦται τῷ ὁρωμένῳ τῶν ἄλλων, οἷον
κινεῖται ὑπὸ[6] κινουμένου ὥστε καὶ ἀντιβλέπων τε-
ταραγμένῳ ταράττεται μάλιστα; ἡ δὲ φθίσις, ὅτι
πνεῦμα φαῦλον ποιεῖ καὶ βαρύ, τάχιστα δὲ τὰ νοσή-
ματα ταῦτα ἅπτεται πάντων, ὅσα τούτου φθειρομένου |
30   γίνεται, οἷον τὰ λοιμώδη; ὁ δὲ πλησιάζων τοιοῦτον
ἀναπνεῖ. νοσεῖ μὲν οὖν, ὅτι νοσῶδες· ἀπὸ μόνου δέ, ὅτι
ἐκπνεῖ, νοσεῖ, οἱ δὲ ἄλλοι ἑτέρως·[7] τὴν αὐτὴν δὲ νόσον,
ὅτι ᾧ ἂν ἀσθενήσῃ, τούτῳ ἀναπνεῖ τοιοῦτον οἷον εἰ
πεπονθὼς ἦν. ἡ δὲ ψώρα μᾶλλον[8] τῶν ἄλλων, οἷον

---

4 ἡμῖν γ : ἡμῶν α β δ   5 ταὐτὸ Marenghi[3] ex Barth. :
αὐτὸ codd.   6 ὑπὸ Richards : ἀπὸ codd.

7 ἑτέρως Yᵃ Ap Xᵃ Pᶜ : ἑτέραν cett. codd.

8 μᾶλλον δ Xᵃ aᵐ p : μόνον cett. codd.

they are moved especially when they smell, and they smell when they are nearby.[8]

7.[9] Why, when we see someone being cut or burned or tortured or experiencing something else that's terrible, do we suffer along in thought? Is it because nature is common to all of us? So, when one sees something of this kind, one suffers along with the person experiencing it, owing to our kinship. Or is it that, just as noses and ears receive certain emanations according to their own capacities, so too does sight experience the same thing from both what is pleasant and what is painful?

8.[10] Why do those who come in contact with consumption, eye disease, and scurvy get infected, but they do not get infected from dropsy, fevers, apoplexy, and others? In the case of eye disease, is it because the eye is most easily moved, and more than the other (*senses*) assimilates itself to what is seen, for instance, it is moved by (*seeing something*) being moved, so that when it looks at (*an eye*) that is disturbed, it too is especially disturbed? In the case of consumption, is it because it makes the breath poor and labored, and those diseases are most quickly contracted which come when the breath decays, for instance the pestilential diseases? The one who comes close inhales this. So he becomes diseased because the breath is diseased; and he gets it from only one person, because the person exhales (*this breath*), while the others exhale differently. And (*he contracts*) the same disease, because he inhales the breath by which he becomes sick, such as he would if he

---

[8] I.e., near the place where the first one urinated.
[9] Cf. *Pr.* 7.5.
[10] Cf. *Pr.* 1.7, 7.4.

35 λέπρας καὶ τῶν τοιούτων, ὅτι ἐπιπολῆς | τε καὶ γλί-
σχρον τὸ ἀπορρέον· τὰ γὰρ κνησμώδη τοιαῦτα. διὸ
αὐτὰ⁹ τῷ ἐπιπολῆς γίνεσθαι καὶ γλίσχρον εἶναι ἅπτεται. τῶν δ' ἄλλων τὰ μὲν οὐχ ἅπτεται, διὰ τὸ μὴ
ἐπιπολῆς γίνεσθαι, τὰ δὲ ὄντα ἐπιπολῆς, ὅτι οὐ¹⁰
προσμένει διὰ ξηρότητα. ||

887b   9. Διὰ τί τὴν αἱμωδίαν παύει ἡ ἀνδράχνη καὶ ἅλες;
ἢ ὅτι ἡ μὲν ὑγρότητά τινα ἔχει; φανερὰ δὲ αὕτη
μασωμένοις τε, κἂν συνθλασθῇ¹¹ χρόνον τινά· ἕλκεται γὰρ ἡ ὑγρότης. τὸ δὴ γλίσχρον εἰσδυόμενον
5 ἐξάγει τὸ ὀξύ. καὶ γὰρ ὅτι | συγγενής, ἡ ὀξύτης
σημαίνει· ἔχει γάρ τινα ὀξύτητα ὁ χυλός. ὁ δὲ ἅλς
συντήκων ἐξάγει καὶ τὴν ὀξύτητα. διὰ τί οὖν ἡ κονία
καὶ τὸ νίτρον οὔ; ἢ ὅτι στύφει καὶ οὐ τήκει;

⁹ αὐτὰ : αὕτη Richards
¹⁰ οὐ om. γ (praeter aᵐ p)
¹¹ συνθλασθῇ Prantl ex Gaza (cf. Pr. 1.38, 863b13) : συντεθῇ
codd.

were already suffering (*from the disease*).[11] Now scurvy is more (*infectious*) than other diseases, for instance leprosy and the like, because the discharge[12] remains on the surface and is sticky; for the itching diseases are of this kind. This is why these are contracted through appearing on the surface and being sticky. But of the others, some are not contracted, because they do not appear on the surface, while others (*are not contracted*), though they are on the surface, because owing to their dryness they do not remain on the surface.

9.[13] Why do purslane[14] and salt stop bleeding gums? Is it because purslane contains some moisture? Now this is obvious to anyone who chews it, or if it is crushed together for some time; for moisture is drawn from it. The sticky material sinks in and draws out the acidity. And indeed, the acidity signifies that there is an affinity;[15] for the juice contains a certain acidity. But salt too drives out the acidity, by melting it. So why don't lye and soda do this? Is it because they cause contraction and not melting?

[11] The text that this line translates is likely corrupt.

[12] This is the same term (τὸ ἀπορρέον) translated "emanation" in the previous chapter.

[13] This chapter is virtually identical to *Pr.* 1.38.

[14] A plant in the family *Portulaca*.

[15] I.e., an affinity between purslane and bleeding gums.

BOOK VIII

INTRODUCTION

Book 8 is a set of twenty-two problems on the cold and its effects on humans. Their subject matter can be subdivided as follows: the cold (3–7, 9, 17, 20), being chilled (1–2, 14, 16, 18–19, 22), and shivering (8, 11–13, 15, 21).

In most cases, no likely source text can be identified. There is one exception: Aulus Gellius (second century AD), in a discussion of the views of Erasistratus on hunger, refers to that author's *Distinctions* (Διαιρέσεων), and ends by quoting the original Greek:

> It is puzzling and necessary to investigate, both in this case[1] and in the case of others who suffer from hunger, why this condition occurs more in winter than in fair weather.
> ἄπορον δὲ καὶ δεόμενον ἐπισκέψεως καὶ ἐπὶ τού-
> του καὶ ἐπὶ τῶν λοιπῶν βουλιμιώντων, διὰ τί ἐν
> τοῖς ψύχεσιν μᾶλλον τὸ σύμπτωμα τοῦτο γίνεται
> ἢ ἐν τοῖς εὐδίαις. (fr. 284 Garofalo)

Either the author of *Pr.* 8.9 was influenced by Erasistratus (early third century BC) or vice versa, or they are both responding to some other source. So Erasistratus' *Distinc-*

---

[1] The reference is unclear, though it may refer to fasting, which had just been discussed.

tions is a possible source for this chapter; and more gener-ally, it is possible that medical writers (including, but not limited to, Erasistratus) were the source for many of these problems.

ΟΣΑ ΕΚ ΡΙΓΟΥΣ ΚΑΙ ΦΡΙΚΗΣ

887b
10
1. Διὰ τί οἱ ῥιγῶντες πελιδνοὶ γίνονται; ἢ διότι τὸ αἷμα πήγνυται διὰ τὸ ψῦχος, πηγνύμενον δὲ μελαίνεται διὰ τὴν ἀπουσίαν τοῦ θερμοῦ; τὸ δὲ λευκὸν τοῦ πυρός. διὸ καὶ τοῖς πρεσβύταις μάλιστα πελιδνοῦται[1] ἡ σάρξ, ὅτι ἐλαχίστην ἔχει θερμότητα. |

15
2. Διὰ τί οἱ ῥιγῶντες καθεύδειν οὐ δύνανται; ‹ἢ›[2] διότι πάντες οἱ ῥιγῶντες μᾶλλον τὸ πνεῦμα κατέχουσιν; ὁ δὲ καθεύδων ἐκπνεῖ μᾶλλον ἢ εἰσπνεῖ, ὥστε χαλεπὸν ῥιγῶντα καθεύδειν· ἅμα γὰρ ποιεῖν τἀναντία ἀδύνατον.

3. Διὰ τί ἐν τῷ ψύχει ὀξύτεροι καὶ οἱ ἀσθενήσαντες |
20 καὶ οἱ λυπούμενοι καὶ οἱ ὀργιζόμενοι; ἢ στιφρότερον ποιεῖ τὸ καταψύχεσθαι;

4. Διὰ τί οἱ ἀθληταὶ δύσριγοι εὖ ἔχοντες; ἢ ὅτι καθαρὰ καὶ εὔπνους ἡ ἕξις καὶ ἀπίμελος; ἡ τοιαύτη δὲ

---

[1] πελιδνοῦται β δ γ : πελιοῦται α
[2] ‹ἢ› Sylburg

244

PROBLEMS ARISING FROM
CHILL AND SHIVERING

1. Why do those who are chilled become livid? Is it because the blood solidifies owing to the cold, and when it solidifies becomes black owing to the absence of heat? For white is characteristic of fire. And this is why among the old especially the flesh becomes livid, because it contains very little heat.

2.[1] Why are those who are chilled unable to sleep? Is it because all those who are chilled hold their breath more? Now the one who is sleeping exhales more than inhales, so that it is difficult for one who is chilled to sleep; for it is impossible to perform opposite actions at the same time.

3.[2] Why are those who are sick and those who are in pain and those who are angry more acute[3] in cold weather? Is it because being cooled makes one stronger?

4.[4] Why are athletes in good condition sensitive to the cold? Is it because their condition is clean and such that they breathe freely and without fat? Now this condition is

---

[1] Cf. *Pr.* 8.22.   [2] Cf. *Pr.* 8.20.   [3] Translators differ considerably over how to interpret ὀξύτεροι ("more acute"): some take the author to be saying that these people are more active or energetic (Forster, Hett, Louis), others that the conditions of these people worsen (Flashar, Marenghi3).   [4] Cf. *Pr.* 8.10.

εὐπαθεστάτη ὑπὸ τοῦ ἀέρος, ὅταν εὐδίοδός τε ᾖ καὶ μὴ
25 ἔχῃ θερμότητα ἐν | αὐτῇ· ἡ δὲ πιμελὴ θερμόν, ἂν μὴ
δίυγρος.

5. Διὰ τί μάλιστα τὰ ἀκρωτήρια ῥιγῶσιν; ἢ διὰ
στενότητα; καὶ οἱ πόροι ἐν αὐτοῖς στενοὶ ὄντες ὀλί-
γαιμοί εἰσιν, ὥστε καὶ ὀλιγόθερμοί εἰσι· τὸ γὰρ αἷμα
θερμόν.

6. Διὰ τί, ἐὰν μετέωροι ὦσιν οἱ πόδες, μᾶλλον
30 ῥιγοῦσιν; | πότερον ὑποπνεῖ μᾶλλον; ἢ ὅτι ἐν ἐλάττονι
γίνεται τὸ αἷμα κάτω, ὥστε τὸ ἄλλο εὐψυκτότερον
ἐκλείποντος τοῦ θερμοῦ;

7. Διὰ τί οἱ παχεῖς σφόδρα, τῆς πιότητος θερμῆς
οὔσης,[3] ῥιγῶσι; ἢ διὰ τὸ μέγεθος τοῦ πάχους, τοῦ μὲν
ἔσωθεν θερμοῦ πόρρω γίνονται τὰ ἔσχατα, τοῦ δὲ ἔξω
ψυχροῦ ἐγγύς; |

35   8. Διὰ τί πταρέντες καὶ οὐρήσαντες φρίττουσιν; ἢ
ὅτι κενοῦνται αἱ φλέβες ἐν ἀμφοτέροις, κενωθέντων δὲ
ὁ ἀὴρ εἰσέρχεται ψυχρός, ὁ ποιῶν φρίττειν;

9. Διὰ τί μάλιστα βουλιμιῶσιν ἐπὶ τῷ ψύχει, καὶ
τοῦ χειμῶνος μᾶλλον ἢ τοῦ θέρους; ἢ διότι ἡ μὲν
888a βουλιμία γίνεται ‖ δι' ἔνδειαν τῆς ξηρᾶς τροφῆς, ἐν δὲ
τῷ ψύχει καὶ τῷ χειμῶνι συστελλομένου τοῦ ἐντὸς
θερμοῦ εἰς ἐλάττω τόπον,[4] θᾶττον ὑπολείπει ἡ ἐντὸς
τροφή· τούτου δὲ γινομένου μᾶλλον βουλιμιᾶν εἰκός.

[3] ῥιγῶσι w R Barth. : om. cett. codd. : post σφόδρα add.
⟨ῥιγοῦσι⟩ Sylburg
[4] τόπον Bonitz (Apᵃ teste Louis) : τοῦτον codd.

most easily affected by the air, since it is permeable and does not have heat in it; but fat is hot, unless it is saturated.

5. Why are the extremities coldest? Is it because of their narrowness? And the passages in them, being narrow, hold little blood, and so they hold little heat; for blood is hot.

6. Why are the feet chillier if they are held up high? Does more air blow beneath them? Or is it because the blood comes to be in a smaller space below, so that the rest (*of the foot*) is more easily cooled when the heat leaves it?

7. Why are bulky people exceedingly chilly,[5] given that fat is hot? Is it because owing to the great size of their bulk, the extremities are far from the internal heat, while the near parts are far from the external cold?

8.[6] Why do people shiver when they have sneezed or urinated? Is it because in both cases the veins are emptied, and having been emptied the cold air enters, which produces shivering?

9.[7] Why do people feel hunger most in the cold, and in winter more than in summer? Is it because hunger[8] occurs due to a lack of dry nourishment, and in cold weather and in winter, when the internal heat is contracted into a smaller space, the nourishment within quickly fails? And when this occurs, hunger is more likely. Now exhaustion

---

[5] Or possibly "Why are exceedingly bulky people chilly," etc.

[6] This is a condensed version of *Pr.* 33.16. Cf. *Pr.* 8.13.

[7] Plutarch seems to refer to this chapter, calling its content Aristotelian (*QC* 6.8 [*Mor.* 694D–E]). Cf. Gell. 16.3, which discusses Erasistratus' similar views on the connection between hunger and the cold.

[8] The word translated "hunger" (βουλιμία, "ox hunger") refers specifically to severe or ravenous hunger.

5 ἡ δ' ἐν τῇ βουλιμίᾳ ἔκλυσις καὶ ἀδυναμία | γίνεται
συντήξεως γινομένης ἐν τῷ σώματι διὰ τὴν τοῦ θερμοῦ ἄθροισιν· ἧς ῥυείσης μὲν εἰς τὸν τῶν σιτίων
τόπον, αὐτὴ τροφὴ γίνεται τῷ σώματι. ἐὰν δ' ἐπὶ τὰς
ἀρχὰς τῆς ἀναπνοῆς ἔλθῃ, ἀφωνία καὶ ἀδυναμία συμ-
βαίνει· ἀφωνία μὲν διὰ τὸ ἐμφράττεσθαι τὸν τοῦ
10 πνεύματος πόρον, ἀδυναμία | δὲ διὰ τὴν τοῦ σώματος
ἀτροφίαν καὶ σύντηξιν. ταχεῖαι δὲ καὶ ἀπ' ὀλίγων αἱ
βοήθειαι γίνονται τοῖς τοιούτοις διὰ τὸ τὴν ἀρχὴν τοῦ
πάθους ἔξωθεν γίνεσθαι. συστέλλον γὰρ τὸ ἐντὸς[5]
ψυχρὸν τὸ θερμὸν ἡμῶν ποιεῖ τὴν βουλιμίαν. καθάπερ
οὖν ἐν τῷ φόβῳ τρέμοντες καὶ ὠχριῶντες, ἀφεθέντες[6]
15 τοῦ | κινδύνου, παραχρῆμα οἱ αὐτοὶ γίνονται, οὕτω καὶ
οἱ βουλιμιῶντες, μικρὰ προσενεγκάμενοι ἐξ ἄρτου,
βίᾳ κινηθέντες ἐκ τῆς φύσεως, μὴ φθαρέντες δέ·
ταχεῖα ἡ ἀποκατάστασις[7] γίνεται. ταὐτὸ γὰρ ἀντέτει-
νεν τήν τε κατὰ φύσιν ἀγωγήν, καὶ καθίστησιν εἰς τὴν
20 φύσιν. ἀφεῖναι οὖν μόνον αὐτὴν δεῖ, | καθάπερ[8] τῶν
παιδίων τὰ ἀντιτείνοντα εἰς τοὔπισθεν τὰ σπαρτία·
καὶ γὰρ ταῦτα ἀφεθέντων τῶν σπαρτίων εὐθὺς πεπτώ-
κασιν ὕπτια.

10. Διὰ τί οἱ γεγυμνασμένοι δυσριγότεροι τῶν
ἀγυμνάστων; πότερον ὅτι τὸ πῖον ὑπὸ τῶν πόνων
25 ἐξῄρηται, τοῦτο δὲ | ἀλέαν παρέχει; θερμὸν γὰρ τὸ

---

⁵ ἐντὸς : ἐκτὸς β Nicasius
⁶ ἀφεθέντες Sylburg : ἀφέντες codd.
⁷ ἀποκατάστασις Apᵇ ᵖᶜ : ἀποκάθαρσις cett. codd.
⁸ ante καθάπερ add. καὶ α γ

and incapacity occur in the case of hunger due to colliquation in the body owing to the collection of heat; this (*liquid*) flows into the space for food, and itself becomes nourishment in the body. But if it reaches the sources of respiration, loss of voice and incapacity follow: loss of voice because the passage of the breath is blocked, incapacity because of the lack of nourishment to the body and colliquation. Now in such cases the treatments are quick and from small (*causes*), because the source of the condition is external. For the internal[9] cold contracts the heat in us and produces hunger. Therefore, just as people tremble and grow pale in the case of fear, but released from the danger they are at once the same (*as before*), so also with those who are feeling hunger, if they take even a little bread, because they have been moved by force from their natural condition, but have not been destroyed: their restoration is rapid. For the same thing both resists the natural tendency and restores us to our natural condition. Therefore it is necessary only to release (*what resists the natural tendency*), just like children who stretch ropes in opposite directions; for when the rope is released, they straightaway fall on their backs.

10.[10] Why are those who have trained in gymnastic exercise more sensitive to the cold than those who are untrained? Is it because fat is removed by exertion, and this provides warmth? For that which is oily is hot. Or is it be-

---

9 If Forster is right, this should read "external" (ἐκτὸς).
10 Cf. *Pr.* 8.4.

ARISTOTLE

λιπαρόν. ἢ ὅτι εὐπνούστερα τὰ σώματα καὶ ἀραι-
ότερα, διὰ τὸ <τὸ>⁹ πῖον καὶ τὸ περίττωμα ἐξῃρῆσθαι,
ὥστε οὐδὲν ἀποστέγειν τὸ ψῦχος; ἢ διὰ τὴν τῶν πόρων
ἀναστόμωσιν¹⁰ τοῖς ἱδρῶσιν οἷον πολλαὶ θύραι ἐξ-
ῄρηνται; φανερὸν δὲ ὅτι οὐχ ἡ αὐτὴ ἕξις πρὸς ὑγείαν
30 καὶ | ἰσχὺν συμφέρει· ἡ μὲν γὰρ πίων, ἡ δὲ ἀραιὰ
φαίνεται οὖσα.

11. Διὰ τί φρίττουσι καὶ τῷ θερμῷ καὶ τῷ ψυχρῷ
προσχεόμενοι; ἄτοπον γὰρ τὰ ἐναντία τοῦ αὐτοῦ εἶναι
αἴτια. ἢ διότι ὑπὸ μὲν τοῦ ψυχροῦ προσχεομένῳ¹¹ τὸ
ἐντὸς θερμὸν σβεννύμενον ποιεῖ τὴν φρίκην, ὑπὸ δὲ
35 τοῦ θερμοῦ τὸ | ἐκτὸς ψυχρὸν ἀντιπεριιστάμενον εἰς ἓν
καὶ ἀθροιζόμενον τῇ φυγῇ ἔσω; ὥστε ὑπὸ τοῦ αὐτοῦ
ἄμφω γίνεται, ἀλλ᾽ ὁτὲ μὲν ὑπὸ τοῦ ἔσω, ὁτὲ δὲ ὑπὸ
τοῦ ἔξωθεν.

12. Διὰ τί φρίττουσιν αἱ τρίχες ἐν τῷ δέρματι; ἢ
ὅταν συσπάσωσι τὸ δέρμα, εἰκότως ἐξανέστησαν;
40 συσπῶσι δὲ | καὶ ὑπὸ ῥίγους καὶ ὑπ᾽ ἄλλων παθῶν. ||

888b   13. Διὰ τί ἐν τῇ τελευταίᾳ προέσει τοῦ οὔρου
φρίττομεν; ἢ ὅτι ἐνόντος μὲν τοῦ ὑγροῦ θερμοῦ πλή-
ρεις¹² ἥ τε κύστις καὶ οἱ περὶ αὐτὴν πόροι, ἐξελθόντος
δὲ ἀέρος ψυχροῦ ἐνέπλησεν; οὐδὲν γὰρ κενὸν δεῖ εἶναι,
5 ἀλλ᾽ ἢ ἀέρος ἢ σώματος | πλήρες. ἄτε οὖν εἰσεληλυ-
θότος ψυχροῦ ἀέρος εἰκότως φρίττειν συμβαίνει.

⁹ <τὸ> Sylburg   ¹⁰ ἀναστόμωσιν Forster : ἀποστόμω-
σιν codd.   ¹¹ προσχεομένῳ Marenghi³ ex Trap. : προσ-
χεόμενοις Forster : προσχεόμενοι codd.
¹² πλήρεις : πλήρης β x Barth.

cause their bodies have a good flow of air and are more porous, because the fat and the residues have been removed,
so that there is nothing to keep out the cold? Or is it due to
the opening of the channels by sweat, as if many doors had
been removed? Now it is evident that the same condition is
not beneficial with a view to health and to strength; for the
former (*requires*) fat, while the latter is manifestly lean.[11]

11. Why do people shiver when they are soaked in either hot or cold water? For it is strange that contrary things
should be the causes of the same result. Is it because, in being soaked by cold water, the extinguishing of the internal
heat produces shivering, but (*in being soaked*) by hot water, the external cold is enclosed in one place and gathered
together by its flight inward? So both are brought about by
the same thing, but in one case the cause is internal, in the
other external.

12.[12] Why do the hairs bristle[13] on the skin? Is it that
when the skin is contracted, it is reasonable that they stand
up? And they contract due to chill and to other conditions.

13.[14] Why do we shiver at the end of an emission of
urine? Is it because, when there is moisture within, the
bladder and the passages around it are full of heat, but
when (*the moisture*) exits they fill up with cold air? For
nothing can be empty, but is full either of air or of something corporeal. Therefore, when the cold air has entered,
it is reasonable that shivering occurs.

---

[11] Or "porous."   [12] This chapter is virtually identical to
Pr. 35.5. Cf. *Pr.* 8.15 and 21.

[13] The same word ($\phi\rho\acute{\iota}\tau\tau o\upsilon\sigma\iota\nu$) translated "shiver" (or "shudder") elsewhere.

[14] Cf. *Pr.* 8.8.

14. Διὰ τί τῶν ῥιγώντων ἡ γλῶττα, καθάπερ τῶν μεθυόντων, πταίει; πότερον ὑπὸ τοῦ ψύχους πηγνυμένη καὶ σκληρυνομένη δυσκίνητος γίνεται, τούτου δὲ

10 συμβαίνοντος οὐ | δύναται σαφηνίζειν; ἢ τῶν ἐκτὸς πυκνουμένων διὰ τὸ ψῦχος εἴσω συρρυὲν τὸ ὑγρὸν ἐξυγραίνει τὴν γλῶτταν; διόπερ οὐ δύναται ἡ γλῶττα τὸ αὑτῆς ποιεῖν, καθάπερ εἴρηται καὶ ἐπὶ τῶν μεθυόντων. ἢ διὰ τὸν ἀπὸ τοῦ ῥίγους τρόμον ἀτάκτου τῆς κινήσεως οὔσης οὐ δύναται τὰ λεγόμενα διαρθροῦν ἡ

15 γλῶττα; διόπερ καὶ πταίει.

15. Διὰ τί τῶν ῥιγώντων ὀρθαὶ αἱ ἐν τῷ σώματι τρίχες γίνονται; ἢ διότι ἀπὸ τῆς καταψύξεως τὸ θερμὸν εἰς τὸν ἐντὸς τόπον ἀθροίζεται, ἐκλείποντος δ' ἐκ τῆς σαρκὸς τοῦ θερμοῦ συνίσταται μᾶλλον, συναγο-

20 μένης δὲ ὀρθότεραι αἱ τρίχες | γίνονται;[13]

16. Διὰ τί τοῦ χειμῶνος τρέχοντες μᾶλλον ῥιγῶμεν ἢ ἑστῶτες; ἢ ὅτι ὁ ἀὴρ ὁ περὶ τὸ σῶμα ἑστώτων μέν, ἐπειδὰν ἅπαξ συνθερμανθῇ, οὐκέτι ἐνοχλεῖ, τρεχόντων δέ, ἀεὶ ἄλλος καὶ ἄλλος προσπίπτει ψυχρὸς ὤν·

25 διόπερ μᾶλλον ῥιγῶμεν. | ἔτι δὲ καὶ κινούμενος ψυχρότερος γίνεται ὁ ἀήρ· τοῦτο δὲ ἐν τῷ τρέχειν μάλιστα συμπίπτει.

17. Διὰ τί ὑποφαύσκοντος μᾶλλον ψῦχος ἢ ⟨τῆς νυκτὸς⟩[14] ἐγγυτέρω τοῦ ἡλίου ὄντος; ἢ ὅτι πλείων

---

13 post γίνονται add. ἢ διότι . . . α (praeter R w), γ

14 ἢ ⟨τῆς νυκτὸς⟩ Flashar ex Pr. 25.5, 938a32 : [ἢ] Bussemaker

14.[15] Why does the tongue of those who are chilled stumble, like that of those who are drunk? Is it because, being solidified and hardened by the cold, it becomes difficult to move, and when this happens it cannot speak clearly? Or is it that when the outer parts thicken owing to the cold, the moisture within flows together and saturates the tongue? This is why the tongue cannot do what is proper to it, as has been said in the case of those who are drunk. Or is it because when the movement is uncontrolled owing to the trembling that comes from chill, the tongue cannot articulate what it says? And this is why it stumbles.

15.[16] Why do the hairs on the bodies of those who are chilled become straight? Is it because as a result of cooling the heat collects in the inner region, and when the heat leaves the flesh, *(the flesh)* becomes more condensed, and as it is brought together the hairs become straighter?[17]

16.[18] Why in the winter are we chilled more while running than while standing? Is it because the air around the body, when we are standing, once it has been heated, no longer causes discomfort, but when we are running, fresh air, which is cold, continually strikes us? This is why we are chilled more *(while running)*. Further, the air is colder when it is moved; and this strikes us most in running.

17.[19] Why is it colder when dawn is breaking than ⟨at night⟩, although the sun is nearer? Is it because the period

---

[15] Cf. *Pr.* 3.31.   [16] Cf. *Pr.* 8.12 and 21.

[17] Some mss. indicate that this chapter did not originally end here.   [18] Cf. *Pr.* 5.17.

[19] Cf. *Pr.* 25.5 and 15.

ARISTOTLE

⟨ὁ⟩[15] χρόνος τῆς τοῦ ἡλίου ἀπουσίας, ὥστε μᾶλλον
30 ἀπέψυκται ἡ γῆ; ἢ ὅτι πρὸς ἡμέραν ἡ δρόσος | πίπτει
ὥσπερ πάχνη, ταῦτα δὲ ψυχρά; ἢ καὶ ταῦτα πίπτει διὰ
τὸ κρατεῖσθαι τὸ ἀναφερόμενον θερμόν, κρατεῖται δὲ
διὰ τὴν τοῦ ἡλίου ἀπουσίαν· διὸ καὶ πλεῖον μὲν
ἀπέχοντος οὐ πίπτει, ἐγγυτέρω δὲ ὄντος πίπτει καὶ
πήγνυται· διότι μᾶλλον ἀπέψυκται ὁ τόπος, πλείω
35 χρόνον τοῦ ἡλίου | ἀπόντος. ἢ ὅτι πρὸς ἡμέραν μᾶλ-
λον τὰ ἐκ νυκτῶν πνεύματα τῆς ψύξεως;[16] ἢ ἡμῖν δοκεῖ
μᾶλλον εἶναι ψῦχος διὰ τὸ πεπέφθαι τὰ σιτία; κενώτε-
ροι δὲ ὄντες δυσριγότεροι. σημεῖον δὲ τὸ μετὰ τοὺς
ἐμέτους μάλιστα ῥιγοῦν.

18. Διὰ τί πονοῦσιν, ὅταν ῥιγῶντας πρὸς τὸ πῦρ
40 φέρωσιν· | ὅταν δὲ κατὰ μικρὸν χλιαίνωσιν, οὔ; ἢ ὅτι
889a ὅλως ἐκ τῶν ἐναντίων ‖ τοὐναντίον γινόμενον μεγάλην
ποιεῖ τὴν μεταβολήν; ὥσπερ ἐπὶ τῶν δένδρων, εἰ μὲν
κατὰ μικρὸν κάμπτοι τις, οὐκ ἂν πονοῖ, εἰ δὲ σφοδρότερον καὶ μὴ κατὰ μικρόν, κλῶνται. εἰ οὖν τὸ ὅμοιον
5 ὑπὸ τοῦ ὁμοίου ἀπαθές, τὸ δὲ θερμὸν τοῦ | ῥιγῶντος
εἴσω συνίσταται καὶ συνέρχεται, τὸ δὲ ὑγρὸν κατα-
λείπεται καὶ τὸ ψυχρόν, τὸ δὲ ἐναντίον τοῦ ἐναντίου
φθαρτικόν, ὥστε ἐὰν μὲν χλιαίνῃ, κατὰ μικρὸν ἐξέρχεται τὸ θερμὸν καὶ ἧττον πονεῖ, ἐὰν δὲ μὴ ἀναχλι-
άνῃ, προσάγει μᾶλλον. |

10 19. Διὰ τί ψυχθέντες μᾶλλον ἀπὸ τῆς αὐτῆς θερμα-

---

15 ⟨ὁ⟩ Bekker
16 ante τῆς ψύξεως add. ⟨αἴτια⟩ Richards

of the sun's absence is great, so that the earth has cooled off more? Or is it because dew falls more toward daybreak, like frost, and these are cold? Or do these also fall because the heat rising (*from the earth*) is mastered, and it is mastered because of the sun's absence? And this is why they don't fall when the sun is farther away, but do fall and solidify when it is nearer: because the region has cooled off more, the greater the period that the sun is away. Or is it because toward daybreak the nocturnal cold winds are more abundant?[20] Or does it *seem* to us to be colder because our food has been concocted? And because we are emptier, we are more sensitive to the cold. A sign of this is that we have the chills most after vomiting.

18. Why do people who are chilled suffer when they are brought to the fire, but when they are warmed gradually they do not? Is it because, generally, one contrary following another contrary produces a great change? Just as in the case of trees, if one bends them gradually they do not suffer, but if it is done more violently and not gradually, they break. Therefore, if like is unaffected by like, and the heat of the one who is chilled combines and collects within, and the moist and the cold are left behind, and a contrary is destructive of its contrary, it follows that if one warms (*another gradually*), the heat comes out gradually and so causes less suffering, but if one does not so warm (*another*), it increases (*the suffering*).

19.[21] Why do we burn and feel pain more by the same

[20] Or, if the addition of αἴτια is correct, "the nocturnal winds tend to be a cause of the cold."

[21] This chapter is virtually identical to *Pr.* 37.4.

σίας καιόμεθα καὶ ἀλγοῦμεν; πότερον διὰ πυκνότητα
στέγει ἡ σὰρξ τὸ προσπῖπτον θερμόν; διὸ μόλιβδος[17]
ἐρίου θερμότερος. ἢ βίαιος γίνεται τοῦ θερμοῦ ἡ δί-
οδος διὰ τὸ πεπηγέναι ὑπὸ τοῦ ψύχους τοὺς πόρους; |

15   20. Διὰ τί οἱ ὀργιζόμενοι οὐ ῥιγῶσιν; ἢ ὅτι ἡ ὀργὴ
τῇ δειλίᾳ ἐναντίον καὶ ὁ θυμός; ἔστι δὲ ἡ μὲν ὀργὴ
ἀπὸ τοῦ πυρός· πολὺ γὰρ τὸ πῦρ κατέχοντες εἴσω
χλιαίνονται. μάλιστα δ' ἔστιν ἐπὶ τῶν παιδίων κατα-
μαθεῖν. οἱ μὲν γὰρ ἄνδρες βλάπτονται, τὰ δὲ παιδία
20   πρῶτον μὲν τὸ πνεῦμα πολὺ | ἀναλαμβάνουσιν, εἶτα
ἐρυθριῶσιν· πολὺ γὰρ εἴσω ὂν τὸ θερμὸν καὶ ἐξυγραῖνον ἐρυθριᾶν ποιεῖ, ἐπεὶ εἴ τις αὐτοῖς πολὺ τοῦ ψυχροῦ
προσχέοι, παύσαιντ'[18] ἂν ὀργιζόμενοι· κατασβεσθείη
γὰρ ἂν αὐτῶν τὸ θερμόν. οἱ δὲ δειλοὶ καὶ φοβούμενοι
τοὐναντίον. ῥιγῶσίν τε γὰρ καὶ ψυχροὶ καὶ ὠχροὶ
25   γίνονται· | ἐκλείπει γὰρ τὸ θερμὸν αὐτοῖς ἐκ τῶν
ἐπιπολῆς τόπων.

21. Διὰ τί, ὅταν φρίξωμεν, αἱ τρίχες ὀρθαὶ ἵσταν-
ται; ἢ διὰ τὸ ἐν ὑγρῷ πεφυκέναι κατακεκλίσθαι;[19]
κρατεῖ γὰρ τοῦ ὑγροῦ τὸ βάρος[20] τῆς τριχός. ἡ δὲ
φρίκη γίνεται ὑπὸ τοῦ ψυχροῦ, τὸ δὲ ψῦχος κατὰ
30   φύσιν πήγνυσι τὸ ὑγρόν.[21] ὅταν | οὖν μεταβάλῃ[22] τὸ
ὑγρόν, ἐξ οὗ πεφύκασιν αἱ τρίχες, καὶ παγῇ, μεταβάλλειν εἰκὸς καὶ τὰς τρίχας. εἰς μὲν οὖν τοὐναντίον

_____

17 μόλιβδος γ δ : μόλιβος α β
18 παύσαιντ' Richards : παύσοιντ' codd.
19 κατακεκλίσθαι Bonitz : κατακεκλεῖσθαι codd. : κατα-
κέκλινται Ross apud Forster

256

heat if we have first been cooled? Does the flesh, owing to its thickness, keep in the heat which it encounters? This is why lead becomes hotter than wool. Or does the penetration of the heat become violent because the passages are solidified by the cold?

20.[22] Why do those who are angry not become chilled? Is it because anger and spiritedness are the opposite of cowardice? Now anger is from fire, for it is by retaining a great deal of fire that they grow warm within. This is observable most of all in children. For men are distressed (*when angry*), but children first draw in deep breaths, and then grow red; for the quantity of heat within being great and causing liquefaction makes them grow red, since if one were to pour a lot of cold water over them they would cease being angry, for their heat would be extinguished. But cowards and those who are afraid are the opposite. For they are chilled, and become cold and pale; for the heat leaves them from the surface regions.

21.[23] Why, when we shiver, do the hairs stand up straight? Is it because they naturally lie down in moisture? For the weight of the hair masters the moisture. But shivering comes from the cold, and the cold naturally solidifies the moisture. Therefore, when the moisture, from which the hairs grow, changes and is solidified, it is likely that the hair will change too. So if they change to the opposite con-

---

[22] Cf. *Pr.* 8.3.   [23] Cf. *Pr.* 8.12 and 15.

---

[20] βάρος Bonitz (cf. 889a34) : βάθος codd.
[21] ὑγρόν Bonitz : θερμόν codd.
[22] μεταβάλῃ : μεταβάλλῃ γ Aᵐ

εἰ μεταβάλλουσιν, ἢ ἐν ταὐτῷ μένουσιν, ἢ ἐπικρα-
τήσει πάλιν ἡ θρὶξ τοῦ ὑγροῦ· οὐκ εἰκὸς δὲ πεπηγότος
καὶ πεπυκνωμένου τοῦ ὑγροῦ τὴν τρίχα τῷ βάρει
35 κρατεῖν. εἰ δὲ | μηδαμόσε κεκλίσθαι δυνατὸν τὴν
τρίχα τῷ τὸ ὑγρὸν πεπηγέναι, λείπεται ἑστάναι ὀρ-
θήν. ἢ διότι ὑπὸ τῆς καταψύξεως τὸ θερμὸν εἰς τὸν
ἐντὸς τόπον ἀθροίζεται; ἐκλείποντος δὲ ἐκ τῆς σαρκὸς
τοῦ θερμοῦ συνίσταται μᾶλλον ἡ σάρξ· συναγομένης
δὲ ὀρθότεραι αἱ τρίχες γίνονται, καθάπερ ἐάν τις εἰς ‖
889b τὴν γῆν ἐμπήξας κάρφος ἢ ἄλλο τι συντάττῃ[23] καὶ
πάντοθεν συνάγῃ τὴν γῆν, μᾶλλον ὀρθοῦται ἢ ἐὰν ἐᾷ
μὴ συνεστηκυῖαν.

22. Διὰ τί οἱ ῥιγῶντες μάλιστα οὐ καθεύδουσιν; ἢ
5 διότι ὁ | ῥιγῶν μᾶλλον κατέχει τὸ πνεῦμα ἢ ἐκπνεῖ, ὁ
δὲ καθεύδων ἐκπνεῖ ἢ εἰσπνεῖ; ἐναντίως οὖν ποιεῖ ἔχειν
τὸ ῥῖγος τῷ καθεύδειν.

23 συντάττῃ : συσσάττῃ Bussemaker (cf. Pr. 25.8, 938b28)

dition, either the hairs remain in the same state or the hair will again master the moisture; but it is not likely that, when the moisture is solidified and thickened, the hair will gain mastery through its weight. Now if the hair can lie down nowhere because the moisture is solidified, it remains for it to stand up straight. Or is it because the heat is collected into the inner region on account of the cooling? And when the heat leaves the flesh, it becomes denser; and as the flesh is brought together the hairs become straighter, just as if someone, fixing a stick or something else into the earth, were to arrange[24] and bring together the earth all around it, it would be straighter than if one left the earth loose.

22.[25] Why do those who are chilled especially not sleep? Is it because the one who is chilled holds his breath more than he exhales, but the one who sleeps exhales more than he inhales? Therefore, chill produces a condition that is contrary to being asleep.

[24] Or, if Bussemaker is right, "pack."
[25] Cf. *Pr.* 8.2.

BOOK IX

INTRODUCTION

This brief book deals with the effects on the body of being struck or beaten. Its chapters can be divided as follows: preventing welts and bruises (1, 6, 9, 10, 12); the color of scars (2, 5, 7, 11—cf. 13, which asks "Why don't hairs grow on scars?"); and, the different effects of blows, especially from a fennel stalk (3, 4, 8, 14). Little can be said about sources for this material, but see the introduction to Book 1 (on medicine).

ΟΣΑ ΠΕΡΙ ΥΠΩΠΙΑ ΚΑΙ
ΟΥΛΑΣ ΚΑΙ ΜΩΛΩΠΑΣ[1]

1. Διὰ τί τοὺς μώλωπας κωλύει τὰ νεόδαρτα δέρματα προστιθέμενα, καὶ μάλιστα κριῶν, καὶ ᾠὰ ἐπικαταγνύμενα; ἢ ὅτι ἄμφω κωλύει τὴν ἄθροισιν τοῦ ὑγροῦ καὶ τὴν ἔπαρσιν; τὸ γὰρ ἀφηλκωμένον ἕλκει ‹καὶ›[2] ἐπαίρεται διὰ τὴν θερμασίαν· τά τε δὴ ᾠὰ διὰ τὴν γλισχρότητα κατακολλῶντα κωλύει | ἐπαίρεσθαι, καθάπερ καὶ τὰ καύματα· ὥσπερ καὶ ἡ κόλλα, καὶ τὰ δέρματα τῇ τε γλισχρότητι προσκολλᾶται, καὶ ἅμα τῇ θερμότητι συμπέττει καὶ παύει τὴν φλεγμασίαν· οὐδὲ γὰρ ἀφαιροῦσιν ἡμερῶν τινων. ἐξάγειν δὲ βούλονται τὴν φλεγμασίαν καὶ οἱ τῷ ἁλὶ καὶ τῷ ὄξει τρίβοντες. |

2. Διὰ τί ἐν μὲν τῷ ἄλλῳ σώματι αἱ οὐλαὶ μέλαιναι, ἐν δὲ τῷ ὀφθαλμῷ λευκαί; ἢ ὅτι ἐναντίαν χρόαν ἡ οὐλὴ λαμβάνει τῇ πρότερον, ὥσπερ πᾶν τὸ νενοσηκός, ἐν τῷ μέλανι δὲ τοῦ ὀφθαλμοῦ τὰ ἕλκη· οὐ μὴν οὐδὲ ἐν τῷ σώματι μέλαιναι εὐθύς, ἀλλ' ἐξ ἀρχῆς

---

[1] μώλωπας : τραύματα Kᵃ Oᵃ
[2] ‹καὶ› Marenghi[3] ex Barth. et Trap. : ‹τὸ ὑγροῦ καὶ› Forster

PROBLEMS CONCERNING
BRUISES, SCARS, AND WELTS

1. Why does the application of newly skinned hides (and especially rams' hides) and broken eggs prevent welts? Is it because both prevent the collection of moisture and so the swelling? For the wounded part attracts (*moisture*) and so swells owing to the heat. Now eggs, because of their stickiness, cause adhesion, and so prevent swelling, as with cauterization; and also like glue, the hides too cause adhesion owing to their stickiness, and at the same time produce concoction through their heat and so stop the inflammation; for they do not remove them for several days. And those who rub (*welts*) with salt and vinegar also want to draw out the inflammation.

2.[1] Why are scars dark[2] on other parts of the body, but light[3] on the eye? Is it because a scar takes on the opposite of its former color, as does everything that's diseased, and the wounds occur in the dark part of the eye? Scars on the body are not dark immediately, however, but are light at

[1] Cf. *Pr.* 9.7.
[2] Or "black" (μέλαιναι).
[3] Or "white" (λευκαί).

25 λευκαί, οὐδὲ ἐν τῷ ὀφθαλμῷ | ἀεὶ λευκαί,[3] ἀλλ᾽ ἀποκα-
θίστανται τῷ χρόνῳ, ἢ ἁπλῶς ἢ εἰς τὸ μᾶλλον.

3. Διὰ τί ὁ νάρθηξ τὰ κύκλῳ τῆς πληγῆς ποιεῖ
ἐρυθρά, τὸ δὲ μέσον λευκόν; πότερον ὅτι ἀποπιέζει τὸ
αἷμα ἐκ τοῦ μέσου, καθὸ μάλιστα προσπίπτει περι-
30 φερὴς ὤν; ἢ ἔδει ἐπανιέναι | διά γε τοῦτο πάλιν; ἀλλ᾽
αἵματος συνδρομὴ τὸ ἐρύθημά ἐστιν, συνδρομὴ δ᾽ εἰς
τὸν πληγέντα τόπον.

4. Διὰ τί τῷ μὲν νάρθηκι σφόδρα τυπτόμενον τὸ
μέσον τῆς σαρκὸς λευκὸν γίνεται, τὸ δὲ κύκλῳ ἐρυ-
θρόν, ξύλῳ δὲ ἐρυθρότερον τὸ μέσον; ἢ ὅτι ὁ μὲν
35 νάρθηξ διὰ κουφότητα, | ἐὰν σφόδρα πατάξῃ, τὸ
ἐπιπολῆς διεσκέδασεν αἷμα, ὥστε ὅθεν μὲν ἐξέλιπεν,
λευκὸν φαίνεται, οὗ δὲ πλέον ἦλθεν, ἐρυθρότερον.
οἰδησάσης δὲ τῆς πληγῆς, οὐ ταχέως ἀποκαθίσταται
τὸ σκεδασθὲν αἷμα διὰ τὸ ὀλίγον τε εἶναι καὶ τὴν
φορὰν εἰς τὸ πρόσαντες εἶναι· πλήθει γὰρ βιασθὲν δεῖ
890a τὴν ‖ παρὰ φύσιν φορὰν ἐνεχθῆναι. διὰ δὲ τῶν σκληρῶν αἱ πληγαὶ διὰ ⟨τὸ⟩[4] βάρος καὶ τὴν ἰσχὺν θλῖψιν
καὶ θλάσιν ποιοῦσιν. θλιβόμενον μὲν οὖν κοῖλον γίνεται, θλώμενον δὲ ἀραιόν· τομὴ γὰρ καὶ διαίρεσίς ἐστι
5 μαλακὴ ἡ θλάσις. | κοίλου δὲ καὶ ἀραιοῦ γενομένου
τοῦ μέσου, φέρεται εἰς αὐτὸ τὸ[5] ἐκ τῶν πέριξ ἐπιπολῆς
αἷμα· κάτω τε γὰρ πέφυκε φέρεσθαι, καὶ εἰς τὰ ἀραιὰ

---

3 λευκαί Bonitz (albae Trap.) : μέλαιναι codd. Barth.
4 τὸ om. codd., add. edd. (teste Marenghi[3], cf. Bekker et
Louis)   5 τὸ Cᵃ : om. cett. codd.

the beginning; nor are they always light in the eye, but that comes about in time, either entirely or for the most part.

3.[4] Why does the fennel stalk produce a red circle in the area of the blow, but with a white center?[5] Is it because it forces the blood out from the center, where it, being round, strikes most of all? Or shouldn't (*the blood*), because of this, go back again? But then the redness is due to a rush of blood, and a rush toward the region that was struck.

4.[6] Why when violently beaten with a fennel stalk does the center of the flesh become white but with a red circle, whereas when beaten with wood the center is redder? Is it because the fennel stalk, owing to its lightness, if it strikes violently, scatters the blood widely on the surface, so that the region from which it leaves becomes white, but where more of it goes becomes redder? And when the region that was struck swells, the scattered blood does not return quickly, because there is not much of it and its course is in an upward direction; for being carried along a course that is contrary to nature requires a great deal of force be imparted. But the blows from hard objects, owing to their weight and strength, produce pressure and crushing. Therefore, being pressured the region becomes hollow, while being crushed it become porous; for crushing is mild cutting and dividing. And when the center has become hollow and porous, the blood from around the surface is carried to it; for it is naturally carried downward and

---

[4] Cf. *Pr.* 9.4.   [5] Xenophon describes fennel stalks being used by soldiers in mock battle (*Cyr.* 2.3, 17–20); they may also have been used for beating children and slaves (see Plu. *Pomp.* 18).   [6] Cf. *Pr.* 9.3 and 8.

τῷ εἴκειν αὐτά. ἀθροιζομένου δ' ἐνταῦθα εἰκότως τοῦ
αἵματος τοῦτο μὲν ἐρυθραίνει, ἃ δὲ ἀπολείπει, λευ-
καίνει. |

10   5. Διὰ τί αἱ οὐλαὶ μέλαιναι τῶν σπληνιώντων; ἢ ὅτι
αἷμα διεφθαρμένον ἔχουσιν διὰ τὴν ἐκ τοῦ σπληνὸς
σύμμιξιν νοσώδους αἵματος καὶ ὑδαρούς; ἡ μὲν οὖν
οὐλὴ τὸ δέρμα λεπτὸν καὶ ἐπιπόλαιον ἴσχει· τὸ δὲ
<αἷμα>,[6] διὰ τὸ ὑδαρὲς καὶ θερμὸν εἶναι μέλαν ὄν,
15   τοιαύτην ποιεῖ τὴν οὐλὴν διαφαινόμενον. | καὶ δὴ
πλεονάκις ἡ οὐλὴ ἐν τούτῳ γίνεται μελαντέρα. γίνεται
δὲ διὰ ταὐτό· δι' ἀσθένειαν γὰρ τοῦ δέρματος καταψύχεται τὸ αἷμα, καὶ ἐξατμίζοντος τοῦ θερμοῦ γίνεται
μελάντερον. ὁμοίως δὲ καὶ τοῖς πρεσβύταις οἵ τε
χρῶτες μελάντεροι γίνονται, καὶ αἱ οὐλαὶ αἱ συγ-
20   γενεῖς | μελάντεραι ἢ νέοις· οἷον ὑπώπιον γὰρ αὐτοῖς
ἅπαν τὸ σῶμα οὐ διὰ λεπτότητα τοῦ δέρματος, ἀλλ'
ὅτι τὸ θερμὸν ἐκλέλοιπεν.

6. Πότερον[7] ὅσα τοῦ αὐτοῦ αἴτια τὴν αὐτὴν ἔχει
δύναμιν εἰς τὸ ποιεῖν ἢ οὔ; λέγω δὲ οἷον ἐπεὶ τὰ
25   ὑπώπια καὶ ὁ | χαλκὸς ἐξαίρει καὶ ἡ ῥαφανὶς καὶ ὁ
κύαμος διαμασώμενος καὶ ὁ πνεύμων καὶ ἡ ἄργιλος
καὶ ἕτερ' ἄττα, τῇ αὐτῇ δυνάμει, ἢ ὁ μὲν χαλκὸς τῷ ἰὸν
εἶναι, τὸν δὲ ἰὸν φαρμακώδη, ὁ δὲ κύαμος καὶ ὁ

6 <αἷμα> Sylburg
7 caput 5 continuatur Aᵐ ‖ ante πότερον lac. suspicor

into the porous regions, which yield to it. And when the blood is collected there, it is reasonable that this turns red, but the region from which it leaves turns white.

5. Why are the scars of those who are splenetic[7] dark? Is it because their blood is corrupted by the mixture of diseased and watery blood from the spleen? So the scar keeps the skin thin and superficial; but the blood, which is dark because it is watery and hot, produces such a scar[8] by showing through (*the skin*). Moreover, the scar in such a case often becomes even darker. And this happens for the same reason: the blood is cooled owing to the weakness of the skin, and becomes darker as the heat vaporizes. In the same way, complexions become darker in old men, and congenital scars are darker than in young men: for the whole body is like a bruise, not because of the thinness of the skin, but because the heat has left.

6.[9] Do all causes of the same effect have the same capacity for producing it, or not? I mean for instance that since copper and radish and mashed bean and sea lung[10] and clay and other things remove bruises, do they do so through the same capacity, or does copper do so through being rusty, and rust is medicinal, whereas bean and sea

---

[7] I.e., people with maladies of the spleen. See Hp. *Morb.* 4.33 and 37, *Af.* 20, *Epid.* 2.1.10, 7.114.   [8] I.e., a dark one.

[9] According to one ms., this is a continuation of ch. 5. That is unlikely, though the unusual beginning to ch. 6 suggests that something might be amiss. I suspect the original opening is missing.   [10] Aristotle says that this animal (literally, "the lung," ὁ πνεύμων) is somewhat like the sponge but differs in being detached (*PA* 681a15–20, cf. *HA* 548a10–11). It is either a type of sea cucumber or jellyfish (and can also be spelled ὁ πλεύμων).

πνεύμων καὶ ἡ ἄργιλος τῷ ἐπισπᾶν ἐφ' αὑτὰ διὰ
30 μανότητα, ἄλλα δὲ δι' ἑτέρας αἰτίας; | ἢ τὸ μὲν
ἔσχατον ἐπὶ πάντων τῶν τοιούτων ταὐτό (πολλὰ γὰρ
καὶ ἐναντία τούτοις, καθάπερ καὶ τὸ θερμὸν καὶ τὸ
ψυχρόν), τὰ δὲ πρὸ τούτων οὐδὲν κωλύει ἕτερα;

7. Διὰ τί αἱ μὲν ἄλλαι οὐλαὶ μέλαιναι γίνονται, αἱ
δὲ ἐν τῷ ὀφθαλμῷ λευκαί; ἢ διότι μεταβάλλουσιν ἐν
35 ᾧ | ἂν ὦσι πρὸς τὰς χροιάς, ἐν δὲ τῷ ὀφθαλμῷ μέλανι
ὄντι γίνονται, ὥστε ἀνάγκη λευκὰς γίνεσθαι;

8. Διὰ τί ἀλγεινοτέρα ἡ πληγὴ τοῦ νάρθηκος ἢ
ἐνίων σκληροτέρων, ἐάν τις κατὰ λόγον σκοπῇ τύ-
πτων; εὐλογώτερον γὰρ τὴν τοῦ σκληροτέρου εἶναι
890b ἀλγεινοτέραν· μᾶλλον γὰρ ‖ τύπτει. ἢ ὅτι ἡ σὰρξ
ἀλγεῖ οὐ μόνον τυπτομένη, ἀλλὰ καὶ τύπτουσα; ὑπὸ
μὲν οὖν τῶν σκληρῶν τύπτεται μόνον (ὑπείκει γὰρ διὰ
τὴν σκληρότητα αὐτῶν), ὑπὸ δὲ τοῦ νάρθηκος ἄμφω
5 αὐτῇ συμβαίνει, τύπτεσθαί τε καὶ διὰ κουφότητα | τοῦ
βάρους τύπτειν μὴ εἴκουσαν, ὥστε διπλασία γίνεται ἡ
πληγή.

9. Διὰ τί ἡ θαψία καὶ ὁ κύαθος τὰ ὑπώπια παύει, ἡ
μὲν ἀρχόμενα, ὁ δὲ ὕστερον, ἐναντία ὄντα; ὁ μὲν γὰρ
κύαθος ψυχρός, ὥσπερ καὶ ὁ ποιητής φησι "ψυχρὸν δ' |

---

11 The Greek does not make clear what is drawn out, though it
must be some material (e.g., moisture, impure blood) that the author believes causes or contributes to bruising.

12 Cf. *Pr.* 9.2.

13 Cf. *Pr.* 9.3–4.

14 It is unclear what the person is considering in proportion. It

lung and clay do so by drawing (*something*) to themselves[11] owing to their loose texture, and other things for different reasons? Or is the ultimate effect in all such cases the same (for they have many opposite qualities among them, such as hot and cold), whereas nothing prevents the earlier effects from being different?

7.[12] Why do other scars become dark, but those in the eye light? Is it because they change in the place where they are with respect to colors, so that those occurring in the eye, which is dark, must be light?

8.[13] Why is the blow from a fennel stalk more painful than from some harder things, if one considers it in proportion in delivering the strike?[14] For it is more reasonable (*to expect*) that the blow of the harder thing would be more painful, for it delivers more of a strike. Is it because the flesh feels pain not only when being struck, but also when delivering the strike? Therefore, by the hard things it is only struck (for it yields owing to their hardness), but by the fennel stalk both effects are produced in it[15]—it is struck, and owing to the lightness of the weight it also delivers the strike without yielding, so that the blow is double.

9.[16] Why do both thapsia[17] and a (*bronze*) ladle stop bruises (the former in the beginning, the latter later), though they are opposites? For the ladle is cold—as the poet says, "He seized cold bronze in his teeth"[18]—whereas

is likely the effect produced, or how hard or soft the striking instrument is (though these may come to the same thing).

[15] I.e., in the flesh.   [16] Cf. *Pr.* 9.10 and 12.

[17] The root of *Thapsia garganica*.

[18] Hom. *Il.* 5.75.

10 ἔλε χαλκὸν ὀδοῦσιν", ἡ δὲ θαψία θερμὸν καὶ καυστι-
κόν. ἢ ὁ μὲν κύαθος ὥσπερ τοῖς μικροψυχοῦσι τὸ
ὕδωρ; ἀπαντῶσα γὰρ ἡ ψύξις κωλύει ἐξιέναι τὸ θερμὸν ἐκ τοῦ αἵματος ἐξ ἐπιπολῆς διὰ τὴν πληγὴν
συνδραμόντος, καὶ ὅταν ἐξέλθῃ τὸ θερμόν, πηγνυ-
15 μένου. ὥσπερ γὰρ ἂν εἰ ἔξω ὂν | πήγνυται, καὶ ἐγγὺς
τοῦ ἔξω τὸ αἷμα, ὅταν ᾖ ὑπὸ τὸ δέρμα· κωλυθέντος δὲ
ἐξιέναι[8] τοῦ θερμοῦ διὰ τὴν ψυχρότητα τοῦ χαλκοῦ
οὐ[9] πήγνυται, ἀλλὰ πάλιν διαχεῖται καὶ ἐπανέρχεται
ὅθεν συνέδραμεν. ἡ δὲ θαψία θερμὴ οὖσα τὸ αὐτὸ
ποιεῖ· κωλύει γὰρ πήγνυσθαι θερμὴ οὖσα. |

20 10. Διὰ τί τὰ ὑπώπια διαλύεται προσέχουσιν τὰ
χαλκᾶ, οἷον κυάθους καὶ τὰ τοιαῦτα; ἢ διότι ψυχρὸν ὁ
χαλκός ἐστιν; κωλύει οὖν τὸ θερμὸν ἐξιέναι ἐκ τοῦ
συνιόντος αἵματος ὑπὸ τῆς πληγῆς, οὗ ἐξελθόντος ἐκ
τοῦ ἐπιπολῆς γίνεται ὑπώπιον. διὸ καὶ ταχὺ δεῖ προσ-
25 τιθέναι πρὶν παγῆναι. καὶ ἡ | θαψία δὲ μετὰ μέλιτος
βοηθεῖ διὰ τὸ αὐτό· θερμὴ γὰρ οὖσα κωλύει ψύχεσθαι
τὸ αἷμα.

11. Διὰ τί ποτε, ὅταν ἐν τῷ αὐτῷ τόπῳ πλεονάκις
ἕλκος γένηται, ἡ οὐλὴ μέλαινα γίνεται; ἢ ὁπόταν
γένηται ἕλκος, πᾶν ἀσθενές ἐστιν τοῦτο, καὶ ὅσῳ ἂν
30 πλεονάκις, τοσούτῳ | μᾶλλον; τὸ δὲ ἀσθενὲς κατ-
εψυγμένον καὶ ὑγρότητος πλῆρες· διὸ καὶ μέλαν φαίνεται, εἴ<περ> τὰ[10] μεγάλα ἕλκη καὶ πολυχρόνια με-

---

8 δὲ ἐξιέναι β : διεξιέναι cett. codd.
9 οὐ β Dˢ Nicasius Barth. : om. cett. codd.

thapsia is hot and burning. Or is the ladle like water on the feeble? For the cold encountering the heat prevents it from leaving the blood on the surface, to which it rushes owing to the blow, and when the heat comes out the blood solidifies. For just as if it solidified on the outside, so the blood solidifies near the outside, when it is under the skin; but as the heat is prevented from escaping owing to the coldness of the bronze, the blood does not solidify, but disperses again and returns to the region from which it came rushing. But thapsia being hot produces the same thing; for being hot, it prevents (*the blood*) from solidifying.

10.[19] Why do bruises disappear with the application of bronze objects, such as ladles and the like? Is it because bronze is cold? Therefore, it prevents the heat from leaving the blood that collects owing to the blow, the exiting of which from the surface results in a bruise. And this is why it must be applied quickly before (*the blood*) is solidified. And thapsia mixed with honey also helps for the same reason: for being hot it prevents the blood from being cooled.

11.[20] Why, when a wound has often occurred in the same place, does the scar become dark? Is it that whenever a wound occurs, the whole area is weak, and the more often this happens the weaker it becomes? Now the weak area is cooled and full of moisture; and this is why it appears dark, if indeed large and old wounds have dark scars.

---

[19] Cf. *Pr.* 9.9 and 12.
[20] Cf. *Pr.* 9.2, 5, and 7.

---

[10] εἴ<περ> τὰ Marenghi[3] : εἰ τὰ codd. (praeter Cᵃ, εἶτα) : εἶτα <τὰ> Forster : καὶ γὰρ Flashar

λαίνας τὰς οὐλὰς ἴσχει. τὸ δὲ πολλάκις λαβεῖν ἕλκος
οὐδὲν ἀλλ᾽ ἢ πολὺν χρόνον ἔχειν ἐστὶν ἕλκος.

12. Διὰ τί ποτε πρὸς τὰ ὑπώπια τοὺς κυάθους
35 προστιθέμεθα; | ἢ διότι, ὅταν πληγῶμεν, ὁ τόπος
καταψύχεται, τὸ δὲ θερμὸν ὑποχωρεῖ; προστιθέμενος
οὖν ὁ κύαθος, ψυχροῦ ὄντος τοῦ χαλκοῦ, διακωλύει τὸ
θερμὸν ἐκπορεύεσθαι.

13. Διὰ τί ἐν ταῖς οὐλαῖς οὐ γίνονται τρίχες; ἢ ὅτι
οἱ πόροι ἐπιτυφλοῦνται ἐξ ὧν αἱ τρίχες, καὶ παραλ-
λάττουσιν; ‖

891a   14. Διὰ τί οἴδημα[11] καὶ πελιώματα λαμβάνουσιν αἱ
πληγαί; ἢ διότι κατὰ τοῦτον τὸν τόπον διασταλέντα
τὰ ὑγρά, εἰς τοὺς πλησίον τόπους προσκόψαντα ἀπο-
πάλλεται πάλιν καὶ τῇ κολλήσει τῶν ὑγρῶν[12] συνήγα-
5 γεν; ἐὰν δὲ καὶ φλέβιά | τινα ῥαγῇ, ὕφαιμος ἡ συν-
δρομὴ γίνεται.

[11] οἴδημα : οἰδήματα β Barth.
[12] τῶν ὑγρῶν Y^a Ap C^a : ὑγρὸν cett. codd.

But to receive a wound often is nothing other than having a wound for a long time.

12.[21] Why do we apply ladles to bruises? Is it because, when we receive a blow, the place is cooled and the heat withdraws? Therefore, applying the ladle when the bronze is cold prevents the heat from going out.

13.[22] Why don't hairs grow on scars? Is it because the passages from which the hairs grow are obstructed and altered?[23]

14. Why do blows cause swelling and livid spots? Is it because the moisture in this region is dispersed, and breaking into the neighboring regions rebounds again, and collects by the adhesiveness of the moisture? And if any veins are broken, there is a rushing together of blood under the skin.

[21] Cf. *Pr.* 9.9–10.
[22] Cf. *Pr.* 10.27 and 29.
[23] Or "displaced."

BOOK X

INTRODUCTION

Book 10 is the longest in the entire *Problems*. Its title is *Epitome of Natural Things* or (more likely) *Epitome of Natural Problems* (Ἐπιτομὴ φυσικῶν)—"Problems" likely being implied, as it is in the other book titles.

Although the heading "natural problems" could include any topics in the study of nature, Book 10 is concerned solely with a subsection of nature, namely animals. In fact, most of the chapters raise questions about issues dealt with in Aristotle's biological writings and/or draw on such works in providing possible answers to these questions. For nearly half of the sixty-seven chapters, possible or probable sources can be identified from Aristotle's biology.[1] Theophrastus' lost works on animals (frs. 350–83 FHSG) may have been another source.[2]

Of what is *Pr.* 10 an epitome (i.e., a summary or abridgement)? Not of other extant books of the *Problems*, for otherwise we would expect much more overlap with chapters from outside Book 10. A number of chapters do

---

[1] Aristotle's biological works are *History of Animals*, *Parts of Animals*, *Generation of Animals*, *Movement of Animals*, and *Progression of Animals*.

[2] See R. W. Sharples, *Theophrastus of Eresus: Sources for His Life, Writings, Thought and Influence*, Commentary Vol. V, *Sources on Biology* (Leiden, 1995), pp. 32–48.

deal with topics also treated outside Book 10: 7 and 1.13–
14; 11 and 14.14; 18 and 33.10; 27 and 9.13; 29 and 9.13; 38
and 11.57; 40 and 11.60; 48 and 34.1; 49 and 34.10; 51 and
31.21; 54 and 33.10. But in only three instances is there
substantial similarity, or near identity, in content: 24 and
4.31; 40 and 11.55; 50 and 31.26.

It is possible that *Pr.* 10 grew out of, or was based on,
some epitome of Aristotle's or, more likely, of Theophrastus'. It seems such works were not uncommon in the
Lyceum. Diogenes Laertius attributes to Aristotle a work
entitled *Epitome of Orators* (2.104) and to Theophrastus
Epitome of Analytics (5.43), *Epitome of Plato's Republic*
(5.43), *Epitome of Laws* (5.44), and—most interesting in
the present case—*Epitome of Natural Things* (Φυσικῶν
ἐπιτομῆς) (5.48 and 9.21) and *Epitome of On Natural
Things* (Περὶ φυσικῶν ἐπιτομῆς) (5.46).[3] Although the
similarity between the last two titles, and that of *Pr.* 10, is
intriguing, as we know nothing of the content of these
Theophrastean works, we can say nothing about any relationship between them and *Pr.* 10.

As for the content of Book 10: Fifty chapters deal with
both humans and other animals—either treating both together (at least implicitly), or contrasting humans with
other animals. Of the remainder, thirteen deal solely with
humans, and merely four with nonhuman animals alone.
Three related topics that are dealt with in a number of
chapters would seem to reveal a major interest in the generation of animals: copulation and generation (9, 13, 24,

---

[3] This last item, however, follows (in Diogenes Laertius' list) a
work called *On Natural Things* (Περὶ φυσικῶν) and so may be a
summary or abridgement of that work.

47, 52, 65); the number and nature of offspring (10, 12, 14, 28, 32, 41, 58, 61); and eunuchs (36, 37, 42, 57). Another topic receiving a great deal of attention is hair and hairiness (21, 22, 23, 25, 27, 29, 53, 62, 63).[4] Topics dealt with in more than one chapter are white leprosy (4, 5, 33, 34), voice (38, 39, 40), eyes (11, 15, 50), and sneezing (15, 54). Here is a sample of topics with a single chapter devoted to them: coughing (1), nosebleeds (2), milk (6), nocturnal emissions (16), urination (20), gallstones (43), belching (44), and excrement (59). There is a lengthy and important chapter contrasting tame and wild animals (45).

[4] A possible source for some of these chapters is Theophrastus' lost *On Hairs* or *On (Types of) Hair* (Περὶ τριχῶν) (DL 5.45). This is speculative, however, as we know nothing about the content of that work.

ΕΠΙΤΟΜΗ ΦΥΣΙΚΩΝ

1. Διὰ τί τὰ μὲν βήττει, τὰ δ᾽ οὔ, οἷον ἄνθρωπος
μὲν βήττει, βοῦς δὲ οὔ; πότερον τῷ εἰς ἄλλο τι
τρέπεσθαι τοῖς | πλείστοις ζῴοις τὸ περίττωμα, ἀν-
θρώπῳ δὲ δεῦρο; ἢ ὅτι ἐγκέφαλον πλεῖστον καὶ ὑγρό-
τατον ἔχει ὁ ἄνθρωπος, ἡ δὲ βὴξ καταρρέοντος γίνεται φλέγματος;

2. Διὰ τί ἀνθρώπῳ μόνῳ τῶν ζῴων αἷμα ῥεῖ ἐκ τῶν
μυκτήρων; ἢ ὅτι ἐγκέφαλον ἔχει πλεῖστον καὶ ὑγρό-
τατον, | ἀφ᾽ οὗ αἱ φλέβες πληρούμεναι τοῦ περιτ-
τώματος διὰ τῶν πόρων προΐενται τὴν ῥύσιν; λεπτότερον γὰρ γίνεται τοῦ αἵματος τοῦ καθαροῦ τὸ
νοσερόν, τοῦτο δέ ἐστι τὸ μιχθὲν τοῖς τοῦ ἐγκεφάλου
περιττώμασιν, καὶ ἔστι καθάπερ ἰχώρ.

3. Διὰ τί τῶν ζῴων τὰ μὲν ὑπὸ σάρκα,[1] τὰ δὲ κατὰ |
σάρκα πίονά ἐστι, τὰ δὲ κατ᾽ ἀμφότερα; ἢ ὅσων μὲν
πυκνὴ ἡ σάρξ, [ὑπὸ σάρκα][2] μεταξὺ τοῦ δέρματος καὶ
τῆς σαρκὸς συστέλλεται ἡ ἰκμὰς διὰ τὸ ταύτῃ εἶναι

891a
10

15

20

---

[1] σάρκα codd. *PPA* Barth. : δέρμα Louis ex Gaza
[2] [ὑπὸ σάρκα] Bussemaker : ὑπὸ δέρμα Sylburg

EPITOME OF NATURAL
PROBLEMS

1. Why do some (*animals*) cough, whereas others do not, for instance a human coughs, but a bull does not? Is it because in most animals the residue[1] is directed to some other part, but in a human it is directed here? Or is it because the human has the largest and moistest brain, and the cough comes from phlegm flowing down?

2. Why, in the human alone of animals, does blood flow from the nostrils? Is it because he has the largest and moistest brain, from which the veins, being filled with residue, emit a flow through the passages? For the diseased blood—i.e., that blood mixed with the residues from the brain—is thinner than clean blood, and is like serum.[2]

3.[3] Why are some animals fat under the flesh,[4] some in the flesh, and some in both places? In the case of those whose flesh is thick, does the fluid collect between the skin and the flesh, because the skin here is naturally loose, and

---

[1] From the brain.

[2] Serum (ἰχώρ) is the watery part of the blood, which is such either because it has not yet been concocted or because it is in the process of decay (see *PA* 651a17–19, *HA* 521b2–3).

[3] Source: *HA* 3.17.

[4] Or, following Louis, "skin."

⟨τὸ δέρμα⟩[3] ἀφεστὸς[4] φύσει· ἢ πεττομένη γίνεται
πιμελή; ὅσα δὲ ἀραιοτέραν[5] ἔχει τὴν σάρκα τό τε
25 δέρμα προσεστός,[6] κατὰ σάρκα πίονα γίνεται. | τὰ δὲ
ἀμφοτέρως ἔχοντα ἐπ᾽ ἀμφότερα[7] πιαίνεται.

4. Διὰ τί οἱ παῖδες καὶ αἱ γυναῖκες ἧττον ἔχουσι
λεύκην τῶν ἀνδρῶν, καὶ τῶν μὲν γυναικῶν αἱ πρεσβύ-
τιδες μᾶλλον; ἢ ὅτι ἡ λεύκη ἐστὶ πνεύματος ἔξοδος,
ἔστι δὲ τὰ μὲν τῶν παίδων οὐκ εὔπνοα σώματα, ἀλλὰ
30 πυκνά, καὶ τὰ | τῶν γυναικῶν ἧττον ἢ τὰ τῶν ἀνδρῶν;
εἰς τὰ καταμήνια γὰρ τρέπεται· δηλοῖ δὲ ἡ λειότης τὴν
πυκνότητα τῆς σαρκός. τὰ δὲ τῶν πρεσβυτέρων καὶ
τῶν γραῶν εὔπνοα· μόνα γάρ, ὥσπερ τὰ παλαιὰ
οἰκοδομήματα, διεστῶσαν ἔχει τὴν σύνθεσιν τῶν μο-
ρίων.[8] |

35 5. Διὰ τί ἄνθρωπος μόνον ἴσχει λεύκην; πότερον
ὅτι λεπτοδερμότατον τῶν ζῴων ἐστίν, ἅμα δὲ καὶ
πνευματωδέστερον;[9] σημεῖον δέ, ὅτι ἡ λεύκη ἐν τοῖς
λεπτοδερμοτάτοις μάλιστα καὶ πρῶτον γίνεται μέρε-
891b σιν. ἢ διὰ ταῦτά τε, καὶ ‖ ὅτι μόνον πολιοῦται τῶν
ζῴων; ἐν γὰρ ταῖς λεύκαις πολιαὶ γίνονται αἱ τρίχες,
ὥστε ἀδύνατον ὅσα μὴ πολιοῦται λεύκην ἴσχειν.

[3] ⟨τὸ δέρμα⟩ Sylburg   [4] ἀφεστὸς Nicasius : ἀφεστὼς
Ap X[a] : ἐφεστὼς Y[a] C[a]   [5] ἀραιοτέραν Sylburg (rariorem
Gaza et Trap.) : δεινοτέραν codd. (duriorem Barth.) : fort.
μανοτέραν Ruelle   [6] προσεστός D L A[m] P[c] Y[a ac] Nicasius :
προεστὼς cett. codd. : προεστός Bekker   [7] ἀμφότερα :
ἀμφοτέροις β   [8] post μορίων add. τὸ σῶμα Y[a] Ap C[a]
[9] πνευματωδέστερον : πνευματωδέστατον Richards

this fluid when concocted becomes fat? But those animals that have more porous flesh and tight skin become fat in the flesh.[5] Now those having both conditions become fat in both places.

4.[6] Why do children[7] and women get the white disease[8] less than men, and among women the old more (*than the young*)? Is it because the white disease is an exiting of breath, and the bodies of children do not have a good flow of air, but are thick, and those of women less so than those of men? For breath is directed into the menses, and the smoothness (*of their bodies*) reveals the thickness of the flesh. But the bodies of older men and old women have a good flow of air; for they alone, just like old buildings, have separations in the construction of their parts.

5.[9] Why does the human alone have the white disease? Is it because he is the thinnest-skinned of animals, and at the same time very full of breath? Now a sign of this is the fact that the white disease occurs most and first on the parts where the skin is thinnest. Or is it for this reason too, i.e., that the human alone of animals turns gray? For in cases of the white disease the hair becomes gray, so that those animals whose hair does not turn gray cannot have the white disease.

---

[5] The text of this and the preceding line is uncertain.

[6] Cf. *Pr.* 10.5, 33, 34.

[7] Or "boys."

[8] I translate ἡ λεύκη "the white disease" throughout; it likely (or usually) refers to vitiligo (also known as "white leprosy"), though that is not entirely clear. Cf. Arist. *HA* 518a12–18, *GA* 784a25–30, *Col.* 797b15–16, Hp. *Prorrh.* 2.43.

[9] Cf. *Pr.* 10.4, 33, 34.

6. Διὰ τί αἶγες μὲν καὶ πρόβατα ἀμέλγονται πλεῖ-
5 στον | γάλα, οὐ μέγιστον σῶμα ἔχοντα, ἄνθρωπος δὲ
καὶ βοῦς ἔλαττον ὡς κατὰ λόγον; πότερον ὅτι εἰς τὸ
σῶμα ἀναλίσκεται, τοῖς δὲ ἄλλοις εἰς τὸ περίττωμα,
τοῖς δὲ προβάτοις καὶ ταῖς αἰξὶ τὸ περιγινόμενον τοῦ
περιττώματος γάλα γίνεται πᾶν; ἢ ὅτι πολυτοκώτερά
10 ἐστι τῶν μεγάλων, ὥστε | πλεῖον σπᾷ περίττωμα διὰ
τὸ πλείω τρέφειν; ἢ δι᾽ ἀσθένειαν τῶν σωμάτων πλεῖον περίττωμα γίνεται κύουσιν αὐτοῖς; τὸ δὲ γάλα
γίνεται ἐκ τοῦ περιττώματος.

7. Διὰ τί τῶν ζῴων τὰ μέν, μεταβάλλοντα τὰ ὕδατα,
μεταβάλλει τὰς χρόας καὶ ὅμοια γίνεται τοῖς ἐκεῖ,
15 οἷον | αἶγες, τὰ δὲ οὔ, οἷον ἄνθρωποι; καὶ ὅλως δὲ διὰ
τί τὰ μὲν μεταβάλλει, τὰ δὲ οὔ, οἷον κόραξ οὐ μεταβάλλει; ἢ ὧν μὲν οὐ[10] κρατεῖ ἡ φύσις τοῦ ὑγροῦ,
ὥσπερ ἡ τῶν ὀρνέων (διὸ καὶ κύστιν οὐκ ἔχει), οὐδέ[11]
μεταβάλλει; καὶ διὰ τί οὐκ αὐτά, ἀλλὰ τὰ ἔκγονα
20 μεταβάλλει; ἢ ὅτι | ἀσθενέστερα τὰ νέα τῶν γεννη-
σάντων;

8. Διὰ τί τὰ ἄρσενα μείζω τῶν θηλειῶν ὡς ἐπίπαν

[10] om. οὐ fort.
[11] οὐδέ Marenghi[4] : οὔτε codd. : οὐ Sylburg

---

[10] I.e., the material that becomes milk. Aristotle's fullest discussion of the nature of milk is in *GA* 4.8. There he says that milk is
a kind of concocted blood. It is one of the useful residues. See also
HA 3.20–21.

6. Why do goats and sheep provide the most milk, though they do not have the largest bodies, while humans and cattle give proportionally less? Is it because (*in humans and cattle*) it[10] is used up on the body, and among the other animals it is used up on residues, but in sheep and in goats all of what remains of the residue becomes milk? Or is it because (*sheep and goats*) have a greater number of offspring than the large animals,[11] so that they draw off more residue because they have more (*offspring*) to nourish? Or is it that, owing to the weakness of their bodies, more residue is formed during their gestation period? And the milk comes from residue.

7.[12] Why do some animals, for example goats, when they change the water (*they drink*), also change their color and become similar to the animals in that (*new*) place, but others, for instance humans, do not? And in general, why do some animals change (*color*), whereas others do not, for example crows do not change? Or is it that the animals the nature of which does not master the moisture—like (*the nature*) of birds (and this is why they don't have a bladder)—do not change?[13] And why do they themselves not change, but their offspring do? Is it because the young are weaker than their parents?

8. Why are males, on the whole, larger than females?[14]

[11] Or possibly, following Hett, "of the large animals, (*sheep and goats*) have the greater number of offspring."

[12] Source: *HA* 3.12. Cf. *Pr.* 1.13–14.   [13] There may be a problem with the text of this sentence. One would expect the animals that *can* master the moisture would not change color.

[14] This is a view expressed often in Aristotle's biology, e.g., at *HA* 538a22–25.

ἐστίν; πότερον ὅτι θερμότερα, τοῦτο δὲ αὐξητικόν; ἢ
ὅτι ὁλόκληρα, τὰ δὲ πεπήρωται; ἢ ὅτι τὰ μὲν ἐν πολλῷ
χρόνῳ τελειοῦνται, τὰ δὲ ἐν ὀλίγῳ; |

25   9. Διὰ τί τὰ μὲν ταχυτόκα τῶν ζῴων ἐστίν, τῶν δὲ
πολυχρόνιος ἡ κύησις; ἢ ὅτι τὰ μακροβιώτερα βραδύτερον πέφυκε τελειοῦσθαι; ἔστι δὲ βραδυτόκα τὰ
μακρόβια. οὐ μέντοι τὰ μάλιστα, οἷον ἵππος ἀνθρώπου βραδυτοκώτερον μέν, ὀλιγοχρονιώτερον δέ. τού-
30   του δὲ αἴτιον ἡ σκληρότης | τῶν ὑστερῶν· ὥσπερ γὰρ
ἡ ξηρὰ γῆ οὐ ταχὺ ἐκτρέφει, οὕτω καὶ ἡ τοῦ ἵππου
ὑστέρα.

10. Διὰ τί τοῖς ἄλλοις ζῴοις τὰ ἔκγονα μᾶλλον τὰς
φύσεις ὁμοιοῦται ἢ τοῖς ἀνθρώποις; ἢ ὅτι ὁ μὲν
ἄνθρωπος πολλαχῶς διατίθεται τὴν ψυχὴν κατὰ τὴν
35   ὁμιλίαν, καθὼς | δ᾽ ἂν ὁ[12] πατὴρ καὶ ἡ μήτηρ δια-
τεθῶσιν, οὕτω ποικίλλεται καὶ τὰ τικτόμενα, τὰ δὲ
ἄλλα ζῷα τὰ μὲν πλεῖστα πρὸς αὐτὸ τοῦτό εἰσιν; ἔτι
δὲ οὐ πληροῦται[13] ὡς ἐπὶ τὸ πολὺ διὰ ταύτην τὴν
ἐπιθυμίαν. ‖

892a   11. Διὰ τί οἱ λευκοὶ ἄνθρωποι καὶ ἵπποι ὡς ἐπὶ τὸ

---

12 ὁ Bekker : ὅ τε codd.
13 πληροῦται : πηροῦται β : fort. πυροῦται ex Trap. (ardent)

---

15 Πηρόω—the root of the word here translated "mutilated"
(πεπήρωται)—means "maim" or "mutilate"; and, at least in Aristotle, πηρόω and related terms can refer to deformities, i.e., animals "mutilated" from birth.
16 Sources: GA 4.6 and 10.

Is it because they are hotter, and this is conducive to growth? Or is it because they are complete, whereas females are mutilated?[15] Or is it because the former grow to perfection over a long time, the latter in a short time?

9.[16] Why do some animals bear their young quickly, whereas the gestation period of others is long? Is it because it is natural for the longer-lived animals to grow to perfection more slowly? And the long-lived are born slowly. This is not true in every case; for instance, the horse bears its young more slowly than the human, but is shorter-lived. Now the reason for this is the hardness of the womb; for just as dry ground cannot produce quickly, so too the womb of the mare.

10.[17] Why in the other animals do the offspring resemble the natures (*of their parents*) more than in humans? Is it because the human, during intercourse, arranges the soul in many ways,[18] and however the father and the mother arranged (*their souls*), in that way the offspring are varied, but with the other animals most are focused on the act itself? And further, they do not become pregnant[19] in most cases owing to this desire.

11.[20] Why do fair-skinned humans and white horses[21] in

17 Aristotle discusses the resemblance of offspring to parents in *GA* 4.3.

18 The phrase "arranges the soul in many ways" is a literal translation, probably meaning something like "is capable of thinking of any number of things" (during intercourse).

19 Or "mutilated" (cf. 10.8) or "inflamed," depending on which ms. reading is correct. The meaning of the line is unclear.

20 Source: *HA* 1.10 and *GA* 779a28–b34. Cf. *Pr.* 14.14.

21 Literally, "white humans and horses."

πολὺ γλαυκοί; ἢ διότι τριῶν χρωμάτων ὄντων τοῖς
ὄμμασιν, μέλανος καὶ αἰγωποῦ καὶ γλαυκοῦ, τῷ τοῦ
σώματος χρώματι καὶ τὸ τοῦ ὀφθαλμοῦ χρῶμα ἀκο-
5 λουθεῖ; τοῦτο | δέ ἐστι γλαυκότης.

12. Διὰ τίνα αἰτίαν οἱ νάνοι γίνονται; ἔτι δὲ μᾶλλον
καθόλου, διὰ τί τὰ μὲν ὅλως μεγάλα, τὰ δὲ μικρά; εἶτα
οὕτω σκεπτέον. δύο δὴ τὰ αἴτια· ἢ γὰρ ὁ τόπος ἢ ἡ
10 τροφή. ὁ μὲν οὖν τόπος, ἐὰν ᾖ στενός, ἡ δὲ τροφή, | ἐὰν
ᾖ ὀλίγη, ὥσπερ καὶ ἤδη γεγενημένων πειρῶνται
μικροὺς ποιεῖν, οἷον οἱ τὰ κυνίδια τρέφοντες ἐν τοῖς
ὀρτυγοτροφείοις. ὅσοις μὲν οὖν ὁ τόπος αἴτιος, οὗτοι
πυγμαῖοι γίνονται. τὰ μὲν γὰρ πλάτη καὶ τὰ μήκη
ἔχοντες γίνονται κατὰ τὸ τῶν τεκόντων μέγεθος, μι-
15 κροὶ δὲ ὅλως. τούτου δὲ αἴτιον, | ὅτι διὰ τὴν στενότητα
τοῦ τόπου συγκλῶμεναι αἱ εὐθεῖαι καμπύλαι γίνονται.
ὥσπερ οὖν οἱ ἐπὶ τῶν καπηλείων γραφόμενοι μικροὶ
μέν εἰσι, φαίνονται δ' ἔχοντες πλάτη καὶ βάθη, ὁμοίως συμβαίνει καὶ τοῖς πυγμαίοις. ὅσοι δὲ διὰ τροφῆς
ἔνδειαν ἀτελεῖς γίνονται, οὗτοι καὶ παιδαριώδη τὰ |
20 μέλη ἔχοντες φαίνονται. καὶ ἐνίους ἰδεῖν ἔστι μικροὺς
μὲν σφόδρα, συμμέτρους δέ, ὥσπερ τὰ Μελιταῖα
κυνίδια. αἴτιον δὲ ὅτι οὐχ ὡς ὁ τόπος ἡ φύσις ποιεῖ.

13. Διὰ τί τῶν ζῴων τὰ μὲν ἐξ ἀλλήλων γίνεται, τὰ

---

22 Or perhaps "gray."
23 Literally, "black," though this surely includes brown eyes.
24 Literally, "goat-eyed."   25 On dwarves and pygmies,
see PA 686b3–31, HA 597a6–9, GA 749a4–6. Such passages may
have been the source for Pr. 10.12.

most cases have light-blue[22] eyes? Is it because there are three colors of eyes—dark,[23] greenish,[24] and light-blue—and the color of the eye follows the color of the body? Now in this case it is light-blue.

12.[25] For what reason are there dwarves? Or more generally, why are some animals as a whole large, while others are small?[26] It is necessary to consider the issue in this way. There are two causes: either space or nourishment. Now the space (*is the cause*) if it is confined, and the nourishment if it is meager, just as they attempt to make animals that have just been born small, e.g., those raising little dogs raised in quail cages. Therefore, in those cases where space is the cause, pygmies come to be. For they have the breadth and the length in the same proportion as their parents, but they are small in general. Now the reason for this is that owing to the narrowness of the space, their straight lines, being crushed, become curved. Therefore, just as the figures (*of animals*) painted on shops are small, though they appear clearly to have (*the correct*) breadth and depth, so it is with pygmies as well. But those who come to be imperfect owing to a lack of nourishment appear clearly to have the parts of children. And it is possible to see some that are extremely small, but well proportioned, like the little Melitaean[27] dogs. The reason is that nature does not produce the same effect as space.

13.[28] Why do some animals come to be from one an-

---

[26] I.e., why are the individuals of a certain kind of animal as a whole large, though some are small?

[27] This likely refers to the Dalmatian island now called Meleda (or Mljet in Croatian).   [28] Cf. *Pr.* 10.65. On spontaneous generation, see *GA* 763a24–16.

δὲ ἔκ τινων συγκρινομένων ὁμοίως τῆς ἐξ ἀρχῆς
25 γενέσεως | αὐτοῖς ὑπαρξάσης; καθάπερ οἱ περὶ φύσε-
ως λέγοντες λέγουσιν καὶ τὴν ἐξ ἀρχῆς γένεσιν τῶν
ζῴων γενέσθαι διὰ τὰς μεταβολὰς καὶ μετακινήσεις
τοῦ κόσμου καὶ τοῦ παντὸς ⟨οὔσας⟩[14] οὕτω μεγάλας·
καὶ νῦν εἴπερ μέλλει πάλιν ἔσεσθαι, τοιαύτας τινὰς
30 ὑπάρξαι δεῖ κινήσεις. ἡ μὲν γὰρ ἀρχὴ | παντὸς ἔργου
μέγιστον· ἥμισυ γάρ. τὸ δὲ σπέρμα ἀρχή. τῶν μὲν
οὖν μικρῶν ὅσα γίνεται μὴ ἐξ ἀλλήλων, αἴτιον ⟨τοῦ⟩[15]
τοιαῦτα γενέσθαι ὥσπερ ἐξ ἀρχῆς ἐγεννήθησαν ἡ τοῦ
σπέρματος μικρότης· τοῦ γὰρ ἐλάττονος καὶ ἡ ἀρχὴ
ἐλάττων. ὥστε ἱκαναὶ καὶ αἱ τούτου μεταβολαὶ πρὸς
35 τὸ γεννῆσαι | αὐτῷ τὸ σπέρμα. ὅπερ συμβαίνει· γίνον-
ται γὰρ ἐν ταῖς μεταβολαῖς μάλιστα. τοῖς δὲ μείζοσι
μείζονος δεῖ καὶ μεταβολῆς.

14. Διὰ τί τὰ μὲν πολύτεκνα τῶν ζῴων, οἷον ὗς,
892b κύων, ‖ λαγώς, τὰ δὲ οὔ, οἷον ἄνθρωπος, λέων; ἢ ὅτι τὰ
μὲν πολλὰς μήτρας καὶ τύπους[16] ἔχει, ἃς[17] καὶ πίμ-
πλασθαι ἐπιθυμεῖ καὶ εἰς ἃ σχίζεται ἡ γονή, τὰ δὲ
τοὐναντίον;

15. Διὰ τί ἐλάχιστον διάστημα τῶν ὀμμάτων ὁ
5 ἄνθρωπος | ἔχει τῶν ζῴων κατὰ μέγεθος; ἢ διότι

14 ⟨οὔσας⟩ Richards
15 ⟨τοῦ⟩ Richards
16 τύπους : τόπους β
17 ἃς β Xᵃ aᵐ p : ἴσους a B Barth. : ἴσας plur. δ

other,[29] whereas others come from the compounding of certain (*elements*), similar to the generation belonging to them at the beginning?[30] Just as those who speak about nature say that the generation of animals from the beginning occurred owing to the changes and alterations in the world and in the universe being so great; so now, if it is to happen again, some such movements must take place. For the beginning of any work is most important: it is half. Now the seed is the beginning. Therefore, the cause of the small animals that do not come to be from one another coming to be as if they had been produced from the beginning is the smallness of seed; for the beginning of the lesser is also less. So the changes even of this are sufficient with a view to producing seed for it. And this is just what happens: for they come to be especially as the result of these changes. But for greater animals there must be a greater change.

14.[31] Why do some animals give birth to many young, like the pig, the dog, and the hare, but others do not, like the human and the lion? Is it because the former have a number of wombs and impressions, which they desire to fill and into which the semen is divided, and the latter are the opposite?

15. Why does the human, of all animals, have the least distance between the eyes in proportion to size? Is it be-

---

[29] This is a highly condensed way of saying "Why do some animals come to be from animals of the same kind having sexual intercourse with one another?"   [30] The author is contrasting normal and spontaneous generation. Much of what follows, however, is unclear.   [31] The source of this chapter is likely *GA* 770b28–772b12. Aristotle there refers to "what was said about these matters in the *Problems*" (772b12).

μάλιστα κατὰ φύσιν ἔχει τῶν ἄλλων, ἡ δὲ αἴσθησις
φύσει τοῦ[18] ἔμπροσθεν; ἐφ᾽ ὃ γὰρ ἡ κίνησις, τοῦτο δεῖ
προορᾶν. ὅσῳ δ᾽ ἂν ᾖ πλεῖον τὸ διάστημα τῶν ὀμμάτων, τοσούτῳ μᾶλλον αἱ ὄψεις ἔσονται ἐν τῷ πλα-
10 γίῳ. εἰ οὖν ἔχειν δεῖ κατὰ φύσιν, | ὅτι ὀλίγιστον δεῖ τὸ
διάστημα εἶναι· οὕτω γὰρ εἰς τὸ πρόσθεν μάλιστα
πορεύσεται. ἔτι δὲ τοῖς ἄλλοις ζῴοις, ἐπεὶ χεῖρας οὐκ
ἔχουσιν, ἀναγκαῖον παρορᾶν εἰς τὰ πλάγια. διὸ πλεῖον διέστηκε τὰ ὄμματα αὐτῶν, καὶ μάλιστα τῶν προβάτων, διὰ τὸ μάλιστα ποιεῖσθαι τὴν πορείαν κύπτον-
τα. |

15   16. Διὰ τί τὰ ἄλλα ζῷα τὰ μὲν οὐκ ἐξονειρώττει, τὰ
δὲ ὀλιγάκις; πότερον ὅτι οὐδὲν ὕπτιον κατάκειται,
ἐξονειρώττει δὲ οὐδὲν μὴ ὕπτιον; ἢ ὅτι οὐκ ἐνυπνιάζει
τὰ ἄλλα ὁμοίως, ὁ δὲ ἐξονειρωγμὸς μετὰ φαντασίας
γίνεται;

17. Διὰ τί τῶν ζῴων τὰ μὲν κινεῖ τὴν κεφαλήν, τὰ
20 δὲ | οὐ κινεῖ; ἢ ὅτι ἔνια οὐκ ἔχει αὐχένα; διὸ ταῦτα οὐ
κινεῖ τὴν κεφαλήν.

18. Διὰ τί ἄνθρωπος πτάρνυται τῶν ζῴων μάλιστα;
πότερον ὅτι τοὺς πόρους εὐρεῖς ἔχει δι᾽ ὧν τὸ πνεῦμα
καὶ ὀσμὴ εἰσέρχεται; τούτοις γὰρ πνεύματος πληρου-
25 μένοις πτάρνυται. | ὅτι δ᾽ εὐρεῖς, σημεῖον ὅτι ἥκιστα
ὀσφραντικὸν τῶν ἄλλων ζῴων· ἀκριβέστεροι γὰρ[19] οἱ

18 τοῦ Richards : τὸ codd.
19 γὰρ scripsi ex [Arist./Alex.] Sup.Pr. 2.51, 4 : δὲ codd.

cause he, much more than the others, is in accordance with
nature, and perception by nature is of what is in front? For
that toward which the movement is directed should be
seen beforehand. Now the greater the distance between
the eyes, the more the organs of sight will face sideways. So
if something should be according to nature, then this distance should be as small as possible; for in this way (*the
sight*) will most of all travel forward. Further, it is necessary for the other animals to see sideways, since they don't
have hands. This is why their eyes have been set apart
more, especially in sheep, because they usually move (*with
their heads*) bent down.

16.[32] Why do some of the other animals not have nocturnal emissions, while some have them rarely? Is it because none of them lies down on its back, and none has a
nocturnal emission except on its back? Or is it because the
other animals do not dream in the same way,[33] but a nocturnal emission (*always*) occurs with imagination?

17. Why do some animals move their heads, and others
not? Is it because some have no neck? This is why they do
not move their heads.

18.[34] Why does the human sneeze most of all animals?
Is it because the passages through which the breath and
odor enter are wide? For it is when these are full of breath
that he sneezes. Now a sign that they are wide is the fact
that he is less able to smell than the other animals. For the

---

[32] Cf. Thphr. *Lass.* 16.   [33] Re. "in the same way" (ὁμοίως): this is often taken here to mean "to the same extent," but the
next clause implies that the author is referring to the *content* of
dreams.   [34] This chapter is virtually identical to *Pr.* 33.10
and very close to [Arist./Alex.] *Sup.Pr.* 2.51. Cf. *Pr.* 10.54.

λεπτότεροι.[20] εἰ οὖν εἰς μὲν τοὺς εὐρεῖς πλέον καὶ
πλεονάκις εἰσέρχεται τὸ ὑγρόν, οὗ πνευματουμένου ὁ
πταρμὸς γίνεται, τοιούτους δὲ μάλιστα τῶν ζῴων οἱ
ἄνθρωποι ἔχουσι, πλειστάκις ἂν πτάρνυντο[21] εἰκότως. |

30 ἢ ὅτι ἐλάχιστοι κατὰ τὸ μῆκος οἱ μυκτῆρες, ὥστε τὸ
θερμανθὲν ὑγρὸν ταχὺ δύναται πνεῦμα γίνεσθαι, ἐν δὲ
τοῖς ἄλλοις διὰ μῆκος καταψύχεται πρότερον;

19. Διὰ τί ἡ γλῶττα οὐδενὸς πιερὰ τῶν ζῴων; ἢ ὅτι
τὸ πῖον πυκνόν, ἡ δὲ γλῶττα ἀραιὰ φύσει ἐστίν, ὅπως
35 τοὺς | χυμοὺς γνωρίζῃ;

20. Διὰ τί τὰ θήλεα συντάσει οὐρεῖ, τὰ δὲ ἄρρενα
οὔ; ἢ ὅτι πορρώτερόν ἐστιν ἡ κύστις ἡ τῶν θηλειῶν,
καὶ εἰς βάθος καὶ εἰς μῆκος; μεταξὺ γὰρ αὐτῶν ἡ
893a μήτρα τῆς ἕδρας καὶ ‖ τῆς κύστεως. ὥστε δεῖται βίας
πλείονος τὸ ἐκπεμπόμενον διά γε τὴν ἀπόστασιν τῆς
μήτρας. βιάζεται δὲ συντεῖνον τῷ πνεύματι.

21. Διὰ τί τῶν ζῴων ὅσα μὴ πέτεται, πάντα ἀπο-
5 βάλλει | τὰς χειμερινὰς τρίχας, πλὴν ὑός; καὶ γὰρ
κύων ἀποβάλλει καὶ βοῦς. ἢ ὅτι θερμότατον ἡ ὗς
ἐστίν, καὶ ἐκ θερμοῦ πεφύκασιν αἱ τρίχες αὐτῇ; τοιοῦτον γάρ ἐστι τὸ λιπαρόν. τῶν μὲν οὖν ἄλλων ἢ διὰ
τὸ ἀποψύχεσθαι τὸ ὑγρὸν ἀποπίπτουσιν, ἢ πέττειν
10 τροφὴν οὐ δυναμένης τῆς οἰκείας θερμότητος. | ‹ἡ δὲ
ὗς› ἢ διὰ τὸ[22] μηδὲν πάσχειν τὴν ὑγρότητα τὴν ἐν
αὐτῇ, ‹ἢ›[23] διὰ τὸ πέττεσθαι καλῶς τὴν τροφήν, οὐκ

[20] λεπτότεροι : λεπτοὶ πόροι Pr. 33.10, 962b12
[21] πτάρνυντο : πτάρνοιντο Sylburg

narrower ones are the more accurate. Therefore, if moisture enters these wide passages in greater quantity and more often, and when it is converted into breath a sneeze occurs, and humans most of all the animals have such passages, it is reasonable that he should sneeze most often. Or is it because his nostrils are especially short in length, so that the heated moisture can quickly become breath, but in the other animals it is cooled beforehand owing to the length of the nostrils?

19.[35] Why is the tongue of animals never fat? Is it because what is fat is dense, but the tongue is naturally porous, so that it may recognize flavors?

20. Why do females strain to urinate, whereas males do not? Is it because in females the bladder is farther away, both in depth and in length? For in them, there is the womb between the buttocks and the bladder. So the expulsion requires more force owing to the distance of the womb. And the force is applied by a straining of the breath.

21. Why do all of the animals that do not fly shed their hair in winter, except for the pig? For both the dog and the bull shed. Is it because the pig is hottest, and in it hair grows from heat? For what is oily is hot. Now in other animals ⟨the hair⟩ falls off either because the moisture is cooled off or because its own heat is not able to concoct nourishment. ⟨But the pig⟩, either because the moisture in it is not affected, ⟨or⟩ because the nourishment is well

[35] On the tongue and the sense of taste, see *PA* 2.17 and *DA* 2.10.

---

22 ⟨ἡ δὲ ὗς⟩ ἢ διὰ τὸ Forster ex Gaza : ἡ δὲ διὰ τὸ κτλ. Nicasius   23 ⟨ἢ⟩ Forster ex Gaza

ἀποβάλλει τὰς τρίχας. ὁπότε γὰρ ἡ αἰτία τῆς ἀπο-
βολῆς ἐστίν, ἱκανὴ ἡ πιότης κωλῦσαι. πρόβατα δὲ καὶ
ἄνθρωποι διὰ πλῆθος καὶ πυκνότητα τῆς τριχὸς ἀπα-
15 θῆ ἐστίν· οὐ γὰρ δικνεῖται | ἡ ψύξις εἰς βάθος, ὥστε
πῆξαι τὴν ὑγρότητα ἢ πέψαι κωλῦσαι τὴν θερμότητα.

22. Διὰ τί τῶν μὲν προβάτων μαλακώτεραι αἱ τρίχες ἀναφύονται τιλλόμεναι, τῶν δὲ ἀνθρώπων σκληρότεραι; ἢ ὅτι τῶν μὲν προβάτων ἐκ τοῦ ἐπιπολῆς
20 πεφύκασιν; διὸ | καὶ ἀλύπως ἐκσπῶνται, μενούσης τῆς
ἀρχῆς τῆς τροφῆς ἀδιαφθόρου, ἥ ἐστιν ἐν σαρκί. τὰ
μὲν οὖν περιττώματα ἀνοιχθέντων ἐξατμίζει μᾶλλον,
τὸ δὲ ἔριον σαρκὸς οἰκείαν τροφὴν λαμβάνει· σὰρξ δὲ
μαλακοῖς καὶ γλυκέσι τρέφεται. αἱ δὲ τῶν ἀνθρώπων
25 τρίχες ἐκ βάθους πεφυκυῖαι | βίᾳ καὶ μετ᾽ ἀλγηδόνος
ἐκσπῶνται. δῆλον δέ· ἐπισπῶνται γὰρ αἷμα. τραυμα-
τιζομένου οὖν τοῦ τόπου συμβαίνει αὐτὸν καὶ οὐλοῦ-
σθαι. διὸ τέλος μὲν συμβαίνει γίνεσθαι τοῖς τιλλομέ-
νοις· ἕως δ᾽ ἂν ἀνίωσι τρίχες, σκληρὰς ἀνιέναι διὰ τὸ
30 τὴν μὲν τροφώδη τῆς σαρκὸς ἐκλελοιπέναι | πᾶσαν
τροφήν, ἐκ περιττωμάτων δ᾽ αὐτὰς γίνεσθαι. σημεῖον
δέ· τῶν μὲν γὰρ πρὸς μεσημβρίαν πάντων σκληραί
εἰσιν αἱ τρίχες διὰ τὸ τὸ ἐκτὸς θερμὸν εἰς βάθος
διικνούμενον ἐξατμίζειν τὴν εὔπεπτον τροφήν, τῶν δὲ
ὑπὸ τὰς ἄρκτους μαλακαί. τούτοις γὰρ ἐπιπολῆς μᾶλ-
35 λόν ἐστιν τό | θ᾽ αἷμα καὶ οἱ γλυκεῖς χυμοί· διὸ καὶ
εὔχροοί εἰσιν.

23. Διὰ τί αἱ μὲν τῶν προβάτων τρίχες ὅσῳ ἂν
μακρότεραι ὦσι, σκληρότεραι γίνονται, αἱ δὲ τῶν

concocted, does not shed its hair. For whenever a cause of shedding is present, the fat is sufficient to prevent it. Now sheep and humans, because of the quantity and thickness of their hair, are unaffected; for the cold does not penetrate deep enough to solidify the moisture or to prevent the heat from concocting it.

22.[36] Why does the hair of sheep grow in softer when it is plucked, while human hair grows in harder? Is it because the hair of sheep grows from the surface? And this is why it is also drawn out painlessly, as the source of the nourishment, which is in the flesh, remains undamaged. So when (the passages) are open the residues evaporate more easily, and the wool receives proper nourishment from the flesh; for flesh is fed by soft and sweet nourishment. But human hair naturally grows from deep down, and is drawn out only by force and with pain. This is clear; for (doing it) draws blood. Therefore, when the region is wounded the result is also that it is scarred. This is why in the end this happens to those who are plucked; but as long as the hair grows again, it grows in hard, because all the nourishment that nourishes the flesh has left it, and it comes to be from residues. And there is a sign of this: the hair of everyone from the south is hard, because the external heat penetrates deep and evaporates the concocted nourishment, but those from the north have soft hair. For with them both the blood and sweet humors are nearer the surface; and this is why they also have good complexions.

23.[37] Why does the hair of sheep get harder the longer it is, whereas human hair gets softer? Is it because the hair

[36] Cf. Pr. 10.23. Source: GA 5.3, esp. 783a1–19. Aristotle discusses hair extensively in GA 5.3–5 and HA 3.10–12.

[37] Cf. Pr. 10.22.

ἀνθρώπων μαλακώτεραι; ἢ ὅτι αἱ τῶν προβάτων, οἵαν
εἴρηται τροφὴν ἔχουσαι, μακρὰν τῆς ἀρχῆς ἀπαρτώ-
40 μεναι ἀτροφώτεραί | εἰσι, καὶ ῥᾳδίως ἐξ αὐτῶν ἐξατμί-
893b ζεται ὑπὸ τοῦ ‖ θερμοῦ ἡ ἐνυπάρχουσα τροφὴ δι'
εὐπεψίαν;[24] ξηραινόμεναι δὲ σκληρότεραι[25] γίνονται·
τὸ γὰρ ὑγρὸν μαλακόν. αἱ δὲ τῶν ἀνθρώπων ἐλάττω
μέν, μᾶλλον δὲ τῆς ἀρχῆς.[26] πέττεται δὲ αὐταῖς μᾶλ-
5 λον διὰ τὸ ἐλάττω εἶναι· πεττομένη δὲ | μαλακωτέραν
ποιεῖ τὴν τρίχα· πάντα γὰρ τὰ πεπεμμένα τῶν
ἀπέπτων μαλακώτερά ἐστιν. ἐκ περιττώματος γὰρ
πλείστου[27] ἡ τοῦ ἀνθρώπου θρὶξ ἢ ἡ τοῦ προβάτου.
σημεῖον δέ· τὰ γὰρ νέα πρόβατα τῶν παλαιῶν μαλα-
κώτερα ἔχει τὰ ἔρια. |

10 24. Διὰ τί οἱ ἄνθρωποι καὶ οἱ ὄρνιθες οἱ δασεῖς λάγνοι εἰσίν; ἢ ὅτι θερμοὶ καὶ ὑγροὶ τὴν φύσιν εἰσίν, δεῖ
δὲ ἀμφοῖν πρὸς τὴν ὀχείαν· τὸ μὲν γὰρ θερμὸν ἐκκρίνει,
τὸ δὲ ὑγρὸν ἐκκρίνεται. διὰ τὸ αὐτὸ δὲ καὶ οἱ χωλοὶ[28]
ἄνδρες· ἡ γὰρ τροφὴ αὐτοῖς ὀλίγη μὲν κάτω ἀφικνεῖ-
15 ται διὰ τὴν | ἀναπηρίαν τῶν σκελῶν, εἰς δὲ τὸν ἐπάνω
τόπον ἔρχεται πολλὴ καὶ εἰς σπέρμα συγκρίνεται.

25. Διὰ τί ὁ ἄνθρωπος χαίτην οὐκ ἔχει; ἢ διότι
πώγωνα ἔχει, ὥστε ἡ ἐκεῖ ἀπελθοῦσα τροφὴ τῆς
τοιαύτης περιττώσεως εἰς τὰς σιαγόνας ἔρχεται; |

[24] εὐπεψίαν : ἀπεψίαν A^m D   [25] σκληρότεραι
Vat.1904^mg Gaza : ξηρότεραι codd.   [26] ἐλάττω μέν ‹ἔχουσι
τὴν τροφήν›, μᾶλλον δὲ τῆς ἀρχῆς ‹ἐγγίγνονται› Forster ex
Gaza : ἐλάττω ‹τροφὴν› μέν ‹δέχονται vel λαμβάνουσι vel
ἔχουσι›, μᾶλλον δὲ τῆς ἀρχῆς ‹τὴν τροφήν› Marenghi[4]
[27] πλείστου : πλεῖον Forster   [28] οἱ χωλοὶ : οἱ ‹ὄρνιθες
λάγνοι καὶ οἱ› χωλοὶ Forster ex Pr. 4.31, 880b4–5

of sheep, obtaining nourishment in the way described,[38] hangs down a long way from its source and is less nourished? So the nourishment present in it is easily vaporized out of it by the heat, because it is easily concocted. As it dries it becomes harder, for moisture is soft. Now human hair (*has*) less (*nourishment*), but (*comes in*) closer to the source.[39] And it is more thoroughly concocted because there is less of it; and being concocted makes the hair softer; for anything that is concocted is softer than what is unconcocted. For human hair comes from residue more abundant than the hair of sheep. And there is a sign of this: young sheep have softer wool than old ones.

24.[40] Why are hairy humans and thick-feathered birds lustful? Is it because they are hot and moist in their nature, and both of these are necessary for copulation? For heat causes excretion, and the moisture is excreted. And for the same reason, lame men as well (*are lustful*);[41] for little nourishment in them passes downward owing to the deformity of their legs, whereas a great deal goes to the upper region and is condensed into seed.

25. Why doesn't man have a mane? Is it because he has a beard, so that the nourishment from such residue, leaving the one place, goes to the jaws?[42]

---

[38] See *Pr.* 10.22, 893a19–20.

[39] The text here is uncertain; Gaza was relied upon to fill in the gaps.   [40] Cf. *Pr.* 4.31.

[41] If we fill in the material from the parallel passage in *Pr.* 4.31, this should be rendered "for the same reason both birds and lame men are lustful."

[42] I.e., the residue that becomes hair does not go to where a mane would be, but instead goes to the jaw and becomes a beard.

20   26. Διὰ τί πάντα τὰ ζῷα ἀρτίους τοὺς πόδας ἔχει; ἢ ὅτι οὐκ ἐνδέχεται κινεῖσθαι μὴ ἑστηκότος τινός, ἂν μὴ ἅλληται; ἐπεὶ τοίνυν ἐκ δυοῖν τινοῖν [κίνησιν]²⁹ ἀνάγκη τῇ πορείᾳ εἶναι, ἔκ τε κινήσεως καὶ στάσεως, ταῦτα [δὲ]³⁰ δύο καὶ ἄρτια ἤδη. καὶ <τὰ>³¹ τετράποδα, δύο ἔτι³² πλείους· τοὺς μὲν γὰρ δύο κινεῖ, οἱ δὲ δύο 25 ἑστήκασιν. καὶ οἱ ἕξ· καὶ τὰ ἄλλα δὲ | δύο ἔτι· τούτων δὲ τὸ μὲν κινεῖται, τὸ δὲ ἕστηκεν.

    27. Διὰ τί τοῖς μὲν ἵπποις καὶ τοῖς ὄνοις ἐκ τῶν οὔλων φύονται τρίχες, τοῖς δὲ ἀνθρώποις οὔ; ἢ διότι τοῖς μὲν ἄλλοις ζῴοις ἐστὶ τὸ δέρμα μέρος τῆς σαρ- 30 κός, ἀνθρώπῳ δὲ καθάπερ | πάθος σαρκός; δοκεῖ γὰρ αὐτῆς³³ τὸ ἐπιπολῆς καταψυχόμενον στερεώτερον γί- νεσθαι, καθάπερ τῶν ἑφθῶν ἀλεύρων αἱ γραῖαι καλού- μεναι. ἐπεὶ οὖν κἀκεῖναί εἰσιν ἄλευρον ἑφθόν, καὶ τὸ τοῦ ἀνθρώπου καλούμενον δέρμα σὰρξ ἂν εἴη. τραυ- ματισθέντος δὲ ἢ τριβέντος ἀνθρώπου μὲν τὴν σάρκα | 35 συμβαίνει πυκνοῦσθαι·³⁴ διὸ ἠλλοιωμένης τῆς ἐπι- πολῆς σαρκὸς οὐ τὴν αὐτὴν φύσιν³⁵ λαμβάνει τὰ τραύματα ἧπερ καὶ ἐκ γενετῆς· ἀλλοιωθείσης δ' αὐτῆς μὴ γίνεσθαι ἔτι τὸ ἐξ αὐτῆς οὐθὲν ἄτοπον, καθάπερ

    29 [κίνησιν] Bussemaker   30 [δὲ] Forster
    31 <τὰ> Marenghi⁴   32 δύο ἔτι Nicasius (cf. 893b25) : διότι codd.   33 αὐτῆς : αὐτοῖς Ap. Cᵃ Xᵃ
    34 ante πυκνοῦσθαι add. φθείρεσθαι καὶ [Arist./Alex.] Sup.Pr. 2.189, 7

26.[43] Why do all animals have an even number of feet? Is it because it is not possible to move if one part is not standing still, unless one jumps? Since, then, it is necessary for progression to come from two things, from both movement and standing, these are two and so already an even number. And the four-footed animals further have two more legs: for they move two, while two stand still. And some animals have six: and in relation to the others[44] there is a further two, and of these one (*of each pair*) moves while the other stands still.

27.[45] Why, in horses and in asses, do hairs grow from scars, but not in humans? Is it because in the other animals the skin is a part of the flesh, whereas in the human it is just like a condition of the flesh? For it seems that the part of it that is on the surface, when it cools down, becomes more solid, just like what is called the crust that forms on boiled wheat meal. Since, then, this crust too *is* boiled wheat meal, so what is called the skin of the human would just *be* flesh. Now when a human is wounded or chafed the result is that the flesh is compressed, so when the surface of the flesh has been altered the wounds do not have the same nature as they did from the beginning; and it is not strange that when it has been altered what had come from it no

---

[43] Cf. *Pr.* 10.30. Source: *IA* 704a14, 708a21–b19.

[44] Likely the four-footed animals, though the text is unclear.

[45] This chapter is virtually identical to [Arist./Alex.] *Sup.Pr.* 2.189. Cf. *Pr.* 9.13 and 10.29.

---

[35] φύσιν : ἐπίφυσιν [Arist./Alex.] *Sup.Pr.* 2.189, 8

καὶ ἐκ τῶν ἀλωπεκιῶν καλουμένων· καὶ γὰρ αὗται τῆς
40 ἐπιπολῆς σαρκὸς φθοραὶ καὶ | ἀλλοιώσεις εἰσίν. τῶν
894a δὲ ὑποζυγίων τριβέντων καὶ ὑγιαζομένων ‖ πάλιν
ἀναπληροῦται τὰ νενοσηκότα μέρη τοῦ σώματος τῶν
αὐτῶν μέν, ἀσθενεστέρων δ' ἢ ἐξ ἀρχῆς ἦν. ἐπεὶ δ'
ἐστὶ καὶ τὸ δέρμα μέρος αὐτῶν, γίνοιντό τε ἂν καὶ
φύοιντο τρίχες (ἐκ δέρματος γὰρ φύονται τρίχες),
5 λευκαὶ δὲ φύονται | διὰ τὸ τὸ δέρμα ἀσθενέστερον
γεγονέναι τοῦ ἐξ ἀρχῆς, καὶ τὴν λευκὴν ἀσθενεστάτην
εἶναι τρίχα.

28. Διὰ τί ἐν μὲν τοῖς ἄλλοις ζῴοις διαμένει ὁμοίως
τὰ δίδυμα θήλεα καὶ ἄρρενα ὄντα, ἐν δὲ τοῖς ἀνθρώποις οὔ; ἢ διότι τούτῳ[36] ἀσθενῆ μάλιστα τὰ δίδυμα;
10 μονοτόκον γάρ ἐστιν. | ἐν δὲ τοῖς διδύμοις παρὰ φύσιν
τὸ θῆλυ γίνεσθαι καὶ ἄρρεν, ὥστε ὃ μάλιστά ἐστι
παρὰ φύσιν, τοῦτο καὶ ἀσθενέστατον.

29. Διὰ τί τοῖς μὲν ἵπποις καὶ τοῖς ὄνοις ἐκ τῶν
οὐλῶν φύονται τρίχες, τοῖς δὲ ἀνθρώποις οὔ; ἢ διότι ἡ
οὐλὴ κωλύει διὰ τὴν πύκνωσιν ἢ διὰ τὸ φθείρειν τὴν
15 τροφήν; τοῖς μὲν | οὖν ἀνθρώποις παντελῶς κωλύει διὰ
τὴν ἀσθένειαν τῆς τριχός, τοῖς δὲ ἵπποις οὐκ ἐκώλυσε,
διέφθειρε δέ.

30. Διὰ τί τοῖς ζῴοις ἄρτιοι πόδες; ἢ ὅτι παντὸς μὲν

---

36 τούτῳ : τούτων Cᵃ

---

46 A disease the main symptom of which is baldness.
47 Literally, "the diseased parts" (τὰ νενοσηκότα μέρη).

longer does so, just as in the case of what is called alope-cia:[46] for these are the destruction and alteration of the surface flesh. But when yoke animals are chafed and then heal, the damaged parts[47] of the body are filled up again with the same things, though they are weaker than they were in the beginning. And since their skin is a part of them, hair would appear and grow (for hair grows from the skin), but it grows in white because the skin is weaker than it was at the beginning, and white hair is the weakest.

28.[48] Why, in the other animals, do the twins survive equally well being female or male, but not in humans? Is it because in the latter case, the twins are especially weak? For the human is (*normally*) the bearer of one child. Now in the case of twins begetting a male and a female is contrary to nature, and so what is especially contrary to nature[49] is also weakest.

29.[50] Why, in horses and in asses, do hairs grow from scars, but not in humans? Is it because the scar prevents this either because of the compression (*of the flesh*) or because of the destruction of the nourishment? Therefore in humans, it prevents this completely because of the weakness of the hair, but in horses it does not prevent this, but impairs it.[51]

30.[52] Why in animals is there an even number of feet? Is

[48] Source: *HA* 584b36–85a3 and *GA* 775a22–27.

[49] I.e., the birth of male and female twins in animals that nor-mally bear one child.   [50] Cf. *Pr.* 9.13 and 10.29.

[51] I.e., in horses, the hair *does* grow in, though it emerges weaker (cf. *Pr.* 10.27, 893b40–94a6), whereas in humans, the hair is too weak to grow in at all.

[52] Cf. *Pr.* 10.26. Sources: *IA* 704a14, 708a21–b19.

τοῦ κινουμένου ἀνάγκη τι ἠρεμεῖν, συνέβαινε δὲ
περιττῶν ὄντων μὴ γίνεσθαι τοῦτο; ὅπερ[37] κατὰ τὴν
20 ἀντιστοιχίαν τῶν ποδῶν | ἦν ἡ κίνησις.

31. Διὰ τί ἐλάττω χρόνον τὰ ζῷα καθεύδει ἢ ἐγρή-
γορεν, οὐ συνεχῶς δέ; ἢ διὰ τὸ μὴ ἅμα πᾶσαν πέττεσθαι τὴν περίττωσιν, ἀλλ' ὅταν τι πεφθῇ, κουφισ-
θὲν διεγείρεται; καὶ πλεονάκις δ' ἐγείρονται, ὅσοις
25 ψυχρὸς ὁ τόπος ὁ πέττων ἐστὶ | τὴν περίττωσιν· ταχὺ
γὰρ παύεται καὶ πολλάκις, ἡ δὲ διάπαυσις ἔγερσίς
ἐστιν. ἡδὺ δέ, ὡς[38] εἰκός, διὰ τὸ ἀνάπαυσιν εἶναι
φαίνεται. ἀλλ' οὐδ' ἐνταῦθα πλείω χρόνον ἡ ἀνάπαυ-
σις γίνεται τῶν κατὰ φύσιν ἔργων· οὐδ' εἰ τὸ ἐσθίειν
ἥδιον τοῦ μή, ὅμως πλείω χρόνον ἐσθίουσιν ἢ ἀσιτοῦ-
σιν. |

30 32. Διὰ τί τῶν ζῴων τὰ μὲν εὐθὺς ἀκολουθεῖ τοῖς
γεννήσασι, τὰ δ' ὀψέ, οἷον ἄνθρωπος, ἢ μόλις ἢ
οὐδέποτε; ἢ διότι τὰ μὲν ταχὺ ἀπολαμβάνει τὸ βαδίζειν,[39] τὰ δ' ὀψέ, καὶ τὰ μὲν ἀναίσθητα τοῦ ὠφελοῦν-
τος, τὰ δὲ ἔχει αἴσθησιν; ὅσα μὲν οὖν ἄμφω ἔχει
35 ταῦτα (λέγω δ' οἷον καὶ αἴσθησιν | τοῦ ὠφελοῦντος
καὶ ἐπιτέλεσιν τοῦ σώματος), ἀκολουθεῖ, τὰ δὲ μὴ
ἄμφω οὐ ποιεῖ τοῦτο· δεῖ γὰρ δύνασθαι καὶ διαισθά-
νεσθαι.

[37] ὅπερ : εἴπερ Nicasius
[38] ὡς Forster : ὡς δὲ β : οὐδὲ cett. codd. : εἶναι Nicasius
[39] τὸ βαδίζειν Richards : τὸ γνωρίζειν codd. (cf. PPA "moving and perceiving")

it because when anything moves something must be at rest, and this could not happen if the number were odd? Movement just is according to the paired arrangement of the feet.

31. Why do animals sleep for less time than they are awake, and do not sleep continuously? Is it because all the residue is not concocted at the same time, but when some is concocted, the animal is relieved and wakes up? And all those (*animals*) in which the region concocting the residue is cold wake more often; for it quickly and often ceases (*to function*), and this cessation involves awakening. Now (*sleep*) seems to be pleasant, as is reasonable, because it is a pause. But the pause here does not last longer than (*the time spent on*) our natural functions; and if eating is more pleasant than not eating, they nevertheless do not spend more time eating than abstaining.

32. Why do some animals follow[53] their parents right away, while some do so later, like the human, or to a small degree or never? Is it because some take to walking[54] quickly, while others are late, and some lack perception of what is beneficial, while others have such perception? Therefore, those that possess both these qualities (I mean perception of what is beneficial, and bodily perfection) follow (*their parents*), but those that do not have both these qualities do not do this. For they must have the (*physical*) capacity and be perceptive.

---

[53] My translation of ἀκολουθεῖ as "follow" is straightforward, though some scholars believe it should here be rendered "imitate" or "obey."   [54] The mss. have γνωρίζειν ("recognizing"). I have adopted Richards' suggestion βαδίζειν ("walking"). The Arabic version has "moving and perceiving," suggesting both.

33. Διὰ τί λεύκη οὐ γίνεται τοῖς ἄλλοις ζῴοις;
πότερον ὅτι τοῖς μὲν ἄλλοις[40] νόσημα, τοῖς δὲ ἀνθρώ-
894b ποις[41] γίνεται διάλευκα ‖ τὰ δέρματα καὶ αἱ τρίχες
αὐτῶν; ἀλλ' ὅμως ἀπορήσειεν ἄν τις διὰ τί ὕστερον οὐ
γίνεται ἀλλ' ἐκ γενετῆς ἡ ποικιλία. ἢ ὅτι τὰ δέρματα
τῶν ἄλλων ζῴων σκληρά, ἄνθρωπος δὲ φύσει λεπτο-
5 δερμότατον; ἡ δὲ λεύκη πνεύματός | ἐστιν ἔκκρισις, ὃ
κωλύεται διὰ τὴν πυκνότητα ἐξιέναι τοῖς ἄλλοις ζῴοις
τοῦ δέρματος.

34. Διὰ τί[42] ἐν μὲν τῇ λεύκῃ πολιαὶ γίνονται, ὅπου
δὲ πολιαί, οὐκ ἀεὶ λεύκη; ἢ διότι αἱ τρίχες ἐκ τοῦ
δέρματος εἰσίν, ἡ δὲ πολιὰ ὥσπερ σαπρότης τις τῶν
10 τριχῶν ἐστιν; ὅταν μὲν | οὖν τὸ δέρμα κάμνῃ, ἀνάγκη
καὶ τὴν τρίχα ἐξ ἐκείνου οὖσαν κάμνειν· ὅταν δὲ ἡ
θρίξ, οὐκ ἀνάγκη τὸ δέρμα.

35. Διὰ τί τῶν ζῴων τὰ μὲν χαλεπά ἐστι μετὰ τὸν
τόκον, οἷον κύων καὶ ὗς, τὰ δὲ οὐδὲν ἐπιδήλως, οἷον
γυνή, πρόβατον; ἢ ὅτι ὅσα μὲν περιττωματικὰ πραέα;
15 ἀπέρχεται γὰρ | ἐν τῷ τόκῳ τὰ λυποῦντα. ὅσοις[43] δὲ
ἀπὸ τῶν εὖ ἐχόντων γίνεται ἡ ἀφαίρεσις, ⟨τούτοις καὶ
ἡ σύντηξις,⟩[44] ὥστε ἡ ἰσχνότης ποιεῖ διὰ τὴν ἕξιν τὴν
ὀργήν, ὥσπερ καὶ αἱ ἀλεκτορίδες οὐ τεκοῦσαι χαλε-
παί, ἀλλ' ἐπῴαζουσαι, διὰ τὴν ἀσιτίαν.

[40] ἄλλοις : ἀνθρώποις Louis ex Gaza
[41] ἀνθρώποις : ἄλλοις Louis ex Gaza
[42] post Διὰ τί add. δὲ Y[a]   [43] ὅσοις : τούτοις A
[44] ⟨τούτοις καὶ ἡ σύντηξις⟩ Marenghi[4] : post ἀφαίρεσις
lac. indic. Hett : ⟨ταῦτα ἐξαγριαίνεται καὶ χαλεπά ἐστιν⟩ Sylburg ex Gaza : ἴσως λείπει ταῦτα χαλεπά X[a mg]

33.[55] Why does the white disease not occur in the other animals? Or is it that the disease *does* exist in other animals, but that in humans their skin and hair become white? Nevertheless, one might raise the question why variation in color (*in animals*) takes place not later but from birth. Or is it because the skin of other animals is hard, but the human is by nature most thin-skinned? Now the white disease is an excretion of breath, which in the other animals is prevented by the thickness of the skin from exiting.

34.[56] Why, in the case of the white disease, does gray hair occur, but where there is gray hair there is not always the white disease? Is it because hair grows from the skin, but gray hair is, as it were, some sort of decay of the hair? So when the skin is afflicted, the hair that grows from it is also necessarily afflicted, but when the hair (*is afflicted*), it is not necessary for the skin to be so.

35.[57] Why are some animals difficult[58] after childbirth, like the dog and pig, but others are not obviously so, like women and sheep? Is it because those that are full of residue are mild? For what causes them pain departs during childbirth. But in those animals from which (*in childbirth*) the drawing off of good material takes place, ‹in these there is also colliquation›,[59] so that their thinness produces ill temper owing to their state, just as hens are not difficult laying an egg, but they are while sitting, owing to the lack of food.

[55] Cf. *Pr.* 10.4, 5, 34.
[56] Cf. *Pr.* 10.4, 5, 33. Source: *GA* 784a25–30.
[57] Source: *HA* 571b10–34.
[58] Or "ill-tempered" ($\chi\alpha\lambda\epsilon\pi\acute{\alpha}$).
[59] Words are likely missing from the text. I translate the suggestion of Marenghi[4].

36. Διὰ τί οἱ εὐνοῦχοι τὰ μὲν ἄλλα εἰς τὸ θῆλυ
20 διαφθειρόμενοι | μεταβάλλουσι; καὶ γὰρ φωνὴν θηλυ-
κὴν ἴσχουσι καὶ ἀμορφίαν[45] καὶ ἀναρθρίαν, καὶ οὕτω
σφόδρα μεταπίπτουσιν ὡς καὶ ἐν τοῖς ἄλλοις ζῴοις τὰ
ἐκτεμνόμενα. ἐναντίως δ᾽ οἱ ταῦροι καὶ οἱ κριοὶ τὰ
κέρατα ἴσχουσι, διότι καὶ τὰ θήλεα ἐναντίως αὐτῶν
25 ἔχει. διὸ οἱ μὲν μείζω ἐκτεμνόμενοι ἴσχουσιν, | οἱ δὲ
ἐλάττω. τὸ δὲ μέγεθος μόνον οἱ εὐνοῦχοι εἰς τὸ ἄρρεν
μεταβάλλουσιν· μείζους γὰρ γίνονται. ἔστι δὲ τοῦτο
τοῦ ἄρρενος· τὰ γὰρ θήλεα ἐλάττω ἐστὶ τῶν ἀρρένων.
ἢ οὐδὲ τοῦτο εἰς τὸ ἄρρεν, ἀλλ᾽ εἰς τὸ θῆλυ; οὐ γὰρ εἰς
πᾶν τὸ μέγεθος, ἀλλ᾽ εἰς τὸ μῆκος μόνον, τὸ δὲ ἄρρεν
30 καὶ εἰς πλάτος | καὶ εἰς βάθος· τότε γὰρ τετελείωται.
ἔτι δὲ ὡς ἔχει τὸ θῆλυ πρὸς τὸ ἄρρεν, οὕτως αὐτοῦ τοῦ
θήλεος ἡ παρθένος πρὸς τὴν γυναῖκα· ἡ μὲν γὰρ ἤδη
γενναία, ἡ δὲ οὔ. εἰς τὴν τούτων οὖν ⟨φύσιν⟩[46] μετα-
βάλλει· ἐπὶ μῆκος γὰρ ταύταις ἡ αὔξησις. διὸ καὶ
35 Ὅμηρος εὖ τὸ "μῆκος δ᾽ ἔπορ᾽ Ἄρτεμις ἁγνή," ὡς | διὰ
τὴν παρθενίαν, ὃ εἶχε, δυναμένης δοῦναι. οὔκουν εἰς

[45] ἀμορφίαν Ap Xᵃ : ὀξύτητα cett. codd.
[46] ⟨φύσιν⟩ Richards

[60] In the *corpus Aristotelicum*, the most sustained discussions
of eunuchs are in the *Problems*: see also 4.3, 10.42, 57, 11.16, 34,
62. Among the genuine works of Aristotle, see *HA* 8(9).50, the
topic of which is animal castration.

[61] This passage can be read in two ways: (1) eunuchs have feminine voices, shapeless bodies (reading ἀμορφίαν), and loose

36.[60] Why do eunuchs, when mutilated, in other respects change into the female? For they have feminine voice and shapelessness and lack of articulation,[61] and so undergo as severe a change as do other animals when castrated. (Now castrated bulls and rams grow horns in opposite ways, because their females are opposite. This is why castrated bulls grow larger horns and rams smaller.) But in respect to size alone, eunuchs change into the male; for they become larger. And this is characteristic of the male, for females are smaller than males. Or is this not a change into the male, but into the female? For it is not a change in every aspect of size, but in height alone, whereas change into the male is in width and depth as well; for this is what it is to be full-grown. Furthermore, as the female is to the male, so within the female gender itself the virgin[62] is to the woman; for the latter is already nobly formed, while the former is not. Therefore, (*the virgin*) changes into the (*nature of women*);[63] for their growth is with respect to height. And this is why Homer speaks well: "Chaste Artemis gave them height,"[64] as being able to give what, in virtue of her virginity, she possessed. Therefore, the eunuch

joints; or (2) (referring solely to speech) eunuchs have feminine, shrill (reading ὀξύτητα), and less articulate voices.

[62] Or "maiden" or "girl."

[63] The text is incomplete. I follow Richards and take there to be an implied φύσιν, i.e., εἰς τὴν τούτων φύσιν ("into their [sc. women's] nature"). If this is correct, then there are two ways to take the passage: (1) the eunuch "changes into their nature" (i.e., the nature of women), or (2) the maiden "changes into the nature of women." The quote from Homer that follows supports the latter.

[64] Hom. *Od*. 20.71.

311

τὸ ἄρρεν κατὰ τὸ μέγεθος μεταβάλλει. οὐ γὰρ εἰς τὸ
τέλειον μεταβάλλει. οἱ δὲ εὐνοῦχοι εἰς μέγεθος τὸ
μῆκος ἐπιδιδόασιν.

37. Διὰ τί οἱ εὐνοῦχοι ἢ ὅλως οὐκ ἴσχουσιν ἢ ἧττον
895a ἰξίας; ‖ ἢ ὅτι μεταβάλλουσι τὴν φύσιν ἐν τῇ ἐκτμήσει
εἰς τὰ ἄγονα; τοιαῦτα δὲ παῖς καὶ γυνή, ὧν οὐδέτερον
ἴσχει ἰξίας, εἰ μή τι σπάνιον γυνή.

38. Διὰ τί μᾶλλον ἄνθρωπος πολλὰς φωνὰς ἀφίη-
5 σιν, τὰ | δὲ ἄλλα μίαν, ἀδιάφορα ὄντα τῷ εἴδει; ἢ[47] καὶ
τοῦ ἀνθρώπου μία φωνή, ἀλλὰ διάλεκτοι πολλαί;

39. Διὰ τί δὲ αὐτὴ ἄλλη, τοῖς δὲ ἄλλοις οὔ; ἢ ὅτι οἱ
μὲν ἄνθρωποι γράμματα πολλὰ φθέγγονται, τῶν δὲ
ἄλλων τὰ μὲν οὐδέν, ἔνια δὲ δύο ἢ τρία τῶν ἀφώνων;
10 ταῦτα δὲ ποιεῖ | μετὰ τῶν φωνηέντων τὴν διάλεκτον.
ἔστι δὲ ὁ λόγος οὐ τὸ τῇ φωνῇ σημαίνειν, ἀλλὰ τοῖς
πάθεσιν αὐτῆς, καὶ μὴ ὅτι ἀλγεῖν ⟨ἢ⟩[48] χαίρει. τὰ δὲ
γράμματα πάθη ἐστὶ τῆς φωνῆς. ὁμοίως δὲ οἵ τε
παῖδες καὶ τὰ θηρία δηλοῦσιν· οὐ γάρ πω οὐδὲ τὰ
παιδία φθέγγονται τὰ γράμματα. |

15 40. Διὰ τί μόνον τῶν ζῴων ἄνθρωπος γίνεται
ἰσχνόφωνον; πότερον ὅτι καὶ ἐνεόν, ἡ δὲ ἰσχνοφωνία
ἐνεότης ἐστίν; ἀλλὰ δὴ καὶ οὐδ᾽ ὅλως πεπλήρωται

---

[47] ἢ wmg R et Gaza : om. cett. codd.
[48] ⟨ἢ⟩ Nicasius

---

[65] The author treats varicocele in men (see *Pr.* 4.20) and vari-
cose veins in women as the same kind of condition.

[66] Cf. *Pr.* 11.57. See also *HA* 4.9.

does not change with respect to size into the male. For he does not change into what is complete. Eunuchs increase in size (*only*) with respect to height.

37. Why do eunuchs generally not have varicocele, or have them less (*than others do*)? Is it because by being castrated they change their nature into that of the sterile? And such are the child and the woman, neither of whom has varicocele, except the woman rarely.[65]

38.[66] Why is a human more able to emit many voices, but the other animals (being not different in kind) are able to emit only one?[67] Or is there one voice for the human as well, but many sorts of speech?

39. But why is this (*voice*) different, while it is not in other animals? Is it because humans pronounce many letters, but of the others some pronounce no letters and some two or three consonants? Yet these consonants combined with vowels produce speech. Now rational speech is signifying something not by the voice, but by certain conditions of it, and not (*merely signifying*) that one is feeling pain or pleasure. And the letters are conditions of the voice. But both children and beasts make themselves understood in the same way, for children cannot yet pronounce the letters.

40.[68] Why does the human alone of the animals stammer? Is it because he alone can also be dumb, and stammering is a sort of dumbness? But of course (*in the case of*

---

67 I suspect "being not different in kind" (ἀδιάφορα ὄντα τῷ εἴδει) was a gloss added to make clear that what is meant is that other (nonhuman) animals *all of one kind* have no more than one voice.

68 Cf. *Pr.* 11.31, 55, and 60. See also [Arist.] *Aud.* 804b26–39.

τοῦτο τὸ μόριον. ἢ ὅτι κοινωνεῖ μόνον⁴⁹ λόγου, τὰ δ᾽
ἄλλα φωνῆς; ἔστι δὲ ἡ ἰσχνοφωνία κατὰ⁵⁰ τὸ ὄνομα
οὐδὲν⁵¹ ἢ οὐ συνεχῶς διεξιέναι. |

20   41. Διὰ τί ἄνθρωπος γίνεται ἐκ γενετῆς χωλὸς
μάλιστα τῶν ἄλλων ζῴων; πότερον ὅτι ἰσχυρὰ τῶν
ἄλλων ἐστὶ σκέλη τῶν ζῴων; ὀστώδη γὰρ καὶ νευ-
ρώδη καὶ τετράποδα καὶ ὄρνιθες ἔχουσιν, οἱ δὲ ἄνθρωποι σαρκώδη· διὰ τὴν ἀπαλότητα οὖν θᾶττον πηροῦν-
25   ται ἐν τῇ κινήσει. ἢ διότι μόνον τῶν ζῴων | πολλοὺς
ἔχει χρόνους τῆς γενέσεως; καὶ γὰρ ἑπτάμηνα καὶ
ὀκτάμηνα καὶ δεκάμηνα γίνεται. τοῖς δ᾽ ἄλλοις εἷς
χρόνος τῆς τελειώσεως γέγονεν οὐ διατρίψας·⁵² τοῖς δ᾽
ἀνθρώποις πολὺς ὁ χρόνος γίνεται τῆς ἐν πλήθει⁵³
διατριβῆς, ὥστε κινουμένων διὰ τὸ ἀπαλὰ εἶναι καὶ
30   θραύεται τὰ ἀκρωτήρια ἐν τῷ |πλείονι χρόνῳ πλείω.

41. Διὰ τί οἱ εὐνοῦχοι ἑλκώδεις τὰς κνήμας ἴσχουσι καὶ σαπράς; πότερον ὅτι καὶ αἱ γυναῖκες, οἱ δ᾽
εὐνοῦχοι γυναικικοί; ἢ τοῦτο μὲν συμβέβηκεν, αἴτιον
δὲ καὶ ταῖς γυναιξὶν ὅτι ἡ θερμότης κάτω ὁρμᾷ; δηλοῖ

---

⁴⁹ μόνον Flashar ex *Pr.* 11.55, 905a21 : μᾶλλον codd.
⁵⁰ κατὰ β : οὐ κατὰ cett. codd.
⁵¹ οὐδὲν Forster : ἐν codd.
⁵² διατρίψας : διατρίψασι Richards
⁵³ πλήθει : μήτρᾳ Richards

---

⁶⁹ The author seems to be saying that although stammering is
a sort of dumbness, it differs from dumbness in that "this part"
(i.e., the organ of speech) is not completely damaged, but rather is
not fully formed.

stammering) this part is not wholly formed.[69] Or is it because the human alone partakes of rational speech,[70] but
the other animals partake of voice? Now stammering, according to its name,[71] is nothing other than the inability to
give an account continuously.

41. Why is a human much more likely to be born lame
than any other animal? Is it because legs of the other animals are strong? For four-footed animals and birds have
bony and sinewy legs, whereas humans have fleshy ones;
therefore, because of their delicateness they are more
quickly maimed by movement. Or is it because humans
alone of animals have many different durations of gestation? For they are born in the seventh month or eighth
month or tenth month.[72] In the other animals, there is one
time for completion and no delay; but in humans, the time
of delay is great in duration,[73] so that when (*the fetuses*)
move, their extremities, owing to being delicate, are also
more likely to become broken during the longer time.

42.[74] Why do eunuchs have wounds and sores on their
legs? Is it because women also have them, and eunuchs are
womanlike? Or while this is the case, is the cause of it in
women also that the heat rushes downward? The gyneco-

[70] Translating Flashar's emendation (μόνον) from the parallel
passage in *Pr.* 11.55 (905a21). If the mss. reading is correct, this
should be rendered "the human partakes of rational speech more
(μᾶλλον)."

[71] ἡ ἰσχνοφωνία comes from ἴσχειν ("to check") and φωνή
("voice").

[72] In addition to the typical cases, born in the ninth month.

[73] Or, following Richards, "the time of delay in the womb is
great."   [74] Cf. *Pr.* 10.37.

315

35 δὲ τὰ γυναικεῖα. διὸ | οὔτε οἱ εὐνοῦχοι οὔτε γυναῖκες
δασεῖς γίνονται, διὰ πολλὴν ὑγρότητα.

43. Διὰ τί τῶν ζῴων οὐδὲν λιθιᾷ ἀλλ᾽ ἢ ἄνθρωπος;
ἢ ὅτι τῶν μὲν ὑποζυγίων καὶ τῶν πολυωνύχων οἱ
πόροι τῆς κύστεως εὐρεῖς εἰσίν; ὅσα δὲ μὴ τὸ πρῶτον,
895b ὕστερον δὲ ζῳοτοκεῖ || ἐν αὑτοῖς, οἷον ἔνιοι τῶν ἰχθύ-
ων, τούτων δὲ οὐδὲν κύστιν ἔχει, ἀλλ᾽ εἰς τὴν κοιλίαν
αὐτοῖς ἡ τοιαύτη συνθλίβεται ὑπόστασις, οἷον καὶ
τοῖς ὄρνισιν, ὥστε ταχὺ καὶ διεξέρχεται κατὰ τὴν
5 ἕδραν. ὁ δὲ ἄνθρωπος κύστιν τε ἔχει καὶ στενὸν | τὸν
καυλὸν ὡς κατὰ μέγεθος. διὰ μὲν οὖν τὸ ἔχειν τοῦτο τὸ
μόριον συνθλίβεται τὸ γεῶδες εἰς τὴν κύστιν (διὸ καὶ
χρώζονται αἱ ἀμίδες ὑπ᾽ αὐτοῦ), διὰ δὲ τὴν θερμότητα
τοῦ τόπου συμπέττεται καὶ παχύνεται μᾶλλον, ἐμμένει
δὲ καὶ αὐξάνεται διὰ τὴν στενότητα τοῦ οὐρητῆρος· οὐ
10 γὰρ δυνάμενα τὰ | γεώδη ὑποστήματα ῥᾳδίως ὑπεξιέ-
ναι, πρὸς ἄλληλα ὑποστρεφόμενα γίνεται λίθος.

44. Διὰ τί οὐκ ἐρεύγεται τὰ ὑποζύγια, οὐδὲ οἱ βόες
καὶ τὰ κερατοφόρα, οὐδὲ οἱ ὄρνιθες; ἢ διὰ ξηρότητα
τῆς κοιλίας; ταχὺ γὰρ ἀναλίσκεται τὸ ὑγρὸν καὶ
15 διηθεῖται· ἐμμένοντος | δὲ καὶ πνευματουμένου γίνεται
ὁ ἐρευγμός. τοῖς δὲ λοφούροις διὰ μῆκος τοῦ αὐχένος

---

75 "The gynecological conditions" (τὰ γυναικεῖα) likely refers
to menstruation.   76 The word I render "cloven-hoofed"
(πολυωνύχων) can also mean "with many claws" (as it does at HA
504a5), but the later reference to birds in this chapter suggests
"cloven-hoofed" is meant here.   77 As Louis point outs, this
refers to ovoviviparous animals (see GA 716b35).

logical conditions[75] show this. This is why neither eunuchs nor women are hairy, because of their abundant moisture.

43. Why do no animals but the human have gallstones? Is it because the passages of the bladder are wider in yoke animals and in cloven-hoofed animals?[76] Now of those animals that bear live young, not at first but later in themselves,[77] as some fish do, none has a bladder, but rather in them this sediment[78] is pressed into the stomach, as it is in the birds as well, so that it quickly passes out through the anus. But the human has a bladder and stem that is narrow in proportion to his size. Therefore, because he has this part, earthy matter is pressed into the bladder (and this is why chamber pots are discolored by it) and, owing to the heat of the region, becomes concocted and thickens more, and remains there and grows owing to the narrowness of the urethra; for as the earthy sediment cannot easily pass out, it swirls around and forms a gallstone.

44.[79] Why do neither yoke animals nor cattle and the (other) horned animals nor birds belch? Is it because of the dryness of their stomachs? For the moisture is quickly expended and filters through; but belching arises when the moisture remains and becomes breath. Now in animals with manes and tails,[80] owing to the length of their

---

[78] I.e., the kind that forms gallstones.

[79] Apollon. *Mir.* 22 quotes from this chapter and refers to "the *Problems* of Aristotle." [80] The Greek for "the animals with manes and tails" (τὰ λοφοῦρα, *HA* 501a6) comes from λόφος (mane) and οὐρά (tail), and could alternatively mean "the animals with tails like manes." Aristotle gives the following examples: horse, ass, mule, jennet (a small Spanish horse), and the so-called Syrian mule (*HA* 490b34–91a6).

ARISTOTLE

εἰς τὸ κάτω ὁρμᾷ τὸ πνεῦμα, διὸ καὶ ἀποψοφοῦσι
μάλιστα. οἱ ὄρνιθες δὲ καὶ τὰ κερατοφόρα οὐ ποιεῖ
οὐδέτερον. οὐδὲ ἐρεύγονται δὲ ὅσα μηρυκάζει, διὰ τὸ
πολλὰς ἔχειν κοιλίας καὶ τὸν καλούμενον κεκρύφαλον·
20 διὰ | πολλῶν οὖν γίνεται καὶ ἄνω καὶ κάτω τῷ πνεύ-
ματι ἡ πορεία, καὶ φθάνει ἀναλισκόμενον τὸ ὑγρὸν
πρὶν ἐκπνευματωθῆναι καὶ ποιῆσαι ἢ ἐρυγεῖν ἢ ψοφῆ-
σαι.

45. Διὰ τί ὅσα μὲν ἥμερα τῶν ζῴων ἐστί, πάντως
καὶ ἄγρια, ὅσα δὲ ἄγρια, οὐ πάντως ἥμερα; καὶ γὰρ
25 ἄνθρωποί | που φαίνονται ἄγριοι ὄντες καὶ κύνες ἐν
Ἰνδοῖς καὶ ἵπποι ἄλλοθι, ἀλλ' οὐ λέοντες ἥμεροι οὐδὲ
παρδάλεις οὐδ' ἔχεις οὐδ' ἄλλα πολλά. ἢ ὅτι ῥᾶον τὸ
φαῦλον καὶ γενέσθαι ἐξ ἀρχῆς καὶ μεταβαλεῖν εἰς
αὐτό; ἡ γὰρ φύσις οὐχ ἡ πρώτη ἀλλ' ἡ ἐν τέλει
30 ἐργώδης τυχεῖν εὐθύς. διὸ πάντα καὶ τὰ ἥμερα | ἄγρια
γίνονται τὸ πρῶτον μᾶλλον ἢ ἥμερα (οἷον παιδίον ἢ
ἀνὴρ παμφάγον καὶ τῷ θυμῷ ζῶν) ἀλλ' ἀσθενέστερα.
ὥσπερ οὖν καὶ ἐπὶ τῶν τῆς τέχνης ἔργων, οὕτως ἔχει
καὶ ἐπὶ τῶν τῆς φύσεως ἔργων. καὶ γὰρ ἐπὶ τούτων
πάντ' ἐστὶ φαύλως εἰργασμένα, καὶ πλείω τὰ φαῦλα,
35 κλίνη καὶ ἱμάτιον | καὶ ἄλλ' ὁτιοῦν. καὶ ὃ μέν ἐστι
καλόν, λαβεῖν ἔστιν ἅπαν καὶ φαῦλον, ὃ δὲ φαῦλον,
οὐ πᾶν καὶ καλόν, οἷον εἴ τις ἐπὶ τῶν ἀρχαίων γρα-
φέων καὶ ἀνδριαντοποιῶν σκοπεῖ τὰ ἔργα· οὐ γὰρ ἦν

---

81 The second stomach of ruminating animals has a netlike
structure.

318

necks, the breath rushes downward, and this is why they break wind most. But birds and horned animals do neither. Nor do ruminating animals belch, because they have many stomachs and the so-called "net";[81] therefore, the course taken by the breath is both up and down through many (*passages*), and the moisture is expended before it is expelled as breath and so causes either belching or breaking wind.

45.[82] Why are all the tame animals in every case found wild as well, but all the wild animals are not in every case found tame? For even humans clearly are wild in some places, as are dogs among the Indians and horses elsewhere, but lions, leopards, vipers, and many others are not tame (*anywhere*). Is it because it is easier (*for an animal*) both to be in a bad condition from the beginning and to change into that condition? For it is not the preliminary nature, but the perfect one, that is difficult to attain directly. This is why all the tame animals too are wild at first rather than tame (for example, a child is more voracious than a man and seethes with anger) but weaker. Therefore, just as it is in the case of the works of art, so it holds for the works of nature as well. For in every one of the former cases, there are things that are badly made, in fact there are more bad (*than good*), whether a bed or a cloak or anything else. And where something is good, it is always possible to find something bad as well, but where something is bad, it is not always possible to find something good as well, for instance, if one considers the works of primitive painters and sculptors. For at that time there was no excel-

[82] Sources: *HA* 488a26–31 and *PA* 643b3–7.

πώποτε οὐδαμῇ γραφὴ σπουδαία οὐδὲ ἀνδριάς, φαῦλα δὲ ἦν. ὁμοίως δὲ καὶ ἡ φύσις φαῦλα μὲν πάντα ‖
896a ποιεῖ, [καὶ πλείους]⁵⁴ καὶ πλείω, σπουδαῖα δ' ἐλάττω,
καὶ οὐ πάντα δύναται. τὸ δὲ ἥμερον βέλτιον, τὸ δὲ
ἄγριον φαῦλον. φύσει δὲ οὐ τῇ ἐξ ἀρχῆς, ἀλλ' ἐφ' ἦν,
οἶμαι, ῥᾷον ποιεῖν⁵⁵ ⟨τὰ⟩⁵⁶ σπουδαῖα καὶ ἥμερα. τὰ δὲ
5 ἐναντία ἢ οὐδέποτε ἢ μόλις, | καὶ ἔν τισι τόποις καὶ ἐν
χρόνοις, ἢ ἄρτι⁵⁷ ἢ ποτέ, ἔν τινι κράσει τοῦ ὅλου,
γίνονται ἥμερα τὰ ζῷα πάντα. τὸ δ' αὐτὸ καὶ ἐπὶ τῶν
φυτῶν πάντων ἐστίν· ὅσα μὲν γὰρ ἥμερα, καὶ ἄγρια,
οὐ πάντα δὲ δύναται ἡμεροῦσθαι, ἀλλ' ὅμως εἰσὶν ἐν
ἰδίᾳ χώρᾳ πρὸς πολλὰ ἰδίως ἐχούσῃ,⁵⁸ ὥστε ἠμελη-
10 μένα καὶ | ἄγρια κρείττω καὶ ἡμερώτερα φύεσθαι τῶν
ἐν ἄλλῃ γεωργουμένων.

46. Διὰ τί τοῖς μὲν ἀνθρώποις οἱ ὀμφαλοὶ μεγάλοι
γίνονται, τοῖς δ' ἄλλοις ζῴοις οὐ φανεροί; ἢ διότι τοῖς
μὲν διὰ τὸ πολὺν χρόνον εἴσω μένειν ἀφαναίνονται
15 καὶ εὐθὺ | τείνονται, ὅλον δ' ἐπανοιδοῦσι τὰ ἕλκη; διὸ
ἔνιοι τῶν ὀμφαλῶν καὶ αἰσχίους εἰσίν· ὁ δὲ ἄνθρωπος
ἀτελὴς ἐξέρχεται, ὥστε ἔφυγροι καὶ ἔναιμοι⁵⁹ οἱ ὀμφαλοὶ ἀκολουθοῦσιν. ὅτι δὲ τὰ μὲν τετελειωμένα τὰ δὲ

---

⁵⁴ [καὶ πλείους] Forster   ⁵⁵ ποιεῖν c D Aᵐ : ποιεῖ cett.
codd.   ⁵⁶ ⟨τὰ⟩ Forster   ⁵⁷ ἄρτι Forster : ἀρτίου codd. :
ἀρτίως Sylburg : ἄρτι οὐ Bussemaker   ⁵⁸ ἐχούσῃ : ἔχοντα Hett   ⁵⁹ ἔναιμοι Ruelle ex Gaza : ἄναιμοι codd.

---

83 This line is unclear. The author is likely saying that most
kinds of animals are rather inferior (humans being the standard of

lent painting or statue anywhere, but there were bad ones. And similarly nature makes every (*kind of*) thing in a bad form, in fact more of them, but fewer excellent ones, and it is unable to make all of them (*excellent*).[83] Now the tame is the better, whereas the wild the bad. It is easier, I suppose, for nature—not nature at the beginning, but that toward which (*the animals develops*)—to make the excellent ones also tame. But the opposite kinds can never (*be tamed*), or seldom, i.e., in certain places and at certain times, either now or later, in some mixture of the whole, all animals become tame.[84] Now the same thing is true in the case of all plants: for those that are tame are also found wild, but not all kinds can be tamed, but nevertheless some, in their own particular soil, have their own particular characteristics in many respects, such that when neglected and wild they grow better and tamer than those which are cultivated in alien soil.

46. Why do navels become large in humans, while in the other animals they are not obvious? Is it because in humans, by remaining in (*the womb*) for a long time, they are withered and stretched outward, and in general the wounds swell? This is why some navels are also uglier. Now humans come out (*of the womb*) imperfect, so that the navels follow wet and bloody.[85] A sign that some animals

superiority), and that even in the case of humans and other higher life forms, nature cannot make every individual excellent.

[84] I take the second half of this cryptic line ("i.e., in certain places" etc.) to be an explanation of the "seldom" (μόλις) that precedes it. Especially obscure is "in some mixture of the whole" (ἔν τινι κράσει τοῦ ὅλου). *HA* 608b29–9a1 may shed some light on this passage.

[85] This likely means wet on the outside and filled with blood.

ἀτελῆ ἐξέρχεται, σημεῖον ὅτι τὰ μὲν εὐθὺς δύναται
ζῆν, τὰ δὲ παιδία ἐπιμελείας δεῖται. |

20   47. Διὰ τί τὰ μὲν τῶν ζῴων ἅπαξ ὀχεύεται, τὰ δὲ
πολλάκις, καὶ τὰ μὲν ὥρα ἔτους, τὰ δ' ὅτε ἔτυχεν,
ἄνθρωπος μὲν ἀεί, τὰ δὲ ἄγρια οὐ πολλάκις, καὶ ὗς
μὲν ἄγριος ἅπαξ, ἥμερος δὲ πολλάκις; ἢ διὰ τὴν
τροφὴν καὶ ἀλέαν καὶ πόνον; ἐν πλησμονῇ γὰρ Κύ-
25   πρις. ἔπειτα τὰ | αὐτὰ ἄλλοθι μὲν ἅπαξ τίκτει, ἄλλοθι
δὲ πλεονάκις, οἷον τὰ πρόβατα ἐν Μαγνησίᾳ καὶ
Λιβύῃ τίκτει δίς. τὸ δ' αἴτιον ἡ πολυχρονία τοῦ τόκου·
οὐ γὰρ ἐπιθυμεῖ ὅταν πλησθῇ, ὥσπερ οὐδὲ τροφῆς τὰ
πλήρη. τὰ δὲ κυοῦντα ἧττον ὀχείας ἐπιθυμεῖ διὰ τὸ μὴ
γίνεσθαι τὴν κάθαρσιν. |

30   48. Διὰ τί τῶν ἀνθρώπων οἱ ἀραιοὺς ἔχοντες τοὺς
ὀδόντας βραχύβιοι ὡς ἐπὶ τὸ πολύ; ἢ ὅτι σημεῖον τοῦ
τὸ ὀστοῦν πυκνὸν εἶναι; ὡς ὁ ἐγκέφαλος ἀσθενὴς οὐκ
εὔπνοῶν, ὥστε ὑγρὸς ὢν τὴν φύσιν ταχὺ σήπεται. καὶ
γὰρ τὰ ἄλλα μὴ κινούμενα καὶ ἀπατμίζοντα. διὸ καὶ
ἄνθρωπος τὴν κεφαλὴν | δασύτατον, καὶ τὸ ἄρρεν τοῦ
θήλεος μακροβιώτερον διὰ τὰς ῥαφάς. δεῖ δὲ ἰδεῖν καὶ
ἐπὶ τῶν ἄλλων.

---

86 See HA 5.8–14, which discusses these and related issues at
greater length. Cf. Plu. Aet. Phys. (Mor. 917B–D).

87 E. fr. 895 (Kannicht). The full line, according to Ath.
(6.270c), is "Cypris is found in fullness, not in being hungry" (ἐν
πλησμονῇ τοι Κύπρις, ἐν πεινῶντι δ' οὔ). "Cypris" is another
name for Aphrodite, here a personification of sexual desire.

88 "Filled" (πλησθῇ) can mean "satisfied" or "pregnant"—
surely the latter here.

come out perfected and others imperfect is that some are capable of living (*on their own*) straightaway, whereas children require supervision.

47.[86] Why do some animals copulate once, but others do so more often, and some copulate during one season of the year, but others whenever they happen to—humans at all times, wild animals not so often, and the wild pig once, the domestic pig often? Is it because of nourishment and warmth and exertion? For "Cypris is found in fullness."[87] Again, the same (*kinds of*) animals bear young once in some regions and many times in others; for instance, the sheep in Magnesia and Libya bear young twice. The reason is the long period of gestation; for nothing feels desire when it is filled,[88] just as what is full does not desire nourishment. Now pregnant animals desire copulation less because purgation does not occur (*during that time*).

48.[89] Why, among humans, are those with porous[90] teeth usually short-lived? Is it because this is a sign of the bone being thick? For the brain is weak if it does not have a good flow of air, such that being moist, it naturally putrefies quickly. Indeed, this is what happens to everything else that neither moves nor evaporates. And this is why the human has a hairy head, and why the male lives longer than the female owing to the (*number of*) sutures.[91] But one must also look at the other (*animals*).[92]

---

[89] Cf. *Pr.* 34.1. Source: *HA* 501b22–24; cf. Hp. *Epid.* 2.6.1.

[90] Or perhaps "well-spaced."

[91] Aristotle believed (erroneously) that men have more sutures in their skulls than women (see *HA* 491b2–6, 516a15–20, *PA* 653a29–b3).

[92] Or (looking ahead to the following chapter) "But one must also consider (*longevity*) in connection with other factors."

49. Διὰ τί δέ ὅσοι τὴν διὰ τῆς χειρὸς τομὴν ἔχουσι
δι' ὅλης, μακροβιώτεροι; ἢ διότι τὰ ἄναρθρα βραχυ-
896b βιώτατα, ‖ ὡς τὰ ἔννγρα; εἰ δὲ τὰ ἄναρθρα βραχύβια,
δῆλον ὅτι τὰ ἠρθρωμένα τοὐναντίον. τοιαῦτα δὲ ὧν
καὶ τὰ φύσει ἄναρθρα μάλιστα ἤρθρωται· τῆς δὲ
χειρὸς τὸ εἴσω ἀναρθρότατον. |

5   50. Διὰ τί τῶν ζῴων ἄνθρωπος ἢ μόνον ἢ μάλιστα
διαστρέφεται; ἢ ὅτι ἢ μόνον ἢ μάλιστα ἐπίληπτον[60] ἐν
τῇ νηπιότητι[61] γίνεται, ὅτε καὶ διαστρέφεσθαι συμβαίνει πᾶσιν;

51. Διὰ τί τῶν ζῴων ἄνθρωπος μάλιστα καπνίζεται;
ἢ ὅτι μάλιστα δακρύει, ἡ δὲ κάπνισις μετὰ δακρύου; |

10   52. Διὰ τί ἵππος ἵππῳ χαίρει καὶ ἐπιθυμεῖ, ἄνθρωπος δὲ ἀνθρώπῳ, καὶ ὅλως δὲ τὰ συγγενῆ τοῖς συγ-
γενέσι καὶ ὁμοίοις; οὐ γὰρ δὴ ὁμοίως ὁτιοῦν[62] ζῷον
καλόν, ἡ δὲ ἐπιθυμία τοῦ καλοῦ. ἔδει οὖν τὸ καλὸν
ἥδιον εἶναι. νῦν δὲ μᾶλλον οὐ πᾶν κάλλος ἡδύ, †τὸ
15   καλὸν καὶ τὸ ἡδύ†[63] οὐδὲ | πᾶσιν[64] ἡ ἡδονὴ ἢ τὸ καλὸν
ἡδύ, οἷον φαγεῖν ἢ πιεῖν ἐστιν ἥδιον ἑτέρῳ καὶ ἀφροδισιάσαι ἄλλῳ. διότι μὲν οὖν ἕκαστον τῷ συγγενεῖ

---

[60] ἐπίληπτον Forster ex Pr. 31.26, 960a10 : ληπτὸν codd.
[61] νηπιότητι : νεότητι Flashar ex Pr. 31.26, 960a10–11
[62] ὁτιοῦν Platt : ὅτι πᾶν codd.
[63] τὸ καλὸν καὶ τὸ ἡδύ codd. (obelis inclusi) : secl. Ruelle
[64] πᾶσιν Yᵃ : πᾶσα cett. codd. ‖ post πᾶσιν add. ⟨ὁμοίως⟩
Forster

---

93 Cf. Pr. 34.10. Source: HA 493b32–94a1.

49.[93] But why are those who have the line[94] across their entire hand long-lived? Is it because the unarticulated animals[95] are the most short-lived, as are the aquatic ones? But if the unarticulated ones are short-lived, it is clear that the articulated ones are the opposite. Now the latter are those in which the parts that are by nature unarticulated are articulated as much as they can be, and the inside of the hand is the most unarticulated part.

50.[96] Why does a human alone of the animals or most of all suffer from strabismus? Is it because he alone or most of all is epileptic in infancy, which in every case is when strabismus occurs?

51.[97] Why is a human of the animals most affected by smoke? Is it because he sheds tears the most, and smoke gives rise to tears?

52. Why does a horse enjoy and desire a horse, and a human a human, and generally animals of the same kind (*enjoy and desire*) animals of the same kind and similar to themselves? For not every animal is equally beautiful, and desire is for beauty. So what is beautiful should be more pleasant. But in actual fact, it is rather the case that not every beauty is pleasant—†the beautiful and the pleasant (*are not the same*)†—nor is the pleasant or the beautiful pleasant to everyone; for instance, eating or drinking is more pleasant to one person and having sex is more pleasant to another. Therefore, why each mates most of all with

---

[94] Literally, "the cut."   [95] Smooth animals, with no or few apparent joints or seams. The author likely has in mind animals like the squid (which Aristotle says is short-lived; see *HA* 550b14).   [96] This chapter is virtually identical to *Pr.* 31.26. Source: Hp. *Epid.* 2.5.11.   [97] Cf. *Pr.* 31.21.

μιγνύμενον μάλιστα καὶ ἥδιστα ἀφροδισιάζει, ἄλλο
πρόβλημα· ὅτι δὲ καὶ κάλλιστον, οὐκ ἔστιν[65] ἀληθές.
ἀλλὰ ἡμεῖς τὸ εἰς τὴν συνουσίαν ἡδὺ οἰόμεθα[66] καλόν, |
20 ὅτι ἐπιθυμοῦντες χαίρομεν ὁρῶντες. καίτοι καὶ ἐπὶ τῶν
ἄλλων ἐπιθυμιῶν ἔχει ὁμοίως· διψῶντες γὰρ ἥδιον
ὁρῶσι τὸ πόμα. τὸ μὲν οὖν πρὸς χρείαν τινὰ καλόν, οὗ
καὶ μάλιστα ἐπιθυμοῦμεν, τοῦτο δοκεῖ ἥδιστον εἶναι,
τὸ δὲ καθ' αὑτὸ οὐκέτι οὕτως. σημεῖον δὲ τούτου·
25 δοκοῦσι γὰρ ἡμῖν | καὶ ἄνδρες καλοὶ εἶναι, <οὐ>[67]
πρὸς τὴν συνουσίαν βλέψασιν. ἆρ' οὖν οὕτως ὥστε
καὶ ἡσθῆναι ὁρῶσι μᾶλλον τῶν εἰς συνουσίαν; οὐδέν
γε κωλύει, εἰ μὴ ἐπιθυμοῦντες τύχοιμεν. οὕτω δὲ πόμα
κάλλιον· εἰ γὰρ διψῶντες τύχοιμεν, ἥδιον ὀψόμεθα.

53. Διὰ τί ποτε τοῦ μὲν ἀνθρώπου τὰ ἔμπροσθεν
30 δασύτερα | τῶν ὄπισθέν ἐστι, τῶν δὲ τετραπόδων τὰ
ὄπισθεν; ἢ ὅτι πάντα τὰ δίποδα τὰ ἔμπροσθεν ἔχει
δασύτερα; οἱ γὰρ ὄρνιθες τὸν αὐτὸν τρόπον τοῖς
ἀνθρώποις ἔχουσιν. ἢ τὰ ἀσθενέστερα μᾶλλον ἀεὶ
σκεπάζειν ἡ φύσις εἴωθεν, ἀσθενὲς δὲ ἕκαστόν ἐστί
35 τινα τρόπον; τῶν δὲ τετραπόδων ἁπάντων | τὰ ὄπισθεν
ἀσθενέστερά ἐστι τῶν ἔμπροσθεν διὰ τὸν τόπον·[68] ὑπὸ
γὰρ τῶν ψυχῶν καὶ καυμάτων μᾶλλον δυνατά ἐστι
πάσχειν· τῶν δὲ ἀνθρώπων τὰ ἔμπροσθεν ἀσθενέ-
στερά ἐστι καὶ τὸ αὐτὸ πέπονθεν. ||

65 οὐκ ἔστιν Sylburg : οὐκέτι codd.
66 οἰόμεθα Bussemaker ex Barth. : ὅτι ὁ μὲν codd.
67 <οὐ> Sylburg   68 τόπον : τρόπον Forster

the same kind of animal and thereby derives the greatest pleasure from sexual intercourse is another issue:[98] it is not because (*the same kind of animal*) is most beautiful. But we think that what pleases us in intercourse is beautiful, because when we feel desire we enjoy seeing (*the object of our desire*). Moreover, in the case of other desires the position is similar; for when we are thirsty, seeing the drink is more pleasant. Therefore, what seems to be most pleasant is that which is beautiful with a view to some purpose, for which we also have a great desire, but this is not so in the case of the beautiful itself. And there is a sign of this: for even men seem to us to be beautiful, when we look at them with‹out› a view to intercourse. Are they so (*beautiful*) as to give us more pleasure than those whom we see with a view to intercourse? Nothing prevents this, if we do not happen to feel desire (*for intercourse*). And so may a drink be more beautiful; if we happen to be thirsty, we shall see it as more pleasant.

53.[99] Why in a human are the front parts hairier than the back, but in four-footed animals the back parts (*are hairier*)? Is it because in all two-footed animals the front has more hair? For birds have this same characteristic that is in humans. Or is it that nature is always accustomed to shield the weaker parts more, and each (*animal*) is weak in some way? For in all the four-footed animals the back parts are weaker than the front parts because of their position, for they can suffer more from both cold and heat; but the front parts of humans are weaker and suffer in the same respects.

---

[98] See *Pr.* 4.15.
[99] Source: *PA* 658a15–24; cf. *HA* 498b19–21.

897a	54. Διὰ τί ἄνθρωπος τῶν ζῴων μάλιστα πτάρνυται;
ἢ ὅτι καὶ κορυζᾷ μάλιστα; τούτου δ' αἴτιόν ἐστιν ὅτι
τοῦ θερμοῦ ὄντος περὶ τὴν καρδίαν καὶ πεφυκότος ἄνω
φέρεσθαι τοῖς μὲν ἄλλοις ζῴοις ἡ κατὰ φύσιν αὐτοῦ
5	φορά ἐστιν ἐπὶ τοὺς | ὤμους, ἐντεῦθεν δὲ ἐξ ἀνακλά-
σεως σχιζόμενον τὸ μὲν ἐπὶ τὸν τράχηλον καὶ τὴν
κεφαλὴν φέρεται αὐτοῦ, τὸ δὲ εἰς τὴν ῥάχιν καὶ τὴν
ὀσφύν, διὰ τὸ ἐπὶ τῆς αὐτῆς εὐθείας εἶναι ταῦτα πάντα
καὶ παρὰ τὴν βάσιν. φερόμενον δὲ ὁμοίως τὸ θερμὸν[69]
10	καὶ τὰ ὑγρὰ μερίζει εἰς αὐτὰ ὁμαλῶς· | ἕπεται γὰρ τὰ
ὑγρὰ τῷ θερμῷ. διὸ οὐδὲ πάνυ κορυζᾷ τὰ τετράποδα
ζῷα, οὐδὲ πτάρνυται· ὁ γὰρ πταρμὸς ἢ πνεύματος
ἀθρόου φορά ἐστιν, ὑγρῶν ἐξατμιζόντων τι μᾶλλον
τοῦ σώματος, ἢ ὑγρῶν ἀπέπτων. διὸ πρὸ τῶν κατάρρων γίνεται, ἃ οὐ συμβαίνει τοῖς ἄλλοις ζῴοις, διὰ τὸ
15	τὴν τοῦ | θερμοῦ φορὰν ὁμαλίζειν ἐν αὐτῷ εἰς τὸ
πρόσθεν καὶ ὄπισθεν. τοῦ δὲ ἀνθρώπου πρὸς ὀρθῇ
πεφυκότος τῇ βάσει, καθάπερ τὰ φυτά, συμβαίνει τοῦ
θερμοῦ φορὰν ἐπὶ τὴν κεφαλὴν γίνεσθαι πλείστην καὶ
σφοδροτάτην. φερόμενόν τε ἐνταῦθα ἀραιοῖ καὶ θερ-
20	μαίνει τοὺς περὶ αὐτὴν πόρους. ὄντες | δὲ τοιοῦτοι
δεκτικοὶ γίνονται τῶν ὑγρῶν μᾶλλον ἢ οἱ κάτω τῆς
καρδίας πόροι. ὅταν οὖν συμβῇ ἐξυγρανθῆναι μᾶλλον
τοῦ δέοντος καὶ καταψυχθῆναι ἔξωθεν, συμβαίνει τὸ
θερμόν, τροφήν τε ἔχον καὶ συστελλόμενον ἐντός,
αὔξεσθαι, αὐξανόμενον δὲ φέρεσθαι ἐπὶ τὴν κεφαλὴν

[69] τὸ θερμὸν Bonitz : τὸ σῶμα codd. : [τὸ σῶμα] Forster

54.[100] Why does a human sneeze most of all the animals? Is it because he also has runny noses most of all? Now the reason for this is that, as heat exists around the heart and is naturally carried upward, in the case of other animals its rush is naturally to the shoulders, and from here, dividing by rebound, part of it is carried to the neck and the head, and part to the spine and the loins, because these parts are all in a straight line and along its base.[101] Similarly, the heat, as it is carried along, also distributes the moisture to the same parts uniformly; for the moisture follows the heat. This is why the four-footed animals do not have runny noses much, and nor do they sneeze: for sneezing is the rush either of collected breath, when the moisture of the body evaporates somewhat more (*than usual*), or of unconcocted moisture. This is why sneezing happens before the discharges, which do not occur in the other animals, because the rush of the heat is divided equally between the fore and hind parts. But since the human, just like plants, is naturally upright from its base, the result is that a substantial and violent rush of heat to the head occurs. Being carried in this direction, (*the heat*) makes porous and heats the passages around this part. Now being such as they are, they are more receptive of moisture than the passages of the heart below. Therefore, when it happens that (*a human*) becomes more full of moisture and more chilled externally than he should be, the result is that the heat, having nourishment and drawing together within, grows, and as it grows it is carried to the head and to

[100] Cf. *Pr.* 10.18 and 33.10.
[101] I.e., these parts are along a line parallel to the ground.

25 καὶ τοὺς ἐν αὐτῇ | πόρους· εἰς οὓς ἀκολουθοῦντα τὰ
ὑγρά, ὄντα λεπτὰ καὶ ἄπεπτα, πληροῖ αὐτοὺς καὶ τοὺς
κατάρρους ποιεῖ, καὶ πταρμοὺς ὁμοίως. ἐν γὰρ ταῖς
ἀρχαῖς τῶν κατάρρων τὸ θερμὸν προαναφερόμενον
τοῦ ὑγροῦ, καὶ πνευματοῦν τοὺς πόρους, τῇ τ᾿ ἐκβολῇ
τοῦ πνεύματος τοὺς πταρμοὺς ποιεῖ καὶ τῇ [πρὸ][70] |

30 τῶν ὑγρῶν ἀναγωγῇ, ἅ ἐστι λεπτὰ καὶ δριμέα. διὸ καὶ
συμβαίνει μετὰ τῶν τῆς κορύζης πταρμῶν ὑδατώδη
ἀπομύττεσθαι. πάντων δὲ τούτων ὁρμησάντων τὰ
συνεχῆ καὶ πάχος[71] ἔχοντα ὑγρὰ ἐφίσταται αὐτοῖς,
καὶ ἐμφράττει τοὺς περὶ τὴν κεφαλὴν καὶ τὴν ῥῖνα

35 πόρους· ὀγκηρότερα γὰρ | γινόμενα καὶ διατείνοντα
ποιεῖ τοὺς περὶ τὴν κεφαλὴν πόνους. σημεῖον δὲ τὸ
μήτ᾿ ἐκτὸς ἢ[72] δι᾿ αὐτῶν πνεῦμα ἀφεῖσθαι. διὸ οὔτε
πτάρνυνται οὔτε ὀσφραίνονται οἱ κορυζῶντες. οἱ δὲ
ἄνευ κορύζης γινόμενοι διὰ μὲν τὰς αὐτὰς αἰτίας
γίνονται, μικρὰς δὲ καὶ ἐλαφρὰς ἀρχὰς λαβόντες.

897b ὥστε ‖ συναχθέντα τὰ ὑγρὰ τῷ θερμῷ, ἐκπνευμα-
τούμενα ὑπ᾿ αὐτοῦ δι᾿ ὀλιγότητα, εἰσπίπτει κατὰ τὰς
ῥῖνας. ποιεῖ δὲ τὸν ψόφον τοῦ πνεύματος οὐχ ἧττον ἡ
βία τῆς φορᾶς ἢ τὸ πλῆθος αὐτοῦ. ἐνεχθέντος γὰρ τοῦ

5 θερμοῦ πρὸς ὀρθὴν πρὸς | τὸν ἐγκέφαλον καὶ προσπε-
σόντος αὐτῷ, ἀνακλᾶται ἐπὶ τὰς ῥῖνας διὰ τὸ τοὺς
ταύτῃ πόρους ἐκτὸς ἀπὸ τοῦ ἐγκεφάλου διατείνειν.
παρὰ φύσιν οὖν τῆς ἐκ τῆς[73] κλάσεως φορᾶς γινο-

---

[70] [πρὸ] Forster ex Gaza
[71] πάχος Forster ex Gaza : πάθος codd.

the passages therein; the moisture follows into them, being light and unconcocted, and fills them and produces discharges, and similarly sneezing. For at the beginning of the discharges the heat, being carried along before the moisture, sends breath through the passages, and by the expulsion of the breath and the withdrawal of the moisture, which is light and pungent, it causes sneezing. And this is why it also happens that after sneezing from a runny nose, watery material is wiped off. Now when all of these have been set in motion, the continuous and thick moisture follows them, and blocks up the passages around the head and nose; for becoming more swollen and expanding they cause pains around the head. A sign of this is the fact that breath can neither pass out of nor through them.[102] This is why those who have runny noses neither sneeze nor use their sense of smell. Sneezes occurring without the nose running occur for the same reasons, but have slight and unimportant origins. So the moisture, being collected by the heat and vaporized by it because of the very small (*amount*), pours down into the nostrils. And the force of the rush of the breath produces the noise no less than its quantity. For when the heat is carried straight up to the head and strikes against it, the heat rebounds to the nostrils because the passages in this region extend out from the brain. Therefore, the rush by the breath from the re-

---

[102] There is probably something wrong with the text here. If Forster's emendation is correct, the line should be rendered "that no breath can pass out through them."

---

72 μήτ' ἐκτὸς ἢ : ἢ om. Bussemaker : μηδὲν ἐκτὸς Forster
73 ἐκ τῆς Bussemaker : ἐκτὸς codd.

331

ARISTOTLE

μένης ἐπὶ τὰς ῥῖνας τῷ πνεύματι, σφοδρὰν συμβαίνει
γίνεσθαι· διὸ ποιεῖ τοὺς ψόφους. τῶν δὲ ἄλλων ζῴων
10 συμβαίνει | μάλιστα κορυζᾶν τοὺς ὄρνιθας διὰ τὸ
μάλιστα ὁμοιόσχημον εἶναι ἀνθρώπῳ· ἧττον δὲ ἢ
ἄνθρωπος πάσχει αὐτό, ὅτι τὰ πολλὰ κάτω ἔχει τὴν
κεφαλὴν διὰ τὸ τὴν νομὴν ἀπὸ τῆς γῆς εἶναι.

55. Διὰ τί τὰ θαλάττια ζῷα τῶν ἐν τῇ γῇ μείζω καὶ |
15 εὐτραφέστερά ἐστιν; ἢ ὅτι ὁ ἥλιος καταδαπανῶν τὰ
περιέχοντα τὴν γῆν ἀφαιρεῖται τὴν τροφήν; διὸ καὶ τὰ
κατακεκλειμένα εὐτραφέστερά ἐστιν. πάντων οὖν τούτων ἀπήλλακται τὰ θαλάττια ζῷα.

56. Διὰ τί ποτε τὰ μὲν ἄλλα ζῷα πλεονάκις τὴν
20 ξηρὰν | τροφὴν ἢ τὴν ὑγρὰν προσάγεται, ὁ δὲ ἄνθρω-
πος τὴν ὑγρὰν ἢ τὴν ξηράν; ἢ ὅτι φύσει ὁ ἄνθρωπος
θερμότατον; πλείστης οὖν καταψύξεως δεῖται.

57. Διὰ τί οἱ εὐνοῦχοι οὐ γίνονται φαλακροί; ἢ ὅτι
πολὺν ἔχουσι τὸν ἐγκέφαλον; τοῦτο δὲ συμβέβηκεν
25 αὐτοῖς διὰ τὸ | μὴ συγγίνεσθαι ταῖς γυναιξίν· ἡ γὰρ
γονή ἐστιν ἀπὸ τοῦ ἐγκεφάλου χωροῦσα διὰ τῆς
ῥάχεως. διὰ τοῦτο δὲ οὖν[74] δοκοῦσι καὶ οἱ βόες οἱ
ἐκτομίαι μεγάλα τὰ κέρατα ἴσχειν, ὅταν ἐκτμηθῶσιν.
δοκεῖ δὲ ἡ αὐτὴ αἰτία εἶναι καὶ ὅτι αἱ γυναῖκες καὶ οἱ
παῖδες οὐκ εἰσὶ φαλακροί. |

30 58. Διὰ τί τὰ μὲν εὐθὺς δύνανται δι᾽ αὑτῶν τρέφε-
σθαι μετὰ τὴν γένεσιν, τὰ δὲ οὔ; ἢ ὅσα ὀλιγοχρονι-
ώτερα τῶν μνήμης δεκτικῶν; διὸ ἅπαντα καὶ τελευτᾷ
θᾶττον.

bound to the nostrils, being contrary to nature, becomes violent; this is why it produces noises. Now of the other animals, birds have runny noses most, because they are the most similar in shape to the human; but they suffer from this less than humans, because for the most part they keep their heads down because their food is from the ground.

55. Why are marine animals larger and better nourished than those on the land? Is it because the sun, consuming the material surrounding the earth, takes away the nourishment? And this is why the (*animals*) enclosed in (*the earth*) are better nourished. Therefore, the marine animals escape all of this.

56. Why do the other animals take in dry nourishment more often than moist, but the human moist more often than dry? Is it because the human is by nature the hottest animal? Therefore he needs the most frequent cooling.

57.[103] Why do eunuchs not become bald? Is it because they have a large brain? Now this happens to them because they do not associate with women; for the semen moves from the brain through the spine. And this, therefore, is why castrated bulls seem to have large horns, once they have been castrated. And it seems to be for the same reason that women and children are not bald.

58.[104] Why are some (*animals*) able to feed themselves immediately after birth, while others are not? Are those that can do so the shorter-lived among the (*animals*) capable of memory? This is why they all also die earlier.

---

[103] Sources: *HA* 518a30–31, 632a4, *GA* 784a6–7. Cf. Hp. *Aph.* 6.28.   [104] Source: *HA* 588b30–89a2.

---

74 δὲ οὖν Bussemaker : δὲ μοι β : δὲ οὐ plur. codd. : δὲ Nicasius

59. Διὰ τί ποτε ὁ μὲν ἄνθρωπος πλείω τὴν ὑποχώ-
ρησιν ποιεῖται τὴν ὑγρὰν τῆς ξηρᾶς, οἱ δὲ ἵπποι καὶ οἱ
35 ὄνοι τὴν | ξηράν; ἢ διότι ταῦτα μὲν τὰ ζῷα πλείονι
τροφῇ χρῆται τῇ ξηρᾷ, ὁ δὲ ἄνθρωπος ὑγρᾷ μᾶλλον ἢ
τῇ ξηρᾷ; πᾶσα δὲ περίττωσις ἀπὸ τῆς τροφῆς ἐστί,
καὶ ἀπὸ τῆς πλείονος πλείω. τὰ μὲν οὖν τῇ ὑγρᾷ
μᾶλλον, τὰ δὲ τῇ ξηρᾷ πλείονι τροφῇ χρῆται· διότι τὰ
μὲν τῶν ζῴων ἐστὶ φύσει ξηρά, τὰ δὲ ὑγρά. τὰ μὲν οὖν
898a τῇ φύσει ‖ ξηρὰ τῆς ὑγρᾶς μᾶλλον ἐπιθυμεῖ, ταύτης
γὰρ ἐνδεέστερά εἰσι, τὰ δὲ τῇ φύσει ὑγρὰ τῆς ξηρᾶς,
ταύτης γὰρ ἐνδεέστερα καθέστηκεν.

60. Διὰ τί ὄρνιθες καὶ ἄνθρωποι καὶ τῶν ζῴων τὰ
5 ἀνδρεῖα | σκληρότερα; ἢ ὅτι ὁ θυμὸς μετὰ θερμότητος;
ὁ γὰρ φόβος κατάψυξις. ὅσων οὖν τὸ αἷμα ἔνθερμόν
ἐστι, καὶ ἀνδρεῖα καὶ θυμοειδῆ· τὸ δὲ αἷμα τροφή. ὅσα
δὲ θερμῷ ἄρδεται τῶν φυομένων, σκληρότερα πάντα.

61. Διὰ τί τέρατα τίκτουσιν μάλιστα τὰ τετράποδα |
10 τὰ μὴ μεγάλα, ἄνθρωπος δὲ καὶ τὰ μεγάλα ἧττον,
οἷον ἵπποι καὶ ὄνοι; ἢ ὅτι πολύγονα ταῦτα, οἷον κύνες
καὶ ὕες καὶ αἶγες καὶ πρόβατα, πολὺ μᾶλλον τῶν
μεγάλων, ἐκείνων δὲ τὰ μὲν ὅλως μονοτόκα, τὰ δὲ ὡς
ἐπὶ τὸ πολύ; τὰ δὲ τέρατα γίνεται ἐπαλλαττόντων τῶν |
15 σπερμάτων ἀλλήλοις καὶ συγχεομένων ἐν τῇ ἐξόδῳ
τῆς γονῆς ἢ ἐν τῇ μίξει τῇ ἐν τῇ ὑστέρᾳ τῆς θηλείας.
διὸ καὶ ὄρνιθες αὐτὰ ποιοῦσιν· τὰ γὰρ ᾠὰ δίδυμα
τίκτουσι, τὰ δὲ τέρατα ἐκ τῶν διδύμων γίνεται, ὧν ἡ
λέκιθος τῷ ὑμένι οὐ διαιρεῖται. |

59. Why does the human produce more moist excrement than dry, whereas horses and asses produce more dry excrement? Is it because these animals take more dry nourishment, whereas the human takes more moist than dry? But all residue is from nourishment, and the greater amount of residue from the greater amount of nourishment. Therefore, some animals take moist nourishment more, others take dry more; this is because some of the animals are dry by nature, others moist. Therefore, the animals that are dry by nature desire moist nourishment, for they are more lacking in this, but the ones that are moist by nature desire dry nourishment, for they stand in greater need of that.

60.[105] Why are birds and humans and the courageous animals the hardest? Is it because spirit involves heat? For fear is a process of cooling. Therefore, those whose blood is hot are courageous and spirited; indeed, blood is (*their*) nourishment. Further, those plants that are watered with warm water are all harder.

61.[106] Why do the four-footed animals that are not large most often bear monsters, but the human and the large (*four-footed animals*), such as horses and asses, do so less? Is it because the former, such as dogs, pigs, goats, and sheep, give birth to many more offspring than the large animals, which generally or for the most part give birth to one? Now monsters come to be when the seeds are mixed up with each other and commingled either in the exiting of the semen or in the mixing in the female's uterus. And this is why birds produce them: for they lay twin eggs, and the monsters come from the twins, in which the yoke is not separated from the membrane.

[105] Cf. *PA* 2.4. [106] Cf. *GA* 769b27–70b27.

20   62. Διὰ τί ἡ κεφαλὴ δασεῖα τῶν ἀνθρώπων μᾶλλον
τοῦ ἄλλου σώματος καὶ οὐ κατὰ λόγον, τοῖς δὲ ἄλλοις
ζῴοις τοὐναντίον; ἢ ὅτι καὶ τῶν ἄλλων τὰ μὲν εἰς
ὀδόντας ἐκδίδωσιν καθ᾽ ὑπερβολὴν τῆς τροφῆς, τὰ δὲ
εἰς κέρατα, τὰ δὲ εἰς τρίχας; ὅσα μὲν εἰς κέρατα, ἧττον
25   τὴν κεφαλὴν | ἔχει δασεῖαν· ἐκεῖ γὰρ ἀνήλωται. ὅσα
δὲ εἰς ὀδόντας, μᾶλλον μὲν τῶν κερατοφόρων (ἔχει
γὰρ λοφιάν), ἧττον δὲ τῶν τοιούτων, οἷον⁷⁵ ὀρνέων.
ἔχουσιν γὰρ ταῦτα καὶ τὴν τῶν ἀνθρώπων.⁷⁶ ὃ <δὲ>⁷⁷
ἐκείνοις πολλαχῇ διὰ πλῆθος, τούτῳ εἰς κεφαλὴν
ἐκδίδωσιν· οὔτε γὰρ οὐδὲν ἔχει, οὔτε πολὺ οὕτως |
30   ὥστε πανταχῇ.

62. Διὰ τί ἄνθρωπος μόνος τῶν ζῴων πολιὰς ἔχει; ἢ
ὅτι τὰ μὲν πλεῖστα τῶν ζῴων ῥυάδα τὴν τρίχα ἀνὰ
πᾶν ἔτος ἔχει, οἷον ἵππος, βοῦς, ἔνια δὲ ῥυάδα μὲν οὐκ
ἔχει, βραχύβια δέ εἰσι, καθάπερ πρόβατον καὶ ἄλλα·
35   οὗ ἡ | θρὶξ ὥσπερ οὐ γηράσκουσα οὐδὲ πολιοῦται. ὁ
δὲ ἄνθρωπος οὐδὲ ῥυάδα ἔχει τὴν τρίχα, μακρόβιόν τέ
ἐστιν, ὥστε ὑπὸ τοῦ χρόνου πολιοῦται.

⁷⁵ οἷον : οἴων Richards
⁷⁶ post τὴν τῶν ἀνθρώπων add. <ὑπερβολὴν τῆς τροφῆς>
Louis : add. <ἔκδοσις> Richards
⁷⁷ <δὲ> Richards

107 Sources: HA 498b16–19 and PA 658b2–10.
108 Either animals that give up the excess nourishment to
teeth, or birds.

62.[107] Why is the head of humans hairier than the rest of the body and not in proportion, whereas in other animals it is the opposite? Is it because among the other animals some give up an excessive amount of nourishment to the teeth, others to horns, and others to hair? Those that give this up to horns have less hair on the head; for (*the available nourishment*) is used up on the horns. And those that give this up to teeth have more hair (*on the head*) than the horned animals (for they have a mane), but less than such animals as birds. For these[108] have the same (*excess of nourishment*) as humans;[109] but whereas in those[110] (*it is distributed*) everywhere because of its quantity, in humans they give this up to the head; for a human neither lacks this nor has enough (*for it to go*) everywhere.

63.[111] Why does the human alone of the animals have gray hair? Is it because most of the animals have hair that sheds every year, such as the horse and bull, whereas some do not, though they are short-lived, like sheep and others—in which case the hair never as it were grows old and so does not turn gray? But the human does not have hair that sheds *and* is long-lived, so that it turns gray over time.

[109] The text is problematic. At the very least, there seems to be a word missing after τὴν τῶν ἀνθρώπων, and none of the suggested emendations are entirely satisfactory. I translate Louis's suggestion: ὑπερβολὴν τῆς τροφῆς ("excess of nourishment") from 898a23. In any case, something like "distribution of excess nourishment" seems to be required.

[110] Either animals that give up the excess nourishment to teeth, or birds.

[111] Sources: *GA* 778a25–27, 780b4–5, 782a11–13.

64. Διὰ τί, ὅσοις τὰ ἀπὸ τοῦ ὀμφαλοῦ κάτω μείζονα
898b ἢ ‖ τὰ πρὸς τὰ στήθη, βραχύβιοι καὶ ἀσθενεῖς; ἢ ὅτι
ἡ κοιλία ψυχρὰ διὰ μικρότητα, ὥστε οὐ πεπτικὴ ἀλλὰ
περιττωματική; οἱ δὲ τοιοῦτοι νοσακεροί.

65. Διὰ τί τὰ μὲν γίνεται τῶν ζῴων οὐ μόνον ἐξ
5 ἀλλήλων, | ἀλλὰ καὶ αὐτόματα, τὰ δ' ἐξ ἀλλήλων
μόνον, οἷον ἄνθρωπος καὶ ἵππος; ἢ κἂν εἰ καὶ μὴ δι'
ἑτέρας αἰτίας, ἀλλ' ὅτι τοῖς μὲν ὀλίγος ὁ χρόνος τῆς
γενέσεως, ὥστε ἡ γεννητικὴ ὥρα ⟨οὐχ⟩[78] ὑπερτείνει
καὶ ἐνδέχεται γενέσθαι ἐν τῇ μεταβολῇ τῶν ὡρῶν, τῶν
10 δὲ πολὺ ἡ γένεσις ὑπερτείνει; | ἐνιαύσιοι γὰρ ἢ δεκά-
μηνοί εἰσιν· ὥστε ἀνάγκη ⟨μὴ⟩[79] γίνεσθαι ἢ ἐξ ἀλλήλων γίνεσθαι.

66. Διὰ τί τῶν Αἰθιόπων οἱ μὲν ὀδόντες λευκοί, καὶ
λευκότεροι ἢ τῶν ἄλλων, οἱ δὲ ὄνυχες οὐκέτι; ἢ οἱ μὲν
ὄνυχες, ὅτι καὶ τὸ δέρμα μέλαν, καὶ μελάντερον ἢ τῶν
15 ἄλλων, | οἱ δὲ ὄνυχες ἐκ τοῦ δέρματος φύονται; οἱ δὲ
ὀδόντες λευκοὶ διὰ τί; ἢ ὅτι ἐξ ὧν τὸ ὑγρὸν ἐξάγει ὁ
ἥλιος ἄνευ τοῦ ἐπιβάπτειν, λευκαίνεται, οἷον καὶ τὸν
κηρόν; τὸ μὲν οὖν δέρμα ἐπιβάπτει, τοὺς δὲ ὀδόντας
οὐκ ἐπιβάπτει, ἀλλὰ τὸ ὑγρὸν διὰ τὴν ἀλέαν ἐξατμί-
ζεται ἐξ αὐτῶν. |

[78] ⟨οὐχ⟩ Nicasius
[79] ⟨μὴ⟩ Nicasius : ⟨ἢ μὴ⟩ Bussemaker : ⟨μὴ ἄλλως⟩ Flashar :
post ἀνάγκη lac. indic. Hett

[112] Cf. *Phgn.* 810b16–18.
[113] It is unclear whether the author is distinguishing different

64.[112] Why are those[113] for whom the parts from the navel downward are greater than those (*from the navel*) toward the chest short-lived and weak? Is it because the stomach is cold owing to its smallness, so that it is not conducive to concoction but is full of residue? And such are unhealthy.

65.[114] Why do some animals come to be not only from one another but also spontaneously, whereas others come to be only from one another, such as the human and the horse? Is it for no other reason but that in some animals the time of generation is short, so that the season of birth is ‹not› protracted and can occur during the change of seasons, whereas in others the generation is protracted a great deal? For it is either a year or ten months, so that they must ‹not› come to be or must come to be from one another.[115]

66.[116] Why are the teeth of the Ethiopians white, and whiter than those of other people, but their nails are not? Are their nails (*not white*) because their skin is dark, and darker than that of other people, and the nails grow from the skin? But why are their teeth white? Is it because whatever the sun extracts moisture from, without dyeing it,[117] becomes white, such as wax? Now it dyes the skin, whereas it does not dye the teeth, but the moisture is evaporated from them owing to the warmth.

---

kinds of animals or kinds of humans, though the latter is more likely.   [114] Cf. *Pr.* 10.13. On spontaneous generation, see *GA* 763a24–16.   [115] The text of this last line is uncertain.

[116] Source: *HA* 517a11–20. See also *SE* 167a10–13.

[117] Literally, "dipping into" (the rare ἐπιβάπτει), which suggests dyeing or gilding, though the author is simply referring to changing color.

20   67. Διὰ τί τὰ μὲν ἀφαιρουμένης τῆς κεφαλῆς
ἀποθνήσκει εὐθὺς ἢ ταχύ, τὰ δὲ οὔ; ἢ ὅσα ἄναιμα καὶ
ὀλιγότροφα, τοῦτο πάσχει; οὔτε τροφῆς γὰρ δεῖται
ταχύ, οὔτε ἐγχεῖται αὐτῶν τὸ θερμὸν ἐν τῷ ὑγρῷ, ὧν
ἄνευ οὐχ οἷόν τε ζῆν τοῖς ἐναίμοις. τούτοις δὲ οἷόν τέ
25   ἐστιν· ἀπνευστὶ ζῆν γὰρ | δύνανται πολὺ μᾶλλον. ἡ δὲ
αἰτία ἐν ἑτέροις εἴρηται.

67.[118] Why do some (*animals*) die immediately or quickly after their head is removed, whereas others do not? Do the animals that are bloodless and require little nourishment experience the latter? For they neither need nourishment quickly, nor is the heat in them diffused into moisture—things without which blooded animals cannot live. But this is possible for the (*bloodless animals*): for they can live longer without breathing. And the reason for this has been stated elsewhere.[119]

[118] Source: *Juv.* 468a20–28, *HA* 531b30–32a5, *PA* 673a10–31.
[119] See *Resp.* 475a20–29.

BOOK XI

INTRODUCTION

The *Vita Hesychii* attributes to Aristotle a work entitled *On Voice* (Περὶ φωνῆς) (no. 164). There is no other evidence for such a work. This may be a reference to *Pr.* 11 (Ὅσα περὶ φωνῆς) or to some other discussion of voice in the *corpus Aristotelicum*—see especially *GA* 5.7, but also *HA* 4.9 and *DA* 2.8. Voice and related topics are also discussed throughout the *De Audibilibus*, in the *Physiognomonica*,[1] and in Theophrastus' *On Music* (as is clear from the longest surviving fragment, fr. 716 FHSG = Porphyry, *On Ptolemy's Harmonics* 1.3). The author of *Pr.* 11 may also have been aware of the Hippocratic *De Carnibus* 18 (on sound and speech). These works form the background for the present book.

GA 5.7 opens as follows:

> Concerning voice (περὶ φωνῆς), that some animals have low voices (βαρύφωνα), while others have

---

[1] The *De Audibilibus* is preserved solely as a long quotation in Porphyry's *Commentary on Ptolemy's Harmonics*. Porphyry attributes the work to Aristotle; modern scholars tend to ascribe its authorship to some other Peripatetic (e.g., Theophrastus, Heraclides, Strato). On voice in the *Physiognomonica* (which scholars generally consider inauthentic), see 806a28–34, b26–27, 807a13–25, b33–35, 813a31–b6.

high voices (ὀξύφωνα),[2] and some are well measured and balanced between the two extremes,
and further, that some are loud-voiced while others
are soft-voiced, and that they differ from one another in smoothness and roughness, and in flexibil-
ity and inflexibility, we must investigate the reasons
for which each of these is so. (786b7–12)

Much of Book 11—which is the third longest in the *Problems*—seems to undertake part of such an investigation.
The subject of one third of the chapters is high and/or low
sounds—which kinds of people produce them, or which
conditions give rise to them (6, 10, 13–21, 24, 32, 34, 40,
47, 50, 53, 56, 61, 62a). A dozen chapters discuss the conditions under which certain sounds are more or less audible
(3, 5, 25, 29, 33, 37, 41, 44, 45, 48, 52, 59), four discuss echoes (7, 8, 23, 51), and three why salt makes a sound when
thrown in fire (26, 42, 43). Seven deal with stammering
(30, 35, 36, 38, 54, 55, 60), six with rough, cracked, broken,
or trembling voices (11, 12, 22, 31, 46, 62b), and three with
deafness and dumbness (1, 2, 4). Two chapters contain fascinating discussions of the development of language in humans (27, 57); equally fascinating are the two devoted to
the differences between sound and light (49, 58). There

---

[2] I consistently translate βαρ- and ὀξυ- by "low" and "high"
(i.e., low-pitched and high-pitched) respectively; but note that
they could also be rendered "deep" and "shrill." The basic (non-
acoustic) meaning of βαρύς is "heavy," of ὀξύς "sharp" or
"pointed."

are two isolated topics: why "some things, such as boxes, make a sound and move suddenly, when nothing perceptible moves them" (28); and the effects of leeks and garlic on voice (39; but cf. 22).

ΟΣΑ ΠΕΡΙ ΦΩΝΗΣ

1. Διὰ τί τῶν αἰσθήσεων ἐκ γενετῆς μάλιστα τὴν ἀκοὴν πηροῦνται; ἢ ὅτι ἀπὸ τῆς αὐτῆς ἀρχῆς εἶναι δόξειεν ἂν ἥ | τε ἀκοὴ καὶ ἡ φωνή; ῥᾷστα δὲ δοκεῖ διαφθείρεσθαι ἡ διάλεκτος, οὖσα εἶδος φωνῆς, καὶ χαλεπώτατα ἐπιτελεῖσθαι. σημεῖον δὲ ὅτι μετὰ τὸ γενέσθαι πολὺν χρόνον ἐνεοί ἐσμεν· τὸ μὲν γὰρ πρῶτον ὅλως οὐδὲ λαλοῦμεν οὐδέν, εἶτα ὀψέ ποτε ψελλίζομεν. διά τε¹ τὸ τὴν διάλεκτον εὔφθαρτον εἶναι, τὴν | αὐτὴν δὲ ἀρχὴν ἀμφοτέρων εἶναι καὶ τῆς διαλέκτου (φωνὴ γάρ τις) καὶ τῆς ἀκοῆς, ὥσπερ καὶ ἐκ² συμβεβηκότος, ῥᾷστα τῶν αἰσθήσεων φθείρεται, καὶ οὐ καθ᾽ αὑτήν, ἡ ἀκοή. τεκμήριον δὲ ἔστι καὶ ἐκ τῶν ἄλλων ζῴων λαβεῖν, ὅτι παντελῶς ‖ εὔφθαρτός ἐστιν ἡ ἀρχὴ τῆς διαλέκτου· λαλεῖ γὰρ οὐθὲν τῶν ἄλλων ζῴων πλὴν ἀνθρώπου, καὶ οὗτοι δὲ ὀψέ ποτε, καθάπερ εἴρηται.

2. Διὰ τί οἱ κωφοὶ πάντες διὰ τῶν ῥινῶν φθέγγονται; | ἢ διὰ τὸ ἐγγὺς εἶναι τοῦ ἐνεοὺς εἶναι;³ οἱ δὲ

---

¹ τε : om. β Nᵃ

898b
30

35

899a
5

PROBLEMS CONCERNING
VOICE

1. Why, of the senses, is hearing most likely to be defective from birth? Is it because both hearing and voice may be thought to come from the same source? Now language, which is a kind of voice, seems to be easily destroyed and most difficult to perfect. A sign of this is the fact that after birth we are dumb for a long time; for at first we cannot talk at all, and then after some time we speak inarticulately. And because language is easily destroyed, and the source is the same for both—for language (being one sort of voice) and for hearing—hearing is as it were incidentally and not in itself easily destroyed of the senses. Now it is possible to get further proof that the origin of language is quite easily destroyed from the other animals; for none of the animals except the human speaks, and he does so only after some time, as we have said.

2.[1] Why do all deaf people speak through their noses? Is it because they are close to being dumb? Now the dumb

[1] Cf. *Pr.* 11.4 and 33.14.

---

[2] καὶ : κἂν Marenghi[2] ‖ ἐκ Sylburg ex Gaza : εἰ codd.

[3] τὸ ἐγγὺς τοῦ εἶναι ἐνεοὺς εἶναι Bekker : τὸ ἐγγὺς τοῦ ἐνεοὺς εἶναι Ruelle

ἐνεοὶ λαλοῦσι διὰ τῶν ῥινῶν· ταύτῃ γὰρ αὐτῶν ἐκπίπτει τὸ πνεῦμα διὰ τὸ τῷ στόματι μεμυκέναι, μεμύ-
κασι δέ, ὅτι οὐθὲν εἰς φωνὴν χρῶνται τῇ γλώττῃ.

3. Διὰ τί μεγαλόφωνοι πάντες εἰσὶν οἱ θερμοὶ τὴν
10 φύσιν; ἢ ὅτι ἀνάγκη καὶ ἀέρα πολὺν καὶ ψυχρὸν ἐν
τούτοις εἶναι; ἕλκει γὰρ τὸ θερμὸν πνεῦμα⁴ πρὸς ἑαυτὸ
[καὶ]⁵ ἀέρα, καὶ πλείω τὸ πλεῖον. ἡ δὲ μεγάλη φωνὴ
γίνεται ἐν τῷ πολὺν ἀέρα κινεῖν, καὶ ὀξεῖα ἐν τῷ
ταχέως, βαρεῖα δὲ ἡ⁶ ἐν τῷ βραδέως. |

15 4. Διὰ τί οἱ κωφοὶ πάντες διὰ τῶν ῥινῶν φθέγγονται; ἢ διὰ τὸ βιαιότερον πνεῖν τοὺς κωφούς; ἐγγὺς
γὰρ τοῦ ἐνεοὶ εἶναι εἰσίν. διίσταται οὖν τῶν μυκτήρων
ὁ πόρος ὑπὸ τοῦ πνεύματος· οἱ τοιοῦτοι δὲ διὰ ῥινῶν
φθέγγονται.

5. Διὰ τί εὐηκοώτερα τὰ τῆς νυκτός; ἢ ὅτι μᾶλλον
20 ἠρεμία | διὰ τὴν τοῦ θερμοτάτου ἀπουσίαν; διὸ καὶ ὡς
ἐπὶ τὸ πολὺ ἀταρακτότερα. ὁ γὰρ ἥλιος ὁ κινῶν.

6. Διὰ τί πόρρωθεν αἱ φωναὶ ὀξύτεραι δοκοῦσιν
εἶναι; οἱ γοῦν μιμούμενοι τοὺς σφόδρα πόρρω ὄντας
καὶ βοῶντας ὀξὺ φθέγγονται καὶ ὅμοιον τοῖς ἀπηχοῦ-
25 σιν, καὶ τῆς ἠχοῦς ὀξύτερος | φαίνεται ὁ ψόφος. ἔστι

---

⁴ τὸ θερμὸν πνεῦμα β : θερμὸν καὶ πνεῦμα cett. codd. : τὸ
πνεῦμα τὸ θερμὸν [Arist./Alex.] Sup.Pr. 2.96, 2
⁵ [καὶ] Jan   ⁶ om. ἡ [Arist./Alex.] Sup.Pr. 2.96, 4

---

² The author uses a word for "talk" (λαλοῦσι), though he must
mean something like "attempt to talk" or "move their mouths as if
talking" or simply "make sounds."

"talk"[2] through their noses; for their breath departs by this way[3] because the mouth is shut, and it is shut, because they do not use the tongue with a view to (*modulating*) the voice.

3.[4] Why are all those who are hot by nature loud-voiced?[5] Is it because there must necessarily be much cold air in them? For the hot breath draws air to itself, and the more so the hotter it is. Now a loud voice occurs when much air is moved, a high voice when (*air is moved*) quickly, and low is the voice when (*it is moved*) slowly.

4.[6] Why do all deaf people speak through their noses? Is it because the deaf breathe more violently? For they are close to being dumb. Therefore the passage of the nostrils is distended by the breath, and such people speak through their noses.

5.[7] Why are nocturnal things easier to hear? Is it because there is more quiet owing to the absence of great heat? And this is why, for the most part, things are more undisturbed. For the sun is the mover.

6.[8] Why do voices seem to be higher from far away? At any rate, those imitating people shouting from a great distance utter higher sounds,[9] similar to those causing an echo, and the sound of an echo appears to be higher. And it

---

[3] I.e., through the nostrils.   [4] Source: Hp. *Epid.* 6.4.19. [Arist./Alex.] *Sup.Pr.* 2.96 is virtually identical to *Pr.* 11.3.

[5] μεγαλόφωνοι—*voce robusta* (Marenghi[2]).

[6] Cf. *Pr.* 11.2 and 33.14.

[7] Cf. *Pr.* 11.33, Plut. *QC* 8.3 (*Mor.* 720C–22F).

[8] Cf. *Pr.* 11.19, 20, 47.

[9] φθέγγομαι ("utter a sound") includes, but is not limited to, the human voice.

δὲ πόρρω, ἀνακλᾶται γάρ. οὐκοῦν ἐπεὶ ὀξὺ μὲν ἐν
ψόφῳ τὸ ταχύ, βαρὺ δὲ τὸ βραδύ,[7] ἔδει βαρυτέρας
πόρρωθεν φαίνεσθαι τὰς φωνάς. τὰ γὰρ αὖ φερόμενα
πάντα βραδύτερον φέρεται ὅσῳ ἂν ἀπέχῃ τῆς ἀρχῆς
πλεῖον, καὶ τέλος πίπτει. πότερ᾽ οὖν ὅτι οἱ μιμούμενοι |
30 ἀμενηνῇ τῇ φωνῇ μιμοῦνται καὶ λεπτῇ[8] τὴν πόρρωθεν
φωνήν; λεπτὴ δὲ βαρεῖα οὐκ ἔστιν, οὐδὲ μικρὸν καὶ
ἀμενηνὸν φθέγγεσθαι βαρύ, ἀλλ᾽ ὀξὺ ἀνάγκη. ἢ οὐ
μόνον οἱ μιμούμενοι διὰ τοῦτο μιμοῦνται, ἀλλὰ καὶ οἱ
ψόφοι αὐτοὶ ὀξύτεροι γίνονται; αἴτιον δὲ ὅτι ὁ ἀὴρ ὁ
35 φερόμενος ποιεῖ τὸν ψόφον· | καὶ ὥσπερ τὸ πρῶτον
ψοφεῖ τὸ κινῆσαν τὸν ἀέρα, οὕτω δεῖ πάλιν ποιῆσαι
τὸν ἀέρα, ἀεὶ <δ᾽>[9] ἄλλον κινοῦντα εἶναι, τὸν[10] δὲ
κινούμενον. διὸ ὁ ψόφος συνεχής, ὅτι ἀεὶ ἐκδέχεται ‖
899b κινοῦντα[11] κινῶν, ἕως ἂν ἀπομαρανθῇ, ὃ ἐπὶ τῶν
σωμάτων ἐστὶ τὸ πεσεῖν, ὅταν μηκέτι δύνηται ὠθεῖν ὁ
ἀὴρ ἔνθα μὲν τὸ βέλος, ἔνθα δὲ τὸν ἀέρα. ἡ μὲν γὰρ
φωνὴ γίνεται ἡ συνεχὴς ἀέρος ὠθουμένου ὑπ᾽ ἀέρος,
5 τὸ δὲ βέλος φέρεται σώματος | ὑπ᾽ ἀέρος κινουμένου.
ἐνταῦθα μὲν οὖν ἀεὶ τὸ αὐτὸ φέρεται σῶμα, ἕως ἂν
καταπέσῃ, ἐκεῖ δὲ ἀεὶ ἕτερος ἀήρ. καὶ πρῶτον ἐλάττω
θᾶττον μὲν κινεῖται, ἐπ᾽ ὀλίγον δέ. διὸ πόρρω ὀξύτεραι
καὶ λεπτότεραι αἱ φωναί. τὸ γὰρ θᾶττον ὀξύ, ὥσπερ
καὶ διηπόρηται. ὥσπερ ἡ αὐτὴ αἰτία δι᾽ ἣν καὶ οἱ μὲν |

---

[7] βαρὺ δὲ τὸ βραδύ Bekker (cf. Gaza) : βαρὺ δὲ τὸ βαρύ x :
βραχὺ δὲ τὸ βαρύ Y^a C^a A^m γ : βραδὺ δὲ τὸ βαρύ w R β
[8] λεπτῇ β Nicasius Gaza : λεπτὴν cett. codd.

is far away, for it is reflected. Therefore, since in sound the quick is high, and the slow is low, voices from far away ought to appear lower. For again, all things that travel travel more slowly in proportion to their distance from the source, and in the end they fall. Is it, then, because those imitating the faraway voice imitate with a feeble and thin voice? But a light voice is not low, nor does a small and feeble one sound low, but it must necessarily sound high. Or is it not merely that those imitating imitate by this means, but that the sounds themselves are higher? Now the reason is that the moving air causes the sound; and just as the first thing moving the air makes the sound, so in turn the air must do this, and continually some air must be the mover and some the moved.[10] This is why sound is continuous, because moving air always succeeds moving air, until (*the motion*) is exhausted, which in the case of bodies is falling, when the air is no longer able to push the missile in the one case and the air in the other. For voice becomes continuous when air is pushed by air, while the missile moves when a body is moved by the air. So in the one case the same body moves continually until it falls, but in the other case different air moves continually. And smaller things move more quickly at first, but over a short distance.[11] This is why voices that are far away are higher and thinner. For what moves more quickly is high—as has already been

---

[10] The text of this line is uncertain.
[11] Or "but for a short time" ($\dot{\epsilon}\pi$' $\dot{o}\lambda\dot{\iota}\gamma o\nu$ $\delta\dot{\epsilon}$).

---

9 $\dot{\alpha}\epsilon\dot{\iota}$ $<\delta$'$>$ Marenghi[2] : $<\kappa\alpha\dot{\iota}>$ $\dot{\alpha}\epsilon\dot{\iota}$ Jan
10 $\tau\dot{o}\nu$: $\tau\dot{o}$ X[a] u : fort. $\ddot{\alpha}\lambda\lambda o\nu$ Barker
11 $\kappa\iota\nu o\hat{\upsilon}\nu\tau\alpha$ Sylburg ex Gaza : $\kappa\iota\nu o\hat{\upsilon}\nu\tau\iota$ codd.

10 παῖδες καὶ οἱ κάμνοντες ὀξὺ φθέγγονται, οἱ δὲ ἄνδρες
καὶ οἱ ὑγιαίνοντες βαρύ. τὸ[12] δὲ τοῖς ἐγγὺς μὴ ἐπίδηλον εἶναι τὴν φωνὴν ἢ βαρυτέραν ἢ ὀξυτέραν
γινομένην, καὶ ὅλως μὴ ὁμοίως ἔχειν τοῖς ῥιπτομένοις
βάρεσιν, αἴτιον ὅτι τὸ μὲν ῥιφθὲν ἐν[13] φέρεται ἀεὶ τὸ
15 αὐτό, ὁ δὲ ψόφος ἀήρ ἐστιν ὠθούμενος | ὑπὸ ἀέρος. διὸ
καὶ τὸ μὲν εἰς ἓν πίπτει, ἡ δὲ φωνὴ πανταχῇ, ὥσπερ ἂν
εἰ τὸ ῥιφθὲν ἅμα φερόμενον ἀπείρως θρυφθείη, καὶ ἔτι
εἰς τοὔπισθεν.

7. Διὰ τί αἱ νεηλιφεῖς οἰκίαι μᾶλλον ἠχοῦσιν; ἢ ὅτι
μᾶλλον ἀνάκλασις γίνεται διὰ τὴν λειότητα; λειότεραι
20 δὲ | διὰ τὸ ἀρραγὲς καὶ τὸ συνεχές. δεῖ δὲ μὴ παντελῶς
ὑγρὰν ἀλλ' ἤδη ξηρὰν λαμβάνειν· ἀπὸ πηλοῦ γὰρ οὐκ
ἔστιν ἀνάκλασις. διὰ ταῦτα γὰρ[14] καὶ τὰ κονιάματα
μᾶλλον ἠχεῖ. συμβάλλεται δὲ ἴσως καὶ ἡ ἀκινησία
τοῦ ἀέρος· ἀθρόος γὰρ ἰὼν μᾶλλον ἀποπλήττεται τὸν
προσπίπτοντα. |

25 8. Διὰ τί, ἐάν τις πίθον καὶ κεράμια κενὰ κατορύξῃ
καὶ πωμάσῃ, μᾶλλον ἠχεῖ τὰ οἰκήματα, καὶ ἐὰν φρέαρ
ἢ λάκκος ᾖ ἐν τῇ οἰκίᾳ; ⟨ἢ⟩[15] ὅτι ἐπεὶ ἀνάκλασις ἡ
ἠχώ, δεῖ περιειλημμένον ἀθρόον εἶναι τὸν ἀέρα, καὶ
ἔχειν πρὸς ὃ ἀνακλασθήσεται, προσπίπτων[16] πυκνὸν

---

12 τὸ : τοῦ Nicasius   13 ἐν Bekker : αἴτιον plur. codd. :
ἐν τι Nᵃ Yᵃ ᵐᵍ : fort. ἐν τι ὂν Bekker

14 γὰρ x Aᵐ γ : δὲ cett. codd.

15 ⟨ἢ⟩ Sylburg

16 προσπίπτων Kᵃ : προσπίπτειν s Oᵃ : προσπῖπτον cett.
codd. : προσπίπτοντα Richards

puzzled over.[12] It's the same reason for which children and those who suffer utter high sounds, but men and healthy people low ones. Now the reason that it is not clear to those nearby whether the voice is becoming lower or higher, and that generally the conditions are not similar to the case of heavy things that are thrown, is that the thing thrown moves as one and the same thing continually, whereas sound is air pushed by air. And this is why the former falls on one spot, whereas the voice falls everywhere, as if the thing thrown were broken into infinitely many pieces as it moved, and even moved backward.

7. Why do newly plastered houses echo more? Is it because there is more refraction owing to the smoothness (*of the surfaces*)? They are smoother because they are unbroken and continuous. However, one should take (*a house*) that is not completely wet, but is already dry; for there is no refraction from damp clay. For it is because of this that stucco echoes more. Now perhaps the immobility of the air also contributes to this; for when the air is massed together it beats back what falls on it with more force.

8.[13] Why, if one buries and puts lids on a large jar or empty pot,[14] the buildings[15] echo more, and also if there is a well or cistern in the house? Is it because, since echo is refraction, the enclosed air must be compact,[16] and have something from which it can be refracted, when it strikes

[12] Perhaps *Pr.* 11.3, 899a13.

[13] Cf. *Pr.* 11.9.

[14] The container is buried but with the opening exposed, upon which a lid is placed.

[15] I.e., the buildings in which the pots are buried.

[16] Or perhaps "the air must be compactly enclosed" (Hett).

30 καὶ λεῖον; οὕτω γὰρ μάλιστα | ἦχος γίνεται. τὸ μὲν οὖν
φρέαρ καὶ ὁ λάκκος ἔχει τὴν στενότητα καὶ τὴν
ἄθροισιν, οἱ δὲ πίθοι καὶ τὰ κεράμια καὶ τὴν πυκνότητα τῶν περιεχόντων, ὥστε ἐξ ἀμφοτέρων τὸ συμ-
βαῖνον. καὶ γὰρ τὰ κοῖλα μᾶλλον ἠχεῖ· διὰ τοῦτο καὶ
ὁ χαλκὸς μάλιστα τῶν ἄλλων. ὅτι δὲ κατορωρυγμένα,
35 οὐθὲν | ἄτοπον· ἡ γὰρ φωνὴ φέρεται κάτω οὐχ ἧττον.
ὅλως δὲ πανταχῇ δοκεῖ καὶ κύκλῳ φέρεσθαι.

9. Διὰ τί δὲ μᾶλλον, ἐὰν κατορύξῃ τις, ἠχεῖ, ἢ ἐὰν
900a μή; || ἢ ὅτι περιστεγόμενα μᾶλλον εἰς αὐτὰ δέχεται
καὶ κατέχει τὸν ἀέρα; συμβαίνει δὲ καὶ τὴν πληγὴν
σφοδροτέραν γίνεσθαι.

10. Διὰ τί τὸ ὕδωρ τὸ ψυχρὸν ἐκ τοῦ αὐτοῦ ἀγγείου
5 ἐκχεόμενον | ὀξύτερον ποιεῖ τὸν ψόφον; ἢ ὅτι θάττων ἡ
φορά; βαρύτερον γάρ. ἡ δὲ θάττων ὀξύτερον ποιεῖ τὸν
ψόφον. τὸ δὲ θερμὸν καὶ τῇ μανότητι καὶ τῇ ἀναφορᾷ
κουφίζει. παρόμοιον δὲ ὅτι καὶ αἱ δᾷδες καιόμεναι
ἀσθενεστέραν τὴν πληγὴν ποιοῦσιν. |

10 11. Διὰ τί τοῖς ἠγρυπνηκόσιν ἡ φωνὴ τραχυτέρα; ἢ
διότι ὑγρότερον τὸ σῶμα διὰ τὴν ἀπεψίαν, καὶ οὐχ
ἥκιστα περὶ τὸν ἄνω τόπον (διὸ καὶ βάρος ἐν τῇ
κεφαλῇ), ὑγρότητός τε περὶ τὸν βρόγχον οὔσης ἀνάγκη καὶ τραχυτέραν εἶναι τὴν φωνήν; ἡ μὲν γὰρ τρα-
15 χύτης διὰ τὴν ἀνωμαλίαν, ἡ δὲ βαρύτης | διὰ τὴν
ἔμφραξιν· βαρυτέρα γὰρ ἡ φορά.

against what is thick and smooth? For echoes occur in these conditions especially. Therefore, the well and the cistern have narrowness and compactness, whereas the jars and the pots have thickness in their sides, so that the same result occurs in both cases. Indeed, hollow things echo more; and for this reason bronze produces more echo than other metals. Now, that (*echoing occurs*) when these are buried is not strange; for the voice carries downward no less (*than in any other direction*). In general, it seems to be carried in all directions and in a circle.

9.[17] But why does it echo more, if one buries (*them*), than if one does not? Is it because when covered they receive and retain the air better in themselves? And the result is that the blow is more violent.

10. Why does cold water make a higher sound (*than hot water*) when poured out of the same vessel? Is it because the movement is quicker? For it is heavier. And what is quicker makes a higher sound. But heat lightens (*the water*) by making it porous and causing it to rise. Similar is the fact that torches when burning produce a weaker blow.

11. Why is the voice rougher in those who have been sleepless? Is it because the body[18] is moister owing to lack of concoction, and not least in the upper parts (which is also why there is heaviness in the head), and as there is moisture around the windpipe the voice must necessarily be rougher as well? For roughness is due to unevenness, while depth is due to obstruction; for the movement is slower.

[17] The present chapter makes sense only in light of the previous one.

[18] Of those who are sleepless.

357

12. Διὰ τί μετὰ τὰ σιτία τάχιστα ἀπορρήγνυται ἡ φωνή; ἢ ὅτι κοπτόμενος μὲν ὁ τόπος ἐκθερμαίνεται, θερμαινόμενος δὲ ἕλκει τὴν ὑγρότητα; πλείων δὲ αὕτη καὶ ἑτοιμοτέρα διὰ τὴν προσφοράν. |

20 13. Διὰ τί οἱ κλαίοντες ὀξὺ φθέγγονται, οἱ δὲ γελῶντες βαρύ; ἢ ὅτι οἱ μὲν ὀλίγον κινοῦσι πνεῦμα δι' ἀσθένειαν, οἱ δὲ σφοδρῶς, ὃ ποιεῖ ταχὺ φέρεσθαι τὸ πνεῦμα; τὸ δὲ ταχὺ ὀξύ· καὶ γὰρ ἀπὸ συντόνου τοῦ σώματος[17] ῥιπτούμενον ταχὺ φέρεται. ὁ δὲ γελῶν
25 τοὐναντίον διαλελυμένος· οἱ δὲ ἀσθενεῖς | ὀξύ, ὀλίγον γὰρ ἀέρα κινοῦσιν· οἱ δὲ ἐπιπολῆς. ἔτι οἱ μὲν γελῶντες θερμὸν τὸ πνεῦμα ἀφιᾶσιν, οἱ δὲ κλαίοντες, ὥσπερ καὶ ἡ λύπη κατάψυξίς ἐστι τοῦ τόπου τοῦ περὶ τὰ στήθη, καὶ τὸ πνεῦμα ψυχρότερον ἀφιᾶσιν. τὸ μὲν οὖν θερμὸν πολὺν ἀέρα κινεῖ, ὥστε βραδέως φέρεσθαι, τὸ δὲ
30 ψυχρὸν ὀλίγον. | συμβαίνει δὲ τοῦτο καὶ ἐπὶ τῶν αὐλῶν· οἱ γὰρ θερμοὶ τῷ πνεύματι αὐλοῦντες πολὺ βαρύτερον αὐλοῦσιν.

14. Διὰ τί οἱ παῖδες καὶ τὰ ἄλλα τῶν ζῴων τὰ νέα ὀξύτερον φθέγγονται τῶν τελείων, καὶ ταῦτα τῆς ὀξύ-

---

[17] σώματος Yª Nª w R x Aᵐ r² Barth. : στόματος β : πνεύματος cett. codd.

---

19 Cf. Pr. 11.22.
20 I.e., the region around which the voice is produced.
21 Cf. Pr. 11.15, 50.
22 As Forster notes, this line (which has troubled editors) makes sense only if it refers to two different types of weepers.

12.[19] Why does the voice crack most readily after food? Is it because this region,[20] when it is struck, heats up, and becoming heated it attracts moisture? And this (*moisture*) is more copious and more available owing to the intake (*of food*).

13.[21] Why do those who weep utter high sounds, whereas those who laugh utter low ones? Is it because some (*who weep*) move a little breath owing to weakness, while others (*who weep move it*) violently, which makes the breath travel quickly?[22] For what is quick is high; and indeed, what is thrown from a body that is taut travels quickly. The one who laughs, by contrast, is relaxed. But the weak are high, for they move little air, and some of them only on the surface.[23] Further, while those who laugh emit hot breath, those who weep—as grief[24] is a cooling of the region around the chest—emit colder breath. Now heat moves much air, so that it travels slowly, but cold moves little. This also happens in the case of *auloi*;[25] for those who play the *aulos* with hot breath play it much lower.

14.[26] Why do children and the young of the other animals utter higher sounds than the fully developed ones,

---

[23] The text may be corrupt; this line is bracketed by Jan and Marenghi[2].

[24] Or "pain" (ἡ λύπη).

[25] I simply transliterate αὐλός (pl. αὐλοί), which has usually been rendered "pipe" or "flute." ("Flute," however, is always wrong.) There were different kinds of *auloi*; all were reed instruments, and most had a double reed, like the modern oboe.

[26] A possible source for this chapter is *GA* 787a28–b19. Cf. *Pr.* 11.16, 24, 34, 62a.

τητος σφοδρότητος οὔσης; ἢ ἡ φωνή ἐστιν ἀέρος
35 κίνησις, καὶ ἡ θάττων | ὀξυτέρα, ῥᾷον δὲ καὶ θᾶττον ὁ
ὀλίγος τοῦ πολλοῦ κινεῖται ἀήρ; κινεῖται δὲ ἢ ἢ συγκρι-
νόμενος ἢ διακρινόμενος ὑπὸ θερμοῦ. ἐπεὶ δὲ ἡ μὲν
εἰσπνοή ἐστι ψυχροῦ εἰσαγωγή, συγκρίνοιτ᾽ ἂν ἐν
αὐτῇ ὁ ἐν ἡμῖν ἀήρ· ἡ δὲ ἐκπνοή, θερμοῦ κινήσαντος
ἀέρα, γίνοιτ᾽ ἂν ἡ[18] φωνή· ἐκπνέοντες γάρ, οὐκ εἰσπνέ-
900b οντες || φωνοῦμεν. ἐπεὶ δὲ τὰ νέα θερμότερά ἐστι τῶν
πρεσβυτέρων καὶ τοὺς ἐν αὐτοῖς πόρους στενωτέρους
ἔχει, ἐλάττω ἂν ἀέρα ἔχοι ἐν ἑαυτοῖς. ὄντος δὲ τοῦ τε
κινουμένου ἐλάττονος καὶ τοῦ κινοῦντος θερμοῦ πλεί-
5 ονος ἐν αὐτοῖς, θᾶττον ἂν δι᾽ ἄμφω | ἡ κίνησις γένοιτο
τοῦ ἀέρος· ἡ δὲ θάττων ὀξυφωνοτέρα ἂν εἴη διὰ τὰ
προειρημένα.

15. Διὰ τί οἱ κλαίοντες ὀξὺ φθέγγονται, οἱ δὲ
γελῶντες βαρύ; ἢ ὅτι οἱ μὲν κλαίοντες συντείνοντες
καὶ συνάγοντες τὸ στόμα φωνοῦσιν; τῇ τε δὴ συν-
10 τονίᾳ κινεῖται ταχὺ ὁ ἐν | αὑτοῖς ἀήρ, καὶ τῷ διὰ
στενοῦ τοῦ στόματος[19] φέρεσθαι θᾶττον φέρεται· δι᾽
ἄμφω οὖν ὀξεῖα γίνεται ἡ φωνή. οἱ δὲ γελῶντες
ἀνέντες τὸν τόνον γελῶσι καὶ κεχηνότες. ἐκπέμποντες
οὖν διὰ τοῦτο εὐρέως καὶ βραδέως τὸν ἀέρα εἰκότως
15 βαρυφωνοῦσιν. |

16. Διὰ τί οἱ ἄγονοι, οἷον παῖδες, γυναῖκες, καὶ οἱ
ἤδη γέροντες καὶ οἱ εὐνοῦχοι, ὀξὺ φθέγγονται, οἱ δὲ
ἄνδρες βαρύ; ⟨ἢ ὅτι⟩ καθάπερ[20] ἡ γραμμὴ καὶ τὰ

[18] ἡ del. Hett   [19] στόματος : σώματος x Aᵐ γ

and this although high pitch implies vehemence? Is it that voice is a movement of air, and the quicker is higher, and a little air moves more easily and more quickly than a great quantity? Now it is moved when it is collected or dissipated by heat. And since inhalation is the drawing in of cold, the air that is in us would be collected in it; but exhalation, when air is moved by heat, would become voice; for we use our voices when exhaling, not when inhaling. Now since the young are hotter than the old and have narrower passages in them, they would have less air in them. And as that which is moved (*in them*) is less, and the moving heat in them is greater, the movement of the air would be quicker for both these reasons; and the quicker (*air*) would be higher for the aforementioned reasons.

15.[27] Why do those who weep utter high sounds, whereas those who laugh utter low ones? Is it because those who weep strain and contract the mouth when they use their voice? Owing to the strain, the air in them is moved quickly, and by traveling through a narrow mouth it travels more quickly; for both these reasons, therefore, the voice becomes high. But those who laugh do so by relaxing the strain and gaping. Therefore, because of this, sending the air out through a wide opening and slowly, they naturally speak with a low voice.

16.[28] Why do those incapable of generation—such as children, women, those already old, and eunuchs—utter high sounds, whereas men utter low ones? Is it be-

[27] Cf. *Pr.* 11.13, 50.   [28] Cf. *Pr.* 11.14, 24, 34, 62a, *Aud.* 803b18–23, 804a8–32, *GA* 787a28–b19.

[20] ⟨ἢ ὅτι⟩ Forster ‖ καθάπερ : καθά που β

ἄλλα λεπτὰ ἓν διάστημα ἔχει, τὰ δὲ παχέα πλείω,
οὕτω²¹ καὶ ἡ λεπτὴ φωνὴ ἓν ἂν ἔχοι διάστημα; ῥᾶον δὲ
20 καὶ ποιῆσαι καὶ κινῆσαι ἐστιν ἓν ἢ | πλείω. ἐχόντων
οὖν τῶν προειρημένων πνεῦμα ἀσθενές, κινεῖ αὐτῷ
ἀέρα ὀλίγον. ἐλάχιστος δέ ἐστιν ὁ ἓν διάστημα ἔχων·
ὃς ἔσται λεπτὸς διὰ τὰ προειρημένα. καὶ ἡ ἀπ᾽ αὐτοῦ
φωνὴ γινομένη τοιαύτη· ἡ δὲ λεπτὴ φωνὴ ὀξεῖά ἐστιν.
οἱ μὲν οὖν ἄγονοι διὰ ταῦτα ὀξύφωνοί εἰσιν· οἱ δὲ
25 ἄνδρες ἰσχύοντες | τῷ πνεύματι πολὺν ἀέρα κινοῦσι,
πολὺς δὲ ὢν βραδέως ἂν κινοῖτο καὶ βαρεῖαν φωνὴν
ποιεῖ. ἐποίει γὰρ ἥ τε λεπτὴ καὶ ἡ ταχεῖα κίνησις
ὀξεῖαν φωνήν, ὧν οὐδέτερον ἐπὶ τοῦ ἀνδρὸς συμβαίνει
γίνεσθαι.

17. Διὰ τί αἱ φωναὶ βαρύτεραι ἡμῖν εἰσὶ τοῦ χει-
30 μῶνος; | ἢ ὅτι παχύτερος ὁ ἀήρ ἐστι τότε, καὶ ὁ ἐν ἡμῖν
καὶ ὁ ἐκτός; παχυτέρου δὲ ὄντος, βραδυτέρα ἡ κίνησις
γίνεται, ὥστε ἡ φωνὴ βαρυτέρα. ἔτι ὑπνωτικώτεροί
ἐσμεν τοῦ χειμῶνος ἢ τοῦ θέρους, καὶ καθεύδομεν
πλείω χρόνον· ἐκ δὲ τῶν ὕπνων βαρύτεροί²² ἐσμεν. ἐν
ᾧ οὖν πλείονα χρόνον καθεύδομεν ἢ ἐγρηγόραμεν |
35 (οὗτος δέ ἐστιν ὁ χειμών), ἐν τούτῳ ἂν εἴημεν βαρυ-
φωνότεροι ἢ ἐν ᾧ τοὐναντίον. τοῦ γὰρ μεταξὺ τῆς
ἐγέρσεως ὄντος ὀλίγου χρόνου, ἡ ἐν τῷ ὕπνῳ ἕξις
γενομένη διαμένει πρὸς τὴν καθύπνωσιν.

²¹ οὕτω Sylburg : ὥστε codd.
²² βαρύτεροί : βραδύτεροί Jan

cause, just as the line and other thin things have only one dimension, while thick things have more, so too the thin voice would have only one dimension? Now it is easier both to produce and to move one thing than it is more (*than one*). Therefore, as the aforementioned people have weak breath, little air moves with it. But what[29] has only one dimension is very small: it will be thin for the afore-mentioned reasons. And the voice coming from it will have such a quality; but the thin voice is high. Those incapable of generation, therefore, have high voices; but men, be-ing strong in breath, move more air,[30] and being more, it would be moved more slowly and produce a low voice. For the thin and quick movement produces a high voice, nei-ther of which qualities occur in the case of a man.

17.[31] Why are our voices lower in winter? Is it because the air—both within us and without—is thicker at that time? And as it is thicker, its movement is slower, so that the voice is lower? Further, we are more inclined to sleep in the winter than in the summer, and we lie asleep a longer time; and coming from sleep we are heavier.[32] So, the period during which we lie asleep for a longer time than we are awake (and this is winter), during that period we should have a lower voice than during the opposite pe-riod. For in the short time between, when we are awake, the condition occurring in sleep persists until fast asleep.

29 The author is referring specifically to air here.

30 Or perhaps "being strong, move more air with their breath."

31 Cf. *Pr.* 11.18, 56, 61.

32 Or, with Jan, "slower" ($\beta\rho\alpha\delta\acute{\upsilon}\tau\epsilon\rho\omicron\iota$). The word translated "heavier" here ($\beta\alpha\rho\acute{\upsilon}\tau\epsilon\rho\omicron\iota$) is the same word rendered "lower" above when referring to voice.

18. Διὰ τί ἐκ τῶν πότων καὶ τῶν ἐμέτων καὶ ἐν τοῖς
901a ψύχεσι ‖ βαρύτερον φθέγγονται; ἢ διὰ τὴν ἔμφραξιν
τοῦ φάρυγγος[23] τὴν γινομένην ὑπὸ τοῦ φλέγματος;
ἐπικατασπᾷ γὰρ ῥευμάτιον εἰς αὐτόν· τοῖς[24] μὲν ὁ
ἔμετος ἢ ὁ πότος, τοῖς δὲ ἡ ὥρα καὶ τὸ συμπλήρωμα,
5 στενώτερον ποιεῖ τὸν φάρυγγα, | ὥστε βραδυτέρα
γίνεται ἡ φορὰ τοῦ πνεύματος. ἡ δὲ βραδεῖα φορὰ
[καὶ][25] βαρεῖαν ποιεῖ τὴν φωνήν.

19. Διὰ τί ἐγγύθεν μὲν ἡ βαρυτέρα μᾶλλον ἐξακού-
εται, πόρρωθεν δὲ ἧττον; ἢ διότι ἡ βαρυτέρα φωνὴ
πλείω μὲν ἀέρα κινεῖ, οὐκ εἰς μῆκος δέ; πόρρωθεν μὲν
10 οὖν ἧττον ἀκούομεν, | διότι ἐπ᾽ ἔλαττον κινεῖται, ἐγ-
γύθεν δὲ μᾶλλον, διότι πλείων ἡμῖν ἀὴρ πρὸς τὸ
αἰσθητήριον προσπίπτει. ἡ δὲ ὀξεῖα πόρρω ἀκούεται,
ὅτι λεπτοτέρα ἐστί, τὸ δὲ λεπτὸν τὴν εἰς μῆκος αὔξησιν ἔχει. λέγοι δ᾽ ἄν τις ὅτι καὶ θάττων ἐστὶν ἡ
ποιοῦσα αὐτὴν κίνησις. εἴη δ᾽ ἂν τοῦτο, εἰ πυκνὸν μὲν
15 στενὸν | δ᾽ εἴη τὸ κινοῦν πνεῦμα τὸν ἀέρα. ὅ τε γὰρ
ὀλίγος εὐκινητότερός ἐστιν ἀήρ (κινεῖται γὰρ ὀλίγος
ὑπὸ τοῦ στενοῦ), καὶ τὸ πυκνὸν πλείους πληγὰς ποιεῖ,
αἳ τὸν ψόφον ποιοῦσιν. ἰδεῖν δ᾽ ἔστι τοῦτο ἐπὶ τῶν
ὀργάνων· αἱ γὰρ λεπτότεραι χορδαὶ ὀξύτεραί εἰσι, τῶν
ἄλλων τῶν αὐτῶν ὑπαρχόντων αὐταῖς. |

20 20. Διὰ τί ἡ φωνὴ ὀξυτέρα φαίνεται τοῖς μακρο-

[23] φάρυγγος : λάρυγγος [Arist./Alex.] Sup.Pr. 2.83, 2
[24] ante τοῖς add. καὶ Sylburg
[25] καὶ seclusi, om. Bekker

18.[33] Why do people utter lower sounds after drinking and vomiting and in cold weather? Is it because of the obstruction of the pharynx[34] due to phlegm? For a small flux is drawn down into it: in some cases the vomiting or drinking, in others the season of the year and the filling (*with phlegm*), make the pharynx narrower, so that the passage of breath becomes slower. And the slow passage produces a low voice.

19.[35] Why is the low (*voice*) more audible from nearby, but less so from far away? Is it because the lower voice moves more air, but not to any distance? So we hear it less from far away, because it is moved less far, but more from nearby, because more air strikes our sense organ. But the high (*voice*) is heard far off, because it is thinner, and what is thin extends to a distance. Now one might also say that the movement producing it[36] is quicker. And this would be so, if the breath moving the air were both dense and narrow. For a little air is more easily moved (for a little is moved by what is narrow), and what is dense produces more impacts, which produce the sound. This can be seen in the case of (*musical*) instruments; for the thinner strings are higher, other conditions being the same.

20.[37] Why does the voice appear higher to those stand-

33 [Arist./Alex.] *Sup.Pr.* 2.83 is virtually identical to this chapter. Cf. *Pr.* 11.17, 56, 61.

34 I translate φάρυγγος "pharynx," though the author may be referring broadly to the windpipe.

35 Cf. *Pr.* 11.6, 20, 47, [Arist./Alex.] *Sup.Pr.* 2.84. Possible sources for this chapter are *Aud.* 803b34–4a28 and Thphr. *On Music* (fr. 716 FHSG).   36 I.e., the high voice.

37 Cf. *Pr.* 11.6, 19, 47, [Arist./Alex.] *Sup.Pr.* 2.93.

τέραν ἀφεστηκόσι, τοῦ ὀξέος ὄντος ἐν τῷ ταχέως
φέρεσθαι, τὸ δὲ μακρότερον[26] φερόμενον βραδύτερον
κινεῖται; ἢ ὅτι ἡ ὀξύτης τῆς φωνῆς οὐ μόνον ἐστὶν ἐν
τῷ ταχέως κινεῖσθαι, ἀλλὰ καὶ ἐν τῷ λεπτότατον[27]
25   ψόφον γίνεσθαι; τοῖς δὲ μακροτέραν | ἀφεστηκόσιν
ἀεὶ λεπτοτέρα ἡ φωνὴ ἀφικνεῖται διὰ τὴν ὀλιγότητα
τοῦ ἀέρος τοῦ κινουμένου. μαραίνεται γὰρ ἡ κίνησις,
μαραινόμενος δὲ ὁ ἀριθμὸς μὲν εἰς τὸ ἓν τελευτᾷ,
σῶμα δὲ εἰς διάστημα ἕν, ὅ ἐστιν ἐν σώματι λεπτότης.
ὁμοίως δὲ καὶ[28] ἐν φωνῇ. |

30   21. Διὰ τί καὶ οἱ γεγυμνασμένοι καὶ οἱ ἀσθενεῖς
ὀξὺ φθέγγονται; ἢ ὅτι οἱ μὲν ἀσθενεῖς ὀλίγον ἀέρα
κινοῦσιν, ὁ δὲ ὀλίγος τοῦ πλείονος θᾶττον φέρεται; οἱ
δὲ γεγυμνασμένοι ἰσχυρῶς κινοῦσι τὸν ἀέρα, ὁ δὲ
ἰσχυρῶς κινούμενος ἀὴρ θᾶττον φέρεται. τὸ δὲ ταχὺ
ἐν φορᾷ ἐν φωνῇ ὀξύ ἐστιν. |

35   22. Διὰ τί τοῖς μετὰ τὰ σιτία κεκραγόσιν ἡ φωνὴ
901b διαφθείρεται; ‖ καὶ πάντας ἂν ἴδοιμεν τοὺς φωνα-
σκοῦντας, οἷον ὑποκριτὰς καὶ χορευτὰς καὶ τοὺς ἄλ-
λους τοὺς τοιούτους, ἕωθέν τε καὶ νήστεις ὄντας τὰς
μελέτας ποιουμένους. ἢ <ὅτι>[29] τὸ διαφθείρεσθαι τὴν
φωνὴν οὐθὲν ἕτερόν ἐστιν ἢ τὸν τόπον διαφθείρεσθαι |
5   καθ᾽ ὃν τὸ πνεῦμα διεξέρχεται; διὸ καὶ οἱ βραγχιῶντες
διαφθείρονται τὰς φωνάς, οὐ τῷ τὸ πνεῦμα γίνεσθαι
χεῖρον, ὃ ποιεῖ τὴν φωνήν, ἀλλὰ τῷ τετραχύνθαι τὴν

---

[26] μακρότερον Yᵃ β Cᵃ Aᵐ [Arist./Alex.] Sup.Pr. 2.93, 2 :
μακροτέρῳ cett. codd.

ing farther away, though high pitch is found in traveling quickly, and what travels a greater distance moves more slowly? Is it because high pitch of voice is found not only in moving quickly, but also in the sound becoming extremely thin? But to those standing farther away the voice always arrives in a thinner state because of the smallness of the air moved. For the movement diminishes, and whereas a diminishing number terminates in one, a diminishing body terminates in one dimension, which in a body is thinness. Now the same is also true in a voice.

21. Why do both those who have taken exercise and those who are weak utter high sounds? Is it because those who are weak move little air, and a little air travels more quickly than a larger amount? But those who have taken exercise move the air powerfully, and powerfully moved air travels more quickly. And what is quick in movement is high in voice.

22.[38] Why is the voice ruined in those who shout after meals? Indeed, we can see that all those who train their voices, such as actors and chorus members and the like, perform their exercises in the morning and when fasting. Is it because the voice being ruined is nothing other than the region through which the breath passes being ruined? And this is why those who have sore throats have ruined voices, not because the breath that produces the voice is inferior, but because the windpipe is roughened. Now this

---

38 Cf. *Pr.* 11.12, *Aud.* 804a18–21.

---

27 λεπτότατον Ya Ca x Xa r t : λεπτότερον β : λεπτὸν τὸν Jan : ἐλάττω τὸν [Arist./Alex.] *Sup.Pr.* 2.93, 4
28 καὶ secl. Bekker   29 ⟨ὅτι⟩ addidi

367

ἀρτηρίαν. ὑπὸ δὲ τῆς θερμασίας τῆς σφοδρᾶς μάλιστα τραχύνεσθαι πέφυκεν ὁ τόπος οὗτος. διὸ καὶ οὔθ'
10 οἱ πυρέττοντες | οὔτε οἱ σφόδρα πεπυρεχότες εὐθὺς
μετὰ τὴν ἄνεσιν τοῦ πυρετοῦ ᾄδειν δύνανται· τετρά-
χυνται γὰρ ὁ φάρυξ αὐτοῖς διὰ τὴν θερμασίαν. ἀπὸ δὲ
τῶν σιτίων εἰκὸς εἶναι τὸ πνεῦμα καὶ πολὺ καὶ θερμόν·
τὸ δὲ τοιοῦτον εὔλογόν ἐστι διεξιὸν ἑλκοῦν τε καὶ
15 τραχύνειν τὴν ἀρτηρίαν· τούτου δὲ συμβαίνοντος | εἰ-
κότως ἡ φωνὴ διαφθείρεται.

23. Διὰ τί, εἴπερ ἡ φωνή ἐστιν ἀήρ τις ἐσχηματισμένος καὶ φερόμενος διαλύεται πολλάκις τὸ σχῆμα, ἡ ἠχώ[30] γίνεται πληγέντος τοῦ τοιούτου πρός τι
στερεόν <καὶ>[31] οὐ διαλύεται αὕτη, ἀλλὰ σαφῶς ἀκού-
20 ομεν αὐτῆς; ἢ ὅτι ἀνάκλασίς ἐστιν, | ἀλλ' οὐ κατάκλα-
σις; οὕτω δὲ τό θ' ὅλον διαμένει, καὶ δύο μέρη ὁμοι-
οσχήμονα ἐξ αὐτοῦ γίνεται· πρὸς ὁμοίαν γὰρ γωνίαν
ἐστὶν ἡ ἀνάκλασις. διὸ καὶ ὁμοία γίνεται ἡ τῆς ἠχοῦς
φωνὴ τῇ ἐξ ἀρχῆς.

24. Διὰ τί τῶν μὲν ἄλλων ζῴων τὰ νέα καὶ νήπια
25 ὀξύτερον | φθέγγονται τῶν τελείων, οἱ δὲ μόσχοι
βαρύτερον τῶν τελείων βοῶν; ἢ ὅτι ἐν ἑκάστῳ γένει τὸ
νήπιον ὅμοιόν ἐστι τῷ ἐν αὐτῷ θήλει; τῶν βοῶν δὲ αἱ
θήλειαι βαρύτερον φθέγγονται τῶν ἀρρένων, οἱ δὲ
μόσχοι ταύταις ὁμοιότεροί εἰσιν ἢ τοῖς ἄρρεσιν· τὰ δὲ
ἄλλα τοὐναντίον. |

[30] ἡ ἠχώ codd. et [Arist./Alex.] Sup.Pr. 2.94, 2 (cf. Pr. 11.51,
904b28) : ἡ <δὲ> ἠχώ <ἡ> Erasmus

region is by nature especially liable to be roughened by excessive heat. And this is why neither those who have a fever nor those who have just had a violent fever are able to sing after the abatement of the fever; for their pharynx has been roughened by the heat. But after meals it is natural that the breath should be considerable and hot; and it is reasonable that such breath, as it passes through, should make the windpipe sore and rough; and when this occurs the voice naturally is ruined.

23.[39] Why, if indeed voice is air that has been given shape and while traveling its shape is often dissolved, does echo occur when such *(air)* strikes against something hard and it is not dissolved, but we hear it clearly? Is it because *(echo)* is refraction, but not dispersion? In this way the whole persists, and two parts that are similar shapes arise from it;[40] for refraction occurs at a similar angle. And this is why the voice of the echo is similar to the original.

24.[41] Why do the young of other animals and infants utter higher sounds than the full-grown ones, but calves utter lower sounds than full-grown bulls? Is it because in each animal kind the infant is similar to the female in it? Among cattle the females utter lower sounds than the males, and calves are more similar to them than to the males; but for the other animals the opposite is true.

[39] This chapter is virtually identical to *Pr.* 11.51 and [Arist./Alex.] *Sup.Pr.* 2.94. Cf. *Aud.* 800a3–7.

[40] I.e., the voice and the echo.

[41] Sources: *GA* 786b14–23, 787a28–b19. Cf. *Pr.* 11.14, 16, 34, 62a.

31 ⟨καὶ⟩ addidi ex [Arist./Alex.] *Sup.Pr.* 2.94, 3

30   25. Διὰ τί, ὅταν ἀχυρωθῶσιν αἱ ὀρχῆστραι, ἧττον
οἱ χοροὶ γεγώνασιν; ἢ διὰ τὴν τραχύτητα προσπίπτουσα ἡ φωνὴ οὐ πρὸς λεῖον τὸ [δὲ] ἔδαφος[32] ἧττον
γίνεται μία, ὥστ' ἐλάττων; οὐ γὰρ συνεχής, ὥσπερ
καὶ τὸ φῶς ἐπὶ τῶν λείων μᾶλλον φαίνει[33] διὰ τὸ μὴ[34]
35   διαλαμβάνεσθαι τοῖς | ἐμποδίζουσιν. ||

902a   26. Διὰ τί ποτε ὁ ἅλς, ὅταν εἰς πῦρ ἐμβληθῇ, ψοφεῖ;
ἢ ὅτι ὁ ἅλς ὑγρὸν ἔχει οὐ πολύ, ὃ ὑπὸ τοῦ θερμοῦ
ἐκπνευματούμενον καὶ βίᾳ ἐκπῖπτον σχίζει τὸν ἅλα;
τὸ δὲ σχιζόμενον ἅπαν ψοφεῖ. |

5   27. Διὰ τί ποτε τῶν παιδίων ἔνια, πρὶν ἥκειν τὴν
ἡλικίαν ἐν ᾗ σαφηνίζειν ὥρα αὐτοῖς, φθεγξάμενα καὶ
σαφῶς εἰπόντα πάλιν ὁμοίως διάγουσιν, ἕως ἂν ἔλθη
ὁ εἰωθὼς χρόνος; ἃ δὴ πολλοὶ τέρατα νομίζουσιν
εἶναι. ἤδη δ' ἔνια λέγεται καὶ εὐθὺς γινόμενα φθέγ-
10   ξασθαι. ἢ ὅτι ὡς μὲν | ἐπὶ πολὺ τὰ πλείω γε[35] τῶν
γινομένων[36] γίνεται κατὰ φύσιν; διὸ ὀλίγοις τοῦτο
συμβαίνει, καὶ φύσει ἅμα κατάλληλα τελειοῦνται· διὸ
καὶ ἀκούει τε ἅμα καὶ φωνεῖ καὶ ξυνίησι κατὰ τὴν
ἀκοὴν καὶ λέγει καὶ σαφηνίζει. οὐ μὴν ἀλλὰ πολλάκις
15   οὐκ ἀπαρτίζει ταῦτα,[37] ἀλλὰ τὰ μὲν | ξυνίησι πρότερον
ἢ τοῦτο τὸ μόριον ἀπολυθῆναι ᾧ διαλέγεται, τοῖς δὲ

---

[32] [δὲ] Sylburg : [τὸ δὲ ἔδαφος] Marenghi[2]
[33] φαίνει Burnel.67 et Gaza : om. cett. codd.
[34] μὴ Dˢ Nicasius et Gaza : om. cett. codd. : ⟨ἧττον⟩
Marenghi[2]   [35] γε Bussemaker : τε codd.
[36] γινομένων : γενομένων Nᵃ w R Xᵃ r u
[37] ταῦτα Richards : τὰ αὐτά codd.

25.[42] Why, when the orchestra is covered with straw, are choruses less able to be heard? Is it due to roughness that the voice striking a ground that is not smooth is less unified, so that (*the voice*) is quieter? For it is not continuous, just as light too shines more on smooth (*surfaces*) because it is not interrupted by impediments.

26.[43] Why does salt make a sound when it is thrown in fire? Is it because salt contains a little moisture, which being evaporated by the heat and escaping with force splits the salt? And what is split always makes a sound.

27. Why do some children, before they reach the age at which it is time for them to articulate clearly, utter sounds and speak clearly, and then once more continue like (*others of their age*), until the usual time (*for speaking*) arrives? In fact, many consider these cases to be abnormal.[44] But already some are said to have uttered sounds immediately upon being born. Is it because for the most part the majority of those being born[45] are according to nature? This is why it happens to few people, and by nature (*our faculties*) develop simultaneously with one another; this is also why at the same time (*the child*) hears and finds his voice and understands what is heard and speaks and articulates clearly. Often, however, these things do not develop together: some understand before the part by which they speak is available, and in others the opposite is true.

---

[42] The text of this chapter is unclear.

[43] Cf. *Pr.* 11.42 and 43.

[44] The word translated "abnormal" (τέρατα) is actually a noun that could be rendered "monstrosities" or "portents."

[45] Or "those who are born," if the other reading is accepted.

ARISTOTLE

τοὐναντίον. ταῦτα μὲν οὖν οὐκ ἂν διαλεχθείη συνετῶς
(ἃ γὰρ ἂν ἀκούσωσι, διαλέγονται), ἀλλ᾽ ὅταν ἥκῃ
καιρὸς ἀμφοῖν, ἀποδιδόασι τὸ κατὰ φύσιν. ὅσοις δὲ
ἔμπροσθεν ἡ κατὰ τὴν ἀκοὴν αἴσθησις διακριβοῦται
20 ἐν τῇ | ψυχῇ ⟨ἢ⟩³⁸ ᾧ πρώτῳ κινοῦσι τὴν φωνὴν καὶ
ποιοῦσι λόγον, τούτοις ἐνίοτε γίνεται ἤδη ξυνιεῖσι
πολλὰ καὶ δύναμίς τις τοῦ μορίου καὶ ἀπόλυσις,
μάλιστα μὲν μετὰ ὕπνον τινά (τούτου δ᾽ αἴτιον ὅτι ὁ
ὕπνος καὶ τὰ σώματα νωθρότερα³⁹ ποιεῖ καὶ τὰ μόρια
25 ἀναπαύσας), εἰ δὲ μή, καὶ ἄλλην μεταβολὴν | λαβόντα
τοιαύτην. πολλὰ δὲ ἔχομεν τοιαῦτα ποιεῖν, ἃ μικρῶν
δεῖται καιρῶν· κἄπειτα οὐκέτι ὁμοίως ἔχει, ὅταν οὕτω
τύχῃ τὸ μόριον ἔχον καὶ ἀπολυθέν. ὅταν ἐπιπολῆς ᾖ
ἐν τῇ αἰσθήσει ὧν ἐκινήθη διάνοια, κατὰ τὴν ἀκοὴν
τοῦτο ἐπανῆλθε καὶ ἐφθέγξατο. πολλάκις δὲ καὶ μέλη
30 καὶ ῥήματα | ἐπέρχεται οὐκ ἐκ προαιρέσεως ἡμῖν· ἀλλ᾽
ἐὰν τὸ πρῶτον προελόμενοι εἴπωμεν, ὕστερον ἄνευ
προαιρέσεως λέγομεν ἢ ᾄδομεν,⁴⁰ καὶ οὐ δύναται ἐκ
τοῦ στόματος ἐξελθεῖν. οὕτω καὶ τοῖς παιδίοις ὅταν
συμβῇ τοῦτο εἰπον,⁴¹ εἶτα πάλιν καταστῇ εἰς τὴν
35 φύσιν ἐκεῖνο τὸ μόριον, ἕως ἂν ἡ ὥρα | ἔλθῃ ἰσχῦσαι
αὐτὸ καὶ ἀποκριθῆναι.

28. Διὰ τί ἔνια ψοφεῖ καὶ κινεῖται ἐξαίφνης, οἷον τὰ

³⁸ ⟨ἢ⟩ Bussemaker ex Gaza   ³⁹ νωθρότερα : νωθρέστε-
ρα Yᵃ Nᵃ w R β Cᵃ x Aᵐ : νωθέστερα Bussemaker
⁴⁰ ᾄδομεν Bekker : οἴδαμεν codd.
⁴¹ εἶπον Forster (dicant Gaza) : ἑπτόν γ : ἐπόν cett. codd. :
λεπτόν Sylburg : ἐπίον Bussemaker

372

Therefore, (*in the latter case*)[46] what they say would not be intelligent (for they merely say what they hear), but when the right time for both (*speaking and understanding*) arrives, they exhibit what is according to nature. But those in whom the sense of hearing develops accurately in the soul before the (*part*) whereby they first set in motion the voice and produce words, in their case the capacity and availability of the part comes when they already understand many things, especially after sleep (the reason for this is that sleep makes bodies and their parts more sluggish by giving them a rest), and if not (*after sleep*), then after undergoing some other such change. Now we can do many such things, which only need slight opportunities; and then the conditions are no longer similar, when the part happens to be in this state of availability. When there are on the surface in the sense things by which a thought has been aroused, on hearing it (*the child*) returns to it and gives utterance to it. Now tunes and phrases often come upon us involuntarily; but if at first we have spoken them voluntarily, later we say or sing[47] them involuntarily, and cannot remove them from our mouths. So too when this occurs in children, they speak,[48] and then this part returns again to its natural condition, until the time arrives for it to grow strong and to become separated.

28. Why do some things, such as boxes, make a sound

---

[46] I.e., the case in which "the opposite is true": those who can converse before they can understand.

[47] Or "know," if the mss. tradition is correct.

[48] Something is likely wrong with the text.

κιβώτια, οὐδενὸς αἰσθητοῦ κινοῦντος; καίτοι κρεῖττον
γέγονε τὸ κινοῦν τοῦ κινουμένου. ὁ δὲ αὐτὸς λόγος καὶ
φθορᾶς καὶ γήρως· ὑπὸ ἀναισθήτου γὰρ φθείρεται τὰ
902b λεγόμενα ὑπὸ ‖ τοῦ χρόνου πάντα. ἢ ὅμοιον τοῦτο τοῖς
σταλαγμοῖς καὶ τοῖς ὑπὸ τῶν ἐκφυομένων αἰρομένοις
λίθοις; οὐ γὰρ τὸ τελευταῖον αἴρει ἢ κινεῖ, ἀλλὰ τὸ
συνεχές. ἐπὶ δὲ τούτου συνέβη ἀναισθήτου ὄντος
5 αἰσθητὴν γίνεσθαι τὴν κίνησιν. οὕτω δὲ | καὶ τὸ
περιεχόμενον αἰσθητοῖς χρόνοις κινεῖται καὶ διαιρεῖται εἰς ἀναίσθητα, τῷ δὲ παντὶ καὶ συνεχεῖ ἐκίνησε
καὶ διέφθειρεν. συνεχὲς δέ ἐστιν οὐκ ἐν τῷ νῦν, ἀλλ᾽ ἐν
τῷ ὡρισμένῳ χρόνῳ ὑπὸ τοῦ νῦν.

29. Διὰ τί οἱ χασμώμενοι ἧττον ἀκούουσιν; ἢ ὅτι
10 τοῦ | ἐξιόντος πνεύματος ἐν τῇ χάσμῃ πολὺ καὶ εἰς τὰ
ὦτα χωρεῖ ἔσωθεν, ὥστε καὶ τῇ αἰσθήσει ἐπίδηλον
εἶναι τὴν κίνησιν ἣν ποιεῖ περὶ τὴν ἀκοήν, μάλιστα δ᾽
ἐκ τῶν ὕπνων; ὁ δὲ ψόφος ἀὴρ ἢ πάθος ἀέρος ἐστίν.
ἀντιπαίοντος οὖν τοῦ ἔσωθεν εἰσέρχεται ὁ ἔξωθεν
15 ψόφος, καὶ ὑπὸ τῆς κινήσεως | καὶ τοῦ ἔξωθεν ψόφου
ἐκκρούεται ἡ κίνησις.

30. Διὰ τί ἰσχνόφωνοι παῖδες ὄντες μᾶλλον ἢ
ἄνδρες; ἢ ὥσπερ καὶ τῶν χειρῶν καὶ τῶν ποδῶν ἀεὶ
ἧττον κρατοῦσι παῖδες ὄντες, καὶ ὅσοι ἐλάττους οὐ
δύνανται βαδίζειν, ὁμοίως καὶ τῆς γλώττης οἱ νεώτε-
20 ροι οὐ δύνανται; ἐὰν δὲ | παντάπασι μικροὶ ὦσιν, οὐδὲ

---

49 Perhaps the author is referring to the creaking of, e.g., a
large wooden chest.

and move suddenly, when nothing perceptible moves them?[49] And yet the mover is stronger than that which is moved. Now the same applies to decay and old age: for the things said to be destroyed by time are destroyed by something imperceptible. Is this similar to dripping water[50] and to stones being lifted by plant growth? For the last (*in a series of actions*) does not raise or move, but the continuous (*series*) does. In this case what is imperceptible results in the movement becoming perceptible. And so too, what is contained in perceptible time is moved in and divided into imperceptible (*parts*), but it moves and destroys by means of the whole and continuous. And continuity is not in the present, but is in the time limited by the present.

29.[51] Why do those who are yawning hear less? Is it because as the breath exits during a yawn, much of it enters the ears from within, so that the movement that it produces around the (*organ of*) hearing is evident to that sense, and especially after sleep? Now sound is air or a condition of air. Therefore, the sound from outside enters while that from inside resists[52] it, and so this motion is checked by the motion and the sound from outside.

30.[53] Why do children stammer more than men? Just as children always have less control over their hands and feet, and those who are even smaller are unable to walk, so too the very young are unable to control their tongue? Now when they are very small, they are unable to utter sounds

---

[50] I assume "dripping water" (τοῖς σταλαγμοῖς) refers to erosion or to the formation of stalagmites and stalactites.

[51] Source: *GA* 781a30–b1. Cf. *Pr.* 11.44, 32.13.

[52] More literally, "strikes back against" (ἀντιπαίοντος).

[53] Cf. *Pr.* 11.35, 36, 38, 54, 55, 60, and see *Aud.* 804b26–39.

φθέγγεσθαι δύνανται ἀλλ' ἢ ὥσπερ τὰ θηρία, διὰ τὸ
μὴ κρατεῖν. εἴη δ' ἂν οὐ μόνον ἐπὶ τοῦ ἰσχνοφώνου,
ἀλλὰ καὶ τραυλοὶ καὶ ψελλοί. ἡ μὲν οὖν τραυλότης τῷ
γράμματός τινος μὴ κρατεῖν, καὶ τοῦτο οὐ τὸ τυχόν, ἡ

25 δὲ ψελλότης τῷ ἐξαίρειν τι, ἢ γράμμα ἢ | συλλαβήν, ἡ
δὲ ἰσχνοφωνία ἀπὸ τοῦ μὴ δύνασθαι ταχὺ συνάψαι
τὴν ἑτέραν συλλαβὴν πρὸς τὴν ἑτέραν. ἅπαντα δὲ δι'
ἀδυναμίαν· τῇ γὰρ διανοίᾳ οὐχ ὑπηρετεῖ ἡ γλῶττα.
ταὐτὸ δὲ τοῦτο καὶ οἱ μεθύοντες πάσχουσι καὶ οἱ
πρεσβῦται· ἧττον δὲ πάντα συμβαίνει. |

30   31. Διὰ τί ἡ φωνὴ τρέμει καὶ τῶν ἀγωνιώντων καὶ
τῶν δεδιότων; ἢ ὅτι σείεται ἡ καρδία τοῦ θερμοῦ
ἐξιόντος; ἀμφοτεράκις δὲ πάσχουσι τοῦτο· καὶ γὰρ
τοῖς ἀγωνιῶσι συμβαίνει καὶ τοῖς φοβουμένοις. σειο-
μένης δὲ, οὐ γίνεται μία ἡ πληγὴ ἀλλὰ πλείους,

35 ὥσπερ ἡ τῶν παρανενευρισμένων | χορδῶν.

32. Διὰ τί οἱ μὲν ἀγωνιῶντες βαρὺ φθέγγονται, οἱ
δὲ φοβούμενοι ὀξύ; ἢ ὅτι τοῖς μὲν φοβουμένοις καταψύχεται ὁ τόπος ὁ περὶ τὴν καρδίαν, κάτω ὁρμῶντος
τοῦ θερμοῦ, ὥστε ὀλίγον ἀέρα κινοῦσιν (ἡ γὰρ ἰσχὺς

903a ἐν τῷ θερμῷ), τοῖς ‖ δὲ ἄνω φέρεται τὸ θερμόν, ὥσπερ
τοῖς αἰσχυνομένοις; δι' αἰσχύνην γὰρ καὶ ἀγωνιῶσιν.
τοῖς δὲ αἰσχυνομένοις ἄνω φέρεται πρὸς τὸ πρόσ-

---

54 I.e., less than it does to children and/or less than it does to
those with speech impediments.   55 Cf. Pr. 11.62b, 27.6–7.
56 Andrew Barker informed me (private correspondence):
"Strings were made from several strands of gut twisted together,
and if the job was done badly there could be lumps on the string,

except in the way beasts do, because of their lack of control. And this (*lack of control*) is involved not only in the case of the stammerer, but lispers and defective speakers are such as well. Lisping is the inability to control a *certain* letter, not any letter, while defective speech consists in omitting some letter or syllable, and stammering comes from the inability to link quickly one syllable to another. But all of these are due to an inability: for (*in these cases*) the tongue does not serve the thought. Now those who are drunk and those who are old experience this same thing: but all of this happens to them less.[54]

31.[55] Why does the voice tremble in those who are anxious and in those who are frightened? Is it because the heart is shaken by the heat exiting? For people experience this in both cases: indeed, it happens in those who are anxious and in those feeling fear. But when the heart is shaken, the impact is not one but many, as in the case of badly twisted strings.[56]

32.[57] Why do those who are anxious utter low sounds, but those who are feeling fear high ones? Is it because in those feeling fear the region around the heart grows cold, as the heat rushes downward, so that little air is set in motion (for strength is in the heat), while in the others the heat travels upward, just as it does in those who feel shame? For people are also anxious through shame. Now in those who feel shame (*the heat*) travels up to the face: a

or discontinuities in the fibres. See *Aud.* 804a37–39, where exactly the same expression occurs, and the resulting 'cracked' or 'broken' sound is compared to that of a cracked horn."

57 [Arist./Alex.] *Sup.Pr.* 2.89 is virtually identical to this chapter. Cf. *Pr.* 11.53.

ωπον· σημεῖον δὲ ὅτι ἐξέρυθροι γίνονται μᾶλλον.
5 συντήκει οὖν καὶ παχὺν ποιεῖ τὸν ἀέρα | ᾧ φθέγγον-
ται· ὁ δὲ τοιοῦτος βραδέως ὠθεῖται, τὸ δὲ βραδὺ ἐν
φωνῇ βαρύ ἐστιν.

33. Διὰ τί εὐηκοωτέρα ἡ νὺξ τῆς ἡμέρας ἐστίν;
πότερον ὥσπερ Ἀναξαγόρας φησί, διὰ τὸ τῆς μὲν
ἡμέρας σίζειν καὶ ψοφεῖν τὸν ἀέρα θερμαινόμενον ὑπὸ
10 τοῦ ἡλίου, τῆς δὲ | νυκτὸς ἡσυχίαν ἔχειν ἅτε ἐκλελοι-
πότος τοῦ θερμοῦ, εἶναι δὲ μᾶλλον ἀκουστὸν μηθενὸς
ὄντος ψόφου; ἢ ὅτι διὰ τοῦ κενωτέρου μᾶλλον ἀκου-
στόν ἐστιν ἢ διὰ τοῦ πλήρους; ἔστι δὲ τῆς μὲν ἡμέρας
ὁ ἀὴρ πυκνὸς ἅτε πεπληρωμένος ὑπὸ τοῦ φωτὸς καὶ
τῶν ἀκτίνων, τῆς δὲ νυκτὸς ἀραιότερος διὰ τὸ ἀπελη-
15 λυθέναι | ἐξ αὐτοῦ τὸ πῦρ καὶ τὰς ἀκτῖνας, σώματα
ὄντα. ἢ ὅτι τῆς μὲν ἡμέρας τὰ σώματα πρὸς πολλὰ
τὴν διάνοιαν ἕλκει· διὸ οὐκ εὐκρινές ἐστι πρὸς τὴν
ἀκοήν; καὶ τῷ πράττειν ἡμᾶς πάντα μᾶλλον ἐν τῇ
ἡμέρᾳ ἢ τῇ νυκτί, καὶ αὐτὴ[42] περὶ τὰς πράξεις ἐστίν.
20 χωρισθεῖσα δὲ αἴσθησις διανοίας | καθάπερ[43] ἀναί-
σθητον πόνον ἔχει, ὥσπερ εἴρηται τὸ νοῦς ὁρᾷ καὶ
νοῦς ἀκούει. νυκτὸς δὲ τῆς ὄψεως ἀργούσης καὶ τῆς
διανοίας μᾶλλον ἠρεμούσης ὁ τῆς ἀκοῆς πόρος μᾶλλον[44] ἀνεῳγμένος, [καθάπερ τῆς ἡμέρας][45] δεκτικὸς
μέν ἐστι τῶν ἤχων ὁμοίως, ἐξαγγελτικὸς δὲ μᾶλλον

42 αὐτὴ Bussemaker ex Gaza : αὐτὰ codd.
43 post καθάπερ add. ὁ νοῦς β
44 μᾶλλον secl. Marenghi[2]
45 [καθάπερ τῆς ἡμέρας] Platt

sign of this is that they become redder. Therefore, (*the heat*) condenses and thickens the air with which they utter sounds; and such air is pushed out slowly, but the slow in voice is low.

33.[58] Why is the night easier to hear things in than the day? Is it as Anaxagoras says,[59] because during the day the air being heated by the sun hisses and makes noise, while at night it is quiet because the heat has ceased, and things are more audible when there is no noise? Or is it because things are more audible through a void than through a filled space? Now during the day the air is dense because it is full of the light and the rays (*of the sun*), but at night it is rarer because the fire and the rays, which are bodies, have gone out of it. Or is it because during the day the bodies draw one's mind to many things; hence we are not discriminating with respect to hearing? Also by our doing all that we do more in the day than in the night, it[60] is concentrated on the actions. But perception separated from mind does as it were an imperceptible amount of work, as is said: "The intellect sees and the intellect hears."[61] But at night when vision is not employed and the mind is more at rest, the passage for hearing, being more open, is equally receptive of sounds, and is more communicative with the mind be-

---

[58] Cf. *Pr.* 11.5, Plut. *QC* 8.3 (*Mor.* 720C–22F).

[59] 59A74 D-K.

[60] I.e., one's mind (if αὐτὴ refers to διάνοια) or one's hearing (if it refers to ἀκοή).

[61] Epicharmus, fr. 249 Kaibel: "Intellect sees and intellect hears: the others are dull and blind" (νοῦς ὁρῆι καὶ νοῦς ἀκούει· τἄλλα κωφὰ καὶ τυφλά).

25 [ἢ]⁴⁶ τῇ διανοίᾳ διὰ τὸ | μήτε αὐτὴν ἐνεργεῖν μήθ' ὑπὸ
τῆς ὄψεως παρενοχλεῖσθαι, καθάπερ καὶ τῆς ἡμέρας.

34. Διὰ τί οἱ ἄγονοι, οἷον παῖδες καὶ γυναῖκες καὶ
οἱ ἤδη γέροντες καὶ οἱ εὐνοῦχοι, ὀξὺ φθέγγονται, οἱ δὲ
ἄνδρες βαρύτερον; ἢ δι' ἀσθένειαν τοῦ κινοῦντος μο-
30 ρίου τὸν ἀέρα; | ὀλίγον γὰρ τὸ ἀσθενὲς κινεῖ, ὁ δὲ
ὀλίγος ταχὺ φέρεται, τὸ δὲ ταχὺ φερόμενον ὀξύ. ἢ
διότι ὁ πόρος ὁ πρῶτος, δι' οὗ ἡ φωνὴ φέρεται, τοῖς
μὲν ἀγόνοις μικρός, ὥστε ὀλίγον ἐξ αὐτοῦ τὸ ὠθοῦν
τὸν ἀέρα, ὀλίγος δὲ ὢν ταχὺ φέρεται δι' εὐρέος τοῦ
35 ἄνω φάρυγγος· ἀκμάζουσι δὲ καὶ ἀνδρουμένοις | δι-
ίσταται οὗτος, ὥσπερ καὶ ‹ὁ›⁴⁷ ἐπὶ τοὺς ὄρχεις, ὥστε
καὶ πλείων ἐστὶν ὁ ὠθούμενος; βραδύτερον οὖν διιὼν
βαρὺς γίνεται.

35. Διὰ τί οἱ ἰσχνόφωνοι οὐ δύνανται διαλέγεσθαι
903b μικρόν; ‖ ἢ ὅτι ἴσχονται τοῦ φωνεῖν, ἐμποδίζοντός
τινος; οὐκ ἴσης δὲ ἰσχύος οὐδ' ὁμοίας κινήσεως ‹οὔσης›,⁴⁸ μὴ ἐμποδίζοντός τε τὴν κίνησιν μηδενὸς καὶ
ἐμποδίζοντος, βιάσασθαι δεῖ. ἡ δὲ φωνὴ κίνησίς
5 ἐστιν· μεῖζον δὲ φθέγγονται μᾶλλον οἱ τῇ | ἰσχύι
χρώμενοι. ὥστ' ἐπεὶ ἀνάγκη ἀποβιάζεσθαι τὸ κωλῦον,
ἀνάγκη μεῖζον φθέγγεσθαι τοὺς ἰσχνοφώνους.

36. Διὰ τί δὲ ἀγωνιῶντες μὲν μᾶλλον ἰσχνόφωνοι
γίνονται, ἐν δὲ ταῖς μέθαις ἧττον; ἢ ὅτι ἀποπληξίᾳ

46 [ἢ] Sylburg
47 ‹ὁ› Platt
48 ‹οὔσης› Richards : ante ἴσης add. ‹οὔσης› Marenghi²

cause the latter is neither itself working nor distracted by vision as it is during the day.

34.[62] Why do those incapable of generation—such as children, women, those already old, and eunuchs—utter high sounds, whereas men utter lower ones? Is it because of the weakness of the part that moves the air? For what is weak moves little air, and a little air travels quickly, and what travels quickly is high. Or is it because the first passage through which the voice travels is small in those incapable of generation, so that what pushes the air from it is small, and there being little air, it travels quickly through the wide upper pharynx, whereas the (*passage*) in those who are in the prime of life and are manly is distended (just like the one to the testicles), so that the air being pushed through is greater too? Therefore, passing through more slowly (*the voice*) becomes low.

35.[63] Why are stammerers unable to speak softly? Is it because they are restrained from using their voice owing to something impeding them? But as the power is not equal and the motion not similar, both when nothing is impeding the motion and when there is an impediment, violent force must be used. Now the voice is a movement; and those who use more power (*when they speak*) utter louder sounds. So, since the hindrance must necessarily be violently overcome, stammerers must necessarily utter louder sounds.

36.[64] Why do people become stammerers more when they are anxious, but less under the influence of drunkenness? Is it because the condition is similar to apoplexy of

[62] Cf. *Pr.* 11.14, 16, 24, 62a, *GA* 787a28–b19.
[63] Cf. *Pr.* 11.30, 36, 38, 54, 55, 60.
[64] Cf. *Pr.* 11.30, 35, 38, 54, 55, 60.

ὅμοιόν ἐστι τὸ πάθος μέρους τινὸς τῶν ἐντός, ὃ ἀδυνα-
10 τοῦσι κινεῖν, | ἐμποδίζοντος διὰ τὴν κατάψυξιν· ὁ μὲν
οὖν οἶνος φύσει θερμὸς ὢν λύει τὴν κατάψυξιν μᾶλλον, ἡ δὲ ἀγωνία ποιεῖ. φόβος γάρ τις ἡ ἀγωνία, ὁ δὲ
φόβος κατάψυξις.

37. Διὰ τί ἔξωθεν εἰς τὰς οἰκίας εἴσω ἀκούεται
μᾶλλον ἢ ἔσωθεν ἔξω; ἢ ὅτι ἔσωθεν ὁ ψόφος διὰ τὸ
15 ἀχανὲς ἰέναι⁴⁹ | διασπᾶται, ὥστε οὐχ ἱκανὸν ἕκαστον
μέρος ἀκουσθῆναι, ἢ ἧττον; ἔξωθεν δὲ ἔσω εἰς ἐλάττω
τόπον καὶ ἀέρα ἑστῶτα ἡ φωνὴ βαδίζουσα ἀθρόα
ἔρχεται, ὥστε μείζων οὖσα ἀκούεται μᾶλλον.

38. Διὰ τί οἱ ἰσχνόφωνοι μελαγχολικοί; ἢ ὅτι τὸ τῇ |
20 φαντασίᾳ ἀκολουθεῖν ταχέως τὸ μελαγχολικὸν εἶναι
ἐστίν, οἱ δὲ ἰσχνόφωνοι τοιοῦτοι; προτερεῖ γὰρ ἡ ὁρμὴ
τοῦ λέγειν τῆς δυνάμεως αὐτοῖς, ὡς θᾶττον ἀκολου-
θούσης τῆς ψυχῆς τῷ φανέντι. καὶ οἱ τραυλοὶ δὲ
ὡσαύτως· βραδύτερα⁵⁰ γὰρ τὰ μόρια ταῦτα τοῖς τοι-
25 ούτοις. σημεῖον δέ· οἰνωμένοι γὰρ | τοιοῦτοι γίνονται,
ὅτε μάλιστα τοῖς φαινομένοις ἀκολουθοῦσι καὶ οὐ τῷ
νῷ.⁵¹

39. Διὰ τί τὰ πράσα συμφέρει πρὸς εὐφωνίαν, ἐπεὶ
καὶ τοῖς πέρδιξιν; ἢ ὅτι καὶ τὰ σκόροδα ἑφθὰ λεαίνει,
τὰ δὲ πράσα γλισχρότητα ἔχει τινά, ῥυπτικὸν δὲ τοῦ
φάρυγγος; |

---

⁴⁹ ἰέναι : εἶναι γ   ⁵⁰ βραδύτερα Vat.1904ᵐᵍ Aᵐ et
Gaza : βραχύτερα cett. codd.   ⁵¹ νῷ Ruelle : λόγῳ D, cf.
Gaza (rationem) : οἴνῳ cett. codd. et Barth.

one of the inner parts, which they cannot move, the impediment being due to cooling? Therefore wine, being hot by nature, tends to dissolve this cooling, whereas anxiety produces it. For anxiety is a sort of fear, and fear is a process of cooling.

37.[65] Why do people hear more inside a house from outside than outside a house from inside? Is it because the noise from inside, going through a vast space, is scattered, so that each part is not strong enough to be heard, or is heard less? But the voice, proceeding from outside into a smaller space and stationary air, enters a compact mass, so that being bigger it is heard more.

38.[66] Why are stammerers melancholic? Is it because being melancholic is following the imagination quickly, and stammerers are such as to do this? For in them the impulse to speak precedes the capacity to do so, as the soul very quickly follows the appearance.[67] The same is true of those who lisp; for in such people these parts[68] are too slow. There is a sign of this: for those who are drunk become such (as to lisp), when they follow the appearances most of all and not their intelligence.

39. Why are leeks helpful with a view to goodness of voice, since this is so even with partridges? Is it because, whereas boiled garlic produces smoothness, leeks have a certain stickiness, and this cleanses the pharynx?

[65] Plutarch attributes this chapter to Aristotle: see *QC* 8.3 (*Mor.* 720C–D).

[66] Cf. *Pr.* 11.30, 35, 36, 54, 55, 60. See also Hp. *Epid.* 2.5.1.

[67] Or "what is being imagined" or "what appears to them" (τῷ φανέντι).

[68] I.e., the organs associated with speech.

30   40. Διὰ τί τὰ μὲν ἄλλα ὀξύτερον φθέγγεται σφο-
δρότερα ὄντα, ὁ δὲ ἄνθρωπος ἀσθενῶν; ἢ διότι ἐλάττω
κινεῖ ἀέρα, οὗτος δὲ ταχὺ διέρχεται, τὸ δὲ ταχὺ ὀξὺν
ποιεῖ τὸν ψόφον;

    41. Διὰ τί ἀκούουσι μᾶλλον κατέχοντες τὸ πνεῦμα
35 ἢ | ἐκπνέοντες; διὸ καὶ ἐν ταῖς θήραις παραγγέλλουσιν
ἑαυτοῖς μὴ πνευστιᾶν. πότερον ὅτι τὸ αἰσθητικὸν ἄνω
ἔρχεται αἰρομένων τῶν φλεβῶν; καθευδόντων γὰρ
κάτω· διὸ καὶ μᾶλλόν τε ἐκπνέουσιν καθεύδοντες ἢ
904a εἰσπνέουσι, καὶ ἀνήκοοί εἰσιν. ‖ ἢ καὶ τὸ αἷμα ἀπέρχεται καταπεπνευκότων,[52] ὥστε κενοῦται τὰ ἄνω;[53]
ἀκούουσι δὲ τῷ κενῷ. ἢ ὅτι ὁ φυσιασμὸς[54] ψόφος τίς
ἐστιν, οὗτος δὲ ἐν τῷ ἐκπνεῖν γινόμενος κωλύει ἀκούειν;

    42. Διὰ τί θᾶττον μὲν ψοφοῦσι καὶ πηδῶσιν οἱ
5 μικροὶ | ἅλες, μείζω δὲ ψοφοῦσι καὶ πηδῶσιν οἱ μεγά-
λοι; ἢ διότι οἱ μὲν ταχὺ σχίζονται (οὐ γὰρ πολὺ ὃ δεῖ
διελθεῖν τῷ πυρί) διὰ τὴν μικρότητα, οἱ δὲ βραδέως;
μεῖζον γὰρ ἔργον τὸ μεῖζον διασχίσαι ἢ τὸ μικρόν.
ψοφεῖ δὲ ὁ μὲν μικρὸς μιχρον (ἡ γὰρ πληγὴ μικρά), ὁ
10 δὲ μείζων μεγάλα, | (μεγάλη γὰρ ἡ πληγή)· ὁ δὲ
ψόφος πληγή ἐστιν. καὶ πηδᾷ δὲ μᾶλλον τὸ ἰσχυ-
ρότερον, ἂν πληγείη· ἧττον γὰρ ἐνδίδωσιν.

<hr />

[52] ἀπέρχεται καταπεπνευκότων Bussemaker (cf. ἀπέρχεται
κάτω καταπεπνευκότων [Arist./Alex.] *Sup.Pr.* 2.97, 5) : ἀνέρχεται ἐκπεπνευκότος codd. : fort. ἀπέρχεται κατεχόντων τὸ
πνεῦμα   [53] ἄνω : κάτω Sept.   [54] ὁ φυσιασμὸς : φύσει ὁ ἀσθμὸς [Arist./Alex.] *Sup.Pr.* 2.97, 6

40. Why do all other (*animals*) utter higher sounds the more vehement they are, whereas the human does so when he is weak? Is it because he moves less air, but this passes through quickly, and what is quick produces a high sound?

41.[69] Why do people hear better when holding their breath than when exhaling? This is why in hunting they advise each other not to breathe. Is it because the perceptual (*faculty*) goes upward when the veins are inflated? For when we are asleep it goes downward. And this is why people sleeping exhale more (*deeply*) than they inhale, and so do not hear. Or does the blood too depart when we breathe (*in and hold our breath*), so that the upper parts are emptied?[70] And we hear (*better*) in what is empty. Or is it because breathing hard is a noise, and when this occurs in exhaling, it prevents hearing?

42.[71] Why do small amounts of salt make a noise and jump more quickly, whereas large amounts make a noise and jump to a greater extent?[72] Is it because the former is split quickly owing to its smallness (for there is not much that the fire must pass through), whereas the latter is split slowly? For it is a greater task to split the greater amount than it is to split the small. Now the small amount makes a small noise (for the impact is small), but the greater amount makes a great noise (for the impact is great); and noise is an impact. But the stronger also jumps more, if it is struck; for it gives way less.

[69] [Arist./Alex.] *Sup.Pr.* 2.97 is virtually identical to this chapter. Cf. *Pr.* 11.48.   [70] Something is probably wrong with the text of this line.   [71] Cf. *Pr.* 11.26, 43.

[72] The context is clearly salt that is heated. Cf. Pr. 11.26.

43. Διὰ τί, ἐὰν εἰς πολὺ πῦρ ἐμβάλῃ τις τὸ αὐτὸ
μέγεθος ἁλός, ἧττον ψοφεῖ ἢ οὐ ψοφεῖ; ἢ ὅτι φθάνει
κατακαυθεὶς πρὶν σχισθῆναι; καίεται μὲν γὰρ τῷ τὸ
15 ὑγρὸν | ἀναλωθῆναι, ψοφεῖ δὲ τῷ σχισθῆναι.

44. Διὰ τί οἱ χασμώμενοι ἧττον ἀκούουσιν; ἢ ὅτι τὸ
πνεῦμα ἐναπολαμβάνουσιν, τὸ δὲ ἀπολαμβανόμενον
πνεῦμα περὶ τὰ ὦτα ἀθροίζεται; σημεῖον δέ· ἐν γὰρ
τοῖς ὠσὶ ψόφος γίνεται ὅταν χασμησώμεθα. τὸ δὲ
20 ἀπολαμβανόμενον | πνεῦμα κωλύει ἀκούειν. ἔτι δὲ καὶ
φωνή τις γίνεται τῶν χασμωμένων· τοῦτο δὲ κωλυ-
τικὸν τοῦ ἀκούειν. καὶ συμπιέζεσθαι ἀναγκαῖον τὰς
ἀκοὰς διασπωμένου τοῦ στόματος.

45. Διὰ τί τῆς φωνῆς (ἐπειδὴ ῥύσις τίς ἐστι) φύσιν
ἐχούσης ἄνω φέρεσθαι, μᾶλλόν ἐστιν εὐήκοος ἄνωθεν
25 κάτω ἢ | κάτωθεν ἄνω;[55] ἢ ὅτι ἡ φωνὴ ἀήρ τίς ἐστι μεθ'
ὑγροῦ; βαρυνόμενος οὖν οὗτος ὑπὸ τοῦ ὑγροῦ φέρεται
κάτω καὶ οὐκ ἄνω· τοῦ γὰρ ὑγροῦ κατὰ φύσιν ἡ κάτω
φορά. διὸ τοῖς κάτω μᾶλλον ἀκούεται. ἢ τοῦτο μὲν
ἐπὶ[56] τῆς τοῦ ζῴου φωνῆς μόνον γίνεται (αὕτη γὰρ
30 μεθ' ὑγροῦ), τὸ δὲ συμβαῖνόν | ἐστι καὶ ἐπὶ τῶν ἄλλων
ψόφων; καθάπερ οὖν ἡ ὄψις, ἐὰν μὲν ἄνωθεν κάτω
προσπέσῃ, τὴν ἀνάκλασιν ἄνω ποιεῖται, κάτωθεν δὲ
ἄνω προσπεσοῦσα ἀνεκλάσθη κάτω, τὸν αὐτὸν τρόπον ἡ φωνὴ ἡ φύσιν ἔχουσα ἄνω φέρεσθαι, προσ-

[55] εὐήκοος ἄνωθεν κάτω ἢ κάτωθεν ἄνω : εὐήκοα τὰ ἄνωθεν κάτω ἢ τὰ κάτωθεν ἄνω [Arist./Alex.] Sup.Pr. 2.90, 2
[56] ἐπὶ scripsi ex [Arist./Alex.] Sup.Pr. 2.90, 5 : ὑπὸ codd.

43.[73] Why, if someone throws the same quantity of salt into a large fire, does it make less noise or no noise? Is it because it is burned up before it is split? For it is burned when the moisture (*in it*) is used up, but it makes a noise when it is split.

44.[74] Why do those who are yawning hear less? Is it because they cut off the breath inside, and the breath that is cut off collects around the ears? There is a sign of this: for a noise occurs in the ears when we yawn. But the breath being cut off prevents hearing. Further, a sort of voice also comes from those who are yawning; and this prevents hearing. And the organ of hearing must necessarily be compressed when the mouth is distended.

45.[75] Why, though the voice (since it is a sort of flowing) naturally travels upward, is it more audible below from above, than above from below? Is it because the voice is a sort of air combined with moisture? Therefore, being weighed down by moisture it travels downward and not upward; for the downward movement of moisture is according to nature. This is why it is heard better by those who are below. Or does this happen only in the case of the voice of an animal (for this is combined with moisture), or is this also the result in the case of other noises? So just as vision, if it strikes below from above, produces a refraction upward, but if it strikes above from below is refracted downward, in the same way the voice, which naturally travels upward, striking the air which opposes it, cannot force

[73] Cf. *Pr.* 11.26, 42.

[74] Source: *GA* 781a30–b1. Cf. *Pr.* 11.29, 32.13.

[75] [Arist./Alex.] *Sup.Pr.* 2.90 is virtually identical to this chapter.

ARISTOTLE

35   κόψασα τῷ ἐξ ἐναντίας ἀέρι, βιάζεσθαι | μὲν οὐ
δύναται πλείονα ὄντα καὶ βαρύτερον, ἀνακλασθεὶς δὲ
ὁ κινηθεὶς ἀὴρ ἐπὶ τοὐναντίον ἠνέχθη κάτω, διὸ κατα-
χεόμενος ἀκούεται μᾶλλον κάτω. τοιοῦτο δὲ καὶ τὸ
περὶ τὴν ἠχὼ συμβαῖνον· ἔστι γὰρ <γὰρ>[57] ἀνάκλασις τῆς
φωνῆς ἐπὶ τοὐναντίον. ‖

904b   46. Διὰ τί μεθυόντων μᾶλλον ἀπορρήγνυται ἡ φωνὴ ἢ νηφόντων; ἢ διὰ τὸ πεπληρῶσθαι ταχέως ἀπορρηγνύασι[58] τὴν φωνήν; σημεῖον δὲ τούτου· οὔτε γὰρ οἱ
χοροὶ μελετῶσιν ἐξ ἀρίστου οὔτε οἱ ὑποκριταί, ἀλλὰ
5   νήστεις ὄντες. ἐν δὲ | τῇ μέθῃ πληρέστεροι ὄντες
εὐλόγως μᾶλλον ἀπορρήγνυνται τὰς φωνάς.

47. Διὰ τί ποτε τῶν ὀξυτέρων φωνῶν πορρώτερον
ἀκούουσιν; ἢ διότι τὸ ὀξὺ ἐν φωνῇ ταχύ ἐστι, θᾶττον
δὲ κινεῖται τὰ βίᾳ μᾶλλον φερόμενα, τὰ δὲ σφοδρό-
10   τερον φερόμενα | ἐπὶ πλέον φέρεται;

48. Διὰ τί κατέχοντες τὸ πνεῦμα μᾶλλον ἀκούομεν;
ἢ ὅτι ἡ ἀνάπνευσις ψόφον τινὰ παρέχει; εἰκότως οὖν
τότε μᾶλλον ἀκούομεν, ὅταν ἥττων ὁ ψόφος ᾖ· ἥττων
γὰρ ὁ ψόφος, ὅταν κατέχωμεν τὸ πνεῦμα. |

15   49. Διὰ τί τὸ μὲν φῶς οὐ διέρχεται διὰ τῶν πυκνῶν,
λεπτότερον ὂν καὶ πόρρω ἰὸν[59] καὶ θᾶττον, ὁ δὲ ψόφος
διέρχεται; ἢ διότι τὸ μὲν φῶς κατ᾽ εὐθεῖαν φέρεται,
ὥστε ἂν ἀντιφράξῃ τι τὴν εὐθυωρίαν, ὅλως ἀποκέκλει-

57 <γὰρ> addidi ex [Arist./Alex.] Sup.Pr. 2.90, 13
58 ἀπορρηγνύασι Sylburg : ἀπορρήγνυσι codd.
59 πόρρω ἰὸν Bonitz : πόρρω ὂν codd. : πορρώ<τερ>ον
Marenghi[2] ex Trap.

388

its way through because the air is greater in quantity and heavier, but the air that is moved is refracted in the opposite direction and carried downward; hence, being poured down, it is heard better below. And this is what happens with the echo as well, ⟨for⟩ it is a refraction of the voice in an opposite direction.

46.[76] Why is the voice of drunken people more broken than that of sober people? Do they break their voice quickly because they are filled? And there is a sign of this: for neither choruses nor actors practice after breakfast, but when fasting. But as people are fuller when drunk, it is reasonable that they break their voices more.

47.[77] Why do people hear higher voices at a greater distance? Is it because what is high in voice is quick, and the things traveling more by force are moved more quickly, and the things traveling violently travel further?

48.[78] Why do we hear better when we hold our breath? Is it because breathing produces a noise? Therefore, it is reasonable that we hear better when there is less noise: for there is less noise when we hold our breath.

49.[79] Why does light not pass through dense things, although it is thinner and goes farther and more quickly (*than sound*), whereas sound does pass through? Is it because light travels in a straight line, so that, if anything obstructs its straight course, it is completely shut off, whereas

---

[76] [Arist./Alex.] *Sup.Pr.* 2.91 is virtually identical to this chapter.

[77] Cf. *Pr.* 11.6, 19, 20.

[78] Cf. *Pr.* 11.41.

[79] Cf. *Pr.* 11.58, 25.9, Strato frs. 30A–B Sharples.

ται, ὁ δὲ ψόφος φέρεται καὶ οὐκ εὐθὺ διὰ τὸ πνεῦμα
20 εἶναι; | διὸ πανταχόθεν ψοφούντων[60] ἀκούομεν, καὶ οὐ
μόνον τῶν κατ' εὐθυωρίαν τοῖς ὠσίν.

50. Διὰ τί ποτε οἱ μὲν γελῶντες βαρὺ φθέγγονται,
οἱ δὲ κλαίοντες ὀξύ; ἢ διότι ἀπὸ τῶν συντόνων ὀξεῖα ἡ
φωνή, τὸ δὲ ὀξύ ἐστιν ἀσθενές; ἄμφω δὲ ταῦτα μᾶλ-
25 λον | τοῖς κλαίουσιν ὑπάρχει· καὶ γὰρ συντέτανται
μᾶλλον οἱ κλαίοντες καὶ ἀσθενέστεροί εἰσιν.

51. Διὰ τί, εἴπερ ἡ φωνὴ ἀήρ τις ἐσχηματισμένος
ἐστί καὶ[61] φερομένη[62] διαλύεται πολλάκις τὸ σχῆμα, ἡ
ἠχώ[63] γίνεται πληγέντος τοῦ τοιούτου πρός τι στερεόν
30 ⟨καὶ⟩[64] οὐ διαλύεται, | ἀλλὰ σαφῶς ἀκούομεν; ἢ διότι
ἀνάκλασίς ἐστιν, οὐ κατάκλασις, τοῦτο δὲ ὅλον ἀφ'
ὅλου; εἶτα τὸ πάθος ἀφ' ὁμοίου· ἀπὸ γὰρ τοῦ ἀέρος
ἀνακλᾶται ἐν τῷ κοίλῳ, οὐκ ἀπὸ τοῦ κοίλου.

52. Διὰ τί ἑνός τε καὶ πολλῶν φθεγγομένων ἅμα
35 οὔτε | ἴσος ὁ φθόγγος, οὔτε ἐπὶ πλεῖον γεγωνόσιν[65] ὡς
κατὰ λόγον εἰς τὸ πόρρω; ἢ ὅτι ἕκαστος τὸν καθ'
αὑτὸν ἀέρα προωθεῖ, ἀλλ' οὐ τὸν αὐτόν, πλὴν ἐπὶ
μικρόν; ὅμοιον δὴ συμβαίνει ὥσπερ ἂν εἰ πολλοὶ μὲν
εἶεν οἱ βάλλοντες, ἕκαστος μέντοι λίθῳ ἑτέρῳ, ἢ οἵ γε
905a πλεῖστοι. οὔτε γὰρ ἐκεῖ πόρρω ‖ οὐθὲν ἀφίξεται βέ-

---

60 ψοφούντων β : ψοφοῦντος A : ψοφοῦντες cett. codd.
61 καὶ om. Sylburg
62 φερόμενος Ross apud Forster (cf. Pr. 11.23, 901b17)
63 ante ἠχώ add. ⟨δ'⟩ Marenghi²
64 ⟨καὶ⟩ addidi ex [Arist./Alex.] Sup.Pr. 2.94, 3
65 γεγωνόσιν : γεγώνασιν Sylburg

sound also travels (*in a course that is*) not straight because it is breath? This is why we hear those making sounds from any direction, and not only those reaching our ears in a straight line.

50.[80] Why do those who laugh utter low sounds, whereas those who weep utter high ones? Is it because the voice coming from those in a state of strain is high, and the high is weak? And both these conditions are present in those who weep: for those who weep are more under strain and weaker.

51.[81] Why, if indeed voice is air that has been given shape and while traveling its shape is often dissolved, does echo occur when such (*air*) strikes against something hard and is not dissolved, but we hear it clearly? Is it because (*echo*) is refraction, not dispersion, and this is a whole from a whole? Further, what it experiences is from something similar; for it is refracted from the air in the hollow thing, not from the hollow thing itself.

52.[82] Why, when one person utters a sound and when many at the same time utter a sound, is the sound not equal, nor does it travel farther in proportion to the number (*uttering sounds*)? Is it because each individual pushes forward his own air, but not the same air, except to a small extent? It's like what would happen if there were many people throwing, but each, or at any rate most of them, threw a different stone. For in that case no missile will

[80] Cf. *Pr.* 11.13, 15.
[81] Cf. *Pr.* 11.23, [Arist./Alex.] *Sup.Pr.* 2.94, and *Aud.* 800a3–7.
[82] Cf. *Pr.* 11.59, 19.2.

λος, ἢ οὐ κατὰ λόγον, οὔτε ἐνταῦθα. οὐ γὰρ ἑνὸς ἡ
τοσαύτη φωνὴ ἀλλὰ πολλῶν. ἐγγύθεν μὲν οὖν κατὰ
λόγον πολλὴ φαίνεται ἡ φωνή (καὶ γὰρ τὰ βέλη
πλείω τεύξεται τοῦ αὐτοῦ), πόρρωθεν δὲ οὐκέτι. |

5   53. Διὰ τί ἀγωνιῶντες μὲν βαρύτερον φθέγγονται,
φοβούμενοι δὲ ὀξύτερον; καίτοι καὶ ἡ αἰδὼς φόβος τίς
ἐστιν. ἢ διαφέρει πολὺ τὸ πάθος; οἱ μὲν γὰρ αἰδού-
μενοι ἐρυθριῶσιν (ἡ δὲ ἀγωνία αἰσχύνη τίς ἐστιν), οἱ
δὲ φοβούμενοι ὠχριῶσιν. φανερὸν οὖν ὅτι τοῖς μὲν
10   φοβουμένοις ἐκλείπει | ἄνωθεν τὸ θερμόν, ὥστε κινεῖ
ἀσθενὲς ὂν ὀλίγον ἀέρα τὸ πνεῦμα, τὸ δὲ ὀλίγον ταχὺ
φέρεται, τὸ δὲ ταχὺ ἐν φωνῇ τὸ ὀξύ· τοῖς δὲ αἰδου-
μένοις ἄνω ἔρχεται τὸ θερμὸν περὶ τὰ στήθη. σημεῖον
δὲ ὅτι γίνονται ἐξέρυθροι. πολὺν δὲ κινεῖ ἀέρα ἡ
15   πολλὴ δύναμις, τὸ δὲ πολὺ βραδέως φέρεται, | τὸ δὲ
βραδὺ ἐν φωνῇ βαρύ.

54. Διὰ τί ἰσχνόφωνοι γίνονται; ἢ αἴτιον ἡ κατάψυξις τοῦ τόπου ᾧ φθέγγεται, ἢ ὥσπερ ἀποπληξία τοῦ
μέρους τούτου ἐστίν; διὸ καὶ θερμαινόμενοι ὑπὸ οἴνου
καὶ τοῦ λέγειν συνεχῶς ῥᾷον συνείρουσι τὸν λόγον. |

20   55. Διὰ τί μόνον τῶν ἄλλων ζῴων ἄνθρωπος γίνεται ἰσχνόφωνον; ἢ ὅτι λόγου κοινωνεῖ μόνον, τὰ δὲ
ἄλλα φωνῆς; οἱ δὲ ἰσχνόφωνοι φωνοῦσι μέν, λόγον δὲ
οὐ δύνανται συνείρειν.

---

83 Cf. *Pr.* 11.32.
84 Cf. *Pr.* 11.30, 35, 36, 38, 55, 60.

travel far, or not in proportion (*to the number of throwers*), nor in the other case (*will sound travel far*). For such a voice is not of one but of many. So from nearby the voice sounds proportionately loud (indeed, a number of missiles will strike the same spot), but at a distance it will not be so.

53.[83] Why do those who are anxious utter lower sounds, but those who are feeling fear higher ones? And yet shame is a sort of fear. Or does the affection differ a great deal? For those who feel shame turn red (and anxiety is a sort of shame), whereas those who are feeling fear turn pale. It is obvious, therefore, that among those feeling fear the heat leaves the upper regions, so that the breath being weak moves little air, but that which is small travels quickly, and what is quick in voice is high; but in those feeling shame the heat around the chest rises. Now a sign of this is the fact that they become red. But a great power moves much air, and a great mass travels slowly, and the slow in voice is low.

54.[84] Why do people become stammerers? Is the cause the cooling of the part with which one utters sounds, which is like the apoplexy of this part? And this is why when they are heated by wine and so by continuous talking they connect their words more easily.

55.[85] Why does the human alone of all the animals stammer? Is it because the human alone partakes of rational speech, but the other animals partake of voice? But stammerers produce voice, though they are unable to string together words.

[85] Cf. *Pr.* 10.40, 11.30, 35, 36, 38, 54, 60. See also *Aud.* 804b26–39.

56. Διὰ τί τοῦ μὲν χειμῶνος ὀξύτερον φθέγγονται
25 καὶ | νήφοντες, θέρους δὲ καὶ μεθύοντες βαρύτερον; ἢ
ὅτι ὀξυτέρα μέν ἐστιν ἡ ταχυτέρα, ταχυτέρα δέ ἐστιν
ἡ ἀπὸ συντεταμένου φωνή; τῶν δὲ νηφόντων καὶ ἐν τῷ
χειμῶνι τὰ σώματα συνέστηκε μᾶλλον ἢ μεθυόντων
καὶ ἐν τῷ θέρει. τὸ γὰρ θερμὸν καὶ αἱ ἀλέαι διαλύουσι
τὰ σώματα. |

30 57. Διὰ τί ἡ φωνὴ ὕστατον τελειοῦται τοῖς ἀνθρώποις τῶν φθεγγομένων; ἢ διότι πλείστας ἔχει διαφορὰς καὶ εἴδη; τὰ γὰρ[66] ἄλλα ζῷα ἢ οὐθὲν γράμμα ἢ
ὀλίγα διαλέγονται. τὸ δὲ ποικιλώτατον καὶ πλείστας
ἔχον διαφορὰς ἀνάγκη ἐν πλείστῳ χρόνῳ ἀποτελεῖ-
σθαι. |

35 58. Διὰ τί ἡ μὲν ὄψις οὐ διέρχεται διὰ τῶν στερεῶν,
ἡ δὲ φωνὴ διέρχεται; ἢ ὅτι τῆς μὲν ὄψεως μία φορὰ ἡ
κατ' εὐθεῖαν (σημεῖον δὲ αἵ τε τοῦ ἡλίου ἀκτῖνες, καὶ
ὅτι ἐξ ἐναντίας μόνον ὁρῶμεν), τῆς δὲ φωνῆς πολλαί;
ἀκούομεν γὰρ πανταχόθεν. ὅταν οὖν κωλυθῇ κατ'
40 εὐθεῖαν ἐκπίπτειν | διὰ τὸ μὴ κατ' ἀλλήλους εἶναι τοὺς
905b πόρους, ἀδυνατεῖ διορᾶν. ‖ ὁ δὲ ἀὴρ καὶ ἡ φωνή, ἅτε
πανταχοῦ φερομένη, διὰ παντὸς διαπίπτει καὶ ἀκούεται. ἐν δὲ τοῖς ὑγροῖς αἱ μὲν ὄψεις διορῶσιν, αἱ δὲ
φωναὶ οὐκ ἀκούονται ἢ μόλις, λεπτοτέρου ὄντος τοῦ

66 γὰρ : δὲ [Arist./Alex.] Sup.Pr. 2.87, 2

---

86 [Arist./Alex.] Sup.Pr. 2.85 is virtually identical to this chapter. Cf. Pr. 11.17, 18, 61.

56.[86] Why do people utter higher sounds in the winter and when they are sober, but lower ones in the summer and when they are drunk? Is it because the quicker (*in voice*) is higher, and the voice that comes from what is taut is quicker? Now among the sober and in the winter, the bodies are more compacted than among those who are drunk and in summer. For heat and warmth relax the body.

57.[87] Why, of the (*animals*) that utter sounds, is voice perfected last in humans? Is it because (*the human voice*) has the greatest number of differences and forms? For the other animals pronounce no letters or very few. Now what is most complex and has the most differences is necessarily perfected in the longest time.

58.[88] Why doesn't sight pass through hard objects, whereas voice does pass through? Is it because the motion of sight is one only, in a straight line (a sign is the rays of the sun, and the fact that we can see them only from the opposite direction), but the motion of sound is in many directions? For we hear from every direction. Therefore, when it[89] is prevented from falling in a straight line because there is no passage between the one and the other,[90] the object is impossible to see through. But air and voice, as they travel in every direction, fall through everything and so are heard. Now sight does see through liquids, whereas voices are not heard or barely are, although liquid is finer

---

[87] [Arist./Alex.] *Sup.Pr.* 2.87 is virtually identical to this chapter.

[88] Cf. *Pr.* 11.58, 25.9, Strato frs. 30A–B Sharples.

[89] I.e., sight or light.

[90] I.e., between the eye and the object.

5 ὑγροῦ ἢ τῆς γῆς, ὅτι οἱ πόροι μικροὶ | καὶ πυκνοὶ καὶ
κατ᾿ ἀλλήλους, ὥστε οὐ κωλύεται ἡ ὄψις εὐθυπορεῖν.
διὰ τοῦτο καὶ διὰ μὲν τῆς ὑέλου διορᾶται πυκνῆς
οὔσης, διὰ δὲ τοῦ νάρθηκος ἀραιοῦ ὄντος οὐ διορᾶται,
ὅτι[67] τῆς μὲν οἱ πόροι κατάλληλοι, τοῦ[68] δὲ παραλλάτ-
τοντες· οὐδὲν δ᾿ ὄφελος εἶναι μεγάλους, ἐὰν μὴ κατ᾿
10 εὐθεῖαν ὦσιν. ἡ δὲ | φωνὴ οὐκ ἀκούεται, ὅτι ἐλάττω τὰ
διάκενα τὰ ἐν τῷ ὕδατι τοῦ ἀέρος, ὥστε οὐ δύναται
δέχεσθαι οὐδὲ διιέναι[69] τὴν φωνήν, ἀλλὰ μόλις τὸν
μετὰ φωνῆς <ἀέρα>.[70] ἡ γὰρ φωνὴ ἀήρ τις. οὐ γὰρ
ἅπαν τὸ μανότερον διτικώτερον, ἂν μὴ καὶ οἱ πόροι
ὦσιν ἁρμόττοντες τῷ διιόντι,[71] ὥστ᾿[72] οὐδὲ συνιτικώ-
15 τερον | εἰς αὑτό, ἂν μὴ δεκτικοὶ ὦσιν οἱ πόροι τῶν
σωμάτων. καίτοι τὸ μανὸν μαλακὸν καὶ δυνάμενον εἰς
αὑτὸ συνιέναι. ἀλλ᾿ ἔνια κωλύεται διὰ τὴν μικρότητα
τῶν πόρων, οἷον ἡ ὕελος· ταύτης γὰρ οὐ συνάγονται,
μανοτέρας οὔσης τοῦ νάρθηκος, διὰ τὴν εἰρημένην
20 αἰτίαν. ὁμοίως | δὲ καὶ τὸ ὕδωρ καὶ εἴ τι ἄλλο τοιοῦτον.
ὥστε καὶ τόδε φανερόν, διότι τοῦ μανοῦ καὶ μαλακοῦ ἢ
ταὐτοῦ ὄντος ἢ παραπλησίου τὴν φύσιν, οὐ τὸ μανότερον μᾶλλον συνάγεται εἰς αὑτό· ἡ γὰρ αὐτὴ αἰτία
πάντων.

59. Διὰ τί γίνεται ἐλάττων μὲν ἡ φωνὴ ἐξαιρου-

---

67 ὅτι Bonitz : ἔτι codd.
68 τοῦ Bonitz : τῶν codd.
69 διιέναι Ruelle ex Gaza : μεῖναι codd.
70 ἀλλὰ μόλις τὸν μετὰ φωνῆς <ἀέρα> Barker : ἀλλὰ μόλις
ἢ (vel ἡ) μετὰ φωνῆς codd. : ἀλλ᾿ ἢ μόνον <ἀέρα> ἢ μετὰ

than earth, because the passages are small and compact
and connected to one another, so that sight is not prevented from passing straight through. And this is why one
sees through glass, which is dense, but one does not see
through a fennel stalk, which is porous, because in the former case the passages are connected to one another, but in
the latter they deviate; and their size is of no advantage,
unless they are in a straight line. But the voice is not heard,
because the empty spaces in the water are too small for the
air, so that they cannot receive the voice or let it through,
but barely the air accompanying voice.[91] For the voice is a
sort of air. For not everything that is looser is easier to pass
through, unless the passages are also suitable to what is
passing through, so that it is not more compressible unless
its passages can receive bodies. And yet what is loose is soft
and compressible. But some things, such as glass, are prevented because of the smallness of their passages; for its
passages are not contracted, although it is looser than the
fennel stalk, for the reason already given. The same is true
of water and any other such thing. So this too is obvious,
that though the loose and soft are the same or similar in nature, what is looser does not admit of more compression;
for the cause is the same in all these cases.

59.[92] Why does the voice become less when (*some of*

[91] There is probably something wrong with the text here.

[92] Cf. *Pr.* 11.52, 19.2. The author seems to be discussing a
chorus.

φωνῆς Marenghi[2] : ἀλλ' ἢ μόλις [ἢ μετὰ φωνῆς] Ruelle (ἢ ante
μόλις Bussemaker)   [71] διόντι Bekker : διέναι β : διέντι
cett. codd.   [72] ὥστ' r u t : ὥσπερ cett. codd.

25 μένων, | ὁμοία δὲ τὸν χαρακτῆρα; ἢ ὅτι ἐμέμικτο
αὐτοῖς, τὸ δὲ μεμιγμένον οὐ τῇ μέν ἐστι τῇ δὲ οὔ, ἀλλὰ
πάντῃ; ὁμοίως οὖν πανταχόθεν ἐξαιρουμένων συνέρχεται [ὁμοίως],[73] ὥστ᾽ ἔλαττόν τε ἀνάγκη καὶ ὅμοιον
εἶναι.

60. Διὰ τί ἰσχνόφωνοι γίνονται; πότερον διὰ θερ-
30 μότητα προπετέστεροί εἰσιν, ὥστε | προσπταίοντες
ἐπίσχουσιν, ὥσπερ οἱ ὀργιζόμενοι; καὶ γὰρ οὗτοι
πλήρεις ἄσθματος γίνονται. πολὺ μὲν οὖν τὸ πνεῦμα
συμβαίνει. <ἢ>[74] διὰ τὴν ζέσιν τοῦ θερμοῦ ἀσθμαί-
νουσιν, διὰ τὸ πολὺ εἶναι καὶ μὴ φθάνειν ὑπεξιὸν τῷ
35 τῆς ἀναπνοῆς καιρῷ; ἢ μᾶλλον τοὐναντίον | κατάψυξις
ἢ θερμότης τοῦ τόπου ᾧ φθέγγεται, ὥσπερ ἀποπληξία
τοῦ μέρους τούτου; διὸ καὶ θερμαινόμενοι ὑπὸ οἴνου
καὶ τοῦ λέγειν συνεχῶς ῥᾷον συνείρουσι τὸν λόγον.

61. Διὰ τί τοῦ χειμῶνος αἱ φωναὶ βαρύτεραι; ἢ ὅτι
παχύτερος ὁ ἀήρ, παχυτέρου δὲ ὄντος βραδυτέρα ἡ
40 κίνησις, | ὥσθ᾽ ἡ φωνὴ βαρυτέρα; ἢ διότι διὰ τῶν
906a στέρνων[75] βραδύτερον ‖ χωρεῖ ὁ ἀήρ, συμφράττεται
δὲ τὸ περὶ τὸν φάρυγγα ὑπό τε τοῦ ψυχροῦ καὶ τοῦ
ἐπιρρέοντος φλέγματος;

62a. Διὰ τί τὰ παιδία καὶ αἱ γυναῖκες καὶ οἱ

---

73 [ὁμοίως] Hett
74 <ἢ> Sylburg
75 στέρνων : στένων [Arist./Alex.] *Sup.Pr.* 2.95, 3

---

93 Cf. *Pr.* 11.30, 35, 36, 38, 54, 55.

those producing it) are removed, whereas its character is similar? Is it because the voice had already been mixed with them, and what is mixed is not so in one part and not the other, but in every part? Therefore, when some of them are removed from every side, (*the sound of the voices*) comes together in the same way, so that it is necessarily both less and similar.

60.[93] Why do people become stammerers? Are they very rushed owing to the heat, so that they stumble and hesitate, just like those who are angry? For these too are full of panting. Therefore, a large amount of breath comes together. Or do they pant because of the boiling of the heat, because it is a large amount and cannot escape before the right time for breathing? Or on the contrary is it a cooling rather than a heating of the part with which one utters sounds, like the apoplexy of this part? And this is why when they are heated by wine and so by continuous talking they connect their words more easily.

61.[94] Why are voices lower in the winter? Is it because the air is thicker, and as it is thicker the movement is slower, so that the voice is lower? Or is it because the air travels more slowly through the chest,[95] and the region around the pharynx is obstructed by both the cold and the phlegm flowing in it?

62a.[96] Why do children, women, eunuchs and those

---

94 [Arist./Alex.] *Sup.Pr.* 2.94 is virtually identical to this chapter. Cf. *Pr.* 11.17, 18, 56.

95 Or, following the reading of [Arist./Alex.] *Sup.Pr.* 2.95, 3, "through narrow (*passages*)."

96 Cf. *Pr.* 11.14, 16, 34, *GA* 787a28–b19. I follow Jan, who divides ch. 62 into two problems. I assume 62b is incomplete.

εὐνοῦχοι καὶ οἱ γέροντες φθέγγονται ὀξύ; ἢ ὅτι θάτ-
5 των κίνησίς ἐστιν | ἡ ὀξυτέρα; ἔστι δὲ τὸ αὐτὸ πλεῖον
ὂν[76] δυσκινητότερον, ὥστε οἱ ἐν ἀκμῇ πλείω συνεπι-
σπῶνται τὸν ἀέρα· οὗτος οὖν βραδύτερον ἰὼν βαρυτέραν παρασκευάζει τὴν φωνήν. ἐν δὲ τοῖς παιδίοις καὶ
εὐνούχοις διὰ τὸ ἐλάττω ἔχειν ἐναντίως.

62b.[77] .... τρέμειν δὲ[78] τοὺς πρεσβύτας οὐ δυναμέ-
10 νους κρατεῖν, ὥσπερ | τοῖς ἀδυνάτοις καὶ παιδίοις,
ὅταν μακρὸν ξύλον λάβωσιν ἀπ' ἄκρου, τὸ ἕτερον
ἄκρον σείεται διὰ τὸ μὴ κρατεῖν. διὰ τοῦτο καὶ οἱ
πρεσβῦται τρέμουσιν.[79] τὸ αὐτὸ δὲ ὑποληπτέον καὶ
ἐπὶ τῶν ἀγωνιώντων καὶ φοβουμένων καὶ ῥιγώντων
15 αἴτιον τοῦ τρόμου τῆς φωνῆς. τοῦ γὰρ ἔχοντος | τὴν
φωνὴν τοιαύτην, ⟨τοῦ θερμοῦ διὰ⟩[80] τῶν τοιούτων
παθῶν εἴσω περιεστηκότος τοῦ πλείστου,[81] λοιπὸν
ὀλίγον ὂν οὐ δύναται κρατεῖν τῆς φωνῆς· διὸ καὶ
σείεται καὶ τρέμει. διὸ καὶ οἱ τεχνικοὶ τῶν συνειδότων
ὅτι ἀγωνιῶσι μικρὸν διαλέγονται ἀπ' ἀρχῆς, καὶ ἄχρι
20 οὗ ἂν καταστῶσιν· μικρᾶς γὰρ οὔσης | τῆς φωνῆς
ῥᾷον κρατοῦσιν.

[76] πλεῖον ὂν β : πλείονος cett. codd.

[77] caput 62b Jan, 62a continuatur in codd. ‖ ante τρέμειν lac.
indicavi   [78] post δὲ add. ⟨δεῖ⟩ Marenghi[2] : add. ⟨ἐικὸς⟩
Bussemaker : add. ⟨συμβαίνω⟩ Ruelle

[79] διὰ τοῦτο—τρέμουσιν C[a] Gaza : om. Ap. : post τρέμουσιν
add διὰ τὸ μὴ (vel μηκέτι) κρατεῖν cett. codd.

[80] ⟨τοῦ θερμοῦ διὰ⟩ Forster ex Gaza   [81] τῶν τοιούτων
⟨ἕνεκεν⟩—τοῦ πλείστου ⟨θερμοῦ⟩ Marenghi[2]

who are old utter higher sounds? Is it because the higher voice is a quicker movement (*of air*)? Now the same thing in larger quantity is more difficult to move, so that those in the prime of life draw in more air; therefore, this air going more slowly produces a lower voice. But the opposite occurs in children and eunuchs, because they have less (*air*).

62b.[97] . . . But old people tremble (*when they speak*) because they cannot control (*their voices*), just as when powerless people and children seize a long plank by the end, the other end shakes because they do not control it. This is also why old people tremble. This same thing must be considered the cause of the trembling of the voice in the case of those who are anxious and afraid and shivering. For in one whose voice is in such a state, since most of the heat has collected within as a result of such conditions, the rest, being small in quantity, cannot control the voice; and this is why it shakes and trembles. This is also why, of those who are aware that they are nervous, the experts[98] speak in a soft voice to begin with, and until they have settled down; for they can control the voice more easily when it is soft.

[97] Cf. *Pr.* 11.31, 27.6–7.

[98] οἱ τεχνικοί ("the experts") can also be rendered "the performing artists" (normally οἱ τεχνῖται), "the orators," and "the teachers." (Gaza has *artium liberalium professores*.) I suspect the author is referring to any of these experts who are nervous when beginning to speak.

BOOK XII

INTRODUCTION

Pr. 12 and 13 are brief books dealing with good odors and bad odors respectively. There is ample evidence for an early Peripatetic interest in the sense of smell and the odors of things: see esp. Aristotle's *De Anima* 2.9 and *De Sensu* 5, and Theophrastus' *De Odoribus*, *CP* 6, and *De Sensibus* (e.g., §§ 85 and 90). In the case of *Pr.* 12, however, the only identifiable sources come from Theophrastus. This may be due to the fact that the author of *Pr.* 12, like Theophrastus, seems to accept the sort of emanation theory of odor that Aristotle rejects (in *Sens.* 5).

Book 12 covers the following topics: the effect of distance on the odor of certain things (1, 2, 4, and 9); the supposed effect of the rainbow on the fragrance of trees (3); the effect of motion on odor (5); the effect of cold on odor (6); the difference, with respect to odor, between burning spices on ash and on fire (7 and 11); the difference in odor of certain types of roses (8); whether smell is smoke or vapor (10); why certain fragrant things are diuretic (12); and, the difference between mixed and unmixed wine with respect to their odors (13).

ΟΣΑ ΠΕΡΙ ΤΑ ΕΥΩΔΗ

1. Διὰ τί τῶν θυμιαμάτων ἧττον αἰσθάνονται πλησίον ὄντες; πότερον ὅτι ἀκρατεστέρα κερασθεῖσα ἡ ἀπόρροια τῷ | ἀέρι ἡδίων, ὥσπερ ἡ σμύρνη τῶν ἰατρῶν; ἢ καὶ τοὐναντίον εἴη ἄν, ὥστε ἀφαιρεῖσθαι τὸ πῦρ τὴν ὀσμὴν διὰ τὸ καίειν; ἡ γὰρ ὀσμὴ θυμιωμένων. διὸ καὶ ἐπὶ τῶν ἀνθράκων οὐκ ὄζει, πορρώτερον δὲ καθαρώτερον φαίνεται καὶ λεπτότατον τοῦτο. |

2. Διὰ τί αἱ ὀσμαὶ ⟨ἐγγύθεν⟩[1] ἧττον εὐώδεις τῶν θυμιαμάτων καὶ τῶν ἀνθῶν;[2] πότερον ὅτι συναπέρχεται τῇ ὀσμῇ καὶ γῆς μόρια, ἃ προκαταφέρεται διὰ βάρος, ὥστε καθαρὰ[3] πορρώτερον γίνεται ἡ ὀσμή; ἢ οὔτε ἐγγὺς οὔσης τῆς ἀρχῆς πλεῖστον γίνεται τὸ ῥέον, οὔτε λίαν πόρρω; τὸ | μὲν γὰρ οὔπω πολύ, τὸ δὲ διασπᾶται.

---

[1] ⟨ἐγγύθεν⟩ Marenghi[5] ex Pr. 12.9, 907a24
[2] post ἀνθῶν add. ⟨ἐκ τοῦ ἐγγύς⟩ Sylburg ex. Gaza
[3] καθαρὰ : καθαρωτέρα vel. ⟨μᾶλλον⟩ καθαρὰ Richards

PROBLEMS CONNECTED
WITH FRAGRANT THINGS

1.[1] Why do people perceive incense less when they are near it? Is it because the emanation, being less powerful when mixed with the air, is more pleasant, like the myrrh of the doctors? Or in fact would the opposite be true, so that the fire by burning it removes the smell? For the smell is from the incense being burned. And this is why there is no odor near the coals, but farther away it appears to be purer and very light.

2.[2] Why are the smells from incense and from flowers ⟨close by⟩ less fragrant? Is it because particles of earth come away with the smell, which travel downward beforehand owing to their weight, so that the smell is pure farther away? Or is what flows (*from it*) greatest neither when the source is nearby, nor when it is very far away? For in the former case it is not yet strong, whereas in the latter it is scattered.

[1] Cf. *Pr.* 12.2, 4, 9. Sources: Thphr. *CP* 6.17, 1–2, *Od.* 12–13.
[2] Cf. *Pr.* 12.1, 4, 9. Sources: Thphr. *CP* 6.17, 1–2, *Od.* 12–13.

3.[4] <Διὰ τί> λέγεται [γὰρ ὡς][5] "εὐώδη γίνεται τὰ δένδρα εἰς ἅπερ ἂν ἡ ἶρις κατασκήψῃ";[6] πότερον [οὖν][7] ἀληθές ἐστιν ἢ ψεῦδος; καὶ εἰ ἀληθές, διὰ <τίν'> αἰτίαν ἂν[8] εἴη τὸ συμβαῖνον; ὅτι μὲν || οὖν οὔτε πάντα οὔτε ἀεί, δῆλον· πολλάκις γὰρ ἡ ἶρις μὲν γέγονε, τὰ δὲ δένδρα οὐθὲν ἐπίδηλα φαίνεται. ὅταν τε γένηται τοῦτο, οὐκ ἐν πάσῃ γίνεται ὕλῃ, ἐπεὶ συμβαίνει γέ ποτε· διὸ καὶ λέγεται. τὸ δ' αἴτιον κατὰ συμβεβηκὸς τῇ ἴριδι ἀποδοτέον, ἄλλως τε καὶ εἰ μή ἐστί τις φύσις ἡ ἶρις, ἀλλὰ τῆς ὄψεως πάθος ἀνακλωμένης. γίνεται δέ, ὥσπερ ἐλέχθη, οὐχ ὁπωσοῦν ἐχούσης τῆς ὕλης τὸ πάθος· οὔτε γὰρ ἐν τοῖς χλωροῖς δένδροις οὔτε ἐν τοῖς αὔοις, ἀλλ' ἐν τῇ ἐμπεπρησμένῃ ὕλῃ φασὶν οἱ νομεῖς μετὰ τὰ ἐπὶ τῇ ἴριδι ὕδατα γίνεσθαι ἐπίδηλον τὴν εὐωδίαν, καὶ μάλιστα οὗ ἂν ἀσπάλαθος ᾖ καὶ ῥάμνος καὶ ὧν τὰ ἄνθη εὐώδη ἐστίν. αἴτιον δὲ τῆς εὐωδίας ἐστίν, ὅπερ καὶ ἐπὶ τῆς γῆς· διαθέρμου γὰρ καὶ διακεκαυμένης οὔσης, ὃ ἂν ἐκφύσῃ, τὸ πρῶτον εὐῶδες

906b (line marker)

5 (line marker)

10 (line marker)

---

4 cap. 2 continuatur codd. et Barth. : nov. cap. *PPA*, Gaza et Casaubon   5 <Διὰ τί> λέγεται [γὰρ ὡς] scripsi (cf. *PPA*), γὰρ om. Casaubon : λέγεται γὰρ ὡς codd.

6 λέγεται—κατασκήψῃ ante πότερον transp. *PPA*, Gaza et Casaubon   7 οὖν seclusi (om. w, del. R1)

8 <τίν'> Sylburg, ἂν w^mg R (teste Marenghi5) : διὰ τί ἂν Marenghi5

---

3 According to the manuscripts, what follows is a continuation of ch. 2. Most editors and translators have attempted to improve the text by dividing ch. 2 of the mss. into two chapters, and trans-

3.[3] ⟨Why⟩ is it said: "The trees upon which the rainbow
has fallen become fragrant"? Now is this true or false? And
if it is true, through what cause would there be this occurrence? Now it is clear that this is true neither for all (*trees*)
nor always; for often the rainbow has come, but nothing
noticeable appears with respect to the trees. And when this
does occur, it does not occur in every wood (since it does
happen sometimes, and this is why it is said). But the cause
should be assigned to the rainbow only incidentally, especially if the rainbow is not a certain nature,[4] but is an effect
of refraction on the organ of sight. Now as was said, this
does not occur whatever the condition of the wood; for it
does not occur in green or in dry trees, but the shepherds
say that the fragrance is noticeable in burned wood after
the rains that come with the rainbow, and especially where
there is camel's thorn and buckthorn[5] and (*plants*) the
flowers of which are fragrant. And the reason for this fragrance is the same as it is in the case of the earth; for when
the earth is thoroughly hot and burned throughout, whatever grows from it has a fragrant odor to begin with. For

posing the first two lines of the new ch. 3. This emendation gets
support from the Arabic version, which also provides a clue to
the original question: "Why do people say that fragrant trees are
agreeable in odor when the rainbow falls on them? Is that true,
and if it is true, what is the cause of that?" (Filius trans.) Source:
Thphr. *CP* 6.17, 6–7.

[4] I.e., not a physical entity (cf. Marenghi[5]: *non è un'entità
fisica*), but an attribute of something.

[5] ἀσπάλαθος likely refers not to plants in the modern genus
Aspalathus but to "Camel's thorn" (*Alhagi maurorum*). ῥάμνος
refers to certain species of buckthorn (genus *Rhamnus*), esp. *R.
graeca* (stone buckthorn) and *R. oleoides* (black buckthorn).

15 ὄζει. τὰ γὰρ πυρούμενά πως τῶν ὑγρότητα | ἐχόντων
ὀλίγην εὐώδη γίνεται· πέττει γὰρ τὸ θερμὸν ταύτην.
διὸ καὶ τῆς ὅλης γῆς εὐωδέστερα τὰ πρὸς τὸν ἥλιον
τῶν πρὸς ἄρκτον ἐστίν. τούτων δὲ τὰ πρὸς ἔω τῶν
πρὸς μεσημβρίαν, ὅτι γεώδης μᾶλλον ὁ τόπος ὁ περὶ
τὴν Συρίαν καὶ Ἀραβίαν ἐστίν, ἡ δὲ Λιβύη ἀμμώδης
20 καὶ ἄνικμος. | δεῖ γὰρ μήτε πολλὴν εἶναι τὴν ἰκμάδα,
ἄπεπτος γάρ ἐστιν ἡ πολλή, μήτε ἄνικμον, οὐ γὰρ
γίνεται ἀτμίς. ὃ συμβαίνει καὶ περὶ τὴν νεόκαυστον[9]
ὕλην καὶ τὸ γένος τοιαύτην ὥστε ἔχειν εὐωδίαν σὺν
αὐτῇ. δηλοῖ δὲ τοῖς ἄνθεσιν· ἀφίησι γὰρ ἐν τούτοις
25 τὴν ὀσμήν. δοκεῖ δὲ ἐν οἷς ἂν ἐνσκήψῃ | ἡ ἶρις
γίνεσθαι, ὅτι οὐδὲν ἄνευ ὕδατος οἷόν τε γίνεσθαι·
βραχεῖσά τε γὰρ ἡ ὕλη καὶ τῷ ἐνόντι θερμῷ πέψασα
τὴν ἐν αὐτῇ γινομένην ἀτμίδα ἀφίησιν. οὔτε πολὺ τὸ
ὕδωρ δεῖ εἶναι· ἐκκλύζει γὰρ τὸ πολὺ λίαν, καὶ
σβέννυσιν τὴν θερμότητα τὴν ἐνυπάρχουσαν ἀπὸ τῆς
30 πυρώσεως. | τὰ δὲ μετὰ τὴν ἶριν ὕδατα οὐ πολλὰ
γίνεται, ἀλλὰ μέτρια ὡς εἰπεῖν. καὶ ἐὰν πολλαὶ γίνων-
ται ἴριδες, οὐ πολὺ γίνεται, ἀλλὰ πολλάκις μὲν, ὀλίγον δέ. διὸ εἰκότως τούτου γινομένου, οὐθὲν ἄλλο
ὁρῶντες διάφορον πλὴν τὴν ἶριν, ταύτῃ τὴν αἰτίαν
προσέθεσαν τῆς εὐωδίας. |

35   4. Διὰ τί τὰ ἄνθη καὶ τὰ θυμιώμενα πόρρωθεν

---

[9] νεόκαυστον γ : νεόκαυτον α β δ

---

[6] I.e., there is moisture, but not too much moisture.
[7] A plant generally, or specifically a tree with flowers.

things containing a little moisture, if they are at all burned
with fire, become fragrant; for the heat concocts this moisture. And this is why over the whole earth what faces the
sun is more fragrant than what faces north. And of the former, what faces east (*is more fragrant*) than what faces
south, for the region around Syria and Arabia is more
earthy, whereas Libya is sandy and without liquid. Indeed,
there must not be a great deal of liquid, for a large quantity
is difficult to concoct, nor must (*the ground*) be without
liquid, for then no vapor comes—which also happens[6] in
the case of newly burned wood and the kind that is such as
to have a fragrance within it. And it is clear in the case of
flowers; for it[7] releases its smell by means of them. But in
the case of (*trees*) upon which the rainbow falls, it seems
that nothing can occur without the presence of water; for
when the wood has been rained upon and then has concocted (*liquid*) by the heat that is in it, it releases the vapor
coming to be in it. But the water must not be in large quantity; for in a large quantity it drenches (*the tree*), and extinguishes the heat that is already present in it as a result of
the burning. Now the waters that come after the rainbow
are not great, but moderate so to speak. Even if there are
many rainbows,[8] there is not a large quantity (*of water*),
but though (*the rain falls*) often, it is in small quantities.
This is why it is reasonable, when this occurs, that, as people see nothing else distinctive except the rainbow, they
ascribe to it the cause of the fragrance.

4.[9] Why do flowers and incense have a more pleasant

---

[8] Presumably in succession.

[9] Cf. *Pr.* 12.1, 2, 9. Sources: Thphr. *CP* 6.17, 1–2, *Od.* 12–13.
Pr. 12.4 and 9 together are similar to [Arist./Alex.] *Supl.Pr.* 2.103.

μᾶλλον ἥδιον ὄζει, ἐγγύθεν δὲ τὰ μὲν ποωδέστερον, τὰ
δὲ καπνωδέστερον; ἢ ὅτι ἡ ὀσμὴ θερμότης τίς ἐστιν
καὶ τὰ εὐώδη θερμά; τὸ δὲ θερμὸν κοῦφον, ὥστε διὰ
μὲν τοῦτο πορρωτέρω ‖ διιόντων ἀμιγεστέρα γίνεται ἡ
ὀσμὴ τῶν συμπαρεπομένων ὀσμῶν ἀπὸ τῶν φύλλων
καὶ τοῦ καπνοῦ, ὄντος ὑδατώδους ἀτμοῦ· πλησίον δὲ
ὄντων, τὰ μεμιγμένα αὐτοῖς συνόζει ἐν οἷς ἐστίν. |

5   5. Διὰ τί πάντα μᾶλλον ὄζει κινούμενα; ἢ ὅτι
ἀναπίμπλησι πλείω ἀέρα ἢ ἡσυχάζοντα; διαπέμπεται
οὖν ἡ ὀσμὴ θᾶττον οὕτω πρὸς τὴν αἴσθησιν ἡμῶν.

6. Διὰ τί τοῦ χειμῶνος ἧττον ὀσφραινόμεθα, καὶ ἐν
τοῖς πάγεσιν ἥκιστα; ἢ ὅτι ὁ ἀὴρ ἀκινητότερός ἐστιν
10   ἐν τῷ ψύχει; | οὔκουν ἀφικνεῖται ὁμοίως ἡ κίνησις ἡ
ἀπὸ τοῦ σώματος τοῦ τὴν ὀσμὴν ἔχοντος διὰ τὴν
δυσκινησίαν τῆς ἀπορροῆς καὶ τοῦ ἀέρος ἐν ᾧ ἐστίν.

7. Διὰ τί δριμύτερον ὄζει τῶν ἀρωμάτων ἐπὶ τέφρας
θυμιωμένων ἢ ἐπὶ τοῦ πυρός, καὶ μᾶλλον καὶ πλείω
15   χρόνον | τὴν αὐτῶν ὀσμὴν ἔχει ἐπὶ τῆς τέφρας θυμιώ-
μενα; ἢ ὅτι ἀπεπτοτέρα ἐστὶν ἡ ὀσμὴ ἐπὶ τῆς τέφρας·
διὸ καὶ πλείω; τὸ δὲ πῦρ, ταχὺ[10] πέττον αὐτῶν τὴν
δύναμιν, ἀλλοιοῖ τὴν ὀσμήν· ἡ γὰρ πέψις ἀλλοίωσίς
ἐστιν τοῦ πεττομένου. |

20   8. Διὰ τί ἥδιον ὄζει τῶν ῥόδων, ὧν ὁ ὀμφαλὸς
τραχύς ἐστιν, ἢ ὧν λεῖος; ἢ ὅτι μᾶλλον ὄζει ἡδὺ ὅσα

[10] ταχὺ : παχὺ Bekker

412

odor at a distance, whereas nearby the former (*smells*) more like grass and the latter more like smoke? Is it because smell is a certain sort of heat and fragrant things are hot? Now heat is light, so that for this reason farther away the smell is less mixed with the concomitant smells spreading out from the leaves and the smoke, which is a watery vapor; but being near by, the mixed (*smells*) give off an odor with the (*plants*) in which they are present.

5.[10] Why do all things have more of an odor when in motion? Is it because they[11] fill up more air than when they are at rest? Therefore, the smell is in this way transmitted more quickly to our sense perception.

6.[12] Why do we perceive smells less in winter, and least of all in frost? Is it because the air is more motionless in the cold? Therefore, the movement from the body containing the smell does not reach as far owing to the difficulty in moving of the emanation and the air in which it is present.

7.[13] Why do spices have a more acrid odor when they are burned on ashes than on fire, and they have their smell more and for a long time when burned on ashes? Is it because the smell is more unconcocted on ashes, and this is why there is more (*of the smell*)? But the fire, quickly concocting their capacity, alters the smell; for concoction is an alteration of what is concocted.

8.[14] Why do roses, the centers of which are rough, have a more pleasant odor than those (*plants the centers*) of which are smooth? Is it because those (*roses*) have a more

---

[10] Cf. *Pr.* 13.12 and [Arist./Alex.] *Supl.Pr.* 2.104.

[11] Or "their odors."   [12] [Arist./Alex.] *Supl.Pr.* 2.101 is a condensed version of this chapter. Source: Thphr. *CP* 6.17, 5.

[13] Cf. *Pr.* 12.11.   [14] Source: Thphr. *HP* 6.6, 4.

τὴν φύσιν ἀπείληφε τὴν αὐτῶν; ἀκανθῶδες δὲ φύσει
τὸ ῥόδον ἐστίν· διὸ μᾶλλον ἔχον τὰ κατὰ φύσιν, ὄζει
ἥδιον.[11]

9. Διὰ τί αἱ ὀσμαὶ ἐγγύθεν ἧττον εὐώδεις καὶ
25 θυμιαμάτων | καὶ ἀνθῶν; ἢ ὅτι πλησίον μὲν συναπο-
φέρεται τὸ γεῶδες, ὥστε κεραννύμενον ἀσθενεστέραν
ποιεῖ τὴν δύναμιν, εἰς δὲ τὸ πόρρω καταφέρεται ἡ
ὀδμή; διὰ ταῦτα δὲ καὶ τριφθέντα τὰ ἄνθη ἀπολλύ-
ουσι τὴν ὀσμήν.

10. Πότερον αἱ ὀσμαὶ καπνὸς [ἢ ἀὴρ][12] ἢ ἀτμίς;
30 διαφέρει | γάρ, ᾗ τὸ μὲν ὑπὸ τοῦ πυρός, τὸ δὲ καὶ ἄνευ
τούτου γίνεται. καὶ πότερον ἀπὸ τῆς αἰσθήσεώς τι
πρὸς ἐκεῖνα ἢ ἀπ᾽ ἐκείνων πρὸς τὴν αἴσθησιν ἀφικνεῖται, ἀεὶ κινοῦν τὸν πλησίον ἀέρα; καὶ εἰ ἀπ᾽ ἐκείνων
ἀπορρεῖ, ἔδει ἔλαττον γίνεσθαι· καίτοι τὰ εὐωδέστατα
ὁρῶμεν μάλιστα διαμένοντα. |

35 11. Διὰ τί δριμύτερον ὄζει μᾶλλον τῶν ἀρωμάτων
ἐπὶ τέφρας θυμιωμένων ἢ ἐπὶ τοῦ πυρός; ἢ διότι
ἀπεπτοτέρα ἡ ὀσμὴ ἐπὶ τῆς τέφρας· διὸ καὶ πλείων;
πολὺ οὖν καὶ τοῦ γεώδους συναναθυμιᾶται καὶ γίνεται
καπνός· τὸ δὲ πῦρ φθάνει ἐκκαῖον τὸ γεῶδες αὐτῶν,
907b ὥστε ἡ ὀσμὴ καθαρωτέρα ‖ καὶ εἰλικρινὴς ἀφικνεῖται
ἄνευ τοῦ καπνοῦ. διὸ καὶ τριβόμενα ἧττον εὐώδη τὰ

---

[11] ὄζει ἥδιον a β : ἥδιστα ὄζει δ γ
[12] [ἢ ἀὴρ] Forster

pleasant odor which (*more*) partake of their nature? Now the rose is by nature thorny; this is why, being more in its natural condition, it has a more pleasant odor.

9.[15] Why are the smells both from incense and from flowers close by less fragrant? Is it because nearby the earthy part is transmitted along with it, so that being mixed it makes the power (*of the smell*) weaker, whereas the smell[16] is carried to a distance? And it is also for this reason that the flowers when rubbed lose their smell.

10.[17] Are smells smoke [or air] or vapor? For it makes a difference, inasmuch as the one is due to fire, while the other comes to be without it. And does something pass from the sense to the objects or from the objects to the sense, continually moving the neighboring air? Indeed, if it emanates from the objects, it should become less; and yet we observe that the most fragrant things last the longest.

11.[18] Why do spices have a more acrid odor when they are burned on ashes than on fire? Is it because the smell is more unconcocted on ashes, and this is why there is more (*of the smell*)? Therefore, much of the earthy material too is burned off with them and becomes smoke. But fire burns out their earthy material beforehand, so that the smell is purer and arrives unmixed, without the smoke. And this is why flowers that are rubbed are less fragrant,

15 Cf. *Pr.* 12.1, 2, 4, and 13.3. Chs. 12.4 and 9 together are similar to [Arist./Alex.] *Supl.Pr.* 2.103. See also Hieronym. fr. 10 White.

16 Without the earthy material.

17 Cf. Arist. *Sens.* 5 and Thphr. *Sens.* 85 and 90.

18 Cf. *Pr.* 12.7, and see also Thphr. *Od.* 13.

ἄνθη· τὸ γὰρ γεῶδες καὶ ἡ τρῦψις κινεῖ καὶ ἡ βραδεῖα
θερμότης οὐ φθείρει.

12. Διὰ τί τὰ εὐώδη οὐρητικὰ καὶ σπέρματα καὶ
5 φυτά; | ἢ ὅτι θερμὰ καὶ εὔπεπτα,[13] τὰ δὲ τοιαῦτα
οὐρητικά; ταχὺ γὰρ λεπτύνει ἡ ἐνοῦσα θερμότης, καὶ
ἡ ὀσμὴ οὐ σωματώδης, ἐπεὶ καὶ τὰ μὴ εὐώδη, οἷον
σκόροδα, διὰ τὴν θερμότητα οὐρητικά, μᾶλλον μέντοι
τηκτικά. θερμὰ δὲ τὰ εὐώδη σπέρματα, διότι ὅλως
10 ἡ ὀσμὴ διὰ θερμότητα γίνεται· ἀλλὰ | τὰ δυσώδη
ἄπεπτά ἐστιν. δεῖ δὲ μὴ μόνον θερμὰ εἶναι ἀλλὰ καὶ
εὔπεπτα, εἰ ἔσται οὐρητικά, ὅπως συγκατιόντα λεπτύ-
νῃ τὰ ὑγρά.

13. Διὰ τί ποτε οἱ κεκραμένοι τῶν οἴνων ἧττον[14]
τῶν ἀκράτων ὄζουσιν; ἢ ὅτι ὁ κεκραμένος ἀσθενέστε-
15 ρος τοῦ ἀκράτου ἐστίν; | τὸ δὲ ἀσθενέστερον[15] ἐπὶ[16]
πάντων ἐξίσταται τοῦ ἰσχυροτέρου. εἶτα ὁ κεκραμένος
ἐστὶν εὐπετέστερος τοῦ ἀκράτου. εὐπετέστερον δέ
ἐστιν ὑπεῖξαι[17] ᾡτινιοῦν, καὶ ἐκλαβεῖν τι τῶν μὴ
ὑπαρχόντων. ὁ μὲν οὖν ἄκρατος ὀσμώδης ἐστίν, ὁ δὲ
κεκραμένος ἄνοσμος.

---

[13] εὔπεπτα Forster (cf. *Pr.* 1.48, 865a20 and 20.16, 924b19) :
λεπτά codd.

[14] ἧττον Forster : θᾶττον codd.

[15] post ἀσθενέστερον add. θᾶττον Louis ex Gaza

[16] ἐπὶ dub. Bekker (cf. Trap. *debilius autem potentiori cedit in
omnibus*) : ὑπὸ a β δ : ἀπὸ γ praeter Xa

[17] ὑπεῖξαι Ross apud Forster : ὑπάρξαι codd.

for rubbing moves the earthy material and the slow heat does not destroy it.

12.[19] Why are fragrant seeds and plants diuretic? Is it because they are hot and easily concocted,[20] and such things are diuretic? For the internal heat liquefies quickly and the smell is not corporeal, since even the ones that are not fragrant, like garlic, are diuretic owing to their heat, though they are more productive of melting. Now fragrant seeds are hot, because the smell generally comes to be owing to heat; but malodorous things are unconcocted. Now if something is to be diuretic, it must not only be hot but also well concocted, in order that it may liquefy the moist elements as they move downward with them.

13.[21] Why do mixed wines have less of an odor than unmixed? Is it because mixed wine is weaker than unmixed? Now the weaker in every case stands aside for the stronger. So mixed wine is more easily affected than unmixed. And to be more easily affected is to yield to anything else, and to receive something that did not originally belong to it. Therefore, unmixed wine has a smell, but mixed wine is odorless.

[19] This chapter is a longer version of *Pr.* 1.48 and virtually identical to 20.16.

[20] Or, following the mss., "light" ($\lambda\epsilon\pi\tau\acute{\alpha}$).

[21] Source: Thphr. *Od.* 11.

BOOK XIII

INTRODUCTION

For the Peripatetic background to the subject matter of *Pr.* 13 (malodorous things), see the opening paragraph of the introduction to Book 12. As in the case of Book 12, the identifiable sources for Book 13 come from Theophrastus.[1]

Pr. 13 covers the following topics: urine (1 and 6); malodorous foods (2); flowers that are rubbed (3); the odor of animals (4); the effect of heat on odor (5); bad breath (7 and 10); sweat (8, 9, and 11); and the effect of motion on odor (12).

---

[1] One partial exception: Arist. *HA* 612a12–15, along with Thphr. *CP* 6.5, 2 and 17, 9, are likely sources for *Pr.* 13.4.

ΟΣΑ ΠΕΡΙ ΤΑ ΔΥΣΩΔΗ

1. Διὰ τί τὸ μὲν οὖρον, ὅσῳ ἂν χρονίζηται ἐν τῷ σώματι, δυσωδέστερον γίνεται, ἡ δὲ κόπρος ἧττον; ἢ ὅτι ἡ μὲν ξηραίνεται μᾶλλον χρονιζομένη (τὸ δὲ ξηρὸν ἀσηπτότερον), | τὸ δὲ οὖρον παχύνεται, πρόσφατόν τε ὂν ὁμοιότερον τῷ ἐξ ἀρχῆς ἐστι πόματι;

907b
25

2. Διὰ τί τὰ δυσώδη τοῖς ἐδηδοκόσιν οὐ δοκεῖ ὄζειν; ἢ διὰ τὸ συντετρῆσθαι τὴν ὄσφρησιν τῷ στόματι κατὰ τὸν οὐρανόν, πλήρης ἡ αἴσθησις γίνεται ταχύ, καὶ τῆς τε ἔσω[1] | οὐκέθ᾽ ὁμοίως αἰσθάνεται (τὸ γὰρ πρῶτον αἰσθάνονται πάντες, ὅταν δὲ ἅψωνται, οὐκέτι, ὥσπερ συμφυοῦς) καὶ ἡ ἔξωθεν ἡ ὁμοία ἀφανίζεται ὑπὸ τῆς ἔσω;

30

3. Διὰ τί τριβόμενα τὰ ἄνθη δυσωδέστερα; ἢ διότι συμμίγνυνται τῇ ὀσμῇ τὸ γεῶδες τὸ ἐν τῷ ἄνθει; |

35

4. Διὰ τί τῶν μὲν ζῴων οὐθὲν εὐῶδές ἐστιν ἔξω τῆς παρδάλιος (αὕτη δὲ καὶ αὐτοῖς τοῖς θηρίοις· φασὶ γὰρ

---

[1] ἔσω : ἔξω Eac A : δυσωδίας [Arist./Alex.] *Supl.Pr.* 2.100, 3

[1] Cf. [Arist./Alex.] *Supl.Pr.* 2.100.

PROBLEMS CONNECTED
WITH MALODOROUS THINGS

1. Why does urine become more malodorous the longer it is in the body, whereas feces becomes less so? Is it because the latter becomes drier by remaining (and what is dry is less putrid), whereas urine becomes dense, and when it is fresh it is more like the liquid it was to begin with?

2.[1] Why do malodorous things seem not to have an odor to those who have eaten (*them*)? Is it because, as the sense of smell is connected to the mouth through the palate, the sense quickly becomes saturated, and so no longer perceives the (*odor*) inside in the same way (for at first everyone perceives, but when they are in contact with it, they no longer do, as if it were part of them) and what is similar outside is obscured by what is inside?

3.[2] Why are flowers that are rubbed most malodorous? Is it because the earthy element in the flower mingles with the smell?

4.[3] Why are no animals fragrant except for the panther (and this is so even to beasts themselves, for people say that

[2] Cf. *Pr.* 12.9, 11, and 13.11. Source: Thphr. *Od.* 13.

[3] Sources: Thphr. *CP* 6.5, 2 and 17, 9, and Arist. *HA* 612a12–15; cf. Thphr. *Od.* 4.

αὐτῆς τὰ θηρία ἡδέως ὀσμᾶσθαι), φθειρόμενα δὲ καὶ
δυσώδη ἐστίν, τῶν δὲ φυτῶν πολλὰ καὶ φθειρόμενα
καὶ αὐαινόμενα ἔτι μᾶλλον εὐώδη γίνεται; πότερον ὅτι
908a τῆς δυσωδίας αἴτιον ‖ ἀπεψία τις περιττώματος; διὸ
καὶ οἱ ἱδρῶτες ἐνίοις καὶ ἐνίοτε τοιοῦτοί εἰσιν, μάλιστα δὲ οἷς μὴ ἀεὶ τοιοῦτοι ἐκ τῶν νόσων γίνονται. καὶ
αἱ φῦσαι δὲ καὶ οἱ ἐρυγμοὶ οἱ τῶν ἀπέπτων δυσώδεις
5 εἰσίν. τὸ αὐτὸ δὲ αἴτιον καὶ τοῦ ἐν ταῖς | σαρξὶ καὶ τῷ
ἀνάλογον· λέγω δὲ ἀνάλογον τὸ ἀντὶ σαρκὸς τοῖς
ἄλλοις ἐνυπάρχον ζῴοις. ἔστι γὰρ καὶ ἐνταῦθα περίττωμα ἐνίοις ἄπεπτον· τοῦτο οὖν ζώντων τε αἴτιον τῆς
δυσωδίας ἐστὶ καὶ φθειρομένων σηπόμενον. διὸ καὶ τὰ
πίονα καὶ ὀστᾶ καὶ τρίχες οὐ δυσώδη ἐστίν, ὅτι τὰ μὲν
10 πέττεται, | τὰ δὲ οὐκ ἔχει ὑγρότητα. τοῖς δὲ φυτοῖς οὐκ
ἔνι περίττωμα. ἢ ἔστι μέν τι καὶ τούτοις, ἀλλ' ὅτι
ξηρὰ καὶ θερμὰ τὰ φυτὰ τὴν φύσιν ἐστίν, ὥστε
εὐπεπτοτέρα ἡ ἰκμὰς καὶ οὐ πηλώδης ἐστὶν αὐτῶν;
δηλοῖ δὲ καὶ τῆς γῆς ἡ ἐν τοῖς θερμοῖς εὐώδης οὖσα,
15 Συρία καὶ Ἀραβία, καὶ τὰ εὐώδη | τἀκεῖθεν, ὅτι ξηρὰ
καὶ θερμά ἐστιν· τὰ δὲ τοιαῦτα ἄσηπτα. τὰ δὲ ζῷα οὐ
τοιαῦτά ἐστι [καὶ θερμά],[2] ὥστε αἵ τε περιττώσεις
ἄπεπτοι καὶ δυσώδεις αὐτῶν εἰσί καὶ ‹αἱ›[3] διαφυσή-
σεις ὁμοίως· καὶ διαφθειρομένων σήπεται ἡ ὑγρότης,
τῶν δὲ οὔ· οὐ γὰρ ἔχουσιν. |

[2] [καὶ θερμά] Hett (non vertit Gaza)
[3] ‹αἱ› Richards

other beasts smell it with pleasure), and when (*animals*) decay they are in fact malodorous, whereas many plants, when they decay and wither, become more fragrant? Is it because the cause of malodorousness is a certain lack of concoction of residue? And this is why sweat in some cases and at some times is such,[4] but especially in those for whom it is not usually such as the result of a disease. Also the winds[5] and belches of those whose (*residue*) is unconcocted are malodorous. And the same thing is also the cause of (*malodorousness*) in the flesh and in what is analogous to it (and by "analogous" I mean what exists in other animals in the place of flesh). For here too there is in some cases unconcocted residue. Therefore, when this putrefies, it is the cause of malodorousness in living and decaying (*animals*). And this is why fat and bones and hair are not malodorous, because the (*fat and bones*) are concocted, and the (*hair*) does not contain moisture. But in plants there is no residue. Or is there some in them too, but plants are naturally dry and warm, so that the fluid in them is easily concocted and not claylike? This is also clear from the earth: this is fragrant in hot places like Syria and Arabia, and the (*plants*) from there are fragrant, because they are dry and hot; and such things do not become putrid. But animals are not like this,[6] so that their residues are unconcocted and malodorous, and similarly their exhalations; and when they decay the moisture putrefies, but this does not happen with (*plants*), for they have no (*residues*).

---

[4] I.e., malodorous.   [5] Or "the breaths" (αἱ φῦσαι)—the author is referring either to expelled gas or to bad breath.

[6] I follow Hett and omit "and hot" (καὶ θερμά) as redundant: it seems to be included in "like this" (τοιαῦτά), i.e., dry and hot.

20   5. Διὰ τί τὰ δυσώδη θερμὰ ὄντα μᾶλλον δυσώδη
ἐστὶν ἢ ἐψυγμένα; ἢ ὅτι ἐστὶν ἡ ὀσμὴ ἀτμὸς καὶ
ἀπορροή τις; ὅ τ᾽ οὖν ἀτμὸς ὑπὸ θερμοῦ γίνεται, καὶ ἡ
ἀπορροή· κίνησις γάρ τίς ἐστιν, τὸ δὲ θερμὸν κινητικόν. τὸ δὲ ψυχρὸν τοὐναντίον στατικὸν καὶ συσταλτι-
25   κὸν καὶ φορὸν δὲ κάτω, τὸ δὲ | θερμὸν καὶ αἱ ὀσμαὶ
πᾶσαι ἀνωφερεῖς διὰ τὸ ἐν ἀέρι τε εἶναι καὶ τὸ
αἰσθητήριον αὐτῶν ἄνω εἶναι, μὴ κάτω· πρὸς γὰρ
ἐγκέφαλον περαίνουσα ἡ ὀσμὴ αἴσθησιν ποιεῖ.

      6. Διὰ τί, ἐάν τις σκόροδα φάγῃ, τὸ οὖρον ὄζει,
ἄλλων δὲ ἐχόντων ἰσχυρὰν ὀσμὴν οὐκ ὄζει ἐδεσθέν-
30   των; πότερον, | ὥσπερ τινὲς τῶν ἡρακλειτιζόντων
φασὶν, ὅτι ἀναθυμιᾶται, ὥσπερ ἐν τῷ ὅλῳ καὶ ἐν
τῷ σώματι, εἶτα πάλιν ψυχθὲν συνίσταται (ἐκεῖ μὲν
ὑγρόν, ἐνταῦθα δὲ οὖρον), ἡ <δ᾽>[4] ἐκ τῆς τροφῆς
ἀναθυμίασις, ἐξ οὗ ἐγένετο αὕτη συμμιγνυμένη, ποιεῖ
τὴν ὀσμήν; αὕτη γάρ ἐστιν, ὅταν μεταβάλλῃ. ἢ ἔδει |
35   καὶ τὰ ἄλλα τοῦτο ποιεῖν, ὅσα ἰσχυρὰς ὀσμὰς ἔχει;
νῦν δὲ οὐ ποιεῖ. ἔτι συγκρινόμενα ἐκ τῆς ἀτμίδος οὐκ
εἰς τὸ ἀρχαῖον ἔρχεται, οἷον οἶνος ἐξ οἴνου, ἀλλ᾽ οὐχ
908b ὕδωρ, ὥστε ‖ καὶ τοῦτο ψεῦδος. ἀλλ᾽ ὅτι μόνον φυσητ-
τικὸν τῆς κάτω κοιλίας τῶν ὀσμὴν ἐχόντων ἰσχυρὰν
ἅμα καὶ οὐρητικήν, τὰ δὲ ἄλλα ἄνω ποιεῖ, οἷον ἡ
ῥάφανος, [καὶ][5] τὰ πνεύματα, ἢ οὐκ οὐρητικά. τούτῳ[6]

4 <δ᾽> Marenghi[5]
5 [καὶ] Forster
6 τούτῳ β Barth. : κάτω cett. codd.

5.[7] Why are malodorous things more malodorous when hot than when they are cooled? Is it because smell is vapor and an emanation? Now vapor is due to heat, and so is an emanation; for it is a form of motion, and heat causes motion. But cold, by contrast, causes stagnation and contraction and movement downward, whereas heat and all smells move upward, because they are in air and their sense organ is above and not below; for smell produces a sensation when it penetrates to the brain.

6. Why, if someone eats garlic, does the urine have an odor,[8] but when other things having a strong smell are eaten it does not have an odor? Is it because, just as some of the Heracliteans say,[9] vaporizing takes place in the body just as it does in the universe, and then when it has cooled again there is condensation (moisture in the one case, urine in the other), and the vaporization from the nourishment, out of which this mixture comes, produces the smell? For smell occurs when there is change. Shouldn't all the other things that have strong smells also produce this result? But in fact they do not do so. Further, what is collected from vapor does not return to its original state—for instance, wine coming from (*the vaporization of*) wine, and not water—so that this too is false. But it is the case that of the things that both have a strong smell and are diuretic, (*garlic*) alone causes the production of wind in the lower stomach; but the others,[10] for instance the radish,

---

[7] Cf. *Pr.* 12.6, 10. Source: Thphr. *CP* 6.17, 5.

[8] It's unclear whether the author means a bad odor or specifically the odor of garlic.

[9] 22A15 and B12 D-K.

[10] I.e., the other things that have a strong smell.

δὲ τρία ὑπάρχει ταῦτα· καὶ γὰρ | οὐρητικόν, καὶ
πνεῦμα ποιεῖ, καὶ τοῦτο κάτω. ὁ δὲ τόπος ὁ πέριξ τὰ
αἰδοῖα καὶ τὴν κύστιν τῶν τοιούτων ἀπολαύει διὰ τὴν
γειτνίασιν, καὶ ὅτι πνευματικός ἐστιν· δηλοῖ δὲ ἡ
συντονία τοῦ αἰδοίου. δῆλον οὖν ὅτι ἀφικνεῖται τὸ
περίττωμα εἰς τὴν κύστιν αὐτοῦ μάλιστα τῶν τοιού-
10 των ἅμα τῷ πνεύματι, | ὃ μιγνύμενον ποιεῖ τοῦ οὔρου
τὴν ὀσμήν.

7. Διὰ τί τὰ στόματα μηδὲν ἐδηδοκότων, ἀλλὰ
νηστευσάντων, ὄζει μᾶλλον (ὃ καλεῖται νηστείας
ὄζειν[7]), φαγόντων δὲ οὔ,[8] ὅτε ἔδει μᾶλλον; ἢ ὅτι,
κενουμένης[9] τῆς κοιλίας, θερμότερος ὁ ἀὴρ γινόμενος
15 διὰ τὴν ἀκινησίαν σήπει τὸ | πνεῦμα καὶ τὰ φλεγμα-
τώδη περιττώματα; ὅτι δὲ θερμότερος γίνεται, σημεῖον ὅτι καὶ δίψαν ποιεῖ ἡ νηστεία μᾶλλον. φαγόντων δὲ
διὰ τὸ ἐλάττων εἶναι ἡ ὀσμὴ τῆς τῶν σιτίων παύεται·
κρατεῖ γὰρ τῆς θερμότητος ἡ τῶν σιτίων θερμότης,
ὥστε μηθὲν πάσχειν. |

20 8. Διὰ τί ἡ μασχάλη δυσωδέστατον τῶν τόπων;
πότερον ὅτι ἀπνούστατός ἐστιν; ἔστι δὲ ἡ δυσωδία ἐν
τοῖς τοιούτοις μάλιστα, διὰ τὸ σῆψιν γίνεσθαι ὑπὸ

---

[7] ὄζειν Sylburg : ὄζει codd.
[8] οὖ a β Barth. : οὐκέτι cett. codd.
[9] κενουμένης β : κινουμένης cett. codd.

---

[11] I.e., garlic.　　[12] I.e., the bladder's, though perhaps the
author meant to refer to the proximity of the region around both
the private parts and the bladder.

produce breaths in the upper (*stomach*) or are not diuretic. But these three things belong to this:[11] It is diuretic, it produces breath, and it does so in the lower (*stomach*). Now the region around the private parts and the bladder experience such things because of its[12] proximity, and because it is full of breath; the rigidity of the private parts makes this clear. It is clear, therefore, that its residue is more likely than that of any other such (*food*) to reach the bladder simultaneously with the breath, and mingling with it affect the smell of the urine.

7.[13] Why do the mouths of those who have eaten nothing, but are fasting, have more of an odor (what is called "having an odor of fasting"), but the mouths of those who have eaten do not, though they should have more of an odor? Is it because, as the stomach becomes empty, the air becoming hotter owing to the lack of motion causes the breath and the phlegmatic residues to putrefy? Now a sign that it becomes hotter is the fact that fasting also produces more thirst. But when people have eaten, because the smell is less than that of the food, it is abated; for the heat of the food masters its heat,[14] so that nothing is experienced.

8.[15] Why is the armpit the most malodorous of regions? Is it because it is the most lacking in air? Now such regions are especially malodorous because putrefaction is brought

---

13 Cf. [Arist./Alex.] *Supl.Pr.* 2.32.

14 Presumably the heat of the air from the stomach.

15 Cf. *Pr.* 2.6 and [Arist./Alex.] *Supl.Pr.* 2.99. Source: Thphr. *Sud.* 9.

τῆς ἡσυχίας τῆς ὑγρότητος.[10] ἢ διότι ἀκίνητος καὶ
ἀγύμναστος;

9. Διὰ τί οἱ τοῦ γράσου ὄζοντες, ὅταν ἀλείφωνται
25 μύρῳ, | δυσωδέστεροι γίνονται; ἢ διότι τοῦτο ἐπὶ
πολλῶν γίνεται, οἷον ὀξὺ καὶ γλυκὺ συμμιχθὲν τὸ
ὅλον γλυκύτερον ἐγένετο; εἶτα πάντες ἱδρώσαντες
δυσωδέστεροί εἰσι· τὸ δὲ μύρον θερμαντικόν ἐστιν,
ἱδρῶτας οὖν παρασκευάζει.

10. Διὰ τί τῶν ἐγκύρτων καὶ κυφοτέρων δυσοσμο-
30 τέρα καὶ | βαρυτέρα ἡ ὀσμὴ τοῦ πνεύματος; ἢ διότι
συγκέκλεισται ὁ τόπος ὁ περὶ τὸν πνεύμονα καὶ
ἀνέσπασται ἐκ τῆς εὐθυωρίας, ὥστε οὐκ εὔπνους,
ἀλλὰ σήπεται ἡ ἰκμὰς καὶ τὸ πνεῦμα μᾶλλον εἴσω
ἐγκατακλειόμενον;

11. Διὰ τί τὰ πολλὰ τῶν μύρων συνεξιδρῶσαι
35 δυσώδη, | ἔνια δὲ ἡδίω ἢ οὐ χείρω; ἢ ὅσα μὲν τῇ
κινήσει ἢ τρίψει[11] μεταβάλλοντα, χείρω ταῦτα,[12] ὅσα
δὲ μή, τοὐναντίον; ἔστι δὲ ἔνια τοιαῦτα, ὥσπερ καὶ
909a τῶν ἀνθῶν, ἐξ ὧν γίνονται ‖ αἱ εὐωδίαι, τὰ μὲν

---

[10] ὑγρότητος scripsi ex [Arist./Alex.] Supl.Pr. 2.99, 3 : ποι-
ότητος a β γ : πιότητος δ   [11] ante τρίψει add. τῇ Cᵃ
Alex.175   [12] ταῦτα Marenghi⁵ : τοιαῦτα codd. : ante
τοιαῦτα add. τὰ Cᵃ

---

[16] Or "the stillness of the fat" or "the quality of stillness," depending on which reading is accepted.
[17] Cf. [Arist./Alex.] Supl.Pr. 2.98. See also Pr. 22.13 and 20.33,
and Thphr. Sud. 10 and Od. 10.

about by the stillness of the moisture.[16] Or is it because it is lacking in movement and exercise?

9.[17] Why do those who have a goatlike odor, when they are anointed with perfume,[18] become more malodorous? Is it because this happens in many cases, for instance, when sharp and sweet are mixed the whole becomes sweeter? Thus everyone is more malodorous after sweating; and perfume is heat-producing, therefore it creates sweat.

10.[19] Why is the smell of the breath worse-smelling and heavier in those who are bent and stooping?[20] Is it because the region about the lungs is constricted and shifted out of a straight position, so that there isn't a free flow of breath, but rather the fluid and the breath enclosed within become putrefied?

11.[21] Why are most perfumes when combined with sweat malodorous, but some are more pleasant or not worse? Do all the things that change owing to movement or friction become worse, but those that do not do the opposite? Now there are some such (perfumes), just as there are some flowers as well, from which fragrances

---

[18] The word translated "perfumes" (μύρων) might also be rendered "ointments" or "unguents" or "myrrh oil." If the author has in mind specifically this last, then he is referring to the oil derived from the dried sap of trees in the genus *Commiphora*, which is used primarily in perfume.   [19] Apollonius (*Mir.* 37) quotes from this chapter, and refers to the *Problems* of Aristotle.

[20] The words I translate "those who are bent and stooping" (τῶν ἐγκύρτων καὶ κυφοτέρων) seem to be near synonyms and likely refer to one class of people, perhaps hunchbacks.

[21] Cf. *Pr.* 2.13, 13.3, 9, 20.33. Sources: Thphr. *Od.* 27–30 and 43.

τριβόμενα ἢ θερμαινόμενα ἢ ξηραινόμενα φαῦλα,
οἷον τὰ λευκόϊα, τὰ δὲ ὅμοια, οἷον τὰ ῥόδα. καὶ τῶν
μύρων δὴ ὅσα ἐκ τοιούτων ἐστί, μεταβάλλει, τὰ δὲ οὔ·
5 διὸ τὸ ῥόδινον ἥκιστα. καὶ δυσώδη δὲ φαίνεται | μᾶλ-
λον ὅσων οἱ ἱδρῶτες δυσώδεις, καὶ διὰ τὸ μίγνυσθαι
τῷ ἐναντίῳ, ὥσπερ τὸ μέλι μετὰ τοῦ ἁλὸς οὐ μᾶλλον
γλυκύ, ἀλλ᾽ ἧττον.

12. Διὰ τί πάντα μᾶλλον ὄζει κινούμενα; ἢ διότι
ἀναπίμπλησι τὸν ἀέρα; διαπέμπεται οὖν θᾶττον ἡ
10 ὀσμὴ πρὸς | τὴν αἴσθησιν.

arise, which when rubbed or heated or dried become foul, such as white violets, while others remain the same,[22] such as roses. And indeed, the perfumes that come from such (*plants*) change, but the others do not, which is why rose perfume changes least. Also (*perfume*) appears to be more malodorous on those whose sweat is malodorous, and this is because it is mixed with its opposite, just as honey mixed with salt is not more sweet, but less.

12.[23] Why do all things have more of an odor when in motion? Is it because they[24] fill up more air? Therefore, the smell is transmitted more quickly to sense perception.

[22] I.e., their odors do not become worse "when rubbed or heated or dried."

[23] Cf. *Pr.* 12.5 and [Arist./Alex.] *Supl.Pr.* 2.104.

[24] Or "their odors."

BOOK XIV

INTRODUCTION

Judging by its title, Book 14 deals with κρᾶσις—the basic meaning of which is "mixing," though it can also mean "temperament" and "climate." This last is its primary meaning in the present book, the topic of which is the effects of climate (in some cases, on temperament).

Although it is difficult to identify with certainty specific sources for each of the chapters of *Pr.* 14, it is clear that the questions they raise reflect the Hippocratic and Peripatetic interest in the effects of climate (or more broadly, locality) on the nature and character of humans and other living beings. The most relevant texts here are the Hippocratic *Airs Waters Places* and Aristotle's *HA* 7(8).28–29 and *Pol.* 7.7.

The subjects of the sixteen chapters making up Book 14 can be described as follows: climate and character (1, 8, 15, 16); climate and longevity (2, 7, 9, 10); various effects of living in wet regions (5, 6, 11, 12); and, miscellaneous (fevers [3], bowlegs [4], stifling heat [13], and eye color [14]).

ΟΣΑ ΠΕΡΙ ΚΡΑΣΕΙΣ[1]

1. Διὰ τί θηριώδεις τὰ ἔθη καὶ τὰς ὄψεις οἱ ἐν ταῖς
ὑπερβολαῖς ὄντες ἢ ψύχους ἢ καύματος; ἢ διὰ τὸ
αὐτό; ἡ γὰρ ἀρίστη κρᾶσις καὶ τῇ διανοίᾳ συμφέρει,
αἱ δὲ ὑπερβολαὶ ἐξιστᾶσιν, καὶ ὥσπερ τὸ σῶμα δια-
στρέφουσιν, οὕτω καὶ τὴν τῆς διανοίας κρᾶσιν.

2. Διὰ τί ἐν τῷ Πόντῳ ὁ σῖτος ἐαθεὶς ἐν τῷ ψύχει
πολλὰ ἔτη γίνεται ἄκοπος; ἢ ὅτι ἐξικμάζεται τὸ ἀλλό-
τριον | ὑγρὸν μετὰ τοῦ θερμοῦ, ὥσπερ ἐν ταῖς σταφυ-
λαῖς; ἔνια μὲν γὰρ ὑπὸ τοῦ ψυχροῦ, ἔνια δὲ ἅμα τῷ
θερμῷ.

3. Διὰ τί ἐν τῇ ψυχροτάτῃ ὥρᾳ[2] οἱ καῦσοι μᾶλλον
γίνονται; ἢ διότι ἀντιπεριίστησι τὸ ψῦχος εἴσω τὴν
θερμότητα; ἐν δὲ τῷ θέρει τοὐναντίον συμβαίνει· τὰ

909a
15

20

---

[1] κράσεις α β : κράσεως γ δ
[2] ὥρᾳ Ruelle cf. Pr. 1.29, 862b26 : χώρᾳ codd.

---

[1] The topic of this chapter is among those discussed in HA
7(8).28–29, Pol. 7.7, and Hp. Aër 12–13, 23–24.
[2] The two occurrences of κρᾶσις in this chapter cover all
three of its meanings: "climate-mix" is my attempt to pack two of

PROBLEMS CONNECTED
WITH CLIMATE

1.[1] Why are those living in conditions of excessive cold or heat beastlike with respect to character and appearance? Is it for the same reason (*in both cases*)? For the best climate-mix benefits thought, but the excesses disturb it, and just as they distort the body, so too do they affect the temperament of thought.[2]

2.[3] Why, in the Pontus, does grain left in the cold remain intact for many years?[4] Is it because the extraneous moisture is evaporated together with the heat, just as it is with grapes? For in some things (*the moisture is evaporated*) by the cold, whereas in others at the same time with the heat.

3.[5] Why do intense fevers occur more during the coldest season? Is it because the cold holds the heat inside? But in the summer the opposite occurs: the inner parts

them into one word, as is called for by the context; κρᾶσις in the sense of "temperament" appears at the end of the chapter.

3 Cf. Thphr. *CP* 4.15.4–16.4, *HP* 8.11.3.

4 Or "left in the cold for many years remain intact . . . "; ἄκοπος ("intact") could also be rendered "not worm-eaten."

5 Cf. *Pr.* 1.20 and 29, and see also Hp. *Morb*. 1.29.

25 εἴσω ψυχρότερα. | ὁ δὲ καῦσος [πυρετὸς]³ τῶν ἔξω
κατεψυγμένων τὰ ἔσωθεν θερμότερα ὑποβάλλει.⁴

4. Διὰ τί οἱ Αἰθίοπες καὶ οἱ Αἰγύπτιοι βλαισοί
εἰσιν; ἢ διότι ὑπὸ τοῦ⁵ θερμοῦ, ὥσπερ καὶ τὰ ξύλα
διαστρέφεται ξηραινόμενα,⁶ οὕτω καὶ τὰ τῶν ζῴων
30 σώματα; δηλοῦσι δὲ καὶ | αἱ τρίχες· οὐλοτέρας γὰρ
ἔχουσιν, ἡ δὲ οὐλότης ἐστὶν ὥσπερ βλαισότης τῶν
τριχῶν.

5. Διὰ τί ἐν τοῖς νοτίοις μᾶλλον θηλυτοκοῦσιν αἱ
ὀχεῖαι; ἢ ὅτι τὸ πλεῖον ὑγρὸν βραδύτερον παχύνεται·
ἐν δὲ τοῖς νοτίοις διὰ τὴν ὑγρότητα τῆς κράσεως
ὑγρότερον τὸ σπέρμα γίνεται. |

35 6. Διὰ τί ἐν τοῖς ἑλώδεσι τὰ μὲν ἐν τῇ κεφαλῇ ἕλκη
ταχὺ ὑγιάζεται, τὰ δὲ ἐν ταῖς κνήμαις μόλις; ἢ ὅτι
βαρεῖα ἡ ὑγρότης διὰ τὸ γεώδης εἶναι, τὰ δὲ βαρέα
εἰς τὸ κάτω ὑποχωρεῖ; τὰ μὲν οὖν ἄνω εὔπεπτα διὰ τὸ
ὑποκεχωρηκέναι εἰς τὸ κάτω, τὰ δὲ κάτω πολλῆς γέμει |
40 περιττώσεως⁷ καὶ εὐσήπτου. ||

909b 7. Διὰ τί οἱ μὲν ἐν τοῖς εὐπνόοις τόποις βραδέως
γηράσκουσιν, οἱ δὲ ἐν τοῖς κοίλοις καὶ ἑλώδεσι ταχέως; ἢ τὸ γῆρας σηπεδών τίς ἐστιν; σήπεται δὲ τὸ

³ πυρετὸς seclusi (cf. Hsch. K 1920 καῦσος· ὁ πυρετός) :
καῦσος hic adjectivum Marenghi³, cf. Hp. Epid. 7.10, [Gal.]
Urin. (19.622K) : post πυρετὸς add. ‹ἐν ᾧ› Sylburg
⁴ ἔσωθεν θερμότερα ὑποβάλλει β (cf. Barth., interiora cali-
diora facit) : ἔσω θερμότητι ὑπερβάλλει cett. codd.
⁵ τοῦ β : om. cett. codd.   ⁶ ξηραινόμενα : θερμαινόμενα β Trap.   ⁷ ante περιττώσεως add. τῆς γ

are colder. And the intense fever makes the parts within warmer, while the outside parts are cool.

4. Why are Ethiopians and Egyptians bowlegged?[6] Is it due to the heat, and just as planks are warped when they become dry, so too are the bodies of animals? Now their hair reveals this as well: for they have curlier hair, and curliness is like a crookedness of the hair.

5.[7] Why is it that in damp regions,[8] copulation is more likely to produce females? Is it because the greater quantity of moisture thickens more slowly? Now in damp regions, owing to the amount of moisture (*characteristic*) of the climate, the seed becomes moister.

6.[9] Why is it that in marshes wounds on the head heal quickly, but those on the legs slowly? Is it because the moisture is heavy owing to its being earthy, and what is heavy moves downward? Therefore, the upper parts are easily concocted[10] because the moisture has withdrawn to the lower parts, but the lower parts are full of many, easily putrefied residues.

7.[11] Why do those living in places with a good flow of air grow old slowly, but those living in hollow and marshy places quickly? Is old age a sort of putrefaction? Now what

---

6 Literally, "twisted" or "crooked" (βλαισοί), though "bow-legged" is a standard meaning of βλαισός.

7 Sources: GA 776b33–35 and HA 573b32–574a3.

8 Or "in regions where the wind comes from the south" (ἐν τοῖς νοτίοις).

9 This chapter is virtually identical to Pr. 1.18.

10 The parallel text of Pr. 1.18 has "cleared out" (ἔκκριτα).

11 See Hp. Aër 7 and Vict. 3.37.

441

ἠρεμοῦν, τὸ δὲ ἐν κινήσει ὂν ἢ ὅλως ἀσαπὲς ἢ ἧττον
5 τοῦτο πάσχει, οἷον τὸ | ὕδωρ. ἐν μὲν οὖν τοῖς ὑψηλοῖς
διὰ τὴν εὔπνοιαν ὁ ἀὴρ ἐν κινήσει ἐστίν, ἐν δὲ τοῖς
κοίλοις μένει. ἔτι δὲ ἐκεῖ μὲν διὰ τὴν κίνησιν ἀεὶ
καθαρὸς ὁ ἀὴρ καὶ ἕτερος γίνεται, ἐν δὲ τοῖς ἑλώδεσι
μένει.

8. Διὰ τί οἱ μὲν ἐν τοῖς θερμοῖς τόποις δειλοί εἰσιν,
10 οἱ | δὲ ἐν τοῖς ψυχροῖς ἀνδρεῖοι; ἢ ὅτι ἐναντίως τοῖς
τόποις καὶ ταῖς ὥραις ἡ φύσις ἔχει, διὰ τὸ ὁμοίως
ἐχόντων ἀνάγκη διακαίεσθαι[8] ταχέως; ἀνδρεῖοι δέ
εἰσιν οἱ τὴν φύσιν θερμοί, δειλοὶ δὲ οἱ κατεψυγμένοι.
συμβαίνει δὲ τοὺς μὲν ἐν τοῖς θερμοῖς ὄντας κατ-
15 εψῦχθαι, τοὺς δὲ ἐν τοῖς ψυχροῖς ἐκτεθερμάνθαι | τὴν
φύσιν. μεγάλοι δὲ ἄμφω εἰσίν, οἱ μὲν ἐν τοῖς ψυχροῖς
διὰ τὴν ἐν αὑτοῖς σύμφυτον θερμότητα, οἱ δ' ἐν τοῖς
θερμοῖς διὰ τὴν ἐν τῷ τόπῳ· ἐν γὰρ τοῖς θερμοῖς καὶ
ὑπὸ τοῦ θερμοῦ αὐξάνονται. τὸ δὲ ψῦχος πιλητικόν
ἐστιν. ἅτε οὖν τῶν μὲν ἐν αὑτοῖς ἐχόντων τὴν ἀρχὴν |
20 τῆς αὐξήσεως σφοδράν, τῶν δὲ οὐ κωλυομένων ὑπὸ
τῆς ἔξωθεν ψυχρότητος, εἰκότως ἐπὶ πολὺ τὴν αὔξησιν
ἐπιδέχονται. οἱ δὲ περὶ ἡμᾶς ἧττον διὰ τὸ ἐλάττω τε
ἔχειν τὴν ἀρχὴν ἐν αὑτοῖς, καὶ διὰ τὸ τοὺς ἐν τοῖς
ψυχροῖς συμπιλεῖσθαι. |

8 διακαίεσθαι : fort. διακναίεσθαι (cf. Pr. 14.16, 910b1–2)

remains still putrefies, but what is in motion does not putrefy at all or does so less, for example water. In high places, therefore, because of the good flow of air, the air is in motion, but in hollow ones it remains still. Further, because of the motion, the air there is always pure and fresh,[12] but in marshy ones it keeps still.

8.[13] Why are those living in hot places cowardly, while those living in cold ones are courageous? Is it because nature is the opposite in places and in seasons, since, if they[14] were the same, people would of necessity be quickly destroyed?[15] Now those who are naturally hot are courageous, whereas those who have been cooled are cowardly. And it happens that those living in hot regions are cooled, whereas those living in cold regions have been heated naturally. And both (classes of people) are large, those in cold places because of the innate heat in them, those in hot ones because of the (heat) inherent in the place; for people grow in the heat and due to the heat. But the cold causes contraction. Therefore, since the former have within themselves the principle of growth to a high degree, whereas the latter are not prevented by the external cold, it is reasonable that they should admit of considerable growth. But those living around us have less (growth), both because they have less of the principle (of growth) in themselves, and because those living in the cold are contracted by it.

---

[12] Literally, "different" (ἕτερος). [13] Cf. *Pr.* 14.16.

[14] I.e., the nature of places (hot or cold) and the nature of seasons (hot or cold). [15] Literally, "burned through" (διακαίεσθαι), though cf. *Mete.* 382b8.

25   9. Διὰ τί μακρόβιοι μᾶλλόν εἰσιν οἱ ἐν τοῖς θερμοῖς τόποις οἰκοῦντες; ἢ διὰ τὸ ξηροτέραν ἔχειν τὴν φύσιν, τὸ δὲ ξηρότερον ἀσαπέστερον εἶναι καὶ πολυχρονι-ώτερον, τὸν δὲ θάνατον οἷον σῆψίν τινα εἶναι; ἢ διότι ὁ μὲν θάνατός ἐστι ψύξις τοῦ ἐντὸς θερμοῦ, καταψύχε-

30 ται δὲ πᾶν ὑπὸ τοῦ | περιέχοντος καὶ ψυχροτέρου; ἔστι δὲ ὁ περιέχων ἀὴρ ἐν μὲν τοῖς ἀλεεινοῖς τόποις θερ-μός, ἐν δὲ τοῖς ψυχροῖς ψυχρός, ὥστε θᾶττον καὶ μᾶλλον φθείρει τὸ ἐν αὐτοῖς θερμόν.

    10. Διὰ τί οἱ ἐν τοῖς θερμοῖς τόποις μακροβιώτεροι;

35 ἢ | ὅτι μᾶλλον τὸ θερμὸν καὶ τὸ ὑγρὸν σώζουσιν; ὁ γὰρ θάνατος ἡ τούτων φθορά.

    11. Διὰ τί ἐν τοῖς ἑλώδεσι τόποις ὑπνωδέστεροι γινόμεθα; ἢ διότι κατεψυγμένοι μᾶλλον ἐν αὑτοῖς ἐσμεν, ἡ δὲ κατάψυξις ἡσυχία τις οὖσα, παρασκευά-

40 ζει ὕπνον, ὁ δὲ ὕπνος | ἐν τῷ ἡσυχάζειν παραγίνεται; ||

910a 12. Διὰ τί οἱ ἐν τοῖς πλοίοις εὔχροοι, ἐπὶ ὕδατος διαιτώμενοι, μᾶλλον τῶν ἐν τοῖς ἕλεσιν; ἢ ἡ ὥρα καὶ τὸ εὔπνουν αἴτιον; ὠχροὺς δὲ τὸ ὕδωρ ποιεῖ, ὅταν σήπηται, ὃ πάσχει δι᾽ ἀκινησίαν· διὸ ἐν τοῖς ἑλώδεσιν ὕπωχροι. |

5   13. Διὰ τί ἐν τοῖς χειμερινοῖς χωρίοις πνίγη σφο-δρὰ γίνεται πολλά, καὶ μᾶλλον ἢ ἐν τοῖς ἀλεεινοῖς; πότερον διὰ τὴν ὑγρότητα τοῦ ἀέρος; ἀπὸ γὰρ τῆς αὐτῆς θερμότητος ὕδωρ θερμότερον γίνεται τοῦ ἀέρος, ὥστε καὶ ὁ ἀὴρ ‹ὁ›[9] ὑγρότερος τοῦ ξηροῦ.[10] ἢ οὐδὲ

9 ‹ὁ› Ross apud Forster
10 ξηροῦ Ross ex Gaza, cf. PPA : θερμοῦ codd.

9.[16] Why are those living in hot places longer-lived? Is it because they have a drier nature, and what is drier is less likely to putrefy and so is longer-lasting, and death is as it were a sort of putrefaction? Or is it because death is a cooling of the internal heat, and everything is cooled by what is surrounding it and colder? But the surrounding air is hot in warm places and cold in cold ones, so that it more quickly and more effectively destroys the heat within them.

10. Why are those living in hot places longer-lived? Is it because they better preserve their heat and moisture? For death is the destruction of these.

11.[17] Why do we become sleepier in marshy places? Is it because we are cooled more in those places, and cooling, being a sort of rest, produces sleep, and sleep accompanies being at rest?

12.[18] Why do those living on board ship have good complexions, spending their time on water, more than those living in marshes? Are the weather[19] and the good flow of air responsible? Now water makes people pale, when it putrefies, which happens because of a lack of movement; this is why people living in marshy regions are pale.

13.[20] Why does extreme stifling heat occur frequently in wintry regions, even more than in warm ones? Is it because of the moisture in the air? For from the same heat water becomes hotter than air, and so the moister air (*becomes hotter*) than the dry. Or is it that the air is not hotter

---

[16] *Long.* 465a9–10, 466b16–18 is the likely source for *Pr.* 14.9 and 10.   [17] Cf. *Pr.* 6.5 and 18.1.

[18] See Hp. *Aër* 7 and *Vict.* 3.37. Cf. *Pr.* 2.30 and 38.3–4.

[19] Or "the season."

[20] Cf. *Pr.* 25.6 and Thphr.(?) *Sign.* 48.

10 ἔστι θερμότερος[11] ὁ ἀὴρ ἐν τοῖς τόποις | τοῖς τοιούτοις,
ἀλλὰ φαίνεται παρὰ τὸ ἐναντίον, ὥσπερ ὁ ἐκ νεφέλης
ἥλιος παρὰ τὸ ἐκ τῆς σκιᾶς θιγγάνεσθαι·[12]

14. Διὰ τί οἱ πρὸς μεσημβρίαν οἰκοῦντες μᾶλλόν
εἰσι μελανόφθαλμοι; ἢ γλαυκὰ μέν ἐστι τὰ ὄμματα
δι᾽ ὑπερβολὴν τοῦ ἐντὸς θερμοῦ, μέλανα δὲ διὰ τὴν
15 τούτου ἀπουσίαν, | ὥσπερ καὶ Ἐμπεδοκλῆς φησίν;
καθάπερ οὖν τῶν πρὸς ἄρκτον οἰκούντων γλαυκὰ
⟨τὰ⟩[13] ὄμματά ἐστι τῷ τὸ ἐντὸς θερμὸν κωλύεσθαι
διεκπίπτειν διὰ τὸ ἐκτὸς ψυχρόν, οὕτω τῶν πρὸς
μεσημβρίαν οἰκούντων τὸ μὲν ὑγρὸν διὰ τὸ περιέχον
θερμὸν οὐκ ἐκπίπτει, τὸ δὲ θερμὸν μηδενὸς ἀντιφράτ-
20 τοντος | ἐκπίπτει, τὸ δὲ λειπόμενον ὑγρὸν μέλαν ποιεῖ·
τῇ γὰρ τοῦ φωτὸς ἀπουσίᾳ τὸ λειπόμενόν ἐστι σκοτῶδες. ἢ τοῖς τοῦ λοιποῦ σώματος χρώμασιν ὁμοιοῦται τὸ ἐν τῷ ὀφθαλμῷ χρῶμα; διὸ τῶν πρὸς ἄρκτον
λευκῶν ὄντων γλαυκὰ τὰ ὄμματα (τοῦ γὰρ λευκοῦ
25 τοῦτο ἐγγὺς τὸ χρῶμα), καὶ τῶν | πρὸς μεσημβρίαν
μελάνων ὄντων μέλανα καὶ τὰ ὄμματα.

15. Διὰ τί οἱ ἐν τοῖς θερμοῖς τόποις σοφώτεροί
εἰσιν ἢ ἐν τοῖς ψυχροῖς; πότερον διὰ τὸ αὐτὸ δι᾽ ὅπερ
καὶ οἱ γέροντες τῶν νέων; οἱ μὲν γὰρ διὰ τὴν ψυχρότητα τοῦ τόπου ἐπανιούσης τῆς φύσεως αὐτῶν θερ-

11 θερμότερος Ross ex Gaza : ξηρότερος codd.
12 θιγγάνεσθαι : φιγγάνεσθαι β : θερμαίνεσθαι Hett
13 ⟨τὰ⟩ Bekker

in such places, but only appears so in contrast to the opposite,[21] just as the sun coming from behind a cloud (*appears hotter*) in contrast to the state of being covered in shadow?

14.[22] Why do those living in the south tend to have dark eyes? Are eyes light-blue because of the excess of internal heat, and dark because of the absence of this, just as Empedocles says?[23] Therefore, just as the eyes of those living in the north are light-blue through the internal heat being prevented from escaping because of the external cold, so the moisture (*in the eyes*) of those living in the south does not escape, because of the surrounding heat, whereas the heat escapes because nothing obstructs it, and the moisture that remains produces the dark color; for in the absence of light, what remains is dark.[24] Or is the color of the eye similar to the color of the rest of the body? This is why, as those living in the north are fair-skinned, their eyes are light-blue (for this color is akin to fair),[25] and as those living in the south are dark, their eyes too are dark.

15.[26] Why are those living in hot places wiser than those living in cold ones? Is it for the same reason for which the old (*are wiser*) than the young? For those (*living in cold places*) are much hotter, because their nature resists ow-

---

[21] Perhaps the author is saying that "in wintry regions" the air on warmer days seems hotter than in other places because of the stark contrast with the air on colder days.

[22] Source: *GA* 5.1 (esp. 779a26–b34).   [23] See 31A91 D-K = Arist. *Sens.* 437b9–14 and *GA* 779b15–20.

[24] Elsewhere in the chapter, "dark" translates forms of the word μέλας (which can also mean "black"). But here, "dark" translates σκοτῶδες (from σκότος), which refers to the lack of light.   [25] Re. "fair-skinned" and "fair": literally, "white."

[26] See *Pol.* 7.7.

30   μότεροί εἰσι πολύ, ὥστε | λίαν μεθύουσιν ἐοίκασιν, καὶ
οὐκ εἰσὶ ζητητικοὶ, ἀλλὰ ἀνδρεῖοι καὶ εὐέλπιδες· οἱ δὲ
ἐν τοῖς ἀλεεινοῖς νήφουσι διὰ τὸ κατεψῦχθαι. πανταχοῦ δὲ οἱ φοβούμενοι τῶν θαρρούντων μᾶλλον ἐπι-
χειροῦσι ζητεῖν, ὥστε καὶ εὑρίσκουσι μᾶλλον. ἢ διὰ
τὸ πολυχρονιώτερον τὸ γένος εἶναι τοῦτο, τοὺς δὲ ὑπὸ
35   τοῦ | κατακλυσμοῦ ἀπολέσθαι, ὥστε εἶναι καθάπερ
νέους πρὸς γέροντας τοὺς ἐν τοῖς ψυχροῖς τόποις πρὸς
τοὺς ἐν τοῖς θερμοῖς οἰκοῦντας;

    16. Διὰ τί οἱ μὲν ἐν τοῖς θερμοῖς τόποις δειλοί
εἰσιν, οἱ δὲ ἐν τοῖς ψυχροῖς ἀνδρεῖοι; ἢ ὅτι ἐναντίως
910b   τοῖς τόποις καὶ || ταῖς ὥραις ἡ φύσις ἔχει, διὰ τὸ
ὁμοίως ἐχόντων διανκαίεσθαι[14] ἂν ταχέως; ἀνδρεῖοι δέ
εἰσιν οἱ τὴν φύσιν θερμοί, δειλοὶ δὲ οἱ κατεψυγμένοι.
συμβαίνει δὴ[15] τοὺς μὲν ἐν τοῖς θερμοῖς ὄντας κατα-
5   ψύχεσθαι (ἀραιοῦ γὰρ ὄντος αὐτοῖς τοῦ | σώματος, τὸ
θερμὸν αὐτῶν ἔξω διεκπίπτει), τοὺς δ' ἐν τοῖς ψυχροῖς
ἐκτεθερμάνθαι τὴν φύσιν διὰ τὸ ἐκ τοῦ ἐκτὸς ψύχους
πυκνοῦσθαι τὴν σάρκα, πυκνουμένης δὲ ἐντὸς συ-
στέλλεσθαι τὸ θερμόν.

[14] διακναίεσθαι β : διακνάεσθαι α γ δ : διακάεσθαι Sylburg
[15] δὴ α β δ : δ' οὖν γ : δὲ x et Barth. (cf. Pr. 14.8, 909b13)

ing to the coldness of the place, so that they're a lot like drunken people, and are not inquisitive, but courageous and cheerful; but those living in warm places are sober because they are cool.[27] And everywhere those who feel fear attempt to inquire more than those who are confident, and so they discover more. Or is it because this race[28] has lasted longer, while the others have been destroyed in the flood,[29] so that the young are to the old just as those living in cold places are to those in hot ones?

16.[30] Why are those living in hot places cowardly, whereas those living in cold ones are courageous? Is it because nature is the opposite in places and in seasons, since, if they[31] were the same, people would be quickly destroyed? Now those who are naturally hot are courageous, while those who have been cooled are cowardly. Of course, it happens that those living in hot regions are cooled (for as their bodies are porous, the heat escapes to the outside), but those living in cold regions have been heated naturally, because the flesh is thickened by the external cold, and when it has thickened the heat is collected within.

[27] The assumption is that whereas the bodies of people living in cold regions work to stay warm, and so are hotter by nature, the bodies of those living in hot regions work to stay cool, and so are cooler by nature.

[28] I.e., the race or class (γένος) of people who live in hot places.

[29] On the idea of an ancient, civilization-destroying flood, see, e.g., Pl. *Lg.* 3.677a–680a, Arist. *Mete.* 339b27ff. and *Pol.* 1329b25ff.

[30] Cf. *Pr.* 14.8.

[31] I.e., the nature of places (hot or cold) and the nature of seasons (hot or cold).

BOOK XV

INTRODUCTION

Book 15 deals with mathematics (chs. 1–3) and astronomy (chs. 4–13). Given the unusual nature of the mss. evidence for the title of this book (see textual n. 1), together with the fact that the opening to ch. 4 is missing, I think it possible that *Pr.* 15 combines (parts of) what were once two separate sets of problems: mathematical ones (ὅσα μαθηματικά) and those connected to celestial matters (ὅσα περὶ τὰ οὐράνια). Such a division, however, may have come late, for according to Aristotle and other early Peripatetics, astronomy is a type of mathematics (and indeed, chs. 4–13, though on celestial matters, are mathematical in nature).

The mathematical problems are fairly basic, raising questions about the name "diameter" (chs. 1–2) and the decimal number system (3). Broadly speaking, the chapters on astronomy all deal with how celestial objects appear to us. This simply is the topic of chs. 4, 7, and 8. But the topics of the others fall under this category as well: shadows from the sun and (in one case) from the moon (5, 9, 10, 13); the effect of sunlight passing through a quadrilateral (6); solar eclipses (11); and parhelia (12).

INTRODUCTION

The sources for most of the chapters of *Pr.* 15 cannot be determined with any certainty or even probability. Aristotle's *Meteorology* 3.2 and 6 seem the clear source for ch. 12. The work of Euclid and Aristarchus may have been sources for some of the others.

ΟΣΑ ΜΑΘΗΜΑΤΙΚΗΣ
ΜΕΤΕΧΕΙ ΘΕΩΡΙΑΣ ΑΠΛΩΣ
ΚΑΙ ΟΣΑ ΠΕΡΙ ΤΑ ΟΥΡΑΝΙΑ[1]

910b
10

1. Διὰ τί διάμετρος καλεῖται μόνη τῶν δίχα διαιρουσῶν τὰ εὐθύγραμμα ἡ ἐκ γωνίας εἰς γωνίαν ἀχθεῖσα γραμμή; ἢ ὅτι διάμετρος δίχα διαιρεῖ, καθάπερ τοὔνομα ὑποσημαίνει, οὐ φθείρουσα τὸ μετρούμενον;

15 ἡ μὲν οὖν κατὰ τὰς συνθέσεις | διαιροῦσα (λέγω δὲ τὰς γωνίας) διάμετρος ἔσται· οὐ γὰρ φθείρει, ἀλλὰ διαιρεῖ, καθάπερ οἱ τὰ στρατιωτικὰ σκεύη διαιροῦντες. ἡ δὲ κατὰ τὰς γραμμὰς σύνθετα τέμνουσα φθείρει· σύγκειται γὰρ τὸ εὐθύγραμμον κατὰ τὰς γωνίας.

2. Διὰ τί διάμετρος καλεῖται; ἢ διότι δίχα μόνη

---

[1] ὅσα μαθηματικῆς μετέχει θεωρίας ἁπλῶς καὶ ὅσα περὶ τὰ οὐράνια scripsi (cf. Barth. *Circa mathematica et circa celestia* et Gaza *eorum quae ad res mathematicas pertinent et ad caelestia*) : ὅσα μαθηματικῆς μετέχει θεωρίας codd. (ante ὅσα add. τὰ δὲ ἔνεστιν Y^a, add. ἀριστοτέλους τὰ δὲ ἔνεστιν Ap) : post θεωρίας add. ἁπλῶς καὶ ὅσα περὶ τὰ οὐράνια, ὅσα περὶ τὰ ἄψυχα, ὅσα περὶ τὰ ἔμψυχα, ὅσα μαθηματικά Y^a Ap

PROBLEMS INVOLVED IN MATHEMATICAL THEORY GENERALLY, AND THOSE CONNECTED TO CELESTIAL MATTERS

1.[1] Why, of those lines dividing rectilinear figures into two parts, is the line drawn from angle to angle alone called a diameter?[2] Is it because the diameter divides into two parts, just as its name implies,[3] without destroying what is measured out? The line dividing at the points of composition (I mean the angles), then, will be a diameter; for it does not destroy (*the figure*), but divides it, just like those dividing military implements. But the line cutting composite figures through their lines destroys them; for a rectilinear figure is constructed at its angles.

2. Why is it called a diameter? Is it because it alone di-

---

[1] See Euc., *El*. 1.Prop. 34, cf. 1.Def. 17.

[2] What we would call the diagonal. In Aristotle, διάμετρος can refer to both the diameter of a circle and the diagonal of a rectilinear figure.

[3] The word διάμετρος comes from διά ("through," "across") and μέτρον ("a measure").

455

20 διαιρεῖ· | ὥσπερ οὖν εἴ τις εἴποι διχάμετρός² ἐστιν. καὶ
διὰ τί³ μόνη τῶν δίχα τοῦτο καλεῖται; ἢ ὅτι κατὰ μέλη
ἢ κέκαμπται μόνη διαιρεῖ, αἱ δὲ ἄλλαι κατὰ πλευράς;

3. Διὰ τί πάντες ἄνθρωποι, καὶ βάρβαροι καὶ
Ἕλληνες, εἰς τὰ δέκα καταριθμοῦσι, καὶ οὐκ εἰς ἄλλον
25 ἀριθμόν, οἷον | β′, γ′, δ′, ε′, εἶτα πάλιν ἐπαναδιπλοῦ-
σιν, ἐν πέντε, δύο πέντε, ὥσπερ ἕνδεκα, δώδεκα; οὐδ᾽
αὖ ἐξωτέρω παυσάμενοι τῶν δέκα, εἶτα ἐκεῖθεν ἐπανα-
διπλοῦσιν; ἔστι μὲν γὰρ ἕκαστος τῶν ἀριθμῶν ὁ
ἔμπροσθεν καὶ ἓν ἢ δύο, καὶ οὗτος⁴ ἄλλος τις, ἀριθμοῦσι δ᾽ ὅμως ὁρίσαντες ἄχρι τῶν δέκα. οὐ γὰρ δὴ
30 ἀπὸ | τύχης γε αὐτὸ ποιοῦντες ⟨πάντες⟩⁵ φαίνονται
καὶ ἀεί· τὸ δὲ ἀεὶ καὶ ἐπὶ πάντων οὐκ ἀπὸ τύχης, ἀλλὰ
φυσικόν. πότερον ὅτι τὰ δέκα τέλειος ἀριθμός; ἔχων
γὰρ πάντα τὰ τοῦ ἀριθμοῦ εἴδη, ἄρτιον, περιττόν,
τετράγωνον, κύβον, μῆκος, ἐπίπεδον, πρῶτον, σύνθε-
35 τον. ἢ ὅτι ἀρχὴ ἡ δεκάς; ἓν γὰρ καὶ δύο | καὶ τρία καὶ
τέτταρα γίνεται δεκάς. ἢ ὅτι τὰ φερόμενα σώματα
ἐννέα; ἢ ὅτι ἐν δέκα ἀναλογίαις τέτταρες κυβικοὶ
ἀριθμοὶ ἀποτελοῦνται, ἐξ ὧν φασιν ἀριθμῶν οἱ Πυθα-

---

² διχάμετρός Sylburg : διάμετρός codd.
³ διὰ τί Bekker : διότι codd.
⁴ οὗτος : οὕτως Ruelle (dub. Bekker)
⁵ ⟨πάντες⟩ Bussemaker

---

⁴ διχάμετρός, from δίχα ("into two parts").
⁵ Aside from works of the Pythagoreans (see e.g. Philolaus
44B11 D-K), possible sources for this chapter are Arist. *Metaph.*
A 5 or some other Peripatetic discussion of the Pythagoreans, or

vides into two parts? Therefore, it is just as if one should
say it is a dichameter.[4] And why, of the lines dividing into
two parts, is it alone called this? Is it because it alone divides where the limbs are bent, whereas the others divide
at the sides?

3.[5] Why do all people, both barbarians and Greeks,
count up to ten, and not to another number, such as 2, 3, 4,
5, and then repeat them again, one-five, two-five, just as
(*they count*) eleven, twelve?[6] Or again, why do they not
stop (*at some number*) beyond ten, and then repeat from
there? For each of the numbers is the preceding (*number*)
plus one or two, and this is some other (*number*), but nevertheless they count by setting the limit up to the tens. For
indeed, it is not from chance that all people plainly do in
truth do this and always; but what is always the case and for
all people is not from chance, but natural. Is it because ten
is a perfect number? For it is a number containing every
kind of number: even and odd, square and cube, length
and plane, prime and composite. Or is it because ten is the
origin?[7] For one and two and three and four become ten.
Or is it because the moving bodies are nine?[8] Or is it because in ten (*compounded*) ratios there are completed four
cubic numbers, from which numbers the Pythagoreans say

some other relevant work known to the Lyceum (e.g. Speusippus,
On Pythagorean Numbers).

[6] Literally, "one-ten" (ἕνδεκα), "two-ten" (δώδεκα).

[7] Or "source" or "principle" (ἀρχή).

[8] And the earth makes ten? According to the Pythagoreans,
the ten moving celestial bodies are the Earth, the Counter-Earth,
the Sun, the Moon, the five planets, and the fixed sphere of the
stars. (See Arist. *Metaph.* 986a8–12.)

γόρειοι τὸ πᾶν συνεστάναι; ἢ ὅτι πάντες ὑπῆρξαν
ἄνθρωποι ἔχοντες δέκα δακτύλους; οἷον οὖν ψήφους
911a ἔχοντες τοῦ οἰκείου ‖ ἀριθμοῦ, τούτῳ τῷ πλήθει καὶ
τἆλλα ἀριθμοῦσιν. μόνοι δὲ ἀριθμοῦσι τῶν Θρᾳκῶν
γένος τι εἰς τέτταρα, διὰ τὸ ὥσπερ τὰ παιδία μὴ
δύνασθαι μνημονεύειν ἐπὶ πολύ, μηδὲ χρῆσιν μηδενὸς
εἶναι πολλοῦ αὐτοῖς. |

5   4. . . . . ὅτι[6] ἡ γῆ κέντρον· ἀεὶ γὰρ ὅμοια τὰ
φαινόμενα ἡμῖν σχήματα. ‹οὐ›[7] δοκεῖ τοῦτο εἶναι, ἐὰν
μὴ ἀπὸ τοῦ μέσου τις θεωρῇ, ἀλλ' ὁτὲ μὲν τρίγωνα,
ὁτὲ δὲ τραπέζια, ὁτὲ δὲ ἀλλοῖα. ἐδόκει ‹δὲ ἄν›[8] ἡ γῆ
μέσον ἡμῖν, εἰ ἀπὸ τούτων ἔνι ἡμᾶς θεωρεῖν. οὔσης
γὰρ σφαιροειδοῦς τῆς γῆς ταὐτὸ κέντρον τούτου καὶ
10   τῆς γῆς | ἔσται. ἡμεῖς δὲ ἐπάνω τῆς γῆς οἰκοῦμεν,
ὥστε οὐκ ἀπὸ τούτου, ἀλλὰ τὸ ἥμισυ τῆς διαμέτρου
ἀφεστῶσιν ἡμῖν τοιαῦτα φαίνεται. τί οὖν κωλύει πλέ-

---

6 ante ὅτι lac. indic. Ruelle, add. *Propter quid apparitiones
figurarum videntur ipsis nobis eedem?* Barth. : cap. 3 continuatur
in Ap : cap. 4 non vertit Gaza

7 ‹οὐ› Bussemaker

8 ‹δὲ ἄν› addidi : ὁτὲ δὲ ἀλλοῖα ‹ἄν› ἐδόκει, ἡ ‹δὲ› γῆ κτλ.
Hett

---

9 I.e., 1, r, r², r³, r⁴, r⁵, r⁶, r⁷, r⁸, r⁹ (see Heath, *Math. in Arist.*, p.
260). It is likely that the Pythagoreans considered the series in
which r=2 and r=3 cosmologically significant: 1 (1³), 2, 4, 8 (2³),
16, 32, 64 (4³), 128, 256, 512 (8³); 1 (1³), 3, 9, 27 (3³), 81, 243, 729
(9³), 2137, 6561, 19683 (27³) (cf. Pl. *Ti.* 35b–36b).

10 Or perhaps "were born with ten fingers."

that the universe is constituted?[9] Or is it because all people began (*counting*) with ten fingers?[10] So having as it were their own number of counters,[11] they count other things with this quantity as well. But a certain race of Thracians alone count up to four,[12] because just like children they cannot remember for long, nor do they use much of anything.

4.[13] . . . because the Earth is a center;[14] for the shapes that appear to us are always the same.[15] This does ⟨not⟩ seem to be so, unless one makes observations from the middle, but sometimes (*they would appear*) as triangles, sometimes as little tables,[16] and sometimes as other things. But we would think the Earth is the middle, if we could make observations from one of these others.[17] For since the Earth is spherical, this[18] and the Earth will have the same center. But we live on the surface of the Earth, so that it is not from the center; rather (*shapes*) of this sort appear to us who are removed by half a diameter (*from the*

---

[11] The word that I render "counters" (ψήφους) refers to pebbles used, *inter alia*, for counting or voting.

[12] I.e., before repeating in the way described earlier.

[13] The opening of this chapter is missing; none of this chapter was translated by Gaza. In Bartholomew's translation, the chapter begins: "Why do the appearances of the shapes (*of the heavenly bodies*) look the same to us?"

[14] Or perhaps "is center (*of the universe*)."

[15] The author may be referring to the shapes of the constellations.

[16] Or "as trapezoids" (τραπέζια).

[17] I.e., other celestial objects (including the constellations).

[18] The universe?

ονος γενομένου τοῦ διαστήματος διαμένειν τὴν τῶν
σχημάτων φαντασίαν;

5.[9] Διὰ τί τοῦ ἡλίου ὁμοτόνως φερομένου, ἐν τῷ
15 ἴσῳ χρόνῳ | οὐχ ἡ αὐτὴ αὔξησις καὶ φθίσις τῶν
σκιῶν; ἢ ὅτι ἴσαι γίνονται αἱ γωνίαι πρὸς τὰ ὁρώμενα,
αἱ ἀπὸ[10] τῶν ἀκτίνων ὑπὸ ταῖς ἴσαις περιφερείαις; εἰ
δ' αὗται καὶ ⟨ἃς⟩[11] ἐμβαλλόμεναι ποιοῦσιν ἀκτῖνες[12]
ἐν τῷ τριγώνῳ, ὅπερ ἔχεται ὑπό τε τῆς πρώτης ἀκτῖ-
20 νος καὶ τοῦ ὁρωμένου καὶ τῆς σκιᾶς.[13] εἰ δ' αἱ | γωνίαι
ἴσαι, ἀνάγκη τὴν πορρωτέρω γραμμὴν τοῦ ὁρωμένου
μείζω εἶναι τῆς ἐγγυτέρω· τοῦτο γὰρ ἴσμεν. διῃρήσθω
οὖν ἡ περιφέρεια εἰς ἴσα ὁσαοῦν πλήθει, ὁράσθω δὲ
τὸ Θ. ὅταν οὖν ὁ ἥλιος ἐπὶ τοῦ Α προσβαλὼν[14] τὸ Θ
ποιήσῃ τινὰ σκιὰν ἐν τῷ ΘΛ,[15] ἀνάγκη δὴ τὴν ἀκτῖνα
25 ἐπὶ τὸ Λ[16] πίπτειν. | ὅταν δ' ἔλθῃ ἐπὶ τὸ Β, ἡ ἀπὸ τοῦ Β
ἀκτὶς ἐντὸς τῆς ΘΛ[17] πεσεῖται, καὶ ὅταν πάλιν ἐπὶ τὸ
Γ μεταβῇ, ὡσαύτως· εἰ δὲ μή, εὐθεῖα εὐθείας διχῇ
ἅψεται. ἐπεὶ οὖν ἴση ἡ ΑΒ τῇ ΒΓ, καὶ αἱ γωνίαι αἱ ὑπὸ
ταύταις[18] αἱ πρὸς τῷ Δ ἴσαι ἔσονται· πρὸς τῷ κέντρῳ
30 γάρ. εἰ τῇδε[19] τοῦ Δ, καὶ ἐν τῷ | τριγώνῳ· κατὰ

[9] ante διὰ tit. scrips. ὅσα περὶ τὰ οὐράνια ἁ Y[a] (ἀριστοτέλους ὅσα περὶ κτλ. Ap), cf. Trap et *PPA*
[10] ἀπὸ Erasmus : ὑπὸ codd.   [11] ⟨ἃς⟩ Forster ex Gaza
[12] ἀκτῖνες Bussemaker : ἀκτῖνας codd.
[13] post σκιᾶς lac. indic. Ruelle
[14] προσβαλὼν Ross apud Forster : προσλαβὼν codd.
[15] ΘΛ Bussemaker : ΘΑ codd.
[16] Λ Bussemaker : Α codd.

center). What, then, prevents the shapes' appearance from persisting given that the distance is considerable?

5. Why, since the Sun travels with the same intensity, is there not the same increase and decrease (*in the length*) of the shadows in the same time period? Is it because the angles to the objects seen—the angles from the rays subtended by equal arcs[19]—are equal? Now if these (*arcs are equal*), so too are (*the angles*) that the rays produce when inserted in the triangle, the one that is contained by the first ray[20] and the object seen and the shadow. And if the angles are equal, the line farther from the object seen must be greater than the one nearer; for this we know. So let the arc be divided into any number of equal parts (A,B,Γ), and let the object seen be Θ.[21] So when the Sun at A strikes Θ and produces a shadow along ΘΛ, the ray must fall on Λ. And when the Sun arrives at B, the ray from B will fall within ΘΛ, and likewise, when it passes to Γ; otherwise, one straight line will touch another straight line at two points. Since AB is therefore equal to BΓ, the angles subtended by them at Δ[22] will also be equal, since they are at the center. But if (*the angles are equal*) on this side of Δ, so (*are those*) in the triangle, since they are vertical an-

[19] Arcs are parts of the circumference (περιφερείαις).

[20] I.e., the ray from the Sun early in the day, hence the lower.

[21] The mss. do not include a diagram, but one can be constructed: see Figure 1 (p. 476).

[22] Δ is the top point of the visible object Θ.

---

[17] ΘΛ Bussemaker : ΘA codd.

[18] ταύταις Forster ex Gaza : ταύτης codd.

[19] τῇδε Bussemaker : δὲ τῇ codd.

κορυφὴν γὰρ ταύταις. ὥστ' ἐπεὶ εἰς ἴσα διαιρεῖται ἡ
γωνία, μείζων ἔσται ἡ ΛΕ[20] τῆς ΕΖ ⟨ἐν⟩ τῇ ΛΘ.[21]
ὁμοίως δὲ καὶ αἱ ἄλλαι ἃς ποιοῦσιν αἱ ἀπὸ τῆς περι-
φερείας ἀκτῖνες. ἅμα δὲ δῆλον καὶ ὅτι κατὰ μεσημβρίαν ἐλαχίστην ἀναγκαῖον εἶναι τὴν σκιάν, καὶ ὅτι
35   αἱ ἐπιδόσεις | τότε ἐλάχισται. μάλιστα γὰρ καθ' ἡμᾶς
ὁ ἥλιος τῆς μεσημβρίας ἐστίν. καὶ πνῖγος γίνεται διά
τε τὴν εἰρημένην αἰτίαν, καὶ ὅτι ἀπνεύματος· ὅταν γὰρ
διακρίνῃ τὸν πρὸς τῇ γῇ ἀέρα, πνεῦμα γίνεται. εἰ οὖν
911b   ἅμα ἐν ἀμφοτέροις ‖ τοῖς ἡμισφαιρίοις, εἰκότως ἂν αἱ
μέσαι νύκτες καὶ ἡ μεσημβρία ἀπνεύματοι εἶεν.

6. Διὰ τί ὁ ἥλιος διὰ τῶν τετραπλεύρων διέχων οὐκ
εὐθύγραμμα ποιεῖ τὰ σχήματα, ἀλλὰ κύκλους, οἷον ἐν
5   ταῖς ῥιψίν;[22] | ἢ ὅτι ἡ τῶν ὄψεων ἔκπτωσις κῶνός ἐστιν,
τοῦ δὲ κώνου κύκλος ἡ βάσις, ὥστε πρὸς ὃ ἂν προσπίπτωσιν αἱ τοῦ ἡλίου ἀκτῖνες, κυκλοτερεῖς φαίνονται;
ἀναγκαῖον μὲν γάρ ἐστι καὶ τὸ ὑπὸ τοῦ ἡλίου σχῆμα
ὑπ' εὐθειῶν περιέχεσθαι, εἴπερ αἱ ἀκτῖνες εὐθεῖαι.
10   ὅταν γὰρ εὐθεῖαι πρὸς εὐθεῖαν προσπίπτωσιν, | εὐθύ-
γραμμον ποιοῦσιν. ἐπὶ δὲ τῶν ἀκτίνων συμβαίνει
τοῦτο· πρὸς εὐθεῖαν γὰρ προσπίπτουσι τὴν τοῦ ῥιπὸς
γραμμήν, ᾗ διαλάμπουσι,[23] καὶ αὗται[24] εὐθεῖαί εἰσιν,
ὥστε πρὸς εὐθεῖαν ἔσται ἡ ἔκπτωσις. ἀλλὰ διὰ τὸ

<hr>

[20] ΛΕ Bussemaker : ΔΕ codd.   [21] ⟨ἐν⟩ τῇ ΛΘ Bussemaker : τῇ ΔΘ codd. : [τῇ ΔΘ] Heiberg apud Heath
[22] ῥιψίν Sylburg ex Gaza : ῥίψεσιν codd.
[23] ᾗ Xᵃ : ἢ plur. codd. ‖ διαλάμπουσι Yᵃ : δι' οὗ λάμπουσι
plur. codd.

gles[23] to them. So, since the angle is divided into equal parts, ΛE will be greater than EZ in $\Lambda\Theta$. And likewise too for the others[24] that the rays from the arc produce. At the same time, it is also clear that at midday the shadow must necessarily be shortest, and that its increases at that time are shortest. For the Sun is most above us at midday. And stifling heat occurs for the reason stated, and because there is a lack of wind; for wind comes when (*the Sun*) disperses[25] the air near the ground. So, if (*the Sun does this*) at the same time in both hemispheres, it is reasonable that midnight and midday should be lacking in wind.

6. Why, when sunlight passes through quadrilaterals, for instance through wickerwork, does it not produce shapes that are rectangular, but circular ones? Is it because the emission of visual rays is a cone,[26] and the base of a cone is a circle, so that whatever object the rays of the Sun fall upon, they appear circular? For the shape produced by the Sun is necessarily contained by straight lines, since the rays are straight. For when straight rays fall on a straight line, they produce a rectilinear figure. This is what happens in the case of the (*Sun's*) rays: for they fall on the line of the wickerwork, which is straight, at the point where they shine through, and are themselves straight lines, so that the emission (*of the rays past the wickerwork*) will be

---

23 I.e., angles at a vertex.

24 I.e., other shadows or lines.

25 Literally, "separates" ($\delta\iota\alpha\kappa\rho\acute{\iota}\nu\eta$).

26 The author holds that the capacity for sight radiates out from the eyes in a conical pattern.

---

24 $\alpha\mathring{v}\tau\alpha\grave{\iota}$ Bekker : $\alpha\mathring{v}\tau\alpha\iota$ codd.

ἀσθενεῖς εἶναι τὰς ἀποσχιζομένας [ἀπὸ]²⁵ τῶν ὄψεων
15 πρὸς τὰ ἄκρα τῶν εὐθειῶν, | οὐχ ὁρᾶται τὰ ἐν ταῖς
γωνίαις· ἀλλ' ὅσον μὲν τῆς εὐθείας ἐνυπάρχει ἐν τῷ
κώνῳ, ποιεῖ αὐτήν, τὸ δὲ λοιπὸν οὐ ποιεῖ, ἀλλὰ λαν-
θάνουσιν αἱ ὄψεις ἐπιπίπτουσαι. πολλὰ γὰρ οὐχ ὁρῶμεν ἐφ' ἃ δικνεῖται ἡ ὄψις, οἷον τὰ ἐν τῷ σκότει.
ὅμοιον δὲ τούτῳ καὶ τὸ τὸ τετράγωνον πολυγωνοειδὲς
20 φαίνεσθαι, ἐὰν | δὲ πλέον ἀφιστῇ, κύκλον. ὄντος γὰρ
κώνου τῆς τῶν ὄψεων ἐκπτώσεως, ἀφισταμένου τοῦ
σχήματος εἰς τὸ πόρρω, αἱ μὲν εἰς τὰς γωνίας ἀπο-
σχιζόμεναι τῶν ὄψεων διὰ τὸ ἀσθενεῖς εἶναι καὶ ὀλί-
γαι οὐχ ὁρῶσι, πλέονος τοῦ ἀποστήματος γινομένου,
αἱ δὲ εἰς τὸ μέσον προσπίπτουσαι, ἀθρόαι καὶ ἰσχυ-
25 ραὶ | οὖσαι, διαμένουσιν. ἐγγὺς μὲν οὖν ὄντος τοῦ
σχήματος δύνανται²⁶ καὶ τὰ ἐν ταῖς γωνίαις ὁρᾶν,
πόρρω²⁷ δὲ αὐτοῦ γινομένου ἀδυνατοῦσιν. διὸ καὶ ἡ
περιφερὴς ἀπαγομένη εὐθεῖα φαίνεται. καὶ ἡ σελήνη
ὑπὸ εὐθειῶν δοκεῖ περιέχεσθαι τῇ ὀγδόῃ, ἐὰν μὴ κατὰ
30 τὸ πλάτος ἀλλὰ κατὰ τὴν περιέχουσαν γραμμὴν | αἱ
ὄψεις προσπίπτωσιν. ἐγγὺς μὲν γὰρ οὔσης τῆς περι-
φερείας δύνανται διακρίνειν αἱ ὄψεις ὅσῳ ἐγγύτερόν
ἐστι θάτερον θατέρου μέρους τῆς περιφερείας· πόρρω
δὲ γινομένης οὐ διαισθάνεται, ἀλλὰ δοκεῖ αὐτῇ ἐξ
ἴσου εἶναι. διὸ καὶ εὐθεῖα φαίνεται. |

35   7. Διὰ τί τῆς σελήνης σφαιροειδοῦς οὔσης εὐθεῖαν

²⁵ [ἀπὸ] Forster (cf. 911b22)
²⁶ δύνανται Sylburg ex Gaza : δύναται codd.

in a straight line. But because the visual rays cut off toward
the extremities of the straight lines are weak, the parts at
the angles are not seen; but all of the straight line that is
within the cone produces this,[27] but the rest does not produce it, rather our visual rays fall on it unnoticed. For we
do not see many things to which a visual ray penetrates,
such as things in the dark. Similar to this is the quadrilateral figure's appearing polygonal, and if we stand farther
off it appears as a circle. For since the emission of visual
rays has a cone shape, when the figure is removed to a distance, if the distance is very great, the visual rays to the angles are cut off and do not see because they are weak and
few (in number); but those that fall on the center persist,
because they are compact and strong. When the shape is
near, therefore, (the visual rays) can see the parts in the
angles, but when (the shape) is far away they cannot. And
this is also why an arc moved farther away appears straight.
And the Moon seems to be enclosed by straight lines on
the eighth day, if the visual rays fall not on its breadth but
on the line enclosing it. For since the arc is near, our visual
rays can distinguish how much nearer one part of the arc is
than the other; but when it is far off it does not perceive it
distinctly, but to our vision (the arc) seems to it to be equal.
And this is why it appears straight.

7.[28] Why, although the Moon is spherical, do we see a

---

[27] I.e., a straight line.   [28] Possible sources for this chapter are Aristarch.Sam. Prop. 5, and Euc. *Opt*. 22. Septalius wrote
of it *"difficillimum est problema."*

---

[27] πόρρω Sylburg ex Gaza : πλεῖον codd. : πλείονος Xª2

ὁρῶμεν, ὅταν ᾖ διχότομος; ἢ ὅτι ἐν τῷ αὐτῷ ἐπιπέδῳ ἡ
ὄψις γίνεται καὶ ἡ τοῦ κύκλου περιφέρεια, ἣν ὁ ἥλιος
ποιεῖ προσβάλλων τῇ σελήνῃ; ὅτε δὲ τοῦτο γένοιτο,

912a εὐθεῖα γραμμὴ ἐφαίνετο ‖ [ὁ ἥλιος].[28] ἐπεὶ γὰρ ἀνάγκη τὸ προσβάλλον τὰς ὄψεις πρὸς τὴν σφαῖραν κύκλον ὁρᾶν, ἡ δὲ σελήνη σφαιροειδὴς καὶ ὁ ἥλιος ὁρᾷ
αὐτήν, κύκλος ἂν εἴη ὁ ὑπὸ τοῦ ἡλίου γινόμενος. οὗτος

5 οὖν ὅταν μὲν ἐξ ἐναντίας ἡμῖν γένηται, ὅλος | φαίνεται
καὶ δοκεῖ πανσέληνος εἶναι· ὅταν δὲ παραλλάττῃ διὰ
τὴν τοῦ ἡλίου μετάβασιν, ἡ περιφέρεια αὐτοῦ κατὰ
τὴν ὄψιν γίνεται, ὥστε εὐθεῖα φαίνεται. τὸ δὲ ἕτερον
μέρος περιφερές, ὅτι ἐξ ἐναντίας κεῖται τῇ ὄψει ἡμισφαίριον, τὸ δὲ τοιοῦτο ἐφαίνετο ἡμικύκλιον. ἀεὶ γὰρ

10 ἡ σελήνη κατ' ἀντικρύ | ἐστι τῆς ὄψεως. ἀλλ' ὅταν ὁ
ἥλιος ἐπιβάλλῃ, οὐχ ὁρῶμεν, καὶ ἀναπληροῦται μετὰ
τὴν ὀγδόην ἐκ τοῦ μέσου, ὅτι ἐπιπαρεξιὼν ὁ ἥλιος
ἐκκλινέστερον ἡμῖν ποιεῖ τὸν κύκλον. οὕτω δὲ τιθέ-
μενος πρὸς τὴν ὄψιν ὁ κύκλος κώνου τομῇ ἐμφερὴς
ἐγένετο. μηνοειδὴς δὲ φαίνεται, ὅταν ὁ ἥλιος μεταβῇ.

15 ὅταν γὰρ | κατὰ τὰ ἔσχατα σημεῖα, καθ' ἃ διχότομος
φαίνεται, ὁ κύκλος ὁ τοῦ ἡλίου γένηται, περιφέρεια
φαίνεται ἡ τοῦ κύκλου. οὐ γὰρ ἔτι κατ' εὐθεῖάν ἐστι τῇ

---

[28] [ὁ ἥλιος] Bowen

[29] Heath, p. 263: "ὅταν ὁ ἥλιος ἐπιβάλλῃ (912a10) must apparently mean 'when the sun first strikes the moon on our side (or
first begins to light it up)', i.e., at new moon."

[30] I.e., the first quarter.

straight (*line*) when it is halved? Is it because our line of sight and the arc of the circle, which the sunlight produces when it falls on the Moon, are in the same plane? Whenever this occurs, it appears as a straight line. That is to say, since what drives our visual rays to a sphere must necessarily lead to seeing a circle, and since the Moon is spherical, and since the Sun looks to it, what comes to be because of the Sun must be a circle. When, therefore, this (*circle*) is facing us, it appears whole and seems to be a full Moon; but when (*the circle*) changes owing to the motion of the Sun, the arc of the circle is along our line of sight and so appears as a straight line. But the other part is round, because a hemisphere lies facing our line of sight, and such an object would appear semicircular. For the Moon is always right along our line of sight. But when the sunlight falls upon it (*along the same line of sight*),[29] we do not see (*the Moon*). And after the eighth day[30] (*the Moon*) fills out the middle, because the Sun as it advances makes the circle incline away from us more. When the circle (*illuminated by the Sun*) is located in this way in relation to our line of sight, it resembles a section of a cone. But (*this circle*) appears crescent-shaped when the Sun changes its position. That is to say, when the circle produced by the Sun is at its extreme points,[31] that is, the points at which the Moon appears cut in half,[32] the (*arc*) of the circle (*produced by the Sun*) appears as a (*full*) circumference.[33] For it is not yet

[31] I.e., when it coincides with the visible hemisphere of the Moon.

[32] I.e., the half facing the observer is entirely dark and the half facing the Sun is entirely illuminated.

[33] The author is explaining the crescent moon.

467

ὄψει, ἀλλὰ παραλλάττει. τούτου δὲ γινομένου, καὶ διὰ
τῶν αὐτῶν σημείων τοῦ κύκλου ὄντος, ἀνάγκη μηνο-
20 ειδῆ φαίνεσθαι. μέρος γάρ τι τοῦ κύκλου | κατὰ τὴν
ὄψιν εὐθύς ἐστι, τοῦ προτέρου[29] ἐξ ἐναντίας ὄντος,
ὥστε τοῦ λαμπροῦ ἀποτέμνεται·[30] εἶθ' οὕτως καὶ τὰ
ἄκρα μένουσιν ἐν τῷ αὐτῷ, ὥστε ἀνάγκη μηνοειδῆ
φαίνεσθαι, μᾶλλον δὲ καὶ ἧττον διὰ τὴν τοῦ ἡλίου
κίνησιν. μεταβαίνοντος γὰρ τοῦ ἡλίου καὶ ὁ κύκλος ὃν
25 ὁρᾷ ἐπιστρέφεται, ἐν τοῖς αὐτοῖς σημείοις | ὤν· ἀπεί-
ρους γὰρ ἐγκλίσεις ἐγχωρεῖ αὐτὸν κλιθῆναι, εἴπερ
γραφῆναι τοὺς μεγίστους κύκλους διὰ τῶν αὐτῶν
σημείων ἀπείρους ἐνδέχεται.

8. Διὰ τί ὁ ἥλιος καὶ ἡ σελήνη σφαιροειδῆ ὄντα
ἐπίπεδα φαίνεται; ἢ ὅτι πάντων[31] ὅσων τὸ ἀπόστημα
30 ἄδηλον, ὅτε | πλεῖον ἢ ἔλαττον ἀφέστηκεν, ἐξ ἴσου
φαίνονται; ὥστε καὶ ἐφ' ἑνὸς μὲν μόρια δ' ἔχοντος, ἂν
μὴ τῇ χρόᾳ διαφέρῃ, ἀνάγκη τὰ μόρια ἐξ ἴσου φαίνεσθαι. τὸ δ' ἐξ ἴσου ὁμαλὸν[32] καὶ ἐπίπεδον ἀνάγκη
δοκεῖν εἶναι.

9. Διὰ τί τὰς σκιὰς ποιεῖ ὁ ἥλιος ἀνίσχων καὶ
35 δύνων | μακράς, αἰρόμενος δὲ ἐλάττους, ἐπὶ τῆς με-
σημβρίας δ' ἐλαχίστας; ἢ ὅτι ἀνίσχων τὸ μὲν πρῶτον
παράλληλον ποιήσει τὴν σκιὰν τῇ γῇ καὶ ἄπειρον, ὡς

---

[29] προτέρου : πρότερον Forster
[30] post ἀποτέμνεται add. ⟨τι⟩ Forster
[31] πάντων : πάντα Bonitz
[32] ὁμαλὸν : ὁμαλὲς Yᵃ

directly in our line of sight,[34] but differs. After this occurs, that is, after the circle (*produced by the Sun*) passes through the same points,[35] (*this illuminated circle*) must appear crescent-shaped. For a certain part of the circle (*which was previously opposite*) is directly in our line of sight, so that (*this part*) of the illuminated circle is cut off. In this way, then, the extremes (*of the visible part of the illuminated circle*) also remain in the same position, with the result that (*the Moon*) appears crescent-shaped, and more or less in accordance with the motion of the Sun. For as the Sun changes position, the circle that it illuminates[36] revolves while it is at the same points;[37] indeed, it is possible for (*this circle*) to incline at an unlimited number of angles, since an unlimited number of great circles can be drawn through the same points.

8. Why do the Sun and Moon, which are spherical, appear to be flat?[38] Is it because all things the distance of which is uncertain, when they are more or less distant, appear at an equal distance? And so, in the case of a single thing with parts, unless they differ in color, the parts necessarily appear at an equal distance. But what is at an equal distance necessarily seems to be level and flat.

9. Why does the Sun produce shadows that are long when rising and setting, but shorter ones as it is ascending and the shortest ones at midday? Is it because when rising, at first (*the Sun*) will produce a shadow parallel to the

[34] Heath, p. 263: "i.e., directly opposite to us behind the moon."　　[35] I.e., as the circle of Moon that always faces us.

[36] Literally, "the circle that it sees."

[37] These points are pivots.　　[38] Or "plane figures" (ἐπί-πεδα)—and, as we'll see, on the same plane.

ἄνισον[33] ὑπερτείνει, ἔπειτα μακράν, ἀεὶ δ᾽ ἐλάττω διὰ
τὸ ἀεὶ τὴν ἀπὸ τοῦ ἀνωτέρου σημείου εὐθεῖαν ἐντὸς
40 πίπτειν; γνώμων τὸ ΑΒ, ἥλιος οὗ τὸ Γ | καὶ οὗ τὸ Δ· ἡ
912b δὲ ἀπὸ τοῦ Γ ἀκτίς, ἐφ᾽ ἧς τὸ ΓΖ, ἐξωτέρω ‖ ἔσται τῆς
ΔΕ.[34] ἔστι δὲ σκιὰ ἡ μὲν ΒΕ ἀνωτέρω ὄντος τοῦ ἡλίου,
ἡ δὲ ΒΖ κατωτέρω·[35] ἐλαχίστη δέ, ὅσῳ ἀνωτάτω ᾖ[36]
καὶ ὑπὲρ τῆς κεφαλῆς.

10. Διὰ τί αἱ ἀπὸ τῆς σελήνης σκιαὶ μείζους τῶν
5 ἀπὸ τοῦ | ἡλίου, ὅταν ἀπὸ τῆς αὐτῆς ὦσι καθέτου; ἢ
διότι ἀνώτερος ὁ ἥλιος τῆς σελήνης; ἀνάγκη οὖν ἐντὸς
πίπτειν τὴν ἀπὸ τοῦ ἀνωτέρω ἀκτῖνα. γνώμων ἐφ᾽ ᾧ
ΑΔ, σελήνη Β, ἥλιος Γ. ἡ μὲν οὖν ἀπὸ τῆς σελήνης
ἀκτὶς ΒΖ, ὥστε ἔσται σκιὰ ἡ τὸ ΔΖ· ἡ δὲ ἀπὸ τοῦ
10 ἡλίου ἡ τὸ ΓΕ, ὥστε ἔσται σκιὰ ἐξ ἀνάγκης | ἥττων·
ἔσται γὰρ τὸ ΔΕ.

11. Διὰ τί ἐν ταῖς τοῦ ἡλίου ἐκλείψεσιν, ἐάν τις
θεωρῇ διὰ κοσκίνου ἢ φύλλων, οἷον πλατάνου ἢ
ἄλλου πλατυφύλλου, ἢ τοὺς δακτύλους τῆς ἑτέρας
χειρὸς ἐπὶ τὴν ἑτέραν ἐπιζεύξας, μηνίσκοι αἱ αὐγαὶ
15 ἐπὶ τῆς γῆς γίνονται; ἢ ὅτι | ὥσπερ δι᾽ ὀπῆς ἐὰν

33 [ὡς ἄνισον] Flashar
34 ΔΕ Bussemaker ex Gaza : ΓΕ codd.
35 κατωτέρω Ross apud Forster : κατωτάτω codd.
36 ὅταν ἀνωτάτω ᾖ Forster : ὅσῳ ⟨ἄν⟩ ἀνωτέρω ᾖ Ruelle

39 The text is uncertain. If Forster, Flashar, and Hett are right,
it should instead read "parallel to the earth and stretching out to
an unlimited distance."

40 I.e., when the Sun is nearer the meridian.

earth and unlimited, as (*the shadow*) stretches out to a distance unequal (*to the object casting it*).[39] Next (*will it produce*) a long shadow, but (*this shadow*) will continually grow shorter because the straight line from the higher point[40] continually falls inside (*the shadow from the lower point*)?[41] Let AB be the gnomon,[42] and let the Sun be where Γ is and where Δ is. The ray from Γ, on which is the line ΓZ, will fall outside the line ΔE. But BE is the shadow when the Sun is higher, and BZ when it is lower;[43] and it is shortest, inasmuch as the Sun is at its highest, that is, overhead.

10. Why are the shadows from the Moon longer than those from the Sun, when (*the shadows*) are from the same perpendicular object? Is it because the Sun is higher than the Moon? The ray from the higher body must, therefore, fall inside (*the ray from the lower*). A gnomon is where AΔ is, the Moon is B and the Sun is Γ.[44] The ray from the Moon, then, is BZ, so that ΔZ will be its shadow; but the ray from the Sun is ΓE, so that its shadow will necessarily be shorter, for ΔE will be its shadow.

11. Why, during eclipses of the Sun, if one makes observations of them through a sieve or through leaves (of a plane tree[45] or another broad-leaved tree, for example) or by joining the fingers of one hand to those of the other, the beams become crescents on the ground? Or is it because if

---

[41] The mss. do not include a diagram, but one can be constructed: see Figure 2 (page 476).

[42] I.e., the pointer of a sundial. Here the pointer is at right angles to the shadow-catching surface, which is flat.

[43] Δ is higher in the Sun's daily course than Γ.

[44] The mss. do not include a diagram, but one can be constructed: see Figure 3 (page 476).   [45] *Platanus orientalis*.

λάμπῃ εὐγωνίου τὸ φῶς, στρογγύλον καὶ κῶνος γίνεται; αἴτιον δὲ ὅτι δύο γίνονται κῶνοι, ὅ τε ἀπὸ τοῦ
ἡλίου πρὸς τὴν ὀπὴν καὶ ὁ ἐντεῦθεν πρὸς τὴν γῆν, καὶ
συγκόρυφοι. ὅταν οὖν ἐχόντων οὕτως ἄνωθεν κύκλῳ
ἀποτέμνηται,[37] ἔσται μηνίσκος ἐξ ἐναντίας ἐπὶ τῆς
20   γῆς τοῦ | φωτός. ἀπὸ τοῦ μηνίσκου γὰρ τῆς περιφε-
ρείας γίνονται αἱ ἀκτῖνες, μικραὶ[38] δὲ ἐν τοῖς δακτύ-
λοις καὶ κοσκίνοις οἷον ὀπαὶ γίνονται· διὸ ἐπιδηλότε-
ρον γίνεται ἢ διὰ μεγάλων ὀπῶν. ἀπὸ δὲ τῆς σελήνης
οὐ γίνονται, οὔτε ἐκλειπούσης οὔτε ἐν αὐξήσει οὔσης
25   ἢ φθίσει, διὰ τὸ μὴ ἀκριβεῖς τὰς ἀπὸ τῶν | ἄκρων
αὐγὰς εἶναι, ἀλλὰ τῷ μέσῳ φαίνειν, ὁ δὲ μηνίσκος
μικρὸν τὸ μέσον ἔχει.

12. Διὰ τί παρήλιος οὐ γίνεται οὔτε μεσουρανοῦν-
τος τοῦ ἡλίου οὔθ᾽ ὑπὲρ τὸν ἥλιον οὔθ᾽ ὑπὸ τὸν ἥλιον,
ἀλλ᾽ ἐκ πλαγίων μόνον; ἢ διότι παρήλιος γίνεται
30   κλωμένης τῆς ὄψεως | πρὸς τὸν ἥλιον, αὕτη δὲ τοῦ
ἀέρος ἡ στάσις, ἐφ᾽ ἧς ἀνακλᾶται ἡ ὄψις, οὔτ᾽ ἐγγὺς
ἂν γένοιτο τοῦ ἡλίου οὔτε πόρρω; ἐγγὺς μὲν γὰρ
οὖσαν ὁ ἥλιος διαλύσει, πόρρω δὲ οὔσης ἡ ὄψις οὐκ
ἀνακλασθήσεται· ἀπὸ γὰρ μικροῦ ἐνόπτρου πόρρω
ἀνατεινομένη ἀσθενὴς γίνεται. διὸ καὶ ἄλλως οὐ γίνε-
35   ται.[39] ἐξ | ἐναντίας τοῦ ἡλίου μὲν οὖν ἐὰν γίνηται καὶ
ἐγγύς, διαλύσει ὁ ἥλιος, ἐὰν δὲ πόρρω, ἐλάττων ἡ ὄψις
προσπεσεῖται. ἐὰν δὲ ἐν τῷ πλαγίῳ, ἔστι τοσοῦτον

[37] οὕτως ἄνωθεν κύκλῳ ἀποτέμνηται : οὕτως ⟨τοῦ⟩ ἄνωθεν
κύκλου ἀποτέμνηται ⟨τι⟩ Forster ex Gaza
[38] μικραὶ Forster ex Gaza : αἱ codd.

472

light shines in this very way through a rectangular opening, it becomes round, i.e., a cone? The reason is that two cones are formed, one from the Sun to the opening and one from there to the ground, and they have the same vertex. So when in these conditions the (*upper*) cone is cut off by a circle above, there will be a crescent of the light on the opposite side on the ground. For the rays come from the arc of the crescent,[46] and there are as it were small openings in the fingers and in sieves. This is why (*the crescent*) is more noticeable than it is through large openings. But (*these crescent-forming rays*) do not come from the Moon, neither as it eclipses (*the Sun*) nor when it is waxing or waning, because the beams from its extremities are not clear-cut, but it shines in its middle, whereas a crescent has a middle that's small.

12.[47] Why does a parhelion not occur when the Sun is at the meridian, or either above the Sun or below it, but only at the sides? Is it because a parhelion occurs when the visual ray to the Sun is reflected, and because this stasis of the air, in which case the visual ray is reflected, can occur neither near the Sun nor far from it? For the Sun will dissolve (*the air*) when it is near, but if it is far away, the visual ray will not be reflected, since if it is stretched out far from a small reflective surface it becomes weak. This is in fact why a halo does not occur. So if (*the stationary air*) is opposite the Sun and nearby, the Sun will dissolve it; but if it is far away, a diminished visual ray will strike it. But when (*the stationary air*) is at the side, the reflective surface can

---

46 Formed when the circle cuts off the upper cone.
47 Sources: Arist. *Mete*. 3.2, 372a10–21, and 3.6.

473

ἀποστῆναι τὸ ἔνοπτρον ὥστε μήτε τὸν ἥλιον διαλῦσαι
μήτε τὴν⁴⁰ ὄψιν ἀσθενῇ⁴¹ ἀνελθεῖν, διὰ τὸ ὑπὸ⁴² τὴν
40 γῆν φέρεσθαι. ὑπὸ δὲ τὸν ἥλιον οὐ γίνεται | διὰ τὸ
913a πλησίον μὲν τῆς γῆς ὄντος διαλύεσθαι ἂν ὑπὸ ‖ τοῦ
ἡλίου, ἄνω δὲ μεσουρανίου τὴν ὄψιν διασπᾶσθαι. καὶ
ὅλως οὐδὲ ἐκ πλαγίας μεσουρανίου γίνεται, ὅτι ἡ ὄψις
†ὑπὸ τὴν γῆν ἐὰν λίαν φέρηται†,⁴³ ὀλίγη ἥξει εἰς τὸ
ἔνοπτρον, ὥστε ἀνακλωμένη πάνυ⁴⁴ ἔσται ἀσθενής. |

5 13. Διὰ τί τῆς σκιᾶς τὸ ἄκρον τοῦ ἡλίου τρέμειν
φαίνεται; οὐ γὰρ δὴ διὰ τὸ φέρεσθαι τὸν ἥλιον·
ἀδύνατον γὰρ κινεῖσθαι εἰς τἀναντία, ὁ δὲ τρόμος
τοιοῦτος. ἔτι δὲ ἄδηλος ἡ μετάβασις, ὥσπερ καὶ τοῦ
ἡλίου αὐτοῦ. ἢ διὰ τὸ κινεῖσθαι τὰ ἐν τῷ ἀέρι; καλεῖ-
10 ται δὲ ξύσματα. φανερὰ δὲ ἔσται ἐν ταῖς | ἀκτῖσι ταῖς
διὰ τῶν θυρίδων· ταῦτα γὰρ κινεῖται κἂν νηνεμίᾳ. ἔκ
τε οὖν τῆς σκιᾶς εἰς τὸ φῶς ἔκ τε τοῦ φωτὸς εἰς τὴν
σκιὰν φερομένων ἀεί, καὶ ὁ ὅρος ὁ κοινὸς τοῦ φωτὸς
καὶ τῆς σκιᾶς φαίνεται κινούμενος παρεγγύς. ἢ γὰρ
15 οἷον σκιὰν ποιοῦσιν, ἢ δὲ φῶς, ἑκατέρωθεν | μεταβάλ-
λοντα⁴⁵ ταῦτα. ὥστε ἡ σκιὰ φαίνεται κινεῖσθαι, οὐ
κινουμένη αὐτὴ οὕτως, ἀλλ' ἐκεῖνα.⁴⁶

---

⁴⁰ μήτε τὴν : τὴν τε D : καὶ τὴν Louis ex Gaza
⁴¹ ἀσθενῇ Forster, cf. 913a4 : ἀθρόαν codd.
⁴² ὑπὸ : πρὸς D
⁴³ ἡ ὄψις †ὑπὸ τὴν γῆν ἐὰν λίαν φέρηται† Flashar, cf. Mete.
378a9–10 ἡ γὰρ ὄψις οὐ πρὸς τὴν γῆν φέρηται
⁴⁴ πάνυ Ruelle : πᾶν plur. codd. : πάντως Cᵃ : πάμπαν
Flashar, cf. Mete. 378a11
⁴⁵ μεταβάλλοντα Forster ex Gaza : μεταβάλλονται codd.

be at such a distance that neither does the Sun dissolve it nor does the visual ray return in a weakened state, because it has gone under the Earth. But (*a parhelion*) does not occur below the Sun because it is dissolved by the Sun when it is near the Earth; and (*it does not occur*) above when (*the Sun*) is at the meridian, because the visual ray is scattered. In fact, it does not occur in general at the side when (*the Sun*) is at the meridian, because if the visual ray †goes too far under the Earth†,[48] it will arrive at the reflective surface[49] in a diminished state, so that when it is reflected it will be very weak.

13. Why does the edge of the shadow cast by the Sun appear to tremble? It is certainly not because the Sun is moving, since it cannot move in opposite directions, and trembling is of this sort. Moreover, the change (*of the shadow's position*) is imperceptible, as is that of the Sun as well. Is it because of the movement of things in the air, called dust particles? Indeed, they will be visible in the rays passing through small openings; for these are in motion even in still air. Therefore, since they are continually moving from the shadow into the light and from the light into the shadow, the common boundary between the light and the shadow visibly moves in nearly the same way, since by changing from side to side, these (*dust particles*) produce as it were a shadow in one place and light in another. Consequently, the shadow appears to move, though it does not itself move in this way, but those (*dust particles*) do.

[48] Like Flashar, I find this phrase suspect.
[49] I.e., the stationary air.

---

[46] ἐκεῖνα D : ἐκεῖναι cett. codd.

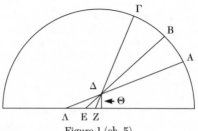

Figure 1 (ch. 5)

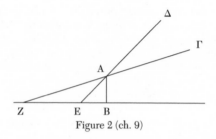

Figure 2 (ch. 9)

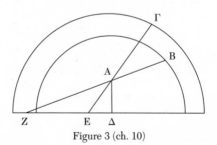

Figure 3 (ch. 10)

BOOK XVI

INTRODUCTION

The focus of Book 16 is largely mechanical and mathematical, and it may have been placed where it is in the *Problems* as something of a continuation of 15. Its chapters cover the following topics: bubbles (1–2); the movement of an object the weight of which is unevenly distributed (3 and 12); rebounding objects (4 and 13); cylinders (5–6); why "magnitudes when divided appear smaller than the whole" (7); the clepsydra (8); why certain things have a rounded shape (9–10); and, the flight of the discus (11).

The sources for these chapters cannot be determined with any certainty or even probability. The author may in some cases have had Euclid in mind, and perhaps there is some connection between the subject matter of chs. 3 and 12 and Strato's *On Lightness and Heaviness* (DL 5.59; see frs. 49–50 Sharples). Ch. 1 mentions "the works on optics," which may refer to a lost work of Aristotle's (see n. 3 to the translation).

ΟΣΑ ΠΕΡΙ ΤΑ ΑΨΥΧΑ

1. Διὰ τί αἱ μὲν βάσεις τῶν πομφολύγων λευκαὶ ἐν |
τοῖς ὕδασι; καὶ ἐὰν ἐν ἡλίῳ[1] τεθῶσι, σκιὰν οὐ
ποιοῦσιν, ἀλλ' ἡ μὲν ἄλλη πομφόλυξ σκιὰν ποιεῖ, ἡ δὲ
βάσις οὐ ποιεῖ, ἀλλ' ἡλίωται κύκλῳ. τὸ δὲ ἔτι θαυ-
μασιώτερον, ὅτι οὐδ' ἐάν τι τεθῇ ξύλον εἰς τὸ ὕδωρ ἐν
τῷ ἡλίῳ . . .[2] τέμνεται ὑπὸ τοῦ ὕδατος ταύτῃ.[3] ἢ οὐ
γίνεται σκιά, ἀλλ' ἡλίῳ διῄρηται | ἡ σκιά; εἰ οὖν σκιά
ἐστιν τὸ μὴ ὁρώμενον, καὶ ὑπὸ τοῦ ἡλίου κύκλῳ ἂν
ὁρῶτο ὁ ὄγκος. τοῦτο δὲ ὅτι ἀδύνατον, δείκνυται ἐν
τοῖς ὀπτικοῖς· οὐδὲ γὰρ τὸ ἐλάχιστον ὑπὸ τοῦ μεγί-
στου ἐνδέχεται ὅλον περιοφθῆναι.

2. Διὰ τί αἱ πομφόλυγες ἡμισφαίρια; ἢ διὰ τὸ ὡς
ἀπὸ | κέντρου πρὸς τὸν ἀέρα φέρεσθαι ἄνω ὁμοίως

913a
20

25

30

---

[1] ante ἡλίῳ add. τῷ Cᵃ
[2] post ἡλίῳ lac. indic. Forster
[3] ταύτῃ Forster : ταῦτα codd.

---

[1] There is a problem with the text; part of this line is likely
missing.   [2] Presumably the bulk of the plank.

[3] According to Diogenes Laertius, Aristotle wrote a treatise
on optics in one book (5.26); another source attributes to him

PROBLEMS CONNECTED
WITH INANIMATE THINGS

1. Why are the bases of bubbles in water white? And if they are placed in sunlight they do not produce a shadow, but the rest of the bubble produces a shadow, whereas the base does not, but is like sunlight in a circle. But what is still more amazing is that even if a plank is placed into the water in the sunlight there isn't . . . it is cut by the water at that point.[1] Or does a shadow not appear, but the shadow is broken up by the Sun? Therefore, if a shadow is that which is not seen, then the bulk[2] would be seen by the Sun in a circle. But that this is impossible has been demonstrated in the works on optics;[3] for the largest object cannot see around the smallest as a whole.[4]

2. Why are bubbles hemispherical? Is it because they are carried upward from the center toward the air equally

a work with the intriguing title τὰ ὀπτικὰ προβλήματα (Vit.Arist.Marc. 4).

[4] It seems impossible to make sense of much of this chapter. On the cryptic last line, Vit.Arist.Marc. 38 may provide some help: "In mathematics (Aristotle held) that the cone of the lines of sight is acute-angled because the line of sight extends further than the magnitude that it sees; and accordingly none of the things seen is simultaneously seen as a whole, and so its axis is larger than its base and the cone turns out to be acute-angled."

πάντῃ· ἀνάγκη δὲ τοῦτο ἡμισφαίριον εἶναι. τὸ κάτω δὲ
ἡμισφαίριον ἀποτέμνεται ὑπὸ τοῦ ἐπιπέδου τοῦ ὑδατώδους, ἐν ᾧ τὸ κέντρον ἐστίν.

3. Διὰ τί τοῖς ἄνισον τὸ βάρος[4] ἔχουσι μεγέθεσιν,
35 ἐάν | τις τὸ κουφότερον κινῇ, κύκλῳ περιφέρεται τὸ
βαλλόμενον, οἷον τοῖς μεμολιβδωμένοις ἀστραγάλοις
συμβαίνει, ἐάν τις βάλλῃ τὸ κουφότερον πρὸς αὑτὸν
στρέψας μέρος; ἢ ὅτι τὸ βαρύτερον ἀδύνατον ἰσοδρομεῖν τῷ κουφοτέρῳ, ἀπὸ τῆς αὐτῆς ἰσχύος ῥιφθέν;
913b ἐπεὶ δὲ ἀνάγκη μὲν πάμπαν κινεῖσθαι, ‖ ἐξ ἴσου δὲ
ἀδύνατον, ὁμοταχῶς μὲν φερόμενα τὴν αὐτὴν οἰσθήσεται γραμμήν, θᾶττον δὲ θατέρου φερομένου κύκλον
ἀνάγκη φέρεσθαι, ἐπειδὴ ἐν τούτῳ μόνῳ τῷ σχήματι
ταῦτα ἀεὶ κατάλληλα ὄντα σημεῖα ἐν ταὐτῷ χρόνῳ |
5 ἀνίσους διέρχεται γραμμάς.

4. Διὰ τί τὰ πίπτοντα ἐπὶ τὴν γῆν καὶ ἀφαλλόμενα
ὁμοίας γωνίας ποιεῖ πρὸς τὸ ἐπίπεδον ἐφ' ἑκάτερα τοῦ
σημείου ᾧ ἥψατο τοῦ ἐπιπέδου; ἢ ὅτι πάντα μὲν φύσει
φέρεται πρὸς ὀρθήν· τὰ μὲν οὖν εἰς ὁμαλὲς πεσόντα,
10 τῇ καθέτῳ | καὶ τῇ διαμέτρῳ προσκρούσαντα τῷ
ἐπιπέδῳ, τοσαύτας ποιεῖ γωνίας ἀφαλλόμενα διὰ τὸ
τὴν μὲν διάμετρον ἴσα διαιρεῖν· τὰ δὲ εἰς τὰ πλάγια
πίπτοντα, οὐ τῇ καθέτῳ προσκρούοντα τῷ χωρίῳ

---

[4] βάρος Ap : βάθος cett. codd.

---

[5] Cf. Pr. 16.12.   [6] Literally, "with leaded knuckle-bones"
(τοῖς μεμολιβδωμένοις ἀστραγάλοις).

in every direction? Now this must be hemispherical. But the lower hemisphere is cut off by the plane of the watery surface, in which the center is situated.

3.[5] Why is it that in magnitudes having unequal weight, if one moves the lighter part, what is thrown revolves in a circle, as happens with loaded dice,[6] if one throws with the lighter part turned toward oneself? Is it because the heavier part cannot move at a pace equal to that of the lighter, when cast with the same strength? And since the whole thing must move, but cannot do so at an equal pace, traveling at the same speed it would be moved in the same line; but with one part traveling more rapidly it must travel in a circle, since it is only in this form that these points[7] that are always opposite can pass along unequal lines in the same time.

4.[8] Why do things that fall to the Earth and rebound make similar angles with the surface on each side of the point at which they touch the surface? Is it because all (*inanimate*) things by nature travel in straight lines?[9] So things that fall on level ground, striking the surface perpendicularly or diametrically,[10] make such angles when they rebound, because the diameter divides (*the surface*)[11] into equal parts. But things that fall on what is slanted, not striking the ground perpendicularly but at a point higher

---

[7] Or "marks" ($\sigma\eta\mu\epsilon\hat{\iota}\alpha$)—perhaps those on a die.

[8] Cf. *Pr.* 16.13.

[9] Or "at right angles" ($\pi\rho\dot{o}s$ $\dot{o}\rho\theta\dot{\eta}\nu$).

[10] I.e., diagonally.

[11] The verb $\delta\iota\alpha\iota\rho\epsilon\hat{\iota}\nu$ seems to require an object. Hett provides "the circle," Forster "the angle at the surface," and Flashar "*die Erde.*" I believe "the surface" is probably implied.

ἀλλὰ τῷ ἀνωτέρω τῆς καθέτου σημείῳ, συμβαίνει
15 πάλιν ἀνωσθέντα ὑπὸ τοῦ πληγέντος τόπου | εἰς τοὐ-
ναντίον φέρεσθαι, τὰ μὲν στρογγύλα, ὅτι ἐν ταὐτῷ⁵
φερόμενα εἰς τοὐναντίον τῆς ἀπώσεως ἐξελίττεται, ἐάν
τε ἠρεμῇ τὸ μέσον αὐτῶν ἐάν τε καὶ τόπον διαλλάττῃ·
τὰ δ' εὐθύγραμμα διὰ τὸ⁶ τὴν κάθετον αὐτὴν⁷ εἰς
τοὔμπροσθεν προσενεχθεῖσαν⁸ ἐκκρούεσθαι, καθάπερ
20 τοῖς τε ξυρουμένοις τὰ | σκέλη συμβαίνει, καὶ ὧν τοὺς
κολύθρους ὑφαρπάζουσιν. πάντες γὰρ οὗτοι εἰς τοὐναντίον καὶ ὄπισθεν ἐπιπίπτουσι, διὰ τὸ ἰσάζειν αὐτὰ⁹
τὴν κάθετον, μετέωρόν τε εἶναι καὶ εἰς τοὔμπροσθεν
ἐκκρούεσθαι· τὰ γὰρ ἐναντία δηλονότι αὐτῆς ὄπισθέν
τε καὶ κάτω συμβαίνει¹⁰ γίνεσθαι, κάτω δὲ φερόμενα |
25 βαρύτερα ἂν εἴη. ὁ οὖν τούτοις πτῶμα, τοῖς ἀφαλλο-
μένοις φορὰν συμβαίνει γίνεσθαι. πρὸς ὀρθὴν μὲν
οὖν οὐδέτερα αὐτῶν ἀφάλλεται διὰ τὸ τὴν μὲν κάθετον
δίχα τῷ βάθει¹¹ διαιρεῖν τὰ φερόμενα, καθέτους δὲ
πλείους πρὸς ταὐτὸ ἐπίπεδον μὴ γίνεσθαι τεμνούσας
30 αὐτάς·¹² ὃ τούτοις συμβήσεται | καθέτου γινομένης
κατὰ τὴν ἔφαλσιν, ᾗ προσέκρουσε τῷ ἐπιπέδῳ τὸ
φερόμενον, διχοτομεῖσθαι πάλιν ὑπ' αὐτῆς αὐτὸ συμβήσεται,¹³ ὥστε ἀναγκαῖον τέμνεσθαι ὑπ' αὐτῆς τὴν

---

5 ταὐτῷ Bussemaker : αὐτῷ codd.
6 τὸ Bussemaker : τε codd.   7 αὐτὴν : αὐτῶν Yᵃ
8 προσενεχθεῖσαν Forster : προσηνέχθη codd.
9 ἰσάζειν αὐτὰ om. Ross apud Forster
10 συμβαίνει : συμβήσεται Yᵃ
11 βάθει Hett : βάρει codd.

than the perpendicular, are pushed back by the place that
was struck and travel in the opposite direction. Spherical
things do this, because traveling in the one direction they
revolve in a direction opposite to that in which they are
pushed back, whether their middle points are at rest or
change position; but rectilinear things do this because the
perpendicular itself is brought forward and then knocked
back, just as happens to those who have their legs knocked
from under them[12] or whose scrotum is pulled down. For
all such people fall in the opposite direction and backward,
because the perpendicular gives them their balance and
this is raised and knocked forward. For clearly it happens
that the opposite of this[13] goes backward and downward,
and traveling downward it would be heavier. Therefore,
what to these people is a fall, in rebounding things becomes movement. Neither of these[14] rebound at right angles because the perpendicular divides traveling things in
two in the direction of their depth,[15] and there cannot be
many perpendiculars to the same surface cutting themselves; what will happen to them if the perpendicular is
formed on the rebound, at the point at which the traveling
thing strikes the surface, is that it will again be cut in two by
the perpendicular, so that the first perpendicular, by which

12 Literally, "to those who have their legs shaved" (τοῖς
ξυρουμένοις τὰ σκέλη).
13 I.e., of the perpendicular.
14 I.e., neither round nor rectilinear things.
15 Or, following the mss., "according to their weight."

---

12 αὐτάς : αὐτάς Bussemaker
13 διχοτομεῖσθαι—συμβήσεται om. Forster

πρώτην κάθετον ὑφ'[14] ἧς ἐφέρετο. ἐπεὶ δ' εἰς τοὐναντίον μὲν οἰσθήσεται, πρὸς ὀρθὴν δὲ οὐκ οἰσθήσεται,
35 λοιπὸν ὀξεῖαν | γίνεσθαι γωνίαν τὴν ἐπὶ θατέρῳ τοῦ
προσπεσόντος τῷ ἐπιπέδῳ σημείου· ὅρος γάρ ἐστιν ἡ
ὀρθὴ τῶν ἐναντίων γωνιῶν.

5. Διὰ τί ὁ μὲν κύλινδρος ὠσθεὶς εἰς εὐθύ τε
φέρεται καὶ γράφει εὐθείας τοῖς ὁρίζουσιν αὐτὸν κύ-
κλοις, ὁ δὲ κῶνος κύκλῳ περιφέρεται, τῆς κορυφῆς
914a μενούσης, καὶ γράφει ‖ τὸν κύκλον τῷ ὁρίζοντι; κύκλῳ
μὲν ἀμφότερα φέρεται, γράφει δ' ἐν τῷ ἐπιπέδῳ ὁ μὲν
κύλινδρος εὐθείας, ὁ δὲ κῶνος κύκλους, διὰ τὸ τοὺς
μὲν ἐν τῷ κώνῳ ἀνίσους εἶναι κύκλους, φέρεσθαι δὲ
5 ἀεὶ θᾶττον τὸν μείζονα τῶν περὶ τὸ | αὐτὸ κέντρον.
φερομένων δὲ ἀνίσως πάντων ἅμα τῶν ἐν τῷ κώνῳ
κύκλων, συμβαίνει τοὺς ἐξωτάτω πλεῖστον ἐν ταὐτῷ
χρόνῳ τόπον καὶ γραμμὴν φέρεσθαι· διὸ καὶ κύκλῳ
φέρονται, γράφονταί τε γὰρ πάντες τῇ αὐτῇ εὐθείᾳ,
καὶ τῆς εὐθείας κύκλῳ μὲν φερομένης οὐ πάντα τὰ ἐν |
10 αὐτῇ σημεῖα ἴσην ἐν ταὐτῷ χρόνῳ γράφει γραμμήν,
εἰς εὐθὺ δὲ φέρει τὴν ἴσην. τοῦ δὲ κυλίνδρου πάντων
ἴσων ὄντων τῶν κύκλων καὶ περὶ ταὐτὸ κέντρον, συμβαίνει τὰ ἅμα τοῦ ἐπιπέδου ἐν αὐτοῖς πάνθ' ἁπτομένοις σημεῖα, φέρεσθαί[15] τε ἰσοταχεῖς κυλιομένους διὰ
15 τὸ τοὺς κυλίνδρους[16] ἴσους εἶναι, | καὶ ἥκειν ἐπὶ τὸ

---

[14] ὑφ' : ἐφ' Ya   [15] συμβαίνει ἅμα τοῦ ἐπιπέδου τὰ ἐν
αὐτοῖς πάνθ' ἁπτομένους σημεῖα φέρεσθαί Forster ex Gaza
[16] κυλίνδρους : κύκλους Bonitz

it traveled, must necessarily be cut by the other. Now since it will be moved in the opposite direction, but will not be moved at a right angle, it remains that the angle on either side of the point where it strikes the surface will be acute; for the right angle is the division between the opposite angles.

5.[16] Why does the cylinder, when pushed, travel straight and describe straight lines with the circles bounding it, whereas the cone travels around in a circle, its vertex remaining still, and describes a circle with the circle bounding it? Both travel in a circle, but the cylinder describes straight lines on a plane surface, while the cone describes circles, because the circles in the cone are unequal, and the larger of the circles around the same center[17] always travel faster. As all of the circles in the cone are traveling at the same time and unequally, the result is that the outermost circles travel over the most space and the longest line; and this is why they travel in a circle, for they are all described by the same straight line, and as the straight line travels in a circle[18] all the points on it do not describe an equal line in the same time, but if it travels straight it does describe an equal line. But as all of the circles of the cylinder are equal and around the same center,[19] it happens that all the (*corresponding*) points on these circles touch the surface at the same time, and as they roll they travel at the same speed, because cylinders are equal,[20]

16 Cf. Euc., *El.* 11.Def. 18 and 21.

17 I.e., the axis of the cone.

18 This is the line of contact of the cone with the plane surface.

19 I.e., the axis of the cylinder.   20 There may be something wrong with the text of this sentence.

ἐπίπεδον πάλιν ἅμα ἐκκυλισθέντα ἕκαστον τὸν αὑτοῦ
κύκλον, ὥστε καὶ τὰς ἐν τῷ ἐπιπέδῳ εὐθείας ἴσας
γίνεσθαι· τῇ γὰρ αὑτῶν ἀφῇ αὐτὰς ἔγραψαν, ὄντες
ἴσοι τε καὶ ἰσοταχεῖς, ἐγίνοντο δὲ εὐθεῖαι αἱ ὑπὸ τῆς
αὐτῆς γραφεῖσαι γραμμῆς εἰς εὐθὺ φερομένης, ὥστε
20 διὰ ταύτας | εἰς εὐθὺ ἂν φέροιτο[17] ὁ κύλινδρος. δια-
φέρει γὰρ οὐθέν, ᾗ [ἡ][18] πρώτη ἥψατο ὁ κύλινδρος τοῦ
ἐπιπέδου γραμμῇ, ταύτῃ ἕλκειν ἐν τῷ ἐπιπέδῳ, ἢ
ἐγκυλίειν αὐτόν·[19] ἀεὶ γὰρ ἴσην καὶ ὁμοίαν γραμμὴν
τῶν ἐν τῷ κυλίνδρῳ συμβήσεται ἅπτεσθαι τοῦ ἐπι-
πέδου, ἑλκομένου τε καὶ κυλιομένου τοῦ κυλίνδρου. |

25   6. Διὰ τί τῶν βιβλίων ἡ τομὴ οὖσα ἐπίπεδος καὶ
εὐθεῖα,[20] ἐὰν μέν τις τέμῃ παρὰ τὴν βάσιν, γίνεται
εὐθεῖα ἀνελιττομένη, ἐὰν δὲ ἐγκλίνας, σκολιά; ἢ ὅτι
συμβαίνει τῶν ἐν τῇ ἑτέρᾳ τομῇ κύκλων ἐν ταὐτῷ
ἐπιπέδῳ ὄντων τὴν ἐγκεκλιμένην τομὴν μὴ παρακει-
30 μένην εἶναι, ἀλλ᾽ ἐν τῇ μὲν | πλεῖον τῇ δὲ ἔλαττον
αὐτῆς ἀπέχειν, ὥστε ἐξελιττομένου οἱ μὲν ἐν ταὐτῷ
ἐπιπέδῳ ὄντες κύκλοι, καὶ τὴν ἀρχὴν ἔχοντες ἐν ταὐτῷ
ἐπιπέδῳ, τὴν ἐξ αὐτῶν ποιήσουσι γραμμὴν ἐξελιττό-
μενοι; ἔστι γὰρ ἡ γιγνομένη γραμμὴ ἐκ τῶν κύκλων
οἵ εἰσιν ἐν ταὐτῷ ἐπιπέδῳ· ὥστε καὶ εὐθεῖα οὖσα ἐν |
35 ἐπιπέδῳ. ἢ δὲ[21] τῆς λοξῆς τομῆς ἐξελιττομένη γραμμὴ
οὐκ οὖσα παρὰ τὴν πρώτην, ἀλλὰ τῇ μὲν πλέον τῇ δὲ

---

[17] ἂν φέροιτο Bussemaker : ἀναφέροιτο codd.
[18] [ἡ] Bussemaker   [19] αὐτόν Bussemaker : αὐτό codd.
[20] καὶ εὐθεῖα om. Cᵃ   [21] δὲ Ruelle : τε codd.

and they reach the surface again as each of its circles revolves at the same time, so that the straight lines (*they describe*) on the surface are also equal; for they describe
them by their contact, being equal and traveling at an
equal speed. Now the lines described by the same line
traveling in a straight direction are straight, so that along
these the cylinder would travel in a straight line. For it
makes no difference whether the cylinder drags over the
surface in a straight line in the position in which it first
touched the surface, or whether it rolls over it; for the result will always be that an equal and similar line from the
(*points*) on the cylinder touches the surface, whether the
cylinder is dragged or rolled.

6. Why, when a book[21] is cut level and straight, if one
cuts it parallel to the base, it will be straight when unrolled,
but if it is cut on a slant, it will be crooked? Is it because the
result is that, though in the previous cut the circles were in
the same plane, the slanting cut is not parallel, but on one
side of the roll it is nearer and on the other side farther
from this,[22] so that when it is unrolled, the circles that are
in the same plane and have their origin in the same plane,
will make, when unrolled, a (*straight*) line of their own?
For the resulting line comes from circles that are in the
same plane, so that, being on a plane, it is also straight. But
the line unrolled from the oblique cut is not parallel to the
first, but is more distant from it on one side and less on the

21 I.e., a papyrus scroll, and thus a cylinder.
22 I.e., the base, which is treated as the first or original cut.

ἔλαττον αὐτῆς διεστηκυῖα διὰ τὸ καὶ τὴν τομὴν οὕτως
ἔχειν πρὸς αὐτήν, οὐκ ἐν ἐπιπέδῳ ἔσται, ὥστε οὐδ'
εὐθεῖα· τῆς γὰρ εὐθείας οὐκ ἔστι τὸ μὲν ἐν ἄλλῳ τὸ δὲ
ἐν ἄλλῳ ἐπιπέδῳ. ||

914b   7. Διὰ τί διαιρούμενα τὰ μεγέθη ἐλάττω φαίνεται
πάντα τοῦ ὅλου; ἢ ὅτι διαιρούμενα μὲν ἀριθμὸν ἔχει
πάντα, μεγέθει δὲ ἐλάττω ἐστὶ τοῦ ἑνός; τὸ μὲν γὰρ
μέγα τῷ κατὰ συνέχειαν εἶναι καὶ ποσόν τι μέγα
5 λέγεται, ὁ δὲ ἀριθμός | τε πᾶς[22] παντὸς μεγέθους
ἀριθμοῦ μείζων. διόπερ εἰκὸς τὸ ὅλον διαιρεθέντων
τῶν μερῶν μεῖζον φαίνεσθαι· τῶν αὐτῶν γὰρ ὄντων
αὐτῶν τὸ μὲν ὅλον τὴν τοῦ μεγέθους ἔχει μᾶλλον
φύσιν, συνεχὲς ὄν, τὰ δὲ μέρη τὴν τοῦ ἀριθμοῦ.

  8. Τῶν περὶ τὴν κλεψύδραν συμβαινόντων τὸ μὲν
10 ὅλον | ἔοικεν εἶναι αἴτιον καθάπερ Ἀναξαγόρας λέγει·
ὁ γὰρ ἀὴρ ἐστιν αἴτιος, ἐναπολαμβανόμενος ἐν αὐτῇ,
τοῦ μὴ εἰσιέναι τὸ ὕδωρ ἐπιληφθέντος τοῦ αὐλοῦ.[23] οὐ
μὴν ἁπλῶς γε αἴτιος· κἂν γάρ τις αὐτὴν πλαγίαν ἐνῇ
εἰς[24] τὸ ὕδωρ, ἐπιλαβὼν τὸν αὐλόν, εἴσεισι τὸ ὕδωρ.
15 διόπερ οὐ λέγεται ὑπ' αὐτοῦ | ἱκανῶς ᾗ αἴτιόν ἐστιν.
ἔστι δὲ αἴτιον μέν, καθάπερ εἴρηται, ὁ ἀὴρ οὗτος δὲ

---

[22] ὁ δὲ ἀριθμός ⟨τῶν μερῶν⟩ πᾶς Forster ex Gaza
[23] αὐλοῦ w Ap[c] Rp[c] E[s] : ἄλλου cett. codd.
[24] ἐνῇ εἰς Sylburg : ἐνῆ εἰς Y[a2] : εἰς Ap. : ἐνεὶς cett. codd.

---

[23] Cf. *Pr.* 17.1.
[24] See *Pr.* 2.1. Hett notes *ad loc.*: "The clepsydra was made of
metal (never of glass), and consisted of a spherical bulb, probably

other, because the (*oblique*) cut bears this relation to the original, so that it will not be in a plane, and therefore not straight either; for one part of a straight line cannot be in one plane, while another is in a different one.

7.[23] Why do all magnitudes when divided appear smaller than the whole? Is it because all divided things have number, but in magnitude each is less than the whole? For what is large is called large by being continuous and a certain size, but the number (*of its parts*) is always greater than the number of the complete whole. So it is reasonable that the whole should appear larger than the divided parts; for though they are actually the same, the whole has more the nature of magnitude, being continuous, while the parts have more the nature of number.

8. Of the things that happen in connection with the clepsydra,[24] the *general* cause seems to be just as Anaxagoras[25] claims: for the air,[26] being enclosed in it, is the cause of the water not entering when the tube is closed. But this is not the cause without qualification: for if one puts it into water at a slant, closing off the tube, the water will enter. So his explanation of how this is the cause is not sufficient. Now air *is* the cause, as has been said; but this, either being

---

flattened at the top (hence the term κωδία, poppy-head), into which was inserted a narrow tube (αὐλός). The upper end of the tube could be closed by a stopcock, or other device (ἐπιλαβεῖν). The bottom of the ball was perforated with small holes (τρυπή-ματα, ἠθμός), through which the water percolated slowly, so long as the stopcock was open."

[25] 59A69 D-K; cf. Arist. *Ph.* 213a24–27.

[26] In this chapter, ἀήρ and πνεῦμα are used interchangeably, and I translate both "air."

ὠθούμενός τε καὶ καθ᾽ ἑαυτὸν φερόμενος καὶ μὴ βια-
ζόμενος ἐπ᾽ εὐθείας πέφυκε φέρεσθαι, καθάπερ καὶ
ἄλλα στοιχεῖα. πλαγίας μὲν οὖν βαφείσης τῆς κλεψύ-
δρας, διὰ τῶν ἐναντίων τοῖς ἐν τῷ ὕδατι τρυπημάτων |
20 ἐπ᾽ εὐθείας μένων ὑπὸ τοῦ ὕδατος ἐξέρχεται, ὑποχω-
ροῦντος δὲ αὐτοῦ τὸ ὕδωρ εἰσέρχεται· ὀρθῆς δὲ εἰς τὸ
ὕδωρ βαφείσης τῆς κλεψύδρας, οὐ δυνάμενος πρὸς
ὀρθὴν ὑποχωρεῖν διὰ τὸ πεφρᾶχθαι τὰ ἄνω, μένει περὶ
τὰ πρῶτα τρυπήματα· σάττεσθαι[25] γὰρ εἰς αὐτὸν οὐ
25 πέφυκεν. σημεῖον δ᾽ ἐστὶ | τοῦ εἴργειν δύνασθαι τὸ
ὕδωρ ἀκινητίζοντα τὸν ἀέρα τὸ ἐπ᾽ αὐτῆς γινόμενον
τῆς κλεψύδρας. ἐὰν γάρ τις αὐτῆς αὐτὴν τὴν κωδίαν
ἐμπλήσας ὕδατος, ἐπιλαβὼν τὸν αὐλόν, καταστρέψῃ
ἐπὶ τὸν αὐλόν, οὐ φέρεται τὸ ὕδωρ διὰ τοῦ αὐλοῦ ἐπὶ
στόμα. ἀνοιχθέντος δὲ τοῦ στόματος οὐκ εὐθὺς ἐκρεῖ |
30 κατὰ τὸν αὐλόν, ἀλλὰ μικροτέρῳ ὕστερον, ὡς οὐκ ὂν
ἐπὶ τῷ στόματι τοῦ αὐλοῦ, ἀλλ᾽ ὕστερον διὰ τούτου
φερόμενον ἀνοιχθέντος. πλήρους τε καὶ ὀρθῆς οὔσης
τῆς κλεψύδρας, ἀνοιχθέντος τοῦ αὐλοῦ εὐθὺς ῥεῖ διὰ
τοῦ ἠθμοῦ, διὰ τὸ ἐκείνου μὲν ἅπτεσθαι, τῶν δὲ ἄκρων
35 τοῦ αὐλοῦ μὴ ἅπτεσθαι. οὐκ | εἰσέρχεται μὲν οὖν τὸ
ὕδωρ εἰς τὴν κλεψύδραν διὰ τὴν προειρημένην αἰτίαν,
ἐξέρχεται δὲ ἀνοιχθέντος τοῦ ὑλοῦ διὰ τὸ τὸν ἐν αὐτῷ
ἀέρα κινούμενον ἄνω καὶ κάτω πολλὴν κίνησιν[26] ποιεῖν τοῦ ἐν τῇ κλεψύδρᾳ ὕδατος. ὠθούμενον δὲ κάτω καὶ

---

[25] σάττεσθαι Bonitz Ind. Arist. 121a24 : ἅττεσθαι codd.

thrust or traveling by itself and not being forced, naturally travels in a straight line, as other elements do. But when the clepsydra is dipped at a slant, the air remains on its straight course through the holes opposite to those in the water and is driven out by the water, and as it recedes the water enters. But when the clepsydra is dipped into the water at a right angle,[27] as the air cannot recede at a right angle because the upper holes are blocked, it remains around the first holes; for it cannot naturally compress into itself. A sign that the air, by not moving, can retain the water is what happens with the clepsydra itself. For if one fills the bulb itself of the clepsydra with water, and closing the tube turns it over on its tube, the water does not travel through the tube to the mouth. Now when the mouth is opened the water does not flow out immediately along the tube, but only after a little time, as it is not at the mouth of the tube, but travels along it later when it is opened. But if the clepsydra is full and at a right angle, when the tube is opened the water flows at once through the strainer,[28] because it touches the strainer but does not touch the extremities of the tube. The water, then, does not enter the clepsydra, for the reason mentioned before, but goes out when the tube is opened because the air moving up and down in it causes much movement of the water in the clepsydra. But when it is thrust downward and itself tends

[27] Or "upright" or "straight" (ὀρθῆς).
[28] I.e., the holes in the bottom of the bulb.

[26] κίνησιν Forster ex Gaza : κένωσιν codd.

αὐτὸ ῥέπον εἰς αὐτὸ εἰκότως ἐκρεῖ, βιαζόμενον τὸν
915a ἐκτὸς ‖ τῆς κλεψύδρας ἀέρα κινούμενόν τε καὶ ὄντα
ἴσον τῇ δυνάμει τῷ ἐπωθοῦντι αὐτὸν ἀέρι, τῇ δὲ
ἀντερείσει ἀσθενέστερον ἐκείνου διὰ τὸ διὰ στενοῦ
αὐτὸν τοῦ αὐλοῦ ῥέοντα θᾶττον καὶ σφοδρότερον ῥεῖν,
5 καὶ προσπίπτειν τῷ ὕδατι. τοῦ δὲ πωμασθέντος | τοῦ
αὐλοῦ μὴ συρρεῖν τὸ ὕδωρ αἴτιον, ὅτι τὸ ὕδωρ εἰσιὸν
εἰς τὴν κλεψύδραν ἐξωθεῖ βίᾳ τὸν ἀέρα ἐξ αὐτῆς.
σημεῖον δέ ἐστι τὸ γινόμενον ἐν ταύτῃ πνεῦμα καὶ
ἐρυγμός. εἰσιόντος δὲ τοῦ ὕδατος, βίᾳ ὠθοῦν συνεισ-
πίπτει εἰς τὸν αὐλὸν αὐτοῦ, καθάπερ τὰ ἐμπιεστὰ[27]
10 ξύλα ἢ χαλκὸς τῇ διαιρέσι πιεζούμενος, μένει | ἄνευ
παντὸς ἄλλου συνδέσμου ⟨ἕως ἂν⟩[28] ἐκκρουσθῇ ἐκ
τοῦ ἐναντίου, καθάπερ τοὺς κατεαγότας ἐπιούρους[29] ἐν
τοῖς ξύλοις ἐκκρούουσιν. συμβαίνει δὲ τοῦτο ἀνοιχθέντος τοῦ αὐλοῦ γίνεσθαι διὰ τὰ προειρημένα. ἢ
οὖν διὰ ταῦτα εἰκός ἐστιν αὐτὸν[30] μὴ ἐκρεῖν, ἢ ἐξιόν-
τος[31] βιαίου ἀέρος καὶ πνευματουμένου. δηλοῖ δὲ ὁ |
15 ψόφος ἐπισπᾶσθαι τῷ πνεύματι τὸ ὕδωρ ἄνω, ὥσπερ
ἐπὶ πολλῶν συμβαίνει γίνεσθαι. ἐπισπώμενον δὲ καὶ
συνεχὲς ὂν αὐτῷ[32] πᾶν τὸ ὕδωρ μένει πιεζούμενον ὑπὸ
τοῦ ἀέρος, ἕως ἂν ἀπωσθῇ πάλιν ὑπ᾽ αὐτοῦ. τῆς δὲ

---

27 ἐμπιεστὰ Yᵃ : πιεστὰ Cᵃ : ἐκπιεστὰ cett. codd.

28 ⟨ἕως ἂν⟩ Bussemaker ex Gaza : post συνδέσμου lac. indic.
Bekker   29 ἐπιούρους Diels (59A69 D-K) : ὁπιούρους
codd. : cuneos Barth.   30 αὐτὸν : αὐτὸ Bussemaker

31 ἐξιόντος : ἐξι⟨έναι κωλύ⟩οντος Diels (59A69 D-K)

32 αὐτῷ : αὐτῶι Diels (59A69 D-K)

in that direction, it naturally flows out, forcing (*its way through*) the air outside the clepsydra, which is moving and is equal in power to the air which is pressing upon it, but weaker than it in resistance, because flowing through the narrow tube it flows more quickly and with more violence, and strikes against the water. And the reason why the water does not flow when the tube is closed is that the water as it flows into the clepsydra forcibly drives the air out of it. A sign of this is the breath and sucking noise that take place in it. But when the water enters, pushing with force it rushes with (*the air*) into the tube, (*and*) just like wood or bronze wedges driven in for splitting, it remains without any other bond, until it is driven out from the opposite direction, just as they knock out broken pegs in timber. This happens when the tube is opened for the aforesaid reasons. For these reasons, then, it is natural that the water does not flow out, or else because air is exiting violently and becomes inflated.[29] The noise shows that the water is drawn up by the air, as also occurs in many other cases. Now all the water, being drawn up and continuous with itself,[30] remains under pressure from the air, until it is pushed back again by it. But since the original water re-

[29] The text of this line is uncertain. If Diels's conjecture is accepted, it should be rendered "because the air violently prevents it and becomes inflated."

[30] Or, following Diels, "with it (i.e., the air)" ($a\dot{v}\tau\hat{\varphi}$ [sc. $\tau\hat{\varphi}$ $\dot{a}\acute{\epsilon}\rho\iota$]), though I think the author is saying that the water, drawn up into the tube, is continuous with itself.

ἀρχῆς μενούσης, καὶ τὸ ἄλλο ἐξ αὐτῆς κρέμαται ὕδωρ
20 ἓν καὶ συνεχές. εὔλογον | δὲ τοῦτο γίνεσθαι· τοῦ γὰρ
αὐτοῦ ἐστι κινῆσαί τε ἐκ τῆς οἰκείας χώρας τι, καὶ
τοῦτο ἴσχειν, ὡς ἐκίνησεν,[33] ἐν πλείονι δὲ χρόνῳ, ἐὰν
ᾖ ὅμοια τῇ δυνάμει τό τε ἔχον καὶ τὸ ἐχόμενον, ἢ τὸ
ἴσχον[34] κρεῖττον, ὅπερ ἐνταῦθα συμβαίνει· πνεῦμα
γὰρ ὕδατός ἐστι κρεῖττον τῇ δυνάμει. |

25 9. Διὰ τί τὰ μόρια τῶν φυτῶν καὶ τῶν ζῴων, ὅσα
μὴ ὀργανικά, πάντα περιφερῆ, τῶν μὲν φυτῶν τὸ
στέλεχος καὶ οἱ πτόρθοι, τῶν δὲ ζῴων κνῆμαι, μηροί,
βραχίονες, θώραξ· τρίγωνον δὲ οὐδὲ πολύγωνον οὔτε
ὅλον οὔτε μόριόν ἐστιν; πότερον, ὥσπερ Ἀρχύτας
30 ἔλεγεν, διὰ τὸ ἐν τῇ κινήσει τῇ φυσικῇ | ἐνεῖναι τὴν
τοῦ ἴσου ἀναλογίαν (κινεῖσθαι γὰρ ἀνάλογον πάντα),
ταύτην δὲ μόνην εἰς αὑτὴν ἀνακάμπτειν, ὥστε κύκλους
ποιεῖν καὶ στρογγύλα, ὅταν ἐγγένηται;

10. Διὰ τί ἐν τοῖς ἐσχάτοις ἀεὶ γίνεται περιφερῆ; ἢ
ὅτι ἡ φύσις ἐκ τῶν ἐνδεχομένων πάντα ποιεῖ ὡς
35 δυνατὸν[35] ἄριστα | καὶ κάλλιστα, τὸ δὲ σχῆμα τοῦτο
κάλλιστον, τὸ αὐτὸ αὑτῷ ὁμοιότατον;

11. Διὰ τί, ἐὰν κύκλος ῥιφθῇ, τὸ μὲν πρῶτον εὐθεῖαν γράφει, παυόμενος δὲ ἕλικα, ἕως ἂν πέσῃ; ἢ
εὐθεῖαν μὲν τὸ πρῶτον ὅτι ὁμοίως ἔνθεν καὶ ἔνθεν ὁ
915b ἀὴρ ἀπορθοῖ; ἴσης ‖ οὖν οὔσης τῆς ῥοπῆς ἔνθεν καὶ

---

[33] ἐκίνησεν Bussemaker : ἐκείνης codd.
[34] ἴσχον Bussemaker ex Gaza : ἴσον codd.
[35] ὡς δυνατὸν om. Cᵃ

mains there, the rest hangs from it, being one and continuous. It is reasonable that this should be so; for it is (*reasonable*) for the same thing both to move something from its proper place, and to restrain it, when it has moved it, and for a longer time, if what is holding and what is held are equal in power, or if what is restraining is stronger, as is the case here; for air is stronger in power than water.

9. Why are the parts of plants and animals that are not instrumental[31] all rounded—of plants the stem and the shoots, and of animals the calves, thighs, arms, and chest—but neither the whole nor a part is triangular or polygonal? Is it, just as Archytas said,[32] because the proportion of equality is present in natural movement (for he said that all things are moved in proportion), but that this proportion alone bends back on itself,[33] so as to make circles and curves, whenever it comes to be?

10. Why are things always rounded at the extremities? Is it because nature makes everything as best and as beautiful as possible from what is available, and this shape is the most beautiful—the one that is most similar to itself?

11. Why, if a circular object[34] is thrown, does it first describe a straight line, but as it comes to a stop it describes a spiral, until it falls? Is it straight at first because the air keeps it aright similarly on one side and the other? Therefore, as the balance is equal on one side and the other, the

---

[31] It is not clear what the author means by instrumental parts here.

[32] 47A23a D-K.

[33] Or "returns to itself" (εἰς αὑτὴν ἀνακάμπτειν).

[34] Clearly a discus, not a ball.

ἔνθεν, ἀνάγκη καὶ τὴν γραμμὴν τοιαύτην εἶναι, ἢ ἴσον
διαιρεῖ τὸν τόπον ἔνθεν καὶ ἔνθεν· τοιαύτη δέ ἐστιν
εὐθεῖα. ὅταν δὲ βρίσῃ ἐπὶ θάτερον μέρος δι᾽ ἀνωμαλίαν τοῦ περισταμένου ἀέρος, οὐκέτι ἴσην γράφει τό
5 τε | ἐντὸς καὶ τὸ ἐκτὸς μέρος, ἀλλ᾽ ἀνάγκη περιφερῆ.

12. Διὰ τί τοῖς ἄνισον τὸ βάρος[36] ἔχουσι μεγέθεσιν, ἐάν τις ⟨τὸ⟩[37] κουφότερον κινῇ τῶν μερῶν, κύκλῳ
περιφέρεται τὸ βαλλόμενον, οἷον τοῖς μεμολιβδωμένοις ἀστραγάλοις συμβαίνει, ἐάν τις βάλλῃ τὸ
10 κουφότερον πρὸς αὑτὸν στρέψας μέρος; ἢ | ὅτι τὸ
βαρύτερον ἀδύνατον ἰσοδρομεῖν τῷ κουφοτέρῳ, ἀπὸ
τῆς αὐτῆς ἰσχύος ῥιφθέν; ἐπεὶ δὲ ἀνάγκη μὲν κινεῖσθαι, ἐξ ἴσου δὲ καὶ ἐπ᾽ εὐθείας ἀδύνατον, ἀνάγκη εἰς
τὸ ἐντὸς φερόμενον κύκλῳ φέρεσθαι· οἷον εἰ ὅλως τι
15 ἦν αὐτοῦ ἀκίνητον διὰ βάρος ἐν μέσῳ, τὸ μὲν πρὸς τῷ
ἀφιέντι εἰς τὸ πρόσθεν ἂν | ἐκινήθη αὐτοῦ μέρος, τὸ δὲ
ὑπ᾽ ἐκεῖνα πρὸς τὸν ἀφιέντα. ἐπεὶ δὲ κινεῖται μὲν τὸ
πᾶν, ἔχει δὲ ἐν μέσῳ τὸ βάρος φερόμενον, ἀνάγκη
ταὐτὸ τοῦτο ποιεῖν.

13. Διὰ τί τὰ φερόμενα ὅταν ἀντιπέσῃ, ἀφάλλεται
εἰς τοὐναντίον ἢ πέφυκε φέρεσθαι, καὶ πρὸς ὁμοίας
20 γωνίας; ἢ | ὅτι οὐ μόνον ἐκείνην φέρεται τὴν φορὰν ἣν
φέρεται κατὰ τὸ οἰκεῖον μέρος, ἀλλὰ καὶ τὴν ὑπὸ τοῦ
ἀφιέντος γινομένην; ἡ μὲν οὖν οἰκεία παύεται, ὅταν εἰς
τὸν οἰκεῖον ἔλθῃ τόπον (ἅπαν γὰρ ἠρεμεῖ ἐλθὸν εἰς ὂν

---

36 βάρος Bussemaker (cf. *Pr.* 16.913a34) : βάθος codd.
37 ⟨τὸ⟩ Richards (cf. *Pr.* 16.913a35)

line too must necessarily be such that it divides the space equally on the one side and on the other; and such a line is straight. But when it is weighed down on one side owing to the unevenness of the surrounding air, the inside and the outside no longer describe an equal line, but it must necessarily be rounded.

12.[35] Why is it that in magnitudes having unequal weight, if one moves the lighter of the parts, what is thrown revolves in a circle, as happens with loaded dice, if one throws with the lighter part turned toward oneself? Is it because the heavier part cannot move at a pace equal to that of the lighter, when cast with the same strength? Now since it[36] must necessarily move, but cannot do so at an equal pace and so in a straight line, when it travels, it must travel in an inward direction and in a circle; just as if, owing to the weight in the middle, part of it had been entirely motionless, the part next to the thrower would have moved forward, but the other side toward the thrower. But when the whole moves, and holds the weight in the center as it travels, it must move in the same way.

13.[37] Why do things that are traveling, when they encounter something, rebound in the direction opposite to that in which they are naturally traveling, and at similar angles? Is it because they travel not only with the impulse for motion that is proper to them, but also with what is imparted to them by the thrower? For the movement proper to them ceases when they reach the proper place (for everything comes to rest when it reaches the place to which

[35] Cf. *Pr.* 16.3.
[36] *Pr.* 16.3 has "the whole thing."
[37] Cf. *Pr.* 16.4.

φέρεται τόπον κατὰ φύσιν), καθ᾽ ἣν δ᾽ ἔχει ἀλλοτρίαν,
25 ἀνάγκη ἔτι κινεῖσθαι, οὐκ εἰς τὸ πρόσθεν | δὲ διὰ τὸ
κωλύεσθαι, ἀλλ᾽ ἢ εἰς τὸ πλάγιον ἢ εἰς τὸ ὀρθόν.
ἅπαντα δὲ ἀποπηδᾷ πρὸς ὁμοίας γωνίας διὰ τὸ φέρεσθαι μὲν ἐνταῦθα οὗ ἡ κίνησις φέρει, ἣν ἐποίησεν ὁ
ἀφείς· ἐκεῖ δὲ πρὸς ὀξεῖαν ἢ πρὸς ὀρθὴν φέρεσθαι
συμβαίνει. ἐπεὶ οὖν τὸ ἀντικροῦσαν κωλύει τὴν εἰς
30 εὐθὺ κίνησιν, ὁμοίως κωλύει τὸ φερόμενον | καὶ τὴν
φορὰν αὐτοῦ. ὥσπερ οὖν ἐν τοῖς κατόπτροις τὸ ἄκρον
τῆς εὐθείας οὗ ξυνέπεσεν ἡ ὄψις φαίνεται, καὶ ἐν τοῖς
φερομένοις οὕτω τὸ ἐναντίον γίνεται· τοσαύτην γὰρ
γωνίαν ἀπέωσται ὅση γίνεται ἡ κατὰ κορυφήν. δεῖ
γὰρ νοῆσαι μετακινουμένην τὴν γωνίαν καὶ τὴν φο-
35 ράν. τούτου δὲ γενομένου φανερὸν | ὅτι πρὸς ὁμοίας
γωνίας ἀνάγκη ἀφάλλεσθαι.

it is traveling according to nature), but, to the extent to which there is an extraneous impulse, it must continue moving, and not forward, because it is checked, but either at a slant or a right angle. Now everything recoils at similar angles because it travels to the point where the movement, which the thrower creates, carries it; and at that point it must be traveling either at an acute angle or a right angle. Therefore, since the resisting (*surface*) prevents its movement in a straight line, it similarly stops both the thing that is traveling and its impulse. So just as in mirrors the image appears at the end of the straight line where it falls, so the opposite takes place in the things that are traveling; for they are pushed back at the same angle as that at the apex. For one should note that both the angle and the impulse are changed. And when this occurs it is evident that it must rebound at similar angles.

BOOK XVII

INTRODUCTION

Judging by their titles and their juxtaposition within the *Problems*, one might conclude that Books 16 and 17 (on inanimate and animate things, respectively) are thematically connected or in some other way related. But except for some minor overlap between 16.7 and 17.1, they are not. Book 16 is fairly long, is filled with textual problems, and its focus is largely mathematical-mechanical. Book 17, by contrast, is the second briefest book in the *Problems*, presents few philological challenges, and consists of three unrelated chapters with a focus quite different from that of 16.

The three chapters of Book 17 deal with these issues: why asymmetrical living things appear larger than symmetrical ones, why living things grow more in length than in breadth or depth, and how the terms "prior" and "posterior" should be understood (in the case of human existence).

I suspect that these three chapters were stuck together rather late in the composition of the extant version of the *Problems*. This does not mean, however, the chapters themselves were composed late.

ΟΣΑ ΠΕΡΙ ΕΜΨΥΧΑ

1. Διὰ τί οἱ ἀσύμμετροι παρ' ἀλλήλους θεωρούμενοι μείζους φαίνονται ἢ καθ' αὑτοὺς μόνους; ἢ ὅτι τὸ σύμμετρόν ἐστιν ‖ ἕν, καὶ ἡ συμμετρία ὅτι μάλιστα ἓν ποιεῖ, τὸ δὲ ἓν ἀδιαίρετον βούλεται εἶναι, τὸ δὲ ἀδιαίρετον ἔλαττόν ἐστιν, ἡ δὲ ἀσυμμετρία[1] κατὰ τὴν διαφορὰν πολλὰ ποιεῖ; καθ' αὑτὰ μὲν οὖν θεωρούμενα μᾶλλον λανθάνει ποῖα ἄττα τὰ μεγέθη ἐστί, παρ' ἄλληλα δὲ οὔ. τὸ μὲν οὖν ἀδιαίρετον ἓν φαίνεται, καὶ ἡ θεωρία μία ἐστὶν αὐτοῦ διὰ τὴν συμμετρίαν· τὸ δὲ ἀσύμμετρον ὡς πολλὰ ὂν θεωρίαν ποιεῖ πλείω, καὶ μείζω φαίνεται τῷ ἓν ὂν πολλὰ φαίνεσθαι· ἔχει γὰρ τήν τε τοῦ μεγέθους κατὰ τὴν συνέχειαν φύσιν, καὶ τὴν τοῦ ἀριθμοῦ κατὰ τὸ ἀνώμαλον τῶν μερῶν. διόπερ εἰκότως τὴν ἐξ ἀμφοῖν αὔξην ἔχον μεῖζον φαίνεται παρὰ τὸ ἁπλοῦν καὶ ἕν.

2. Διὰ τί ἐπὶ μῆκος μᾶλλον τὰ ζῷα καὶ τὰ φυτὰ

916a

5

10

---

[1] ἀσυμμετρία Bussemaker ex Gaza : συμμετρία codd.

PROBLEMS CONNECTED
WITH ANIMATE THINGS

1.[1] Why do those who are asymmetrical look larger when next to others,[2] than when they are by themselves? Is it because the symmetrical is a unity, and symmetry most of all produces unity, and unity tends to be indivisible, and the indivisible is smaller, whereas asymmetry produces multiplicity in accordance with its diversity? When things[3] are seen by themselves, therefore, their sizes tend to escape notice, but not when they are next to others. So the indivisible appears to be a unity, and because of its symmetry the impression it makes is one; but the asymmetrical, as though it were many, makes more of an impression, and it appears larger by appearing to be many although it is a unity. For it has the nature of size, in accordance with its continuity, and of number, in accordance with the inequality of its parts. Hence it is reasonable that, having an increase in both these characteristics, it appears larger in comparison with what is simple and a unity.

2. Why do animals and plants grow more in length? Is it

---

[1] Cf. *Pr.* 5.25, 16.7, 30.4.   [2] I.e., those who are symmetrical. There may be something wrong with the text here (esp. ἀλλήλους).   [3] The author is speaking either of things generally or of asymmetrical things specifically.

φύεται; ἢ ὅτι τὸ μῆκος μὲν τρὶς αὔξεται, τὸ δὲ πλάτος
δίς, τὸ δὲ βάθος ἅπαξ; ἔστι γὰρ μῆκος τὸ ἀπὸ τῆς
15 ἀρχῆς πρῶτον, | ὥστε μόνον τε αὔξεται, καὶ ἅμα τῷ
πλάτει πάλιν γινόμενον, καὶ τρίτον ἅμα τῷ βάθει. τὸ
δὲ πλάτος δίς, καθ᾿ ἑαυτό τε καὶ ἅμα τῷ βάθει.[2]

3. Πῶς τὸ πρότερον καὶ τὸ ὕστερον δεῖ λαβεῖν;
πότερον ὥσπερ ἡμῶν οἱ ἐπὶ Τροίας καὶ ἐκείνων οἱ πρὸ
20 αὐτῶν καὶ | ἀεὶ οἱ ἐπάνω πρότεροί εἰσιν; ἢ εἴπερ ἀρχή
τίς ἐστιν καὶ μέσον καὶ τέλος τοῦ παντός, καὶ ὅταν
γηράσκων τις ἐπὶ τὸ πέρας ἔλθῃ καὶ πάλιν ἐπανα-
στρέψῃ ἐπὶ τὴν ἀρχήν, τὰ δὲ ἐγγυτέρω τῆς ἀρχῆς
πρότερα, τί κωλύει ἡμᾶς ἐν τῷ πρὸς τὴν ἀρχὴν εἶναι
25 μᾶλλον; εἰ δὲ τοῦτο, κἂν πρότεροι εἴημεν. ὥσπερ | ἐπὶ
τοῦ οὐρανοῦ καὶ ἑκάστου τῶν ἄστρων φορᾷ κύκλος τίς
ἐστιν, τί κωλύει καὶ τὴν γένεσιν καὶ τὴν ἀπώλειαν τῶν
φθαρτῶν τοιαύτην εἶναι, ὥστε πάλιν ταῦτα γίνεσθαι
καὶ φθείρεσθαι; καθάπερ καὶ φασὶ κύκλον εἶναι τὰ
ἀνθρώπινα. τὸ μὲν δὴ τῷ ἀριθμῷ τοὺς αὐτοὺς ἀξιοῦν
30 εἶναι ἀεὶ τοὺς γινομένους εὔηθες, | τὸ δὲ τῷ εἴδει
μᾶλλον ἄν τις ἀποδέξαιτο· ὥστε κἂν αὐτοὶ πρότεροι
εἴημεν, καὶ θείη ἄν τις τὴν τοῦ εἱρμοῦ τάξιν τοιαύτην
εἶναι ὡς πάλιν ἐπανακάμπτειν ἐπὶ τὴν ἀρχὴν καὶ
συνεχὲς ποιεῖν καὶ ἀεὶ κατὰ ταὐτὰ ἔχειν. τοὺς γὰρ
ἀνθρώπους φησὶν Ἀλκμαίων διὰ τοῦτο ἀπόλλυσθαι,

---

[2] βάθει w Rpᶜ : μεγέθει cett. codd.

---

[4] Sources: *Metaph.* Δ 11, GC 338b14–19, and Strato *On Prior*

because increase in length is triple, in breadth double, and in depth single? For length is primary and from the beginning, such that *(at first)* it alone increases, *and* it again occurs at the same time as breadth, and thirdly at the same time as depth. But breadth is double, by itself and at the same time as depth.

3.[4] How should one understand the terms "prior" and "posterior"?[5] As the people of Troy[6] are prior to us, and those before them are prior to them, and so on for those even prior to them? Or if indeed there is a beginning, a middle, and an end of the universe, and when someone old he reaches the limit and turns back again to the beginning, and those things that are nearer the beginning are prior, what prevents us from being nearer to the beginning? If this is true, then even we should be prior. Just as with the movement of the heavens and of each of the stars there is a circle, what prevents the birth and death of perishable things from being this way, so that they are born and destroyed again? And so they say human life is a circle. Indeed, to claim that those coming into being are always the same *in number* is absurd, but one would more likely accept that they are the same *in form*. So we too should ourselves be "prior," and one could assume the arrangement of the series to be such that it curves back to the beginning and produces continuity and always acts in the same way. For Alcmaeon[7] says that humans die because of

and Posterior (frs. 15–16 Sharples). See also *Phys.* 4.14.

[5] Or "before" and "after." The author is clearly concerned with these terms as they apply to human existence generally.

[6] I.e., from the time of the Trojan War.

[7] 24B2 D-K; cf. A12.

35 ὅτι οὐ δύνανται τὴν | ἀρχὴν τῷ τέλει προσάψαι,
κομψῶς εἰρηκώς, εἴ τις ὡς τύπῳ φράζοντος αὐτοῦ
ἀποδέχοιτο καὶ μὴ διακριβοῦν ἐθέλοι τὸ λεχθέν. εἰ δὴ
κύκλος ἐστίν, τοῦ δὲ κύκλου μήτε ἀρχὴ μήτε ηπέρας,
οὐδ' ἂν πρότεροι εἶεν τῷ ἐγγυτέρω τῆς ἀρχῆς εἶναι,
οὔθ' ἡμεῖς ἐκείνων οὔτ' ἐκεῖνοι ἡμῶν.

this, that they cannot connect the beginning to the end—cleverly spoken, if one accepts that he is speaking figuratively and does not want what he said to be taken literally. Now if it is a circle, and the circle has neither beginning nor limit, they would not be prior by being nearer the beginning,[8] nor would we be prior to them nor they to us.

[8] I.e., if human life is a circle, etc., those from the time of the Trojan War would not be prior by being nearer the beginning.

BOOK XVIII

INTRODUCTION

The key word in the title (φιλολογία) does not mean "philology" in the modern sense of the science or study of language per se. That is not the topic of *Pr.* 18. Nor is the topic studiousness or love of learning (one meaning of φιλολογία), though that is closer. Rather, I take the word (which does not appear elsewhere in the book) to mean "love of (or interest in) literature or letters" (cf. *Rh.* 2.23, 1398b14)—including rhetoric, which is in fact the most prominent topic of *Pr.* 18.

The chapters of *Pr.* 18 contain the following topics: reading and sleepiness (1 and 7); contentious arguments (2 and 8); rhetorical speeches (and the use of paradigms, stories, and enthymemes in them) (3); differences between oratory and other occupations (4–6); and, the kinds of historical accounts people enjoy hearing (9–10). The background for much of this book is Aristotle's *Rhetoric*, though the author may be drawing on or referring to Aristotle's logical works and *Poetics* as well.

ΟΣΑ ΠΕΡΙ ΦΙΛΟΛΟΓΙΑΝ

916b   1. Διὰ τί τοὺς μέν, ἐὰν ἄρξωνται ἀναγινώσκειν,
ὕπνος λαμβάνει καὶ μὴ βουλομένους, τοὺς δὲ βουλομένους ποιεῖ ἐγρηγορέναι,[1] ὅταν λάβωσι τὸ βιβλίον;[2]

5   ἢ ὅσοις μέν εἰσι πνευματικαὶ | κινήσεις διὰ ψυχρότητα
φύσεως ἢ μελαγχολικῶν χυμῶν, δι᾽ οὓς περίττωμα
γίνεται πνευματικὸν ἄπεπτον διὰ ψυχρότητα; τούτοις
ὅταν μὲν κινῆται ἡ διάνοια καὶ μὴ νοήσῃ ἐπιστήσασά
τι, ἐκκρούεται τῇ ἑτέρᾳ κινήσει οὔσῃ καταψυκτικῇ, διὸ
μᾶλλον καθεύδουσιν. ὅταν δὲ ἐρείσωσι πρός τι ἐν τῇ

10   διανοίᾳ, | ὅπερ ἡ ἀνάγνωσις ποιεῖ, κινοῦνται ὑπὸ τῆς
θερμαντικῆς κινήσεως οὐκ ἐκκρουομένης ὑπ᾽ οὐδενός,
ὥστε οὐ δύνανται καθεύδειν. τῶν δὲ κατὰ φύσιν ἐχόντων ὅταν στῇ πρὸς ἓν ἡ διάνοια καὶ μὴ μεταβάλλῃ
πολλαχῇ ἰσχυροτάτη οὖσα, ἴσχεται[3] καὶ τὰ ἄλλα ὅσα

15   ἐστὶ περὶ τὸν τόπον τοῦτον, ὧν ἠρέμησις | ὁ ὕπνος
ἐστίν. ὅταν δὲ στῇ καὶ οἷον κοπιάσῃ ὁ νοῦς, βαρύνει

---

     [1] ποιεῖ ἐγρηγορέναι Bussemaker ex Gaza (cf. Pr. 18.7,
917a19) : προσεγρηγορέναι Bekker : προεγρηγορέναι codd.

     [2] post βιβλίον lac. indic. Ruelle

     [3] ἴσχεται : ἴσταται Forster (cf. Pr. 18.7, 917a30)

PROBLEMS CONNECTED
WITH THE LOVE OF LETTERS

1.[1] Why is it that in some people, if they begin to read, sleep overtakes them when they don't want it to, whereas others, who want to sleep, are made to be awake when they take up a book? Is it because in the former, there are pneumatic movements owing to a coldness that is natural or from melancholic humors, owing to which the pneumatic residue becomes unconcocted because of coldness? In such people, when the intellect is moved but does not think with concentration, it is checked by the other movement,[2] which cools, which is why they are more likely to sleep. But when they fix on something in the intellect, which is what reading does, they are moved by a hotter movement, which is unchecked by anything, so that they cannot sleep. Now for those who are in a natural state, when the intellect, being very strong, stands at one point[3] and does not change in many directions, all the other (*activities*) in this region are restrained, and their immobility is sleep. And when thought is stationary and as it were fa-

[1] Cf. *Pr.* 18.7.

[2] Presumably, the movement of pneumatic residues.

[3] Or perhaps "focuses on one subject."

τὴν κεφαλὴν ὢν ἐν αὐτῇ καὶ ποιεῖ τὸν ὕπνον. κινουμένης δὲ τῆς ψυχῆς κατὰ φύσιν οὐ καθεύδει· ζῇ γὰρ
τότε μάλιστα. τὸ δ' ἐγρηγορέναι τοῦ ζῆν ⟨μᾶλλον⟩[4]
αἴτιόν ἐστιν ἢ τὸ καθεύδειν. |

20   2. Διὰ τί οἱ ἐριστικοὶ λόγοι γυμναστικοί εἰσιν; ἢ
ὅτι ἔχουσι τὸ νικᾶν ἢ ἡττᾶσθαι πυκνόν; φιλονείκους
οὖν εὐθὺς ποιοῦσιν· καὶ γὰρ νικῶντες διὰ τὸ χαίρειν
προάγονται μᾶλλον ἐρίζειν καὶ ἡττώμενοι ὡς ἀναμα-
χούμενοι. καὶ οἱ ἐν τοῖς ἄλλοις ἀγῶσι ταὐτό· διὸ καὶ
25 μαχόμενοι καὶ ἥττους ὄντες πολλάκις | οὐ βούλονται
διαλύεσθαι.

  3. Διὰ τί τοῖς παραδείγμασι χαίρουσιν οἱ[5] ἄνθρωποι ἐν ταῖς ῥητορείαις καὶ τοῖς λόγοις μᾶλλον τῶν
ἐνθυμημάτων; ἢ ὅτι τῷ τε μανθάνειν χαίρουσι καὶ τῷ
ταχύ; ῥᾷον δὲ διὰ τῶν παραδειγμάτων καὶ τῶν λόγων
30 μανθάνουσιν· ἃ γὰρ ἴσασιν, | ἔστι ταῦτα καὶ ἐπὶ
μέρους, τὰ δὲ ἐνθυμήματα ἀπόδειξίς ἐστιν ἐκ τῶν
καθόλου, ἃ ἧττον ἴσμεν ἢ τὰ μέρη. ἔτι οἷς ἂν μαρτυ-
ρῶσι πλείους, μᾶλλον πιστεύομεν, τὰ δὲ παραδείγμα-
τα καὶ οἱ λόγοι μαρτυρίαις ἐοίκασιν· αἱ δὲ διὰ τῶν
μαρτύρων ῥᾴδιοι πίστεις. ἔτι τὸ ὅμοιον μανθάνουσιν
35 ἡδέως, τὸ δὲ παράδειγμα | καὶ οἱ μῦθοι τὸ ὅμοιον
δεικνύουσιν.

---

4 ⟨μᾶλλον⟩ Bonitz ex Gaza (cf. Pr. 18.7, 917a24–25)
5 οἱ Y[a] Ap. X[a] : om. cett. codd.

---

4 Cf. Pr. 18.8. At SE 165b7–8, Aristotle writes: "Contentious
arguments are syllogisms or apparent syllogisms that come from
what appear to be reputable opinions (ἐνδόξων) but are not."

tigued, it weighs down the head (being in it) and produces sleep. But when the soul moves according to nature, it does not sleep; for then especially it is alive. But being awake is the cause of life rather than being asleep.

2.[4] Why are contentious arguments suitable for exercise? Is it because they involve frequent victories and defeats? Therefore they immediately produce a love of victory: indeed, victorious people are induced by their enjoyment to compete again, and those who are defeated are such as to renew the fight. And those engaged in other contests are the same; this is why when people are fighting and being defeated, often they do not want to resolve it.

3.[5] Why do people enjoy paradigms[6] and stories[7] more than enthymemes[8] in rhetorical speeches? Is it because they enjoy learning, and quickly? But they learn more easily by paradigms and stories; for what they come to know are these particular things, but enthymemes are demonstrations from universals, which we know less than particulars. Further, we are more inclined to believe what many bear witness to, and paradigms and stories are more like witnesses; and the proofs that come from witnesses are easy (*to obtain*). Further, people learn with pleasure what is similar,[9] and paradigms and tales display similarities.

[5] Cf. *Rh*. 1356b21–23.   [6] Or "examples" ($\pi\alpha\rho\alpha\delta\epsilon\acute{\iota}\gamma\mu\alpha$-$\sigma\iota$). Paradigms are rhetorical inductions; see esp. *Rh*. 2.20, which may be a source for this chapter.   [7] The last line of this chapter makes clear that the author is treating synonymously οἱ λόγοι and οἱ μῦθοι (which I translate "stories" and "tales" respectively). Aristotle treats stories and paradigms together in *Rh*. 2.20.

[8] I.e., rhetorical syllogisms; see esp. *Rh*. 2.22, which may be a source for this chapter.

[9] Perhaps the author means "what is familiar."

4. Διὰ τί ῥήτορα μὲν καὶ στρατηγὸν καὶ χρηματιστὴν λέγομεν δεινόν, αὐλητὴν δὲ καὶ ὑποκριτὴν οὐ λέγομεν; ἢ ὅτι τῶν μὲν ἡ δύναμις ἄνευ πλεονεξίας (ἡδονῆς γὰρ στοχαστική ἐστι), τῶν δὲ πρὸς τὸ πλεο-

917a νεκτεῖν; ῥήτωρ γὰρ καὶ στρατηγὸς ‖ καὶ χρηματιστὴς ἀγαθός ἐστιν ὁ δυνάμενος πλέον ἔχειν, ἡ δὲ δεινότης μάλιστα ἐν τῷ πλεονεκτεῖν ἐστίν.

5. Διὰ τί τὸν φιλόσοφον τοῦ ῥήτορος οἴονται δια-φέρειν; ἢ ὅτι ὁ μὲν τί ἐστιν ἀδικία, ὁ δὲ ὡς ἄδικος ὁ

5 δεῖνα, καὶ ὁ μὲν | ὅτι τύραννος, ὁ δὲ οἷον ἡ τυραννίς;[6]

6. Διὰ τί, ἅπερ ἄν τινες προέλωνται, ἐνδιατρίβουσι τούτοις ἐνίοτε φαύλοις οὖσι μᾶλλον ἢ ἐν τοῖς σπου-δαιοτέροις, οἷον θαυματοποιὸς ἢ μῖμος ἢ συρικτὴς μᾶλλον ἢ ἀστρονόμος ἢ ῥήτωρ εἶναι ἂν βούλοιτο ὁ

10 ταῦτα προελόμενος; ἢ ὅτι βούλονται | μὲν ἔνιοι τὰ σπουδαιότατα μεταχειρίζεσθαι, διὰ δὲ τὸ μὴ πιστεύ-ειν ἑαυτοῖς ὡς δυνησομένοις, διὰ τοῦτο οὐ πράττου-σιν; ἢ ὅτι ἐν οἷς οἴεται ἕκαστος κρατιστεύειν, ταῦτα προαιρεῖται; ὃ δὲ αἱρεῖται, καὶ ἐπὶ τοῦτ' ἐπείξεται, νέμων τὸ πλεῖστον ἡμέρας αὑτῷ μέρος, ἵνα αὐτὸς

15 αὑτοῦ τυγχάνει κράτιστος ὤν. | ὅ τι δὲ ἄν τινες ἐξ ἀρχῆς προέλωνται καὶ οἷς ἂν συνεθισθῶσιν, οὐδὲ κρίνειν ἔτι δύνανται τὰ βελτίω· διέφθαρται γὰρ ἡ διάνοια διὰ φαύλας προαιρέσεις.

---

6 ὁ μὲν τί τύραννος, ὁ δὲ ποῖον ἡ τυραννίς Richards

---

10 πλεονεξία ("gaining more") can refer to gaining more un-

4. Why do we say an orator, a general, or a businessman is clever, but we do not say this of an *aulos* player or an actor? Is it because the power of the latter does not involve gaining more[10] (for it aims at pleasure), whereas the power of the former is with a view to gain? For an orator, a general, or a businessman is good if he can gain more, and cleverness is found especially in gaining more.

5.[11] Why do people think the philosopher is better than the orator? Is it because the former says what injustice is, whereas the latter says that so-and-so is unjust, and the latter says that someone is a tyrant, whereas the former says that tyranny is such and such?

6. Why do some people spend their time in activities, which they have chosen, that are sometimes base, rather than in more serious ones—e.g., the one choosing these things would want to be a conjurer or mime or a pipe player rather than an astronomer or an orator? Is it because some want to engage in the most serious activities, but do not do so because they don't trust themselves to be able to? Or is it because each chooses that in which he thinks he can excel? Now what he picks "he is enthusiastic about, and devotes most of each day to it, in order that he may surpass himself."[12] But what people have chosen from the beginning and become accustomed to, they can no longer judge with respect to what is best, for their intellect has been corrupted by their base choice.

---

justly or to gaining more without qualification; it can apply to winning an argument or a battle as well as to accumulating wealth.

[11] This chapter is a shorter version of *Pr.* 30.9.

[12] This is a quote from or paraphrase of E. *Antiop.* (fr. 183 Nauck); cf. *Rh.* 1371b31–34.

7. Διὰ τί τοὺς μέν, ἂν ἄρξωνται ἀναγινώσκειν,
ὕπνος λαμβάνει καὶ μὴ βουλομένους, τοὺς δὲ βουλο-
20 μένους οὐ⁷ ποιεῖ δύνασθαι, | ὅταν λάβωσι βιβλίον; ἢ
ὅσοις μέν εἰσι πνευματικαὶ κινήσεις διὰ ψυχρότητα
φύσεως ἢ μελαγχολικῶν χυμῶν, δι᾽ οὓς περίττωμα
γίνεται πνευματικὸν ἄπεπτον διὰ ψυχρότηατ; τούτοις
ὅταν μὲν κινῆται ἡ διάνοια καὶ μὴ νοῇ ἐπιστήσασά τι,
ἐκκρούεται ἡ ἑτέρα κίνησις, διὸ μᾶλλον μεταβάλ-
25 λοντες | πολὺ τὴν διάνοιαν καθεύδουσιν. ἡττᾶται γὰρ
ἡ πνευματική. ὅταν δὲ ἐρείσωσι πρός τι τὴν διάνοιαν,
ὅπερ ἡ ἀνάγνωσις ποιεῖ, κινοῦνται ὑπὸ τῆς πνευματι-
κῆς κινήσεως, οὐκ ἐκκρουομένης ὑπ᾽ οὐδενός, ὥστε οὐ
δύνανται καθεύδειν. τῶν δὲ κατὰ φύσιν ἐχόντων ὅταν
30 στῇ πρὸς ἓν ἡ διάνοια καὶ μὴ | μεταβάλλῃ πολλαχῇ,
ἵσταται καὶ τὰ ἄλλα ὅσα περὶ τὸν τόπον, ὧν ἠρέμησις
ὁ ὕπνος ἐστίν. ἑνὸς γὰρ κυρίου στάντος, ὥσπερ ἐν
τροπῇ, καὶ τὰ ἄλλα μόρια ἵστασθαι πέφυκεν. φύσει
γὰρ ἄνω τὸ κοῦφον φέρεται, τὸ δὲ βαρὺ κάτω. ὅταν
οὖν ἡ ψυχὴ κινῆται κατὰ φύσιν, οὐ καθεύδει· †τούτω
35 γὰρ ἔχει†.⁸ | ὅταν δὲ στῇ καὶ οἷον κοπιάσῃ, ὁ μὲν νοῦς
μεταβάλλει, καὶ ἄνω τὰ σωματώδη πρὸς τὴν κεφαλὴν
ἰόντα ποιεῖ τὸν ὕπνον. δόξειε δ᾽ ἂν ἡ ἀνάγνωσις
κωλύειν καθεύδειν. ἔστι δὲ οὐ διὰ τὸ νοεῖν (ὥρισται
γὰρ τότε μᾶλλον ἡ ψυχή), ἀλλὰ διὰ τὸ μεταβάλλειν ἡ

⁷ οὐ post βουλομένους Ross apud Forster (cf. Pr. 18.1,
916b3–4) : οὐ ante βουλομένους codd.

⁸ †τούτω γὰρ ἔχει† Flashar : ζῇ γὰρ τότε μάλιστα Forster ex
Pr. 18.1, 916b17–18

7.[13] Why is it that in some people, if they begin to read, sleep overtakes them when they don't want it to, whereas others, who want to sleep, are made unable to, when they take up a book? Is it because in the former, there are pneumatic movements owing to a coldness that is natural or from melancholic humors, owing to which the pneumatic residue becomes unconcocted because of coldness? In such people, when the intellect is moved but does not think with concentration, the other movement is checked, so that, the intellect undergoing a great change, they are more inclined to sleep. For the pneumatic (*movement*) is defeated. But when they fix the intellect on something, which is what reading does, they are moved by pneumatic movements, which are unchecked by anything, so that they cannot sleep. Now for those who are in a natural state, when the intellect stands at one point[14] and does not change in many directions, all the other (*activities*) in the region stand still, and their immobility is sleep. For when a single leader stands still, as in a rout, the other units naturally come to a standstill as well. For by nature the light travels upward, and the heavy downward. Therefore, when the soul moves according to nature, it does not sleep; †for this is its condition†.[15] And when it is stationary and as it were fatigued, thought undergoes change, and the bodily elements rising to the head produces sleep. Now reading might seem to prevent sleep. But wakefulness is due not to the thinking (for then the soul is more concentrated),[16] but

13 Cf. *Pr.* 18.1.   14 Or "focuses on one subject."

15 Perhaps we should adopt the reading from ch. 1: "for then especially it is alive."

16 Literally, "divided" or "defined" or "limited" (ὥρισται).

917b ἀγρυπνία, ἐπεὶ καὶ νοήσεις αἱ τοιαῦται ‖ ἄγρυπνοί
εἰσιν, ἐν αἷς ζητεῖ ἡ ψυχὴ καὶ ἀπορεῖ, ἀλλ' οὐκ ἐν αἷς
ἀεὶ θεωρεῖ· ἐκεῖναι μὲν γὰρ ἀοριστεῖν ποιοῦσιν, αὗται
δὲ οὔ.

8. Διὰ τί ἐν τοῖς ἐριστικοῖς οὐκ ἔνεστιν ἀδολεσχία;
5 ἢ ὅτι | συλλογισμός ἐστι φαινόμενος, ἐν ὀλίγοις δὲ ὁ
συλλογισμός; καὶ ἐὰν μηκύνῃ, χρόνου γινομένου ὁ
παραλογισμὸς δῆλος, καὶ ἔστιν ὃ ἔδωκεν ἀναλαβεῖν.

9. Διὰ τί ποτε τῶν ἱστοριῶν ἥδιον ἀκούομεν τῶν
περὶ ἓν συνεστηκυιῶν ἢ τῶν περὶ πολλὰ πραγματευ-
10 ομένων;[9] ἢ διότι | τοῖς γνωριμωτέροις μᾶλλον προσ-
έχομεν καὶ ἥδιον αὐτῶν ἀκούομεν; γνωριμώτερον δέ
ἐστι τὸ ὡρισμένον τοῦ ἀορίστου. τὸ μὲν οὖν ἓν ὥρισται, τὰ δὲ πολλὰ τοῦ ἀπείρου μετέχει.

10. Διὰ τί ἡδόμεθα ἀκούοντες τὰ μήτε λίαν παλαιὰ
μήτε κομιδῇ νέα; ἢ διότι τοῖς μὲν πόρρω ἀφ' ἡμῶν
15 ἀπιστοῦμεν, | ἐφ' οἷς δὲ ἀπιστοῦμεν οὐχ ἡδόμεθα, τὰ
δὲ ὥσπερ ἔτι αἰσθανόμεθα, καὶ περὶ τούτων ἀκούοντες
οὐχ ἡδόμεθα;

---

[9] πραγματευομένων : πεπραγματευομένων Y[a]

to the changing, since those acts of thinking are wakeful in which the soul investigates and questions, and not those in which it continuously contemplates; for the former cause a lack of concentration, whereas the latter do not.

8.[17] Why is verbosity not present in contentious arguments? Is it because (*such an argument*) is an apparent syllogism, and the syllogism consists in few (*words*)? And if it is prolonged, as time passes the fallacy becomes clear, and it is possible to take back what one conceded.

9.[18] Why do we listen to historical accounts organized around one (*event*)[19] with more pleasure than those that deal with many? Is it because we pay more attention, and listen with more pleasure, to what is more easily comprehended? But the limited is more easily comprehended than the unlimited. Now what is one is defined, whereas what is many partakes of the infinite.

10. Why do we enjoy hearing what is neither very old nor quite new? Is it because we disbelieve[20] what is far away from us, and we do not enjoy what we disbelieve, whereas the latter as it were we still perceive, and we do not enjoy hearing about such things?

[17] Cf. *Pr.* 18.2 (and see n. 4).
[18] *Po.* 7–9 may contain the source for this chapter.
[19] Or perhaps "one subject" (the Greek simply has ἕν, "one").
[20] Or "distrust."

BOOK XIX

INTRODUCTION

"Of all the books the most interesting and the most important is the XIXth." So says Hett in the introduction to his Loeb edition of the *Problems*. Judging by the amount of attention *Pr.* 19 has received (easily more than any other book—a fact reflected in the textual notes), this is an opinion shared by many scholars who have worked on the *Problems*. According to the title, its topic is ἁρμονία—a word too versatile to be represented consistently by any one English word or phrase. For the most part, it refers to a scale or system of tuning or to a mode of music. As a title for *Pr.* 19, its most accurate English counterpart is "music." I transliterate the term throughout.

Andrew Barker provides a good overall description of *Pr.* 19 in his brief opening remarks on it in the first volume of *Greek Musical Writings*:

> Book XIX contains problems concerning music: together with Book XI (problems to do with the physics of sound and the physiology of voice-production) it is an important source for aspects of both theory and practice. Some of the questions it raises . . . relate directly to harmonic or acoustic theory. Of the ones concerned with the more practical aspects of music and with musical ethos, some again demand a familiarity with detailed points of theory. . . . Many

529

of the "solutions" offered are confused, weak, or simply silly. They are often of value none the less for the small items of information that they dispense in passing. . . . The collection is a jumble of odds and ends, some broken beyond repair, but one that is well worth sifting.[1]

Pr. 19.39 and 42, he says, "are of special interest, both for the sophistication of their arguments, and for the way in which they hint at a theory of pitch certainly developed out of Pythagorean and Platonist beginnings, but distinct from the theories of relative velocity or 'force' that are usual in this tradition."[2]

The various topics of this "jumble of odds and ends" are difficult to classify, and there is a fair amount of overlap. More than half the chapters concern a wide variety of issues connected to acoustic or harmonic theory (2–4, 8, 11–15, 17–26, 33, 35a–37, 39b, 41, 42, 45, 46, 48–50). Ten chapters deal with music's capacity to evoke emotions and especially to give pleasure (1, 5, 6, 9, 10, 16, 38, 39a, 40, 43); and a related topic—music's connection to ethical character—is the focus of two chapters (27 and 29). A half dozen treat the history of music (7, 28, 31, 32, 44, 47).

Music theory was widely discussed before and during the era in which Aristotle and his followers worked. It is therefore difficult (if not impossible) to distinguish

---

[1] Andrew Barker, *Greek Musical Writings*, vol. 1, *The Musician and His Art* (Cambridge, 1984), and vol. 2, *Harmonic and Acoustic Theory* (Cambridge, 1989). The passage quoted is from vol. 1, p. 190. I have found both volumes extremely helpful in understanding, translating, and annotating *Pr.* 19.

[2] Barker, *Greek Musical Writings*, vol. 2, p. 85.

sources on which the author(s) of *Pr.* 19 were drawing from texts taking similar approaches to the same issues. In any case, here are such sources or companion texts: Plato's *Republic* 3 and 7, *Laws* 2 and 7, Aristotle's *Politics* 8, the Peripatetic *De Audibilibus*, Theophrastus' works on music,[3] Aristoxenus' *Elementa Harmonica* and *Elementa Rhythmica*,[4] the *Sectio Canonis* attributed to Euclid,[5] and [Plutarch] *On Music* (which, though late, is based on fourth-century sources).

[3] *Harmonics*, *On Music*, and *On the Musicians*, none of which is extant. For what remains of them, see frs. 714–726 FHSG.

[4] Aristoxenus (fourth century) is especially interesting, as he joined the Lyceum sometime after 330 but before Aristotle's death in 322.

[5] Annotated translations of the Peripatetic *De Audibilibus*, Theophrastus' long fragment on harmony, Aristoxenus' *Elementa Harmonica* (and what remains of the *Elementa Rhythmica*), and the *Sectio Canonis* can all be found in Barker, *Greek Musical Writings*, vol. 2, chs. 5–8.

ΟΣΑ ΠΕΡΙ ΑΡΜΟΝΙΑΝ

1. Διὰ τί οἱ πονοῦντες καὶ οἱ ἀπολαύοντες αὐλοῦν-
ται; ἢ | ἵνα οἱ μὲν ἧττον λυπῶνται, οἱ δὲ μᾶλλον
χαίρωσιν;

2. Διὰ τί πορρωτέρω ὁ αὐτὸς τῇ αὐτῇ φωνῇ γεγωνεῖ
μετ᾽ ἄλλων ᾄδων καὶ βοῶν ἢ μόνος; ἢ ὅτι τὸ ἀθρόως τι
ποιεῖν ἢ θλίβειν ἢ ὠθεῖν οὐ τοσαυταπλάσιόν ἐστιν
ὅσος ὁ ἀριθμός, ἀλλ᾽ ὥσπερ ἡ γραμμὴ ἡ δίπους οὐ
διπλάσιον ἀλλὰ τετραπλάσιόν | τι γράφει, οὕτω τὰ
συντιθέμενα πλέον ἰσχύει κατὰ τὸν ἀριθμὸν ἢ ὅταν ᾖ
διῃρημένα; ἀθρόων οὖν ὄντων μία γίνεται ἡ τῆς φωνῆς ἰσχὺς καὶ ἅμα ὠθεῖ τὸν ἀέρα, ὥστε πολλαπλά-
σιον προϊέναι· καὶ γὰρ ἡ ἐκ πάντων φωνὴ μιᾶς ἑκά-
στης πολλαπλάσιος. |

917b
20

25

PROBLEMS CONNECTED
WITH *HARMONIA*

1.[1] Why do those who are suffering and those who are enjoying themselves both have the *aulos* played to them? Is it so that the former will feel less grief, while the latter will feel more pleasure?

2.[2] Why does the same person with the same voice project further when singing or shouting with others than when he is alone? Is it because with respect to doing something as a group—pressing or pushing—the number[3] is not proportionate (*to the number of people involved*), but just as a line two feet long describes something not twice but four times as great, so things that are put together are stronger in relation to their number than when they are separated? When people are a group, then, the strength of their voice becomes one and pushes the air at the same time, so that it goes forward many times further; and indeed, the voice proceeding from all is many times greater than from each one.[4]

[1] Cf. *Pol.* 1341a18–b8.
[2] Cf. *Pr.* 11.52, 59.
[3] I.e., the amount of what is achieved.
[4] I.e., from the sum of each taken individually.

30   3. Διὰ τί τὴν παρυπάτην ᾄδοντες μάλιστα ἀπορρήγνυνται, οὐχ ἧττον ἢ τὴν νήτην καὶ τὰ ἄνω, μετὰ
δὲ διαστάσεως[1] πλείονος; ἢ ὅτι χαλεπώτατα ταύτην
ᾄδουσι, καὶ αὕτη ἀρχή; τὸ δὲ χαλεπὸν διὰ τὴν ἐπί-
τασιν καὶ πίεσιν τῆς φωνῆς· ἐν τούτοις δὲ πόνος·
πονοῦντα δὲ μᾶλλον διαφθείρεται. |

35   4. Διὰ τί δὲ ταύτην χαλεπῶς, τὴν δὲ ὑπάτην ῥᾳδίως;
καίτοι δίεσις ἑκατέρας. ἢ ὅτι μετ’ ἀνέσεως ἡ ὑπάτη,
καὶ ἅμα μετὰ τὴν σύντασιν[2] ἐλαφρὸν τὸ ἀναχαλᾶν;[3]
διὰ ταὐτὸ δὲ ἔοικεν [καὶ] τὰ πρὸς μέσην λεγόμενα
⟨καὶ⟩ πρὸς τρίτην[4] ἢ παρανήτην. †δεῖ γὰρ μετὰ συν-
918a   νοίας καὶ καταστάσεως οἰκειοτάτης ‖ τῷ ἤθει πρὸς
τὴν βούλησιν. τοῦ δὲ δὴ μετὰ συμφωνίας τίς ἡ αἰτία;†[5]

───────

    [1] διαστάσεως : διατάσεως Eichtal-Reinach

    [2] σύντασιν Ruelle : σύστασιν codd.

    [3] ἀναχαλᾶν Jan : ἄνω βάλλειν codd. : κάτω βάλλειν
Eichtal-Reinach   [4] [καὶ] τὰ πρὸς μέσην λεγόμενα ⟨καὶ⟩
πρὸς τρίτην Barker : καὶ τὰ πρὸς μίαν λεγόμενα πρὸς ταύτην
codd. (βίαν pro μίαν Bussemaker)

    [5] δεῖ γὰρ—ἡ αἰτία; codd. (obelis inclusi) : post γὰρ lac.
indic. Marenghi[1]

───────

    [5] Cf. *Pr.* 11.12, 46.

    [6] Hett's note *ad loc.*: "Cf. *DA* 804b11, where the word [*par-
hypatê*] is explained as 'the sound made by the voice when there is
no longer strength enough to expel the breath with force.' The
notes of the octave beginning at the lowest are *hypatê, parhypatê,
lichanos, mesê, paramesê, tritê, paranêtê, nêtê.* This passage must
mean singing the interval from *hypatê* to *parhypatê*, for there can

3.[5] Why does singing *parhypatê*[6] most of all make the voice break,[7] no less than singing *nêtê* and the higher notes, though (*in the latter cases*) the interval is greater? Is it because they sing this (*interval*) with great difficulty, and this is a starting point?[8] Now the difficulty is due to the straining and compression of the voice; and there is an effort in these; and since they require an effort, they are more likely to fail.

4. But why do (*they sing*) this[9] with difficulty, though *hypatê* easily? And yet there is (*only*) a *diesis*[10] between them. Is it because singing *hypatê* involves relaxation, and immediately after the strain the slackening is light work? For the same reason what is said about *mesê* and about *tritê* or *paranêtê* seems (*to be the case*).[11] †For one must (*proceed*) with the reflection and calm most appropriate to the ethical character (*of the piece*), with respect to the intention.[12] But what, then, is the cause of what (*is composed*) with concord?†

be no *special* difficulty attached to the singing of any note. If this [interpretation] is correct, which is uncertain, Aristotle must be referring to the enharmonic scale in which the interval between *hypatê* and *parhypatê* is a quarter tone—admittedly most difficult to sing. This interpretation is supported by the next problem."

[7] Or "waver."   [8] I.e., the first interval in the scale.

[9] I.e., *parhypatê*.   [10] Here, this refers to a quarter tone.

[11] Barker comments (private correspondence): "It's hard to make any case for seeing the next two sentences as continuations of the same line of thought as in what precedes them (or indeed as being coherently connected with one another). I suppose they may be random marginal jottings, or the remnants of a lost problem, or maybe bits displaced from elsewhere in the text."

[12] One's own intention, or that of the composer.

5. Διὰ τί ἥδιον ἀκούουσιν ᾀδόντων ὅσα ἂν προεπι-
στάμενοι τυγχάνωσι τῶν μελῶν, ἢ ὧν μὴ ἐπίστανται;
5 πότερον ὅτι | μᾶλλον δῆλος ὁ τυγχάνων ὥσπερ σκο-
ποῦ, ὅταν γνωρίζωσι τὸ ᾀδόμενον, τοῦτο δὲ ἡδὺ θεωρεῖν; ἢ ὅτι ⟨ἧττον⟩ ἡδὺ⁶ τὸ μανθάνειν; τούτου δὲ
αἴτιον ὅτι τὸ μὲν λαμβάνειν τὴν ἐπιστήμην, τὸ δὲ
χρῆσθαι καὶ ἀναγνωρίζειν ἐστίν; ἔτι καὶ τὸ σύνηθες
ἡδὺ μᾶλλον τοῦ ἀσυνήθους. |

10 6. Διὰ τί ἡ παρακαταλογὴ ἐν ταῖς ᾠδαῖς τραγικόν;
ἢ διὰ τὴν ἀνωμαλίαν; παθητικὸν γὰρ τὸ ἀνωμαλὲς
καὶ⁷ ἐν μεγέθει τύχης ἢ λύπης, τὸ δὲ ὁμαλὲς ἔλαττον
γοῶδες.

7. Διὰ τί οἱ ἀρχαῖοι ἑπταχόρδους ποιοῦντες ἁρμονίας τὴν ὑπάτην ἀλλ' οὐ τὴν νήτην κατέλιπον; πότε-
15 ρον τοῦτο ψεῦδος | (ἀμφοτέρας γὰρ κατέλιπον, τὴν δὲ
τρίτην ἐξῆρουν), ἢ οὔ, ἀλλ'⁸ ὅτι ἡ βαρυτέρα ἴσχει⁹ τὸν
τῆς ὀξυτέρας φθόγγον, ὥστε μᾶλλον ἡ ὑπάτη ἀπεδί-
δου τὸ ἀντίφωνον ἢ ἡ νήτη, ἐπεὶ τὸ ὀξὺ δυνάμεως
⟨σημεῖον⟩¹⁰ μᾶλλον, τὸ δὲ βαρὺ ῥᾷον φθέγξασθαι;¹¹

---

⁶ ἢ ὅτι ⟨ἧττον⟩ ἡδὺ Richards : ἢ ὅτι ⟨τὸ θεωρεῖν μᾶλλον⟩
ἡδὺ ⟨ἢ⟩ Bonitz   ⁷ om. καὶ fort.   ⁸ ἀλλ' secl. Hett
⁹ ἴσχει Lambeth.1204 : ἰσχύει cett. codd.
¹⁰ ⟨σημεῖον⟩ Ruelle (cf. Pr. 19.37, 920b25–26)
¹¹ [ἐπεὶ τὸ—φθέγξασθαι] Jan

---

¹³ Cf. Pr. 19.40.   ¹⁴ ἡ παρακαταλογή (recitative) is
"something between melodic singing and speech" (Barker, *Greek
Musical Writings*, vol. 1, p. 191n. 4).   ¹⁵ Or "evokes emotions in extreme calamity or grief," if the καὶ is omitted.
¹⁶ Cf. Pr. 19.32, 47.

5.[13] Why do people listen with more pleasure to people singing melodies they happen to know beforehand, than to ones that they do not know? Is it because the ⟨*singer*⟩ hitting his target, as it were, is more obvious when they recognize what is being sung, and this is pleasant to contemplate? Or is it because it is less pleasant to learn ⟨*than to contemplate*⟩? Now the reason for this is that ⟨*learning*⟩ is the acquiring of knowledge, while ⟨*contemplation*⟩ is using and recognizing ⟨*what one knows*⟩. And further, the familiar is more pleasant than the unfamiliar.

6. Why is recitative[14] in songs tragic? Is it because of the contrast? For the contrast evokes emotions and is found in extreme calamity or grief,[15] while uniformity is less mournful.

7.[16] Why did the ancients, when they made a seven-note *harmonia*, leave in the *hypatê* but not the *nêtê*?[17] Is this false (for they did leave in both, but cut out *tritê*), or is it not ⟨*false*⟩, but it is the case because the lower note contains[18] the sound of the higher note, so that *hypatê* yields the answering sound better than *nêtê*, since the high note is a sign of more power, and the low note is easier to utter?

[17] Hett's note *ad loc.*: "There seems a confusion of thought here. The heptachord was older than the octachord, and it would therefore be more true to say that ancient musicians *added nêtê* when they made an eight-note scale. They may, however, have played an octave on seven strings which would have involved omitting one of the intermediate notes." Barker informs me that this last sentence is too cautious: on the heptachord spanning a full octave, see Nicomachus *Harm.* 3, 5, and 9, and Philolaus fr. 6a Huffman.

[18] Or "prevails over" if we follow the mss. tradition.

8. Διὰ τί ἡ βαρεῖα τὸν τῆς ὀξείας ἴσχει[12] φθόγγον;
20 ἢ | ὅτι μεῖζον τὸ βαρύ; τῇ γὰρ ἀμβλείᾳ ἔοικεν, τὸ δὲ
τῇ ὀξείᾳ γωνίᾳ.

9. Διὰ τί ἥδιον τῆς μονῳδίας ἀκούομεν, ἐάν τις
πρὸς αὐλὸν ἢ λύραν ᾄδῃ;[13] καίτοι πρόσχορδα[14] καὶ τὸ
αὐτὸ μέλος ᾄδουσιν ἀμφοτέρως· εἰ γὰρ ἔτι μᾶλλον τὸ
25 αὐτό, πλέον | ἔδει πρὸς πολλοὺς αὐλητάς καὶ ἔτι ἥδιον
εἶναι. ἢ ὅτι τυγχάνων δῆλος τοῦ σκοποῦ μᾶλλον, ὅταν
πρὸς αὐλὸν ἢ λύραν; τὸ δὲ πρὸς πολλοὺς αὐλητὰς ἢ
λύρας πολλὰς οὐχ ἥδιον, ὅτι ἀφανίζει τὴν ᾠδήν.

10. Διὰ τί, εἰ ἡδίων[15] ἡ ἀνθρώπου φωνή, ἡ ἄνευ
30 λόγου ᾄδοντος | οὐχ ἡδίων ἐστίν, οἷον τερετιζόντων,
ἀλλ' αὐλὸς ἢ λύρα; ἢ οὐδ' ἐκεῖ, ἐὰν μὴ μιμῆται,
ὁμοίως ἡδύ; οὐ μὴν ἀλλὰ καὶ διὰ τὸ ἔργον αὐτό. ἡ μὲν
γὰρ φωνὴ ἡδίων ἡ τοῦ ἀνθρώπου, κρουστικὰ δὲ μᾶλλον τὰ ὄργανα τοῦ στόματος, διὸ ἡδίονα[16] ἀκούειν[17] ἢ
⟨τὸ⟩[18] τερετίζειν. |

35 11. Διὰ τί ἡ ἀπηχοῦσα ὀξυτέρα; ἢ ὅτι ἔλαττον,
ἀσθενεστέρα γινομένη;

---

[12] ἴσχει Lambeth.1204 : ἰσχύει codd.
[13] πρὸς αὐλὸν ἢ λύραν ᾄδῃ : πρὸς ἕνα αὐλὸν ἢ λύραν ᾄδῃ
ἢ πρὸς δύο Monac.361 Berol.148   [14] πρόσχορδα Jan :
πρὸς χορδὰς codd.   [15] ἡδίων : ἥδιον Ap.   [16] ἡδίονα
Barker : ἥδιον codd.   [17] ἀκούειν : κρούειν Jan : fort. ᾄδειν
ex Gaza   [18] ⟨τὸ⟩ Barker

---

[19] Or "prevails over" if we follow the mss. tradition.
[20] The Greek for "high" and "acute" is the same.

8. Why does the low note contain[19] the sound of the high note? Is it because the low note is greater? It is like the obtuse angle, whereas the latter is like an acute angle.[20]

9.[21] Why do we listen with greater pleasure to a solo song, if one sings it to the accompaniment of one *aulos* or one lyre?[22] Yet in both cases[23] they sing the same melody (*as the instruments*) note for note. For if there is more of the same thing, it ought to be still more pleasant when accompanied by many *aulos* players. Is it because (*the singer*) hitting his target is more obvious when (*he sings*) to one *aulos* or lyre? And the accompaniment of many *aulos* players or many lyres is not more pleasant, because it obscures the song.

10. Why, if the human voice is more pleasant (*than an instrument*), is the voice of one singing without words, like one babbling, not more pleasant, but an *aulos* or lyre is? Or in the latter case do we not get as much pleasure, unless it is imitative? (Of course, this is also dependent on the actual execution.) For although the human voice is more pleasant, the instruments strike a note better than the mouth, hence they are more pleasant to hear than is humming.[24]

11. Why is the voice echoing back[25] higher (*than the original*)?[26] Is it because, being smaller, it becomes weaker?

---

[21] Cf. *Pr.* 19.43.   [22] In contrast to the accompaniment of two or more *auloi* or lyres.   [23] I.e., whether accompanied by one instrument or more than one.   [24] The text of this last line likely needs emending.   [25] ἡ ἀπηχοῦσα (sc. φωνή).

[26] Hett's note *ad loc.*: "It is apparently true that in certain circumstances an echo is an octave higher than the original."

12. Διὰ τί τῶν χορδῶν ἡ βαρυτέρα ἀεὶ τὸ μέλος λαμβάνει; †ἂν γὰρ ἐάσῃ τὴν παραμέσην δέον συμψῆλαι τῇ μέσῃ, γίνεται τὸ μέλος οὐθὲν ἧττον· ἐὰν δὲ τὴν

40 μέσην, δέον ἄμφω | ψῆλαι, οὐ γίνεται.†[19] ἢ ὅτι τὸ βαρὺ
918b μέγα ἐστίν, ὥστε κρατερόν, ‖ καὶ ἔνεστιν ἐν τῷ μεγάλῳ τὸ μικρόν; καὶ τῇ διαλήψει δύο νῆται ἐν τῇ ὑπάτῃ γίνονται.

13. Διὰ τί ἐν τῇ διὰ πασῶν τοῦ μὲν ὀξέος ἀντίφωνον γίνεται τὸ βαρύ, τούτου δὲ τὸ ὀξὺ οὔ; ⟨ἢ⟩[20] ὅτι

5 μάλιστα μὲν ἐν ἀμφοῖν | ἐστιν τὸ ἀμφοῖν μέλος, εἰ δὲ μή, ἐν τῷ βαρεῖ· μεῖζον γάρ;

14. Διὰ τί λανθάνει τὸ διὰ πασῶν καὶ δοκεῖ ὁμόφωνον εἶναι, οἷον ἐν τῷ φοινικίῳ καὶ ἐν τῷ ἀνθρώπῳ;[21] τὰ γὰρ ἐν τοῖς ὀξέσιν ὄντα οὐχ ὁμόφωνα, ἀλλ' ἀνάλο-

10 γον ἀλλήλοις | διὰ πασῶν. ἢ ὅτι ὥσπερ ὁ αὐτὸς εἶναι δοκεῖ φθόγγος διὰ τὸ ἀνάλογον; ⟨τὸ δὲ ἀνάλογον⟩[22] ἰσότης ἐπὶ φθόγγων, τὸ δὲ ἴσον τοῦ ἑνός. ταὐτὸ δὲ τοῦτο καὶ ἐν ταῖς σύριγξιν ἐξαπατῶνται.

---

[19] ἂν γὰρ ἐάσῃ—ψῆλαι, οὐ γίνεται Monro : ἂν γὰρ δέηται ᾆσαι τὴν παραμέσην σὺν ψιλῇ τῇ μέσῃ γίνεται τὸ μέσον οὐθὲν ἧττον ἐὰν δὲ τὴν μέσην δέον ἄμφω ψιλὰ οὐ γίνεται codd.

[20] ⟨ἢ⟩ Sylburg
[21] ἀνθρώπῳ : ἀτρόπῳ Xᵃ mg et Gaza
[22] ⟨τὸ δὲ ἀνάλογον⟩ Forster ex Gaza

12.[27] Why does the lower of the strings[28] always take the melody? †For if one omits *paramesê* when one should have played it with *mesê*, the melody is there nonetheless; but if one omits *mesê* when one should have played both, it is not.† Is it because the low is large, so that it is strong, and the small is present in the large? Indeed, in division there are two *netai* in the *hypatê*.[29]

13. Why is it that in the octave[30] the low is a correspondent of the high, but the high is not a correspondent of the low?[31] Is it because, at best, the melody of both is in both, but if not, it is in the low, for it is greater?

14. Why does the octave escape notice and seem to be in unison, as in the "Phoenician"[32] and in the human (*voice*)? For the higher notes are not in unison (*with the lower*), but are analogous to each other at the octave. Is it because, due to the analogy, they seem as if they were the same note? Now in the case of sounds, analogy is equality, and the equal is characteristic of the one. People are deceived in this same way also in the case of panpipes.

---

27 Cf. [Plut.] *Mus.* 19 (*Mor.* 1137B–D). Hett's note *ad loc.*: "The meaning of this problem is obscure and indeed with the ms. text nothing can be made of it. For the purpose of the present translation Monro's emendation has been accepted."

28 Or "notes" (χορδῶν).

29 This refers to dividing the string in two, i.e., stopping it in the middle.

30 For an account of why the Greek for "octave" is διὰ πασῶν (rather than δι᾽ ὀκτώ), see *Pr.* 19.32.

31 I translate ἀντίφωνον "correspondent" (see n. 39 below). It is not clear what this question is asking.

32 Likely a lyre, with "arms" made from the horns of an animal (according to Hdt. 4.192; see also Ath. 636b, 637b).

15. Διὰ τί οἱ μὲν νόμοι οὐκ ἐν ἀντιστρόφοις ἐποι-
οῦντο, αἱ δὲ ἄλλαι ᾠδαὶ αἱ χορικαί; ἢ ὅτι οἱ μὲν νόμοι
15 ἀγωνιστῶν ἦσαν, | ὧν ἤδη μιμεῖσθαι δυναμένων καὶ
διατείνεσθαι ἡ ᾠδὴ ἐγίνετο μακρὰ καὶ πολυειδής;
καθάπερ οὖν καὶ τὰ ῥήματα, καὶ τὰ μέλη τῇ μιμήσει
ἠκολούθει ἀεὶ ἕτερα γινόμενα. μᾶλλον γὰρ τῷ μέλει
ἀνάγκη μιμεῖσθαι ἢ τοῖς ῥήμασιν. διὸ καὶ οἱ διθύ-
ραμβοι, ἐπειδὴ μιμητικοὶ ἐγένοντο, οὐκέτι ἔχουσιν
20 ἀντιστρόφους, | πρότερον δὲ εἶχον. αἴτιον δὲ ὅτι τὸ
παλαιὸν οἱ ἐλεύθεροι ἐχόρευον αὐτοί· πολλοὺς οὖν
ἀγωνιστικῶς ᾄδειν χαλεπὸν ἦν, ὥστε ἐν ⟨μιᾷ⟩ ἁρμονίᾳ[23]
μέλη ἐνῇδον. μεταβάλλειν γὰρ πολλὰς μεταβολὰς τῷ
ἑνὶ ῥᾷον ἢ τοῖς πολλοῖς, καὶ τῷ ἀγωνιστῇ ἢ τοῖς τὸ
ἦθος φυλάττουσιν. διὸ ἁπλούστερα ἐποίουν αὐτοῖς
25 τὰ | μέλη. ἡ δὲ ἀντίστροφος ἁπλοῦν· εἷς ῥυθμὸς[24] γάρ
ἐστι καὶ ἑνὶ μετρεῖται. τὸ δ' αὐτὸ αἴτιον καὶ διότι τὰ

---

[23] ἐν ⟨μιᾷ⟩ (vel ά) ἁρμονίᾳ Chabanon : ἐν ἁρμονίᾳ Ap. CᵃXᵃ :
ἐναρμόνια cett. codd.
[24] εἷς ῥυθμὸς Jan : ἀριθμὸς codd.

---

[33] The basic meaning of *nomos* is "custom" or "law." For one
account of why this term was applied to a kind of song, see *Pr.*
19.28. Barker writes: "*Nomoi* were always solo pieces. . . . We hear
of them most frequently as items performed at competitive festi-
vals. . . . They were grouped into four classes: kitharodic (songs accompanied by the singer on a *kithara*), kitharistic (instrumental
solos for *kithara*), aulodic (songs accompanied by the *aulos*), and
auletic (instrumental solos for *aulos*)" (*Greek Musical Writings*,
vol. 1, p. 249).

15. Why were *nomoi*[33] not composed in antistrophes,[34] whereas the other songs (the choral ones) were? Is it because *nomoi* were for professional competitors, who being already able to perform imitations and exert themselves for a sustained period, their song became long and multiform? Like the words, then, the melodies too followed the imitation in being continually varied. For it was more necessary to imitate by means of the melody than by means of the words. And this is why the dithyrambs, when they became imitative, no longer had antistrophes, as they did before. Now the reason is that in the old days the free men themselves performed in the choruses; hence it was difficult for many to sing together like professional competitors, so that they sang melodies in a single *harmonia*; for it is easier for one person to execute many modulations than it is for many, and it is easier for the professional competitor than it is for those who preserve the character (*of the music*).[35] That is why they composed simpler melodies for them.[36] Now the antistrophic melody is simple: for there is one rhythm and one meter.[37] And it is for the same

34 Presumably, the claim is that they were not written in corresponding lines of strophe (literally, a turning), sung by one part of the chorus, and antistrophe (literally, a turning back), sung by the other in response.

35 The latter ("those who preserve the character") likely refers to the chorus.

36 Barker comments: "The writer's point is that citizen-choruses couldn't be relied on to negotiate these changes in structure, and their songs were therefore composed without modulations, remaining in the same *harmonia* throughout" (private correspondence).

37 Literally, "it is measured by one thing" (ἑνὶ μετρεῖται).

μὲν ἀπὸ τῆς σκηνῆς οὐκ ἀντίστροφα, τὰ δὲ τοῦ χοροῦ
ἀντίστροφα· ὁ μὲν γὰρ ὑποκριτὴς ἀγωνιστὴς καὶ
μιμητής, ὁ δὲ χορὸς ἧττον μιμεῖται. |

30   16. Διὰ τί ἥδιον τὸ ἀντίφωνον τοῦ συμφώνου; ἢ ὅτι
μᾶλλον διάδηλον γίνεται τὸ συμφωνεῖν ἢ ὅταν πρὸς
τὴν συμφωνίαν ᾄδῃ; ἀνάγκη γὰρ τὴν ἑτέραν ὁμο-
φωνεῖν, ὥστε δύο πρὸς μίαν φωνὴν γινόμεναι ἀφανί-
ζουσι τὴν ἑτέραν.

17. Διὰ τί ⟨ἐν τῷ διὰ⟩ πέντε[25] οὐκ ᾄδουσιν ἀντί-
35 φωνα; ἢ ὅτι οὐχ ἡ αὐτὴ | ἡ σύμφωνος [τῇ συμφωνίᾳ][26]
ὥσπερ ἐν τῷ διὰ πασῶν; ἐκείνη γὰρ ⟨ἡ βαρεῖα⟩[27] ἐν
τῷ βαρεῖ ἀνάλογον, ὡς ἡ ὀξεῖα ἐν τῷ ὀξεῖ· ὥσπερ οὖν
ἡ αὐτή ἐστιν ἅμα καὶ ἄλλη. αἱ δὲ ἐν τῷ διὰ πέντε καὶ
διὰ τεττάρων οὐκ ἔχουσιν οὕτως, ὥστε οὐκ ἐμφαίνεται
ὁ τῆς ἀντιφώνου φθόγγος· οὐ γάρ ἐστιν ὁ αὐτός. |

40   18. Διὰ τί ἡ διὰ πασῶν συμφωνία ᾄδεται μόνη;

---

[25] ⟨ἐν τῷ διὰ⟩ πέντε Eichtal-Reinach : ⟨διὰ⟩ πέντε Bojesen :
⟨διὰ⟩ πέντε ⟨καὶ διὰ τεττάρων⟩ Gevaert-Vollgraff ex Gaza (*in
diapente et diatessaron*)

[26] [τῇ συμφωνίᾳ] Eichtal-Reinach : ⟨ἐν⟩ τῇ συμφωνίᾳ
Ruelle : τῇ συμφωνίᾳ codd. : τῇ συμφωνῷ Jan

[27] ⟨ἡ βαρεῖα⟩ Gevaert-Vollgraff

---

[38] Cf. *Pr.* 19.34, 35a, 39a, 41.

[39] I follow Barker in translating τὸ ἀντίφωνον "correspondence." Barker comments: "In the *Problems* the expression almost always refers to the octave, but it seems not to *mean* 'octave'.
It means rather 'sounding a corresponding note', that is, one me-

reason as well that ⟨*songs*⟩ performed on the stage are not antistrophic, while those performed by the chorus are antistrophic; for the actor is a professional competitor and imitator, while the chorus does less imitating.

16.[38] Why is correspondence[39] more pleasant than consonance?[40] Is it because being consonant is more obvious than when one sings to a consonant accompaniment?[41] For one of the notes must be in unison, so that two notes played against one voice obscure the other note.[42]

17. Why do they[43] not sing in correspondence in the fifth? Is it because the concordance is not the same ⟨*in the fifth*⟩ as it is in the octave? For there[44] the low note has an analogous position in the low range, as the high note has in the high range: it is, as it were, simultaneously the same and different. But ⟨*the concordances*⟩ in the fifth and the fourth are not ⟨*analogous*⟩, so that the sound of the correspondence is not apparent; for it is not the same.

18.[45] Why is the octave concord alone used in singing?

lodically equivalent to the original" (*Greek Musical Writings*, vol. 1, p. 193 n. 27).

[40] From Hett's note: "Consonance refers to the other two harmonies acknowledged by Greek music—the fourth and fifth. In some passages consonance covers the octave harmony as well."

[41] From Hett's note: "The [consonant] accompaniment consists of two notes: one in unison with the singer and the other a fourth or fifth higher."

[42] Eichtal-Reinach (pp. 37, 44–45) maintain that the question posed in this chapter and the response that follows it are in fact not related and were erroneously put together.

[43] I.e., "choruses singing at two pitches" (Barker, *Greek Musical Writings*, vol. 1, p. 194 n. 30).   [44] I.e., in the octave.

[45] Cf. *Pr.* 19.39b.

919a μαγαδίζουσι ‖ γὰρ ταύτην, ἄλλην δὲ οὐδεμίαν. ἢ ὅτι
μόνη ἐξ ἀντιφώνων ἐστὶ χορδῶν, ἐν δὲ ταῖς²⁸ ἀντιφώνοις, καὶ τὴν ἑτέραν ἐὰν ᾄδῃ, τὸ αὐτὸ ποιεῖ; ἡ γὰρ
μία τρόπον τινὰ τὰς ἀμφοτέρων ἔχει φωνάς, ὥστε καὶ
5   μιᾶς ᾀδομένης ἐν ταύτῃ τῇ ‖ συμφωνίᾳ ᾄδεται ἡ
συμφωνία, καὶ ἄμφω ᾄδοντες, ἢ τῆς μὲν ᾀδομένης τῆς
δὲ αὐλουμένης, ὥσπερ μίαν ἄμφω ᾄδουσιν. διὸ μόνη
μελῳδεῖται, ὅτι μιᾶς ἔχει χορδῆς φωνὴν τὰ ἀντίφωνα.

19. Διὰ τί δὲ ταῖς ἀντιφώνοις τοῦτο μόναις ὑπάρ-
10   χει; ἢ ‖ ὅτι μόναι ἴσον ἀπέχουσι τῆς μέσης; ἡ οὖν
μεσότης ὁμοιότητά τινα ποιεῖ τῶν φθόγγων, καὶ ἔοικεν ἡ ἀκοὴ λέγειν ὅτι ἡ αὐτὴ καὶ ὅτι ἀμφότεραι
ἔσχαται.

20. Διὰ τί, ἐὰν μέν τις τὴν μέσην κινήσῃ ἡμῶν
ἁρμόσας τὰς ἄλλας χορδάς καὶ χρῆται τῷ ὀργάνῳ, οὐ
15   μόνον ὅταν ‖ κατὰ τὸν τῆς μέσης γένηται φθόγγον,
λυπεῖ καὶ φαίνεται ἀνάρμοστον, ἀλλὰ καὶ κατὰ τὴν
ἄλλην μελῳδίαν, ἐὰν δὲ τὴν λιχανὸν ἤ τινα ἄλλον
φθόγγον, τότε φαίνεται διαφέρειν μόνον, ὅταν κἀκείνῃ
τις χρῆται; ἢ εὐλόγως τοῦτο συμβαίνει; πάντα γὰρ τὰ
20   χρηστὰ μέλη πολλάκις τῇ μέσῃ ‖ χρῆται, καὶ πάντες
οἱ ἀγαθοὶ ποιηταὶ πυκνὰ πρὸς τὴν μέσην ἀπαντῶσιν,
κἂν ἀπέλθωσι, ταχὺ ἐπανέρχονται, πρὸς δὲ ἄλλην

---

²⁸ ταῖς : τοῖς Xᵃ Cᵃ

46 Hett's note *ad loc.*: "According to Athenaeus [14.634C] the
magadis was an ancient instrument containing twenty strings,
upon which two octaves could be played."

For people magadize[46] in this concord, but in no other. Is it because it alone comes from corresponding notes, and in corresponding notes, and whichever of them one sings, one produces the same result? For the one note contains in a certain way the sounds of both, so that when even one is sung in this concord the concord is sung, *and* when they sing both—or when one is sung and the other played on the *aulos*, as if they both sing one note. This is why only that note is the melody, because the corresponding notes have the sound of a single note.

19. But why does this[47] exist in the corresponding notes alone? Is it because these alone are equidistant from the *mesê*?[48] This intermediate position, then, produces a certain similarity of sounds, and the hearing seems to indicate that they are the same note and that both are extremes.

20.[49] Why is it that if one shifts *mesê* after tuning the other strings and then uses the instrument, the note is painful and seems out of tune not only when *mesê* is played but also in the rest of the melody, while if one shifts *lichanos* or any other note, it appears to differ only when one uses that note?[50] Or is it reasonable that this occurs? Indeed, all good melodies make frequent use of *mesê*, and all good composers have constant recourse to *mesê*, and if they leave it, they quickly return to it, but not to any other

---

[47] I take it, having the sound of a single note.

[48] In fact, *mesê* is not equidistant from the ends of the octave, for it is the fourth of eight notes.

[49] Cf. *Pr.* 19.36.

[50] Barker comments: "The note *mesê* was certainly in some sense fundamental in Greek melodies, but its exact function is unknown" (*Greek Musical Writings*, vol. 1, p. 195 n. 39).

οὕτως οὐδεμίαν. καθάπερ ἐκ τῶν λόγων ἐνίων ἐξαι-
ρεθέντων συνδέσμων οὐκ ἔστιν ὁ λόγος Ἑλληνικός,
οἷον τὸ τέ καὶ τὸ καί, ἔνιοι δὲ οὐθὲν λυποῦσιν, διὰ τὸ
25 τοῖς μὲν ἀναγκαῖον | εἶναι χρῆσθαι πολλάκις, εἰ ἔσται
λόγος, τοῖς δὲ μή, οὕτω καὶ τῶν φθόγγων ἡ μέση
ὥσπερ σύνδεσμός ἐστι, καὶ μάλιστα τῶν ἄλλων,[29] διὰ
τὸ πλειστάκις ἐνυπάρχειν τὸν φθόγγον αὐτῆς.

21. Διὰ τί τῶν ᾀδόντων οἱ βαρύτερον ᾄδοντες τῶν
30 ὀξὺ | ᾀδόντων, ἐὰν ἀπᾴδωσι, μᾶλλον κατάδηλοι γίνον-
ται; ὁμοίως δὲ καὶ[30] τῷ ῥυθμῷ οἱ ἐν τῷ βραδυτέρῳ[31]
πλημμελοῦντες κατάδηλοι μᾶλλον. πότερον[32] ὅτι
πλείων ὁ χρόνος ὁ τοῦ βαρέος, οὗτος δὲ μᾶλλον
αἰσθητός, [ἢ][33] ὅτι ἐν πλείονι χρόνῳ πλείω αἴσθησιν
35 παρέχει, τὸ δὲ ταχὺ[34] καὶ ὀξὺ λανθάνει διὰ τὸ | τάχος.

22. Διὰ τί οἱ πολλοὶ μᾶλλον ᾄδοντες τὸν ῥυθμὸν
σώζουσιν ἢ οἱ ὀλίγοι; ἢ ὅτι μᾶλλον πρὸς ἕνα τε καὶ
ἡγεμόνα βλέπουσι, καὶ βραδύτερον[35] ἄρχονται,[36]
ὥστε ῥᾴδιον[37] τοῦ αὐτοῦ τυγχάνουσιν; ἐν γὰρ τῷ
τάχει ἡ ἁμαρτία πλείων. ||

919b   23. Διὰ τί διπλασία τῆς νήτης ἡ ὑπάτη;[38] ἢ πρῶτον

---

[29] ἄλλων Stumpf : καλῶν codd. : κώλων Gevaert-Vollgraff
[30] καί : κἂν Ruelle   [31] βραδυτέρῳ Bonitz : βαρυτέρῳ
codd.   [32] πότερον secl. Marenghi[1]
[33] [ἢ] Eichtal-Reinach   [34] ταχὺ : βαρὺ Ruelle
[35] βραδύτερον β, cf. Pr. 19.45, 922a33 : βαρύτερον cett.
codd.   [36] ἄρχονται : ἔρχονται Eichtal-Reinach : ὀρχοῦνται Graf   [37] ῥᾴδιον : ῥᾷον Bekker, cf. Pr. 19.45, 922a33
[38] τῆς νήτης ἡ ὑπάτη Wagener apud Gevaert-Vollgraff : ἡ
νήτη τῆς ὑπάτης codd.

note to the same extent. Just as if certain conjunctions are removed from the words (*of the Greek language*), such as τέ and καί, the language is no longer Greek, while some words are not painful (*if they are removed*), because some words must be used frequently, if there is to be language, while other words need not be, so too *mesê* is, as it were, a conjunction among notes, and is so most of all the notes, because its sound is involved most often.

21.[51] Why is it that of those who are singing, if they sing out of tune, the ones singing lower pitches are more noticeable than those singing high ones? And similarly with rhythm[52] those who are out of tune in a slower[53] rhythm are more noticeable. Is it because the time taken by the low note is longer, and this is more perceptible, because in a longer period of time it furnishes more sense perception, whereas what is quick and so high-pitched escapes notice because of its quickness.

22.[54] Why do many people singing together preserve the rhythm better than a few? Is it because they look more to one person who is their leader, and begin[55] more slowly, so that they easily strike the same moment? For in what is quick the error is greater.

23.[56] Why is *hypatê* double *nêtê*? Is it primarily because

51 Cf. *Pr.* 19.26, 46.   52 Or "with time" (τῷ ῥυθμῷ).
53 Or "lower," with the mss.   54 Cf. *Pr.* 19.45.
55 Or "go" (with Eichtal and Reinach) or "dance" (with Graf). This problem concerns a large chorus.
56 Barker comments: "The theory of ratio underlying this passage (originated by the Pythagoreans and used by both Plato and Aristotle) is most carefully worked out in the Euclidean *Sectio Canonis*" (*Greek Musical Writings*, vol. 1, p. 196 n. 44).

549

μὲν ὅτι ἐκ τοῦ ἡμίσεος ἡ χορδὴ ψαλλομένη καὶ ὅλη
συμφωνοῦσι[39] διὰ πασῶν; ὁμοίως δὲ ἔχει καὶ ἐπὶ τῶν
συρίγγων· ἡ γὰρ διὰ τοῦ μέσου τῆς σύριγγος τρή-
5   ματος φωνὴ τῇ δι' ὅλης | τῆς σύριγγος συμφωνεῖ διὰ
πασῶν. ἔτι ἐν τοῖς αὐλοῖς[40] τῷ διπλασίῳ διαστήματι
λαμβάνεται τὸ διὰ πασῶν, καὶ οἱ αὐλοτρύπαι οὕτω
λαμβάνουσιν. [ὁμοίως δὲ καὶ τὸ διὰ πέντε τῷ ἡμιολίῳ.][41] ἔτι[42] οἱ τὰς σύριγγας ἁρμοττόμενοι εἰς μὲν
τὴν πάτην ἄκραν τὸν κηρὸν ἐμπλάττουσι, τὴν δὲ
10 νήτην μέχρι | τοῦ ἡμίσεος ἀναπληροῦσιν. ὁμοίως δὲ
καὶ τὴν διὰ πέντε τῷ ἡμιολίῳ καὶ τὴν διὰ τεττάρων τῷ
ἐπιτρίτῳ διαστήματι λαμβάνουσιν. ἔτι δὲ[43] ἐν τοῖς
τριγώνοις ψαλτηρίοις τῆς ἴσης ἐπιτάσεως γινομένης
συμφωνοῦσι διὰ πασῶν, ἡ μὲν διπλασία οὖσα, ἡ δὲ
15 ἡμίσεια τῷ μήκει. |

24. Διὰ τί, ἐάν τις ψήλας τὴν νήτην [νήτην][44]
ἐπιλάβῃ, ἡ ὑπάτη μόνη δοκεῖ ἀντηχεῖν; ἢ ὅτι συμ-

39 συμφωνοῦσι Xa Ap : συμφωνοῦσα Ca Ya

40 αὐλοῖς Wagener apud Gevaert-Vollgraff : ἄλλοις

41 ὁμοίως—ἡμιολίῳ secl. Gevaert-Vollgraff (cf. Gaza)

42 ἔτι Wagener apud Gevaert-Vollgraff : ὅτι codd.

43 δὲ Marenghi[1] : καὶ Jan : εἰ Ya Ca Ap : οἱ Xa : αἱ Bojesen ex
Gaza

44 alterum νήτην om. Bekker, secl. Forster

57 "Pipes" (συρίγγων) here refers not specifically to panpipes
(as it does in 19.14) but either to wind instruments generally (the
view of Forster) or more likely to a specific wind instrument,
namely, a pipe with finger holes and no reed (the view of Barker).

when the string is plucked at half its length and as a whole they produce the concord of the octave? And the same holds as well in the case of pipes:[57] the sound through the hole in the middle of the pipe produces the concord of the octave with the sound through the whole pipe. Further, in *auloi*[58] the octave is obtained by the double distance—indeed, the *auloi*-borers obtain it in this way. Further, those who tune panpipes mold wax into the end of the *hypatê* (*pipe*), but fill the *nêtê* (*pipe*) up to the middle.[59] And similarly, they obtain the fifth with a hemiolic distance and the fourth with an epitritic distance.[60] And further, in triangular harps, when the tension (*of the strings*) is equal, they produce the concord of the octave when one (*string*) is double in length, while the other is half.

24.[61] Why, if one plucks *nêtê* and then damps it, does *hypatê* alone seem to sound in answer? Is it because the

---

[58] Or "in the others (i.e., wind instruments)," following the mss.

[59] Barker comments: "In its usual form, the pipes of this instrument were of equal length, fixed together with wax to form a rectangular shape. . . . The different pitches were created, as described here, by filling up different proportions of the lower part of each pipe with wax" (*Greek Musical Writings*, vol. 1, p. 196 n. 46).

[60] Barker comments: "Hemiolic ratio is 3: 2, epitritic 4: 3. The 'hemiolic distance' is two thirds of the length, the 'epitritic' is three quarters" (*Greek Musical Writings*, vol. 2, p. 93 n. 50).

[61] Cf. *Pr.* 19.42. From Hett's note *ad loc.*: "A poem in the *Anthology* (I 46) contains the words 'When I have just twanged the *hypatê* with the plectrum on the right, *nêtê* on the left will vibrate automatically'. . . ."

φυῆς μάλιστα γίνεται τῷ φθόγγῳ ὁ ἀπὸ ταύτης ἦχος
διὰ τὸ σύμφωνος εἶναι· τῷ οὖν συναυξάνεσθαι τῷ
ὁμοίῳ φαίνεται μόνος, οἱ δὲ ἄλλοι διὰ μικρότητα
ἀφανεῖς. |

20   25. Διὰ τί μέση καλεῖται ἐν ταῖς ἁρμονίαις, τῶν δὲ
ὀκτὼ οὐκ ἔστι μέσον; ἢ ὅτι ἑπτάχορδοι ἦσαν αἱ
ἁρμονίαι τὸ παλαιόν, τὰ δὲ ἑπτὰ ἔχει μέσον;

    26. Διὰ τί ἐπὶ τὸ ὀξὺ ἀπᾴδουσιν οἱ πλεῖστοι;
πότερον ὅτι ῥᾷον ὀξὺ ᾆσαι ἢ βαρύ; ἢ ὅτι χεῖρον τοῦ
25 βαρέος, ἁμαρτία | δέ ἐστι τοῦ χείρονος πρᾶξις;

    27. Διὰ τί τὸ ἀκουστὸν μόνον ἦθος ἔχει τῶν αἰσθη-
τῶν; καὶ γὰρ ἐὰν ᾖ ἄνευ λόγου μέλος, ὅμως ἔχει ἦθος·
ἀλλ' οὐ τὸ χρῶμα οὐδὲ ἡ ὀσμὴ οὐδὲ ὁ χυμὸς ἔχει. ἢ
ὅτι κίνησιν ἔχει μόνον, οὐχί[45] ἣν ὁ ψόφος ἡμᾶς κινεῖ;
30 τοιαύτη | μὲν γὰρ καὶ τοῖς ἄλλοις ὑπάρχει· κινεῖ γὰρ
καὶ τὸ χρῶμα τὴν ὄψιν· ἀλλὰ τῆς ἑπομένης τῷ τοιούτῳ
ψόφῳ αἰσθανόμεθα κινήσεως. αὕτη δὲ ἔχει ὁμοιότητα
ἔν τε τοῖς ῥυθμοῖς καὶ ἐν τῇ τῶν φθόγγων τάξει τῶν
ὀξέων καὶ βαρέων, οὐκ ἐν τῇ μίξει. ἀλλ' ἡ συμφωνία
35 οὐκ ἔχει ἦθος. | ἐν δὲ τοῖς ἄλλοις αἰσθητοῖς τοῦτο οὐκ
ἔστιν. αἱ δὲ κινήσεις αὗται πρακτικαί εἰσιν, αἱ δὲ
πράξεις ἤθους σημασία ἐστίν.

[45] μόνον οὐχί : μονονουχί Ap[a] (teste Louis) ‖ μονονουχί
codd. (teste Marenghi[1])

---

[62] Cf. *Pr.* 19.44.   [63] "*Mesê*" means "mean" or "intermediate."   [64] Cf. *Pr.* 19.46.
[65] I.e., as Hett renders it, "sing sharp."
[66] Cf. *Pr.* 19.29. This chapter is referred to by Gellius 1.11 and

sound from this (*string*) coalesces especially with this note, because it is concordant with it? In being increased, then, by what is similar, it alone is apparent, while the others are imperceptible owing to their smallness.

25.[62] Why is *mesê*[63] so called in the *harmoniai*, given that there is no mean of eight? Is it because in the old days the *harmoniai* were heptachords, and seven does have a mean?

26.[64] Why do most people sing out of tune toward the higher?[65] Is it because it is easier to sing high than low? Or is it because (*the high*) is worse than the low, and error is doing what is worse?

27.[66] Why does what is heard, alone of perceptible objects, possess ethical character? Indeed, even if a melody is without words, it nonetheless possesses ethical character; but neither color nor smell nor flavor possess it. Is it because (*what is heard*) alone possesses movement, though not that which the sound moves in us? For such movement exists in the other (*perceptible objects*) too—indeed, even color moves our sight; but we perceive a movement that follows this sort of sound. This movement has a likeness (*to ethical character*) both in the rhythms and in the arrangement of high and low notes, not in their mixture. But consonance has no ethical character.[67] This character, however, does not exist in the other perceptible objects. But these movements are connected with action, and actions are signs of ethical character.

attributed to Aristotle. *Pol.* 8.3 and 5 are possible sources for this chapter.

[67] Barker comments: "Moral character is represented by movement from note to note, not by notes played simultaneously" (*Greek Musical Writings*, vol. 1, p. 197 n. 55).

28. Διὰ τί νόμοι καλοῦνται οὓς ᾄδουσιν; ἢ ὅτι πρὶν
ἐπίστασθαι γράμματα, ᾖδον τοὺς νόμους, ὅπως μὴ
920a ἐπιλάθωνται, ‖ ὥσπερ ἐν Ἀγαθύρσοις ἔτι εἰώθασιν;
καὶ τῶν ὑστέρων οὖν ᾠδῶν τὰς πρώτας[46] τὸ αὐτὸ
ἐκάλεσαν ὅπερ τὰς πρώτας.[47]

29. Διὰ τί οἱ ῥυθμοὶ καὶ τὰ μέλη φωνὴ οὖσα ἤθεσιν
ἔοικεν, οἱ δὲ χυμοὶ οὔ, ἀλλ᾽ οὐδὲ τὰ χρώματα καὶ αἱ
5 ὀσμαί; | ἢ ὅτι κινήσεις εἰσὶν ὥσπερ καὶ αἱ πράξεις;
ἤδη δὲ ἡ μὲν ἐνέργεια ἠθικὸν καὶ ποιεῖ ἦθος, οἱ δὲ
χυμοὶ καὶ τὰ χρώματα οὐ ποιοῦσιν ὁμοίως.

30. Διὰ τί οὐδὲ ὑποδωριστὶ οὐδὲ ὑποφρυγιστὶ οὐκ
ἔστιν ἐν τραγῳδίᾳ ⟨τὸ⟩[48] χορικόν; ἢ ὅτι οὐκ ἔχει
10 ἀντίστροφον; ἀλλ᾽ ἀπὸ σκηνῆς· | μιμητικὰ[49] γάρ.

31. Διὰ τί οἱ περὶ Φρύνιχον ἦσαν μᾶλλον μελο-
ποιοί; ἢ διὰ τὸ πολλαπλάσια εἶναι τότε τὰ μέλη ἐν
ταῖς τραγῳδίαις τῶν μέτρων;

32. Διὰ τί διὰ πασῶν καλεῖται, ἀλλ᾽ οὐ κατὰ τὸν

---

[46] πρώτας : προτέρας Richards
[47] ὅπερ τὰς πρώτας secl. Eichtal-Reinach
[48] ⟨τὸ⟩ addidi
[49] μιμητικὰ Wagener apud Gevaert-Vollgraff : μιμητικὴ
codd.

---

[68] Greek for "laws" is νόμοι.
[69] A Scythian tribe. See Hdt. 4.100–104.
[70] The text of the last line is possibly corrupt, but the meaning
is nevertheless clear: they called the first (or perhaps foremost or
earlier) of their later songs (the *nomoi*) the same thing as the laws
that they (even earlier) used to sing.
[71] Cf. *Pr.* 19.27.

28. Why are the *nomoi* that people sing so called? Is it because before they knew how to write, they sang their laws,[68] so as not to forget them, as is still the custom among the Agathyrsi?[69] And so they called the first of their later songs the same thing as their first songs.[70]

29.[71] Why do rhythms and melodies, which are sound,[72] resemble ethical character, while flavors do not, nor colors and odors? Is it because they are movements, as actions too are? Now activity is ethical[73] and produces ethical character, but flavors and colors do not act in this way.

30.[74] Why is the choral part in tragedy neither in Hypodorian nor in Hypophrygian?[75] Is it because they do not admit of antistrophic (*song*)?[76] But they are used from the stage, since they are imitative.

31. Why were those around Phrynichus[77] primarily songwriters? Is it because at that time there were many times more songs in tragedies than (*spoken*) metrical lines?[78]

32.[79] Why is it called "*dia pasôn*," but not "*di' octô*" ac-

---

[72] Or "voice" ($\phi\omega\nu\dot{\eta}$).

[73] Or perhaps "indicative of ethical character" ($\dot{\eta}\theta\iota\kappa\grave{o}\nu$).

[74] Cf. *Pr.* 19.48.

[75] On the nature of the Hypodorian and Hypophrygian scales, see *Pr.* 19.48, which deals at greater length with the same problem.

[76] See *Pr.* 19.15.

[77] I.e., the early Athenian tragedian Phrynichus and his contemporaries.

[78] Hett's note *ad loc.*: Arist. *Po.* 4, 1449a17 "mentions that Aeschylus among other reforms of tragedy assigned the leading part to the dialogue."

[79] Cf. *Pr.* 19.47.

15 ἀριθμὸν | δι᾽ ὀκτώ, ὥσπερ καὶ διὰ τεττάρων καὶ διὰ
πέντε; ἢ ὅτι ἑπτὰ ἦσαν αἱ χορδαὶ τὸ ἀρχαῖον; εἶτ᾽
ἐξελὼν τὴν τρίτην Τέρπανδρος τὴν νήτην προσέθη-
κεν, καὶ ἐπὶ τούτου ἐκλήθη διὰ πασῶν, ἀλλ᾽ οὐ δι᾽
ὀκτώ· [δι᾽]⁵⁰ ἑπτὰ γὰρ ἦν.

33. Διὰ τί εὐαρμοστότερον ⟨ἀπὸ τοῦ ὀξέος⟩⁵¹ ἐπὶ τὸ
20 βαρὺ ἢ | ἀπὸ τοῦ βαρέος ἐπὶ τὸ ὀξύ; πότερον ὅτι τὸ
⟨μὲν⟩⁵² ἀπὸ τῆς ἀρχῆς γίνεται ἄρχεσθαι; ἡ γὰρ μέση
καὶ ἡγεμὼν ὀξυτάτη τοῦ τετραχόρδου.⁵³ τὸ δὲ οὐκ ἀπ᾽
ἀρχῆς ἀλλ᾽ ἀπὸ τελευτῆς. ἢ ὅτι τὸ βαρὺ⁵⁴ ἀπὸ τοῦ
ὀξέος γενναιότερον καὶ εὐφωνότερον;

34. Διὰ τί δὶς μὲν δι᾽ ὀξειῶν καὶ δὶς διὰ τεττάρων οὐ
25 συμφωνεῖ, | δὶς διὰ πασῶν δέ; ἢ ὅτι οὐ δὶς⁵⁵ δι᾽ ὀξειῶν
οὐδὲ δὶς⁵⁶ διὰ τεττάρων . . . ἐστίν,⁵⁷ τὸ δὲ διὰ τεττάρων
καὶ διὰ πέντε . . .⁵⁸

35a. Διὰ τί ἡ διὰ πασῶν καλλίστη συμφωνία; ἢ ὅτι
ἐν ὅλοις ὅροις οἱ ⟨ταύτης⟩⁵⁹ λόγοι εἰσίν, οἱ δὲ τῶν

---

50 [δι᾽] Ruelle   51 ⟨ἀπὸ τοῦ ὀξέος⟩ Bekker

52 ⟨μὲν⟩ Wagener apud Gevaert-Vollgraff

53 ἡ γὰρ—τετραχόρδου secl. Eichtal-Reinach ‖ τετραχόρδου Sylburg ex Gaza : παραχόρδου codd.

54 ante τὸ βαρὺ add. ἐπὶ fort.

55 οὐ δὶς B A E Apᵃ : οὐδεὶς x Aᵐ D Lambeth.1204 : ἡ δὶς
cett. codd. et Eˢ

56 οὐδὲ δὶς B A E Apᵃ x Aᵐ D Lambeth.1204 : οὐ δὶς cett.
codd.   57 ante ἐστίν lac. indic. Ruelle : ante ἐστιν add.
ἐπιμόριόν Jan

58 post πέντε lac. indic. Ruelle

59 ⟨ταύτης⟩ Sylburg ex Gaza

cording to its number, like *dia tettarôn* and *dia pente*?[80] Is it because there were originally seven strings? Then Terpander took away *tritê* and added *nêtê*,[81] and in his time it was called "*dia pasôn*," but not "*di' octô*," since there were seven (*strings*).[82]

33. Why is it more fitting[83] to pass ‹from high note› to low than from low to high? Is it because the former is to begin at the beginning? For the *mesê* or "leader" is the highest note of the tetrachord. But the latter (*is to begin*) not at the beginning but at the end. Or is the low note from the high nobler and more euphonious?

34.[84] Why are a double fifth[85] and a double fourth not concordant whereas a double octave is? Is it because neither a double fifth nor a double fourth is . . . , but a fourth and a fifth are . . . ?

35a. Why is the octave the most beautiful concord? Is it because its ratios are between whole terms, whereas the

80 Barker comments: "*Dia pasôn*, 'through all [the strings]' is the normal term for 'octave'. *Di' oktô* means 'through eight', *dia tettarôn* 'through four' (the interval of a fourth), and *dia pente* 'through five' (the interval of a fifth). (*Greek Musical Writings*, vol. 1, p. 198 n. 61, brackets in the original).

81 Despite Terpander's revisions, the number of strings remained seven. On Terpander (seventh century BC), see [Plu.] *Mus.* (*Mor.* 1132c–35d).

82 Or, with the mss., "since it was *di' hepta.*"

83 Or "more harmonious" (εὐαρμοστότερον).

84 The text of this chapter is clearly incomplete or otherwise corrupt. Cf. *Pr.* 19.41, which presents a longer, complete, though no different, answer to this same initial question. See also Aristox. *Harm.* 2.45.   85 Δι' ὀξειῶν is an alternative (esp. Pythagorean) term for the fifth.

ἄλλων οὐκ ἐν ὅλοις; ἐπεὶ γὰρ διπλασία ἡ νήτη τῆς
30 ὑπάτης, οἷα[60] ἡ νήτη | δύο, ἡ ὑπάτη ἕν, καὶ οἷα[61] ἡ
ὑπάτη δύο, ἡ νήτη τέσσαρα, καὶ ἀεὶ οὕτως. τῆς δὲ
μέσης ἡμιόλια. τὸ γὰρ διὰ πέντε ἡμιόλιον οὐκ ἐν
ὅλοις ἀριθμοῖς ἐστίν· οἷον γὰρ ἓν τὸ ἔλαττον, τὸ
μεῖζον τοσοῦτον τε[62] καὶ ἔτι τὸ ἥμισυ. ὥστε οὐχ ὅλα
πρὸς ὅλα συγκρίνεται, ἀλλ᾽ ἔπεστι μέρη. ὁμοίως δὲ |
35 καὶ ἐν τῷ διὰ τεττάρων ἔχει· τὸ γὰρ ἐπίτριτόν ἐστιν
ὅσον τεμεῖν, ὅ⟨λον⟩[63] καὶ ἔτι ἓν τῶν τριῶν[64] [ἐπίτριτόν
ἐστιν].[65] ἢ ὅτι τελεωτάτη ἡ ἐξ ἀμφοτέρων οὖσα, καὶ
ὅτι μέτρον τῆς μελῳδίας. . . .[66]

35b.[67] Διὰ . . . παντὸς τοῦ φερομένου ἡ κατὰ μέσον
920b κίνησις σφοδροτάτη, ‖ ἀρχομένου δὲ καὶ λήγοντος
μαλακωτέρα; ὅτε δὲ σφοδροτάτη ἡ κίνησις, καὶ ἡ
φωνὴ ὀξυτέρα τοῦ φερομένου. διὸ καὶ χορδαὶ ἐπιτεινό-
μεναι ὀξύτερον φθέγγονται· θᾶττον γὰρ ἡ κίνησις
5 γίνεται. εἰ[68] δὲ φωνὴ ἢ ἀέρος ἢ ἄλλου τινὸς | φορά, τὴν

[60] οἷα Sylburg : ὅσα codd.   [61] οἷα Sylburg : ὅσα codd.
[62] τε Bekker : δὲ codd.
[63] τεμεῖν ὅ⟨λον⟩ Marenghi[1] : τεμεῖν ὅ codd. : fort. τ᾽ ἐκεῖνο
Bekker   [64] τριῶν Bojesen ex Gaza : τεττάρων codd.
[65] [ἐπίτριτόν ἐστιν] Ruelle
[66] post μελῳδίας lac. indic. Ruelle
[67] cap. 35b Eichtal-Reinach, 35a continuatur in codd. : cap.
35b non vertit Gaza ‖ post διὰ lac. indic. Eichtal-Reinach : ante
διὰ lac. indic. Ruelle ‖ capitis initium deperditum ita restituere
tentavit Eichtal-Reinach, διὰ ⟨τί ἡ φωνὴ ἀνὰ μέσον ὀξυτάτη;
ἢ ὅτι⟩ παντὸς κτλ. : Marenghi[1], ⟨διὰ τί ἡ νήτη ὀξυτάτη; ἢ ὅτι
κατὰ μέσον φθέγγεται τῆς ὑπάτης καὶ⟩ διὰ παντὸς κτλ.

ratios of the others are not between wholes? Indeed, since *nêtê* is double *hypatê*, if *nêtê* is two, *hypatê* is one, and if *hypatê* is two, *nêtê* is four, and so on always. But it is hemiolic of *mesê*.[86] For the fifth, being hemiolic, is not in whole numbers: for example, if the lesser term is one, the larger is that and also the half in addition. Consequently, a whole (*number*) is not being compared to a whole, but parts are added. And the same thing is the case with the fourth: for the epitritic is dividing in this amount, a whole and one third in addition. Or is it because the (*concord*) composed out of both is the most perfect, and because the measure of the melody. . . .[87]

35b.[88] Why . . . when anything is traveling the movement is most violent in mid-course, but is gentler when beginning and slowing down? And when the movement is most violent, the sound of the thing that's traveling is higher. And this is why strings that are tightly stretched make a higher sound; for their movement is quicker. Now if sound is a movement of air or something else, it must be

[86] See *Pr.* 19.23.

[87] Or, if the chapter ends here (as in Gaza), "because it is the measure of the melody?"

[88] Cf. *Pr.* 11.23 and 51. Hett's note *ad loc.*: "The mss. make [19.35a and b] one Problem, which is most unsatisfactory. The second part is certainly a new Problem, but its statement is missing in all the mss. and in the Latin translation[s]." Eichtal and Reinach's speculation about the missing opening is on the right track: "Why is the sound highest in the middle of the note? Is it because," etc.

---

68 εἰ Bussemaker : ἡ codd.

ἀνὰ μέσον τὸν πόρον ὀξυτάτην δεῖ γίνεσθαι. ὥστε εἰ
τοῦτο μὴ συμβαίνοι,[69] οὐκ ἂν εἴη φορά τινος.

36. Διὰ τί, ἐὰν μὲν ἡ μέση κινηθῇ, καὶ αἱ ἄλλαι
χορδαὶ ἠχοῦσι φθειρόμεναι,[70] ἐὰν δὲ αὖ ἡ μὲν μένῃ
τῶν δ' ἄλλων τις κινηθῇ, ⟨ἡ⟩[71] κινηθεῖσα μόνη φθεί-
10 ρεται;[72] ἢ ὅτι τὸ ἡρμόσθαι | ἐστὶν ἁπάσαις τὸ [δὲ][73]
ἔχειν πως πρὸς τὴν μέσην [ἁπάσαις],[74] καὶ ἡ τάξις ἡ
ἑκάστης ἤδη δι' ἐκείνην; ἀρθέντος οὖν τοῦ αἰτίου τοῦ
ἡρμόσθαι καὶ τοῦ συνέχοντος οὐκέτι ὁμοίως φαίνεται
ὑπάρχειν. μιᾶς δὲ ἀναρμόστου οὔσης, τῆς δὲ μέσης
μενούσης, εὐλόγως τὸ κατ' αὐτὴν ἐκλείπει μόνον·[75]
15 ταῖς γὰρ ἄλλαις | ὑπάρχει τὸ ἡρμόσθαι.

37. Διὰ τί τοῦ ἐν φωνῇ ὀξέος ὄντος κατὰ τὸ ὀλίγον,
τοῦ δὲ βαρέος κατὰ τὸ πολύ (τὸ μὲν γὰρ βαρὺ διὰ τὸ
πλῆθος βραδύ,[76] τὸ δὲ ὀξὺ δι' ὀλιγότητα ταχύ), ἔργον
μᾶλλον ᾄδειν τὰ ὀξέα ἢ τὰ βαρέα; καὶ ὀλίγοι τὰ ἄνω
20 δύνανται ᾄδειν, | καὶ οἱ νόμοι ὄρθιοι καὶ οἱ ὀξεῖς
χαλεποὶ ᾆσαι διὰ τὸ ἀνατεταμένοι εἶναι. καίτοι ἔλαττον ἔργον τὸ ὀλίγον κινεῖν ἢ τὸ πολύ, ὥστε καὶ ἀέρα.
ἢ οὐ ταυτό γε ὀξύφωνον εἶναι φύσει καὶ τὸ ὀξὺ ᾄδειν;

[69] συμβαίνοι Sylburg : συμβαίνει codd.
[70] φθειρόμεναι Stark apud Helmholtz, Lehre v.d. Tonemp-
findungen : φθεγγόμεναι codd.
[71] ⟨ἡ⟩ Sylburg
[72] φθείρεται Stark apud Helmholtz, Lehre v.d. Tonemp-
findungen : φθέγγεται codd.
[73] [δὲ] Forster : δὲ codd. : τε Jan
[74] [ἁπάσαις] Forster ‖ τὸ δὲ—ἁπάσαις om. Ap

highest in the middle of its course. Consequently, if this were not the case, ⟨sound⟩ would not be a movement of anything.

36.[89] Why, if *mesê* is shifted, is the sound of the other strings ruined as well, but if on the other hand *mesê* stays still and one of the other strings is shifted, only the one that is shifted is ruined? Is it because for all strings, being in tune *is* standing in a certain relation to *mesê*, and the position of each is already determined by it? So when the cause of their being in tune and of what holds them together is removed, it[90] no longer seems to be the same. Now when one string is out of tune, but *mesê* stays still, it is reasonable that what relates to that string alone fails, since the others remain in tune.

37.[91] Why, though the high in voice goes with the small, and the low goes with the large (since the low is slow because of the large quantity ⟨of air⟩, while the high is quick because of the small quantity), is it more work to sing high notes than to sing low ones? Indeed, few can sing the upper notes, and the Orthian *nomoi* and the high ones are difficult to sing because of the strain involved. Yet it is less work to move a small quantity than to move a large one, and so it is with air as well. Or is being naturally high-voiced not the same as singing high notes? Rather all natu-

---

89 Cf. *Pr.* 19.20.
90 I.e., the position of each string in relation to *mesê*.
91 Cf. *GA* 5.7.

---

75 ἐκλείπει μόνον Bojesen : ἐκλειπόμενον codd. : ἐκλειπόμενον ⟨φαίνεται μόνον⟩ Marenghi[1]
76 βραδύ Sylburg : βαρύ codd.

ἀλλὰ φύσει μὲν ὀξύφωνα ἅπαντα δι᾽ ἀσθένειαν, τῷ μὴ
25 δύνασθαι πολὺν κινεῖν ἀέρα ἀλλ᾽ ὀλίγον. ὁ δ᾽ ὀλίγος
ταχὺ φέρεται, ἐν δὲ τῷ ᾄδειν τὸ ὀξὺ δυνάμεως σημεῖον. τὸ μὲν γὰρ σφοδρῶς φερόμενον ταχὺ φέρεται, διὸ
τὸ ὀξὺ δυνάμεως σημεῖον. διὸ καὶ οἱ εὐεκτικοὶ⁷⁷ ὀξύ-
φωνοι. καὶ ἔργον τὰ ἄνω ᾄδειν· τὰ δὲ βαρέα ῥᾷον.⁷⁸

38. Διὰ τί ῥυθμῷ καὶ μέλει καὶ ὅλως ταῖς συμ-
30 φωνίαις χαίρουσι πάντες; ἢ ὅτι ταῖς κατὰ φύσιν
κινήσεσι χαίρομεν κατὰ φύσιν; σημεῖον δὲ τὸ τὰ
παιδία εὐθὺς γενόμενα χαίρειν αὐτοῖς. διὰ δὲ τὸ ἔθος
τρόποις μελῶν χαίρομεν. ῥυθμῷ δὲ χαίρομεν διὰ τὸ
γνώριμον καὶ τεταγμένον ἀριθμὸν ἔχειν καὶ κινεῖν
35 ἡμᾶς τεταγμένως· οἰκειοτέρα γὰρ ἡ τεταγμένη κίνησις φύσει τῆς ἀτάκτου, ὥστε καὶ κατὰ φύσιν μᾶλλον.
σημεῖον δέ· πονοῦντες γὰρ καὶ πίνοντες καὶ ἐσθίοντες
τεταγμένα σώζομεν καὶ αὔξομεν τὴν φύσιν καὶ τὴν
δύναμιν, ἄτακτα δὲ φθείρομεν καὶ ἐξίσταμεν αὐτήν·
921a αἱ γὰρ νόσοι τῆς τοῦ σώματος οὐ⁷⁹ κατὰ φύσιν
τάξεως κινήσεις εἰσίν. συμφωνίᾳ δὲ χαίρομεν, ὅτι
κρᾶσίς ἐστι λόγον ἐχόντων ἐναντίων πρὸς ἄλληλα. ὁ
μὲν οὖν λόγος τάξις, ὃ ἦν φύσει ἡδύ. τὸ δὲ κεκραμένον
5 τοῦ ἀκράτου πᾶν ἥδιον, ἄλλως τε κἂν αἰσθητὸν ὂν
ἀμφοῖν τοῖν ἄκροιν ἐξ ἴσου τὴν δύναμιν ἔχοι⁸⁰ ἐν τῇ
συμφωνίᾳ ὁ λόγος.

---

⁷⁷ εὐεκτικοὶ Ross apud Forster : ἑκτικοὶ A B x Aᵐ D Eᵃᶜ :
εὐκτικοὶ cett. codd.

⁷⁸ ῥᾷον Jan : κάτω codd. : ἧττον Ruelle

⁷⁹ οὐ om. Gaza   ⁸⁰ ἔχοι : ἔχῃ Bussemaker : ⟨ἔχῃ
τοῦτο δ᾽⟩ ἔχει Ross apud Forster

rally high-voiced things are so owing to weakness, by not being able to move much air but only a small quantity, and a small quantity travels fast, but in singing the high is a sign of power. For what is traveling violently travels quickly, which is why the high is a sign of power. And this is why those in good health[92] have high voices. Indeed, it is work to sing the upper notes; but the low ones are easier.

38.[93] Why does everyone enjoy rhythm and melody and in general all concords? Is it because we naturally enjoy natural movements? Now a sign of this is that children enjoy these straightaway from birth. And we enjoy different types of melody because of habituation. But we enjoy rhythm because it has a recognizable and orderly number and moves us in an orderly fashion; for orderly movement is naturally more akin to us than disorderly movement, and so is more natural. And here is an indication of this: by exercising and drinking and eating in an orderly fashion we preserve and improve our nature and power, but in a disorderly fashion we ruin and derange it: for diseases are movements of the order of the body not in accordance with nature. But we enjoy concord, because it is a mix of opposites standing in proportion to one another. Therefore, proportion is an order that is naturally pleasant. Now anything that is mixed is more pleasant than what is unmixed, especially if, being perceptible, the proportion in the concord has the power in the two extremes equally.

---

92 Or, with the mss., "those who are frantic" (οἱ ἐκτικοὶ).

93 Cf. *Pr.* 19.39a. See Pl. *Lg.* 653d–e, 664e–665a, and Arist. *Po.* 4.

39a. Διὰ τί ἥδιόν ἐστι τὸ ἀντίφωνον[81] τοῦ ὁμο-
φώνου; ἢ <ὅτι>[82] καὶ τὸ μὲν ἀντίφωνον σύμφωνόν ἐστι
διὰ πασῶν; ἐκ παίδων γὰρ νέων καὶ ἀνδρῶν γίνεται τὸ
10 ἀντίφωνον, οἳ διεστᾶσι τοῖς | τόνοις ὡς νήτη πρὸς
ὑπάτην. συμφωνία δὲ πᾶσα ἡδίων ἁπλοῦ φθόγγου (δι᾽
ἃ δέ, εἴρηται), καὶ τούτων ἡ διὰ πασῶν ἡδίστη· τὸ
ὁμόφωνον δὲ ἁπλοῦν ἔχει φθόγγον.

39b.[83] <Διὰ τί> μαγαδίζουσι [δὲ] ἐν τῇ διὰ πασῶν
συμφωνίᾳ; <ἢ> ὅτι[84] καθάπερ ἐν τοῖς μέτροις οἱ πόδες
15 ἔχουσι πρὸς αὑτοὺς λόγον ἴσον πρὸς | ἴσον ἢ δύο
πρὸς ἓν ἢ καί τινα ἄλλον, οὕτω καὶ οἱ ἐν[85] τῇ συμφωνίᾳ φθόγγοι λόγον ἔχουσι κινήσεως[86] πρὸς αὑτούς;
τῶν μὲν οὖν ἄλλων συμφωνιῶν ἀτελεῖς αἱ θατέρου
καταστροφαί εἰσιν, εἰς ἥμισυ τελευτῶσαι· διὸ τῇ
δυνάμει οὐκ ἴσαι εἰσίν. οὖσαι δὲ ἄνισοι, διαφορὰ τῇ
20 αἰσθήσει, καθάπερ | ἐν τοῖς χοροῖς, ἐν τῷ καταλύειν
μεῖζον ἄλλων φθεγγομένοις ἐστίν. ἔτι δὲ ὑπάτη συμβαίνει[87] τὴν αὐτὴν τελευτὴν τῶν ἐν τοῖς φθόγγοις
περιόδων ἔχειν. ἡ γὰρ δευτέρα τῆς νεάτης πληγὴ τοῦ
ἀέρος ὑπάτη ἐστίν. τελευτώσαις δ᾽ εἰς ταὐτόν, οὐ
ταὐτὸν ποιούσαις, ἓν καὶ κοινὸν τὸ ἔργον συμβαίνει |
25 γίνεσθαι, καθάπερ τοῖς ὑπὸ τὴν ᾠδὴν κρούουσιν· καὶ
γὰρ οὗτοι τὰ ἄλλα οὐ προσαυλοῦντες, ἐὰν εἰς ταὐτὸν

---

[81] ἀντίφωνον Bojesen ex Gaza : σύμφωνον codd.

[82] <ὅτι> Jan   [83] cap. 39b Eichtal-Reinach, cf. Gaza : 39a
continuatur in codd.   [84] <Διὰ τί> μαγαδίζουσι [δὲ] ἐν τῇ
διὰ πασῶν συμφωνίᾳ; <ἢ> ὅτι κτλ. Eichtal-Reinach

[85] ἐν om. Marenghi[1]

39a.[94] Why is correspondence more pleasant than unison? Is it because correspondence is concordance in the octave? For correspondence arises from (*the combination of voices of*) young children and men, who are separated in pitch as *nêtê* is from *hypatê*. Now every concord is more pleasant than a simple sound (we have already explained why),[95] and of these the octave is the most pleasant, whereas unison has a simple sound.

39b.[96] Why do people magadize in the concord of the octave? Is it because just as in meters the feet have a ratio to each other of equal to equal or two to one or even some other, so too the notes in a concord have a ratio of movement to each other? In the case of the other concords the termination of one or the other notes is incomplete, ending halfway; this is why they are not equal in power. But being unequal, there is a difference in how they are perceived, as there is in choruses, when in concluding some sing louder than others. And further, it happens that *hypatê* has the same ending of the periodic (*movements*) in its notes. For the second blow on the air made by *nêtê* is *hypatê*. But since they finish on the same note, though they do not accomplish the same thing, the function they perform is one and common, like those who accompany a song on an instrument. And indeed, though these (*accompa-*

[94] Cf. *Pr.* 19.16, 38.

[95] See *Pr.* 19.16, 18, 19.

[96] I follow Gaza and many editors in dividing *Pr.* 19.39 into two chapters. Cf. *Pr.* 19.18.

---

[86] post κινήσεως add. ⟨ἢ τελευτῆς⟩ Marenghi[1] ex Gaza

[87] post συμβαίνει add. τῇ νεάτῃ Forster ex Gaza

καταστρέφωσιν, εὐφραίνουσι μᾶλλον τῷ τέλει ἢ λυποῦσιν ταῖς πρὸ τοῦ τέλους διαφοραῖς, τῷ [τὸ]⁸⁸ ἐκ
διαφόρων τὸ κοινόν, ἥδιστον⁸⁹ ἐκ τοῦ διὰ πασῶν⁹⁰
30 γίνεσθαι. τὸ δὲ μαγαδίζειν | ἐξ ἐναντίων φωνῶν. διὰ
ταῦτα ἐν τῇ διὰ πασῶν μαγαδίζουσιν.

40. Διὰ τί ἥδιον ἀκούουσιν ᾀδόντων ὅσα ἂν προ-
επιστάμενοι τύχωσι τῶν μελῶν, ἢ ἐὰν μὴ ἐπιστῶνται;
πότερον ὅτι μᾶλλον δῆλός ἐστιν ὁ τυγχάνων ὥσπερ
35 σκοποῦ, ὅταν | γνωρίζωσι τὸ ᾀδόμενον, γνωριζόντων
δὲ ἡδὺ θεωρεῖν; ἢ ὅτι συμπαθής ἐστιν ὁ ἀκροατὴς τῷ
τὸ γνώριμον ᾄδοντι; συνᾴδει γὰρ αὐτῷ. ᾄδει δὲ πᾶς
γεγηθὼς ὁ μὴ διά τινα ἀνάγκην ποιῶν τοῦτο. ||

921b   41. Διὰ τί δὶς μὲν δι᾽ ὀξειῶν ἢ δὶς διὰ τεττάρων οὐ
συμφωνεῖ, δὶς διὰ πασῶν δέ; ἢ ὅτι τὸ μὲν διὰ πέντε
ἐστὶν ἐν ἡμιολίῳ λόγῳ, τὸ δὲ διὰ τεττάρων ἐν ἐπιτρίτῳ; ὄντων δὲ ἡμιολίων τριῶν⁹¹ ἑξῆς ἀριθμῶν ἢ
5 ἐπιτρίτων, οἱ ἄκροι πρὸς | ἀλλήλους οὐδένα λόγον
ἕξουσιν· οὔτε γὰρ ἐπιμόριοι οὔτε πολλαπλάσιοι ἔσονται. τὸ δὲ διὰ πασῶν ἐπειδή ἐστιν ἐν διπλασίῳ λόγῳ,
δὶς τούτου γινομένου ἐν τετραπλασίῳ λόγῳ ἂν εἶεν οἱ

⁸⁸ [τὸ] Forster
⁸⁹ post ἥδιστον add. ὃν Forster
⁹⁰ ἐκ τοῦ διὰ πασῶν secl. Marenghi¹
⁹¹ τριῶν : δυοῖν Bojesen

⁹⁷ I.e., those notes that the singer alone sings.
⁹⁸ Cf. *Pr.* 19.5.
⁹⁹ Cf. *Pr.* 19.34. See also Aristox. *Harm.* 2.45.

nists) do not play the other notes,[97] if they conclude on the same note, they cause more delight at the end than they cause offense with the differences before the end, because after the diversity of notes the common note, arising from the octave, is most pleasing. Now magadizing comes from contrary sounds. For this reason people magadize in the octave.

40.[98] Why do people listen with more pleasure to people singing melodies they happen to know beforehand, than if they do not know them? Is it because the (singer) hitting his target, as it were, is more obvious when they recognize what is being sung, and when they recognize this it is pleasant to contemplate? Or is it because the listener is sympathetic with the one singing what is recognized? For he sings it with him. And everyone enjoys singing who is not obliged to do this.

41.[99] Why is a double fifth or a double fourth not concordant whereas a double octave is? Is it because the fifth is in a hemiolic ratio and the fourth in an epitritic one?[100] Now where there are three numbers in succession in hemiolic or epitritic ratio, the extremes will have no ratio to one another, since they will be neither epimoric nor multiple.[101] But since the octave is in a double ratio, when this is doubled the extremes would be in a quadruple ratio to one

[100] The hemiolic ratio is 3: 2, the epitritic 4: 3.

[101] The hemiolic ratio of three numbers in succession is n: $3/2$ n: $(3/2)^2$ n—e.g., 4: 6: 9; the epitritic ratio of three numbers in succession is n: $4/3$ n: $(4/3)^2$ n—e.g., 9: 12: 16. An epimoric ratio is n+1: n, a multiple ratio mn: n. The point is that there is no epimoric or multiple ratio between the extreme numbers (4 and 9 in the first example, 9 and 16 in the second).

ἄκροι πρὸς ἀλλήλους. ὥστ᾽ ἐπεὶ συμφωνία εὐλόγως[92]
ἐχόντων φθόγγων πρὸς ἀλλήλους ἐστίν, λόγον δὲ οἱ
10 μὲν τὸ | δὶς διὰ πασῶν διάλειμμα ἔχοντες πρὸς ἀλλή-
λους φθόγγοι ἔχουσιν, οἱ δὲ τὸ δὶς διὰ τεττάρων ἢ δὶς
διὰ πέντε οὐκ ἔχουσιν, οἱ μὲν δὶς διὰ πασῶν σύμ-
φωνοι εἶεν ἄν, οἱ δ᾽ ἕτεροι οὔ, διὰ τὰ εἰρημένα.

42. Διὰ τί, ἐάν τις ψήλας τὴν νήτην ἐπιλάβῃ, ἡ
15 ὑπάτη | μόνη δοκεῖ ὑπηχεῖν; ἢ ὅτι ἡ νεάτη λήγουσα
καὶ μαραινομένη ὑπάτη γίνεται; σημεῖον δὲ τὸ ἀπὸ
τῆς ὑπάτης τὴν νεάτην δύνασθαι ᾄδειν· ὡς γὰρ οὔσης
ἀντῳδῆς ⟨τῆς⟩[93] νεάτης, τὴν ὁμοιότητα λαμβάνουσιν
ἀπ᾽ αὐτῆς. ἐπεὶ δὲ καὶ ἠχὼ τίς[94] ἐστιν [ἀφή ἐστι
20 φωνῆς][95] τῆς νεάτης ληγούσης, ⟨καὶ⟩[96] ἦχος | ὧν ὁ
αὐτὸς τῷ τῆς ὑπάτης φθόγγῳ κινεῖται,[97] εἰκότως τῇ
ὁμοιότητι τὴν ὑπάτην ἡ νήτη δοκεῖ κινεῖν. τὴν μὲν γὰρ
νεάτην ἴσμεν οὗ κινεῖται ἐπιληφθεῖσα· τὴν δὲ ὑπάτην
αὐτὴν ὁρῶντες ἀκατάληπτον οὖσαν, καὶ φθόγγου αὐτῆς ἀκούοντες, ταύτην οἰόμεθα ἠχεῖν. ὅπερ ἐπὶ πολ-
25 λῶν ἡμῖν συμβαίνει, | ἐφ᾽ ὧν μήτε τῷ λογισμῷ μήτε
τῇ αἰσθήσει δυνάμεθα εἰδῆσαι τὸ ἀκριβές. ἔτι εἰ
πληγείσης τῆς νεάτης μάλιστα ἐντεταμένης συμβαί-

---

[92] εὐλόγως Stumpf : εὔλογον codd. : λόγον Bojesen

[93] ἀντῳδῆς ⟨τῆς⟩ Ross apud Forster : αὐτῆς ᾠδῆς codd. :
αὐτῆς ⟨τῆς⟩ ᾠδῆς Louis

[94] ἠχὼ τίς Barker : ἠχὼ φωνή τίς Ap : ἠχὼ ᾠδῇ τίς cett.
codd. : ἠχὼ ἀντῳδῇ τίς Ross apud Forster   [95] ἀφή ἐστι
φωνῆς seclusi : ἀφή ἐστι secl. Ross apud Forster : ἀφή ⟨γὰρ⟩
ἐστι Marenghi[1] : ἀφ᾽ ἧς pro ἀφή Bussemaker

another.[102] So, since there is concord when notes are in a good ratio to one another, and the notes containing the interval[103] of the double octave have ⟨such⟩ a ratio to one another, while those containing the intervals of the double fourth or double fifth do not, those containing the double octave would be consonant, while the others would not be, for the reasons given.

42.[104] Why, if one plucks *nêtê* and then damps it, does *hypatê* alone seem to resound? Is it because *nêtê*,[105] when ceasing and dying down, becomes *hypatê*? A sign of this is that it is possible to sing *nêtê* from *hypatê*; for as it is an answering song to *nêtê*, people grasp the similarity from it. And since ⟨*hypatê*⟩ is also an echo of *nêtê* as it fades away, and an echo that is the same as the note of *hypatê* is set in motion, it is reasonable because of its similarity that *nêtê* seems to set *hypatê* in motion. Indeed, we know that *nêtê* is not moving, as it is has been damped; but seeing that *hypatê* itself is not damped down, and hearing its note, we think that it is sounding. This happens to us in many cases in which we are unable to know the exact ⟨*truth*⟩ either through reasoning or through sense perception. Again, it would not be surprising if, when a very tightly stretched

102 A double ratio is 2:1, a quadruple ratio 4:1.

103 I.e., the extremes.

104 Cf. *Pr.* 19.24.

105 For some reason, the author (or an early scribe) here switches to an alternative spelling of *nêtê* (νεάτη instead of νήτη). Both spellings are used throughout this chapter.

---

96 ⟨καὶ⟩ addidi

97 κινεῖται Gevaert-Vollgraff : κινεῖ codd.

νει τὸν ζυγὸν κινεῖσθαι, οὐθὲν ἂν εἴη θαυμαστόν.
κινηθέντος δὲ πάσας τὰς χορδὰς συγκινεῖσθαι καί
τιν' ἦχον ποιεῖν οὐκ ἄλογον. ταῖς μὲν οὖν ἄλλαις ὁ τῆς |
30 νεάτης φθόγγος ἀλλότριός ἐστι καὶ λήγων καὶ ἀρχό-
μενος, τῇ δὲ ὑπάτῃ λήγων ὁ αὐτός. οὗ προστεθέντος
τῇ ἰδίᾳ αὐτῆς κινήσει, ἐκείνης δόξαι πάντ' αὐτὸν εἶναι
οὐθὲν ἄτοπον. ἔσται δὲ μείζων ἢ ὁ κοινὸς τῶν λοιπῶν
χορδῶν ἦχος, ὅτι αἱ μὲν ὑπὸ τῆς νεάτης καθάπερ
35 ὠσθεῖσαι μαλακῶς ἤχησαν, ἡ | δὲ νεάτη πάσῃ τῇ
αὑτῆς δυνάμει, οὖσα αὐτῶν σφοδροτάτη. ὥστε εἰκότως καὶ τὸ δευτερεῖον αὐτῆς κρεῖττον ἂν εἴη ἢ τὸ τῶν
ἄλλων, ὥστε καὶ βραχείας κινήσεως αὐταῖς γεγενη-
μένης.[98] ||

922a 43. Διὰ τί ἥδιον τῆς μονῳδίας ἀκούομεν[99] ἐάν τις
πρὸς αὐλὸν ἢ ⟨πρὸς⟩ λύραν[100] ᾄδῃ; ἢ ὅτι πᾶν τῷ
ἡδίονι μιχθὲν ἥδιον ἔτι[101] ἐστιν; ὁ δὲ αὐλὸς ἡδίων τῆς
λύρας, ὥστε καὶ ἡ ᾠδὴ τούτῳ μιχθεῖσα ἢ λύρᾳ[102]
ἡδίων ἂν εἴη, ἐπεὶ τὸ μεμιγμένον τοῦ ἀμίκτου ἥδιόν |
5 ἐστιν, ἐὰν ἀμφοῖν ἅμα τὴν αἴσθησίν τις λαμβάνῃ.
οἶνος γὰρ ἡδίων τοῦ ὀξυμέλιτος διὰ τὸ μεμῖχθαι
μᾶλλον αὐτοῖς τὰ ὑπὸ τῆς φύσεως μιχθέντα ἢ ⟨τὰ⟩[103]
ὑφ' ἡμῶν. ἔστι γὰρ καὶ οἶνος ὁ μικτὸς[104] ἐξ ὀξέος καὶ

98 ὥστε—γεγενημένης D : ὥστε καὶ βραχείας κινεῖσθαι
ὡς αὐτῆς τε γεγενημένης cett. codd. (secl. Marenghi[1]) : ἄλλως
τε καὶ βραχείας κινήσεως αὐταῖς γεγενημένης Sylburg ex
Gaza

99 ἀκούομεν Xᵃ (cf. Pr. 19.9, 918a23) : ἐστὶν cett. codd.

100 ante λύραν add. ⟨πρὸς⟩ Jan : add. ⟨ἐάν πρὸς⟩ Forster

nêtê is struck, the bridge is set in motion. And it would not be unreasonable if, when (*the bridge*) is set in motion, all the strings moved with it and produced a sound. Now the sound of *nêtê* is alien to the others both when it is ceasing and when it is beginning, whereas it is the same as *hypatê* when it is ceasing. This being added to the particular movement of (*hypatê*) itself, it is not strange that it would seem to be entirely that note. And it will be louder than the combined sound of the remaining strings, because those that have so to speak been driven by *nêtê* sound softly, whereas *nêtê* sounds with all its own power, being the most violent note of them. So it is reasonable that its secondary (*sound*) too would be stronger than that of the others, inasmuch as just a small movement has occurred in them.[106]

43.[107] Why do we listen with greater pleasure to a solo song, if one sings it to the accompaniment of an *aulos* than to a lyre? Is it because anything mixed with what is more pleasant is more pleasant still? The *aulos* is more pleasant than the lyre, so that a song mixed with the former would be more pleasant than one mixed with a lyre, since the mixed is more pleasant than the unmixed, if one grasps the perception of both elements at the same time. For wine is

---

[106] There are likely problems with the text of this last line.
[107] Cf. *Pr.* 19.9.

---

[101] τῷ ἡδίονι μιχθὲν ἥδιον ἔτι Forster : τὸ ἥδιον μιχθὲν ἡδίονι ἔν codd.   [102] λύρᾳ Bojesen : λύρα codd.

[103] ⟨τὰ⟩ Jan

[104] οἶνος ὁ μικτὸς codd. (ὁ οἶνος ὁ μικτὸς C^a teste Louis) : ὁ οἶνος μικτὸς Sylburg

γλυκέος χυμοῦ. δηλοῦσι δὲ καὶ αἱ οἰνώδεις ῥοαὶ κα-
10 λούμεναι. ἡ μὲν οὖν ῳδὴ καὶ ὁ αὐλὸς | μίγνυνται
αὐτοῖς δι᾿ ὁμοιότητα (πνεύματι γὰρ ἄμφω γίνεται)· ὁ
δὲ τῆς λύρας φθόγγος, ἐπειδὴ οὐ πνεύματι γίνεται ἢ
ἧττον αἰσθητὸν ἢ ὁ τῶν αὐλῶν, ἀμικτότερός ἐστι τῇ
φωνῇ· ποιῶν δὲ διαφορὰν τῇ αἰσθήσει ἧττον ἡδύνει,
καθάπερ ἐπὶ τῶν χυμῶν εἴρηται. ἔτι ὁ μὲν αὐλὸς
15 πολλὰ τῷ αὑτοῦ ἤχῳ | καὶ τῇ ὁμοιότητι συγκρύπτει
τῶν τοῦ ῳδοῦ ἁμαρτημάτων, οἱ δὲ τῆς λύρας φθόγγοι
ὄντες ψιλοὶ καὶ ἀμικτότεροι τῇ φωνῇ, καθ᾿ ἑαυτοὺς
θεωρούμενοι †καὶ ὄντες αὐτοῖς†[105] συμφανῆ ποιοῦσιν
τὴν τῆς ῳδῆς ἁμαρτίαν, καθάπερ κανόνες ὄντες αὐτῶν. πολλῶν δὲ ἐν τῇ ῳδῇ ἁμαρτανομένων, τὸ κοινὸν
20 ἐξ ἀμφοῖν | ἀναγκαῖον χεῖρον γίνεσθαι.

44. Διὰ τί [τῶν μὲν ἑπτά][106] μέση καλεῖται, τῶν δὲ
ὀκτὼ οὐκ ἔστι μέσον; ἢ ὅτι ἑπτάχορδοι ἦσαν αἱ
ἁρμονίαι τὸ παλαιόν, τὰ δὲ ἑπτὰ ἔχει μέσον; ἔτι
ἐπειδὴ τῶν μεταξὺ τῶν ἄκρων τὸ μέσον μόνον ἀρχή
25 τίς ἐστιν (ἔστι γὰρ[107] τῶν <εἰς >[108] θάτερον | τῶν ἄκρων
νευόντων ἔν τινι διαστήματι[109] ἀνὰ μέσον [ὂν][110] ἀρ-

---

[105] καὶ ὄντες αὐτοῖς codd. (obelis inclusi) : ὄντες αὐτοῖς secl.
Barnes ‖ αὐτοῖς : αὐτοὶ Ross apud Forster   [106] [τῶν μὲν
ἑπτά] Bojesen : τῶν μὲν ἑπτὰ codd. : τῶν μὲν ὀκτὼ Hett
[107] γὰρ om. Ruelle   [108] <εἰς> Bussemaker
[109] διαστήματι : συστήματι Ruelle   [110] [ὂν] Barker

---

[108] A mixture of vinegar and honey.
[109] See *Pr.* 20.3, 923a14, 9, 923b29, and e.g. [Arist.] *Plant.*
821a36, Thphr. *CP* 1.9, 2.   [110] I.e., we perceive the sounds

more pleasant than oxymel[108] because things mixed by nature are more mixed in themselves than are things mixed by us. Indeed, wine too is the mix of bitter and sweet flavor; and the so-called "winelike pomegranates"[109] reveal this as well. So the song and the *aulos* mix with each other because of their similarity, since they both come to be through breath; but the sound of the lyre, either because it does not come to be through breath or because it is less perceptible than the sound of *auloi*, is less mixed with the voice; and producing a distinction in the perception,[110] it is less pleasant, as has been said in the case of flavors. Furthermore, the *aulos* by its own sound and by its similarity (*to voice*) conceals many of the mistakes of the song, whereas the sounds of the lyre, being bare[111] and less mixed with the voice, being observed in themselves †and existing by themselves†, make the mistake in the song obvious, being as it were a measuring rod for them. Now when there are many mistakes in the song, the combined effect of both (*lyre and voice*) must be worse.

44.[112] Why is *mesê* so called, given that there is no mean of eight? Is it because in the old days the *harmoniai* were heptachords, and seven does have a mean? Further, since of the (*points*) between the extremes the middle alone is a sort of starting point (for there is a starting point in the middle (*between*) those inclining toward one or the other

of the lyre and of the voice as distinct.   [111] Barker comments: "*Psiloi*. The word is commonly used of instrumental music unaccompanied by the voice. Here the voice accompanies it, but is isolated from it by its incapacity to mix" (*Greek Musical Writings*, vol. 1, p. 202 n. 89).   [112] Cf. *Pr.* 19.25. There are major problems with the text of this chapter.

χή), τοῦτ᾽ ἔσται μέση.[111] ἐπεὶ δ᾽ ἔσχατα μὲν[112] ἐστὶν
ἁρμονίας νεάτη καὶ ὑπάτη, τούτων δὲ ἀνὰ μέσον οἱ
λοιποὶ φθόγγοι, ὧν ἡ μέση καλουμένη μόνη ἀρχή
ἐστι θατέρου τετραχόρδου, δικαίως μέση καλεῖται.

30 τῶν γὰρ μεταξύ τινων ἄκρων τὸ | μέσον ἦν ἀρχὴ
μόνον.

45. Διὰ τί οἱ πολλοὶ ἄδοντες σώζουσι μᾶλλον τὸν
ῥυθμὸν ἢ οἱ ὀλίγοι; ἢ ὅτι μᾶλλον πρὸς ἕνα τε καὶ
ἡγεμόνα βλέπουσι, καὶ βραδύτερον ἄρχονται,[113] ὥστε
ῥᾷον τοῦ αὐτοῦ τυγχάνουσιν; ἐν μὲν γὰρ τῷ τάχει

35 πλείων γίνεται ἡ ἁμαρτία, | συμβαίνει δὲ τῷ ἡγεμόνι
προσέχειν τοὺς πολλούς· ἰδιαζόμενος δὲ οὐδεὶς ἂν
αὐτῶν διαλάμψειεν ὑπεράρας τὸ πλῆθος. ἐν δὲ τοῖς
ὀλίγοις μᾶλλον διαλάμπουσιν· διὸ καθ᾽ αὑτοὺς ἐν
αὑτοῖς μᾶλλον ἀγωνίζονται ἢ πρὸς τὸν ἡγεμόνα.

46. Διὰ τί ἐπὶ τὸ ὀξὺ ἀπᾴδουσιν οἱ πλεῖστοι; ἢ ὅτι
922b ῥᾷον ‖ ὀξὺ ᾆσαι ἢ βαρύ; ἄδουσι γοῦν ὀξὺ μᾶλλον, καὶ
ἐν ᾧ ἄδουσιν, ἁμαρτάνουσιν.

47. Διὰ τί οἱ ἀρχαῖοι ἑπταχόρδους ποιοῦντες τὰς
5 ἁρμονίας τὴν | ὑπάτην ἀλλ᾽ οὐ τὴν νήτην κατέλιπον; ἢ
οὐ τὴν νήτην[114] ἀλλὰ τὴν νῦν παραμέσην καλουμένην

---

[111] μέση Jan : μέσον codd.
[112] μὲν Jan : μέσον codd. : [μέσον] Louis
[113] ἄρχονται : ὀρχοῦνται Forster
[114] νήτην Bojesen : ὑπάτην codd.

of the extremes in any interval), this[113] will be *mesê*. And since *nêtê* and *hypatê* are the extremes of the *harmonia*, while the remaining notes are in the middle of them, of which the one called *mesê* alone is the starting point of the next tetrachord, it is right that it should be called *mesê*. For (*as we have seen*) of the points between two extremes the middle alone was a starting point.

45.[114] Why do many people singing together preserve the rhythm better than a few? Is it because they look more to one person who is their leader, and begin more slowly, so that they easily strike the same moment? For in what is quick the error is greater, whereas many people pay attention to the leader; and none of them would shine through by being conspicuous and rising above the majority. But in a small group (*individuals*) shine through more; this is why they compete among themselves rather than look to their leader.

46.[115] Why do most people sing out of tune in a high (*voice*)? Is it because it is easier to sing high than low? At any rate, they are more inclined to sing high, and so they make mistakes in what they sing.

47.[116] Why did the ancients, when they made the seven-note *harmoniai*, leave in the *hypatê* but not the *nêtê*? Or did they remove not *nêtê* but the (*string*) now called *para-*

---

113 I.e., the middle that is a sort of starting point.
114 Cf. *Pr.* 19.22.
115 Cf. *Pr.* 19.21 and 26.
116 Cf. *Pr.* 19.7 and Aristox. *Harm.* 1.24.

ἀφῄρουν καὶ τὸ τονιαῖον διάστημα; ἐχρῶντο δὲ τῇ
ἐσχάτῃ τῇ μέσῃ¹¹⁵ τοῦ ἐπὶ τὸ ὀξὺ πυκνοῦ· διὸ καὶ
μέσην αὐτὴν προσηγόρευσαν. ἢ ὅτι ἦν τοῦ μὲν ἄνω
τετραχόρδου τελευτή, τοῦ δὲ κάτω ἀρχή, καὶ μέσον
εἶχε λόγον τόνῳ τῶν ἄκρων; |

10   48. Διὰ τί οἱ ἐν τραγῳδίᾳ χοροὶ οὔθ᾽ ὑποδωριστὶ
οὔθ᾽ ὑποφρυγιστὶ ᾄδουσιν; ἢ ὅτι μέλος¹¹⁶ ἥκιστα
ἔχουσιν αὗται αἱ ἁρμονίαι, οὗ δεῖ μάλιστα τῷ χορῷ;
ἦθος δὲ <ἔχει>¹¹⁷ ἡ μὲν ὑποφρυγιστὶ πρακτικόν, διὸ
καὶ ἔν [τε]¹¹⁸ τῷ Γηρυόνῃ ἡ ἔξοδος καὶ ἡ ἐξόπλισις ἐν
15   ταύτῃ πεποίηται, ἡ δὲ ὑποδωριστὶ μεγαλοπρεπὲς | καὶ
στάσιμον, διὸ καὶ κιθαρῳδικωτάτη ἐστὶ τῶν ἁρμο-
νιῶν. ταῦτα δ᾽ ἄμφω χορῷ μὲν ἀνάρμοστα, τοῖς δὲ
ἀπὸ σκηνῆς οἰκειότερα. ἐκεῖνοι μὲν γὰρ ἡρώων μιμη-
ταί· οἱ δὲ ἡγεμόνες τῶν ἀρχαίων μόνοι ἦσαν ἥρωες, οἱ
δὲ λαοὶ ἄνθρωποι, ὧν ἐστιν ὁ χορός. διὸ καὶ ἁρμόζει
20   αὐτῷ τὸ γοερὸν | καὶ ἡσύχιον ἦθος καὶ μέλος· ἀνθρω-
πικὰ γάρ. ταῦτα δ᾽¹¹⁹ ἔχουσιν αἱ ἄλλαι ἁρμονίαι,
ἥκιστα δὲ αὐτῶν ἡ [ὑπο]φρυγιστί.¹²⁰ ἐνθουσιαστικὴ

¹¹⁵ τῇ ἐσχάτῃ τῇ μέσῃ Cᵃ : τῇ ἐσχάτῃ μέσῃ cett. codd. :
μέσῃ τῇ ἐσχάτῃ Jan
¹¹⁶ ante μέλος add. <τὸ> Forster, <τοιοῦτον> Richards
¹¹⁷ <ἔχει> Sylburg
¹¹⁸ [τε] Gevaert-Vollgraff
¹¹⁹ δ᾽ : μὲν Wagener apud Gevaert-Vollgraff
¹²⁰ [ὑπο]φρυγιστί Bojesen

mesê and the interval of the tone? So they used *mesê* for
the last note of the *pyknon*[117] in the high (*pitched*) part,
and this is why they named it *mesê*. Or is it because *mesê*
was the end of the upper tetrachord, and the beginning of
the lower one, and had in pitch the relationship of a mean
between extremes?

48.[118] Why do choruses in tragedy sing neither in Hypodorian nor in Hypophrygian? Is it because these *harmoniai* have the least melody, which is most necessary to the
chorus? Now the Hypophrygian has a character of action,
and this is why in the *Geryone*[119] the marching out and the
arming (*episodes*) are composed in this manner, while the
Hypodorian has a magnificent and steadfast character, and
this is why of the *harmoniai* it is most suited to kithara
song. But these (*harmoniai*) are both inappropriate to the
chorus, and more suitable to the (*actors*) on the stage. For
the latter are imitators of heroes; but in the old days the
(*chorus*) leaders alone were heroes, while the people, of
whom the chorus consists, were humans. And this is why a
mournful and quiet character and melody are appropriate
to it; for (*the chorus*) is human. Now the other *harmoniai*
have these,[120] but the Phrygian has them least, since it is

---

117 In a note on *pyknômata* (Pl. *Rep.* 531a4), Barker writes
that *pyknon* "is used by Aristoxenus to designate the pair of small
intervals at the bottom of an enharmonic or a chromatic tetrachord" (*Greek Musical Writings*, vol. 1, p. 56 n. 3).

118 Cf. *Pr.* 19.30, and see *Pol.* 8.7.

119 Probably refers to a lost poem by Stesichorus (lyric poet,
ca. 600–550 BC), on Heracles' quest for Geryon's cattle.

120 I.e., the harmonies that are neither Hypodorian nor Hypophrygian have the characteristics appropriate to the chorus.

γὰρ καὶ βακχική. . . .[121] κατὰ μὲν οὖν ταύτην πάσχο-
μέν τι· παθητικοὶ δὲ οἱ ἀσθενεῖς μᾶλλον τῶν δυνατῶν
εἰσί, διὸ καὶ αὕτη ἁρμόττει τοῖς χοροῖς· κατὰ δὲ τὴν
25 ὑποδωριστὶ | καὶ ὑποφρυγιστὶ πράττομεν, ὃ οὐκ οἰ-
κεῖόν ἐστι χορῷ. ἔστι γὰρ ὁ χορὸς κηδευτὴς ἄπρα-
κτος· εὔνοιαν γὰρ μόνον παρέχεται οἷς πάρεστιν.

49. Διὰ τί τῶν τὴν συμφωνίαν ποιούντων φθόγγων
ἐν τῷ βαρυτέρῳ τὸ μαλακώτερον;[122] ἢ ὅτι τὸ μέλος τῇ
30 μὲν αὑτοῦ | φύσει μαλακόν ἐστι καὶ ἠρεμαῖον, τῇ δὲ
τοῦ ῥυθμοῦ μίξει τραχὺ καὶ κινητικόν; ἐπεὶ δὲ ὁ μὲν
βαρὺς φθόγγος μαλακὸς καὶ[123] ἠρεμαῖός ἐστιν, ὁ δὲ
ὀξὺς κινητικός, καὶ τῶν ταὐτὸ μέλος ἐχόντων εἴη ἂν
μαλακώτερος[124] ὁ βαρύτερος [ἐν ταὐτῷ μέλει][125] μᾶλ-
λον· ἦν γὰρ τὸ μέλος αὐτὸ[126] μαλακόν. |

35 50. Διὰ τί ἴσων πίθων καὶ ὁμοίων, ἐὰν μὲν ὁ ἕτερος
κενὸς ᾖ, ὁ δὲ ἕτερος εἰς τὸ ἥμισυ διάμεστος, διὰ
πασῶν συμφωνεῖ ἡ ἠχώ; ἢ ὅτι διπλασία γίνεται
[καὶ][127] ἡ ἐκ τοῦ ἡμίσεος τῆς ἐκ τοῦ κενοῦ; τί γὰρ
διαφέρει τοῦτο ἢ ἐπὶ τῶν συρίγγων; δοκεῖ γὰρ ἡ

---

[121] post βακχική lac. indicavi : add. ⟨μάλιστα δὲ ἡ μιξολυ-
διστί⟩ Bojesen ex Gaza (at vero mixolydius nimirum illa
praestare potest)
[122] μαλακώτερον : μελικώτερον Eichtal-Reinach
[123] μαλακὸς καὶ secl. Marenghi[1]
[124] μαλακώτερος : μελικώτερος Eichtal-Reinach
[125] ἐν ταὐτῷ μέλει seclusi
[126] αὐτὸ Cᵃ : αὐτῷ cett. codd.
[127] [καὶ] Bojesen

inspirational and Bacchic, (*and the Mixolydian certainly has them most of all*).[121] Under the influence of this (*harmonia*),[122] therefore, we are affected in a certain way; and the weak are affected more than the strong, which is why even this one is appropriate to choruses; but under the influence of the Hypodorian and Hypophrygian we *act*, which is not suitable to a chorus. For the chorus is an inactive attendant, since it merely offers goodwill to those who are present (*on the stage*).

49. Why, among the notes that make up the concord, is the softer (*quality*) in the lower (*note*)?[123] Is it because the melody is in its own nature soft and tranquil, but through the mixture with rhythm it becomes rough and conducive to movement? Now since the low note is soft and tranquil, while the high note is conducive to movement, it follows that of the (*two notes*) having the same melody, the lower would tend to be softer; for (*as we have seen*) the melody itself is soft.

50.[124] Why is it that of (*two*) vessels equal (*in size*) and similar, if one is empty while the other is half full, the (*combined*) sound gives an octave concord? Is it because the sound from the half is double that from the empty? Indeed, what difference is there between this and the case

[121] There is likely a gap in the text here. The phrase I add is based on Gaza's translation. The author may have gone on to say more about why the Mixolydian harmony (on which see *Pol.* 1340b1) has these characteristics most of all.

[122] The author seems to be referring to the Phrygian, not the Mixolydian, harmony.   [123] It is difficult to make sense of the Greek here. I follow a suggestion of Barker.

[124] Cf. Hippias 18A13 D-K (= Theon Sm. 59.4–21).

θάττων κίνησις ὀξυτέρα εἶναι, ἐν δὲ τοῖς μείζοσι ‖
923a βραδύτερον ὁ ἀὴρ ἀπαντᾷ, καὶ ἐν τοῖς διπλασίοις
τοσούτῳ, καὶ ἐν τοῖς ἄλλοις ἀνάλογον. συμφωνεῖ δὲ
διὰ πασῶν καὶ ὁ διπλασίων ἀσκὸς πρὸς τὸν ἥμισυν.

of panpipes? For the quicker motion seems to be higher (*pitched*), whereas the air meets[125] more slowly in larger spaces, and in things double the size it does so that much more slowly, and proportionately in other cases. A double-sized wineskin also gives an octave concord with one of half the size.

[125] There is no indication as to what the air meets ($\dot{\alpha}\pi\alpha\nu\tau\hat{\alpha}$)— the wall of the container, in the one case, the outside air, in the case of the panpipes.